ROY HATTERSLEY

The Devonshires

The Story of a Family and a Nation

VINTAGE BOOKS
London

Published by Vintage 2014

2 4 6 8 10 9 7 5 3 1

First published in Great Britain in 2013 by
Chatto & Windus

Vintage
Random House, 20 Vauxhall Bridge Road,
London SW1V 2SA

www.vintage-books.co.uk

Addresses for companies within The Random House Group Limited can be
found at: www.randomhouse.co.uk/offices.htm

The Random House Group Limited Reg. No. 954009

A CIP catalogue record for this book
is available from the British Library

ISBN 9780099554394

The Random House Group Limited supports the Forest Stewardship
Council® (FSC®), the leading international forest-certification organisation.
Our books carrying the FSC label are printed on FSC®-certified paper. FSC is
the only forest-certification scheme supported by the leading environmental
organisations, including Greenpeace. Our paper procurement policy can be
found at www.randomhouse.co.uk/environment

Typeset in Sabon LT Std by Palimpsest Book Production Ltd,
Falkirk, Stirlingshire

Printed and bound in Great Britain by
CPI Group (UK) Ltd, Croydon CR0 4YY

THE DEVONSHIRES

Roy Hattersley was elected to Parliament in 1964. He served in Harold Wilson's government and in Jim Callaghan's cabinet. In 1983 he became deputy leader of the Labour Party. A weekly columnist with the *Guardian* (for twenty-five years), the *Daily Mail*, *Punch* and the *Spectator*, he has published twenty-two books, including *A Yorkshire Boyhood* and *In Search of England* as well as much acclaimed biographies of John Wesley, William and Catherine Booth and, most recently, David Lloyd George. Roy Hattersley has been Visiting Fellow of Harvard's Institute of Politics and of Nuffield College, Oxford. In 2003 he was elected a Fellow of the Royal Society of Literature.

Contents

List of Illustrations

First Section

Portrait of Sir William Cavendish at 44 years (National Trust Images / Hawkley Studios)

Bess of Hardwick as a young woman, English School, 1550s (The Devonshire Collection National Trust Photographic Library / Angelo Hornak / Bridgeman Art Library)

Mary, Queen of Scots, possibly Rowland Lockey, c.1578 (National Trust Images)

Lady Arbella Stuart aged 13, Rowland Lockey, 1589 (National Trust Photographic Library / John Hammond / Bridgeman Art Library)

William Cavendish, First Duke of Newcastle, after Sir Anthony Van Dyck (Private Collection / Bridgeman Art Library)

Bolsover Castle (John Bethell / Bridgeman Art Library)

Lismore Castle, published in 'Building News', English School, 1858 (Private Collection / Bridgeman Art Library)

William Cavendish, First Duke of Devonshire, Sir Godfrey Kneller, c.1680-85 (Reproduced by permission of Chatsworth Settlement Trustees / Bridgeman Art Library)

Thomas Hobbes, English School, 1676 (National Trust Photographic Library / John Hammond / Bridgeman Art Library)

Lancelot Capability Brown, Nathaniel Dance-Holland (Burghley House Collection / Bridgeman Art Library)

Second Section

Henry Cavendish, c.1851 (Universal History Archive / UIG / Bridgeman Art Library)

William Cavendish, Fifth Duke of Devonshire, Anton von Maron (Reproduced by permission of Chatsworth Settlement Trustees / Bridgeman Art Library)

Georgiana, Duchess of Devonshire, Thomas Gainsborough, c.1785-87 (Reproduced by permission of Chatsworth Settlement Trustees / Bridgeman Art Library)

Portrait of the Right Honourable Earl Grey K.G., Henry Hetherington Emmerson, 1848 (Tyne & Wear Archives & Museums / Bridgeman Art Library)

Lady Elizabeth Foster, Sir Joshua Reynolds (Reproduced by permission of Chatsworth Settlement Trustees / Bridgeman Art Library)

A Gaming Table at Devonshire House, Thomas Rowlandson, 1791 (The Metropolitan Museum of Art / Scala)

Babble, Birth and Brummagem, Theobold Chartrem, 1880 (Private Collection)

William Spencer Cavendish, Sixth Duke of Devonshire, Sir Thomas Lawrence (Reproduced by permission of Chatsworth Settlement Trustees / Bridgeman Art Library)

Sir Joseph Paxton, Henry Perronet Briggs, 1836 (Reproduced by permission of Chatsworth Settlement Trustees / Bridgeman Art Library)

Spencer Compton Cavendish, Marquess of Hartington, later Eighth Duke of Devonshire, Sir John Everett Millais (Reproduced by permission of Chatsworth Settlement Trustees / Bridgeman Art Library)

Lord Frederick Cavendish, 1877 (Rischgitz / Getty Images)

The assassination of Frederick Cavendish and Thomas Henry Burke, 1882 (Hulton Archive / Getty Images)

LIST OF ILLUSTRATIONS

Hardwick Hall (Bridgeman Art Library)

Chatsworth House and the Emperor Fountain (Neil Holmes / Bridgeman Art Library)

Devonshire family tree

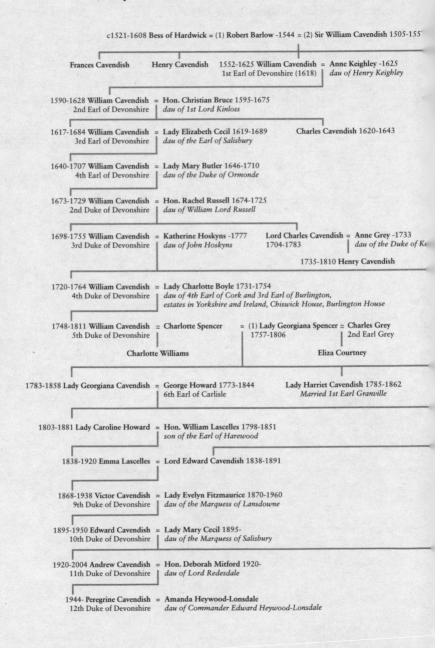

c1521-1608 Bess of Hardwick = (1) Robert Barlow -1544 = (2) Sir William Cavendish 1505-155?

Frances Cavendish   Henry Cavendish   1552-1625 William Cavendish = Anne Keighley -1625
1st Earl of Devonshire (1618) | *dau of Henry Keighley*

1590-1628 William Cavendish = Hon. Christian Bruce 1595-1675
2nd Earl of Devonshire | *dau of 1st Lord Kinloss*

1617-1684 William Cavendish = Lady Elizabeth Cecil 1619-1689   Charles Cavendish 1620-1643
3rd Earl of Devonshire | *dau of the Earl of Salisbury*

1640-1707 William Cavendish = Lady Mary Butler 1646-1710
4th Earl of Devonshire | *dau of the Duke of Ormonde*

1673-1729 William Cavendish = Hon. Rachel Russell 1674-1725
2nd Duke of Devonshire | *dau of William Lord Russell*

1698-1755 William Cavendish = Katherine Hoskyns -1777   Lord Charles Cavendish = Anne Grey -1733
3rd Duke of Devonshire | *dau of John Hoskyns*   1704-1783 | *dau of the Duke of Ke?*

1735-1810 Henry Cavendish

1720-1764 William Cavendish = Lady Charlotte Boyle 1731-1754
4th Duke of Devonshire | *dau of 4th Earl of Cork and 3rd Earl of Burlington,
estates in Yorkshire and Ireland, Chiswick House, Burlington House*

1748-1811 William Cavendish ≃ Charlotte Spencer   = (1) Lady Georgiana Spencer ≃ Charles Grey
5th Duke of Devonshire | 1757-1806 | 2nd Earl Grey

Charlotte Williams   Eliza Courtney

1783-1858 Lady Georgiana Cavendish = George Howard 1773-1844   Lady Harriet Cavendish 1785-1862
6th Earl of Carlisle | *Married 1st Earl Granville*

1803-1881 Lady Caroline Howard = Hon. William Lascelles 1798-1851
son of the Earl of Harewood

1838-1920 Emma Lascelles = Lord Edward Cavendish 1838-1891

1868-1938 Victor Cavendish = Lady Evelyn Fitzmaurice 1870-1960
9th Duke of Devonshire | *dau of the Marquess of Lansdowne*

1895-1950 Edward Cavendish = Lady Mary Cecil 1895-
10th Duke of Devonshire | *dau of the Marquess of Salisbury*

1920-2004 Andrew Cavendish = Hon. Deborah Mitford 1920-
11th Duke of Devonshire | *dau of Lord Redesdale*

1944- Peregrine Cavendish = Amanda Heywood-Lonsdale
12th Duke of Devonshire | *dau of Commander Edward Heywood-Lonsdale*

= (3) Sir William St Loe -1565   = (4) George Talbot 1528-1590
                                           6th Earl of Shrewsbury

Charles Cavendish = (2) Katherine Ogle   Elizabeth Cavendish = Charles Stuart   Mary Cavendish = Gilbert Talbot
1553-1617   1570-1629   1555-1582   1556-1632   7th Earl of
                                                                  Shrewsbury

William Cavendish   Charles Cavendish 1595-1654   Arbella Stuart
1593-167̄ ,   1575-1615
Duke of Newcastle

1754-1834 **George Cavendish** = **Lady Elizabeth Compton** 1760-1835
1st Earl of Burlington (2nd creation)   *heiress to the Earls of Northampton*
                                      estates in Sussex

2) **Lady Elizabeth Foster**
759-1824

     Caroline St Jules   **Augustus Clifford**

William Spencer George Cavendish 1790-1858   1783-1812 **William Cavendish** = **Hon. Louisa O'Callaghan**
6th Duke of Devonshire   *dau of Lord Lismore*

1812-1840 **Lady Blanche Howard** = **William Cavendish** 1808-1891
                               2nd Earl of Burlington (2nd creation)
                               7th Duke of Devonshire

1833-1908 = **Louise von Alten** 1832-1921   1836-1882 = **Lady Lucy Littelton**
Spencer Compton Cavendish   *Duchess of Manchester*   **Lord Frederick Cavendish**   *dau of Lord Littelton*
8th Duke of Devonshire

1917-1944 **William Cavendish** = **Kathleen Kennedy** 1920-1948
    Marquess of Hartington   *sister of President Kennedy*

Acknowledgements

During my early teens, each of our family summers invariably included a series of 'days out'. One of them was always an excursion to Chatsworth. The journey across Sheffield and into Derbyshire – two tramcars and a bus – took most of the morning. So we ate our lettuce and tomato sandwiches in the park before visiting the house – by which time I was more than ready to go home. I was impressed by neither the pictures nor the furniture. All that lightened my afternoon was the sight of the *trompe-l'oeil* violin which was 'hanging' from a door in the north wall of the State Music Room. It 'hangs' there still. Several times during the last three years, I have taken a break from working my way through the Chatsworth archives and, in order to relive that moment of adolescent wonder, joined the visitors who were making their way through the state rooms. I owe the Duke of Devonshire far more than the unpaid entrance fees. Without his generosity in allowing me regular access to his family papers, *The Devonshires* could not have been written and I would not have enjoyed the particular pleasure of reading the historically important but neglected correspondence of the Eighth Duke of Devonshire, 'Harty-Tarty'. The Duke was also kind enough to read, and improve, the 'Afterword' – a twentieth-century postscript to the 500-year story.

James Towe, the Archivist/Librarian at Chatsworth – together with Stuart Band and Andrew Peppitt, the 'archivists emeritus' – provided far more help than simply retrieving the documents which I wanted to examine, a task which they accomplished with unfailing patience. They all possess an extraordinary knowledge of Devonshire history which they happily shared with me. Andrew Peppitt read the penultimate draft of the whole book and, as well as correcting numerous errors, made valuable suggestions for its improvement

Philip Riden of the School of History in the University of Nottingham allowed me to read and quote from papers he had written on Bess of Hardwick's immediate descendants, as well as providing general guidance about the origins of the families which came together to create the dynasty. Professor Keith Burnett, FRS – the Vice-Chancellor of the University of Sheffield – gave me individual tuition on the work of Henry Cavendish, the scientist who 'measured the weight of the world.' My recent discovery of word-processing spared Cynthia Shepherd, my personal assistant for almost twenty years, the tedium of typing innumerable drafts. But she corrected grammar and spelling, identified contradictions and repetitions and made sense of the notes and references. Penny Hoare, my editor at Chatto, made suggestions which enabled me greatly to improve the flow of the text.

I am also grateful for original material which was made available (online) by the Fogler Library, Maine, USA, and I am indebted to the University of Nottingham for permission to quote from its collection of Portland Papers. The London Library was, as always, indispensable. Included among the books it lent to me were – much to my surprise – a biography of Cardinal Wolsey, written immediately after his death, a memoir of the First Duke of Newcastle, written by his wife in 1667, and *The Lives of All the Earls and Dukes of Devonshire*, written by Mr Grove of Richmond in 1764.

My gratitude for all the help which I received, during the three years in which I wrote *The Devonshires*, is boundless. Of course, the errors and omissions which undoubtedly remain are entirely my responsibility.

Author's Note

Family histories, by their nature, are stories about generations of characters with identical names. Ten consecutive Earls and Dukes of Devonshire were baptised William Cavendish. The problem of clearly identifying members of the nobility is compounded by their habit of changing names as a result of inheriting titles. Thus Spencer Compton Cavendish became first the Marquis of Hartington and then the Eighth Duke of Devonshire. Naturally enough, contemporary documents used whichever name was appropriate when they were written. In the hope of avoiding confusion I have identified some characters by name more often than is usual and in more detail than is customary – 'the Marquis of Hartington, soon to become the Duke of Devonshire'.

What follows contains quotations from documents which were written over a period of five centuries. For much of that time there was neither standard spelling nor standard grammar. Even in the nineteenth century the notes which were sent, almost hourly, between politicians were littered, as are texts today, with abbreviations and errors which the writer lacked either time or inclination to correct. As long as the meaning is clear, I have always quoted verbatim. Nor have I followed strange usages with the explanation 'sic'. Had I done so, sic would have become one of the most frequently used words in the book.

THE DEVONSHIRES

CHAPTER 1

Before Bess

Andrew Cavendish, the Eleventh Duke of Devonshire, told me that he had not expected to survive the war. In the spring of 1944, he was a company commander in the Third Battalion of the Coldstream Guards – part of General Alexander's Eighth Army which was fighting its way north through Italy in the long and bloody Battle of the Gothic Line. As a racing enthusiast, he judged his chances of returning home to be 'very long odds indeed'. Coldstream officers, he explained, wore fawn rather than khaki trousers. As a result, they could be identified and picked off by German snipers. I asked the obvious question. Why did they not abandon what was surely no more than an affectation, and revert to regulation uniform? Before he replied, the Duke paused in astonishment. 'We weren't going to let the Germans tell us what to wear.'

The Duke had encapsulated, in a single sentence, all that is best and worst in the English aristocracy. He had also demonstrated the extraordinary confidence in way of life and standard of behaviour that comes from membership of a family which has been famous, rich and powerful for five hundred years or more. The Eleventh Duke was not an arrogant man. So another, often quoted, example of his self-assurance may be apocryphal. But if – when asked if he belonged to Pratt's Club – he really did answer, 'No. It belongs to me', he was expressing a minor example of a greater truth. The Devonshires stamped their indelible mark on England. They helped to make it as it made them. Other families – the Russells, the Stanleys, the Cecils – played equally notable parts at moments in history. But the Devonshires endured. The family administered the dissolution of the monasteries, fought but failed to save Charles I, schemed successfully to depose James II, and produced a Prime Minister in the eighteenth century and, in the nineteenth, a politician who was described by John Buchan in *The Three Hostages* as 'the epitome of Englishness'. They also built great houses, patronised the arts and, from time to time, scandalised respectable society.

Yet – despite what they had already achieved – when, in the seventeenth century, William Cavendish became Earl of Devonshire, the family felt so insecure about its origins that it employed a 'pedigree maker' to trace its nobility back beyond the reign of Henry VII, the Welsh parvenu who, in 1485, defeated the Plantagenets on Bosworth Field and founded the Tudor monarchy.

The indisputable proof of noble lineage was the discovery of a blood line which stretched back to men who landed with William the Conqueror or fought with Henry V at Agincourt. The Devonshires' 'pedigree maker' knew his duty. He obligingly provided both a Norman and an Angevin knight – with equally dubious provenance. So the Cavendish story begins with a confusing mixture of fact and fiction. The family was happy to accept the inventions as historical truth.

The first myth was built around Robert Gernon. He possessed the essential qualification of mention in the *Domesday Book* and because of his kinship with a Ralph de Gernon – who lived in Essex, but was Lord of Bakewell in the Peak – established the necessary territorial connection. It was then necessary to find a suitable descendant who could relate Gernon to the Tudor Cavendishes. The pedigree maker found two – thus making it more difficult to expose his work as a fraud. One nominee was a Gernon descendant called Robert de Cavendish who, in 1226, contested the ownership of 6 acres of land along the Essex/Sussex border.[1] The only real evidence to support his claim to membership of the dynasty was his passion for the acquisition of land – an obsession which, for the next five hundred years, was a defining Cavendish preoccupation. The second contender was a Gernon who was said to have changed his name in order to inherit Cavendish Manor in Suffolk. In 1359, Cavendish Manor was certainly owned and occupied by a Sir John Cavendish – a busy and successful lawyer who became a judge. But the records show that he bought, rather than inherited, property and that he had no connection with the Gernons of the *Domesday Book*.

There is some circumstantial evidence to suggest a connection between Sir John and the Cavendish family. The College of Arms cannot identify the origin of the Cavendish crest, since it only began to compile 'a central register of Arms . . . when Henry VIII introduced a tax for having them in 1530'. But the College also reports that 'Sir John Cavendish, Chief Justice temp. Edward III, bore Sable three bucks heads cabossed Argent'. Three bucks still emblazon the Cavendish shield. They decorate the flag which flies over Chatsworth when the Duke is at home. Whether or not the connection could be confirmed, the 'Chief Justice temp. Edward III' was an ideal ancestor for a family of Tudor placemen. The Devonshires did not need much persuasion to accept him as their own.

Sir John Cavendish became the rising star of the Plantagenet judiciary. During the 1360s, he was a tax collector for Essex and Suffolk – a remunerative, but not exalted, position for a Cambridge graduate and ambitious lawyer to occupy. He soon made up lost ground. In 1366 he became sergeant – a senior counsel – and by 1371 he was puisne judge in Common Pleas, inferior in rank only to a chief justice. A year later he became a justice of the King's Bench. The sagacity which had contributed to his success was demonstrated by his refusal to rule on whether or not a female claimant was still a minor or old enough to inherit property. 'There is no man in England who would rightly adjudge her age or her full age, for all women who are of the age of thirty want to be thought to be eighteen'.[2] In 1377, on the accession of Richard II, he was appointed Chief Justice with a salary of one hundred marks a year. In 1380 he was elected Chancellor of Cambridge University.

The necessary Agincourt connection was provided by Sir John's younger son, another John. He was said to have been rewarded for his service on Saint Crispin's Day 1415 by his appointment as Brouderer (embroiderer) of the King's Wardrobe at the Court of Henry V. The award of needle-working rights was a strange way to recognise valour in battle and the improbability of the legend is confirmed by documents of the time which suggest that no one of that name ever held the title.[3] The Cavendish genealogists attributed the discrepancy to a mistake by the record-keepers. The soldier who fought in the war against the French was certainly their invention. No one called Cavendish appears in the roll of knights who fought at Agincourt. It is unlikely that the pedigree maker built the Devonshire claim to nobility on an archer or one of the humble men-at-arms who stood shoulder to shoulder to repel the French charge.

In 1381, the poll tax – Richard II's method of raising money to finance the Hundred Years War – provoked a revolt against the whole feudal system. On Blackheath in London, the Lollard priest, John Ball, preached the gospel of revolution to the gathering of rebellious Kentish bondsmen. His text was a question: 'When Adam delved and Eve span, who was then the gentleman?' Its message was reinforced by his sermon. 'From the beginning all men were created alike and our bondage and servitude came by unjust oppression . . . Cast off the yoke of bondage and recover your liberty.' What came to be called the Peasants' Revolt demanded the commutation of servile dues and taxes, the limitation of rents and the repeal of the Statute of Labourers which held down wages by law. In *Piers Plowman*, the greatest poem of the Middle Ages, William Langland wrote that half of England 'cursed the King and all his Council . . . for making such laws as labourers grieve'. That was a reflection of a hatred which created a lethal hostility to tax collectors and lawyers. The second John Cavendish was such a man.

In June 1381, as Wat Tyler and his Kentish followers marched on

London, John Wraw, a Suffolk priest, led a related revolt which began at Liston – 10 miles away from the home of Chief Justice Cavendish. When news of the rising reached him, he hid his plate and valuables in the Liston church tower and fled to Ely. Neither the judge nor his property was spared. The church was looted and the manor sacked before the rebels marched on Bury Saint Edmunds and destroyed the monastery. On the following day – as much by chance as by intention – they captured Cavendish at Lakenheath. He was about to make good his escape across the Brandon River when Katherine Garner, a boat-woman with revolutionary inclinations, cut loose the ferry and allowed it to float downstream beyond his reach. The mob by which he was captured beheaded him on the spot – making him one of the few members of the family (religious and civil wars notwithstanding) to meet a violent death. They carried his head to Bury Saint Edmunds and set it on a spike in the market place, next to that of his friend, John of Canterbury, prior of the abbey. According to legend, they were arranged in a way which created the impression that the priest was hearing the Chief Justice's much-needed confession.[4]

The myths which grew up around the kernel of truth in the story included the claim that the East Anglian mob was motivated by more than general hatred of tax collectors. The legend describes the mobsters as 'incensed in a more than ordinary degree against the Chief Justice, his son having killed the notorious Watt Tyler'. So they 'dragged him into Bury market place and there beheaded him'.[5] It is easy to understand why the Tudor Cavendishes welcomed such a dramatic episode being included in their pedigree – particularly since it is a tale of martyrdom endured by a man who supported the Crown against the rebellious peasantry. Unfortunately, the story has a flaw. In fact, the Chief Justice was beheaded many miles from Bury and on the day before Wat Tyler's death. Wat Tyler's assassin was Jenan or Ralph Standish.

If the Chief Justice was connected to the Cavendishes who became the Devonshires by more than their decision to copy his coat of arms, a link must have existed between him and a humble tradesman. A trades letter-book for 1312 describes Stephen Cavendish, a mercer, as 'the son of Watre de Ewelle, late apprentice of Walter de Cavendish', a guildsman of the same trade.[6] The connection is confirmed by the practice – begun by Stephen Cavendish and continued by his son and grandson – of endowing the church of St Thomas the Martyr at Acton, and stipulating, in their wills, that they be buried within its walls. St Thomas was the church of the Mercers' Company. The likelihood is that the former Stephen de Ewelle changed his name to Cavendish in order to gain some sort of financial or social advantage from his master. Whatever the reason, the Tudor Cavendishes' choice of forebear was not descended from a Norman knight. He was the protégé of a Plantagenet draper.

In his autobiography, Andrew Devonshire, the Eleventh Duke of Devonshire – a man incapable of real malice – wrote that Harold Macmillan ('Uncle Harold' by marriage) acted like, and would like to have been thought of as, a Trollopian grandee, but in reality was a Galsworthian businessman. The merchant who longed to be an aristocrat was not a new phenomenon in the Devonshire family. Several generations passed before they accepted their mercer origins. And for four hundred years the inventions about old nobility were accepted by men who might have been expected to recognise their implausibility. In 1851, the biography of Henry Cavendish – published in tribute to his scientific genius – blandly asserted that a Norman 'who had assisted William the Conqueror in his invasion of the realm . . . was the founding father of the dynasty'.

The dynasty did not have a founding father. It had a founding mother – Bess of Hardwick the four-times-married country girl who ruthlessly built the House of Cavendish. But the name was bequeathed to her descendants by her second husband, William Cavendish – son of George Cavendish, who had contested claims against his inheritance with uninhibited ferocity and, by 1525, had established uncontested ownership of the Cavendish property. The acquisitive instinct was in the Cavendish blood. It produced Cavendish tradition which George Cavendish could claim to have originated. He married money.

George Cavendish's first wife, Alice Smith, was the daughter of a Suffolk neighbour who brought to her marriage a dowry of local land and property in Bedfordshire and Buckinghamshire. Three sons of the marriage survived: William, Thomas and George, the oldest of the brothers who – like his father before him – inherited the whole estate, after winning lawsuits brought against him by his dead mother's relations. His fortune was sufficient to maintain him in dignity for life. But he chose public service of a sort. In or about 1525, the year of his father's death, he became gentleman usher to Cardinal Thomas Wolsey, Archbishop of York, Lord Chancellor for life, twice Henry VIII's nominee for the papacy and the man who, above all others, made Tudor England a great power in the world. George Cavendish remained with Wolsey beyond the Cardinal's fall from royal grace in 1529. He was still in attendance when Wolsey died in Leicester in 1530 and he remained faithful to his old master's memory for the rest of his life. Immediately after Wolsey's death he was called before the Privy Council to confirm or deny rumours that the Cardinal's last words had been an incitement to treason. His answers were an object lesson in how to reconcile loyalty and self-preservation. 'My Lord of Norfolk spoke to me first . . . "How say ye it is reported that your master spoke certain words, even before his departure from this life; the truth whereof I doubt not ye know" . . . "Forsoot" quoth I. "I was so diligent attending more to the preservation of his life than I was to note and mark every word that he spake: and, sir, indeed he spoke many idle words, as men in such extremities do, the which I cannot now remember."[7]

Surprisingly for an inquisition which thought it worth exhuming the last words of a dying man, the equivocation was accepted as proof that Cavendish was a loyal servant of the King as well as true to the memory of his old master. In consequence, he was offered employment both by Henry VIII and the Duke of Norfolk. Both offers were declined. All he asked for was a horse and a cart in which he could carry his chattels back to Suffolk. By the King's command he was given six of the dead Cardinal's best horses, a wagon, 5 marks for his expenses, £10 for wages due and an ex gratia grant of £20.

The rest of his life was spent in quiet retirement – perhaps because he was out of sympathy with the King's refusal to accept the authority of the Pope. His second wife was the niece of Thomas More who, although once the obedient servant of Henry VIII, had opposed the King's determination to flout the judgment of Rome and marry Anne Boleyn. There is no evidence to suggest that she shared her uncle's view that King Henry could not – legally and legitimately – annul his marriage to Catherine of Aragon. But the fact that she knew and occasionally met More was enough to put her life and freedom in jeopardy. Cavendish passed his time writing a biography of Wolsey which – more because of fashion than prejudice – was not published for more than a century after it was completed and then only in garbled and compressed form. For years its provenance was disputed. Then, in 1814, the Reverend Joseph Hunter – an antiquarian most famous for his *History of Hallamshire* – pronounced in Cavendish's favour. His judgement was supported by Samuel Weller Singer, whose 1821 edition omitted a number of laudatory poems which Cavendish had added in an appendix. The preface explained why. 'It is to be regretted that [the] artless narrative of facts in prose should have evoked the muse [of verse] in vain.'

Whatever the quality of either the poetry or the prose, the biography leaves no doubt that George Cavendish remained devoted to his deposed and discredited master. His *Life of Cardinal Wolsey* is unstinting in its praise of a man who 'executed his office . . . so justly and exactly that he was held in great estimation'.[8] There are passages in which the encomium is slightly double-edged. 'In fullness of time he served all their turns, so they had their purposes and he had their good will.'[9]

But, surprising for an era in which past allegiances were rarely forgiven, his loyalty did not prejudice the new regime against him. Indeed it may have counted in his favour. For it is reasonable to suppose that it was thanks to him that, after Wolsey's fall, his brother William Cavendish was employed by Thomas Cromwell – Master of the Rolls, Keeper of the Privy Seals, Vicar General and, for almost ten years, after the King, the most powerful and feared man in England.

Unlike his brother, George, William Cavendish had neither attended Cambridge nor registered at Gray's Inn. Apart from that, nothing else is known about his life and work before 1531, the date in which he is first mentioned in Cromwell's papers.[10] A year later he was assisting Cromwell in the dissolution of the monasteries.

The process had begun long before Cromwell became the instrument of the King's greed. As early as the end of the fifteenth century Bishop Alcock of Ely had closed the nunnery of Saint Radegund in Cambridge, on grounds of the dissolute lifestyle of the sisters, and Bishop Fisher of Rochester had dissolved two Kentish houses for the same reason. The Saint Radegund building had become Jesus College and Bishop Fisher had spent the income from Kent on funding St John's College in the same city. But what had begun as a genuine reform became a method of financial royal expenditure, first in the reign of Henry VII and then, more extensively, in the interest of his son. Some of the money was put to good use. Wolsey, acting on the authority of a papal bull, dissolved a score of monasteries and used the money so acquired to build schools and colleges in Ipswich and Oxford. The pattern was firmly established with the closure of Christchurch in Aldgate.[11] But it was Cromwell who spread the process throughout the kingdom and diverted capital, endowments and revenue to the royal treasury. The surrender of the previous incumbents was accepted, on Thomas Cromwell's behalf, by William Cavendish.

In 1533, parliament created the Court of Augmentation to give the dissolution the trappings of legitimacy – usually by providing a pension for the monks and nuns while expropriating the monasteries and convents. Three years later William Cavendish became one of its auditors on a salary of £20 a year which was increased by the profit that he was allowed to make on the sale of the property. Most of his work was done in the Midlands and the Home Counties, though there were occasional excursions further afield. From time to time he sent accounts of his activities to the courts. They usually emphasised the difficulty of his work and the success with which his duties had been discharged. 'Saint Sepulchres of Canterbury' proved 'very arduous and painful to gather and receive.'[12] At Little Harlow the prioress took 'her discharge like a wise woman'.[13] But at Saint Albans the prior 'began to wax melancholy, saying that his friends counselled to die rather than to surrender'.[14] The godly man did not accept their advice. Instead he made an arrangement by which he leased most of the abbey to Cavendish and kept the rest – as his personal possession.

There is no doubt that William Cavendish exploited his position for personal gain, in a way which modern society would regard as corrupt. But in Tudor England such abuse was not so much accepted as expected, as long as the malfeasance remained within moderate limits. From time to time Cavendish was accused, with inconclusive results, of going too far – or allowing his greed to become too obvious. In 1533 Robert Farrington, a Cambridge scholar, complained that he had been cheated of 4 marks which were rightfully his due.[15] Five years later Cavendish was found to have accepted unauthorised gifts of plate from the Abbot of Merrivale, who hoped that what amounted to a bribe would guarantee that his abbey was not sequestrated. In the same year Cavendish was indicted for claiming unjustified expenses – the invoice for £34 16s 8d being 'written in his own hand and being without the knowledge of the clerks'.[16] He was excused the expenses fraud after making a humble apology and attributing the discrepancy to what he described as an error built on a misunderstanding. In 1540 he was judged to be 'guilty of malpractice during his audit at Darley, Pipewell, Merrivale, Lilleshall and Stafford'.[17] Once more, censure was not followed by punishment. By then he had achieved a status which guaranteed that he would be acquitted of all but the most serious indictment. He had evolved from auditor to henchman.

In the summer of 1538 he had arranged – by methods which he did not reveal to the court – for a Lincolnshire priest to give evidence in the trial of Henry Litherland, the Vicar of Newark. Litherland was convicted of treason and executed. Cavendish had exposed a traitor. A man who could perform such service to the Crown would not be prevented from acquiring valuable property – in the course of duty – on terms so favourable that the transaction amounted to theft. Cavendish was in an ideal position to gratify his passion for land. It is impossible to distinguish between those of his numerous land deals which were acquired honestly (at least by the standards of the time) and those which even Tudor England would have condemned as illegal. But many of the grants of local land which followed his official duties were authorised recompense for his success in filling the King's coffers.

In one way and another he acquired Northaw Manor in Hertfordshire[18] together with the associated properties including rectories in Cardigan and Berwick. That was no more than a beginning. By 1538 his inventory of property included the site of the Grey Friars monastery in Stafford, related premises in Stoke and, most significantly as it turned out, abbey granges in Lilleshall – where he had conducted an audit which was subsequently said to be corrupt. Apart from Henry VIII himself, the major benefactors of the dissolutions were the Talbots, the Russells and the Dorsets. But other families – less exalted in Tudor times – built their subsequent fame and fortune on the plunder of holy houses. Thanks to Sir William, the Cavendishes were among them.

Within two days in 1540, William Cavendish was dealt a double blow. Margaret, his wife, died on June 9 and on June 10 Thomas Cromwell was arrested. A bill of attainder – certifying that Cromwell had committed treason by promoting the marriage between Henry and Anne of Cleves – was passed on June 29 and he was executed a month later. William survived both tragedies with remarkable ease. Death was accepted with equanimity in sixteenth-century England. Close connection with a convicted traitor was less easily brushed aside. But Cavendish not only avoided banishment or imprisonment. He was promoted. In August, less than two months after Cromwell's death, he was appointed one of the three commissioners who were to support and assist the Lord Treasurer in Ireland. He was allowed 13s 4d a day for living expenses. The senior commissioner received 20s.

The commissioners were appointed to survey the King's land, to award portions of it as a sign of royal esteem (where appropriate and in anticipation of the Irish parliament being reconvened) and to advise on the possibility of reducing the number of Irish military garrisons. They were also charged with examining the accounts of Sir William Brabazon, the Vice-Treasurer, who was suspected of corruption beyond even the tolerance of the Tudor Court. Inevitably, their remit was extended to supervising the dissolution of the Irish monasteries. Anthony St Ledger, the Deputy of Ireland, told the King that 'Mr Cavendish took great pains in your said service . . . And I note him to be such a man who little feareth the displeasure of any man.'[19] Cavendish was also – despite the occasional discrepancies in his accounts, which were almost certainly not the result of incompetence – judged to be a man of precise intellect and careful judgement.

After three years of arduous and uncongenial labour – only interrupted by a brief return to England in 1541 during which Cavendish married his second wife, Elizabeth Parker of Pollingford in Suffolk – the two surviving Irish commissioners reported that their work was done. The Dublin parliament had met and declared Henry to be King of Ireland. Cavendish resumed work in the Office of Auditor in the Court of Augmentations, supervising the disposal of recently vacated monastic land and property. Then, in 1546 tragedy struck again. His second wife died in childbirth.

Once more personal grief was assuaged by professional success. An instruction to audit the monasteries in Boulogne was suddenly countermanded. Cavendish was immediately to become Treasurer of the Chamber – in effect managing the King's private accounts – on a salary of £100 a year, as much again in living expenses, £20 to pay clerks, £10 for boat hire (transport between the Tower of London and Hampton Court) and another £10 for office expansion. Equally important, in terms of both prestige and opportunities, he would become a figure in the Court of Henry VIII and would even occasionally attend meetings of the Privy Council itself.

Perhaps the demand that Cavendish should provide weekly statements of account was no more than good financial practice. But it is possible that he brought with him a reputation for dubious dealing. Whatever the reason, he was required to demonstrate his probity and efficiency. He responded in the grand manner by immediately preparing an hitherto unheard-of estimation of the office's overall financial position. Debts of £14,000 were outstanding, leaving him so short of funds that he would be able to discharge only the most pressing debts. A precise statement was impossible since his predecessor, who had not been given the account books, had bequeathed him records which were not up to date. The Privy Council was satisfied with the explanation and, as a matter of routine, issued him warrants to spend the King's money as he thought fit.

William Cavendish – one of the 'Gentlemen of Hertfordshire' who, in 1546, were chosen to attend the Admiral of France when he visited England – became a figure of consequence in Tudor England. His success, indeed his survival, was only partly attributed to his ruthless ambition and flexible principles. He was fortunate to be in the right places at the right times and his luck survived the death of Henry VIII in 1547. Cavendish remained – offices and prestige intact – in the service of the new King, Edward VI. All in all, it was an eventful year. In the notebook* in which he recorded both notable public and significant private events, he wrote: 'Memorandum. That i was married unto Elizabeth Hardwick, my third wife, in Leicestershire at Bradgate House, the 20th of August in the first year of King Edward 6 at 2 of the clock after midnight, the domynical letter B†.'

---

* The notebook was lost. It was last seen in Welbeck Abbey in 1946.
† The letter – related to the date on which the first Sunday in January fell – was used in church calendars.

CHAPTER 2

Four Weddings and . . .

Elizabeth Barlow – Bess of Hardwick – was the daughter of John Hardwick, a Derbyshire yeoman who farmed 450 acres in his native county and earned rent for another 100 acres in Lincolnshire.[1] His ancestors had inhabited the Hardwick area since the end of the fourteenth century as tenants of the Savages of Stainsbury to whom they were probably related by marriage. They lived in a large farmhouse that was protected, on one side, by a sheer drop down to the River Doe Lea. With the passage of the years, it came to be called Hardwick Hall. The Hardwicks – John and his wife, born Elizabeth Leake of nearby Haslam – had four daughters and a son. Sources disagree about when their daughter Elizabeth was born. The evidence points to sometime between February 1521 and May 1522*. Her only brother, James, was born in 1526 and was barely a year old when his father died at the age of forty-one. In consequence the whole family was the object of attention from the Office of Wards.

Henry VII had devised an ingenious way of raising revenue which Henry VIII implemented with undisguised enthusiasm. The gentlemen of England were required to place themselves at the service of their sovereign when the safety of the realm was threatened. Anyone unpatriotic enough to inherit a family estate before he was old enough to bear arms had to compensate for the gap which his infancy left in the line of battle. The compensation was the contribution of some of his inheritance towards the upkeep of the royal household. John Hardwick married late in life and – on the reasonable assumption that he would die before his son came of age – determined to frustrate the Tudor laws of inheritance. He left all his land and property in the hands of a trust which was to administer the estate for the twenty years before James, his son, came of age. Meanwhile, the income was to be used for the benefit of his widow and the welfare of his children with suitable dowries (between 40 and 60 marks [£30 to £40]) being provided for each of his daughters. That, he felt certain, would be enough to find them husbands 'of a middling sort'.[2]

---

*The conclusion of the latest research by Philip Ridden of Nottingham University.

The whole arrangement was so obviously a contrivance that it is hard to imagine why John Hardwick believed that it would be allowed to stand. But, initially, it was. The legal system of the day required that an Inquisition Post Mortem enquired into the nature, and general purposes, of the trust. Surprisingly it found the arrangement a legitimate attempt efficiently to manage Hardwick's legacy rather than a contrivance to avoid (or even evade) paying the King his rightful dues. Unfortunately for the Hardwick family, the Office of Wards was not so easily convinced. It insisted that the Feodracy – its investigative arm – re-examine the case. Three commissioners were appointed.

> Henry VIII by Grace of God, King of England and France, defender of the faith and Lord of Ireland to his beloved and faithful John Gyfford and his beloved John Vernon Esquire and Anthony Babbington esquire, greetings . . . Know that we have assigned to you . . . to enquire by the oath of true men of Derby . . . by whom the truth of the matter can be better known, what lands and tenements John Hardwick of Hardwyke Hall deceased . . . held both in demand and in service in the county aforesaid on the day which the same John Hardwyck died.[3]

Two of the commissioners, John Vernon of Haddon Hall and Anthony Babbington, were friends and neighbours. That may account for the length of time which the deliberations took and for the acceptance, in evidence, of clearly bogus claims about John Hardwick's having disposed of his property long before he died. John Hardwick had failed to sign all the necessary documents.[4] But, even had the formalities been observed, the case would have gone against him. Whatever their inclinations, the commission had no choice but to conclude that his estate had, in effect, passed into the possession of his only son, an infant, and was, in consequence, forfeit to the Crown.

The surveyor, who was employed by the Commission, estimated that the value of the contested property was £20 a year. No doubt influenced by the members who were John Hardwick's friends, he recommended that the widow be treated leniently. The Office of Wards decided that a quarter of the legacy was to be used as a jointure for Amy Racheford – a young lady whose *locus standi* remains a mystery. John Bugby, a courtier with the title 'Officer of the Pantry', bought another quarter for £20 which was to be paid to the Crown in three annual instalments. He was also granted the wardship of the Hardwick daughters, an obligation which carried with it the right to profit from their marriage settlements. Half of the land – including Hardwick Hall – was kept in the King's possession. Elizabeth continued to live in the Hall – either by grace and favour or on payment of a peppercorn rent – and rented back half of what had been her land from the Office of Wards.[5] Nobody was satisfied with the outcome. According to John Bugby – who made an official complaint to the commission – John Lecke and Henry Marmyon (the two original executors of John Hardwick's will) had reacted to their exclusion from its bequests by attacking Hardwick Hall and breaking all its windows.[6] The story was a malicious invention.

Infant destitution is one of the myths which helped to create the legend that still surrounds Bess. During the years which followed the death of her first husband, Elizabeth Hardwick (née Leake) – Bess's mother – did not live in grinding poverty. But both her income and her place in society substantially deteriorated. The only way to improve her circumstances was to remarry. Unhappily the man she chose – or the only husband available – was Ralph Leche, the younger son of the Leches of nearby Chatsworth. Leche's father – also Ralph – was, or was about to become, a man of substance. He had negotiated land sales with Thomas Cromwell on behalf of Derbyshire smallholders and had acted as agent for the Earl of Shrewsbury during the purchase of additions to his family's property. In 1535 he was appointed 'a commissioner to enquire into the spirituality of the county [of Derbyshire] recently transferred from Pope to King'.[7] But the younger Ralph – either because of a temporary change in political fashion or his father's parsimony – had nothing to contribute to the marriage except an annuity (variously estimated at £6 13s 4d and £10 13s 4d a year) and the income from some scattered lands in the south of Derbyshire. Imprisoned for debt in 1538 and 1544, he died in 1549.[8]

According to Elizabeth, Leche deserted her and her children. Whether or not that complaint was justified, he certainly failed to provide the security which his union with Elizabeth was supposed to bring. In consequence, Bess – his stepdaughter – was brought up in an atmosphere of regret and resentment that the family's right to place and property had somehow been snatched away. No doubt that contributed to the creation of what one of her detractors called 'a woman of masculine understanding and conduct'.[9] It certainly made her mother and stepfather eager to find her a suitable husband. Bess was still young when, in the spring of 1543, she was betrothed to thirteen-year-old Robert Barlow* – the son of a close neighbour, a distant relative, and a young man of substantial means.

The evidence suggests that Bess was motivated by neither love nor the need for security but pity. Nathaniel Johnson, the seventeenth-century

---

* Some contemporary papers refer to him as Barley.

Yorkshire antiquarian, wrote that he was 'told by some ancient gentleman [that] Mr Barlow lay sick of a Chronic Distemper. In which time this young gentlewoman, making many visits upon account of them being neighbourhood in the country and out of kindness to him being very solicitous to afford him all the help she was able to do him in his sickness, ordering his diet and being then young and handsome he fell in love with her.'[10] The circumstances of their meeting, if not the nature of her affection, is not in doubt. Bess met Robert Barlow when she was in service – part maid and part lady-in-waiting – either in the household of Frances Grey, wife of the Marquis of Dorset, or 'in London attending Lady Zouche'. Both women were Bess's distant relatives.

There followed, on April 24 1543, one of the unconsummated adolescent marriages by which the Tudor aristocracy secured advantageous alliances – leaving the 'bedding' to follow when the happy couple reached a suitable age. So the wooing and wedding may not have been as romantic as Johnson's account suggest. And the antiquarian slightly spoilt his own story – and provided evidence to support the sceptics – by repeating an unsubstantiated allegation made a century earlier. 'She took such advantage of [Barlow's] great affection for her that, for lack of issue by her, he settled a large inheritance of land upon herself and her heirs, by which his death in a short time after, she fully enjoyed.'[11] But whether Bess's intention was to exploit or comfort Barlow their union constituted the first episode in a matrimonial saga in which Bess is represented as always marrying for money rather than love. Horace Walpole even presumed to describe the attribute which enabled her to profit from each marriage.

> Four times the nuptial bed she warmed,
> And every time so well performed,
> That when death spoiled each Husband's billing,
> He left the widow every shilling.

Tudor portraits are notoriously unflattering. So the earliest known likeness of Bess, painted in about 1560* when she was in her mid-thirties, may do her less than justice. But it certainly does not suggest that – even at the time of her first marriage – she was a ravishing beauty. In so much as appearance is an indication of character, it confirms her reputation as a woman of single-minded determination and iron will – not attributes which the Tudor gentry always found

---

* It is still to be seen in Hardwick Hall.

attractive in women. The portrait does reveal, beyond doubt, the extent of her aspiration. She is dressed, quite literally, like a queen – black velvet gown, lined with fur and decorated with pearls. Whatever attracted Barlow to Bess and Bess to him, the importance of the marriage is clear. It was the first of Bess's great matrimonial leaps from obscurity on a modest income to the fame and wealth which made her, after Queen Elizabeth, the greatest lady in all England.

Barlow was denied the opportunity to advance his bride towards the status which she was determined to achieve. He died on December 19 1544. The right to inherit what money Robert Barlow had left was put in doubt by his early death. He was still a minor and his father was still alive. So for the second time in her young life, Bess's prospects were in jeopardy of forfeit to the Office of Wards – or the Court of Wards as it had become. And a second possible impediment imperilled her inheritance. According to the Duchess of Newcastle, wife of Bess's grandson, Barlow had 'died before they were bedded together, they both being very young'. If that was so, Bess's inheritance rights were extinguished by the fact that the marriage – not being consummated – was a fiction. Bess was in good company. The arguments which ended in the Reformation turned on the same point. If Prince Arthur – the eldest son of Henry VII who died in youth before he succeeded to the throne – had failed to consummate his marriage to Catherine of Aragon, there was no impediment to her becoming his brother's wife and Queen to Henry VIII. But if, in his own coarse words, Arthur had 'spent the [wedding] night in Aragon' the marriage was invalid and Anne Boleyn was the true Queen of England.

Virgin or not, Bess claimed a 'widow's dower' – one third of the income which was earned by her late husband's estate. The Barlow family and Sir Peter Frecheville of Stavely – who had bought the wardship of George Barlow, Robert's twelve-year-old brother and natural heir – contested her claim. Bess – in her seventeenth year – began the first of the long, numerous and complicated legal actions which were to be a feature of her life. No doubt with the help of her mother – who had already suffered at the hands of the Office of Wards – she took her case to court. Frecheville argued first on a point of law (probably that the marriage was never consummated) that Bess had no entitlement. Then he claimed that part of the rent, included in Bess's demands, was for property leased, rather than owned, by the Barlow family. The case dragged on.

In the autumn of 1545, Frecheville offered a compromise – 'a small recompense . . . at his pleasure',[12] subject to Bess's undertaking to abandon all other claims on the Barlow property. The widow – impelled by desperate need rather than satisfaction – was at first inclined to accept. But her resentment at what she thought an injustice was strong enough to make her, on second thoughts, decide to fight rather than compromise. So the adjudication was left to the court. Bess won. She was awarded 'the third part of the manor of Barlow with 80 messuages [houses], 7 cottages, 880 acres of land, 260 acres of meadows, 550 acres of pasture, 320 acres of woods, 400 acres of furze and heath and £8.10.0 rent with appertances and sundry properties in the villages of Barley, Barley Lees, Dronfield and Hulmfield'.[13] It was not the fortune that a recital of the judgment suggests. But it did provide an income of about £30 a year. The settlement left Bess secure though not prosperous, but she chose again to become a 'gentlewoman' in a noble house. She joined the household of Henry Grey, the Marquis of Dorset, at Bradgate House. If she went into service with the object of meeting a man who would make a suitable husband, her plan succeeded. At Bradgate she met William Cavendish. Knighted and made a member of the Privy Council by Henry VIII, he had been promoted from the Court of Augmentation to become Treasurer of the King's Chamber – a more remunerative as well as a more distinguished position for which he had paid the King £1,000. And he had retained, under Edward VI, all the offices which he had been granted by Henry VIII. So, despite the discrepancy in ages – she was twenty and he was forty-two – Sir William was an attractive proposition to a young woman who was looking for status and security and he, 'being somewhat advanced in years', married Bess 'chiefly for her beauty'. To dispute that judgement is not to denigrate Bess's real, if unconventional, charm. And there is no other plausible explanation of their mutual attraction. Whatever it was that brought them together, Bess and Sir William were married at Bradgate in 1547, eight months after the death of Henry VIII.

Initially the Cavendishes lived in Sir William's increasingly dilapidated Northaw Manor in Hertfordshire and his London house in Newgate Street to the north of the old Saint Paul's Cathedral. From the start they meant to move up in the world. Their financial and social progress was meticulously recorded in Sir William's lost notebook and can be judged by the godparents who graced the christenings which were a regular feature of their lives. In 1548, ten months after the marriage, 'Frances, my 9th child and the first by the said woman was born on Monday between the hours of 3 and 4 at afternoons viz 18 June Anno 2 R[ex] E[dward] 6. The dominical letter G.' The principal godmother was Lady Frances Grey – the daughter of the late Charles Brandon, Duke of Suffolk, and his wife Princess Mary, favourite sister of the late King Henry VIII after whom, despite a period of estrangement, he had named the *Mary Rose*. The principal godfather was the new Duke of Suffolk, Brandon's thirteen-year-old son. In 1544, Elizabeth Barlow, née Hardwick, was the widow of a Derbyshire yeoman who had not, at his death, come of age. Four years later, her daughter's godmother was, albeit distantly, in line of succession to the thrones of England and France.

Bess's second daughter, Temperance, was born a year later. She died in infancy – but not before she had been baptised in the presence of godparents who were as least as illustrious as those who had attended her sister's christening. They were the Countess of Warwick, whose son was to marry Lady Jane Grey (the reluctant claimant to Queen Mary Tudor's throne), and the Earl of Shrewsbury. But their eminence was nothing as compared with the distinction of the godparents who, in 1550, witnessed the baptism of Henry, the first Cavendish son. The Earl of Warwick was joined by the Duke of Suffolk and the Princess Elizabeth – while her brother Edward and sister Mary lived childless, third in line to the throne of England. William, the Cavendishes' second son, boasted almost as illustrious godparents as his older brother. William Paulet (the Lord Treasurer), the Countess of Northampton and the Earl of Pembroke all swore to bring him up in the true Christian religion.

At the start of their marriage, Bess and William Cavendish – although lavish spenders as their place in society required – lived well within their means. Their annual income included rents worth £250, annuities of £400 and favours of one sort or another which were sold for a, not unnaturally, undisclosed sum. Their total expenditure was £340.[14] So, for a while, they lived in prudent affluence. Their income grew as Bess took increasing charge of the Northaw estate and, as a first step to improving its efficiency, enclosed what had previously been common land. But so did their expenditure. London was full of strange delights – including exotic foods – that Bess had not previously experienced. And her husband came to believe that conspicuous consumption was essential to the preservation of his status.

It was not, however, an attempt to economise which prompted the decision to leave Northaw Manor and Hertfordshire in favour of Derbyshire. Nor was it, as romantics have suggested, purely the result of the young wife's longing for home and her elderly and indulgent husband's reluctance to frustrate her hopes. It was political prudence that made them move to the then wild and remote Peak. From the beginning of the sickly King Edward's reign, it was clear that Catholic Mary would one day inherit the throne and no one knew how determined she would be to impose the 'true religion' on England. But there was always the fear – as her succession grew more certain – that, even if she forgave the part that Cavendish had played in the despoliation of the religious houses, there would be fanatics at her court who were still looking for heretics to burn. Derbyshire was first a refuge and then the hope of permanent stability and security.

On June 30 1549, Sir William Cavendish bought the manor of Chatsworth from Thomas Agard at a bargain price. Two years earlier, Agard had bought the house from Francis Leche, nephew of Bess's stepfather, Ralph Leche, and husband of her sister Alice. Francis Leche had discovered that his wife was unfaithful and had sold the property, for virtually nothing, in order to avoid its being inherited by sons who, he suspected, were not his. He then changed his mind and claimed that the sale was invalid. The legal dispute which followed further depressed the price. Of course Bess – shrewd beyond her years – knew the financial consequences of her sister's conduct. Agard's son, who was short of capital, was forced to sell the property. On his wife's advice Sir William made a derisory offer. It was accepted.

The £600 purchase included, as well as Chatsworth itself, several nearby manors, land in the associated parishes and substantial acres in Repton and the Trent Valley.[15] It was the first episode in what, for Sir William and his wife, was an orgy of acquisition. Early in 1550 they bought the manor of Ashford in the Wye Valley and the rectory at Edensor – both only a few miles from Chatsworth. In June 1552 Northaw Manor itself and all the Cavendish land in Hertfordshire, Middlesex, Wales and East Anglia was exchanged with King Edward for four principal estates and four smaller properties in Derbyshire including Doveridge and Meadowpleck. The deal also brought them land as far away as Devon. But Derbyshire had become their kingdom.

King Edward VI died in 1553 and Mary Tudor became Queen of England. Within weeks of her accession, a rebellion was raised in the name of Lady Jane Grey and the Protestant faith. It was the product of frustrated ambition. For years the Grey family had hoped that their daughter Jane would marry the young King. But as his health deteriorated and it became clear that he would not long survive, they conspired with the Duke of Northumberland in a plot for the studious and innocent sixteen-year-old Jane to usurp the throne. Her tenuous claim to the succession – great-granddaughter of Henry VII and Edward's cousin – was reinforced when the enfeebled Edward was persuaded to nominate her as his successor. In May 1553, in preparation for her accession, Jane was married to Guildford Dudley, Northumberland's youngest son, with the intention that he would rule the kingdom in his wife's name. Two months later Edward died and Jane – with the endorsement of the Protestant faction at Court – was proclaimed Queen of England. She reigned for nine days.

Mary, supported by her sister Elizabeth and 'innumerable companies of common folk',[16] rallied her forces in East Anglia and marched on London. As Northumberland led Jane's army out of London to meet them, he passed Northaw Manor, once the home of the resolutely Protestant Sir William Cavendish – a friend of the Greys and father of Northumberland's godson. Even though he was in Derbyshire – far away from the turmoil of near civil war – Cavendish must have feared that the doomed rebellion marked the end of his pomp and prosperity. He had inherited a £200 legacy from Edward VI, a sure sign that he was close to the men who had surrounded the young Protestant King – many of whom favoured Jane Grey and were ready to fight for her. Although he had played no part in the plot (and there was no evidence to suggest that his Protestant friends had even asked him to do so) he was associated with its perpetrators. And the part that he had played in the dissolution of the monasteries and the confiscation of their properties – some of which he had subsequently acquired – was, in itself, enough to put his life and liberty in danger. A purge of Jane Grey's sympathisers might well have led him to the Tower and the block.

Cavendish decided his only hope lay in proving that he had been loyal to Queen Mary when her future was in doubt – even though he cannot have had much hope that his stratagem would succeed. So, despite the absence of supporting evidence, he announced that he had spent £700 in raising a band of fighting men to help in the defeat of the usurper, Jane. And, against all probabilities, the Queen believed him. He was reappointed Treasurer of the Chamber. Even more surprisingly, six months after the rebellion – when Charles (his third son) was born – Queen Mary agreed to become the boy's godmother. The price that Cavendish paid for the unexpected honour was apostasy. The child was baptised according to the rites of the Catholic Church. No doubt Mary thought that the christening was a sign of repentance. In fact it was no more than proof of Sir William's will to survive at any cost.

Although the Cavendishes were secure in Queen Mary's affection, they remained committed to Derbyshire. They bought more local land in Baslow and Beeley and although they sold property in Gridlow, Goatscliffe and Youlgreave, Sir William – by then a Justice of the Peace – had become a figure in the county. Keeping up appearances at Chatsworth – with some time spent in London – proved more expensive than life divided between London and Northaw. Bess's account book for eleven weeks, in late 1555, shows that, in addition to wages and household expenditure, Sir William spent £352. One grocery bill – from Robert Harrison for 'all thynges from the begynynge of the world to thys day' – came to £6 11s 10d.[17] Annual expenditure amounted to £2,000 a year – not allowing for increased gambling losses which were the inevitable result of Sir William's association with the aristocracy. But the greatest expenditure was incurred by the passion which earned Lady Cavendish the sobriquet of 'Building Bess'. It was an obsession which she shared with her husband. During his lifetime, Sir William was an enthusiastic partner in the enterprise which came to be an essential part of creating the Cavendish dynasty – the building, and constant rebuilding, of Chatsworth House.

Little is known of the original building apart from its location on the hill above the then turbulent waters of the Derwent. The Cavendishes built on the same site. They began work during December 1551 when Roger Worde, a master mason, was paid 20 shillings to design a new house.[18] It was not finished for almost fifty years. What came to be called Elizabethan Chatsworth was drawn, in some detail, during 1699, in preparation for the first Duke of Devonshire's major rebuilding. It was a 'tall square structure . . . of a surprising height' with four – or, in places, five – storeys enclosing a courtyard.[19] 'At each of its corners was a large square turret . . . An impression of severity . . . was further emphasised by a heavy breastwork of massive towers in the foreground.' Although 'forbidding of aspect',[20] it was clearly intended to be more a palace than a fortress. In 1555 Cavendish wrote to John Thynne – owner and builder of Longleat – asking for the loan of his 'connynge plaisterer . . . which hath in your hall made diverse pendents and other pretty things' and added, in a note of clear impatience, that his own hall was 'yet unmade'.[21] While the work was still going on, he and Bess began to furnish the house with a splendour which they thought appropriate to their undeniably improving social position.

Seven large symmetrical ponds were dug in the land by which the house was surrounded. Their main purpose was drainage. But they were decorated with arched bridges and fountains and, on an island in one of them, what is now called Queen Mary's Bower was built. Together with the Stand (or Hunting Tower as it became known) it was, for many years, regarded as a relic of Elizabethan Chatsworth. It is now accepted as a Victorian folly.

Sir William's success – indeed his survival – during the reign of 'Bloody Mary' can be attributed to a combination of cunning and competence. Yet, although for most of his career he was regarded as a loyal, efficient and conscientious public servant, he ended his life submerged in the suspicion of corruption and allegations of incompetence. In the summer of 1557 Queen Mary – determined to send troops to reinforce her husband Philip of Spain in his war against France – demanded that every department of state made savings and that the money which was pared from their budget be contributed to the cost of the expedition. That led to an unexpected audit of Sir William's account books. When the Privy Chamber ledgers were examined, it was discovered that he had not issued, or even prepared, a formal statement of accounts 'for his entire period of office from February 1546 until . . . 1557, both as Treasurer of the Chamber and a member of the Court of General Surveyors'. He was accused of using public money for private purposes, told to account for the £5,237 5s 0¼d which was missing from the royal coffers and instructed that from then on his books would be subject to regular audit.

It took six months for the books to be examined fully and returned to Cavendish.[22] They were accompanied by a claim for the return of the money (which the auditors alleged he owed the Crown) and an instruction to attend the Privy Council to account for his actions and hear its adjudication on how the matter was to be resolved. His claim that he was too ill to attend the Council in person was almost certainly genuine and accepted as such by his inquisitors. An almost immediate amendment to the injunction gave permission for a clerk to represent him at the proposed tribunal – a strong indication that Cavendish would escape the severe punishment that he might have expected. But, although he was not to lose his head, it seemed probable that he would lose his job and possible that he would lose most of his possessions. On October 12 Robert Bestnay, his secretary, accompanied by two clerks, delivered what must have been a hurried response to the charges. It was impossible to deny that the books did not balance, but Bestnay insisted that the blame lay elsewhere. So he read out a plea from his master for royal forgiveness. 'I . . . humbly beseech Her Majesty, pitying my condition . . . to pardon and allow all things.' He had been 'most truly deceived to [his] great grief'. So to 'Her Majesty's merciful consideration' he humbly submitted himself. Were Queen Mary's grace not to be bestowed upon him his whole family, including his 'innocent children', would be 'utterly undone and like to end [their] days in no small penury'.[23]

An inventory of detailed excuses followed. Thomas Knot, a clerk who had been inherited from his predecessor (but had remained in his service), had absconded leaving debts of £1,200 and taking £500 with him. Warwick (by then executed for high treason despite abandoning

Jane and denouncing her as a traitor) had, on the unlawful accession of his daughter-in-law, prevented him from entering his office. He had lent money to sundry other servants of Henry VIII, Edward VI and the Queen herself, none of which had been repaid. The list went on and on until it concluded with what he clearly thought would guarantee a sympathetic response – the details of the expense which he had gladly incurred in raising a battalion of troops to fight for the Queen during her brief usurpation by Lady Jane Grey.

Sir William did not live to hear the Privy Council's response. He died, aged fifty-two, in London on October 25 1557. Although, surprisingly, he had made no will, six months before his death he had put all his Derbyshire lands in trust for the use of himself and his wife in their lifetimes before being passed on, in various portions, to his children. Thus the Office of Wards had no dominion. But, although his land and property were worth more than he claimed in his submission to the Privy Council, Bess – with six children of her own and two stepchildren, all under age – was not left a fortune. And the Privy Council required her to repay what her husband, as a result of corruption or incompetence, owed to the sovereign.

A bill requiring the repayment of all debts to the Crown was introduced into parliament in January 1558. It passed all its stages in the House of Lords and was given a Second Reading in the Commons. Bess – warning that, if it became law, it would 'not only undo me and my poor children but a great number of others'24 – in her attempts to have it annulled was assisted by Sir John Thynne of Longleat. The extent of his intervention is not known. But in March, Queen Mary – probably more anxious to protect her debtor friends than penalise her duplicitous servants – ordered that the bill be abandoned. A similar bill was put to parliament in March 1559. It made the same progress and met the same fate. So the threat of immediate ruin was averted. But by then the world had changed. Elizabeth had succeeded her sister on the throne of England and Bess of Hardwick had married for the third time.

Both changes – royal and matrimonial – worked to Bess's immense advantage. Elizabeth remembered that while still a princess with an uncertain future she had been invited to serve as godmother to one of Bess's sons. The circle within which Bess and her second husband had moved firmly linked the Cavendishes to the Protestant cause, allowing the brief obeisance to Catholicism to be accepted as an expedient rather than an expression of genuine doubt about the Reformation. But it is easier to understand why Bess wanted to be at Court than it is to imagine why the Queen chose to bestow favours on the widow of a minor official – particularly one who was still burdened with the debt incurred by her dead husband's mismanagement of his office. The answer that commends itself to the romantic historians is that the attraction of Bess's personality transcended all other considerations. It is much more likely that Bess benefited from Elizabeth's notorious weakness for flattery. Whatever the cause of Elizabeth's patronage, there is no doubt that her protégée worked to maintain it with single-minded determination.

Bess was again living beyond her means. In the year that followed her second husband's death, she enjoyed an income of £300 a year from rents alone – considerably more than her living expenses. But she also had debts to the Crown of £5,000.[25] That was, in itself, a reason for continuing her life at Court. Proximity to the Queen would be enough to protect her from being pauperised by enforced repayment. And Bess had special additional reasons for welcoming the chance to establish herself in the higher reaches of society. It was a prospect which would have commended itself to any impecunious (and comparatively young) widow of her time. Life in society offered the hope of finding a husband who would enable her to take the next step towards the status for which she craved. During her second matrimonial fishing trip Bess caught Sir William St Loe, Chief Butler of England and Captain of the Queen's Yeomen Guard. Lady Cavendish became Lady St Loe in the autumn of 1559.

William St Loe was a professional soldier who had made his name in Ireland. In 1548 he been appointed Lieutenant of the King's Forts in Leinster and had discharged his duties with such distinction that, at the age of twenty-eight, he was knighted and granted an annuity of £40. In 1553, he became Keeper of the Horse to Edward VI and, after the death of the King, served as Gentleman Attendant to Princess Elizabeth. His association with the Protestant cause was so close that in 1554 he had been accused of complicity in Thomas Wyatt's rebellion against Queen Mary – the last folly of the conspirators who had plotted to make Lady Jane Grey queen. He was imprisoned in the Tower along with the Princess Elizabeth herself and was, no doubt, fearful – as she must have been – that he would follow Jane Grey to the block. 'The Nine Day Queen' had been spared execution when her father-in-law was beheaded. But Wyatt's abortive rising had convinced Mary that, while Jane lived, she would remain the pretender around whom the Protestants rallied. Elizabeth was released into house arrest after eight weeks, but St Loe spent four months in the Tower and seven in the Fleet Prison before he was paroled on 'oath of good bearing' and on the payment of a £200 fine. The experience bound him to the Princess Elizabeth with the bonds of mutual fear and suffering.

In November 1558, when Mary Tudor died, St Loe was called back into the service of Elizabeth and became an obvious candidate for preferment in a Court which had to be purged of men who had supported Mary, Catholicism and Spain. As Chief Butler of England, St Loe did little more than perform the occasional ceremonial duty and supervise the royal cellar. But as the Captain of the Guard, he was the protector of Queen Elizabeth's life and safety. Elizabeth must have trusted him completely. And she expressed her confidence in material terms. St Loe was granted a life annuity of 100 marks, 50 marks a year payable from customs dues, various wardships and gifts of land. Bess's third marriage confirmed both her prosperity and her place in the heart of Elizabethan England.

The betrothal of Sir William St Loe and Lady Cavendish was announced in July 1559 and the marriage took place on August 27 – a date chosen by the Queen as a sign of her patronage and approval. The groom was a widower of forty and on the death of his father in the previous year, he had become a comparatively rich man. All Bess had to set against St Loe's wealth and guaranteed income was the rents she received from the heavily encumbered Chatsworth estate and debts to the Crown of £5,000. Materially, as well as in terms of status, Bess got the better of the bargain. In consequence of their marriage. Bess became a Lady of the Privy Chamber – probably as a wedding gift from the Queen – and acquired more stepchildren. St Loe had two, as yet unmarried, daughters.

The St Loes might have become a happy family had not St Loe been suddenly indicted in the Exchequer Chamber – unaccountably along with his wife – on the charge of withholding money from the Treasury.[26] Such changes in fortune were common in Elizabethan England. So were sudden pardons – one of which the Queen granted St Loe on the payment of £1,000. On the evidence of his three surviving letters to his wife – written to his 'own sweet Bess' when, to his regret, court duties kept them apart – he would have gladly have paid ten times as much to avoid a prison sentence which denied him the pleasure of her company. In February 1560 he nearly lost her for ever.

Sir William St Loe's brother, Edward, was certainly disreputable and dishonest and probably guilty of a series of murders which he had committed in the hope of financial gain. In 1558, he had married Bridget Scutt, the second wife and widow of a tailor to Henry VIII. The wedding to St Loe had taken place barely a month after the death of the bride's first husband. Doubts about his probity increased with the discovery that he had spent the four weeks between funeral and marriage buying his bride's inherited property at discretionary prices.

The revelation that Bridget was three months pregnant with Edward's child added to the suspicion that Scutt had been poisoned by his wife or her lover. Six weeks after her second marriage, Bridget herself died – in the words of Sir William St Loe, before her time – meaning that the unborn child died too. Edward remained single, though not celibate, for six months. Then he married Margaret, the daughter of Bridget Scutt's first marriage.

Sir John St Loe – the head of the family – was disgusted by his son's behaviour and virtually disinherited him. After his father's death, Edward contested the will with the claim that Sutton Court, the ancestral home, had been promised to his wife for her lifetime. In an attempt to avoid an internecine lawsuit, Sir William St Loe – to whom the house had been bequeathed – offered his brother the Sutton Court stewardship with residential rights for life. Edward accepted the offer and visited his brother in London in order, he said, to pay his respects to Bess, the new Lady St Loe. On the day after he left, Bess was taken ill. The symptoms suggested poisoning and a suitable remedy was applied and proved successful. Enquiries at the house in which Edward had stayed identified a 'conjuror and magician' who, together with a distant St Loe cousin, was held exclusively responsible. Edward St Loe escaped even censure.

Although Sir William and Lady St Loe were said to be devoted to each other, circumstances forced them to spend much of their lives apart. The Queen was unyielding in her demands that courtiers should be at court whether it sat in London, Windsor or Oxford – though she seemed more reluctant to lose the company of men than women. Bess was equally obdurate in her determination to spend her time in Derbyshire supervising the building work at Chatsworth rather than supporting her husband in his official duties. Occasionally she made the journey to London, but her letters leave no doubt that she was more unhappy about leaving the house than she was about being separated from her husband. When she was away, her steward was bombarded with instructions. Work had to be completed on time. 'As for the other mason . . . if he will not apply his work, you know he is no meet man for me.' Bills must be paid promptly but carefully checked. 'If he do tell you that he is any penny behind for work done . . . he doth lie like a false knave.'[27] Completing the new Chatsworth had become such an all-absorbing obsession that, when she was there, she could spare no time for writing to her husband and a servant was deputed to send him news of life in Derbyshire. St Loe was desolate. 'My own, more dearer to me than I am myself. Understand it is no small fear or grief to me . . . my continual nightly dreams, besides my absence hath troubled me, but chiefly that Hugh Alsop cannot satisfy me in what estate thou or thine is. Therefore I pray thee, as thou dost love me, let me shortly hear from thee.'[28]

The constant protestations of affection were reinforced by a more tangible expression of the love that lasts beyond the grave. In December 1564, Sir William St Loe was suddenly taken ill. Bess, at Chatsworth, rushed south. He died before they were reunited – leaving only his will as consolation. 'In consideration of the natural affection, mutual love and assured good will which I have ever perceived and found in my entirely beloved wife . . . I do give and bequeath to her . . . all manner [of] my leases, farms, plate, jewels, hangings, implements of household, debts, goods and chattels, whatever, to have, hold, use and enjoy to her own proper use and behalf.'[29] To reinforce his wife's sole claim on his estate – an extraordinary arrangement in Tudor England – St Loe made Bess his sole executor, stipulated that after her death what was left of his bequest was for 'her heirs forever' and, to protect her against all possible challenge, also gave her, post mortem, all he owned by deed of gift. The wisdom of what might have seemed an unnecessary precaution was made clear by the discovery that Edward St Loe had nursed his brother during the last days of Sir William's fatal illness.

The immediate assumption was that Sir William had been poisoned. Although nothing could be proved, the suspicions were increased when Edward claimed that, shortly before his death, Sir William had given him 'a lifetime interest' in Sutton Court and that he possessed an indenture confirming the gift. The possible loss of Sutton Court – already in Edward's possession through the grant of stewardship – could be contested at leisure. The more immediate concern was the news that Margaret Norton – St Loe's younger daughter by his first marriage – was contesting the whole will. The Court of Probate dismissed her claim. But, although Bess's finances were secure, her reputation had suffered permanent damage. She had become the scheming widow who denied her late husband's daughters the legacy which they had the moral, if not the legal, right to expect. Whatever the merits of the complaints against Bess, they coloured, for ever, the assessment of her character. And her fourth marriage – both its circumstances and its progress – was taken to confirm her grasping nature and her belief that love was less important than land and the creation of a dynasty more important than a happy family.

Bess spent most of 1565 at Chatsworth, to which she proposed to add a third floor of state rooms. By then she was in possession of a substantial fortune, made up of the Cavendish and St Loe inheritances and, though it provided only a fraction of her income, her widow's dower from the Barlow family. Her three sons were at Eton and her eldest daughter was married. Only Elizabeth, aged ten, and Mary, aged nine, were still at home. She had a place at Court and influential friends. There was no need to look for a wealthy husband. She had become a catch in her own right. But, when she returned to London in August 1566, there was already talk of an impending marriage. At first the gossip nominated Henry Cobham – the brother-in-law of Bess's best friend. Then it was rumoured that 'either Lord Darcy or Sir John Thynne shall marry my Lady St Loe'.[30] The gossips were wrong. Some time between early February and late March 1568, Bess married George Talbot, the Sixth Earl of Shrewsbury.

Bess and Shrewsbury had known each other for years. Sheffield Castle, Shrewsbury's home, was 15 miles from Chatsworth and, although his family (the Talbots) and hers (the Barlows) were divided by rank and wealth, they were inevitably linked by the sale of land, one to the other, and when marriage to Sir William Cavendish had improved Bess's social standing, Shrewsbury had been godfather to their daughter, Temperance. Shrewsbury's first wife, the daughter of the Earl of Rutland to whom he had been betrothed when he was eleven, had died in early 1567. It had been a dynastic marriage designed to bring together vast tracts of the Midlands. Much of Bess's estate was similarly adjacent to Shrewsbury land and the chance to extend his domain must have been near to irresistible. Bess, on the other hand, was acquiring further status. Shrewsbury offered her the prospect of advancement into the ancient aristocracy. No woman with an insatiable desire to rise could possibly have rebuffed his proposal. At first, as their letters show, there was a genuine mutual attraction. But, different though their motives were, their love was certainly reinforced by self-interest.

The Earl of Shrewsbury owned land in Derbyshire, Nottinghamshire, Shropshire, Staffordshire and Yorkshire as well as Sheffield Castle, Wingfield Manor, Worksop Manor and Buxton Hall. At the time of the dissolution of the monasteries, his family had acquired Welbeck and Rufford Abbeys and had leased Tutbury Castle and its abbey from the Crown. As a mark of the part he had played in putting down the Pilgrimage of Grace – the Yorkshire-and-Lincoln-based revolt against the desecration of the northern abbeys – the Fifth Earl had been granted property which had previously belonged to the Basingwerk Monastery in County Flint. The defeat of the Catholic peasantry in 1537 had been an inglorious victory. The troops recruited by Shrewsbury and Norfolk had defeated the ragged army only after its leaders had been tricked into believing that Henry would meet some of their demands. But the grants had not only been a mark of gratitude for halting an insurrection which came near to toppling the King. The Crown saw 'the enhancement of [the Shrewsburys'] local power as a guarantee of their continued loyalty and the stability of their country'.[31] Between them, Bess and the Sixth Earl of Shrewsbury owned thirty-seven manors in the north of England.[32] Their land was mostly 'a vast extent of rough grazing . . . used for all the said purposes of ploughing, mowing and pasture as required where mere subsistence rivalled stock breeding as the great object of husbandry'.[33] But its size – combined with increasingly important deposits of lead and coal – ensured that George Talbot was head of one of the richest families in the land. And its strategic location made the Earl of Shrewsbury's support essential to Elizabeth's determination to unify England under her reign.

Shrewsbury's vast wealth and power were complemented by his immense status. He was a Knight of the Garter, Lord Lieutenant of Yorkshire, Derbyshire and Nottinghamshire, Chief Justice of Eyre and Chamberlain in Receipt of the Exchequer and, as the Sixth Earl of Shrewsbury at a time when dukedoms had fallen out of royal favour, the second most senior peer of the realm. Bess, although unable to claim noble lineage, was at least as well regarded at Court. During one of Bess's absences from London, Queen Elizabeth was uncharacteristically fulsome about the new Countess. 'I have been glad to see my Lady St Loe, but am now more desirous to see my Lady Shrewsbury. I hope my Lady doth know my good opinions of her . . . I assure you there is no Lady in this land I better love or like.'[34] Bess worked hard to remain in the Queen's good graces. One Christmas gift, although extravagantly expensive, was more notable for the trouble which she took in ensuring that it would please the royal recipient. Ladies-in-waiting were consulted. Lady Cobham's suggestion of £50 in a gold cup was turned down as lacking in originality. Bess's eventual choice, a cloak 'embroidered with pretty flowers and leaves with sundry colours', was such a success that 'five hundred pounds . . . would not have been so well taken'.[35] At the beginning of her fourth marriage, Bess felt prosperous and successful as well as – a matter of less consequence – loved by her husband,.

Letters between the Earl and his new Countess confirm that, at the outset of their relationship, a bond of mutual affection held their marriage together. But the practical advantages which both parties saw in the union were confirmed by an arrangement which, though not unusual at the time, leaves no doubt that both bride and groom hoped to create a mighty dynasty. Before the wedding took place, Henry Cavendish

(Bess's seventeen-year-old son) was betrothed to Grace Talbot (Shrewsbury's eight-year-old daughter) and Gilbert Talbot (Shrewsbury's fifteen-year-old second son) was betrothed to Mary Cavendish (Bess's twelve-year-old daughter). Hunter, in his *History of Hallamshire*, claims that Bess made the intermarriage of the families a requirement which had to be fulfilled before 'she would consent to be raised to the bed of the first Peer of the Realm'.*[36] Whether or not Hunter was right, the arrangement, at the time when it was made, was certainly mutually convenient. But not even the convenience lasted.

What seemed, by the standards of the time, an ideal match, deteriorated into a series of disputes over land and property, accusations and counter-accusations about the withholding of due payments, refusal of admission to the family homes and the physical assault by the servants of one party on the servants of the other. The arguments became so rancorous and so public that the Queen set up a commission to arbitrate between the warring parties. When it failed to achieve a reconciliation, Elizabeth issued a formal rebuke. 'The place we hold requires . . . that we do not suffer in our realm two persons of your degree and quality to live such a life of discord.'[37] Periods of reluctant and half-hearted reconciliation followed – more armed neutrality than peace. But by then the Earl had taken up with Eleanor Britton, his housekeeper, and Bess's emotional energy was expended on her building projects at Chatsworth. As the marriage progressed, everything which had seemed so right at its beginning had gone wrong. Shrewsbury was even short of money. He was suffering from the penury which was special to his class – a shortage of ready cash. He had huge capital assets, mostly land. But that did not prevent what, to Shrewsbury, must have been constant humiliation.

Frances Pierpoint (née Cavendish), his widowed stepdaughter, was asked to agree that her annuity would have to be withheld 'for want of credit'.[38] Thomas Baldwin, the Earl's agent, complained that he could not settle all the bills in the London account.[39] Creditors were invited to accept that for a year they would receive only the interest on loans rather than the scheduled repayment. The principal cause of Shrewsbury's sudden financial collapse can be precisely identified. Gilbert – his second son, Bess's son-in-law and, on the death of Francis Talbot, heir to the earldom – had lost vast sums in speculation and his debts had become a charge on the whole estate. Two other factors contributed to the Earl's near bankruptcy. One was Bess's extravagant

---

* Hunter's table of precedence was nearly right. At the time there was one duke – Norfolk. Shrewsbury was the premier earl.

spending both on building and the furnishing of what she built. The other – and by far the most corrosive in its effect on the Shrewsbury fortune – was the Earl's appointment as guardian, during her imprisonment in England, of Mary Stuart, Queen of Scotland and briefly Queen of France. Mary's royal status made Shrewsbury's duties as warder both difficult and expensive. For Queen Elizabeth insisted that her cousin be treated as a queen as well as a prisoner. Mary's character guaranteed that Shrewsbury would fail to meet both royal demands – and that his already strained relationship with his wife would be stretched to breaking point.

CHAPTER 3

. . . An Execution

Bess of Hardwick was twenty-one or -two when Mary Stuart was born on Friday December 8 1542. The two women were separated by race, religion and class as well as by age. Yet, for fifteen years, they lived in passionate companionship – first as devoted friends and then as bitter enemies. For much of that time the future of the Tudor monarchy rested in the uncertain hands of Bess of Hardwick and her husband.

Six days after she was born Mary Stuart had become Queen of Scotland. Her father James V – though sickly by nature and dissipated by inclination – had made no provision for a sudden succession. So his death was followed by a bitter dispute about who should act as Regent until the infant queen came of age. The Protestant and pro-English Earl of Arran was appointed. But he was not the only influence on young Mary's early years. Her mother, Mary of Guise, the daughter of one of France's most powerful families, remained loyal to her birth and upbringing. So, from the start, Mary Queen of Scots was embroiled in the dynastic and denominational disputes which dominated the politics of sixteenth-century Britain.

Mary was barely four months old when she made her debut in the conflict between Scotland and England which, sixty years later, was to be resolved by her son's union of the two crowns. Henry VIII believed that he could make her a link in the chain which would bind England and Scotland together. Nobles, captured during her father's defeat in his last foray south, were released from the Tower of London on the understanding that Mary would be brought to England and kept there until she was old enough to marry Prince Edward, the heir apparent. Despite Henry's threats, the pro-French faction at the Scottish court first delayed and then repudiated the betrothal. And by the time of Mary's coronation as Queen of Scotland in the Chapel Royal at Stirling – throughout which she, prophetically, howled and wailed – her mother was in firm control of the nine-month-old queen's destiny. Whatever chance Mary had of enjoying a secure and peaceful life was destroyed on that day. From then on she, or the people who called themselves her followers and friends, became the enemies of Protestant England. Her death warrant was effectively signed before her first birthday.

In 1558 – after what amounted to a Scottish civil war, in which France intervened on the side of Mary of Guise and her Catholic followers – Mary married the Dauphin of France. A year later her husband was Francis II and she was the Queen of both the nations in 'the auld alliance'. Francis died in 1560 and the double Queen returned to Scotland where, in 1566, she married her first cousin, Henry Stuart, Lord Darnley. Her second marriage did produce a son and heir, but – like her first – lasted barely a year. In February 1567 – after the attention of the servants was diverted by an explosion in the garden of their house at Kirk o'Field – Darnley was found strangled.

James Hepburn, Fourth Earl of Bothwell, was charged with murder but acquitted by an intimidated jury. Mary's complicity seemed to be confirmed by her refusal to respect the conventions of mourning and her open association with the man who, it was still generally assumed, had killed her husband. What followed is the stuff of melodrama. Bothwell, a married man, concluded that he could only become consort – and virtual King of Scotland – if he took Mary by force. So he abducted and either seduced or raped her – conduct which, since she was Queen of Scotland, was treason, whether or not it was criminal assault. Bothwell's personal version of 'rough wooing' worked. Mary remained an increasingly willing prisoner for twelve days. Then, in quick succession, Bothwell was divorced, awarded new orders of chivalry and betrothed to the Queen. They married on May 14 1567, three months after Darnley's death. A year later, Bess married the Earl of Shrewsbury and accepted the obligation to support and succour him for better and for worse. The worst of all turned out to be Mary Queen of Scots.

An alliance of Scottish peers – who called themselves the Confederate Lords – had already decided that their country's fate must not be left in Mary's unreliable hands. Their strength and determination grew with Bothwell's increased pretensions until their opposition amounted to open rebellion – which they called a campaign to free the Queen from the captivity in which she was held by her husband. Mary rallied what support she could still command and, foolishly if bravely, chose to confront her 'liberators'. Defeat was inevitable. So was Mary's isolation.

Mary fled south to England in 1568. But the world had moved on since the time when Henry VIII had hoped to make her his daughter-in-law. Edward, once her intended husband, had succeeded his father, reigned for six years and died. Then the succession had passed to his half-sister, Mary Tudor, who, in turn, was succeeded on November 17 1558 by her half-sister, Elizabeth. While the Virgin Queen remained unmarried and childless, Mary Stuart – her second cousin and, like her, a direct descendant of Henry VII – was her undoubted heir. In Tudor England, to be a heartbeat away from the throne was to be regarded as a potential regicide. But, in addition to her right of succession, Mary posed a particular and potent threat. English Catholics, unreconciled to the Reformation, disputed Elizabeth's right to reign. The Pope had refused to annul Henry's marriage to Catherine of Aragon despite the King's claim that she had not been the true – that is to say, consummated – wife of his brother, Arthur. So, according to Rome, Anne Boleyn had never been more than Henry's mistress and Elizabeth – the issue of the irregular union – was a bastard with no right to the succession. That made Mary Stuart already the true Queen of England.*

Mary – although an unlikely saint and martyr – was an icon around which rebellious Catholics could rally. She could not be left free in a still divided England. First she was imprisoned in Carlisle, then in Bolton Castle in Wensleydale. While she was there, Elizabeth and her Council considered how to deal with their unwelcome guest. They agreed that if she formally abandoned the Catholic faith and openly acknowledged Elizabeth as Queen of England, the accusation that she had murdered her second husband – substantiated by the 'Casket Letters' which, if they were genuine, confirmed her guilt – could be overlooked. Then some mutually acceptable agreement would be possible. Queen Elizabeth believed devoutly in the divine right of monarchs. So she was reluctant to execute a queen – either for treason or murder – if there was an alternative which left her secure on the throne of England. The alternative on which Queen and Council decided was built around George Talbot, Sixth Earl of Shrewsbury and Bess of Hardwick's fourth husband. He, they were sure, would keep the Scottish Queen safe, secure and separated from her enemies.

At first – thinking of enhanced status rather than onerous obligation – Shrewsbury was desperate for Elizabeth to confirm that he was to be appointed royal warder. During the first week in December 1568 he wrote to Bess, with undisguised excitement, 'This present Monday morning I [had audience with] the Queen in her garden. With as good words as I could wish, [she told me] that ere long I should perceive that she did trust me as she did few [others]. She would not tell me wherein, but I doubt not that it was about the custody of the Scot's Queen.'[1] As was usual, his message ended on a domestic note. He was grateful for

---

* Catherine had conveniently died in 1536, the year in which Anne Boleyn was executed. Henry was therefore free to marry Jane Seymour and produce a son who became Edward VI, the indisputable King of England.

the gift of pudding and venison. On the 13th of the month, he was confident enough to write home with the news that he was 'Now certain that Scots Queen is coming to Tutbury in my charge'.[2] On January 26, he received written confirmation together with written instructions about the manner in which his duty was to be performed.[3] They included the injunction that he 'must, by no pretence . . . allow [Mary] to gain rule over him or practice for her escape' and remember that 'with devices of towels or toys at her chamber windows or elsewhere or in the night, a body of her agility and spirit may escape'.[4] The warning should have made him realise how dangerous, as well as exacting, the role of Mary's gaoler would be.

There is no doubt that Queen Elizabeth had confidence in Shrewsbury. But it was not only the high esteem in which he was held that prompted her to make him Mary's custodian. He was the owner of seven great houses – some of them better described as castles – which were conveniently situated in the remote North Midlands, equally distant from Edinburgh and London. He was still rich and could overcome his temporary shortage of cash by selling land. Alternatively he could raise the credit which was always available to the nobility. So the notoriously mean Elizabeth could expect him to pay for much of Mary's upkeep. And – as premier Earl of England, with only the Duke of Norfolk senior to him in the order of precedence – he seemed the man most qualified to meet the royal injunction that Mary, 'being a Queen of our blood', had to be treated 'with the reverence and honour meet for a person of her state and calling'[5] and, at the same time, prevent her from either escaping or encouraging her followers to revolt.

Mary's temperament and health made his task impossible to fulfil. She was clever, devious, proud, courageous and either chronically sick or a hypochondriac. Her frequent vomiting was probably a symptom of porphyria, though she may have suffered from what we today call bulimia. All in all, Mary seemed destined to disturb the fragile tranquillity in the Shrewsbury household.

Tutbury – the house in which Mary was initially lodged – was neither owned by Shrewsbury nor situated in the North Midlands. It was an old manor house in Staffordshire which the Earl rented as a shooting lodge but never used. Bess had wanted Mary to be moved from Bolton to Sheffield Castle. But the Privy Council insisted – for reasons which it did not reveal – on Tutbury. So work was set in hand to make it habitable. 'I have', Bess told Queen Elizabeth, 'caused workmen to make forthwith . . . all such things . . . most needful to be done before her coming.'[6] Turkish carpets, chandeliers, tapestries and furniture – including velvet-covered chairs embroidered with cloth of gold – were sent from Sheffield Castle and Chatsworth. They were augmented by plate and cutlery from the Tower of London. Mary, who arrived on February 4 1569, after a cold and arduous journey which she barely survived, was not impressed. She described her new home as 'rather like a dungeon for base and abject criminals rather than the habitation fit for a person of my quality . . . It is so damp that you cannot put any piece of furniture in that part without it being, in three or four days, covered in mould.'[7] At least Mary was greeted in a manner befitting her station. Elizabeth, Lady St Loe, Countess of Shrewsbury, was at the gate waiting to welcome her not as a prisoner but as an honoured guest.

Two months later, Mary was moved to more congenial surroundings at Wingfield Manor, one of the Earl's more spacious Derbyshire houses. At the time, she was fantasising about marriage to the Duke of Norfolk – a union which, she hoped, would reconcile her to Elizabeth since the idea had been suggested by Elizabeth herself before Mary married Bothwell. Attempts to revive the plan foundered when the Scottish parliament ruled that Mary's marriage to Bothwell was legal and extant. When Elizabeth discovered Mary's designs, her anger was not assuaged by the knowledge that the idea was more fantasy than plot. In her fury, the Queen held Shrewsbury responsible for the treacherous thoughts which she claimed were the result of his negligence. Norfolk was sent to the Tower of London and Mary was returned to Tutbury with the Earl of Huntingdon sent – much to Shrewsbury's chagrin – to assist in the business of keeping the Queen of Scots safe.

Despite her displeasure, Elizabeth remained determined that her royal kinswoman should be treated like a queen – but a queen who was a prisoner. It was Shrewsbury and Bess – without Huntingdon's assistance – who had to work out a way of reconciling both elements of Mary's dual role. The task was beyond them – as it would have been beyond anybody – and was complicated by Elizabeth's reluctance to pay the full cost of her cousin's upkeep. Elizabeth decreed that Mary's household was too large and therefore unnecessarily expensive. Shrewsbury was required to negotiate or enforce a reduction. He failed. At the beginning of Shrewsbury's stewardship, Mary's retinue was cut to thirty servants. But during the first two years of her captivity, it grew to forty-eight. He was more successful in fulfilling the injunction that 'her diet must be kept at the former rate'[8] – meaning the high quality and extensive choice to which she had been accustomed. Obedience to that instruction made Mary a costly guest. Although she ate very little, her status required that she be presented with lavish meals. They usually consisted of 'two courses of sixteen dishes each' and included 'four or five dishes of the daintier sort'.[9] And her ladies-in-waiting enjoyed almost equal treatment. Shrewsbury's annual bill for fuel, wine and spices had, he calculated or claimed, risen to £1,000. The same sum was, he complained, paid out each year as a result of 'the loss of plate, the buying of pewter and all manner of household stuff, which is by them' (by which he meant Mary's retinue) 'exceedingly spoilt and wilfully wasted'.[10]

It took months of pleading and patient negotiation – no doubt with their own health and comfort as much in mind as Mary's – for Shrewsbury and Bess to persuade the Queen and Council that Tutbury must, once more, be left to rot. In November 1570 – after a brief stay at Chatsworth – the Scots' Queen arrived at Sheffield Castle, where she was to remain for most of what was left of her fifteen-year imprisonment.

Both in Sheffield and in Chatsworth – to which she was taken from time to time – her accommodation was reminiscent of her days of pomp and power. Her apartments included a 'privy chamber' and a 'presence chamber' in which she received guests while sitting on a high-backed chair that, because it was elevated on a dais, looked like a throne. Ladies-in-waiting sat on low stools as they had done in Holyrood Palace. The implication of majesty was emphasised by the Cloth of State – an unambiguous symbol of monarchy – which hung above Mary's chair. Worst of all, when – to cut both costs and pretensions – her household was eventually reduced, she was allowed to make one addition to the stipulated number. He was known as Sir John Morton but, whatever his true name, he was a Roman Catholic priest.

Although Mary enjoyed some of the privileges of royalty, in one particular she chose not to act with the hauteur expected of the Lord's Anointed. It had been assumed that she would want to emphasise her independence from her English captors, by paying for at least part of her upkeep with a contribution from her French pension. On that assumption the Court promised to pay Shrewsbury £52 a week towards her board and lodging. Mary refused to supplement the official allowance in any way. But the Court's grant remained at £52 a week. The Privy Council had promised that it would be paid to Shrewsbury by a clerk who would travel each month from London for that explicit purpose. Often he arrived late and sometimes he did not arrive at all.

Shrewsbury negotiated an additional payment to cover the cost of extra security at times of suspected danger – 6d a day for the twenty-four extra guards that Elizabeth's advisers thought necessary. He always employed fifty and – to guarantee their loyalty – paid them, collectively, £400 a year above the agreed rate.[11] Mary's enforced stay in Derbyshire was calculated to cost Shrewsbury, in total, about £30 a day – of which Elizabeth paid less than a quarter. Yet in 1575, Elizabeth cut the allowance to £30 a week and in 1580 she cut it again – much to the alarm of her more sagacious advisers who warned that it was folly to alienate Mary's gaoler.

Sir Francis Walsingham – then Queen Elizabeth's 'spymaster' – bravely advised that 'to have so special a charge committed to person discontented, everybody seeth stands no way to policy'. But his protest was ignored and he was left praying 'that the abatement of charges towards the nobleman who has charge of the bussom serpent has not lessened his care in keeping her'.[12] It did not make him a worse gaoler than he was before the cut in the allowance. But it did increase his neurosis about the cost of keeping Mary driving him to bankruptcy. The continual anxiety about money certainly contributed to the increasing tension between Shrewsbury and Bess. But the real and lasting damage to the marriage was done by the Earl's absolute, and probably wilful, failure to observe Elizabeth's strictures on the subject of the proper relationship between captor and captive.

Shrewsbury was enjoined by Elizabeth not to allow his conduct to be influenced by Mary's famous beauty and notorious charm and, if he felt sympathy for her, to recall 'the apparent presumption against her for murdering her husband'. After Nicholas White – a servant of William Cecil (soon to become Lord Burghley), the Queen's Principal Secretary of State – met Mary, he thought it necessary to warn his master about her seductive charm. 'She has withal an alluring grace . . . Fame might move some to relieve her, and glory joined with gain might stir others to adventure much for her sake.'[13] It was the general view that Mary was irresistible, which prompted Elizabeth to make her second piece of good advice to Shrewsbury absolutely explicit. 'Should she be sick or wish to speak to his wife, the Countess, he shall permit the latter to come to her rarely and no other gentlewoman shall be permitted to visit.'[14]

There was never the slightest chance that Bess, one of the great social climbers of English history, would have a queen – albeit a queen with a tarnished crown – under her roof without spending a great deal of time in her company and becoming her effusive, if not always genuine, friend. They were never as close as Mary later suggested, but in the early years of her captivity, she wrote in her day book 'had I been her own Queen [Bess] could not have done more for me'.[15] Bess's acts of friendship were carefully calculated to promote and preserve her own interests. So it is inconceivable that Mary was promised, as she later claimed, that if her life was threatened, the Countess of Shrewsbury would help her to escape.[16] Mary – being a romantic – confused deference with respect and flattery with affection.

The two women did spend a great deal of time together, much of it as a result of their mutual interest in the pastimes which enlivened the humdrum existence of all Tudor ladies of quality. Both women embroidered with pleasure and skill and they spent long hours working on tapestries which they often emblazoned with motifs that reflected their changing moods. Mary's needlework included a hanging on which she had worked the motto 'One, like a lioness' – a reference to her son, James Stuart, 'the sorry child who had been torn away from her arms'.[17] Not surprisingly, she did not use her needlework to commemorate her decision to make the boy a usurper by revoking her declaration of abdication after he had been proclaimed the King of Scotland. The Delphic rubric, 'In the end is my beginning', embroidered at a time of depression, may have been an error. She had been doomed from birth. 'In the beginning was my end' would have been more appropriate.

Some of the Scottish Queen's embroidery was overtly political and, in consequence, consciously reckless. In an age when poets and artists depicted Elizabeth as a shining star or rising sun, Mary embroidered eclipses and signed them with the monogram 'MR' (Maria Regina). One piece of work – based on a plate from Gesner's *Icones Animalium* – portrayed a tabby cat threatening a mouse. The crown on its bright orange head left no doubt by whom the design had been inspired. A panel which depicted a vine – one side laden with fruit and the other barren – was more than an insulting reference to the Queen's childless state. The embroidery included a hand, holding a bill-hook in the act of pruning the fruitless branches – a clear reference to the need to rid the state of a sovereign who could not produce an heir.[18] Fortunately, at the time of Mary's most imaginative creations she and Bess were at least feigning friendship. So Queen Elizabeth remained ignorant of her prisoner's enthusiasm for a rare form of needlework – offensive embroidery.

Bess also used her needlework to express her emotions – though she, wisely, embroidered personal rather than political messages. One of her pieces included symbols which represented the names of her previous husbands – Barlow, Cavendish and St Loe – surrounded by tears and the assurance, in Latin, that 'quenched flames live on'.[19] Perhaps she was already beginning to feel the dissatisfaction with Shrewsbury which was later to turn into hatred. If Shrewsbury noticed his wife's nostalgic embroidery, he showed no sign of concern about her excursions into romantic melancholy. He had other things on his mind.

Shrewsbury knew that, despite his high rank and exalted position – if he valued his life and freedom – he dare not offend Queen Elizabeth. Yet the task with which he was charged was beyond him. As the years passed and he failed – either out of sympathy or incompetence – to maintain the level of security that Elizabeth and her Court demanded, his protestations of devotion grew increasingly fervent and farcical. As early as the summer of 1569, when he was asked to account for disquieting rumours that his captive was being treated with too much leniency, he did no more than vehemently refute the allegation. Five years later – when Elizabeth's hopes of a concordat with Mary had almost vanished and fears of a Catholic insurrection had grown – Shrewsbury's protestations of good faith bordered on the hysterical. 'I know her to be a stranger, a Papist, my Enemy.'[20] Then he added, 'What hopes can I have of good of her for either myself or my country?' Fortunately for the Earl, Queen Elizabeth had no talent for linguistic exegesis. Careful analysis of the rhetorical question suggests that his loyalty was the product of self-interest. Had there been a chance that Mary might, one day, still ascend the throne, his 'hopes' might have made him more sympathetic towards her.

Perhaps because he suspected that Elizabeth – or more likely Walsingham's army of spies – recognised his inconstancy, Shrewsbury regularly sent to Court embarrassingly unconvincing examples of his fidelity. He reported that he had christened his own grandchild rather than allow visitors, who might be Catholic spies, into the house.[21] The protestation had quite the opposite effect from the one which he intended. Cecil responded with the almost equally bizarre – though no doubt true – accusation that, far from the Earl's houses being in quarantine, Mary was being exhibited in Derbyshire like an animal in a zoo. According to the indictment, a guest at Chatsworth had been asked if he had ever seen the Scottish Queen and, when he replied that he had not, was promised sight of her before his visit ended.[22] But despite doubts about Shrewsbury's assiduity – and suspicions about the common sense with which he discharged his duties – he remained the best candidate for the job of gaoler. He was as loyal as any of the alternatives and sufficiently self-protective, almost until the end of his life, to make a show of meeting the Queen's wishes. Most important, he could, with a struggle, find the money to pay the bills.

Throughout Mary's early years at Chatsworth and in Sheffield Castle, Queen Elizabeth's advisers – most notably Walsingham – argued for the Scottish Queen to be moved to more secure, and therefore less congenial, accommodation. Elizabeth – so determined to respect her cousin's regal status that she had threatened war with Scotland when Mary was first deposed – regularly rejected their advice until she was convinced that the threat from Mary's supporters was not only real but imminent. Only once, before then, was Elizabeth prepared to move Mary away from the deferential supervision of the Earl of Shrewsbury. After an abortive Catholic rising in Yorkshire the royal prisoner was briefly imprisoned in Coventry. But, long after all realistic hope of compromise was dead, Elizabeth still harboured hopes of avoiding offence against the holy laws which protected the Lord's Anointed. It was a dangerous course to follow. From the moment at which Mary arrived from Scotland, her English supporters – mostly Catholic, but some no more than hopeful opportunists – plotted her rescue. Sometimes Mary co-operated with the plotters. Sometimes they acted without her knowledge or consent. Either way Mary was responsible. Her presence in England made plots against Elizabeth, of one sort or another, inevitable.

Even the remote Peak District was not as free from Catholic subversion as the Queen and her Council had hoped. Two months after the publication of the papal bull *Regnans in Excelsis* – which excommunicated Elizabeth and therefore released her subjects from all obligation to loyalty – Sir Thomas Gerrard, a Derbyshire Catholic squire – conspired with two of his neighbours, Francis and George Rolleston, to spirit Mary west via the Isle of Man. One of the Rolleston brothers met John Beaton, the master of Mary's household, on the high moors above Chatsworth and was told that Mary would not be party to their plans since she 'nothing doubted but that the Queen's Majesty, at the request of the Kings of Spain and France, would restore her to her former dignity'.[23] Elizabeth's spies heard reports of both the conspiracy and Mary's over-optimistic assumption. It was agreed that Mary's rejection of attempted rescue by Derbyshire rurals confirmed that she had abandoned all thought of a coup. And the confident Court chose neither to punish nor even admonish Shrewsbury for allowing the failed conspirators access to his prisoner.

Less than a year later, Mary – belatedly conscious that her hopes of royal rehabilitation were vain – actually encouraged a rebellion which was being promoted by Roberto Ridolfi, a Florentine banker with a history of Catholic intrigue. When Ridolfi offered to approach the Pope and the King of Spain with the suggestion that they should declare a holy war against England, Mary invited him to assure both men that large numbers of loyal English Catholics were waiting for the call to arms and would rise up in support of an invasion. She also contacted Norfolk – recently freed from the Tower of London where he had been imprisoned since the revelation of her marriage plans – and told him that she still expected to become his wife. Norfolk responded cautiously but was implicated in the plot by inclusion in the list of supporters which Ridolfi sent by letter to Rome. The courier – John Leslie, Bishop of Ross – was intercepted at Dover and under torture not only confessed everything but added his own list of lurid inventions. Mary, he said, had poisoned her first husband, been complicit in the murder of the second, tried to kill the third and would, had Norfolk married her, also have disposed of him. Shrewsbury – although he had failed to intercept Mary's messages – was again absolved of negligence, but was required – as a punishment for Mary – to reduce her number of servants to sixteen. Norfolk was treated more severely. He was tried for treason, convicted and sentenced to death.

Shrewsbury, Lord High Steward of England, was required to preside over Norfolk's trial – in the knowledge that, once it had ended with the predestined result, he would resume his duties as gaoler to the woman who had hoped to marry the condemned man. While he performed his judicial task, Sir Ralph Sadler took his place as Mary's custodian. The Queen of Scots chose to regard a locum as beneath her dignity and ignored him. The substitute told Walsingham that his presence was 'such a trouble to Mary Stuart that she rarely comes out of her chamber. I rarely come to her.'[24] But he added that 'Lady Shrewsbury is rarely from her'. Bess did not match intimacy with tact. Norfolk was condemned to death on January 16 1572. When the news reached Sheffield two days later, it was compassion, rather than cowardice, which prompted Sadler to ask Bess to tell Mary, for he assumed that she would discharge the doleful duty with the sensitivity of a friend. He was wrong.

Sadler reported to Cecil that when Bess entered Mary's room she 'found her all beweeping and mourning'.[25] The Queen of Scots, a regular recipient of secret messages from her supporters in London, already knew that Norfolk was to die. Bess was not easily flustered. But embarrassment is the only possible excuse for her reaction to Mary's anguish. Despite knowing its cause, she asked her supposed friend the reason for her distress. Mary 'knew her ladyship could not be ignorant of the cause and of how deeply she must be grieved for her friends who fared worse for her sake'.[26] She then lamented the part she had played in Norfolk's destruction. His death would, she said, be the result of irritation she had caused Elizabeth by constantly complaining about her detention and her separation from her son.

Clearly it was the proposal of marriage, rather than complaints about living conditions, which had sealed Norfolk's fate. And perhaps Bess intended no more than to assure Queen Mary that there was no reason to believe that her expressions of resentment and regret had contributed to the Duke's conviction. But attempt at comfort amounted to the opinion that Norfolk deserved to die. Mary could 'be sure that, whatever she had written to the Queen's majesty could do the Duke neither good nor harm touching his condemnation . . . If all the offences and reasons had not been great and plainly proved against him, those noblemen who sat on his trial'[27] would not have found him guilty of treason. Bess knew that every word of the conversation would be reported to the Privy Council. Her comments were intended to convince Cecil of her loyalty, not Mary of her innocence.

Mary – who was inconstant in every aspect of her life – quickly recovered her composure. The expressions of grief and remorse were forgotten and – in the most brutal language – she recanted the confession that she was, even in part, responsible for Norfolk's destruction. 'What the Duke of Norfolk and others have done she sayeth she cannot tell. Let them answer for themselves.'[28] She too was conscious that her reactions were being noted and would be described to men who were anxious to find evidence of treason. Even so, her behaviour was hardly proof of an inclination to fidelity. And it did not succeed in its assumed objective. Despite what amounted to a disclaimer, Mary was accused of sundry crimes and treacheries – complicity in the Ridolfi Plot, approval of the papal bull, *Regnans in Excelsis*, encouraging the invasion of England and claiming the English crown. She refused to recognise the Commission which examined her. Parliament, convinced of her guilt, would have passed a Bill of Attainder, and thus opened the way for her execution, had Elizabeth not intervened. Shrewsbury was left to guard a woman who was generally supposed to be plotting treason.

Mary's only punishment was the deprivation, by Act of Parliament, of the right of succession to the throne of England. By imposing so light a penalty, Elizabeth was certainly rejecting the advice of Cecil and Walsingham and – according to them – defying the wishes of her people. After the massacre of Saint Bartholomew's Day in 1572 – the treacherous murder of 3,000 Huguenots in Paris – Elizabeth's advisers warned of the popular assumption that Mary, the kinswoman of the Guise family who had instigated the slaughter, would gladly dispose of English Protestants in the same way. Cecil told Shrewsbury that 'all men cry out of your prisoner'.[29]

In the light of that advice it was madness for Shrewsbury to allow

Mary the freedom to make excursions outside the grounds of Sheffield Castle. Perhaps he was literally suffering from a mental disorder which impaired his judgement. For at more or less the same time that he proposed to ease the condition of Mary's imprisonment he took a decision which, he almost immediately realised, was financial folly.* Letters and other documents, written at about the same time, confirm that he was at least lucid. And soon after the mistake was made he came to realise the extent of his error. It was then that – distraught by the extent of his losses – he was forced to respond to the Scottish Queen's demands that she be allowed more liberty.

It had always been necessary – in order to meet the requirements of health and hygiene – for Mary to spend a few days each month outside the castle which was her prison. The building possessed neither sanitation nor means of refuse disposal. To save its inhabitants from typhus, the building had to be evacuated from time to time while the pits of ordure, rotting vegetables and rancid meat were dug out and their contents carted away. So Mary was usually moved from Sheffield Castle itself to temporary accommodation in the nearby manor house – fit for a Queen before Mary's arrival and extended during her stay to provide convenient and secure habitation during the times when her permanent apartments needed 'sweetening'. But she still agitated to be allowed to ride in open countryside and occasionally – particularly during her visits to Chatsworth – her wish was granted. In 1572 her demands for more freedom were cunningly convoluted with the plea that she be allowed to take the healing waters at Saint Anne's well in Buxton, or Buckstones as it was then called.

Some of Mary's servants were allowed more freedom than their mistress. So it is likely that it was through them that the Scottish Queen first heard of the Buxton spa. She may have been told of, or even read, a treatise published in 1572 by a Doctor Jones. It described the healing properties of Buxton's mineral-impregnated water which the sick and the lame had drunk – and bathed in – since Roman times. More recently the spring had been enclosed in a chapel which was dedicated to its patron saint and, at the height of the Reformation, Thomas Cromwell had denounced the well as a manifestation of Papist idolatry.[30] Everything in Mary's character – religion which was difficult to separate from superstition, hypochondria and cunning – encouraged her determination to visit Buxton and take the cure. Fortunately, Dr Jones, being a physician, had described the efficacious effects of the

---

* For details, see p. 85.

water in purely scientific terms and therefore made its use possible even for good Protestants.

According to Doctor Jones's contemporary account, after her husband acquired rights to the well, Bess was proposing to market the water with a scale of charges – £3 10s 0d for a duke and 12d for a yeoman – which related to the patient's ability to pay. Since there was only one duke in all England she could not have expected much revenue from customers at the top end of the social scale. But, if Jones was correct, that might not have unduly concerned her since the whole enterprise was, he wrote, intended to be a charity. That might have come as a surprise to Edmund Lodge who, in his nineteenth-century *Illustrations of British History*, described Bess as 'a builder, a buyer and seller of estates, a money lender, a farmer and a merchant of coals and timber'.[31] But whatever the commercial basis on which the well was run, Mary – constantly in pain and distress from illnesses caused by stress and restriction – grew increasingly desperate and determined to test its healing powers.

Initially, Shrewsbury was entirely opposed to Mary's making an excursion to Buxton. It was only 16 miles from Chatsworth. But the journey was across open moorland – exactly the sort of country in which Gerrard had met the Rolleston brothers to plot Mary's escape. The claim that St Anne's healing waters were essential to her health was implausible. She was already applying cures, similar to those provided by the well, by bathing in herb-impregnated water and sometimes even white wine – at his expense. But Mary was insistent and the Earl either became sympathetic or was too weak-minded to sustain his objection. So he asked Elizabeth's permission for his prisoner to be allowed to make the excursion. The Queen consulted Cecil and Cecil consulted the Privy Council who decided that the Queen herself must make the decision. Shrewsbury reinforced his request with accounts of Mary's deteriorating health and of his own indisposition which would, he explained, much benefit from the waters which he could not sample unless he took his prisoner with him. While the deliberations were going on, Mary – in anticipation of a favourable decision – was moved to Chatsworth. Permission was granted and in August 1573 Mary made her first visit to Buxton.

For the next ten years the Scottish Queen took the cure almost every summer. The excursions were preceded by protracted correspondence between Shrewsbury and the Privy Council during which the Queen often expressed doubts which were as much the result of her mood as of an assessment of the need for uncompromising security. In 1577 she changed her mind after permission had been granted and again instructed Shrewsbury to take Mary from Buxton to Tutbury. The order was revoked after the intervention of Bess who was, at the time, making one of her rare appearances at Court. Mary was allowed to visit Buxton during the next two summers, but in 1580, permission was refused, much to the distress of Bess who was already presiding over the social gathering that the well attracted. Shrewsbury promised, by way of consolation, wine from Wingfield.[32]

Buxton offered Mary more than cloudy, tepid and bitter-tasting water. Shrewsbury and Bess had made it into a holiday resort. The bath-house was, in effect, an hotel from which she organised a programme of social activities with eating and drinking as their main attraction. The men competed at archery and bowls and the women played what would now – at least in France – be called *boules*. The Shrewsburys worked hard and successfully to make the spa fashionable. Cecil was there in 1575 and the Earl of Leicester – once Elizabeth's choice as a safe husband for Mary – took the waters in 1577 and 1584. Mary met them both, but spent most of her days at Buxton in a lodge,* which had been specially built to ensure her comfort and security. But Mary's weeks of relative freedom were rare and usually brought to a sudden end when Cecil or Walsingham began to suspect or pretended that a new plot was being hatched to effect her escape. Mary's last visit was in 1584. Before she left – in an act of unusual prescience – she used her diamond ring to scratch a parting message on a window pane, 'Buxton, perchance I shall visit thee no more. Farewell'.[33]

Until then, Buxton provided some relief for Shrewsbury as well as for his prisoner. But the years during which Mary was in his care took their toll on his mental health as well as on his money and his marriage. Bess was increasingly required to run the estate and manage the family's affairs. It was a task for which she was well equipped, but one which she did not always discharge as her husband would have wished. Fear that money which was rightly his was being expropriated by his wife and stepsons became an obsession.

Bess managed her own affairs with the skill that established her reputation as a businesswoman and with a single-minded concentration on her personal wealth which suggested that she was less than wholly committed to her fourth marriage. By 1584, her annual income – including the settlements which followed the deaths of previous husbands and rent from lands she had leased from the Crown – was probably £5,000. William and Charles, her second and third sons,

---

* It is now the Old Hall Hotel.

began to add to their estates. William, his mother's favourite, spent £25,000 on land in twelve years.[34] Shrewsbury believed that many of the purchases were financed by money which was rightly his and that his wife was the effective owner of the property – even though, as a married woman, all she owned was legally at her husband's disposal. The suspicion that his wife was preparing for her fourth widowhood by investing in property which would become hers when he died was, in itself, enough to drive the Shrewsburys apart. The Earl's anxieties about money – far greater than his situation justified – made Bess's success in surreptitiously acquiring land all the more intolerable. During the Queen of Scots' imprisonment in Sheffield and at Chatsworth Bess changed from loving wife to vengeful termagant. In 1568, Bess was 'my own sweetheart . . . my dear . . . my own'. Ten years later she was 'my wicked and malicious wife . . . my enemy'.[35]

The Shrewsburys' final separation was occasioned, if not caused, by a triviality. In 1577, the Earl of Leicester – sick, fat and not at all the romantic figure whom dramatists portray as Elizabeth's lover – spent some days at Chatsworth after a visit to the Buxton spa. Bess had arranged that, while she and her husband played hosts in Derbyshire, various small repairs and improvements were made to Sheffield Castle. On their return to Yorkshire, Bess discovered that the men, who were to be employed to carry out the work, had been refused lodgings by the Keeper of the Earl's Wardrobe. Asked to over-rule and rebuke his servant, Shrewsbury refused and, after angry exchanges with his wife, left the castle.

The whole affair might have been forgotten had it not become entangled with a dispute between the Earl and his son, Gilbert Talbot, which was even more trifling – and certainly more demeaning – than an argument about carpenters' accommodation. When Gilbert married Bess's daughter Mary, he had received gifts of furniture from both his father and his mother-in-law, but had complained that Shrewsbury, in contrast to Bess, had been less than generous. Shrewsbury believed that Charles Cavendish – Bess's son and Gilbert's best friend – had fermented the argument about wedding presents as part of a plot to turn his children against him. In his tortured mind, the dispute about his wife's workmen had been engineered by his son and son-in-law as an extension of the wedding gift dispute.

Brooding about what he believed to be a family conspiracy, Shrewsbury decided that by leaving Sheffield Castle he had conceded victory to Bess. So he returned to demand an apology for her conduct. By the time he got back to Sheffield his wife had gone – nobody was sure where – and he concluded that Gilbert and Charles had arranged her departure in order to humiliate him. Both men were innocent. Bess, as Gilbert tried to convince his father, had left Sheffield in order to avoid another confrontation. Shrewsbury, not persuaded, decided on direct action. According to the law of England, whatever his wife earned or owned was his by right. All that Bess claimed to possess she only held 'on trust' and that trust had been forfeited by her disloyal conduct. So he reclaimed his property by force of arms. A raid on Chatsworth – Shrewsbury leading forty armed men – broke down the doors and looted the house. A few nights later, William Cavendish – Bess's second son – led a retaliatory attack on Sheffield Castle and took back what he could find of his mother's possessions. The recovery of her property did not lessen Bess's anger. And what slight chance there was of reconciliation was extinguished with the rumour – growing in currency at Court – that the Earl of Shrewsbury was committing adultery with Mary Queen of Scots.

During the early years of Mary's imprisonment, Bess had been sufficiently confident of her husband's fidelity to make – slightly barbed – jokes about the possibility that her husband had become infatuated by the Scottish Queen. A letter, which she sent to Shrewsbury in 1577, refers to Mary as his 'charge and love'[36] and while at Court, in the same year, she answered the Queen's enquiry about Mary's conduct with a reply which she clearly did not mean Elizabeth to take seriously: 'She cannot do ill while she is with my husband and I begin to grow jealous, they are so great together.'[37] But Mary was regarded as a *femme fatale* and, inevitably, there was speculation about whether Shrewsbury would be able to resist her seductive charms. In 1569, when Mary was on the way to Tutbury, Nicholas White had told the Court that 'she hath withal an alluring grace, a pretty Scottish accent and a searching wit clouded with mildness'.[38] Years of imprisonment had diminished, though not extinguished, her charm. The Scottish Queen's attraction – fatal to her and half a dozen men whom she infatuated – combined with the gossip to make Bess fear that she was not only being betrayed but, far worse, made to look a fool by a woman half her age.

The stories grew in number and increased in improbability. One suggested that Mary had conceived Shrewsbury's child – a slander which developed into the allegation that, over the years, she given birth to two of his children. A collection of lewd verses, which purported to describe the couple's intimate moments, was passed from hand to hand at Court and only suppressed when Shrewsbury, initially against the wishes of his wife, sued the perpetrators for libel. Bess was, or claimed to be, distraught at the consequent public ridicule. Mary Queen of Scots believed that it was the apparently outraged Countess who was herself responsible for the defamation and asked for an audience with the Queen to protest her innocence and demand that the culprit be punished. As always, the request for a meeting was rejected. She then gave the French Ambassador a new explanation for the increasingly repeated calumnies. Bess's relations were slandering her in order to damage Shrewsbury. The most outrageous – though by no means most improbable – theory about the story's origins came from some of Mary's friends. They believed that the culprit was Queen Elizabeth or men working on her orders to discredit the Scottish Queen. They told Mary that the scurrilous stories were 'the final poison that your enemies have reserved, not to poison your body but your reputation'.³⁹

Formal redress, although unlikely, was Mary's last hope. She wrote to Cecil with the demand that the Privy Council should endorse her right to clear her name. But she was capable of neither moderation nor caution. Recklessly she ended her letter with the warning that the Queen should not take Bess's loyalty for granted. Her accusation was justified by examples of what she claimed that Bess was saying about Elizabeth – which she demanded be shown to her 'sister queen' together with the assurance: 'I protest that I answered rebuking the said lady for believing or speaking so licentiously of you as a thing that I do not at all believe.'⁴⁰ Whether or not Bess's accusations were Mary's invention, most of them were wholly implausible. But one was almost certainly true. It is more likely than not that Leicester was the Queen's lover, as well as her true love. And it is at least possible, as Bess was said to have claimed, that at some moment during their tempestuous relationship, Elizabeth had agreed to marry him.

Gossip about Leicester was rife at Court and it was encouraged by Elizabeth's behaviour towards him. Repeating the stories about that relationship was nothing like so dangerous as the suggestion that the Queen was 'not like other women' – a discovery which Bess might have made while she was a lady-in-waiting. If, as Mary charged, Bess had said or implied that Elizabeth had a physical deformity – anticipating Ben Jonson's specific claim that the Queen had an obstruction which 'made her uncapable of man . . . though she tried many' – she was asserting that Elizabeth was incapable of producing an heir. That suggestion was profoundly inflammatory in a nation still apprehensive about a return to dynastic wars.

Most of the allegations which Mary attributed to Bess were accusations of promiscuity. The list was extensive. 'Firstly, that one to whom she said you had made a promise of marriage before a lady in your chamber, had made love to you an infinite number of times with all the licence and intimacy which can be used between man and wife.' Elizabeth was insatiable and 'would never lose [her] liberty to make love and always have [her] pleasure with new lovers'.[41] She had slept with Sir Christopher Hatton and treated him amorously in public, had been seen in her chemise enticing the Duke of Alençon into her bedchamber and had kissed Jean de Simier in full view of the Court as well as having 'taken various indecent liberties with him'.[42] The suggestion that she had behaved improperly with Simier was particularly offensive. He was the Duke of Alençon's Master of the Wardrobe and had been in England to woo Elizabeth on behalf of his master. Mary then added, for good measure, that Bess had attempted to marry her granddaughter, Arbella, to James VI of Scotland and make her the future Queen of England.

The litany of accusations ended with an open charge of treason which, since it was bound up with astrology, would have particularly exercised a superstitious Queen and her Court. According to Mary, Bess – relying on an 'old book' – had prophesied Elizabeth's violent death and 'the succession of another Queen which she interpreted as myself'.[43] One allegation, if it was ever made, was certainly justified. Bess was said to have reported that the Queen expected, and received, flattery from her courtiers which amounted to idolatry. The letter ended with an offer. If Elizabeth agreed to meet her – an unrealised hope that she entertained throughout her imprisonment – Mary would supply an even longer list of Bess's treachery.

Elizabeth did not reply to the letter and probably never received it. Cecil may have kept it from her or perhaps Mary drafted the letter but lost her nerve before it was sent. But there is a third possibility. In November Mary discovered that Bess – and her sons – had been summoned to the Privy Council to answer the charge of slandering her husband. Elizabeth might well have thought it expedient to punish Bess by finding her guilty of false testimony against Shrewsbury rather than arraign her for misdemeanours which could only result in publicising scandal which Mary was said to be spreading. Shrewsbury – anxious that nothing would prevent his wife from answering to the Privy Council for her treatment of him – would certainly have supported that decision. For him, exposing Bess's failure as a wife was far more important than rooting out her treason. And he had no doubt that he could rely on the Privy Council to condemn her. He was wrong.

Bess was acquitted. The drama with which she conducted her defence – swearing on oath that she and her sons had never spread 'false scandalous lies' about Mary bearing Shrewsbury's child[44] – ended with a *coup de théâtre* which proved more effective than all the evidence against her. She fell to her knees and swore that Mary – her devoted friend – had always 'deported herself in honour and chastity'.[45] Mary's morals – though no doubt of interest to the Privy Council – were not the subject of the inquiry. But in the emotion of the moment Bess was found not guilty.

By the time that the Privy Council pronounced Bess innocent, Mary was no longer in Shrewsbury's keeping. On August 4 1584 Sir Ralph Sadler had relieved the Earl of his 'heavy burden'. Sadler, who had deputised as gaoler during the Norfolk trial, was an easy-going septuagenarian, who had been Henry VIII's ambassador to Scotland when Mary was a baby, and he admitted a residual affection for his prisoner. However, he faithfully obeyed his instruction to move his prisoner from Sheffield to Wingfield Manor and then on to the dreaded Tutbury. Once she was there, the regime was relaxed to a point which far exceeded anything that Shrewsbury allowed. Mary was permitted to go hawking unguarded. It was not only Mary who found the new arrangement preferable to the old. Shrewsbury thanked the Queen for having 'freed him from two she devils, the Queen of Scotland and his wife'.[46]

For some time Shrewsbury's behaviour had been unpredictable to the point of eccentricity and his often irrational conduct certainly contributed to a decision to relieve him of his custodial duties. During her last months in which Mary was his prisoner, he took her to see the progress which was being made on his new house at Worksop. The excursion was, in itself, a reckless abdication of his responsibilities and he compounded the offence by allowing (or perhaps even arranging) a meeting with the Earl of Rutland – his first wife's brother and, more significantly, a devout Catholic. That he escaped even censure and remained the Queen's 'good old man' suggests that she regarded him as no longer wholly answerable for his conduct. There was much evidence to support that view.

Keeping Mary safe for fifteen years – in the comfort of a queen – was enough, in itself, to drive a potentially unstable man into fits of madness. But during Shrewsbury's last years his life was composed of trouble and tragedy. He was short of money and he suffered from arthritis and gout. His son, Francis, died and was succeeded as heir to the earldom and Talbot property by Gilbert – in his father's view an ingrate who had allied himself with Bess during the many matrimonial crises. Gilbert's son George – on whom his grandfather doted despite his differences with Gilbert himself – suffered a fatal attack of convulsions. The result of the strife and suffering was a change in the Earl's personality. He became obsessed with saving small sums of money and spent – indeed wasted – his time attempting to arrange unlikely marriages between distant relatives and persons of power and influence. His eccentricity was occasionally as vicious as it was pathetic. He failed to persuade his son Gilbert to leave his wife and thus escape from the dominance of his mother-in-law but succeeded in arranging for the rent from St Loe properties in Somerset and Gloucester to be paid to him rather than to Bess.

Despite presiding over a generally adulterous Court, Queen Elizabeth often took it upon herself to intervene in the marriage disputes of its members. Leicester – an unlikely marriage guidance councillor – was asked to adjudicate in the increasingly bitter Shrewsbury conflict. His conclusion that Bess was a loving wife was no more likely to result in a reunion than it was accurate. The Earl and Countess had become temperamentally incompatible. Bess, who was never a compliant spouse by nature, had begun openly to compete with her husband for power and influence. For years their individual building projects had resulted in a not very friendly rivalry. As early as 1575, Shrewsbury had complained that Bess was hindering his work by employing most of the craftsmen in the area. She had made no attempt to accommodate his concerns. Seven years later, at the time when Shrewsbury could not afford to finish the work on Worksop Manor, Bess chose to exhibit the difference in their financial status by beginning – without her husband's knowledge or approval – a flurry of essentially decorative new building at Chatsworth.

So, because of his other heavy burdens, relief from the misery of being Mary's guardian did nothing to restore the composure which years of domestic conflict had undermined. At the first meeting of the Privy Council after the Scottish Queen left his care, he demanded that the other members publicly confirm their absolute confidence in his loyalty to the Queen. Then he opposed the election of his stepson, Sir Charles Cavendish, as Knight of the Shire of Nottingham and suggested that one of his own sons be chosen in his place. He justified his objection to Sir Charles by giving a garbled, and profoundly biased, report of the 'attack' on Sheffield Castle which had followed his attempt to 'reclaim his property' that had been 'illegally removed to Chatsworth'. Sir Charles was arrested and remained in gaol until Bess provided the Privy Council with a more accurate account of the incident.

Sir Ralph Sadler did not remain Mary's custodian for long. War with Spain seemed unavoidable. Colleges at Douai and Rome were dedicated to 'returning England to the true faith' and the faithful assured their French and Spanish patrons that if there was an invasion Catholics throughout the country would rise in its support – led by exiled priests who had, secretly, returned home. Unjustified boasts in Paris and Madrid were matched by unreasonable fears in London. They were usually built around the news that another Jesuit priest had been found fermenting treason. One of them, Edmund Campion, announced that 'a league of all the Jesuits of the world' would descend on England with 'an enterprise' which, since 'it is of God cannot be withstood' and he was taken so seriously that Leicester himself interrogated him before he was subjected to routine torture. There was a continual fear that the Avenging Fire – depicted in the picture over the altar in the English College in Rome as certain to engulf England – would be ignited when Mary was rescued or escaped. In consequence it was essential to prevent her from sending or receiving messages – a task which was never successfully accomplished.

In April 1585, a new attempt to cut the lines of seditious communication was made by the appointment of a new custodian, Sir Amias Paulet, a passionate anti-Catholic and natural authoritarian. He dismissed the laundresses – the traditional suspects whenever evidence of a message was discovered – instructed Mary to remove her Cloth of State from above her chair and refused permission for her to leave the house with the not altogether wise explanation that 'under cover of giving alms . . . she has won the hearts of the people'.[47] England was preparing for a subversion-backed invasion. Yet the Queen and her Privy Council were still willing to spend time in an attempt to reconcile the warring Shrewsburys: 'We have long desired for your own good and quiet that all matters of dispute between the countess, your sonnes and you might be brought to some good composition.'[48] The Queen needed the great families of England to be at peace with themselves so that they were ready for war with the nation's enemies. In November 1585, the Queen commissioned two Midland worthies – Sir Francis Willoughby of Wollaton Manor and Sir John Manners of Haddon Hall – to inquire into the Shrewsbury marriage.

After six months of deliberation, the commission ruled on various debts, claimed to be outstanding by the Earl and his stepsons. In a judgment which blamed them both but was clearly more critical of Shrewsbury, they ordered that 'all suits against the Countess must cease' and that none of her tenants should be displaced.[49] The ruling was conveyed to Shrewsbury with a letter from the Queen which – while leaving no doubt that the instructions must be obeyed – was equally clear that Elizabeth attributed Shrewsbury's behaviour to 'variances [which had] greatly disquieted him' and required 'repose, especially of the mind'.[50] The Earl rejected the findings and Bess refuted all suggestions that she had contributed to the Earl's disturbed condition. They were both called before Walsingham and Cecil to give an account of the way in which they intended to respond to the commission's findings. Peace of a sort was restored – reinforced by the Queen's decision that the Earl would be fined £4,000 if he molested Bess. Shrewsbury still pressed Bess to pay her supposed debts. But in the summer of 1586, the Queen and Court – and even the incompatible Shrewsburys – had to turn their minds to more serious matters.

Walsingham – always convinced that while Mary lived, the kingdom was in peril – had at last found evidence of a plot that made Elizabeth reconsider the divine right of queens not to be tried for treason. Anthony Babington, who had once been Shrewsbury's page, had conspired with Bernardino de Mendoza – Spanish Ambassador to the Court of Saint James's until he was expelled from England – to combine the assassination of Elizabeth and the uprising of English Catholics with the support of a Spanish invasion. Walsingham's agents, who had infiltrated the conspiracy, provided irrefutable proof that Mary – by then moved to Chartley Castle – had agreed to the whole plan. The evidence included a letter which she had hoped to smuggle out of Chartley in a beer barrel. Brewing was adjudged to be so conducive to subversion that the brewing was moved from both Chartley and Chatsworth to Burton-on-Trent – where it has flourished ever since.

Elizabeth still hoped that the prematurely aged and increasingly infirm Scottish Queen would die of natural causes but, after days of argument, agreed she should be tried for treason and – after further indecision – that the trial should be held in Fotheringhay Castle in Northampton. The commission, whose verdict was not in doubt, consisted of twenty-four Privy Councillors and men of rank. Shrewsbury was invited to preside. The Lord Chancellor, hearing that the Earl had described himself as too ill to take part, told him, menacingly, 'I would advise you not to be absent.'[51] The Earl heeded the warning and was rewarded for his loyalty by being chosen to tell Mary that she had been sentenced to death. On the morning of Monday January 8 1587 he sat on a stool close to the block and, in the moments before the execution, exhorted Mary to heed the words of the Protestant priest who prayed for her heavenly redemption. Then he broke down in tears.

George Talbot, Sixth Earl of Shrewsbury, died on November 18 1590 – apparently at peace with the world and in the company of Eleanor Britton, his housekeeper who, through most of the years of tribulation, had been his mistress. A year before, on the death of Peter Barlow, he had purchased all the land which remained in the ownership of the Barlow family. Despite the estrangement, Bess inherited a third of his estate. Combined with the receipts from the jointures of other husbands, Bess's dower income was, in consequence, something between £7,000 and £10,000 a year. She had become – after only the Queen – the richest woman in England. Gilbert Talbot, the Earl's heir, was not so lucky. He had to raid Eleanor Britton's house to recover the family plate and was obliged to contest in court the ownership of land which he had taken for granted his father would leave to him.

Perhaps, as he compared his mother-in-law's condition to his own, he regretted taking her part against his father. Bess's prosperity had become obvious – indeed was flaunted – even before her husband died. She proclaimed her prosperity by not only building a new wing and adding two storeys to Old Hardwick Hall, but also by planning a new house nearby – designed by Robert Smythson, the architect employed at Longleat. It still stands, in almost exactly the state in which it was designed, overlooking the Lea Valley and proclaiming the rank and status of its builder by the huge stone initials which crown its towers – ES for Elizabeth Shrewsbury.

When the frenzy of building was at its height, 375 workmen toiled under Bess's close supervision. One of her notes of instruction reads: 'Because the walls rise and be not well, nor all of one colour, they must be whited in the plasterer's charge.'[52] And she was as impatient as she was meticulous. Special machinery was constructed to facilitate the cutting of hard stone. Glaziers – who normally only polished panes and fitted them to windows – were employed, in times of shortage, to make glass on the site. Bess could have lived happily in the Old Hall or in any of the other properties which she acquired, in an orgy of buying, during her last decade.* But she chose to move into Hardwick New Hall on Monday October 4 1597 (two years before the building was finished) and use the Old Hall as an annexe. She was beginning to feel that time was running out.

Ironically, the woman who had so carefully planned a dynasty could not look forward, with any certainty, to the succession and the security of the property in which she placed such store. Chatsworth was entailed to Henry, her oldest son, who – through his marriage to Shrewsbury's daughter, Grace – should have made the major contribution to the noble line. Yet, although he was father to several bastards, he had not produced the necessary heir. His mother called him 'my bad son Henry' and was as much offended by his gambling as by his promiscuity.

---

* They included Stainsby Manor, estates in Stavely, Clowne and Bolsover, small manors in Lartington, Cotherstone, Claxby and Cleasby, various rectories and avowsons – some as far away as County Durham.

William, her favourite son, remained close. He lived with her, in Hardwick, through both his marriages. It fell to him to continue the Cavendish line. But before he received his inheritance, Bess had come to the dangerous conclusion that perhaps even greater glory awaited the Cavendish family.

CHAPTER 4

A Cavendish Queen?

It fell to Geoffrey Talbot – stepson of Bess of Hardwick, Mary Stuart's occasional friend – to carry the news of the Scottish Queen's death to the Court. Elizabeth claimed and perhaps, in the emotion of the moment, actually believed that she had not intended the immediate discharge of the death warrant which she had gladly signed. But whatever her anguish about the execution of an anointed queen, she must have taken consolation in the thought that she had eliminated the only pretender to the English throne who combined the claims of blood and birth with the inclination to challenge her authority. Mary's self-destructive support for the Babington Plot had, at least in part, been the result of the discovery that James, her son, had concluded an alliance with Elizabeth – the acceptance that he was successor rather than immediate claimant in return for an allowance of £400 a year. But James had been brought up a Protestant. And the Church of Rome did not lightly abandon its hope of returning England to the 'true religion'. Achieving that ambition depended on finding a Catholic claimant to the crown.

The essential qualification was descent from Henry Tudor – through either of his daughters, the Princesses Margaret and Mary. Margaret, the older of the sisters, had married James IV of Scotland and was, therefore, a queen in her own right. Her second husband, following the death of the King, was the Sixth Earl of Angus. Their daughter, another Margaret, married the Fourth Earl of Lennox and with him produced two sons. One was Henry Stuart, Lord Darnley, the husband of Mary Queen of Scots. The other was Charles Stuart, who confusingly became the First Earl of Lennox by the third creation. It was his daughter, Arbella, on whom rebellious Catholics eventually pinned their hopes. At the moment that a coup seemed possible she was third in line to the English throne. Arbella's mother was Elizabeth Cavendish, the daughter of Bess of Hardwick, the Countess of Shrewsbury.

Arbella inherited as much trouble as royal blood. At the time when both Henry VIII's daughters, Mary and Elizabeth, were declared illegitimate, her grandmother had been heir presumptive to the English throne. Yet she had become betrothed, without the King's permission, to Thomas Howard. She was sent to the Tower and parliament passed the Act which required men and women of the blood royal to obtain the sovereign's permission before marriage. When the birth of Prince Edward provided an heir apparent to Henry VIII, Margaret was released. Howard died shortly afterwards and it was then that she was contracted in a marriage of political convenience, to Matthew Stuart, the Fourth Earl of Lennox. Stuart was a pro-English Catholic, who spent many years at Queen Mary Tudor's Court and retained his power and influence after the accession of Elizabeth in 1558.

In 1564, the Earl of Lennox returned to Scotland, but the Countess – who had become one of Bess's closest friends – remained in England. A year later she was again committed to the Tower after arranging, without royal approval, the marriage of Lord Darnley, her elder son, to Mary Queen of Scots. Darnley was murdered in 1567. Lennox – who had been made regent to James, Mary's infant son – was assassinated in 1571 and in November 1574 the Countess was released from the Tower. She immediately asked permission to visit Scotland and see her fatherless grandchild – the son of Mary Queen of Scots. The French Ambassador had no illusions about the real object of her journey. 'I greatly suspect that she has no other purpose than to transfer the little prince into England.'[1] But, in one of the idiosyncratic decisions which were a mark of her character, Queen Elizabeth agreed to Margaret's request with the proviso that she did not visit her daughter-in-law, the Scottish Queen, on the way north. The order was obeyed. The Dowager Countess did not call at Chatsworth, but she and her nineteen-year-old son – the Earl of Lennox after his father's assassination – broke their journey at Rufford Abbey in Nottinghamshire. Bess travelled 20 miles east to be reunited with her old friend, taking with her – as a travelling companion – her twenty-year-old unmarried daughter, Elizabeth. Margaret was unwell. So the whole party remained at Rufford for almost a week. It was long enough for Elizabeth Cavendish and Charles Stuart to fall in love. Royal blood flowed in both Charles's and Elizabeth's veins. Once again the Lennox family defied the Royal Marriages Act.

The Earl of Shrewsbury was determined to avoid both blame and responsibility. The explanation which he sent to Lord Burghley got near to defending the match, but he made clear, with the words 'as my wife tells me', that he was doing no more than repeating Bess's view that 'they hath tied themselves upon [their] own liking as they cannot part'.[2] His letter to Queen Elizabeth was more explicit. 'The marriage was dealt in suddenly and without my knowledge . . . My wife finding . . . that the young gentleman was inclined to love within a few days acquaintance, did her best to further her daughter in this match, without having therein any other intent or respect than reverent duty towards your Majesty.'³ He was almost certainly right. Bess – despite her dynastic ambitions – had more sense than to believe that the remote chance of a Cavendish queen justified conduct which, although beginning in romance, could end in high treason. Her motive in encouraging the match was clear. Elizabeth – Bess's only unmarried daughter – had recently been rejected by a minor member of the Huntingdon family and her mother worried that she would go, a spinster, into old age.

The Queen took it for granted that Margaret, Countess of Lennox was motivated by more than her romantic disposition. She had told Lord Burghley that her 'son . . . entangled himself so that he could have no other'.⁴ But Elizabeth, unwilling to believe the story, ordered her back to London and again sent her to the Tower. The lament, 'Thrice have I been cast into prison, not for matters of treason but for love matters',⁵ was disingenuous. She was imprisoned because she had form. The Dowager Countess of Lennox was a known intriguer.

Within three months of marriage, Elizabeth Cavendish – the new Countess of Lennox – was pregnant, a happy event which, irrationally, was taken to confirm the political innocence of the young couple's alliance. The baby, a girl, was born on November 10 1575 and christened Arbella. Tudor portraits of children are notoriously unflattering. So Arbella may not have been quite as unprepossessing as the picture, painted when she was twenty-three months old, suggests. Even if it was a true likeness, what she lacked in beauty she made up in character and conduct. In January 1577, when she was barely a year old, Elizabeth Wingfield – Bess's half-sister – described her as a 'good child'.⁶ And it seems that she actually improved. Ten years later she assured the child's grandmother that 'Lady Arbella is so good a child as can be'.⁷ Her virtue was not rewarded.

Charles Stuart, Earl of Lennox, died of consumption in April 1576 eighteen months after his marriage to Elizabeth Cavendish. Arbella, their daughter, was barely six months old. According to Scottish law, Elizabeth should have inherited both his English and his Scottish lands and Arbella should have succeeded to his title. But the new regent of Scotland – governing on behalf of the young James, Arbella's cousin – immediately expropriated both the earldom and the Scottish property and placed them at the boy King's disposal. Mary Queen of Scots, who had toyed with the idea of willing the Scottish Crown to Arbella's father, tried to insist that justice be done. 'I give my niece, Arbella, the Earldom of Lennox, held by her late father and enjoin my son as my heir and successor to obey my will in this particular.'⁸ But when the twelve-year-old James deposed the regent and assumed the throne, he preferred to elevate the elderly Bishop of Caithness. At Bess's suggestion, Queen Elizabeth sent a message to the Scots supporting Arbella's claim to the earldom and the Scottish land. But her sympathy did not extend to making a personal sacrifice. While the dispute was going on, the Dowager Countess Lennox died and was given the funeral in Westminster Abbey which was deemed suitable to Henry Tudor's granddaughter. It was arranged by the Court and paid for by Queen Elizabeth, who then announced that she was expropriating the Lennox's English lands to cover the cost. Elizabeth Lennox, the dead Countess's daughter-in-law, was left destitute. The Shrewsburys – despite Bess's later protestations of affection and concern – had not provided her with a dowry. It seemed that all that was left of the whole Lennox inheritance was the family jewels which the Dowager Countess had left explicitly to Arbella and were in the safe keeping of Thomas Fowler, the executor of her will.

Arbella never received them. The will was explicit. On the death of the Dowager, Thomas Fowler should have given the jewels to Elizabeth Lennox who was to remain their custodian until her daughter's fourteenth birthday. A year later they were still in Fowler's possession. The Queen of Scots sent him a stern instruction to hand them, without delay, to her 'right well-beloved cousin'. Fowler ignored the order. Instead, he left for an undisclosed destination in Scotland and reported that he was robbed of the jewels on the way.[9] Eventually they followed an unknown route into the possession of King James. He kept them.

Only Bess stood between the Lennoxes and absolute poverty. She could easily have afforded to keep both her daughter and granddaughter in the level of luxury which she herself enjoyed. But that was not Bess's way. Instead she persuaded Burghley and Walsingham to petition Queen Elizabeth with the request that they be granted a state pension. Some time during 1577, the request was granted. The Queen agreed to pay £200 a year to Arbella and £400 to Elizabeth, her mother. It was her last act of generosity towards the family. Elizabeth Lennox died in 1582. During her last days she had sent a message to Burghley, Leicester, Walsingham and Hatton. It begged them to 'continue their wanton favours to the small orphan'.[10] Bess took the more practical course of asking that the £400 pension, which had been granted to her daughter Elizabeth, be transferred to Arbella. Neither request was granted. But by making it, Bess conceded that Arbella was her responsibility and, in effect, a member of her household. It was not the ideal environment in which to rear an easily disturbed teenage girl.

By the time of Arbella's 'adoption' the Earl and Countess of

Shrewsbury were living apart – united only by mutual animosity. So Arbella lived surrounded by hatred and fear – enough, in itself, to destroy what little feeling of personal security a recently orphaned child was likely to enjoy. And she lived under a second cloud. At an age when girls were betrothed long before puberty, Arbella had yet to be found a suitable husband. In normal circumstances that would have been a task which her grandmother enjoyed. But Arbella was not a normal child. She was – if the blood line was the only test – next in line to the throne of England after Mary Queen of Scots, her aunt by marriage, and James VI of Scotland, her cousin. What was more, unlike them, she had been born in England and in consequence was, according to some authorities, entitled to precedence over the Scottish claimants. That meant that every possible 'match' was judged by its potential effect on Arbella's prospects as a pretender to the Crown.

All sorts of unlikely possibilities were discussed. In 1581, there was talk of an engagement to Esme Stuart, a distant relative of young King James whose only qualification was his acquisition of the Lennox land and earldom, which had been surrendered by the Bishop of Caithness.[11] The advantage of reuniting Arbella with the title and property which were rightly hers was more than outweighed by Esme's personal unsuitability. He was forty and Arbella was ten. Worse still, he was a Catholic and virulently anti-English. Four years later, there were rumours that Arbella would marry James himself. But although the match would have ended all disputes about the succession, it might have encouraged the belief that such obvious claimants to the throne had no need to wait for it to be vacated. Bess decided to find a husband for her granddaughter, purely on her own initiative. It was a task to which she turned with more enthusiasm than discretion.

Bess must have known that Queen Elizabeth would only approve a marriage which both suited the Queen's caprice and contributed to the political interests of England. Yet – whether she initiated them or not – she became embroiled in plans for Arbella's future which might have been designed to cause offence. On March 4 1584 Lord Paget told the Earl of Northumberland that 'the Queen should be informed of the practices between Leicester and the Countess [of Shrewsbury] for Arbella'.[12] The 'practices' to which he referred were negotiations – including the exchange of portraits – about the possibility of ten-year-old Arbella's being betrothed to the Earl of Leicester's four-year-old son by Lettice Knollys. Paget clearly had no doubt that the purpose of the proposed union was the creation of a new dynasty with claims to the throne. He was not alone in that belief. When Mary Queen of Scots heard of the proposed match, less than three weeks after the news reached the Court, she immediately seized the opportunity both to ingratiate herself with Queen Elizabeth and to damage Bess. 'Nothing ever alienated the Countess from me more than the vain hope she has conceived of setting the Crown on her grand-daughter Arbella's head, even by marrying her to the Earl of Leicester's son. Divers tokens have been exchanged between the children.'[13]

Before the rumour could grow into an accusation the Leicester boy died. From then on, the search for a suitable suitor was pursued with more circumspection – which meant that Arbella became a pawn in the dynastic game. In a Court which was riddled by intrigue and infested by suspicion, there was always the fear that she would become infatuated by an adventurer who made her the rallying point for rebellion. As a result, for much of her life she was almost as much a prisoner as Mary Queen of Scots. Bess, Countess of Shrewsbury, was again the gaoler.

Despite the knowledge that she would be called to account by Queen Elizabeth when her granddaughter showed signs of independent thought or action Bess allowed Arbella to visit her aunt and uncle-by-marriage,* the new Earl and Countess of Shrewsbury. The Countess, Mary Talbot, was a 'recusant' who flaunted her continued Catholicism by refusing to attend Church of England services. Yet despite her Popish sympathies – and the difference in their ages – Mary Talbot became something approaching a much-needed friend. But the friendship, welcome though it was to the often lonely Arbella, added to the Court's concerns about her future. When Arbella flirted with rebellion – always against the restraints which were imposed upon her rather than the monarch, the established Church or the state – her association with Mary Talbot contributed to the suspicion that she was being manipulated by Rome. In fact she never gave any indication that she possessed pronounced religious views – either Catholic or Protestant. But while Mary Queen of Scots was alive almost everything that Arbella did was seen through the prism of possible treason.

In June 1587, five months after the execution of Mary Queen of Scots, Arbella – despite having moved one place closer to the throne – was invited to Court. The reason is unknown. The rational explanation is that cultivation of Arbella's goodwill seemed more expedient than alienating her affection. But the likelihood is that – like so many of the decisions taken by Elizabeth – Arbella's rehabilitation was purely the result of a royal whim.

---

* Because of the Byzantine marriages arranged by Bess and the Sixth Earl for their children, he was also her step-uncle.

Arbella was an instant success. But the seeds of her eventual social destruction had already been sown by her grandmother who had instructed, since her childhood, that she be addressed as 'Your Highness'. Her self-esteem was encouraged by an early invitation to sit next to the Queen at dinner. Perhaps she was entitled to be treated like royalty. But, in a court where pretensions were regarded as a mark of disloyalty, it was a dangerous right to exercise. At first the airs and graces did Arbella no harm. She was cultivated by Lord Burghley who 'spoke openly and directed his speech to Sir Walter Raleigh, greatly in her commendation'.[14] His aside that he 'wished she were fifteen' was, we must presume, related to his plan for her to be betrothed to Rainutio Farnese, the son of the Duke of Parma, the Spanish Governor-General of the Netherlands. The arrangement was intended as a gesture towards Philip of Spain which, it was hoped, would promote a swift end to the war in the Spanish Netherlands. The plan was endorsed by Queen Elizabeth, and Burghley instructed his agents to enquire into Farnese's political suitability. Nicholas Hilliard, the Queen's portraitist, was commissioned to paint a miniature to be sent to the prospective bridegroom as proof of Arbella's youthful attractions. Before the deal could be done, the Duke of Parma was relieved of his command and, since the marriage had no purpose other than the creation of a direct line into the Spanish high command, the idea was abandoned. From start to finish, Arbella was not consulted.

Although all the plans came to nothing the possibility of Arbella being married for reasons of state made her a figure of apparent consequence. Her new status stimulated James, or his counsellors, into adding a further insistence to the demand that Queen Elizabeth should acknowledge him as her 'lawful and nearest successor to the Crown, failing her bodily succession', so as 'to remove all suspicion of her evil meaning, specially after the infernal proceedings against his dearest mother'. He also demanded that Elizabeth should demonstrate her goodwill by granting him 'some lands in England . . . with the title of Duke'.[15]

Arbella remained at Court for a year, but – to emphasise that she was a guest, not a resident – her personal effects were never brought to London from Chatsworth. Her decision to lodge with the known recusants Gilbert and Mary Talbot fuelled new, and even more wild, speculation about her future. It was rumoured that Queen Elizabeth had told the wife of the French Ambassador, 'Look well to her: she will be even as I am and a lady mistress. But I will have gone before.'[16] James began to fear that he had a credible rival. Before the year ended, he demanded, in anticipation of his elevation, that the law should stipulate that 'The Lady Arbella shall not be given in marriage without the King's consent'.[17] Had he been familiar with the laws of the country which was to become his kingdom, he would have known that, being of the – admittedly diluted – blood royal, she was already under that obligation.

Although Arbella's first visit to Court was an undoubted success, her second ended in disaster. Some time in July 1588, Armada year, Elizabeth decreed that the whole Cavendish family must leave London. With an invasion imminent, it was thought expedient to move Catholic sympathisers, no matter how well connected, out of the capital. But the real cause of the expulsion was Arbella's behaviour. The Venetian Ambassador to London told the Doge, 'The Lady Arbella displayed such a haughtiness that she soon began to claim first place and one day, going into chapel, she herself took such precedence of all the princesses who were in her Majesty's suite . . . At this time, the Queen in indignation ordered her back to her private existence.'[18] And, years later, Arbella herself admitted that, long ago, she had committed an indiscretion, as a result of which it had 'pleased hir Majesty that I should be disgraced in the Presence at Greenwich'.[19] Arbella had not accepted the rebuke with good grace. She had denounced 'the most ridiculous world' into which she had been translated and added, bitterly, 'If ever there was such a virtue as courtesy at Court, I marvel at what has become of it.'[20] Thanks to her grandmother's influence, Arbella had developed ideas above even her station.

Despite the inauspicious reason for her swift return north, Arbella settled well in Derbyshire – perhaps too well if Nicholas Kinnersley, her steward, is to be believed. For, although she was 'merry' and ate 'her meat well', she 'went not to school'.[21] Kinnersley took the view that only Bess's arrival at Wingfield Manor, where Arbella was temporarily accommodated, could restore proper discipline to the household. However, Bess was preoccupied with other family matters. While London rejoiced at what turned out to be the temporary defeat of the Armada and Leicester wrote to Shrewsbury in Derbyshire to describe Queen Elizabeth's address to her troops at Tilbury, Bess was waging a war of her own on her husband's relatives. When the old Earl of Shrewsbury died in 1590, the new Earl had immediately contested his will with the claim that his sons should receive more and his widow less.

Bess's relations with Arbella were undoubtedly complicated by her suspicion that both Talbots – including her daughter, Mary – were no longer her loyal friends. Combined with Arbella's strange position in society – part royal favourite and part suspected rallying point for rebellion – the friendship encouraged the absurd rumour that Arbella had secretly married. The bridegroom – who, it seems, knew no more of the betrothal than his bride – was Harry Percy, Earl of Northumberland. The suggestion that he had become Arbella's husband caused particular consternation. Harry Percy was a Catholic. Then there was talk of her marrying Ludovic Stuart, the son of Esme who had been touted ten years earlier as a possible husband and who, according to his father, 'longeth for Arbella'. A marriage with either of the Stuarts was thought plausible because it would have reunited Arbella with the Lennox jewels.

Arbella spent most of the sixteenth century's last decade in Derbyshire, but there was a long visit to London with the whole Talbot-Shrewsbury families, during which she made several appearances at Court. She was there at Christmas 1592 when she received a Christmas message from her cousin James – either the result of a guilty conscience (occasioned by another refusal to return the Lennox jewels) or the belief that, as Elizabeth's reign drew to its close, it was prudent for him to make a friend of his cousin. The message was redolent with insincerity. 'As the strict band of nature and blood, whereby we are linked [one] to another craveth a most entire goodwill . . . so we have of a long time carried a most earnest desire to contract that acquaintance by letters, as witness of the conjunction of hearts . . .'[22]

Whether or not life at Court was enjoyable to Arbella, it was certainly expensive. Courtesy required the exchange of lavish gifts and there was what amounted to a competition in the display of extravagant finery. In 1591, Bess had spent £200 on jewellery, including 'five little jewels' at 14s a piece and 'one of a bee' for 6s 8d, and £100 to hire the Bishop of Bristol's barge to take her family down the Thames to Court in Greenwich Palace.[23] Entries in her account books record the purchase of silk, lace and perfumed gloves – all intended to make a show. Arbella, again popular at Court, added to the cost. Mary Talbot told her mother that 'the Queen asked very carefully' after Arbella.[24] Royal commendations meant that sixteen-year-old Arbella deserved – indeed required – to be indulged. Elizabeth Wingfield wrote to Bess, in distress with the news that the tailor had only 5¼ yards of green velvet when 7 were needed to make a dress for 'as good a child as can be'.[25]

Bess, whose extravagance knew no bounds, would have gladly continued to squander part of her substantial fortune on a life illuminated by proximity to Gloriana. But the Queen, or her counsellors, again changed their view about the best way to ensure that Arbella did not become a threat to the tranquillity of the realm. She was once more sent back to remote Derbyshire. One letter from Bess to Burghley assured him that she was kept under the strictest supervision. 'Arbella walks not late. At such time as she takes the air it shall be near the house and well attended. She goes not to anybody's house at all. I see her almost every hour of the day and she lieth in my bed-chamber.'[26]

It was not long before the Privy Council felt that its caution had been vindicated. A captured Jesuit – who had defied the statute which prohibited, on pain of death, members of his society from entering England – had confessed that there was a plot for 'two Scotch Catholics to convey Arbella out England by stealth'.[27] It was not clear if the intention was to make her a puppet queen or to prevent her claiming the throne in advance of a genuine Catholic pretender. Sir William Stanley – an exiled zealot, quoted by the priest as the authority for the kidnap story – was reputed to have told the Spanish Court that 'one young lady, yet unmarried, was the greatest fear [that Rome] had, lest she should be proclaimed queen, that it should happen that her Majesty should happen to die'.[28] Had the stories been true, Arbella would have enjoyed the unusual distinction of being both the Protestant and Catholic favourite candidate to usurp the throne of England. Burghley must have regarded the stories as fantasies but their repetition could only inhibit the peaceful and orderly transition from monarch to monarch. The peace and safety of the realm required undisturbed progress towards the eventual accession to the English throne of James VI of Scotland.

Burghley – and Robert Cecil, his increasingly powerful son – realised that, although exiled to Derbyshire, Arbella might still be vulnerable to the machinations of Catholic dissidents. The county had been a hotbed of willing martyrs. In 1588, the Earl of Shrewsbury himself had arrested Nicholas Garlick and Robert Ludlam in Padley Manor House at Hathersage, 10 miles from Chatsworth, and – not least because they had converted a convicted murderer on their way to the scaffold – their martyrdom had encouraged open antagonism to the established Church. It was the age of spies and counter-spies. A network of agents reported to Robert Cecil on the machinations which surrounded Arbella Stuart. Their reports gave different accounts of the role which potential rebels hoped she would play. None of them said that she encouraged or, indeed, knew much about, the proposed treason. But an informer by the name of Barnes, describing the hopes of irreconcilable Catholics, warned that 'all platforms fell to the ground on the death of the Queen of Scots . . . They harp much on Lady Arbella, despairing of the King of Scots.'[29] And Arbella's family made both the Cecils nervous by expecting her to be treated like royalty.

A pamphlet, entitled 'A Conference About the Next Succession to the Crown of England', claimed that Arbella was disqualified by the double illegitimacy which was the consequence of both her parents being formally betrothed to other suitors before they married. Even more improbable was the fear, said to be felt by James himself, that 'the Queen of England would persuade the French King . . . either to divorce or kill his wife and to marry himself with the Lady Arbella to bring him into the succession of England'. There were reports that Henri IV of France had said 'neither would I refuse the Princess Arbella of England if, as is publicly said, the crown of England really belongs to her',[30] and even the suggestion that Robert Cecil meant to make her his wife as the sure and certain way of becoming King. Arbella believed that James himself encouraged stories of one improper relationship by 'unprincely and unchristian giving ear to the slanderous and unlikely surmise of the Earl of Essex and me'.[31] That rumour was potentially lethal as well as scurrilous. The relationship was long over and probably innocent. But Essex was Elizabeth's new favourite and, at the same time, was known to covet the throne.

In fact, what little chance of the succession Arbella had once possessed had been extinguished. The delegation that came from Scotland, bearing James's congratulations on Elizabeth's suppression of the Essex rebellion, had signed a secret agreement with the elder Cecil. On the Queen's death, the thrones of England and Scotland would be united. But in order to ensure a smooth transition, it was still necessary to make sure that Arbella was not contracted to a reckless adventurer. Or that she gave any comfort to traitors. Arbella was incapable of observing the necessary discipline.

In 1601, the Earl of Essex – after he had compounded the offences of military incompetence, political ineptitude and personal impropriety with open rebellion – was tried for treason, found guilty and executed. Recklessly, Arbella ignored the inglorious record and announced that he died 'Unbound because he was a prince'. The moral she drew from what she saw as heroic defiance was expressed in a rhetorical question which, although close to gibberish, signified a loyalty to Essex rather than to the Queen: 'Shall my hands be bound in helping myself from this distress?'[32] But it was not only romantic illusions that fed Arbella's discontent. In her late twenties she was, at best, treated like a child. At worst she lived, as the Venetian Ambassador described, 'not so much a prisoner but, so to speak, buried alive'.[33] Her incarceration was becoming increasingly difficult to bear. She spent her days in Hardwick – where the building of the new hall had been completed – reading, working on her embroidery and growing more and more resentful about the restrictions which statecraft and circumstances had imposed upon her. Escape became an obsession.

James Starkey – one of the several Protestant priests in Bess's household – became Arbella's confidant. She told him that being tired of being 'bobbed and her nose played withal' like a naughty child, she had 'thought of all means she could to get from home' where she was 'hardly used in despiteful and disgraceful words'.[34] She had a plan. It involved a message being taken to London. Starkey was asked to take it. The inducement, which she hoped would secure his help, probably acted as a deterrent. He was promised a prosperous living when her 'time came'. That sounded as if the revolution was on its way. Starkey's anxiety turned to panic when he discovered that the message had to be conveyed verbally to the Earl of Hertford's attorney. He withdrew his offer of help. John Dodderidge, one of Bess's oldest retainers, was persuaded, with some difficulty, to take Starkey's place. He carried the message that amounted to the suggestion that Arbella should marry Edward Seymour, the Earl's sixteen-year-old grandson – an idea that Dodderidge was instructed to say had come from Arbella's uncles, William and Henry Cavendish.

The idea was deeply dangerous as well as ridiculous. Hertford was the son of Edward Seymour, Duke of Somerset, brother to Henry VIII's third wife and the disgraced Lord Protector who had ruled England during the reign of Edward VI. Hertford had married, without permission, Catherine Grey – sister of the executed Lady Jane – a union which Elizabeth had refused to recognise since that would have enabled his children and grandchildren to trace their blood line back to Henry VII. Tenuous though Seymour's claim to the succession undoubtedly was, it would have been strengthened by marriage to Arbella. But that was of no concern to Arbella. All she wanted was to escape from her grandmother. The extent of her desperation was exemplified by the manic, and self-defeating, detail in which she set out her plan. Edward Seymour and a companion were to gain entrance to Hardwick by pretending they were looking to buy land and were then to confirm their identity by showing her a letter written by the long-dead pretender to the throne, Lady Jane Grey!

Hertford chose prudence over chivalry and reported Dodderidge's stuttered message to Robert Cecil. The result was an official inquiry conducted at Hardwick by Sir Henry Brounker, an elderly and remarkably benevolent court official. It concluded that the Cavendish brothers were in no way involved and that Arbella's offence was caused by 'vanity and love of herself rather than want of duty and contempt'. The report concluded, indulgently, that it was 'not strange for a young lady to err'.[35] Perhaps his judgement was tempered by Dodderidge's diagnosis of Arbella's real complaint. He attributed the whole affair to 'wits throughout disordered either from fear of her grandmother or conceit

of herself'.[36] Although Arbella escaped without punishment, the consequences of the incident can only have driven her nearer to the edge
of reason and intensified the distressing scrutiny of all that she did.
Invitations from her aunt Mary Talbot were intercepted by Cecil's
agents, who returned counterfeit replies which were intended to
convince Arbella that she had even been rejected by her only friend.
Bess, who had long grown weary of her granddaughter's company,
was so unnerved by the affair that she wrote to the Queen with a plea
and a warning. 'I am desirous and most humbly beseech your Majesty
that she may be placed elsewhere . . . I cannot now assure myself of
her as I have done.'[37] The Queen did not respond. So, much to Bess's
distress, she remained a gaoler.

By the end of 1602, grandmother and granddaughter were both
near to breaking point. Arbella regarded Bess as 'the greatest enemy
she hath'. So it may be that the warning sent to the Queen in January
1603 was the product of a conspiracy between two women with a
mutual passion to escape each other. There was, Bess claimed, 'another
match in working, but who the party should be' she could not say.
'Sometimes she will say she can be taken away off my hands if she so
wills.'[38] The liberating hero was a figment of Arbella's imagination. He
was described in a rambling statement – six pages long – that she sent
to Bess on February 2 that year. Clearly she wanted and expected the
news of a new liaison to be passed on to Burghley.[39] Her phantom
lover – who was certainly not Edward Seymour – was described as a
man so loyal that he would rather abandon Arbella than 'incurre hir
Majesties displeasure'. Yet he had persuaded her to 'enter into some
great action' to win herself repute and test the Queen's affection. Four
days later she changed tack and asked for relaxation of the rules which
governed her conduct rather than boasting that rescue was at hand.

In reaction to Arbella's lapse into fantasy, Robert Cecil wrote to Bess
with the advice that it would be best not subject her granddaughter to
'any extraordinary restraint'. In a letter to John Stanhope, the Vice-
President of the Council, Arbella requested an interpretation of Cecil's
wishes and asked if it 'be in her Majesty's pleasure I should well have
the company of some young lady or gentlewoman for my recreation'
and whether or not 'it be her Highness pleasure to allow me that liberty
(being on 6 February 27 years old) to choose my choice of abode'.[40]
The letter concluded with an offer to reveal her secret lover's name to
the Queen – a dramatic flourish that did not obscure its real purpose.
Above all else, Arbella wanted to live apart from her grandmother.

Cecil and Stanhope were more alarmed than reassured by what was
obviously the emotional outpouring of a disturbed and distressed young

woman. So Brounker was sent back to Hardwick to conduct another examination. Arbella's response included the bizarre 'admission' that her secret lover was 'the Kinge of the Scottes'.[41] On the day that she recorded her answers to Brounker's cross-examination she also wrote to him the first of a series of letters which confirmed her anguish. There were eight letters in ten days. One, written on February 25 1603, the second anniversary of Essex's execution, included her lament for her old friend. Much of what she wrote was barely comprehensible. But there is no doubt that she believed that she was, in some way, being victimised because of her relationship with Queen Elizabeth's fallen favourite. 'They are dead whom I loved. They have forsaken me whom I trusted . . . I am dangerous to my most guiltless friends . . . How dare others visit me in distress when the Earl of Essex, then in the highest favour scarse dare steale a salutation in the Privy chamber?'[42] Arbella boasted that she had remained faithful to the 'noble friend who graced [her] . . . in his greatest and happiest fortune', even though he knew that the relationship could only result in the 'eclipsing [of] part of her Majesty's favours from him'.[43] All the letters were a sad combination of apologies and complaints and they all – directly or by implication – made clear that her object was freedom from her grand-mother's tyranny. She hoped that after she had endured her punishment she would be allowed to 'leave all troubles behind . . . and go into a better place than hir Majesty hath provided these last 27 years'.[44] To 'reobtaine hir majesties favour and have [her] dear and due liberty' she was prepared to promise 'never to marry while i live'.[45]

Nobody believed her. Indeed the offer was taken to be the first move in a devious stratagem. Bess complained that her granddaughter's conduct was undermining her health and Scaramelli, the Venetian Ambassador, told the Doge that the Queen had taken to her bed suffering from the same 'vexation'. Brounker, being a reasonable man, might well have attributed the talk of a forbidden marriage to the 'distemper of the brain' which he had detected in the disturbed young woman had he not, by chance, seen her uncle, Henry Cavendish, in the company of Henry Stapleton, a Catholic zealot who had taken lodgings in Mansfield, 10 miles from Chatsworth. Stapleton, Brounker discovered, had ridden north together with forty armed men – one of whom, significantly, had, behind his saddle, a pillion which he attempted to hide under a cloak. Suspicions turned into certainty when it was discovered that Richard Owen, Arbella's page, had visited Stapleton.

At about ten o'clock on the morning of March 9 1603, two men rode up to the gates of Hardwick House. At about the same time, Henry Cavendish and Stapleton arrived at Ault Hucknall parish church and asked the vicar for the keys to the tower – from the top of which Hardwick was in clear view. The vicar refused the request but allowed the two men to spend the morning in the vicarage. At about noon, Arbella 'Came forth from her chamber, went towards the gates, as she said intending to walk, but being persuaded it was dinner time, did stay'.[46] The message, carried by a servant to Ault Hucknall, contained neither explanation nor apology, only the bald statement, 'She cannot come out this day.' All that can be said for certain is that, when the time came, she lacked either the wish or the will to attempt an escape.

Henry Cavendish and Stapleton did not give up quite so easily. They rode to Hardwick and boldly asked for permission to see Arbella. Henry Cavendish, being a member of the family, could not – in Bess's judgement – be denied entry to the house but she 'would not suffer Stapleton to come within the gates'.[47] After a brief conversation, niece and uncle left the great hall and crossed the courtyard. Arbella spoke to Stapleton through the grille in the gatehouse door and then attempted to leave but the porter refused to let her go. After a not very emphatic protest, Henry Cavendish announced that he would return the next day and Bess, having decided that she had done all that courtesy required, told him that he would not be allowed through the gate. And so the escapade ended. Henry Cavendish – more motivated by resentment of his mother's clear preference for his brother William than either disapproval of the reigning monarch or enthusiasm to install a new one – lost interest in the whole enterprise. Arbella calmly accepted – with detached resignation – that the always doomed escape attempt had failed.

Faced with irrefutable evidence of a plot to defy the wishes of his sovereign lady, Brounker reacted with remarkable moderation. A warrant was issued, requiring all Derbyshire magistrates to prohibit 'unlawful assemblies and disorderly attempts' and, at the suggestion of Robert Cecil, the invitation for Henry Cavendish to explain himself to the Privy Council was conveyed in a 'friendly letter' rather than a summons. William Cavendish, as always at home with his mother, was exonerated of any involvement in the escapade as he was 'a weak man for such purposes'. Arbella was, however, to be held in greater security. Sir Francis Leake of Rufford Abbey and Sir John Manners of Haddon were instructed to assist in ensuring her safe keeping.

The discovery that the plotters had planned to take Arbella by sea from Hull to Scotland convinced Brounker that the worst that could be expected was another dash for liberty, not a plot to seize the throne. He concluded that Stapleton was 'a very wilful papist' and that a new urgency had been added to Arbella's plans for freedom by the assumption that the Queen would soon die, but there was 'no fear of any new practice . . . unless the opinion of her Majesty's sickness, which is here too common, draws on some sudden resolution'.[48] That conclusion combined complacency and – for a courtier and confidant – a strange ignorance of the true state of the Queen's health. At Hardwick, Arbella locked herself in her room while Brounker wrote his report. In Chatsworth House, Bess wrote a new will, disinheriting Arbella. In London, Robert Cecil, who had succeeded his father at the Queen's right hand, was drafting the proclamation that Queen Elizabeth would be succeeded by James VI of Scotland as the English sovereign.

Queen Elizabeth died on March 23 1603 – accompanied, as was inevitable, by new rumours of Papist rebellion. They included the suggestion – based on nothing more than his sudden departure from London – that Lord Beauchamp, the father of the man to whom Arbella had made her unexpected proposal, was to be Rome's standard-bearer. On May 5, James – who must have realised that he faced no serious opposition – set out on his stately progress from his old to his new kingdom. On his way south, he stayed with the Earl and Countess of Shrewsbury at Worksop Manor – either without knowing or caring about Mary Talbot's Catholic inclinations. Perhaps Mary spoke up for her niece. Or it may be that he believed the propaganda – spread by his supporters – that Arbella could never be queen because she was mad. Whatever the reason, he decided 'to free our cousin from the unpleasant life which she has led in the house of her grandmother with whose severity and age, she being a young lady, could hardly agree'.[49] The choice of residence was still not to be hers. But West Park in Bedfordshire – home of the Earl of Kent, a distant relative – was a great deal more congenial than Hardwick.

The Queen's death did nothing to reduce Arbella's bitter resentment of the way in which she had been treated. As Elizabeth's nearest female relative she was entitled to be chief mourner at the state funeral. She declined the invitation on the principle that, having often been denied audience in Elizabeth's lifetime, she was not going to pay court after her death. James – who himself had forbidden the wearing of mourning black – was not inclined to make an issue of the insult to his royal predecessor. Indeed he invited Arbella to Court when it assembled at Greenwich. From then on she was treated as a princess of the blood royal. Often she was included in the Court as it moved from palace to palace in the hope of escaping the plague. Usually she lived with the Shrewsburys. Often, when the Court was not meeting, she stayed with the Marchioness of Northampton at Sheen. Life improved. Then, in July 1603, she was unwittingly enmeshed in a real plot to kill the King.

There were two plots that summer. The first, the 'Bye Plot', was intended to do no more than kidnap James and hold him prisoner until he agreed to end the persecution of Catholics and Catholicism. The second, the 'Main Plot', planned the assassination of the King and his replacement, with the aid of a Spanish invasion, by Arbella Stuart whose always distant claim to the throne had become more remote with the birth of James's son. But the rebels – many of them motivated more by disappointment and envy than by religious conviction – were not interested in legitimacy. They simply wanted to replace James.

Doubts still remain about the extent of Walter Raleigh's involvement in the 'Main Plot'. But in the early summer of 1603 he was certainly consumed by the resentment which follows rejection. During Elizabeth's fading years he had been reinstated as Captain of the Guard. After openly rejoicing when his bitter rival Essex was executed for high treason, he had regained something like his old position at Court together with the emoluments that Elizabeth's favour always provided. All that counted against him when James became King. One of James's Scottish noblemen was appointed Captain of the Guard and Raleigh lost the income from the ownership of wine and woollen broadcloth monopolies as well as the income from tin mined in the Cornish stanneries. He was summarily evicted from his grace-and-favour house in the Strand and it was returned to the Bishop of Durham – whose predecessor had been dispossessed during the dissolution of the monasteries. On his way to join a royal hunting party at Windsor, he was stopped and told that the King did not wish to ride with him and that, instead, he must appear before the Privy Council on the charge of high treason.

Arbella featured in two of the indictments. Raleigh was accused of attempting to 'entice' Arbella to write to the King of Spain with the usual assurances that an uprising would follow an invasion.[50] And he was charged with plotting to secure Spain's victory by making Arbella queen.[51] The accusation that Raleigh was in league with Spain was clearly absurd. In fact, the trial and conviction which followed were instigated as much by Robert Cecil's determination to eliminate all opposition to a negotiated peace with Spain as genuine belief in Raleigh's guilt. Such perfidy was common in both Tudor and Stuart England. More unusual was the effort to which the prosecutors went to absolve Arbella Stuart from all blame.

There is no doubt that she could have been included in the indictment. Lord Cobham – the true begetter of the 'Main Plot' and a man of notoriously poor judgement – had invited her to write to the King of Spain and the Duke of Savoy, asking them to support the coup. She had ignored the request. But, faced with clear evidence of treason, Cecil did not usually make such nice distinctions between the perpetrators and those whom they implicated. Yet when, in the course of the trial, the Attorney General mentioned Arbella's name, the Secretary of State intervened to urge him to 'not scandal the innocent by confusion of speech. She is as innocent as any man here.'[52] Then the Earl of Nottingham, who sat next to Arbella in the gallery of the court, called out, 'The Lady doth here protest, on her Salvation, that she never dealt in any of these things.'[53] After that, Raleigh's complete, if ungallant and self-contradictory, exoneration seemed superfluous. Arbella, he said, was 'a woman with whom he had no acquaintance and one of whom what he saw he never liked'.[54]

Raleigh – as Cecil had always intended – was convicted and sentenced to death. Then he was reprieved and sent to the Tower* where he remained for thirteen years until he was released to lead a doomed expedition up the Orinoco – still in search of El Dorado. Arbella was not just exonerated. At Court she was inexplicably exalted above all except the royal couple and their children. When, on January 25 1604, James made the triumphant 'progress' through London which had been postponed from coronation year because of the plague, Arbella was in the third carriage, immediately behind the Queen. The way in which Arbella was treated raised suspicions that she had, somehow, been complicit in the exposure of the plot – a theory which was supported by her sudden receipt of Cecil's patronage.

King James and his Queen, Anne of Denmark, were as benevolent as their chief minister. Arbella was appointed Carver to the Queen – a role which carried prestige as well as the actual duty to carve at formal meals. She bore the Queen's train when Anne went to chapel and became godmother to the King's new daughter, Mary. There was again talk of marriage – now with the approval of the King. The candidates included Count Maurice of Nassau – a suggestion which was abandoned to avoid imperilling peace with Spain – and Ulric, Duke of Holstein. King Sigismund III of Poland was said to have made a formal proposal. Like the unauthorised unions – which had been rumoured ten years before – they all came to nothing.

In the years of her rehabilitation, Arbella had constant access to the King – the ambition of all courtiers. She watched, with him, performances by the King's Men, a band of players which included William

---

* Imprisonment in the Tower did not always mean years spent in a fetid dungeon. Prisoners of rank and distinction were accompanied by their servants and occupied suites of rooms.

Shakespeare. Her pleas for an increased 'pension' were initially refused but then agreed. She asked for £2,000 a year and was given £666 but eventually it was increased to £1,000. Arbella's improved status at Court had encouraged her grandmother to forgive her the sins which had once made her presence intolerable and to give her land which earned enough rent to increase her annual income to £3,000. Bess must have felt, though there is no record of her expressing, delight at one element of her granddaughter's success. Uniquely, Arbella persuaded the King to give her a blank 'patent of nobility' which she could award to anyone she chose. She used it to award a peerage to her uncle William. The creation of Baron Cavendish made Arbella one of the true begetters of the Cavendish dynasty.

Despite the privileges which she enjoyed, Arbella Stuart soon became again disenchanted with life at Court where, after a few months, she realized that her freedom was barely greater than it had been in Derbyshire. James spent lavishly and expected those around him to do the same and, although he was probably the most intellectual sovereign in British history, he was also one of the most debauched. Arbella found the heavy drinking and the public dalliance with his male favourites uncongenial. Hunting, an obsession everyone at Court was expected to share, bored her. So Hardwick acquired attractions which it had not possessed when she lived there. In the spring of 1605, she returned – after two years' absence – to Derbyshire. Although she bore a letter from the King commanding Bess to treat her granddaughter with her 'former bounty and love',[55] it was not a successful reunion. Bess replied, more offended than chastened, that she 'had sufficiently expressed her good measure and kindness', but, nevertheless, gave Arbella a gold cup worth £100 and £300 in coin.

Rebellion – and rumours of rebellion – continued to haunt the Court. Prince Henry – the heir to the throne – was suspected of attempting to work with the dead Earl of Essex's son to revive the Elizabethan war party and prevent a rapprochement with Spain. Fears that there was a Catholic plot to make Princess Elizabeth – James's eldest daughter – a puppet queen, spawned a fantasy that Arbella would become the Protestant figurehead in the subsequent civil war. A 'gunpowder plot' was detected when one of the conspirators warned a friend against attending parliament on November 5. In Derbyshire, far away from the intrigues and alarums of the Court, the Cavendish family were plotting against each other and fighting their own civil war over land and property. It intensified, rather than abated, when Bess, Dowager Countess of Shrewsbury, died on February 13 1608.

The previous month, Arbella – restored to the glory of the Court

– had been at a performance of Ben Jonson's *Masque of Beauty*, in attendance on the Queen. The ever-vigilant Venetian Ambassador reported on the splendour of the occasion. But Arbella, at least according to her own estimation, was still living in penury. Her application to be given the right to license hide imports from Ireland was refused, but she was granted Irish licensing rights for brewing, the selling of wine and aqua vitae and the sale of oats to travellers in England. And she made £800 by selling Mary Stuart memorabilia to her aunt Mary Talbot. The sale was an indication of the new Countess of Shrewsbury's abiding sympathy for the Catholic cause and Arbella's cold heart.

It was a condition which she admitted. When she bought a house in Blackfriars, she wrote to Gilbert Talbot: 'For want of a nunnery, I have retired myself to the friars.'[56] However, she felt sufficiently part of the world – and had enough money, self-confidence and freedom – to make an almost regal tour of Yorkshire and Derbyshire. 'My lady Arbella will be in Sheffield some day this week . . . Fish must be watered for there will be an extreme great multitude in hall every day.'[57] But the new life did not last. It was her fate to be pursued by rumours and allegations built on exaggerations of small truths. There was talk of a secret compact to marry the Duke of Moldavia and that, under the influence of Mary Talbot, she had become a secret Catholic. Arbella was again examined by the Privy Council, once more found blameless and restored to Court yet again. Her second rehabilitation was confirmed by the King's gift of a cupboard of plate worth £200 and with it 100 marks to pay her rising debts. Despite her professed reticence, she had acquired the expensive habits of the circle in which she moved. Her household included twenty-two servants as well as the usual ushers and ladies-in-waiting.

The rehabilitation was brief. In February 1610 it was reported that a man was making visits to Arbella's chambers at Court and she was 'again called before the Lords upon a new marriage which she had in hand to be concluded . . . with [William Seymour] the second son of Lord Beauchamp'.[58] It was Arbella's second romantic excursion with the family. But, as the Privy Council realised, it was far more significant than her attempt to arrange marriage with the Earl of Hertford's sixteen-year-old grandson. Seymour himself was cross-examined by the Privy Council and, chivalrously, took all the blame for a liaison which, paradoxically, he claimed to have initiated for unchivalrous reasons. He was a younger son who had to make his own way in the world and Arbella was 'a lady of great honour and virtue and as [he] thought of great means'.[59] He added that he believed that Arbella was free to marry and, almost certainly only speaking for himself, that their proposed union always depended on gaining the King's consent. Once more the case against Arbella was dismissed. Cecil had come to believe not only that she did not aspire to the throne but that she had lost either desire or hope of ever marrying. He was wrong.

In fact Arbella, aged thirty-five, was keener on the marriage than the twenty-two-year-old Seymour. Either natural inclination or reaction against the attention of the Privy Council had encouraged Seymour to have second thoughts. But chivalry, of a sort, continued to guide his conduct and he told a friend that 'he found himself bound, in conscience by reason of a former pledging of his faith, to marry her'.[60] Arbella clearly remained determined and undeterred. The first week in May was occupied by the celebrations which surrounded Prince Henry's inauguration as the Prince of Wales. At the actual installation, Arbella sat in the Court of Requests with the King's second son, the future Charles I, and his sister Elizabeth, by then the Princess Royal. Barely more than a fortnight later, at about four o'clock on the morning of Wednesday June 22 1610 – shortly after the King's sudden departure from Greenwich – Arbella Stuart and William Seymour were married.

The wedding party – six witnesses as an insurance against claims that the marriage was not valid – arrived at Arbella's chambers before midnight. The ceremony did not begin for several hours because of either the difficulty in finding a co-operative priest or the reluctance of the witnesses to accept the lie that the King had been told and approved. The marriage was common knowledge at Court by July 8. On that day, William Seymour was summonsed to appear before the Privy Council and sent to the Tower. Next day Arbella was placed under house arrest. The witnesses – members of the couple's households – were confined in the Marshalsea prison. Arbella returned to her old habit of compulsive letter-writing. First she wrote to her uncle, Gilbert Talbot, who – although a Privy Councillor – had not signed her arrest warrant.[61] Then there were letters to Lady Jane Drummond, the First Lady of the Bedchamber, the Queen herself and finally to the Privy Council. They apologised for the grief which she had caused the King, but not for the marriage.

For the rest of the year – during which there was the mistaken belief that Arbella was pregnant – she, and her husband, remained the King's prisoners. Then, on Twelfth Night 1611, Arbella was called before the Privy Council again. It was decided that she should be 'sent to Durham, and there committed and confined to that Bishop's charge with intent that she and her husband shall not come together'.[62] The party – prisoner and escorts – set off north in March. They paused at Highgate.

At Barnet – after they had completed the next stage of their journey – Doctor Mountford, President of the Colleges and Arbella's personal physician – said his patient was too ill to continue the journey. King James sent Doctor Hammond, his own physician, to examine her. She was pronounced well enough to travel. The tension was too much for the Bishop of Durham who was accompanying the party. He collapsed with nervous exhaustion and was sent to recover in Bath. Hammond announced that they would leave Barnet on June 5. On June 3 Arbella escaped.

For some time the wife of Arbella's chaplain, who was her privy chamber guardian, had allowed her to make evening excursions. On the evening of the escape, Arbella's supposed captor had helped to disguise her as a man and sent her off – she believed or claimed to believe – to say goodbye to William Seymour for ever. What followed does great credit to Arbella's determination and stamina. After she left her quarters, she walked south for about a mile. She was then met on the road by a confederate with horses. They rode together 14 more miles to Blackwall, where she expected to meet Seymour. His luggage and his friends were there. He was not.

Arbella decided to continue her journey of escape as planned. So the whole company – missing only its leading man – rowed to Leigh where it was intended that they should embark on the ship that would take them to France. That, like William Seymour, was missing. Bribes, offered to the crew of another vessel, were refused in the belief that Arbella was Moll Cutpurse, a notorious highwaywoman. But the crew did direct the party of apparent desperadoes to a boat which was waiting 2 miles downshore. It was the ship which had been chartered to take them to France. Arbella refused to set sail in the hope that, if they waited, William Seymour would soon join them.

William Seymour had left his lodgings on time, but he was so late arriving at Blackwall that he decided that Arbella would be half-way to France before he reached the Channel. So he made his way to the coast and – in his case offering a successful bribe – hired a boat and sailed straight to Calais. He arrived safely. But the confusion had confounded Arbella. Edward Rodney, one of the escape party, left a farewell letter with Seymour's brother, Francis. Suspecting that an escape plot had been planned, Francis rushed to the Tower to warn against what he regarded as pure folly. It was too late to counsel caution. William Seymour had already left. Prudently – at least in terms of his own safety – Francis reported William's absence to the Lieutenant-Governor.

Once the alarm was raised, events took their inevitable course. Everyone who was suspected of aiding or abetting the escape was arrested. Mary Talbot, Countess of Shrewsbury, was sent to the Tower and Gilbert, the Earl of Shrewsbury, resigned from the Privy Council. Seymour was beyond capture, but Arbella – who could have escaped had she not waited for her husband – was still at sea. The Earl of Nottingham, Lord High Admiral of England, argued that it was expedient as well as compassionate to let her go. But King James ordered her arrest. A naval pinnace, the *Adventurer*, caught up with her in mid-Channel. It fired thirteen shots before her ship turned back. Immediately she landed in Sheppey, Arbella Stuart was arrested. She was back in the Tower within the day.

William Seymour settled in Bruges under the protection of Archduke Albert, the Governor of the Netherlands. King James rejected his petition that Arbella should be allowed to join him. When it was suspected that she intended to leave the country without permission, Mary Talbot, who was said to have encouraged her defiance, had the pardon – which was granted so that she could nurse her sick husband – revoked. Arbella's other friends lost nerve or patience. Cecil, who had continued to befriend her, withdrew his patronage. Lord Cavendish, who owed Arbella his title, and Henry, his brother, simply ignored their niece's existence.

During the next four years Arbella slipped slowly into madness. In the belief that she would be invited to the wedding of Princess Elizabeth and the Elector Palatine of Bohemia she bought several new gowns, one of which cost £1,500. By 1613, the best that could be said of her was that 'she was restrained of late, though they say her brain continues to be cracked'.[63]

At the beginning of 1615, she began to refuse food. By May she lived in a semi-conscious daze. Arbella Stuart died on September 25 that year. The six doctors who performed the post-mortem agreed that she had starved herself to death. She was embalmed, and – as befitted her royal status – buried in Westminster Abbey in the vault that already contained the remains of Mary Queen of Scots and Henry, the young Prince of Wales, whose death had left Prince Charles heir apparent to the throne. She had written her own epitaph. When she sent Mary Stuart's book of hours as a present – probably to William Seymour – she inscribed the title page, 'Your most unfortunate Arbella Stuart'.

CHAPTER 5

The House Divided

In the first week of January 1608, Grace Cavendish – wife to Bess of Hardwick's 'bad son' Henry – wrote to Sir John Harpur of Swarkestone to ask his advice about a negotiation between her husband and his brother, William – by then, thanks to the help of Arbella Stuart, a peer of the realm. William was the son on whom Bess had built her dynastic ambitions and the major beneficiary of the complicated financial arrangements which his mother had negotiated with the Earl of Shrewsbury at the time of their marriage. Because of his louche habits, financial irresponsibility and lack of filial respect – aspects of his character which brother William made a point of exposing – Henry, although the oldest son and natural heir, was excluded from the gifts and bequests. But his mother could not deny him all the rights of primogeniture. So Chatsworth – though not its stock and contents – was bequeathed to him.

Henry, extravagant and short of money, had, for some time, wanted to sell the reversionary rights to the Chatsworth estate. William – ambitious and solvent – had been just as eager to buy. But they could not agree a price. William had offered £5,000 at once and £500 a year for as long as their mother lived. Henry had asked for £6,000 immediately and £500 a year for four years, whether Bess lived or died.[1] Clearly Grace had doubts about the whole deal. So did Harpur. But before he replied, he deemed it his duty to show Grace's letter to her brother, Gilbert Talbot, Seventh Earl of Shrewsbury.

Harpur was puzzled by the size of the offer. William Cavendish – who, for years, had hoped to acquire his brother's property – had never before thought it worth more than £3,000. Gilbert had no doubt about the reason for the increase. The value of the Chatsworth land would multiply with Bess's death and the consequent freedom to sell it on the open market. William knew, or ought to have known, that the end could not be long delayed. Bess was so ill that she was 'not able to walk the length of chamber between two servants'.[2] The loving and faithful son was already preparing for the unhappy event by attempting to buy the land before its value increased with his mother's death.

Shrewsbury 'had heard' that William's men had been told 'to be in readiness to drive away all her sheep and cattle . . . immediately upon her death . . . How like it is that when she is thought to be in danger, your good brother will think it time to work with you.'[3] William, he added gratuitously, had 'till of late . . . been of some hope to have seen your end before hers . . .'. Now it was clear that Bess would die first. After that it was hardly necessary to add, 'I wish and advise you to take no hold of any offer that shall be made unto you.'[4] Even so, Henry was reluctant to abandon an agreement which would allow his debts to be paid and, he hoped, guarantee his brother's friendship 'with no expectations of suits or law brabbles between us'.[5] However, he wrote to Gilbert to tell him that 'out of affection' and as proof that he valued his advice, he would refuse the offer. The conclusion of the letter made clear why he had tried to represent his decision as an indication of his respect for the Earl. 'In consequence' of his decision, he wrote, 'my wife and I need your help'.[6] The loan for which he hoped was not forthcoming and the offer was not resisted for long.

William's hopes were motivated by avarice and Henry's fears were influenced by his chronic, but increasingly desperate, shortage of money. But the underlying animosity was fuelled by the bitter internecine warfare which was complicated by the intermarriage of the Cavendishes and Talbots. Henry Cavendish – Bess's oldest son and the husband of Grace Talbot – had sided with his father-in-law during the old Earl's disputes with his wife. William had dutifully supported his mother, until she forfeited his affections by favouring his brother Charles. Gilbert Talbot, the new Earl, was married to Mary Cavendish and, because he was Charles's bosom friend, was – at first – his mother-in-law's ally in her feud against his father. Then, towards the end of her life, Bess had forfeited his affections by – according to the complaint he made to the Chancery Court – felling timber and sinking coal mines on Talbot land. Mary Talbot (née Cavendish) had – thanks to her Catholic inclinations – been estranged from her mother until the year before Bess's death. Eventually even Charles was alienated by Bess's resentment of his friendship with his brother-in-law. The disputes were embittered by avarice, jealousy and pride and intensified by the litigious inclination of all the parties. Gilbert Talbot's attempts to challenge the terms of the old Earl's will had been frustrated by Bess 'buying up' the lawyers he engaged to represent him in court.[7]

Bess died in the depth of the coldest winter in living memory. The Thames froze over and in Derbyshire workmen were unable to melt enough ice to mix the mortar needed to continue the rebuilding of Hardwick.[8] Bess's suggestion that they should use ale rather than water was deemed impracticable. The desperation of her proposal encouraged the myth that a gypsy had prophesied that she would die when she could no longer build. However, the beneficiaries of her estate were too busy with material matters to spend much time on whimsy. When it was clear that the end was near, there were unseemly arguments at the bedside of the dying woman. No one disputed that Bess 'did by word of mouth will and bequest to her son Sir Charles Cavendish either the som of £4000 or 4000 marks of money'.[9] But she also bequeathed £100 to a beneficiary, unknown to her relatives, who kept watch on her last hours. 'It was then told her either by Lord Cavendish or some other person present that she might not nor could not give it . . .'[10] Charles remained disinherited apart from the deathbed gift. But she did 'by word of mouth, will £2000 to Wylkyn son of Lord Cavendish and £2000 to his daughter Frances [and she] said in presence of Lord and Lady Katherine Cavendish she would give Sir Charles Cavendish £4000 or £5000' for Charles's children.

Within hours of Bess's death, Gilbert Talbot, Earl of Shrewsbury – her stepson and son-in-law – sent an instruction to his bailiffs. Tenants of the land which was held by his stepmother for her lifetime must prepare to pay their rents to him next quarter day and all Bess's 'gentlemen servants' and ladies-in-waiting were to be evicted from Wingfield Manor. William, the principal beneficiary of those parts of Bess's estate which remained in her gift, patiently waited to receive the reward for his years of love and loyalty. Charles took consolation in the bequests made by Bess to his children. Henry inherited entailed Chatsworth, but remained on the edge of bankruptcy, the penalty for a reputation which he did not altogether deserve.

Henry Cavendish was born on December 12 1550 and had enjoyed what, at the time, must have seemed the most auspicious of beginnings. The Princess Elizabeth, the future Queen of England, was his godmother – in itself, enough to confirm his status as one of fortune's favourites. When, at the age of seventeen, he was betrothed to eight-year-old Grace Talbot, daughter of his stepfather, the Earl of Shrewsbury, he was expected to lay the foundations of a dynasty which united birth and wealth. His education began after his marriage – first at Eton – the beginning of a Cavendish tradition which, with a couple of exceptions, survived into the twentieth century – and then at Grays Inn. Like all young gentlemen of the period, he made the Grand Tour – in his case with Gilbert Talbot immediately after his prospective brother-in-law's betrothal to his sister. Most significant of all, at the age of fourteen – even before either his betrothal or his exposure to the adult world – he was appointed bailiff of the castle and manor of Tutbury.

That was a clear indication of what was expected of him in future years. His mother's hopes were never realised.

Henry's marriage contract, and arrangements related to it, assigned to him land owned or controlled by his father-in-law and he enjoyed a substantial inheritance from his father. In his early manhood, he acquired more property by purchase and prudent exchange. But certainly from 1580 onward, and probably before, he was raising money through mortgages and by 1585 he had debts of £3,000.[11] In that year he told Sir Amias Paulet – the temporary gaoler of Mary Queen of Scots – that he would rent out his house at Tutbury for use as a royal prison while he was 'straitly lodged' in a smaller house 4 miles away.[12] The reason for his penury is not clear. But it was obvious, long before he made that desperate offer, that Henry Cavendish was never going to be the heir that Bess wanted him to be. His principal interests were women, horses and dicing. Love of music was one of his few attractive characteristics.

In 1572 – at the age of twenty-two – Henry Cavendish was, thanks to his family's influence, elected Knight of the Shire of Derbyshire. He was – for the same reason – re-elected four times. None of the parliamentary journals of the time even mention him. So we must assume that, throughout his years in parliament, he neither said nor did anything of consequence. He was, for a time, a soldier of fortune – though his fortune was mixed. A letter which he wrote to his mother after she had received reports of his misconduct claimed that he only heeded the call to arms in order to regain her good opinion. 'For me, I little regarde reports nor study to please every man. I have attained to please those I seeke if I please your Ladyship. For others I little esteme to please theare fantasyes . . .'[13] The allegation that he had left Derbyshire for London 'to playe at dyce, to seeke ease and dalliance or for any other vain delyghte' was, he insisted, a cruel libel. He had visited the capital 'to seeke vyrtu and honour in armes'[14] – a claim supported by his early record. He served in Ireland in 1573 and was commended for his soldierly qualities in an account of the campaign sent from Essex to Shrewsbury. Essex ended his commendation with the hope that Henry Cavendish would again serve under his command. Five years later, in a letter of introduction to Walter Davidson, the English agent in the Low Countries, the Earl of Leicester described him as his 'very dear friend' who was taking a company of 500 men to Holland, where they would fight for the Protestant cause under the Prince of Orange.[15] Admittedly, he 'had no great experience in wars, yet [he was] to be esteemed for his earnest desire to serve'.[16] Walsingham added his own endorsement to the other testimonials.

Henry Cavendish's performance must have disappointed his sponsors. First there was the suspicion that he planned to divert his men from Belgium to Scotland in a foray which was more concerned with booty than with honour. Then, when the Low Countries expedition was confirmed or renewed, he proved so inefficient that Walsingham apologised for sending over so incompetent an officer. When the company which he had raised played a conspicuous part in the victory over the Spaniards at Rijmenam in August 1578, he was unaccountably absent. He was probably on his way to Paris where – according to Sir Amias Paulet, by then the English Ambassador – he spent too much time in the company of John Leslie, the Bishop of Ross and an acknowledged supporter of Mary Queen of Scots.

His exploits in the Low Countries made him famous enough to be confused with Thomas Cavendish – a distant relative, associate of Sir Walter Raleigh and manic depressive who was the second man to circumnavigate the globe. In 1586, Bernardino de Mendoza, the Spanish Ambassador in London, wrote to tell King Philip that the latest English attempt to sail round the world was to be led by 'Sir Harry Cavendish, son of the Countess of Shrewsbury who served as a colonel with the Flemish rebels'. Three years later he did set out on an expedition. Nobody noticed it until 'Fox, his servant' published a journal entitled *Mr Harrie Cavendish: His Journey to and from Constantinople*. Surprise that he could afford such an enterprise led to first the suspicion that it had been financed by his mother and – since Bess regarded the pursuit of adventure as an activity far inferior to the acquisition of land and property – the consequent assumption that it had a commercial purpose. However, the servant's account makes no mention of business. The pleasures which it described included visits to Venice, which was 'a foul stinking place', and Sofia, where the travellers were relieved to be only spat at rather than stoned.

On his return Henry was – wilfully, his mother must have believed – a constant source of trouble. Sometimes the difficulties he caused were local. There were complaints to the Privy Council about 'sondrie foule abuses and outrages' committed against William Agard of Foston which resulted in Henry Cavendish being bound over to keep the peace. On other occasions – and far more dangerous in an age when whole families were punished for one member's indiscretions – he was politically reckless to the point of exhibiting his sympathy for Mary Queen of Scots; and he was interrogated, though adjudged to be innocent, during the investigations which followed the exposure of the Bye Plot to kidnap King James and hold him prisoner until he agreed to end the persecution of Catholics.

Henry was certainly guilty of treason against his mother. In 1584, he sided with his stepfather in the domestic disputes which destroyed the Shrewsbury marriage and was ejected from Chatsworth. It was then that, believing that Bess was unnecessarily harsh in her treatment of Arbella Stuart, he had helped to organise the (inevitably incompetent) plot for her to escape from Hardwick. It was his multiple disloyalty that prompted Bess's first decision – retracted and then confirmed – to cut him out of her will. He was reported to have greeted the news that he had been disinherited with a torrent of abuse against his mother, during which he 'charged her to be a harlot to some of his men'.[17] Bess must have been almost as offended by the discovery that he was locally known as 'the Common bull of Staffordshire and Derbyshire'[18] – a tribute to characteristics that led him to father at least eight illegitimate children. But worst of all, he exhibited none of the qualities which would have equipped him to build on the foundations which Bess had assembled. Fortunately, the second Cavendish son inherited his mother's acumen. Six months after Bess's death Henry sold his brother most of his inheritance for £8,000 and in October 1616 he died without legal heir. Chatsworth, in its entirety, then passed to William Cavendish.

Charles, Bess's third son, was, at least initially, a different – and a more dangerous – sort of disappointment. After he came down from Cambridge he was suspected of being in league with Mary Queen of Scots. Their association was said to have been confirmed by a mysterious request for Mary to write a letter – subject unknown – on his behalf and her even more mysterious refusal to oblige. That he was at least a Catholic sympathiser was not in doubt and it was feared that, together with Mary – his sister, who was to become the Countess of Shrewsbury – he had a malign influence on Gilbert, his brother-in-law and the future Earl. Robert Bainbridge – admittedly a rabid anti-Papist who had been one of the earliest advocates of Mary Stuart's execution – complained that Gilbert Talbot was 'always at [Cavendish's] elbow' in a friendship that was looked on with suspicion because Charles's 'first wife was a papist by Birth and so continued and his second wife is thought to be no better'.[19]

In the early summer of 1581 he had behaved in what was to become the best Cavendish tradition by marrying money. Margaret Kitson, a wealthy and prominent recusant, was, together with her sister, joint heir presumptive to her father's fortune. She died the following year, shortly after her husband was knighted as a reward for services in the Low Countries. Sir Charles did not marry again for ten years. Then, for the second time, he found a wealthy bride – Katherine, the daughter of the Seventh Lord Ogle, a border baron. The marriage, like so many

Devonshire unions, proved immensely profitable. Lord Ogle died without a male heir and his land was divided between his daughters, Katherine and Jane, the wife of Edward Talbot, Charles's stepbrother. The Talbots died childless and all of the Ogles' Northumbrian land reverted, via Katherine, to Charles Cavendish. Charles was first invited to Court when his mother was in Derbyshire and he fulfilled the duty of a good son by writing home to Chatsworth with fashionable London gossip. It was Charles who reported that Arbella had made her first curtsey to Queen Elizabeth. His letters home were most welcome when they contained good news about his mother's continuing negotiations to buy land. He was able to report that two gentlemen with estates for sale 'both answered that your Ladyship should have it before any and that about three weeks hence, Master Clyford meaneth to be in Buxton and will there speak with you'.[20]

The decade between the two weddings was filled with the disputes between Shrewsbury and his stepsons about land. On April 22 1572 the Earl had signed a deed which gave his stepsons, William and Charles Cavendish, all the lands which – though once belonging to Bess – had become his when she forfeited her property rights by becoming his wife. At the time he had foolishly thought that the apparent act of generosity was a bargain, since it relieved him of obligations which he had incurred under the marriage settlement, including 'great Somes of money, which he, the said Earle, Standeth Chargeable to pay . . . to the yonger children of the said Countess' when they came of age, and also absolved him of the duty to pay Bess's debts and protected him from 'other weighty Consyderations'.[21] The land-rich and cash-poor Earl had sacrificed his long-term interests for immediate financial relief from payments which were much smaller than the income from the land which he had wantonly given away.

Realising his error, Shrewsbury accused his stepsons of misappropriation. William and Charles Cavendish countered their stepfather's accusation with the double defence that no land had been misappropriated and that they were justified in expropriating it because of the Earl's own financial malpractices. Tenants on land which was indisputably theirs had been bullied into paying rents to Shrewsbury, a bad husband who had failed to pay his due allowance to his wife. In consequence, they were forced to support their mother. The brothers' first estimate of the cost of the Earl's malpractices was £4,000. Then they announced that the expenditure which he had forced upon them had been increased by the cost of repairing wilful damage, done at Chatsworth by the Earl's men, and the payment of wages to additional servants who had been recruited to deter future attacks after lead mills and woodland had been destroyed. It was then that Shrewsbury responded with the accusation that both William and Charles had made slanderous statements against him – concerning his relationship with Mary Queen of Scots. Family and friendship counted for nothing as compared with property in the creation of a dynasty, not of blood, but of power and wealth.

When it was clear that the families would not resolve their own disagreements, Queen Elizabeth – who, despite her other preoccupations, always found time to interfere in the private life of her Court – set up a commission, under the Lord Chancellor, to settle the dispute between Shrewsbury and his stepsons as she had tried to resolve the differences between Shrewsbury and his wife. The parties submitted claims and made accusations which grew more bitter as they became more puerile. A sort of settlement was negotiated which – since it required the brothers to pay public homage to their stepfather – was adjudged to be a victory for the Earl of Shrewsbury, even though they relinquished no land. But, privately, the dispute continued until the Earl died. Then Charles Cavendish, who had subdued his acquisitive instincts in the public dispute during the old man's lifetime, began to acquire land again. Some was bought in the open market. Some was the gift of his mother – the reward for taking her part against her husband. And some was sold to him, on favourable terms, by the new Earl of Shrewsbury, his brother-in-law.

For Charles Cavendish, the elevation of his old friend Gilbert Talbot to the Shrewsbury earldom heralded a new area of prospects and preferment. In 1584, the Sixth Earl had frustrated Charles's ambitions to represent Derbyshire in parliament because of fear that he would use his influence to protect Bess's interests. The Seventh Earl ensured that in 1593 Charles was elected Knight of the Shire for Nottingham – even though he was accused of possessing little or no land in the county. John Stanhope – a Nottingham landowner who believed that the honours which were showered on the new Earl of Shrewsbury and his friends, including a knighthood for Charles Cavendish, should have been bestowed on him – made an official complaint.

Stanhope and Gilbert Talbot had been close friends. After the death of his father, the new Earl of Shrewsbury had replied to Stanhope's condolence letter with the request that he reported Court gossip about the likely recipients of the honours and appointments which had been left vacant. Both the Fifth and Sixth Earls of Shrewsbury had been Earl Marshal of England. The Seventh Earl desperately wanted to keep the distinction in the family, but he feared that other contenders were pressing their claims. Gilbert's fears were justified. He was made a Knight of the

Garter but denied the coveted title of Earl Marshal, and, when he was nominated as Lord Lieutenant of Derbyshire, he found to his surprise that Sir Thomas Stanhope, John's brother, was also a candidate. He assumed – rightly or wrongly – that his rival's interests were being promoted by the man he had regarded as his agent. Gilbert Talbot, always quick to anger, vowed to frustrate Stanhope's ambition, and Charles Cavendish – claiming to hear his friend the Earl of Shrewsbury had been libelled – challenged Stanhope to a duel. Duels and challenges to duels were to become a feature of Cavendish life.

Charles Cavendish's challenge was accepted and a date and place agreed. But when the combatants arrived at the meeting place, Henry Nowell – Cavendish's second – 'searching Mr Stanhope's doublet . . . found it of great thickness and so hard quilted that [he] could hardly thrust through it . . . Sir Charles offered to fight in his shirt' and, in what was clearly meant to be a sign of contempt, 'sent word that he would lend Mr Stanhope his waistcoat'.[22] Stanhope declined the offer and the duel was abandoned. Whatever the decision to withdraw says about Stanhope's courage, it clearly entitled him to argue that he was the more reluctant of the two potential participants. Yet it was Stanhope, not Cavendish, who was imprisoned in the Marshalsea prison for disobeying the Privy Council's edict against duelling.[23] He was released after a week, following an undertaking to keep the peace. He immediately demonstrated his continuing animosity by asking the Star Chamber to adjudicate in a long-standing, but dormant, dispute with the Cavendish–Shrewsbury partnership. His attempts to build a weir across the River Trent were, he claimed, constantly sabotaged by Gilbert and his brother-in-law, Charles.

While the complaint was still being heard, the defendants decided that their cause would best be served by direct action. During September 1593, 'a troop of the Earl of Shrewsbury's and Sir Charles Cavendish's men went up and down Cheapside seeking and enquiring for Mr Stanhope . . . Sixteen of this company having swords, daggers and gauntlets and seven or eight of them bucklers, entered the tavern in Fleet Street called the Three Tons, shouting "Yonder comes Stanhope. To it! To it!"'[24] Jaques, one of Stanhope's men, was injured in the subsequent affray. The Earl of Shrewsbury was above censure, but Charles Cavendish was committed to the Marshalsea. He was released after depositing a bond which would be forfeit if, within twelve months, Jaques died. Mary, Countess of Shrewsbury, rallying to the support of her husband and brother, revealed a remarkable talent for meaningless abuse – no doubt inherited from Bess, her mother. On her instruction, her servant, Humphrey Chedell, carried a message to Sir Thomas Stanhope. It described his brother, John, as 'more wretched, vile [and] miserable than any creature living and for your wickedness become more ugly in shape than the vilest toad' and added that, 'without great repentance, he would be damned perpetually in Hell's fire'.[25] The messenger flinched from repeating the most offensive parts of the diatribe but did bring himself to say that, although the Countess did not wish for Stanhope's death, she hoped 'that all the plagues and miseries that befall any man may light upon such a caitiff' as him.[26]

Charles Cavendish was sufficiently apprehensive about the conse-quences of Jaques' death to transfer much of his property to his sister on a twenty-one-year lease. Jaques survived. So did the animosity between the Cavendishes and the Stanhopes. As late as June 1599, when Charles – together with his two Ogle brothers-in-law – was inspecting building work on the new house at Kirkby in Hardwick, his party was attacked by Stanhope and a band of twenty armed men. Outnumbered, Charles and the Ogles attempted to flee. But Charles's horse fell and he was shot where he lay. He suffered 'a wound in the point of the buttocks' and 'a ball in the shoulder'.[27] Escape being then impossible, Cavendish and his men decided to stand and fight. Six of their assailants were unhorsed, two killed and two more seriously wounded. Then Cavendish reinforcements arrived. 'John Stanhope who was the hindmost in all the fight was the foremost in running away, carrying all his hirelings with him . . . They left behind them six good geldings, whereof some are worth twenty pounds apiece, two or three cloaks, five rapiers, two pistols, one sword and dagger and some of their hats, all of which are safely kept by Sir Charles.'[28]

Perhaps Charles Cavendish and his servants were thought to have over-reacted. Or it may be that Stanhope was still enjoying the indul-gence granted to those who made regular appearances at Court. Whatever the reason, Sir Charles, although not the aggressor, received an admonition from the Privy Council. 'The Queen has been informed of the late incident between you and Mr Stanhope. This is to warn you at your peril against further disorder on the part of yourself, friends or servants.'[29] She was, however, sufficiently sympathetic to send Mr Clownes, her surgeon, to examine the shoulder wound from which Chesterfield doctors had been unable to extract the ball. To no avail, he meddled 'with a probe'.[30]

In 1604, conscious that Stanhope would continue to harass him, and fearful that he might not receive the protection of the law if he reacted or retaliated, Charles Cavendish decided to abandon the house he was building at Kirkby in Hardwick and make his home at Welbeck

– the former Premonstratensian abbey on the edge of Sherwood Forest which he had leased from Gilbert Talbot in 1597. The decision was taken and implemented so quickly that a wall of the proposed new house at Kirkby was left unfinished. Welbeck was a couple of miles away from the flamboyant Worksop Manor which the Sixth Earl had built as a sign of his magnificence. Gilbert and Charles had become neighbours as well as friends.

Welbeck whetted Charles's appetite for venerable property. In 1608, Gilbert Talbot leased him Bolsover Castle – 15 miles from Chatsworth – for a thousand years. In 1613 Charles bought it outright together with manor houses and land which stretched from Chesterfield to the Nottingham border. By then he had decided to demolish what was left of the old Norman building and employ Robert Smythson – the architect of Worksop Manor and the new Hardwick Hall – to design a fantasy. At its centre was the Little Castle, a mock-Norman keep which contained anachronistic panelled rooms with elaborately painted ceilings. Below it was a 'vast bailey laid out for tilting'.[31] Sir Charles Cavendish was a romantic who, in his declining years, dreamed of a return to the age of chivalry. It was a characteristic which, along with the unfinished new castle, he bequeathed – with disastrous consequences – to his son William.

The Bolsover tilting ground was never the site of a tournament. But the prudence of the decision to move to Welbeck was confirmed when Sir Charles demonstrated inability to avoid trouble even when Stanhope and provocation were 50 miles away. In December 1611, he was once more called before the Privy Council and charged with offences against a freeman, Otto Nicholson. When he refused to answer the 'bill of complaint', land in his possession in Sherwood Forest was confiscated. But, in the years ahead, the land surrounding Bolsover Castle was to more than compensate for the loss. Coal had been mined from Cavendish land and used to smelt Cavendish iron since before Bess's time. More than a hundred years after the Bolsover folly was built, 'black gold' from Derbyshire began to fuel the furnaces of England's Industrial Revolution. Providence and geology were kind to the Cavendishes.

Henry and Charles Cavendish were absorbed in the acquisition of power and wealth. William Cavendish – Bess's 'good son' – was obsessed by it. He was almost exactly a year younger than his 'bad' brother, Henry, and – according to his teachers – certain to 'be learned for he doth study and apply his books both day and night. There is no need to call him for going to his books.'[32] His education, at Eton and Clare Hall, Cambridge, was – according to contemporary sources – followed by two elections to parliament.[33] He represented Liverpool and

Newport, but mystery surrounds the names of possible patrons who were an indispensable requirement for service in the Elizabethan House of Commons. One aspect of his existence is, however, beyond doubt. He was devoted, and unequivocally loyal, to his mother. Even after his first marriage, he lived with Bess and became, in effect, her steward. Much of his energy was spent on finding and buying – often on his mother's behalf – land which was likely to increase in value. In 1583 he bought the whole of the Hardwick Hall estate in her name. It was another bargain. Bess's brother had been declared bankrupt, and his property was in the hands of the receivers.

It was not only his commercial acumen that made William Bess's favourite son. When, at the bitter height of the Shrewsburys' estrangement, the Earl had attempted to occupy Chatsworth by force, the famously aggressive Charles Cavendish had taken refuge in the tower of the parish church. The studious and prudent William had attempted to hold them off with pistol and halberd and, having failed to deter the invaders, mounted the expedition to retrieve the stolen goods from Sheffield Castle.

William was notoriously 'careful'. He had been knighted in 1580, but reluctance to pay the necessary price of further distinction held back greater honours. 'Cavendish waits hard . . . for his barony . . . but he will not prevail . . .'[34] Even when it became known that his niece Arbella had obtained 'a promise for one of her uncles to be made a baron', it was thought 'not very likely to be William for he is sparing in his gratuity'.[35] Peerages were usually bought for a high price. But in May 1605 he became Baron Cavendish and on August 7 1618, while he was attending the King in Wiltshire, he was created Earl. He chose the title Devonshire – probably for no better reason than that the names of places with which he was associated were already registered in the College of Arms. Ennoblement cost him £10,000. It was a price which he could easily afford. He was enjoying the benefits of early investment in the Virginias and Bermuda and he had become a member of the Company of the City of London for the Plantation of the Somers Islands. To facilitate his regular visits to London, he had built an extra wing on Leicester Abbey, which he used as a staging post on his way south.

The new Earl of Devonshire had no doubts about his obligations to promote the interests of the dynasty. So 'Wylkyn', his oldest son – baptised William but given the sobriquet to distinguish him from all the other Cavendishes with the same Christian name – had to be weaned away from the wild ways of his Derbyshire childhood and prepared for the role which awaited him. In 1608 it was decided that the necessary improvement was most likely to be brought about by a tutor who would teach him to live like a gentleman as well as Latin and Greek. The Principal of Magdalen Hall, Oxford, recommended the appointment of a young scholar who had recently graduated from that college. His name was Thomas Hobbes.

Wylkyn was eighteen. The proposed new tutor was only two years older. That was, according to John Aubrey, an added qualification since it was adjudged that the young pupil 'would profit more in his learning if he had a scholar of his own age to wait on him than if he had the information of a grave doctor'.[36] In November 1608, Hobbes – his ideas on the relationship between the state and the individual still not developed – accompanied Wylkyn from Cambridge to Hardwick. It was the beginning of what, as the family hoped, became a close friendship – though it was not, in every particular, the sort of friendship which they intended. Much of their time together was spent in what Wylkyn described in a book of essays as 'all field delights, as hunting, riding, hawking'.[37] It is not clear if Hobbes enjoyed country pleasures or if he merely indulged his pupil – though he certainly came to regret that, because of his neglect of books during his early days in Derbyshire, he lost much of his capacity to read Greek and Latin on sight.[38] However, one of his tasks must have been unequivocally uncongenial. According to Aubrey, Wylkyn 'who was a waster, sent [Hobbes] up and down to borrow money and to get gentlemen to be bound to him, being ashamed to speak for himself'. In the process, his tutor 'took colds, being wet in the feet'.[39]

Notwithstanding these privations, Hobbes clearly benefited from the association. Thanks to the Cavendish connection he made three grand tours – the first with Wylkyn, the second with Gervase Clifton, a neighbour and family friend, and the third with Wylkyn's son, yet another William. The first excursion, though the date is in doubt, probably took place in the autumn of 1614. By then, Wylkyn – though only twenty-four and regarded as still in need of the 'finishing' that the continental tour provided – had become one of Derbyshire's Members in what was called the Addled Parliament. It lasted for only eight weeks, during which time Wylkyn made one speech and was formally rebuked for reading from a prepared text – a habit which was forbidden, though practised, until parliamentary procedures were 'modernised' at the end of the twentieth century.

Within weeks of the dissolution tyro and tutor were in Venice. It was November 1615 before they reached Paris on the return journey from an excursion which had been more rewarding for Hobbes than for Wylkyn. Hobbes's Aristotelian view of the world had been moderated by exposure to the laws of planetary motion as advanced by Galileo and Kepler – theories which also influenced his views on religion. 'If a man going down a pair of stairs, by chance his foot should slip' but he regains his footing, after having 'called upon Saint Francis or Saint Carlo', he is inclined 'to make a miracle of it'.[40] Hobbes's complaint was not simply about the lack of reason in that assertion. He believed that attributing miraculous powers to saints diminished the glory of God.*[41] In Venice, the Doge's refusal to accept the temporal authority of the Pope chimed exactly with Hobbes's developing view that all power should reside – if necessary as a result of the subject's willing sacrifice – in the hands of a secular monarch.

Back home the maturing student and the tutor who had become his unlikely friend turned their attention to commerce. In June 1622, Wylkyn who – through his father's influence – had become a governor of the Virginia Company – gave Hobbes a single share in what was a fast-failing enterprise. Each shareholder, no matter how few or how many shares he held, enjoyed the same voting rights. Hobbes's duty was to increase the strength of the Sandys Faction which Wylkyn supported in opposition to the Smythe Faction whose members were – according to the Sandyites – ruining the company. It was a view which Wylkyn held so strongly that in March 1623 he expressed his criticisms in terms which libelled one of its most powerful supporters, Robert Rich, Earl of Warwick. The immediate result was the indictment of Wylkyn and Sandys himself for ignoring a Privy Council instruction to keep the peace. After a brief period of house arrest, they were released, allowing Wylkyn to attend the July meeting of the Virginia Company – at which the Earl of Warwick accused him of lying.

Wylkyn, believing with some justification that his honour had been impugned, challenged the Earl to a duel. Warwick accepted. Duelling had been outlawed in England. So, it was agreed that satisfaction should be secured in the Netherlands on August 1. Wylkyn's wife Christian was a close friend of the Countess of Warwick. The two women made a joint submission to the Privy Council which proposed that the would-be duellists should be arrested before one of them killed the other. The proposal was accepted and arrest warrants issued. Warwick eluded capture long enough to travel as far as Ghent. Wylkyn got no further than Shoreham-on-Sea. The melodrama spluttered out, but Hobbes was left to reflect on the moral that the Virginia Company dispute exemplified. In *Behemoth* he denounced all merchants as 'the

---

* The same point was made in *Leviathan* in 1651.

first to encourage rebellion' with no other interest than 'to grow excessively rich by buying and selling'.

The specific criticism did not reflect his judgement about the merchant venturers' conduct. John Donne, in a sermon to the Virginia Company, had argued that land not occupied by permanent inhabitants was available to anyone who could take it. In *Leviathan*, Hobbes contended that aboriginal Americans lived in a state of nature where nothing was, intrinsically, 'thine or mine'. So acquisition, in itself, establishes the right to ownership. It was a philosophy which appealed to Cavendish prejudices. But it was the sovereign rights of 'princes' which most exercised Hobbes and, since there was no agreement about its extent, drove England along the road to civil war.

James I died on March 27 1625. William Cavendish, the Earl of Devonshire, was one of the fourteen 'assistant to the chief mourner'. He was supported by his household including Wylkyn, his son, and Thomas Hobbes. Both Houses of Parliament were summoned to meet in April in order to begin the new reign with a reassertion of their prerogative over the right to raise excise duties. After some argument the Commons agreed to signify what had once been its routine and automatic agreement to the royal request for 'supply' – but only for one year. King Charles announced his intention to ignore the time limit and began to finance his extravagant expenditure through forced loans – the cause of profound discontent when employed by Elizabeth I, so certain to sow the seeds of rebellion against a monarch who was neither as popular nor as powerful. Wylkyn, the Lord Lieutenant of Derbyshire, was responsible, within the county, for the loans' collection. Initially he refused even to pay his own dues and his was the first signature on a letter to the Privy Council from the Derbyshire justices which declined to make 'a free gift' to the King.[42]

On the advice of Thomas Hobbes – who believed that power, in itself, legitimised the King's authority – he eventually, and reluctantly, did his fiscal duty. So he was in good standing with the King and Court when, in February 1626, his father died and he became the Second Earl of Devonshire. It was a distinction which he did not hold for long. Wylkyn died, aged thirty-eight, on June 20 1628. His widow was barely thirty.

Christian Bruce was the daughter of the Earl of Kinloss, a close friend of the King. She had brought to her marriage a dowry of £100,000. At the time of the betrothal Christian was twelve years old. Wylkyn, aged eighteen, was devoted to one of Bess's young attendant ladies and the couple were known to be lovers. It was in that knowledge that his Uncle Henry – who saw married life in carnal terms – wrote to the Earl of Shrewsbury after the elaborate wedding celebrations, which followed hard on Bess's death, were concluded, 'Helas por Wylkyn, he desyred and deserved a woman already groene. They were bedded together to his great punishment some 11 hours.'[43] Christian was far better than Wylkyn deserved. Second only to Bess in the pantheon of strong and ruthless Cavendish women, by force of personality – combined with an almost spiritual belief in the obligation to protect the family – she was to save Chatsworth from becoming a casualty of the Civil War.

With Wylkyn's death, Hobbes's real job – resident friend – disappeared. The new Earl, a boy of ten, was adjudged by his mother to be too young for a tutor. Hobbes was offered a place in the Cavendish household, but the employment of an 'instructor' convinced him that he was 'too much disregarded'[44] for him to remain, with dignity, at Chatsworth. As a valedictory rebuke, he dedicated his translation of Thucydides' *Peloponnesian War* to 'one now in heaven' and he took employment with Sir Gervase Clifton, a neighbour of the Welbeck Cavendishes, whose difficult son needed a reliable tutor to accompany him on the Grand Tour. Hobbes proved unfitted to the task of restraining a headstrong youth. Indeed he barely tried to do his duty. Instead he pursued his latest intellectual obsession, geometry. While in Geneva, 'Hobbes was in a gentleman's house in which a copy of Euclid's *Elements* lay open on a desk'[45] at proposition 47, Pythagoras' theorem. His first reaction was to reject the notion that the square on the hypotenuse equalled the sum of the squares on the other two sides. After he convinced himself that it did, Euclid rather than his young charge had first claim on his attention.

Despite his negligence the Grand Tour continued without major disaster until he was called back to England to resume service with the Derbyshire Devonshires. The Third Earl, having reached the age of fourteen, was adjudged to be old enough to need a tutor. Or, as Hobbes would have it, Christian – the Dowager Countess – having rectified family fortunes by winning all the thirty lawsuits in which she claimed the ownership of contested land, had decided that she could afford to pay his salary. By November 1630 he was back in Hardwick Hall.

Christian, the Dowager Countess, and her son were soon at odds about money. The Third Earl, yet another William, believed that he had inheritance rights which protected the family fortune from claims made against it by his father's multiple creditors. His mother – more prudent – wanted to pay off the family debts before William began the new orgy of spending which his character made inevitable. Mother and son both sought remedy in the courts and each one asked Thomas Hobbes for advice. He responded to each of them without telling the other and published a thesis which justified his acting on behalf of both parties. William was urged 'not to commence any action against' his mother. For this advice he 'neither received nor demanded, nor expected any reward but the testimony of having performed the part of a faithful tutor'.[46] It was by the display of such piety that Hobbes remained on good terms with both the Dowager Countess and the Earl. In the spring of 1633 he was with the family when William Cavendish travelled to Welbeck Abbey to join in the festivities which marked Charles I's visit to Nottinghamshire. The King brought with him a huge entourage.* So entertaining his peripatetic Court was an expensive privilege. The royal visit to Welbeck cost almost £2,000, the equivalent of at least £1 million at twenty-first-century prices. But the Stuarts – even Charles I, the saint and martyr whose rectitude is commemorated in village churches by the royal coat of arms above the rood screen – expected the lavish hospitality that they believed regal status justified. It was by meeting royal expectations that the Cavendishes of Welbeck and Bolsover temporarily rose above the Cavendishes of Hardwick and Chatsworth in the ranks of the nobility.

---

* It included five surgeons. One of them was William Harvey, who discovered the human circulation system.

CHAPTER 6

Wrong but Romantic

Charles I had left London on May 13 1633 to begin the 'progress' north which was to end with his being crowned King of Scotland in Stirling. It took him seven days to get to Welbeck Abbey where 'the Court were received and entertained . . . in such a wonderful manner and in such an excess of feasting as had scarce ever been known in England'. The King was so impressed that he suggested that a similar event be organised for Queen Henrietta Maria,[1] who – since she had chosen not to leave London – had missed all the fun. So William Cavendish at once offered to make 'the King and Queen a more stupendous entertainment'.[2] In the meantime, to prove the depth of his affection, he moved out of the abbey for the duration of the visit and left it at the King's exclusive disposal.

William Cavendish of Welbeck was born some time towards the end of 1593, four years before Gilbert Talbot, the Seventh Earl of Shrewsbury, gave his father the long lease on Welbeck Abbey. Charles, his elder brother, died soon afterwards. In or about 1595, his mother gave birth to a third son – also christened Charles – who was born with some sort of physical handicap. Aubrey described him as a 'little week and twisted man'[3] and Clarendon wrote that 'in this unhandsome or homely habitation there was a mind and a soul lodged that was very lovely and beautiful; cultivated and polished by all the knowledge and wisdom that arts and science could supply it with'.[4] But, notwithstanding his personal merits, his opportunities were limited by his deformity. So, 'nature not having adapted him for the court nor the camp. He betook himself to the study of mathematics, wherein he became a great master'.[5] That initially left gallantry and chivalry to be the exclusive preserve of his elder brother, William, whose commitment to those virtues was to lead to his elevation, then his downfall and eventually his ascent to the highest rank of nobility.

William Cavendish was always the King's man – unthinking in his loyalty. He embodied many of the virtues and vices which we now associate with Stuart England. Sir William Warwick, a contemporary in the service of King Charles I, described him as 'a gentleman of grandeur, generosity, loyalty and a steady forward courage' but added that 'his edge had too much of the razor to it, for he had the tincture of a romantic spirit'.[6] He lacked the native wit that helped so many members of his family through hard times. So his life was destined to consist of a series of heroic disasters.

In 1608 – at the then not unusual age of fourteen – William Cavendish entered St John's College, Oxford, where his tutors 'could not persuade him to read or study much'.[7] It seems that the same was true of Thomas Wentworth, an exact contemporary. Both men left without degrees. Wentworth registered at the Inns of Court and Cavendish joined the Royal Mews, where he pursued what was to become his lasting preoccupation. When affairs of state were over, battles fought and lost, exile ended and respect restored, it was his prowess with horses which he remembered with most pride. 'I have practiced since I was ten years old, have rid with the best masters of all nations, heard them discourse at large and tried their various ways, have read all . . . in a word, all that has been writ upon that subject good or bad.'[8]

In June 1610, his royal connection having been established in the mews, he was invited to be one of the five young attendants on Prince Henry when he was invested as Prince of Wales. When the ceremony was over, each of the young men was made a Knight of the Bath. At the age of sixteen, William had been awarded his first honour. He celebrated in the royal tilt-yard – now Horse Guards' Parade. It seems unlikely that he spared much thought for his benighted cousin, Arbella, also a guest at the Prince of Wales's inauguration. She was about to embark on her self-destructive marriage to William Seymour.

For the new knight, greater distinction was swiftly to follow. In 1612, together with his brother Charles and his cousin Lord Cavendish (of the Derbyshire branch of the family), Sir William was invited to join the diplomatic mission to Savoy which, while expressing King James's love and respect for Duke Charles Emmanuel, was also instructed to discuss the possibility of marriage between the Duke's daughter and Henry Prince of Wales. In the wholly laudatory biography which she published after his death, Margaret Lucas, his second wife, claimed that the Duke promised William that 'if he would stay with him he would not only confer on him the best titles of honour that he could but would give him an honourable command in war',[9] but that Sir Henry Wotton, who led the mission, 'would not leave him behind without his parents' consent'.[10] On the mission's return, the Prince of Wales, although unable to show any enthusiasm for the official choice of bride, pronounced himself ready to marry whomever his father chose. His filial devotion was never tested. On November 6 1612, he died of a fever which, his surgeons ruefully agreed, was the result of late-night bathing in the Thames. The stage was set for the succession of Prince Charles and the turmoil over the divine right of kings which his character, religion and wife made inevitable.

Unusually for a young aristocrat – and virtually unknown among Devonshires – William was not subject to family pressure to contract an early and materially advantageous marriage. And, at least according to his second wife's biography, it was not his habit to go 'whoring and wenching'. Margaret Lucas did draw attention to a youthful 'gallantry' which had previously not been noticed. 'I knew him not addicted to any manner of vice except that he had been a great lover and admirer of the female sex; which whether it be so great a crime as to condemn him for it, I'll leave to the judgement of young gallants and beautiful ladies.'[11] In his old age, he was to boast that, whether or not he was attracted to women, women were attracted to him. He celebrated his irresistible charm in what he believed to be poetry.

> Maid, wife or widow, which bears the grave style,
> Cavendish but name him and I know she'll smile.

Among William's later efforts are couplets and stanzas which seem to reveal a clear desire to establish an amorous reputation. It is best not to ponder the *double entendre* of

> What though my youth's decline; I am afraid
> You'll think me a Patriarch with my handmaid.

Other salutations to real or imaginary mistresses contain a less ambiguous image. One lady is 'the only wonder of the high Peak'. Another is 'Queen' of the Derbyshire uplands. What appears to be an appeal to a reluctant candidate for seduction is more straightforward:

> Forbidden fruit, dost thou not long to taste?
> The mid-trees knowledge, plucked below thy waist.

Some of the conquests, no doubt, were the figment of an old man's imagination. But Ben Jonson – although paid to eulogise – was probably justified in extolling his swordsmanship, even though the verse does not scan.

A quick and dazzling motion; when a pair
Of bodies meet like rarefied air . . .
All this, my lord, is valour: this is yours
And was your father's, all your ancestors!

Jonson's contention that 'there was never a subject more beloved than he' must be open to some doubt. So must the insistence that a man who bought so many titles and, in middle age, was shamelessly desperate for royal recognition, could legitimately be described as 'hating pride and loving humility'. But – thanks to his many portraits – we know that his wife's description of his 'outward shape . . . neat and exactly proportioned, his stature of middle size and his complexion sanguine' – is more or less correct.[12]

Although Sir Charles Cavendish had been disinclined to attend parliament himself, he had thought it only fitting that his son should take a seat in the House of Commons and in 1614 he arranged for William to represent East Retford. Three years later Sir Charles died. On October 24 1618 William married his first wife, Elizabeth, the nineteen-year-old widow of the Earl of Suffolk's third son. His choice was made 'to his own good liking and his mother's approving'.[13] Elizabeth was just as independently minded. She chose William in preference to Kit Villiers, the brother of the King's favourite. Elizabeth's attractions included an income of £3,000 a year and £7,000 in cash. But there is no doubt that – true to his temperament – he made a love match. William's second wife graciously and accurately acknowledged, 'God made him happy in marriage.'[14]

William's father had stipulated, in his will, that he must be buried not in the parish church which served his home in Welbeck Abbey but in Bolsover within the shadow of his castle folly. His alabaster effigy portrays him as a knight in armour and is decorated by a memorial verse composed by Ben Jonson.

Let such as justly have outlived all praise,
Trust in the tombs, their careful friends do raise . . .
It will be matter loud enough to tell
Not when I died, but how I lived – farewell.

William, his son, accepted that advice and began to live the good life by completing the building of Bolsover Castle as a filial duty. It was an obligation which he gladly accepted. On the first floor of the Little Castle, the ceiling of the main room was embellished with golden stars and the walls were decorated with paintings of biblical scenes. One of the adjacent rooms was given a black-and-white marbled floor, a second was decorated with images of pagan deities and a third featured Christ's ascent into heaven accompanied by cherubs and angels. Altogether it was a revelation of Sir William's latent romantic temperament which, when it fully emerged, would spring to life in support of the most doomed of lost causes, Charles I's crown and kingdom.

At the age of twenty-three William Cavendish became a person of substance with estates in Nottingham and nearby Derbyshire and property in the West Country which had once belonged to Sir William St Loe, his grandmother's third husband. And he was yet to inherit the Ogle land in Northumbria to which his mother had retired on the death of her husband. Brother Charles, the 'little twisted man' who was bequeathed a portion of his father's estate, employed the apparently indispensable John Smythson to build him a castle of his own at Slingsby, near Malton in Yorkshire, and retired there, in Aubrey's words, to spend his time 'with books and learned men'.

William chose country rather than town and attended parliament only rarely. He still lived, for most of the time, in Derbyshire and entertained himself and his neighbours with such rural delights as the country afforded. His passion remained horses. Only now and then 'would he go up to London for some short time to wait on the King'.[15] But he wanted to hold office in his own county and was willing to change his ways in order to obtain it. Aristocratic hauteur was put aside and he began to canvass his friends to find which of them was prepared to advance his cause at Court.

Emboldened by the Prince of Wales's agreement to be godfather to his second and only surviving son, William decided that the time had come to invest in the conspicuous consumption which was a mark of success in Jacobean England. Naturally enough, he chose to express his wealth by indulging his passion for horses and horsemanship. Between 1623 and 1625 he built the stables at Welbeck Abbey. They were designed and constructed on such a monumental scale that it is hard to blame Ben Jonson for using an overblown metaphor to describe them. Jonson declared that their size and splendour almost made him long to be a horse and

. . . when I saw the floor and room,
I looked for Hercules to be the groom.

In seventeenth-century England commoners of great wealth expected to buy their way into the nobility. King James had hunted in Sherwood

Forest in the summer of 1618 and so enjoyed the sport that he returned there the following year. So William had at least two opportunities to say or hint that he was ready to patronise His Majesty's most fruitful enterprise, the sale of honours. Reminiscing when he was old, he boasted of his elevation being the reward for his hospitality. It was not. Nor was it bought in the usual way. He was, uniquely, made a peer to avoid a protracted dispute over a bequest.

Edward the Eighth Earl of Shrewsbury had died suddenly (which was a seventeenth-century hazard) and without issue – leaving Sir William a substantial bequest. Mary, the Dowager Countess of Shrewsbury – widow of Gilbert the Seventh Earl and William's aunt – had asked him to be an executor of her husband's will. He retained that responsibility, without much thought, when the Earl determined the disposition of his legacy. So Sir William became both an executor and a legatee. The Earl of Arundel – the husband of a Talbot cousin who was also named in the will – contested the settlement on the grounds of conflicting interests. He suggested that the two men meet at Court to resolve their disagreement. That meant that King James – copying Queen Elizabeth's habit of interfering in domestic disputes between members of the nobility – would, if necessary, nominate an adjudicator to divide the inheritance. William – at the King's suggestion – agreed to sacrifice part of what he believed had been willed to him in return for being made a viscount. The Letters Patent were blatantly explicit. 'The parliament has now resolved . . . for the accommodating of disputes between the heyrs of the late Earl of Shrewsbury and Sir William Cavendish, nephew of the Earl of Devonshire who hath been entitled to some of those lands by the Countess of Shrewsbury . . . as an expedient to create the said Sir William, at the request of the heyres above mentioned, Viscount Mansfield which is now done by patent.'[16] He was not the only man in James I's England to be ennobled for reasons which were unconcerned with merit. But William Cavendish's elevation was unusual in so much as the recipient was not required to pay for his promotion. It was not King James's habit to distribute coronets and ermine free of charge.

The new Viscount – from then on Mansfield rather than Cavendish – found the House of Lords more congenial than the Commons. But he remained – in the estimation of the more seriously minded members of the Court – too enthusiastic in the pursuit of his old pleasures. William Laud, then Bishop of Saint David's, complained that on Good Friday 1624, he had seen him 'running at tilt to practice' and that 'with the shock of the meeting, his horse, weaker or testy, tumbled over and over and brake his own neck'. The bishop noted, without any obvious relief, that 'The lord had no great harm' but added the rhetorical question 'Should not this day have other employment?'[17] King James seemed to find no cause for complaint. In the autumn of that year he was back at Welbeck for the hunting. It was his last visit. He died on March 27 1625 and was succeeded by his son. The accession of Charles I to the throne of England made civil war – a conflict between King and Commons – inevitable. It was to be a time when William Cavendish, by then Viscount Mansfield, was able to display the best and worst of his character.

The first parliament of the new reign opened in June. William Laud had forgotten or forgiven the time wasted in tilting and commended the new Viscount Mansfield to King Charles. It was a decision which Laud never repented. His will included the bequest of his 'best diamond ring, worth £140 or there abouts . . . to my much honoured friend'.[18] The King took Laud's advice. Mansfield was at last made Lord Lieutenant of Nottinghamshire and given leave of absence from the House of Lords to enable him to improve the efficiency of the county militia. The appointment stimulated a previously dormant interest in military affairs which was to grow with the years and he set about the task with a determination to do a good job. As is always the case with new commanders, he felt obliged to draw attention to the failures of his predecessors. There was, he reported, a shortage of gunpowder. But he decided not to levy a local tax to pay for increased supplies. That decision was a mistake. A year later there were enough working muskets but as 'for pikes and corselets, there were not above six in the whole county as right as they should be'.[19] Nottinghamshire had grown so unused to subscribing to the upkeep of the militia that he thought it easiest to pay the cost of improvement himself. By August 1627 he had 100 men trained and ready to embark in Hull for Copenhagen where they would serve Charles Stuart's uncle, the King of Denmark. The pattern of conduct which was to be reproduced in his subsequent military career was beginning to emerge. Zeal was combined with incompetence. A month after the company set out for Hull he was instructed to send a further platoon of 50 men to Plymouth. They were four days south on their march when he realised that twelve of them should have been archers.

Although he discharged his martial duties with real pleasure, other obligations were performed with resigned reluctance. He was embarrassed by the instruction to search the house of Gervase Markham – a respected neighbour – after it had been reported (probably maliciously) that the old man was a Catholic and potential regicide who was storing gunpowder. King Charles, like his father, was raising revenue by the sale of knighthoods and peerages. So Mansfield was required to be an honours broker. A letter to George Villiers, Duke of Buckingham and the King's dominant adviser, suggests that he was expected to tell his cousin, Henry Pierpoint, that he would have to increase his offer before an award could be made. Haggling was not to his taste. 'He sayeth that Doctor Moore treated with him in King James times about Honor and tolde him that if he woulde be a Baron he might be for 4000£ . . . He sayeth further that he is not a moneyde man and I believe it . . . I think that if your Lo.p did speake with him in London, he might be brought to good terms.'[20] The embarrassment with which he raised royal revenue was not held against him. On March 7 1628 he was created Baron Cavendish of Bolsover and Earl of Newcastle-upon-Tyne – a title which he took because of his anticipated ownership of the Ogle lands. From then on Mansfield was Newcastle.

Newcastle's uncle – the Second Earl of Devonshire, William Cavendish of Hardwick and Chatsworth – died a few weeks after his nephew's elevation. He was succeeded by his son, a boy of ten, who – it was assumed – would one day become Lord Lieutenant of Derbyshire. Until he came of age, Newcastle, his second cousin, was required to act as locum. As with Nottingham so with Derbyshire. The new commander found equipment in poor condition, the militia below strength and local landowners reluctant to contribute to the cost of improvement. He had begun to enjoy playing at soldiers. It was to prove a dangerous hobby and one to which he was not suited. But he proved at least assiduous in calling the counties he controlled to arms. That was just as well. He had, in effect, become military commander of most of the East Midlands.

Charles I reigned for eleven years without the assistance of parliament. For much of the time, Newcastle was preoccupied with family matters. His first son died in infancy. A second was born and the line secured. Contentment gave way to the ambition to perform on a bigger stage. He began to attend Court more regularly and, in or about 1630, built a house on the site of a ruined Benedictine nunnery in Clerkenwell, then a fashionable rural retreat, outside the capital but in easy reach of society. He developed friends in high places in addition to William Laud, by then Bishop of London and soon to become Archbishop of Canterbury. After the assassination of Buckingham – Charles's closest confidant – the King had, disastrously, come to regard Queen Henrietta Maria as his chief adviser. The Queen approved of Newcastle. Unlike the ladies of her bedchamber Henrietta Maria enjoyed riding and she admired his horsemanship.

Newcastle also enjoyed the advantage of having no pronounced religious belief. The Queen's papal agent sent an exasperated message to Rome, describing him as 'too indifferent. He hates the Puritans, he laughs at the Protestants and has little confidence in the Catholics.' But in a Court rent by religious disagreement, his indifference protected him from the danger that any strong commitment would have created. As he grew to feel increasingly at home, he began to behave as other courtiers behaved. He patronised Van Dyck, attended the fashionable theatre (while arranging an increase in pension for his old and outmoded friend, Ben Jonson) and sent gifts to the King. He felt in such favour that, when Thomas Strafford was appointed Lord Deputy in Ireland, Newcastle hoped to succeed him as Lord President of the Council of the North. Strafford kept both offices. So it was with relief as well as pleasure that Newcastle discovered that he was 'lively in the memory of the King' and that he was 'appointed to attend [him] into Scotland'.[21]

The message was not what it seemed. Newcastle was 'appointed' to attend upon the King *on his way* to Scotland. And it was in the discharge of that duty that he organised the 'excess of feasting' at Welbeck. Leaving the abbey to the exclusive accommodation of Charles and his Court was no great sacrifice. At Bolsover the Little Castle had just been finished. A terrace of apartments, nearly 100 yards long, commanded the edge of the western escarpment. It would be Newcastle's pleasure to welcome Charles to the ideal setting for the entertainment that was to be held in the Great Court which had replaced Bolsover's medieval outer bailey. The occasion was such a success that he must have begun to believe the rumour – although it originated with the notoriously inventive Venetian Ambassador – that he was to be made Master of Horse. Again, despite his obvious suitability for the post, he was disappointed.

For a while he buried his frustration in the pastimes of a cultivated Stuart gentleman. His time at Court had gained him the reputation of a patron of the arts. John Ford had dedicated the *Chronicle History of Perkin Warbeck* to him and James Shirley paid him the same compliment when he wrote *The Traitor*. Shirley and Newcastle were the joint authors of two plays, *The Country Captain* and *The Variety* – a considerable improvement on the masque he had written without the assistance of a professional playwright. His excursion into devotional poetry, *A Divine Meditation upon receiving the Blessed Sacrament on Christmas Day, 1637*, resembled the work of Donne and Milton only in its title. It may be that the 'indifference to religion', which the papal legate had observed, made his religious work lack conviction. But the quality of the result was less important than the therapeutic effect of its production. Building was the traditional Cavendish therapy. When Newcastle was downcast, he always turned to composition for consolation. In 1667, near to the nadir of his fortunes, he was joint author with John Dryden of *Sir Martin Mar-all*, a Restoration comedy – of sorts.

In the 1630s, speculation about the material and mystical world provided almost as much a refuge from the ungrateful world as literature. It was the decade during which Thomas Hobbes most frequently visited Welbeck and, under his influence, Newcastle considered whether 'it was possible to make man fly as birds do . . . by the help of artificial wings', and decided that it was not. He also examined the proposition that there 'were none but imaginary witches' and concluded that anyone who made 'it their religion to worship the devil' could be so described.[22] Hobbes – who recognised the importance of showing interest in all his master's enthusiasms – wrote, with a remarkable show of interest as well as of authority, a pamphlet entitled *Considerations Touching the Faculty or Difficulty of the Motions of a Horse on Straight Lines and Circular*. He and Newcastle also discussed genuine scientific subjects. The Earl had already conducted experiments with his chaplain to determine the composition of the sun and to discover the reasons that it radiated heat and light. Hobbes, being a better philosopher than a physiologist, convinced him that 'light is a fancy of the mind caused by motion in the brain'.[23] There is no doubt that Newcastle took his scientific education seriously. When passing through London, Hobbes thought it his 'first business' to seek 'for Galileo's Dialogues . . . at taking my leave of your lordship. I undertook to buy it for you.'[24] The two men became so close that – even as Hobbes took the young Chatsworth Cavendish on the Grand Tour – he was ruminating about the possibility of one day moving to Welbeck, there to continue his own studies without interruption. And on July 29 1636 he presumed to suggest a way in which Newcastle could avoid future disappointment when preferment did not come his way. 'I am sorry your Lordship [has had] not so good dealing in the world as you deserve. But, my Lord, he that will venture to sea must resolve to endure all weather, but for my part I love to keep a'land. And it may be your Lordship now will do so too.'[25]

Although for a time further cast down with both real and imaginary sickness, Newcastle – unlike Bunyan's shepherd boy – was not prepared to take refuge in the notion that he who is down need fear no fall. However, soon after his arrival in Ireland, Strafford received an agonised letter which, at first, suggested that his old friend had accepted Hobbes's advice. Newcastle had been 'put in hope so long' that he would 'labour no more of it'. Nor would he, ever again, ask his friends for help.[26] By the end of the letter his mood had changed and he again was asking for Strafford to recommend him for a place suitable to his status. His cronies at Court did their best. After the death of Lord Carlisle, they pressed – without success – for Newcastle to replace him as Gentleman of the Bedchamber.

By the spring of 1636, frustrated hope had elevated disappointment into a persecution complex. On April 8, he told his wife, 'There is nothing that I can either say or do or here [sic] but it is a crime and I find a great deal of venom against me.'[27] The complaint that 'they cry me down more than they ever cried me up' was followed by a revelation of his most recent ambition. 'They say absolutely that another shall be for the Prince.' Newcastle wanted to be appointed Governor to the Prince of Wales.

On April 15 hope revived. 'It is believed absolutely that I must be about the Prince.'[28] There was also speculation – perhaps more by him than others – that he would become a Knight of the Garter. By May 23 he was in anguish again. 'I find it a lost business.'[29] There followed almost a year of anxiety. Then, in March 1637, the message for which Newcastle longed – but of which he almost despaired – arrived. The King had 'been pleased, in his gracious opinion' of Newcastle, to make him 'the only gentleman of the Prince's bedchamber'.[30] His appointment 'in so weighty a business' was not to be attributed to the good offices of his friends. Charles told Newcastle that he had 'no particular obligation to anyone whatsoever . . . but merely to the King's and Queen's Majesties alone'.[31]

Newcastle was to become head of a large and virtually independent establishment which included Doctor Brian Duppa, Bishop of Chichester, as tutor and the Marquis of Hamilton as Master of Horse. However it turned out that the Prince of Wales was still subject to the sort of supervision that less exalted children experience. 'I am sorry', wrote Queen Henrietta Maria to her son 'that I must begin my first letter by chiding you because I hear that you will not take phisicke.'[32] Newcastle was on a brief visit to Welbeck when the admonitory letter was received, but – although his mother was on hand – the prince thought it right to make his excuses to his governor rather than to her. 'My Lord, I would not have you make me take too much Phisicke: for it doth allwaies make me worse and I think it will do the like to you . . . Make haste to return to him that loves you.'[33] The obvious affection that the letter reveals may, in part, have been the result of Newcastle's theory of royal education. The regime which he believed best prepared the future king to meet his destiny must have been more to the young man's liking than the assiduous study of the classics. Newcastle was determined that the Prince of Wales would not 'become too studious. Too much contemplation spoils action.' Nor was he to be turned into 'a living dictionary'. He could not be both 'a good contemplative man and a good commonwealth man'. The memorandum in which the Royal Governor's philosophy was set out emphasised the importance of good manners, accomplished horsemanship and a knowledge of history so as to understand 'the errors and the excellence of both Kings and subjects'. Newcastle also warned against too much religious devotion. 'One may be a good man but a bad king' and in consequence follow in the footsteps of misguided monarchs who by 'seeming to gain the Kingdome of Heaven have lost their own'.[34] It was advice which Newcastle could have given, with profit, to the Prince's father, Charles I.

Newcastle had barely begun his duties as Governor when, to his delight, he was called by the King temporarily to abandon pastoral care in favour of more martial employment. Charles I had instructed the Church in Scotland to accept and employ a new prayer book which had been prepared by bishops under the guidance of Archbishop Laud. The result was one of the several 'covenants' by which the religious Scots expressed both their independent theological view and their refusal to be governed by edicts from London. The General Assembly of the Kirk declared the Scottish episcopacy abolished – an act of rebellion which Charles could not ignore. His standing army was small and badly equipped. So to raise a force which was large and competent enough to subdue the rebellious Scots, he appealed to his nobility to subscribe men and money. Newcastle 'lent his Majesty £10,000 and raised himself a volunteer troop of horse which contained 120 knights and gentlemen of quality'.[35] He proposed to lead it into battle himself and – in tribute to his young master – called it 'the Prince of Wales' Troop'. His plan seemed to be endorsed by the King's decision that the troop 'should be independent and not commanded by any general officer'.[36]

Unfortunately the King either failed to mention his decision to the Earl of Holland, who commanded the whole expedition, or the royal edict was received but ignored. When the army advanced against the Scots' hastily raised forces, the Prince of Wales Troop was placed at the rear of the column. Newcastle objected, but Holland was unmovable. Pride was swallowed, but the Prince of Wales's colours were furled. To fly them in such a place in the order of battle would, in Newcastle's opinion, have been a slight to the heir apparent. The outcome of the engagement imposed a far greater indignity on the whole House of Stuart. Holland, the King's amateur general, faced Alexander Leslie, an experienced officer from the Thirty Years War. The fatuous demand that the Scots should surrender or withdraw was rejected and the English immediately retreated south across the border and the 'Covenanters' survived to fight another day. When the army was disbanded, Newcastle concluded that it was proper for him to demand satisfaction for the insult he and his troop had suffered. Holland was challenged to a duel. It was prohibited by the King. The Cavendish tradition of duels which were proposed but never took place was upheld.

Thomas Strafford had spent all his time in Ireland methodically offending all the vested interests which exploited Ireland and its people. The pressure to replace him as Lord Deputy had become so powerful that even a strong sovereign would have found it hard to resist. But Charles's authority had collapsed to the point at which parliament refused 'to grant supply' and finance his household. It was an escalation of the sporadic parliamentary war which had broken out in his father's reign and was, in reality, less about money than power. James had challenged parliament's authority when it stood in the way of his comfort and security. Charles believed that he had a divine right to impose his will on the Houses of Lords and Commons. Strafford's fall was a by-product rather than a consequence of the conflict.

Thanks to his obdurate nature rather than his royalist sympathies, Strafford treated parliament with such contempt that King Charles's most determined opponents regarded him as the most dangerous of their enemies. He might have survived their animosity had he not already alienated the Anglo-Irish establishment by exposing their corruption and challenging their hegemony by encouraging new settlers. Before his doom was certain, King Charles in a reckless show of loyal bravado made Strafford the Earl of Wentworth. The House of Commons responded to what amounted to a challenge by indicting the new Earl for high treason – a constitutional novelty, since his offence was against parliament rather than the King. He was imprisoned in the Tower and named in a Bill of Attainder – the prelude to conviction and execution.

There were many royalists – including Sir John Suckling the soldier poet – who were reluctant to sacrifice Strafford without a fight. Some of them hoped to negotiate a settlement with parliament. The bolder spirits were undoubtedly ready, perhaps anxious, to test the will and strength of the House of Commons in battle by riding to Strafford's rescue. The King's enemies inevitably elevated the rescue plans to the status of a full-scale plot, designed to bring the army south from the Scottish border and use it to suppress the rebellious parliament. Charles

– exhibiting signs of appropriate guilt and anguish – bowed to the will of parliament and signed Strafford's death warrant. So the King authorised an execution which was the punishment for being loyal to the King. Newcastle watched the drama unfold with both regret and morbid fascination. He could not have expected that it would end with his own implication in a plot to frustrate the will of parliament.

There is no doubt that Newcastle's name had been mentioned as a potential leader of what came to be called the Army Plot. On the evidence of his character and conduct, it was reasonable to expect him to sympathise with the extremists who wanted the army to restore the King's absolute rule. And he was certainly asked to ride north in the hope that he would demonstrate the legitimacy of the enterprise by bringing the Prince of Wales with him. But whether or not Newcastle ever considered joining – or even offering to lead – what turned out to be an entirely abortive enterprise, he certainly played no active part in it. But parliament came to believe that he was one of the conspirators.

On May 25 1640, the House of Lords resolved that 'the Earls of Newcastle and Carnarvon and the Lord Bishop of Chichester shall be attended with this order and that their Lordships be desired to repair unto the Lords' Committee . . . to take examination concerning certain late practices concerning the Army of the North'.[37] No offence was discovered because no offence had been committed by the men who were named in the indictment. The Lords had little option than to give Newcastle leave again 'to attend upon the Prince of Wales'. But parliament – convinced that he believed in the supreme and unfettered authority of the King – waited for an opportunity to protect the heir apparent from his insidious influence. It came a month later when the Prince fell from his horse in Hyde Park and broke his arm. Newcastle did not wait to be accused of negligence. 'Having hitherto attended the Prince, his master, with all faithfulness . . . [he] was privately advised that parliament's design was to take the government of the Prince from him, which he apprehending as a disgrace to himself, wisely prevented'[38] by resigning his office and retiring to the country. Much to Newcastle's gratification – and the fury of parliament – the King demonstrated continued royal confidence by making him a Gentleman of the Bedchamber. From then on he justified, in every particular, the description of a royalist gentleman, immortalised in *1066 And All That* – wrong but romantic.

For a while, Newcastle had time to spare for family matters. Elizabeth, his fourteen-year-old second daughter, was married to the eighteen-year-old son and heir of the Earl of Bridgwater, after which he 'settled himself with his lady, children and family' at Welbeck 'to his great satisfaction with intent to have continued there, rested under his own vine and managed his own estate'.[39] The alacrity with which he responded to the King's next call suggests otherwise – though the circumstances of the time might well have made even the most reluctant royalist realise that the time had come to fight or perish.

Parliament had issued the Great Remonstrance against Charles and was, according to rumour, about to impeach Henrietta Maria. The King, in turn, had instructed the Attorney-General to arraign John Pym for high treason and been rebuffed by Speaker Lenthall when he had attempted to arrest the five ringleaders of the parliamentary revolt against his proposals for increased taxation. In anticipation of the conflict to come, the Commons had moved from Westminster to the Guildhall and the Court had left Whitehall first for Windsor and then for Hampton Court. Charles I was not the most provident of English monarchs, but on January 11 1641, he wrote to his 'trusty and well beloved cussen and counceller' Newcastle, with instructions that leave no doubt that he was preparing for troubles ahead. 'We, being confident of your affection and fidelity . . . do Command you upon your Duty and Allegiance, immediately upon the sight hereof to repair in person with all possible speed to our town of Hull and to take our town of Hull and all our magazines there into your care and government.' It was a task which a wiser man would have realised could only end in failure and humiliation – even had it been entrusted to a soldier of experience and proven tactical judgement.

Newcastle was charged with responsibilities which far exceeded those of a civic governor. He was instructed to 'take into the said town of Hull the Regiment of Sir Thomas Mettam, or any other force that you shall think necessary for the defence of that place . . . and not to forsake or deliver up the sayd place upon any command whatsoever other than under our own hand'.[40] Despite possessing neither aptitude nor experience for real soldiering, Newcastle was to organise the military protection of Hull against the anticipated occupation by the King's enemies in the East Riding of Yorkshire.

The new recruit responded to the call by 'hastening from his house, where his family were all at their rest'.[41] In his haste, Newcastle either ignored or overlooked the order to secure the governorship of Hull with the support of Mettam's regiment and whatever other troops he could recruit along the way. Instead of arriving in force, he chose to enter Hull disguised as Sir John Savage, a private citizen. Once inside the gates he introduced himself to the Mayor as the Earl of Newcastle and announced that he had become Governor of the City. His arrival was not received with great rejoicing. 'I am here in Hull according to your Majesty's commands, but the town will not admit of me by no means. So I am very flat and out of countenance, but will stay here until I know your Majesty's further pleasure, which I hope I shall soon do.'[42]

Within two days the news of the debacle had reached London. The Commons demanded the Lords 'to show under which warrant' the Earl was claiming to govern the city and port and the Lords demanded his immediate return. Before Newcastle had time to reply, parliament had appointed its own governor, Sir John Hotham, who – the Commons explained with gratuitous offence – was valued 'more highly than the King's nominee'. Hotham, assuming that Newcastle would deny his authority, began to raise an army with the object of taking the city by force. The Mayor of Hull, in the hope of keeping a neutral peace, ordered the city gates closed. Soldiers, whatever their allegiance, were to be denied entry into Hull.

There is no way of knowing how Newcastle – with neither troops nor legitimate authority to back his claim to control the city – would have responded to the Lords' injunction to return to London. For the King lost his nerve and ordered him to 'observe such directions as he should receive from the Parliament then sitting'.[43] When the Commons examined his claim to govern Hull, Newcastle, honourably, took full responsibility for his decision to 'disguise himself under another name', but – either out of prudence or incompetence – neglected to explain why he had been sent to Hull in the first place. The Commons must have realised that the King had wanted Hull fortified in preparation for the conflict which was to come, but once the will of parliament was accepted, Members were content not to pursue the point. Newcastle, with mixed feelings of regret and relief, became a private citizen again.

The King knew that although parliament was quiet, it was not content. So he continued to make preparations for the final challenge to his authority which could not long be delayed. Queen Henrietta Maria left for Holland, taking with her the crown jewels. Charles himself moved north to York – from which city he made an expedition to Hull. On his arrival he suffered being refused entry into the city by Hotham – who nevertheless sank to his knees and swore his loyalty to the Crown even as he closed the gates. The time had come for Charles to call again on those of his supporters whose devotion was not in doubt. Newcastle was appointed Governor of Newcastle upon Tyne and 'the four counties next adjoining'. With civil war approaching, it was not an easy task to fulfil. 'He neither found any military provision . . . nor generally any great encouragement from the people.'[44] However, he did his duty, though he might 'have secured himself as others did either by neutrality or adherence to the rebellious party'.[45]

The idea that other nobles might, honestly and sincerely, disagree with the King was beyond the comprehension of men like Newcastle. Yet there were many peers who objected, on constitutional principle, to 'personal rule'. The Earls of Essex, Holland and Northumberland fought with the parliamentary army. The Earls of Hertford, Dorset and Southampton opposed Charles's absolutism in argument, if not by force of arms. Their dilemma was personified by Viscount Falkland who – incapable of taking up arms against the King, but certain that Charles would lead England to destruction – sought, and found, death in the Battle of Newbury. The Third Earl of Devonshire – Newcastle's cousin at Chatsworth – followed a less heroic course. He left the country.* In contrast, Newcastle became a gentleman general.

The first 'engagement' in which Newcastle led his Durham militia was an expedition to subdue a riot in Durham, where coal miners – sympathetic to parliament – had refused to accept the King's authority. He was not inclined to be lenient. Restoring order cost the lives of eleven miners. Tynemouth and Shields had to be garrisoned and defended and, after July 2 1642 – when the fleet declared that it owed allegiance to parliament – kept open to provide a safe haven for whichever ships the northern royalists retained under their command. He needed more troops. The trained bands were persuaded or pressed into becoming regular soldiers. The Bishop of Durham was instructed to make sure that all sermons preached within his diocese were supportive of the King. Newcastle was anticipating the civil war which had become inevitable.

On August 22 1642, King Charles I raised his standard in the shadow of Nottingham's ruined castle. The staff from which the royal colours flew broke in the strong wind. That was taken by superstitious Royalists as an augury of defeat. But the real indication of the doom which lay ahead was the disappointingly small number of supporters who, in what was thought to be a Royalist stronghold, turned out to cheer Charles on his way.[46] Sir Francis Wortley was appointed to raise men and money in Derbyshire, a task which he interpreted as requiring him to plunder the homes of known parliamentary supporters.[47] The Civil War, with all its internecine brutality, had arrived in Cavendish country.

---

* An account of his prudence appears in chapter eight.

CHAPTER 7

The Business of Yorkshire

In October 1642 – six weeks after Charles I raised his standard in Nottingham – Sir John Gell's parliamentary volunteers marched south out of Chesterfield, defeated Wortley's Royalist forces at Wirksworth and occupied Derby. In the course of his advance he captured Wingfield Manor and made it a parliamentary garrison.[1] But to the north in Yorkshire, the war began slowly – indeed for several months it did not begin at all. The Royalist Lord Lieutenant met Lord Fairfax – the undisputed champion of the parliamentary cause – and agreed that the three Ridings would remain neutral. The King believed that Fairfax was buying time in order to recruit soldiers and that parliament's generals, in other parts of the country, were limiting engagements to skirmishes while they did the same. Fearing that they would soon be outnumbered, Royalists followed suit.

Newcastle was particularly well positioned to assemble an army. In the north, he had more connections than his name alone. His maternal grandfather had been Lord Ogle and Northumberland was Ogle country. Newcastle's mother had inherited the smaller portion of the Northumbrian estate but the Ogle peerage, which went into abeyance when her father died, was revived in her interest and that of her heirs. William Cavendish inherited the Ogle title as well as Ogle land. So he was able to send 'for all his tenants and friends in those parts and presently raised a troop of horse consisting of 120 and a regiment of foot'.[2] He augmented his appeal to the local patriotic instinct with bribery, coercion and the promise of glory. He had intended that they would wear a uniform, or livery, of bright red. But because no dye was available, his soldiers wore and – when the war came – fought in bleached wool. They became known as the Whitecoats. The unintended distinction added to their fame.

The recruitment of an elite force of gentlemen and their tenants – the beginning of the slow evolution of Newcastle from courtier to Lord General of the North – was easy enough. But raising a force of the size that the King needed was more difficult. It could only be achieved in the north by the enlistment of men whose religious sympathies enabled Newcastle's detractors to accuse him of leading 'a Popish army'.[3] The

Earl, unnerved by the accusation, asked the King if Catholics were eligible to serve in His Majesty's colours. Charles's reply was based on the demands of hard necessity rather than the virtues of religious tolerance. 'The rebellion has grown to that height that I must tell you that I must not look what opinion men are who at this time are able and willing to serve me. Therefore I do not only permit, but command you to make use of all my loving subjects without examining their consciences.'[4] The need to recruit whoever was available became even more urgent when the Yorkshire truce was denounced by Sir John Hotham, broken by his son, who made raids on York, and then – after the appointment of Lord Fairfax as Parliamentary Commander for the county – formally abandoned. The Royalists of Yorkshire responded to the prospect of open warfare by appealing to the only loyal grandee they knew. Newcastle was invited to march south from the border. He did not reply in the romantic language of the true Cavaliers. Who, he asked, would pay the cost of the proposed expedition?

Newcastle could not have been more frank. 'I was very sorry you pleased to leave out the article for the officers' pay . . . Last night when I was going to bed there came colonels and lieutenant colonels who said they heard that you had left it out, and for their parts that they must think that if you were so cautious not to grant it on paper before we came in, they doubted very much of it in money when we were there.'[5] Unless he could be sure that his soldiers would be paid, he feared they would resort to looting and plunder. For once, practicality had taken precedence over chivalry.

The necessary assurances were provided and Newcastle led 800 men south. Seventeenth-century generals, although innocent of formal military training, normally rose to command after some experience in the field. Newcastle had none. His lieutenant general, the Earl of Newport, had previously heard the noise of battle but only in defeat and most notably when he was taken prisoner at La Rochelle during the disastrous attempt to support a Huguenot rising. He faced Captain Hotham – son of Sir John and, like his father, a professional soldier – at Piercebridge on the Tees. But numbers are sometimes more important than experience. Although Hotham tried to halt the Royalists' progress, Newcastle's larger force swept on, without further sight of the enemy, to York.

Lord Fairfax and the main body of parliament's northern army was 10 miles away at Tadcaster and his son, Sir Thomas Fairfax, upstream on the River Wharfe at Wetherby with a smaller force. Newcastle decided to attack Tadcaster at once. He chose to divide his forces – leading the assault from the east himself while Newport, after a forced march to cut off Wetherby, advanced from the North. It was universally agreed that the plan was 'ill-executed'.[6] Newport did not arrive until the battle was half over.

A romantic myth suggests that Sir Thomas Fairfax sent the Earl of Newport a letter that ended with the counterfeit signature 'Will Newcastle' and, according to the legend, instructed him 'to stay till he was sent orders next morning'. A year later, Newport defected from the Royalist cause. So he may have chosen to be late. Whatever the cause of the delay, it put the outcome of the battle in doubt. Newcastle chose to attack alone and drove Fairfax out of Tadcaster. But he had not enough men to turn Fairfax's defeat into a rout. The parliamentary army retired in good order to the wool towns of the West Riding.

The Royalist forces moved on south and established new head-quarters at Pontefract. Some of Newcastle's troops were sent into Nottinghamshire to help establish crossings over the River Trent. The King was delighted. 'The services I have received from you hath been so eminent, and is so likely to have so great an influence on all my affairs, that I need not tell you that I shall never forget it, but always look upon you as a principal instrument of keeping the crown upon my head.'[7] Gratitude blinded his judgement. 'The business of Yorkshire I account almost done.'

Within a week of Newcastle receiving Charles's letter, parliamentary forces had reoccupied Leeds. A convoy of much-needed munitions, bound for Newcastle's camp at Pontefract, was intercepted and captured. Fairfax regrouped and prepared for a new offensive. There was, however, some good news for the Royalists in the north. Sir John Hotham – offended by what he described as the 'Anabaptist' piety of some parliamentary commanders – began secret negotiations with Newcastle. And James King, the Lord Eythin – a soldier of fortune who had served Gustavus Adolphus in Sweden – joined the King's cause. He immediately organised an expedition which recaptured much of the arms convoy. But, despite the improvement in the Royalist fortunes, Newcastle decided to retire to York and begin to improve its fortifications. It was a sure sign that, perhaps subconsciously, he recog-nised the frailty of the Royalist position. Making preparations for withstanding a siege was more important than planning to advance.

Three weeks after the work began, a messenger from the East Riding coast brought Newcastle the news that Queen Henrietta Maria – who had, for some time, wanted to return from Holland to England – had landed at Bridlington and was on her way to York. She had brought with her 250 wagon-loads of ammunition and £80,000 in gold. Newcastle – by chance on the road, half-way between York and the coast, when the message reached him – hurried off to greet her and take delivery of the much needed powder and shot.

A force of local militia was assembled on the quay to greet the Queen and guarantee her safety. Their duties involved no more than lining up for inspection. The East Riding was cavalier country and the royal party were all safely ashore before the ships of the parliamentary navy, unable to prevent the landing, bombarded the town. A hundred cannon were directed at the Queen's lodgings. At one point of the bombardment she confirmed her suitability to sit on an English throne at the side of an English monarch by insisting on braving the bombardment and returning to the town to rescue her dog.

The Queen and Newcastle met 3 miles inland in the conveniently vacated house of a local parliamentary-supporting grandee. Henrietta told Newcastle that she was destitute – the £80,000, being earmarked for the Royalist cause, was not for her personal use. So 'Her Majesty, having some present occasion for money', her host 'presented her with £3,000 sterling, which she graciously accepted'.[8] It was money which the Earl of Newcastle could not afford and almost certainly had to borrow. But a cavalier could not shrink from either death or debts in the service of the King.

Henrietta Maria regarded the bombardment of Bridlington as an attack on her royal person and therefore proof that parliament was not conducting the war according to the rules of chivalry. Newcastle, discreetly silent in the presence of the Queen, held the unexpressed view that the bombardment of a convoy which carried military supplies, as well as the Queen, was only to be expected. That was the considered view of a man for whom chivalry was an absolute obligation. Thanks in part to him, much of the Civil War in the North was fought as a contest between gentlemen. Both Newcastle and Lord Fairfax prided themselves on their gallantry – and wrote to each other emphasising their elevated views on the profession of arms. When Fairfax made accusations of improper conduct by the Royalist forces, Newcastle replied with a 'declaration' which extolled the virtues of their 'ancestors who used not to spend time scratching each other out of holes, but in open fields'. His affection for the old-fashioned pitched battle was not just the result of his inclination to nostalgia. The old way – ranks of infantrymen, firing at each other on open ground until they were mown down by cavalry – 'set a period to the suffering of the people'. Fairfax's response was more bellicose than compassionate. As soon as he found an opportunity to offer 'battel to his Lordship . . . [he] would take it for a great honour to do him that service'.[9] In one form or another, the correspondence continued in that archaic tone for as long as the two men confronted each other. Often the letters related to encounters which, whether won or lost, were followed by the sort of note with which party guests record their thanks for an enjoyable evening. 'I have received the noble favour which your Lo'p was pleased to do me, your poor servant . . .' wrote Fairfax after one skirmish.[10]

The younger Hotham – in an attempt either to convert Newcastle to parliament's cause or as a preparation for his own apostasy – tried to convince the Earl that he was so ill thought of at Court that he was in danger of ignominious dismissal from the command of the King's northern forces. Several letters passed backwards and forwards between them across the battle lines. In April 1643 – after correspondence which included the promise to 'do anything which might favour his Majesty's service in the peace of the kingdom' – Hotham added, almost casually, that 'within this four days some very near her Majesty spoke such words of contempt and disgrace of you as truly for my part I could not hear them repeated with patience'.[11] Newcastle demanded to know how the disturbing intelligence had been obtained and Hotham obliged. His reply, as is so often the case with rumours, quoted a third-hand source. His father had been told of 'words spoken by my Lady Cornwallis'. The accusation was that Newcastle was 'a sweet general, lay in bed until eleven o'clock and combed until twelve, then came to the Queen, and so the work was done. General King (Lord Eythin) did all the business.'[12]

Undoubtedly there was some dissatisfaction at Court with Newcastle's performance. 'He liked the pomp and authority of a general well and preserved the dignity of it to the full; and for the discharge of the outward state and circumstances of it, in acts of courtesy, affability, bounty and generosity he abounded . . . But the substantial part and fatigue of a general he did not in any degree understand (being utterly unacquainted with war) nor could submit to.'[13] He was a man of 'invincible courage' but once the battle was over, 'he retired to his delightful company, music or his softer pleasures, to all of which he was so indulgent, and to his ease, that he would not be interrupted upon any occasion soever'.[14] In a letter to Sir Edward Nicholas, the King's private secretary, Lord Clarendon said that Newcastle was 'as fit to be a general as a bishop'.[15]

After Lord Eythin joined the Royalist cause, Newcastle had one genuine soldier on his staff. But the rest of his officers were as inexperienced as their commander-in-chief. His General of Ordnance was his son, by courtesy known as Viscount Mansfield, a man of barely twenty. Mansfield was supported by a Lieutenant General of Ordnance

– William Davenant who, having been granted the state pension which Jonson had received until he was disabled by a stroke, was regarded as the unofficial Poet Laureate. Whatever the quality of his verse, he was certainly a better poet than a soldier. The General of Horse, Lord Goring, was an alcoholic and Newcastle's Lieutenant General was Charles Cavendish, his twenty-two-year-old cousin and the younger brother of the Earl of Devonshire. The essentially amateur approach to war was a convention which parliament chose not to follow. A propaganda leaflet, distributed in the north, described Newcastle – with puritanical disdain – as 'at best but a playwright, one of Apollo's whirligigs'.[16] It is astonishing that he won as many battles as he did.

In March 1643 the House of Commons formally decided to impeach Newcastle and expressly exclude him from any amnesty which might be agreed when the war was over. He greeted the news that he had become a renegade with pride. Parliament had recognised his devotion to the King. He was less successful in the field. Sir Thomas Fairfax recaptured Tadcaster in January, but in March he was convincingly defeated at Seacroft Moor. After a Royalist victory on Tankersly Moor, Fairfax reoccupied the wool towns of the West Riding and recaptured Wakefield. A few days later, Newcastle received the news that his wife had died. The Civil War was briefly abandoned while, on April 19 1643, he attended the funeral in Bolsover. On his return north, Newcastle briefly laid siege to Leeds and then prepared to push south to Nottingham and Derbyshire. The plan was abandoned when Sir Thomas Fairfax – at the head of 1,100 men – defeated 3,000 Royalist troops at Wakefield and captured the arsenal. The Queen was only 50 miles away in York.

The Queen, fearful of capture and unnerved by the news that parliament intended to charge her with treason and popery, left York to join her husband in Oxford. Lodging in Newark on her way south, she sent Newcastle an extraordinary message. 'The King is still expecting to be besieged . . . He told me to command you absolutely to march to him, but I do not send it to you, since I had taken a resolution with you that you remain.'[17] The Queen's confidence in his strategic judgement encouraged Newcastle to mount another aggressive campaign. His judgement was vindicated. After a long and bitter battle, the badly outnumbered parliamentary army, commanded by Sir Thomas Fairfax, was beaten on Adwalton Moor. Gradually the Royalists reoccupied all of Yorkshire except Hull. During the long retreat Fairfax made a stand at Bradford. He was surrounded and fought his way out, but his wife – too sick to travel with the army – was captured by the advancing Royalist troops. Newcastle entertained her in a manner appropriate to her station until she could be reunited with her husband.

Newcastle moved on to Lincolnshire and recaptured Lincoln and Gainsborough where his victory was marred by an accident which typified the *grand guignol* quality of some royalist excursions. The parliamentary garrison – which had captured Lieutenant General Robert Pierpoint, Earl of Kingston – evacuated the town, taking their prisoner with them. The first stage of the retreat was by pinnace down the River Trent. It had not sailed far when the approaching Royalist troops saw and recognised Kingston. To halt the pinnace's progress and secure Pierpoint's escape, they opened fire. Kingston and his servant were killed. Their captors escaped.

It was at Gainsborough that Charles Cavendish – younger brother to the Earl of Devonshire and nominally Newcastle's Lieutenant General of Horse – met his heroic death. He had rushed to the King's side within days of the royal standard being raised in Nottingham, but whether he rode to join the Army of the North out of love for the King or love of battle is in doubt. During his Grand Tour he had caused an affray in Paris, absconded and then chosen to travel through the East alone and unsupervised. According to John Aubrey, he was 'so eager to see Babylon' that he volunteered 'to March in the Turk's army'.[18] He certainly saw himself as a professional soldier. By the time that the Civil War broke out he had already fought with the French army in Luxemburg and the Prince of Orange against the Spaniards. Whatever his motives for fighting, he always fought bravely.

At the beginning of the Civil War he had ridden with the King's Own Troop, an elite band of nobles of whom it was said 'the revenues of those in that single troop would buy the estates of my Lord Essex and all the officers in his army'.[19] But, by its nature, what amounted to a royal bodyguard could not be in the thick of the fight. So before the Battle of Edgehill, Charles Cavendish had agitated to be moved to the right flank, where he arrived just in time to take part in the reckless charge by which Prince Rupert – King Charles's headstrong nephew – almost contrived to lose the day. He was offered the command of the Duke of York's Troop in the Prince of Wales' Regiment but refused the commission because he disliked the colonel. Impertinence and audacity being closely related, he obtained an audience with the King and proposed his own promotion. He asked to be given a command and suggested that it should be financed from a donation that his brother had made to Royalist funds. The King agreed.

In terms of valour, if not judgement, Colonel Cavendish more than justified the King's confidence. In the spring of 1643 he first captured Grantham and then defeated Sir John Hotham at Ancaster and went on first to storm, then to take, Dunnington and Burton upon Trent. In July, the Earl of Newcastle sent him, and his regiment, to join the siege of Gainsborough. *Mercurius Aulicus*, the Royalist broadsheet, describes the action which followed in a detail that undermines its general conclusion about Charles Cavendish's tactical brilliance. He advanced on Gainsborough in command of '30 troops of horse and dragoons' and, discovering that he was confronted by '24 troops of horse and dragoons', decided to split his forces and attack the enemy with half his strength 'leaving all the rest for reserve'. His decision, 'being observed by the rebels', enabled the parliamentary troops 'to get between' him and his reserve and the '16 troops . . . being wearied with frequent watches'[20] were routed. The reserves eventually cut their way through and won the day, and 'Lord Willoughby of Parham forthwith yielded Gainsborough to the King's party'.[21]

Colonel Cavendish did not survive the battle. He 'unhorsed by a blow to the head'. Captain-Lieutenant Berry, Oliver Cromwell's adjutant, offered him quarter – a courtesy which was usually available to fallen officers. But, because he was 'a person of great valour and conduct', he refused to yield and, according to legend, 'died magnanimously . . . throwing the blood that ran from his wounds in their faces of those that shed it'.[22] He was twenty-three. Thirty years after the Civil War was over, the Reverend William Naylor – preaching the sermon at the funeral of the Countess of Devonshire – thought it right to eulogise her son. 'Two things this commander did not know. He knew not how to fly away. He knew not how to ask quarter.'[23]

After both Gainsborough and Lincoln had surrendered, Newcastle felt strong enough to attempt the removal of Fairfax from Hull, parliament's one remaining stronghold in the north. But as he prepared to return to Yorkshire, he received a despatch from the King which – this time directly rather than through the Queen – instructed him to turn south and join with the Royalist forces there. Newcastle decided to stand by his original plan and march his army away from Oxford rather than towards it. His judgement was reinforced by a message from Henrietta Maria. The King had again proposed that he should abandon the north. 'He has written to me to send you word to go to Suffolk, Norfolk or Huntingdonshire. I answered him that you were a better judge than he of that and that I should not do it. The truth is they envy your army.'[24] The 'they' of whom she spoke were the gallants who surrounded Prince Rupert of the Rhine, most of whom had recently arrived in England to add their swords to the Royalist cause. They had joined an army with a fatally confused chain of command.

Once he was aware of the King's wishes, Newcastle, although

determined not to obey, had no choice but to respond. No doubt emboldened by the Queen's support, he replied that 'he had not enough strength to march and to leave Hull securely blocked up'. What was more, 'the gentlemen of Yorkshire, who had the best regiments and were among the best officers in the country utterly refused to march south until Hull was taken'.[25] Charles sent Sir Philip Warwick, a Royalist MP who was acting as the King's Secretary in Oxford, to plead with Newcastle to change his mind. The emissary came to the unflattering conclusion that the reluctance to move was not based on military considerations. When Warwick showed Newcastle the King's commission – 'three or four words under the King's hand, written on a piece of white sarsenet [silk]' – his reaction was 'very averse' to the royal wishes. The messenger judged that his reluctance 'to be joined to the King's Army or to serve under Prince Rupert' was the result of hubris. He was Lord General of the North and had 'designed himself to be the man who should turn the scale and to be a self-subsisting and distinct army wherever he was'.[26]

Newcastle's will prevailed. He left a part of his army in Lincolnshire but moved most of it back into Yorkshire where, after taking Beverley, he laid siege to Hull. Warwick – no doubt instructed by the King to report on the Lord General's performance – followed him north. In September, he found the Royalist earthworks so full of mud that he 'conceived that those without [the city] were more likely to rot than those within'.[27] Newcastle reacted with a splendid exhibition of aristocratic insouciance, as well as a surprising knowledge of Catholic theology. 'You often hear us called the Popish army. But you see that we trust not in good works.'[28]

The parliamentary army was not in a joking mood. On October 11, Fairfax sallied out of Hull and routed the Royalists who surrounded the city; and Oliver Cromwell – then no more than a parliamentary general of horse – inflicted a heavy defeat on the Royalist troops who had been left in Lincolnshire, occupied Gainsborough again and recaptured Lincoln. Newcastle retired to York with what – after death and desertion – was left of his forces. On October 27 he received the gratifying and consoling news that, far from being out of favour or in danger of paying the price of disobedience, he had – in recognition of his great victory on Adwalton Moor – been elevated from Earl to Marquis of Newcastle, a distinction to which the titles of Baron Bertram and Bolsover and Baron of Bothal and Hepple had been added.

He was held in even higher esteem by the Queen. When the Marquis of Hertford was appointed Groom of the Stole to the King and 'must cease to be governor to Prince Charles,' Henrietta Maria wrote to

Newcastle to say that she did not want to appoint his successor without hearing Newcastle's opinion of the candidates; she added that, to show the world her high regard, she wished to arrange for him to occupy an official position at Court. Which would he prefer, Chamberlain or Gentleman of the Bedchamber? The greatest compliment she left until last. 'If I had chosen to act ceremoniously, I should have written to you by another' but such formality was inappropriate from one who regarded herself as his 'faithful and very good friend'.[29]

Rumours that Cromwell was advancing from Lincolnshire into Nottinghamshire and Derbyshire – mistaken though they proved to be – enabled Newcastle to spend the Christmas of 1643 at home in Welbeck Abbey after recapturing Wingfield Manor and its garrison and re-establishing the King's authority in Bolsover and Chesterfield. Prudently he decided that Derby was too well fortified to justify the loss of life and ammunition which would be wasted on its assault. While he was at home he received a message from the Marquis of Hamilton. The long-feared Scottish invasion was about to begin. Hamilton advised the immediate occupation of Carlisle and Berwick.

Newcastle – his sense of honour being stronger than his common sense – could not believe in the threat. The King had negotiated an agreement with the Scottish lords who – being gentlemen – would not, in Newcastle's opinion, break their word. Therefore there was no need to take immediate action. Nevertheless, as a matter of courtesy, he wrote to the King to ask for advice and instruction. The delay was disastrous. Before Charles replied, the Scots had crossed the border and occupied Berwick.

Royalists in Yorkshire reacted to the news with the demand that the King's army in the Midlands return north. They accompanied their plea with a promise to raise 10,000 men to reinforce the troops that would be redeployed from Nottinghamshire and Derbyshire. Newcastle believed that honour required him 'to preserve those parts which were committed to his care',[30] even though he doubted that the reinforcements would be mobilised and was not sure that he could defeat the enemy even if they were. If that was so, while his sense of duty was as acute as ever, his judgement was far better than was usual. As he made his way back through Yorkshire towards the border, 'he found not one man raised to assist him . . . nor an intention of raising an army' to support him.[31] He made camp in York while he considered how his mission would be best accomplished.

While he was there, he was joined by Sir Charles Lucas, Charles Cavendish's successor as Lieutenant General of Horse. Lucas was a cavalry commander of some experience and a diehard Royalist who had declared for the King in Nottingham on the first day of the war and then served under Prince Rupert in the West Country. He was a valuable addition to Newcastle's command, but Newcastle's letter of thanks to the Prince for releasing Lucas was courteous to the point of obsequiousness – an inclination which was to prejudice both his relationship with Rupert and the whole Royalist cause. There were six 'Your Highnesses' in 100 words. 'I am infinitely bound to you for giving Sir Charles Lucas leave to come to this army and to come with so many horse.'[32] A postscript expressed Newcastle's pleasure at the discovery that Will Legg – a soldier who had accompanied him on his first expedition to Hull – was 'much in favour' with the Prince.

Newcastle was naturally and genuinely inclined to defer to royalty. But the letter's formal deference hid his doubts about the success of the relationship. As the war progressed Newcastle certainly felt increasing regret, and probably growing resentment, that Prince Rupert – a man in his twenties – assumed authority over him. In theory both men – Rupert as General of the Horse and Newcastle as Lord General in the North – held autonomous commands and were subordinate only to the King. But their formal relationship was never defined. The result was a statement which, despite its formal loyalty, revealed Newcastle's resentment. 'I would never make the least scruple in obeying the grandson of King James.'[33]

On January 28 1644, the Royalists left York and again marched north, despite the danger of being trapped between the Scots moving south and Fairfax's army advancing from Hull in the east. Newcastle was outnumbered. His letter to Prince Rupert, written on the day he set out, estimated that his 8,000 horse and foot would confront more than 14,000 Scots. In fact the invading army numbered over 21,000 – infantry, cavalry and dragoons. Yet, for the first three months of the year, Newcastle – though short in numbers – held off the Scots who had little experience of battle and suffered from low morale. Inconclusive engagements were fought in County Durham and, on March 24, the Scots were forced back into Sunderland and Newcastle-upon-Tyne. But, knowing that his forces were too weak to drive on to complete victory and that the Scots would soon successfully regroup, Newcastle wrote an agonised letter to Prince Rupert. It was dramatically explicit. The Royalists could not, for long, withstand the enemy's weight of numbers. 'If your Highness does not please to come hither, and that very soon, the great game of your uncle's cause will be endangered if not lost.'[34]

Some time in March 1644, Newcastle – told that his critics were calling for his dismissal – offered to resign his command. The King rejected the resignation with an appeal to his patriotism and his vanity.

'If either you or my Lord Ethlyn leave my service, I am sure the north is lost.' There was no 'tyme for long discourses'. That may be the reason why the King's spelling was eccentric even by the standards of the day. However, the message could not have been clearer. The Scots, the King wrote, were not Newcastle's only enemies. 'I must tell you in a word' that 'you must as much contemn the impertinent or malitious tongues of those that ar or profess to be your friends as well as you despyse the sword of an equall ennemie'. After a homily about constancy being the chief virtue, the King signed himself 'Your most asseured reall and constant frend'.[35] But friendship alone was not enough. Newcastle needed reinforcements. When he appealed directly to Charles, the royal response was a sobering platitude. 'We, like you, cannot always do what we want.' The letter concluded with a promise of help which was so qualified that it amounted to an outright rejection. 'You may be assured of all assistance from hence that may be without laying ourselves open to imminent danger.'[36]

A week later, the critics at Court had real reason for complaint. The Royalist reverse outside Selby was less a defeat than a disaster. Newcastle claimed that the Governor of the town had been left with enough forces to defend his territory but, although he had orders not to challenge the enemy, chose to meet the Fairfaxes' troops in pitched battle. However the engagement began, it ended with the Governor 'utterly routed and himself taken prisoner'.[37] After consulting the professional soldiers who were a belated addition to his staff, Newcastle decided that he could not remain exposed from attack on two flanks. He therefore decided to leave the counties of Durham and Northumberland to the Scots, with the not altogether confidently expressed intention 'immediately to march into Yorkshire with his army to preserve (if possible) the city of York out of enemy hands'.[38]

Newcastle's advance guard arrived at York on April 16 and began preparations for a long siege in the knowledge that he would be outnumbered by more than four to one. The odds were lengthened when the Earl of Manchester – commanding the army of parliament's Eastern Association with Oliver Cromwell as his lieutenant general – arrived to reinforce the Fairfaxes. On May 31 – with food supplies running out – Newcastle asked permission for ladies to pass through the lines to comfort and safety. Manchester rejected the request, but opened negotiations about the honourable surrender of the city. Newcastle later insisted that he was only playing for time and that neither he nor his troops ever contemplated capitulation. While the talks were taking place, the city wall was mined under St Mary's Tower and Manchester's troops entered York for the first time. They were beaten back. But it was growing increasingly clear that, without help, Newcastle could not hold out for much longer.

By June 15, King Charles had accepted that capture of York was both a real risk and a blow from which his cause might not recover. He therefore wrote to Prince Rupert, who, after recruiting in Wales and victories in Lancashire, was hovering in the north-west. The King's letter was composed in emotional language which was certain to inflame the combustible Prince's romantic passions. It was also open to several different interpretations.

If York be lost I shall esteem my crown a little less, unless supported by your sudden march to me and a miraculous conquest in the South before the effects of the Northern power can be found here; but if York be relieved, and you beat the rebel armies of both kingdoms which are before it, then but other ways not, I may possibly make a shift upon the defensive to spin out time until you come to assist me.[39]

The order that followed was equally confusing but even more inflammatory.

All new enterprises laid aside, you immediately march, according to Your first intention, with all your force to the relief of York; but if that be either lost or having freed themselves, or that for want of powder you cannot undertake that work, that you immediately march with your whole strength directly to me and my army, without which, or you having relieved York by beating the Scots, all the success you can afterwards have most infallibly will be useless to me.[40]

At the Court in Oxford, Sir John Colepepper confirmed his reputation as a brave, as well as moderate, loyalist by telling the King the unpalatable truth. 'Before God, you are undone, for upon this peremptory order he will fight, whatever comes on't.'[41] He was right. From then on, Rupert regarded caution as a betrayal of the King.

On receipt of the orders, Rupert set out at once for York and, by outmanoeuvring Fairfax and Manchester, was able to reach the outskirts of the city without facing the parliamentary army. On July 1 1644 the same William Legg who had served with Newcastle when the Lord General attempted to claim Hull for King Charles arrived at the city as the Prince's herald. Newcastle sent him back to his general with a sycophantic greeting which assured Rupert that the enemy had fled in fear of his arrival. He also 'sent some persons of high quality to attend His Highness and invite him into the city to consult with him'.[42] Rupert did not want consultations. He wanted to issue orders. The parliamentary forces had reacted to his arrival by withdrawing to Tadcaster. He had no doubt that the initiative was with him and he would soon lead the Royalist army to a conclusive victory.

The Prince ordered the Lord General to regroup his forces and join him, outside York, early the next morning. Lord Eythin – who had served with Rupert before and blamed his impetuosity for the defeat in the Low Countries at Vlotho – warned Newcastle against following the Prince's reckless plan. But Newcastle believed that he had a duty to obey. He instructed his officers to round up his hungry soldiers – many of whom were pillaging and looting along what had previously been the parliamentary front line – and prepare for battle.

It took some time for Newcastle to muster his cavalry. So it is not certain at what time the column rode, through Micklegate, out of York. Newcastle and his sons – who were required, by their father, to prove their loyalty by fighting, and if necessary dying, for the King – were with the rearguard in the Lord General's coach. The advance guard arrived on the great expanse of rough moorland, on which the Prince had determined the battle would be fought, at some time between nine o'clock and noon. Rupert's greeting was neither tactful nor polite. 'My Lord, I wish you had come sooner with your forces.'[43] The infantry, under Eythin's command, had left York after Newcastle's departure and, since they moved more slowly than the cavalry, had not reached the rallying point several hours after Newcastle's arrival. Initially Rupert rejected Newcastle's proposal that the battle should not be joined until they were reinforced by 'four thousand as good foot as there are in the world'.[44] Then, to general surprise, he accepted the wisdom of the advice and – to even greater amazement – said that, when his full force was assembled, the two generals who were to serve under him would be asked to offer their opinion of his battle plans.

When the meeting took place, Newcastle said nothing, but Eythin was brutally frank. 'By God, sir, it is very fine on paper, but it is no such thing in the field.'[45] In his judgement, the Royalist battle lines were too close to the entrenched parliamentary position and occupied unfavourable ground. Rupert, unusually emollient, offered to make changes, but Eythin told him it was too late and added, to emphasise his point, 'Sir, your forwardness lost us the day in Germany when you yourself were taken prisoner.'[46] There followed a bitter exchange of charge and counter-charge which only ended with Newcastle, who did not approve of such unseemly conduct, making a pretty little speech. It left no doubt about his loyalty but was less reassuring about his confidence in the success of Rupert's plans. 'Happen what would, he would not shun the fight for he had no

William Cavendish
'Little feared the displeasure of any man'

MARIA · REGINA

Bess of Hardwick
'A woman of masculine understanding and conduct'

(*Facing page*) Mary Queen of Scots
'She has, withal, an alluring grace'

ARBELLA STVARTA
COMITISSA LEVINIÆ
ÆTATIS SVÆ 13 ET 4
ANNO DÑI 1589

'Your most unfortunate Arbella Stuart'

William Cavendish, First Duke of Newcastle
'As fit to be a general as a bishop'

Bolsover Castle
A medieval fantasy with a tilt yard – built five hundred years after tilting went out of fashion

Lismore Castle
Bought, at a knock-down price, from Walter Raleigh shortly before his execution

William Cavendish, First Duke of Devonshire
'The guardian of our liberties'

Thomas Hobbes
'Only a prince who rules by law deserves obedience'

Capability Brown
He wanted Chatsworth to imitate Arcadia

other ambition but to live and die a loyal subject of His Majesty.'[47] When Newcastle and the Prince reconnoitred the parliamentary lines on the brow of the hill, Rupert announced that the enemy would not be ready to fight that day. He was reassured that he had gained, and still sustained, the initiative. His optimism was boundless. 'My Lord,' he said to Newcastle, 'I hope we shall have a glorious day.'[48]

However, it was not clear what part in the glory the Lord General would play. Other generals and lieutenant generals were given specific commands – sectors of the battle line and divisions of the Royalist army. But Newcastle was left to fight like an unattached gentleman volunteer. He had, in effect, been relieved of his command.

For most of the afternoon there were inconclusive skirmishes between outposts of the contending forces. But in early evening, Rupert, certain that the battle would be next day, announced that he would return to his headquarters to eat his supper and suggested, either out of kindness or contempt, that Newcastle should retire to his coach and rest. The Lord General had barely lit his pipe when the noise of gunfire drowned the sound of the thunderstorm which had broken over Marston Moor. The battle had begun.

Within moments, Newcastle was armed and in the saddle. He assembled a troop of equally unattached gentlemen and told them, 'If you follow me, I shall lead you the best I can and show you the way to honour.'[49] Newcastle fought bravely and well – though the story that, during a bout of hand-to-hand combat, his sabre was broken but he fought on with his page's ceremonial sword is an invention. Fortunes ebbed and flowed. At one stage of the battle the Royalists were so near to winning that reports of victory were sent to Oxford and London. But Lieutenant General Oliver Cromwell led a decisive charge of the parliamentary cavalry. The Royalists were routed. Many of them ran. Amongst those who stood and fought were Newcastle's Whitecoats. They were virtually wiped out.

What was left of the Royalist army had no choice but to retreat. Rupert only escaped capture by hiding in a beanfield. The Marquis of Newcastle was the last general to abandon the fight – leaving behind, on the field of battle, the coach in which he had made his stately progress from York. When it was searched by soldiers of the parliamentary army, they found the letters in which Sir John Hotham and his son had given Newcastle cause to believe that they were prepared – if the terms were right – to abandon the Commonwealth and fight for the King. They became the principal evidence in the indictment for treason which followed and ended, in January 1645, with the execution of both men – father on one day and son on the next.

Whatever is the truth about the time at which Newcastle decided to flee rather than fight, he certainly arrived back in York after the Prince. He therefore had the doleful duty of reporting how the day had ended. He did not soften the blow. All, he said, was lost. There then followed a conversation between Newcastle, the Prince and Eythin – described again as General King – which Rupert recorded in his diary.

Says General King, 'What will you do?' Says the Prince, 'I will rally my men.' Says General King, 'Now what will you, Lord Newcastle, do?' Says Lord Newcastle, 'I will go to Holland', looking upon all as lost. The Prince would have him endeavour to recruit his forces. 'No', says he, 'I will not endure the laughter of the Court.' King said he would go with him.[50]

Newcastle and his household – about seventy people in total – left for Scarborough the next day in the company of Eythin and escorted by a troop of dragoons. Both Newcastle and Eythin were bound for Hamburg but they chose to sail in different ships – almost certainly a sign of the recriminations which followed defeat. Eythin went on to Sweden, where Queen Christiana – for whom he had previously won great victories – gave him a peerage and a pension. Newcastle remained in Hamburg. As he left England he had asked his steward how much money they were taking with them and was told £90. He accepted the news philosophically. There would have to be some reductions in his establishment. But he knew that the nobility can live on credit the world over – as long as they live in style. So immediately he landed he borrowed £160 and bought nine Holstein horses. The following week he bought a coach.

Included in his entourage was his younger brother the mathematician Charles Cavendish, 'the little crooked man' who, despite his 'shrunken frame . . . charged the enemy, in all battles, with as keen a courage as could enter the heart of a man'.[51] At Marston Moor – squire to his brother's knight – he had charged like a ghost from the medieval Bolsover which the Cavendishes of Welbeck had so lovingly rebuilt. And he followed Newcastle into exile as he had followed him into battle.

Although, much to the delight of Puritan pamphleteers, Newcastle was reported as living in reduced circumstances, he was faring far better than the cause which he had abandoned. York surrendered two weeks after the Battle of Marston Moor and the parliamentary army swept south, capturing Bolsover and Welbeck on their way. But it was still a gentlemen's war – for the gentlemen if not for the rank and file who fought with them. At Welbeck, where the family plate had been hidden under the brewhouse, Newcastle's daughters – Jane and Elizabeth – were allowed to remain, undisturbed, in residence. By the spring of the following year, even the city of Exeter was judged to be in danger and Henrietta Maria, leaving her infant daughter in the care of Lady Dalkeith, had found a safe haven in Paris, where she stayed in the Louvre with her sister-in-law, Anne of Austria, the Dowager Queen of France. From there, on November 20 1644 she wrote a letter to Newcastle which, while affectionate, was clearly not meant to exonerate him from the charge of inconstancy. 'I shall assure you of the continuance of my esteem for you, not being so unjust as to forget past services on present misfortunes.'[52]

Eight days later, King Charles wrote to Newcastle in even more generous terms. 'The misfortune of our Forces in the North, we know is resented as sadly by you as the loss of soe considerable portion of our country deserves.' There followed a promise to 'recompense those that have with soe great affection and courage . . . assisted us in the time of our greatest necessity and troubles'. The letter ended with the promise that if 'in the means time' the King could 'express the reality' of his good intentions, he would 'most readily do it'.[53] However, there was no suggestion that Newcastle might be rescued from penury by the repayment of some of the money which he had lent to help to finance the war and allow the Queen, after her return from Holland, to live in comfort.

Newcastle was not a man to think ill of royalty – even less to hold grudges against the Lord's Anointed. So when he discovered that the Queen was in Paris, it was only a matter of time before he joined her Court. He arrived on April 20 1645, bringing with him his nine Holsteins, seven of which he gave Henrietta Maria as a token of his abiding affection. The reunion was recalled by his second wife in the biography which she wrote after his death. 'It was my fortune to see him the first time, I being then one of the Maids of Honour to her Majesty.'[54]

CHAPTER 8

For King and Cavendish

Margaret Lucas was twenty-three when she met Newcastle. And she was unhappy. She had not enjoyed being a maid of honour and for two years had been ostracised by her colleagues entirely, according to her own account, because of her determination to retain her chaste reputation. 'I had heard that the world was likely to lay aspersions even on the innocent, for which I durst neither look up with my eyes, nor speak, nor be any way sociable.'[1] As a result, she was 'thought a Natural Fool' by other courtiers – but not by the Earl of Newcastle.

The marriage of Margaret and the Earl of Newcastle was a love match which both families opposed. Margaret – brother of Sir John Lucas who fought at Marston Moor and was created Lord Lucas by Charles I – was advised against marrying a discredited Royalist general who lived in exile and on credit. There was some doubt about whether or not his intentions were entirely honourable. 'Good friends' counselled her that Newcastle had 'assured himself to many but was constant to none'.[2] And Henrietta Maria did not approve of her ladies-in-waiting entering into liaisons which she had not arranged. Newcastle was expected, by his family as well as his creditors, to find a bride who was prepared to squander her family's fortune on buying a title. It says much for his devotion to Margaret that even as he was attempting to arrange rich marriages for his sons – 'hoping by that means to provide for them and himself'[3] – he chose to marry a woman who was not a great heiress.

Margaret believed that Newcastle made the great sacrifice because of her irresistible charms. She described herself as 'tender . . . chaste both by nature and education . . . seldom angry . . . naturally bashful . . . neither spiteful, envious nor malicious'.[4] She admitted to ambition – 'neither for beauty, wit, titles, wealth or power but as they are steps to raise me to Fame's tower'.[5] It was an ambition which – to her credit – she attempted to realise by writing rather than basking in the reflected glory of her husband's title. She wrote poetry and plays which were much applauded by fashionable society though derided by more discerning critics. Samuel Pepys described *The Humorous Lovers* as 'the most ridiculous thing that ever was wrote'.[6] Before they met, he was given a less than complimentary description of her appearance. She was said to wear a 'velvet cap, her hair about her ears, many black patches because of pimples about her mouth, naked necked without anything about it and a black just-au-corps'.[7] But after he first saw her, admittedly from a distance, Pepys conceded that at least 'she seemed a very comely woman'.*[8]

Margaret Lucas's artistic pretensions and unusual appearance were related. Confidence in her creative ability led her to boast that she 'took great delight in attiring fine dressing and fashion, especially such fashions as I did invent myself, not taking that pleasure in the fashions as was invented by others'.[9] However, despite her 'attic dress and her deportment so unordinary',[10] Margaret Lucas suited the Earl of Newcastle. She was of especially great assistance in his determined efforts to spend money which he did not possess.

In Paris, after their marriage, credit from tradespeople was augmented by loans from friends – £1,000 each from the Earl of Devonshire and the Marquis of Hertford and a gift of £2,000 from the Queen. Even so, when – at Henrietta Maria's request – Newcastle left Paris to join the Prince of Wales in the Netherlands, the Queen's controller and treasurer had to accept responsibility for his unpaid debts. For most of the time in Rotterdam and Antwerp he lived equally grandly – although he briefly experimented with thrift by living in an inn before he rented 'a house belonging to the famous picture drawer, Van Rubens'.[11] According to his wife, he made Antwerp the fashionable refuge of Royalist émigrés. And the attention which he was afforded by the Prince of Wales – Charles II after the imprisonment and execution of his father – gives some credibility to the claim. But it was because of his horsemanship that, during his years of exile, he became famous throughout Europe.

In Paris he had bought two Barbary horses. In Antwerp he bought six more. They were the central attraction of the riding school in which he taught amazing feats of what would now be called dressage. Charles II and Don John of Austria visited his ménage and after five years of acclaimed and triumphant display he published *La Méthode et Invention Nouvelle de dresser les Chevaux* – a manual of horsemanship illustrated with engravings of the Marquis himself, sometimes demonstrating the art of dressage and sometimes in allegorical poses as he rode in the

---

* Recently she has become a hero to feminist historians who exalt her for the invasion of previously male preserves. One actually described her as amalgamating the qualities of Georges Sand and Diana Princess of Wales – not, in everybody's opinion, a commendation.

company of the gods. When the Restoration seemed at hand, he wrote to Edward Nicholas, the Royalist Secretary of State, 'My services to my Lord Chancellor and tell him that now I hope . . . to see him take possession of the Chancery, and upon one of my horses of ménage, which will be the quietest, safest, surest he or any man can have.'[12] Newcastle was certainly a better horseman than a general.

At least, poor tactician though Newcastle was, he chose to fight. His second cousin, William Cavendish, the Third Earl of Devonshire, did not. 'When he found matters were brought to such extremity that he could no longer stem the tide he retired beyond the sea to wait a more favourable turn of affairs.' His decision was universally blamed on his mother, the Dowager Countess. Christian Bruce had married the Second Earl when she was twelve. Her husband had died in 1628, leaving his young wife with three children and considerable debts. The widow immediately set about restoring the family fortunes with a ruthless determination that allowed for no compromise. Hobbes – an expensive luxury she could not afford – was discharged.* Parliament was persuaded to pass an Act which disentailed some of the Cavendish land. It was sold and the proceeds averted family bankruptcy. When the Great Civil War began she was not in a mood to sacrifice the financial stability, achieved by force of her strong personality, on the altar of absolute monarchy. Her son was not in the habit of defying her wishes. According to the courtier De L'Isle and Dudley 'Every one perceives that he dares not eat or drink but how she appoints.'[13] The charge against the Third Earl of Devonshire is cowardice in the face of his mother.

Until he made the fateful decision to leave the country, the Third Earl of Devonshire had been – in his way – just as loyal to the King as the Earl of Newcastle. In the House of Lords he had voted against the Bill of Attainder that preceded the Earl of Strafford's indictment, prison and death and he 'would not consent to the condemnation of William Laud',[14] when the Archbishop was accused of attempts to revive ritualism in the Anglican Church. He had declined Queen Henrietta Maria's invitation to play an active part in the Royalist faction which she hoped to create in parliament, but he had followed the King and Court to York. It was there that he subscribed to Royalist funds rather than personally participating in the defence of the King. He proposed to raise a troop of cavalry for Royalist service. The offer illustrated the temperamental differences which separated the cousins.

---

* He was recalled in 1630 when the family income had been increased by other expedients.

Newcastle would have wanted to lead the charge himself. Devonshire was content to finance the enlistment of the men and pay for the upkeep of their horses.

If his hope was to disguise his support for the King, the stratagem failed. He was expelled from the House of Lords and a warrant was issued for his arrest. It was then that, in the belief that he had done enough for King and country, he decided to submit to the 'importunity, or rather commands, of his mother who, being a Lady of exquisite discernment, used exquisite arguments to convince him that he might still be of service to the Royal Cause without ruining his family'.[15] The alternative description of his behaviour is that he fled the country. He was, however, not exiled for long.

When Charles Cavendish, the Third Earl of Devonshire's younger brother, died in glory outside Gainsborough, the Dowager Countess Christian reacted to her loss with a combination of uncontrollable grief and careful calculation. It was time for her eldest son to return to England and make his peace with Parliament. He could not have given his support to the King's enemies. That would have been dishonourable and, what was even more important, imprudent. No one knew how the war would end. The Cavendish family still hoped that the Royalists would be victorious. But it was possible, at the same time, to insure against the King's defeat. That could be done by 'composition' – the agreement to make an immediate payment to the parliamentary cause which guaranteed that land and property would not be confiscated if the Royalists lost the war. Christian was for the King by instinct and upbringing. She was also a personal friend of Queen Henrietta Maria. It was said that she would have gladly risked her own life to save Charles. But she was not prepared to risk her family's inheritance. So she proposed an arrangement which – since the parliamentary army was in immediate need of funds to fight the war – she knew would benefit her enemies. Christian believed that the interests of the House of Cavendish transcended those of the House of Stuart.

So William Cavendish the Third Earl of Devonshire returned to England and took up residence, with his mother, at Latimers, his house in Buckinghamshire. Such were the strange ways in which the Civil War was fought that neither guilt nor embarrassment prevented Christian from offering the King refuge in Leicester Abbey after the Battle of Naseby, when it was clear that the Royalists had lost the war. While the Earl was negotiating with the parliamentary leadership about the cost of absolution, the King – transported through England as a prisoner of Cromwell's New Model Army – was the Earl's guest at Latimers.

Composition had become such an established, indeed an accepted, practice that even the ever loyal Marquis of Newcastle agreed that his brother, Sir Charles Cavendish, and his wife, the Countess, should leave him in Holland and return to England in the hope of negotiating an arrangement which would save Welbeck and Bolsover as well as part of Sir Charles's estates in Yorkshire, Lincolnshire and Northumberland. For them the task was far harder than it had been for the Earl of Devonshire. Both of the brothers had fought with the Royalist army. In consequence, their property had been sequestrated before the negotiations began.

Charles, the 'weak and twisted man',[16] was, at first, unwilling to enter into what he regarded as a dishonourable arrangement, even though, unless he agreed to composition, all his temporarily confiscated property would be permanently forfeit. His immediate instinct was to reject the offer of what he regarded as a dishonourable arrangement. But he was persuaded that it was his duty to negotiate a deal which would save his brother, sister-in-law, nephews and nieces from a life of penury. So he accepted the Cavendish precept that safeguarding the family and its property transcended all other obligations. In May 1649, while still in Holland, he applied 'to compound for his delinquency' and was discharged on the payment of £2,048 6s 8d.[17] The agreement was then revoked on the grounds that he had left the country. So, putting aside considerations of dignity and honour, Sir Charles set sail with his sister-in-law to strike a bargain with the men who, four months earlier, had executed the King.

The Commonwealth – even before Oliver Cromwell evolved from Lord Protector into virtual King – was a stern and authoritarian regime. Dissent was suppressed. Allegations of corruption were pursued with the zeal, and sometimes the hysteria, that had once been employed against witches. Immodesty in dress and behaviour was regarded as sinful. All signs and symbols of Popish sympathies were prohibited. In some villages the 'steeple houses' were closed. It was a bad time to be an aristocrat with Catholic sympathies and royal connections. The survival of so many is a mark of their resilience. Those who made an early peace with the Commonwealth prospered most. Those who fought for the King and went into exile with family fared the worst. Sir Charles and the Duchess of Newcastle must have landed in England with forebodings which approached a feeling of despair that their immediate experience could only have served to confirm.

They arrived so short of funds that they could not afford to travel further towards London than Southwark and they lodged there while a servant was sent ahead to the City to raise credit. No one was willing to lend cash to a returning Royalist fugitive. So Sir Charles pawned his gold watch to provide money for their immediate needs. When he appeared before the Committee for the Compounding of Delinquents, he told them – all pride exhausted – that he had left the country after Marston Moor because of ill-health rather than on account of reluctance to live under the Commonwealth. The obvious invention was laughed out of court. But it was agreed that he could compound for £4,500. Then the assessors had second thoughts and demanded £5,000 – which Sir Charles paid with money raised by selling as much of his land as was necessary to ensure that he did not lose it all.[18]

At first, the Marchioness – not too timid but certainly too haughty to advance her own cause – asked her brother, Lord Lucas, to apply to the committee for the help which was said to be available to the impoverished wives and children of humbled Royalists. The application – which it was, perhaps, unwise to entrust to a defeated Royalist general – was rejected on the grounds that the Earl of Newcastle, having commanded the Army of the North, had committed a particularly grave offence against parliament. And it was ruled for good measure that, by marrying a delinquent *after* he had taken up arms against parliament, Margaret had forfeited all right to compassionate consideration. Margaret was certain that she could have obtained a better outcome herself. So she went in person to Goldsmiths Hall where the committee met and appeared before it to advance her own cause. Her appeal was rejected in such categorical language that, when the hearing was over, she could only bring herself to utter one sentence to her brother-in-law: 'Take me from this ungentlemanly place.'[19]

Newcastle's son tried to save some of his inheritance by edging away from his father's Royalist record. His application for 'Discharge of Delinquency' claimed that, at the outbreak of hostilities, he had, without success, asked first for permission to attend parliament and then for leave to travel abroad. He further affirmed that although he had been obliged to follow his father during the early years of the war and had – from time to time – worn a sword, he had never actually assisted the Royalist cause. Remembering that the applicant had enjoyed the title of General of Ordnance in the Army of the North, the committee – not unreasonably – rejected his appeal. The Cavendishes of Welbeck were extremists – all of them extreme in their loyalty and some of them extreme in their apostasy.

Then Margaret, having been rebuffed on her own account, responded, with typical indomitability, by assisting Charles in the major task of saving Welbeck Abbey and Bolsover Castle by the only method open to him – buying them back from the owners to whom they had been sold by the Commonwealth. The task was made more daunting by the discovery that the new owner of Bolsover Castle had begun to demolish the outer walls and was selling the stone for new building. But Sir Charles did his fraternal duty, sold more of his own property and both rescued and restored the castle.

It was Charles's last service to the family. When Margaret received a message from Antwerp, telling her that Newcastle was gravely ill, his brother was too sick to make the urgent journey to Holland. By the time that the Countess arrived – having made the crossing alone – she found, in a mixture of relief and irritation, that her husband was restored to good health. But back in England, Charles 'fell into a slow decline' and died. The obsequies included the sort of tribute which is always received, and sometimes deserved, by those who overcome great handicaps. He was described as 'one of the most extraordinary persons of that age in all the endowments of the mind' with 'all the disadvantages in his person, which was not only of so small a size that it drew the eyes of men upon him . . . but in his unhandsome or homely habitation there was a soul lodged that was very lovely and beautiful'. And his intellect was said to be no less admirable than his character. 'He was a great philosopher [and] an excellent mathematician' who 'corresponded with Gassendus and Descartes'.[20]

Aubrey, with a fine disregard for medical science, even as practised in the seventeenth century, attributed his death to 'scurvy contracted by hard study'. He also claimed – without adding much collateral evidence – that when the solicitor who was the executor of his will died, Charles Cavendish's 'incomparable collection' of mathematical manuscripts was sold 'by weight to the paste board makers for waste paper'.[21] To the end Charles did what was expected of Bess's grandchildren and contributed to the concentration of wealth on the head of his branch of the family. His property, having been reclaimed from the Commonwealth by composition, was disposed of as his will required. It was inherited by his elder brother.

Despite that windfall, Newcastle continued to live on credit, but in the manner in which both he and his wife thought was the due reward of those who enjoy an elevated station in society. Margaret noted – with no sign of resentment – that, although she was sending money from London to Antwerp, her husband's standard of living was far higher than hers. When the exiled Charles II – King-in-Exile since his father's execution in 1649 – visited Antwerp two years before the Restoration, Newcastle was host to a sumptuous banquet and ball which featured – for additional entertainment – verses and songs which he had written himself. Among the guests were James, Duke of York, and his sister, Mary, Princess of Orange. Newcastle was not to know that there were three future British sovereigns under his rented roof. But he must have felt that if or when the Restoration came, he would enjoy a place at the centre of the Court, despite his reduced circumstances.

His hopes were not realised. Charles II was in The Hague when the combined Houses of Parliament invited him to return to England. Newcastle hurried from Amsterdam to pledge his fealty. The Duke of York offered him passage home in one of the ships which had been chartered for the royal homecoming. Uncharacteristically, he declined. Perhaps he had a premonition that there would be no place for him within the royal inner circle. And so it turned out. But although Newcastle was not to be numbered among the King's intimates, he would receive occasional requests for advice. Before Charles left Holland, he asked his old mentor if General Monck – the architect of the Restoration – should have his wish granted and be made Master of Horse. The question must have caused Newcastle great pain. For that was the office for which he longed, above all others. It was also the job for which – in so much as it involved any serious duties – he was eminently qualified. But he selflessly replied that Monck was 'A person . . . worthy of any favour that His Majesty could bestow upon him . . .' and went towards the ship which was to transport him to England.[22]

The frigate which he had hired for the journey was so old that some of his entourage feared that she would sink before she reached port and refused to sail in her. The leaking hulk was becalmed for so long in the Channel that there were fears in London that their caution had been justified. When Margaret – who left a week later, after assuring her creditors that the debts would now be discharged – arrived in London, she found her husband's 'lodgings . . . not fit for a person of his rank and quality'.[23] She suggested a move north to the comfort of Welbeck Abbey. At first the Earl rejected the idea. But then – realising that London had nothing more to offer him – he convinced himself and announced that he had acquired a 'great desire to live a country life'.[24] Before he left he told the King: 'I am not ignorant that many believe I am discontented, and 'tis probable they'll say I retire through discontent. But I take God to witness that I am in no kind of ways displeased.'[25] So – gracious as a true cavalier and loyal as an unquestioning Royalist – he kissed the King's hand and retired from Court for ever.

After the Restoration, estates which had already been forfeit to the Commonwealth, as part of a composition deal, were granted, by Act of Parliament, to the Duke of York to dispose of as he wished. Margaret insisted that her husband was deeply grateful that 'much of the land which had previously been his' was 'graciously restored'. However, her biography of her husband complains, on three separate occasions, of the sacrifice that Newcastle had made when he lent the King – never to be returned – £10,000. The third mention concludes with an exasperated note. At the time of the loan he had arranged the marriage of his daughter. To provide her a dowry of £12,000, he had to raise a loan, 'at interest, the use of which he paid for many years after'.[26]

Margaret's full calculation of Newcastle's losses always assumed the most and worst. But the total cannot have been much less than £1 million. Annual rents of £22,393 10s 1d were forfeited during the eighteen years of civil war and exile, producing a total loss of £403,083. Adding the interest that might have accrued increases the figure to £733,579. The value of 'trees cut down from woods left standing' added another £45,000 to the losses. Together with the expense of lawsuits, the theft of plate and the destruction of corn, the total cost of Newcastle's unswerving allegiance was calculated to be £941,303.[27] Newcastle's fidelity to the King was not matched by the devotion of those who should have felt a similar obligation to him. As well as the 'rents which . . . fell into the hands of the enemy' he lost much of the portion which might have been saved because of the 'cozenage of his tenants and officers'.[28]

Despite being close to bankruptcy, Newcastle – as well as beginning to restore the damage done to Welbeck Abbey during the Civil War – bought Nottingham Castle and began to rebuild and restore it at great cost. It was meant to be proof of his continued grandeur. But only progress up the orders of nobility conferred honour and dignity, Newcastle still longed for the recognition – which meant the rank – that he believed his service to the Crown justified. Some time in early 1664, he wrote to the King with a direct request. Charles's reply, dated June 7, was wholly sympathetic but offered no hope of immediate preferment.

The King had chosen to forget that he was literally in Newcastle's debt. The huge loans that had been made to James I had never been redeemed and Newcastle had never been paid the pension – estimated to be worth £4,000 – for which he had qualified as Gentleman of the Bedchamber. So – feeling that he was in a position of strength – he approached the King again. His second letter was a direct request for a dukedom. For eight months he waited in increasing despair. Then, on March 16 1665, letters patent were issued that created him Earl Ogle and Duke of Newcastle upon Tyne. There were to be twenty dukes among Bess of Hardwick's descendants. William Cavendish of Welbeck enjoyed the distinction of being the first.

Relying on the historical truth that dukedoms were originally the preserve of royalty, Newcastle began to refer to himself as a prince. The assumed title appears in his second work on horsemanship – the enthusiasm to which he returned in his declining years. The sequel did not enjoy the success of the first manual. The title – *A New Method and Extraordinary Invention to Dress Horses and Work them, According to Nature; as also to Perfect Nature by the Subtlety of Art; which was never found out but by the thrice noble, high and puissant Prince William Cavendish* – cannot have done much to promote sales. But publication made him feel part of the literary establishment of which he had always been a patron. Jonson and Shirley were dead. But Dryden's *The Mock Astrologer* was dedicated to the Duke with a fulsome tribute to his contribution to English poetry – as patron of Dryden and Davenant.

Margaret – who proclaimed herself to be poet, dramatist and philosopher – thought that her intellectual distinction was confirmed by her status as author of thirteen volumes of verse and plays as well as the publication of disquisitions on the nature and the purpose of existence. None of her work had the slightest merit, except in her own estimation. But she became notorious because of her pretensions – one of which was the claim that she was a superior playwright to Shakespeare because, unlike him, she invented her own plots rather than relying on Plutarch. In the spring of 1667, when she advertised her intention of visiting London, for the first time since the brief stay after her return from Antwerp, Pepys wrote that 'there is as much expectation of her coming to court, that so many people may come to see her as if she were Queen of Sheba'.[29] Two weeks later, he saw her for himself. She was in 'a large black coach, adorned with silver instead of gold, and so white curtains and everything in black and gold'.[30]

So although Newcastle never achieved his ambition to become Master of Horse, he was elevated to the highest rank of nobility to which a commoner can ascend and his wife became a celebrity. The Duchess survived until 1676, the Duke two years longer.* They lie side by side in Westminster Abbey within a tomb which is embellished with an epitaph that the Duke wrote himself. He did no more than describe

---

* The Duke was succeeded by his second son, who died without a male heir. The title became extinct, but was revived when the Second Duke's daughter married John Holles, Earl of Clare. He too died without a male heir. His daughter married William Bentinck, Duke of Portland, and a new dynasty – the Cavendish-Bentinck – was founded.

himself as 'Loyall' – not, perhaps, out of modesty but because he thought there could be no greater accolade. His wife, however, was afforded a long panegyric – 'wise, wittie and learned . . . a Loving and carefull wife'. It contains the encomium for her family which has come to describe the state of bliss which cavaliers – the romantic tendency within the Royalist ranks – believed themselves to inhabit. 'All the brothers were valiant and all the sisters virtuous.'

CHAPTER 9

Leviathan Awakes

After the Restoration, the Earl of Devonshire – Newcastle's Cavendish cousin, across the county border at Chatsworth in Derbyshire – chose to follow the Welbeck example and spend his time in the country rather than at Court. It was a matter of choice not necessity. He had quickly been forgiven his desertion. One of the only two of his letters to be preserved in the archives at Chatsworth records his pleasure at the speed at which he was restored to recognition. 'I have been but a week home and already received messages from his Majestie.'[1] In the weeks which followed, Charles II treated him with surprising courtesy and made him Lord Lieutenant of Derbyshire, an act of implicit forgiveness which his friends, ungraciously, dismissed as an appointment 'which his large possessions and interests in the county entitled him to'.[2] He was also made steward of both Tutbury (of Mary Stuart memory) and the High Peak. His obvious joy at being treated as a person of importance makes his insistence that he had become an enthusiastic countryman sound as if he was as anxious to reassure himself as he was to convince his friends. A letter, written from Hardwick to invite a Colonel Cooke to Derbyshire, contains the proviso, 'I can entertain you with nothing serious. I can only tell you that I have grown a perfect lover of sports . . . I hope my cousin has grown grave and serious for I am turned more jockey than he ever was.'[3]

The enthusiasm for all things equestrian – another Cavendish tradition – was probably genuine. But it was not true to say that it absorbed all his time and energy. He had developed such an interest in science and philosophy that the delights of country living began to pall. He became a founder member of the Royal Society, together with Christopher Wren, Robert Boyle and the diarist John Evelyn. But despite his new friends and his long-felt determination to stay safe and secure he remained true to Thomas Hobbes, his old tutor, who in his declining years had become a deeply controversial figure. During the Commonwealth and Restoration Hobbes had, by the expression of his views on the good society, managed to alienate Royalists and then parliamentarians in equal measure.

Commentators – who confused his philosophical speculation with opportunism – condemned him in a single sentence. Hobbes 'was so great a temporiser, that every form of government and every kind of religion that prevailed were to him the same'. He certainly changed sides. That was consistent with his political philosophy. He believed that legitimacy depended upon the possession of power. But while he changed from monarchist to parliamentarian and back again he was constant to a fault in his devotion to the families which employed him and in his gratitude for the access they provided to the extensive Hardwick Hall Library.*

His loyalty knew no limits. His ludicrously favourable judgement on *Plays Writen by the Thrice Noble, Illustrious and Excellent Princess the Lady Marchioness of Newcastle* exposed him to the sort of ridicule that was heaped on the author. Pepys dismissed the writing of 'Mad Madge' as the ramblings of a 'conceited, ridiculous woman'.[4] Hobbes judged Margaret's collected works to be 'filled throughout with more and truer ideas of virtue and honour than any book of morality' he had read. It was the product of a 'high and noble mind endued with virtue since its infancy'. He could not possibly have believed that to be true.

Like the Earl of Devonshire, then his master, Hobbes had left England when the Civil War was at its height, eventually settling in Paris on the fringes of Queen Henrietta Maria's exiled Court and instructing the young Charles II in mathematics. He stayed abroad for eleven years – far longer than the Earl who had been his patron. But the close connection was never broken. Indeed his advice remained so important to the family that the appointment of a new tutor for the seven-year-old Devonshire heir was postponed until Hobbes had pronounced on the sort of education which was essential for a young man of position and property in the new world which Cromwell was creating. Hobbes's view had not changed with the times. 'That which is requisite for my young Lord is the Latin tongue and the mathematics, I mean while he is young. For other knowledge – of the passions and manners of men, of the nature of government, the reading of history or poets . . . he is, and will be a great while, too young.'[5]

Three years later, in 1651, Hobbes published his great work, *Leviathan, or the Matter, Form and Power of the Commonwealth, Ecclesiastical and Civil*. It contained his famous conclusion about civilised existence. Man, he contended, was not, inherently, a social being. So the state of nature, far from being idyllic, offered only the

---

* Some of the works are listed in Quentin Skinner's *Hobbes and Republican Liberty* (Cambridge University Press, 2008).

'continual fear and danger of violent death' and a life which is 'solitary, poor, nasty, brutish and short'. To escape from barbarity men have to lay down 'articles of peace' and 'confer all their power and strength upon one Minister or Assembly' to ensure that the articles are enforced. A doctrine which could be interpreted as justifying an absolute monarchy would have suited the Royalist taste had it not been for a proviso which Hobbes added to his basic contention. The 'Minister or Assembly' only possesses legitimacy for as long as the 'strength and power', conferred by the people, is exercised in the successful protection of order and tranquillity. Supporters of the Stuart cause suspected that Hobbes's analysis led to the conclusion that Charles I had been too weak to rule and that the authority which was essential to restoring respect for the 'articles of peace' required Cromwell to become King Oliver. It is unlikely that the Earl of Devonshire shared that view.

On his return to England Hobbes wrote a justification of his theory in what amounted to a case study of the ruinous consequences of a weak monarch. *Behemoth* – in some of its printed editions subtitled *The History of the Civil Wars of England* – did not, as he hoped and expected, endear him to the Restoration Court. It was the timing of the book's publication, rather than its contents, which caused alarm. Charles II was trying to persuade a sceptical House of Commons that he accepted its authority to grant or refuse his requests for 'supply'. The publication, at that moment, of a book which set out to justify the assumption of supreme authority would have offended parliamentarians, no matter who had been the author. But *Behemoth* had been written by a man who had, albeit briefly, been the King's tutor and – had it been published when it was written – would have been regarded as a declaration of constitutional war. Hobbes was still on good enough terms to ask the King for permission to publish, but was 'flatly refused'.[6] *Behemoth* was only published – against the wishes of the author as well as his sovereign – a year after Hobbes's death.

In the circumstances of the time it was much to the Earl of Devonshire's credit that Hobbes remained his pensioner and continued to live with the Cavendish family even when they left Chatsworth House for Hardwick Hall in October 1679. He was with them when, in December that year, he died. By then the Earl had almost completely abandoned the Court and parliament. He was one of the few peers to ignore the vote on 'exclusion' – the denial of public office to Catholics and Catholic sympathisers. What might have been contented detachment was turned into loneliness and isolation by his almost total alienation from his son and heir. When the Third Earl died in November 1684, it seemed – to superficial observers – that the lavish funeral, on which the new Earl had insisted, was assumed to be proof that he would, from then on, accept the obligations which birth had imposed upon him. In fact the size and nature of the ceremony surrounding the burial was intended to be a reproof to his sovereign. William Cavendish believed that his father should have been made a duke. So, although the King had denied the Earl that honour his son had determined that his father should be buried in a manner that was appropriate to the status to which he had been entitled.

CHAPTER 10

The Wayward Whig

The Third Earl of Devonshire chose not to accept Hobbes's advice about the most appropriate early education for his son. From childhood, the young William Cavendish was instructed, by a succession of tutors, in all the subjects with which a gentleman of taste and breeding should, according to the *mores* of the time, be familiar. The extent to which he benefited from their tuition must remain in doubt. For what his early biographers called his aesthetic susceptibilities produced no more than some very bad poetry and the rebuilding of Chatsworth House which, when he imposed his will on the professional architects, improved the strength rather than the appearance of the building. The William Cavendish who was to become the Fourth Earl and First Duke of Devonshire owes his important place in English history, not to his contribution to the cultural life of the nation but to the central part he played in the inexorable progress towards the Glorious Revolution of 1688 and the Bill of Rights by which it was followed. He was never the leader of the movement which claimed — which much justification — to have saved England's 'ancient liberties' from the tyranny of an absolute monarchy. But as well as playing a crucial supporting role, William Cavendish – in almost everything he did – embodied the spirit, as well as the ideas, which held together the variety of the men who brought about the changes. Those men came to call themselves Whigs. And William Cavendish's wayward youth was, in its way, as much a part of the Whig tradition as the passion for parliamentary government which preoccupied his middle age.

The Whigs have been described in many ways. Doctor Johnson claimed that the first Whig was the devil. Other observers have judged, with more justification, that it is impossible to define Whiggery simply by setting out the principles which Whigs followed or the policies which they supported. Whigs were united by an attitude to life. Men of inherited power and wealth believed that they were endowed from birth with more than a fortune. They were bequeathed a duty to protect the interests of the nation in which they, and their families, prospered. Sir Lewis Namier – the historian of Hanoverian England – wrote that Whigs were united by 'one immutable, unchanging element, the

overriding, absolute belief in property' and argued that the feeling of
obligation was increased by the emotions which sprang from the
ownership of vast estates. Certainly most Whig grandees were great
landowners. But they were also united by an idea of responsible government. Whigs were not instinctive democrats. Land was the physical
manifestation of the country which it was their duty and their right
to rule. They did not believe that the people of England should be
given the power to protect themselves against arbitrary government.
The Whigs were, themselves, prepared to risk land and life to provide
that protection – ideally by assuming office. And Whigs possessed
another common characteristic. Wealth and status not only required
them to be the champions of liberty. It entitled them to live according
to their own inclinations – irrespective of the beliefs, conventions and
perhaps even the domestic laws of the time.

Lord Macaulay, whose admiration for the Whigs was boundless,
found it hard to criticise William Cavendish, the Fourth Earl of
Devonshire. But he admitted that even 'his eulogists, unhappily, could
not claim that his morals had escaped untainted from the widespread
contagion of the time'.[1] The contagion to which he referred was forni-
cation. The simple fact – half hidden under Macaulay's censure – was
that the dashing, arrogant, intemperate William Cavendish was a typical
seventeenth-century Whig and therefore felt no obligation to respectability. The virtues which he eventually displayed in his service to the
state and the vices which enlivened his private life were two sides of
the same coin. William Cavendish was a man who lived according to
his own rules. To say that he was guided by his conscience would be
to extend the usual meaning of that word. To understand his contribution to English history it is necessary to understand his wayward
character.

Lord Cavendish – as William, being son and heir to an earl, was
known – was blessed by an upbringing which was a near perfect
prelude for embodying, in almost every particular, all that it meant to
be a Whig. Born on January 25 1640, he was too young to be required
to choose between King and parliament in the Great Civil War and,
thanks to his father's return to England and rapprochement with the
Commonwealth in 1645, he was able to enjoy a peaceful and prosperous boyhood, divided between Latimers, the house which the Earl
preferred, and Roehampton, where his grandmother, the Dowager
Countess Christian, held court. In 1657, a few months before his
eighteenth birthday, he set out on the almost compulsory Grand Tour,
accompanied by François de Prat, his third tutor, who – as had been
the case with Hobbes and his father – was barely older than the youth

he chaperoned. There were rumours – not taken seriously in Chatsworth – that while attempting to cross from France to Italy by sea, they had been abducted by pirates. Both men returned to England, safe and well, in 1661. During their absence, Charles II had been restored to the throne of England.

Cavendish was one of the four young noblemen who carried the King's train at the coronation and shortly after his twenty-first birthday in the same year he was returned, on his father's nomination, as Member of Parliament for Derbyshire. A few weeks earlier he had been betrothed to Mary Butler, the fifteen-year-old second daughter of the Duke of Ormonde. A year passed before he visited Kilkenny Castle for the performance of the actual wedding ceremony. But having made the journey, he remained in Ireland – despite his obligations in the Commons – until the summer of 1663. Then, after he had accompanied the King to Oxford – and been created a Master of Arts by special decree – he returned briefly to wife and parliament and then left both to fight against the Dutch under the Duke of York. Cavendish, then in his twenty-fifth year, did not concern himself with the merits of the conflict. Fighting under royal colours was a fashionable way to spend a month or two. And, as a young man, William Cavendish lived à la mode.

As the years passed, conviction superseded convention. Cavendish became a passionate advocate of ending the Dutch Wars, although he knew that withdrawing English troops from their place in the line of battle alongside the French would have a dire effect on Charles's income. At first he simply accepted that as the necessary consequence of neutrality. But as his interest in politics developed, he came to believe that limiting the King's income – and therefore his freedom of action – was, in itself, an essential objective. It was not the most popular cause at Court. The policy which Cavendish came to pursue to the point of obsession was the foundation stone on which his whole political philosophy was built. Denying the Crown the 'Supply' it needed to pursue policies of which the Lords and Commons disapproved, became the Whig way of edging England a little closer to parliamentary democracy.

William Cavendish's growing concern for what he saw as the public good was in stark contrast to a private life devoted to self-indulgence. Horace Walpole described him as 'a patriot among the men and a gallant among the ladies' meaning that even in an age of sexual licence he was a notable libertine. The eulogies that accompanied his death in 1707 – speaking of his virtue as well as of his abilities – provoked an unknown pamphleteer into writing *The Hazards of a Deathbed Repentance* which listed all the sins for which he was said to have asked forgiveness. None of his detractors questioned his courage or his charm. Some of them blamed his failings on his good looks. Lord Macaulay described him as 'in wealth and influence second to none of the English nobles'. That was no more than an exaggeration. The claim that 'the general voice designated him as the finest gentleman of his time' and that 'his magnificence, his taste, his talents, his classical learning, his high spirits, his grace and the urbanity of his manners were all admired by his enemies'[2] was an invention. But it was proof of the mark that he made on society.

Trouble followed Cavendish wherever he went and, more often than not, was a welcome companion. In 1669, when Ralph Montagu was appointed English Ambassador to Paris, William Cavendish went with him – much to the distress of his numerous creditors. When the two men visited the opera they sat, as was the custom for persons of distinction, on the side of the stage. However, they were not too far away from the rest of the audience for Cavendish to be insulted – no one was ever quite sure how or why – by two drunken French army officers. In classic style, he struck one of them across the face. Both the officers drew their swords. Cavendish did the same and, in the fight which followed, received several superficial wounds. He might not have survived with his life had not Montagu's Swiss servant caught him round the waist and thrown him into the orchestra pit. As it was, he badly injured his arm. The incident did wonders for his reputation. In England the occasion was exploited to illustrate the superiority of the Anglo-Saxon race.

> However the French may pique themselves on their national politeness and charge the proud Insularities (as they are pleased to call us) with the behaviour of roughnecks and barbarians, I venture to affirm that had the same incident happened to one of their country – we will not say at our Opéra-bouffe, but even at Sadler's Wells or the Bear Garden – the whole company to a man would have resented the affront and treated the aggressors as they deserved.[3]

The French opera audience which witnessed the incident was unlikely to have been as censorious of the two soldiers as patriotic English opinion thought appropriate. But the Paris authorities responded with suitable severity. The French officers were arrested and sent to the Bastille, where they remained until Devonshire himself interceded on their behalf and obtained their release. Magnanimity is always admired. Sir William Temple, the British minister in The Hague, wrote with his congratulations. 'I can assure your Lordship, all that can be said to your advantage on this occasion is the common discourse here; and not disputed by the French themselves, who say you have been as generous in excusing your enemies as in defending yourself.'[4]

Age and increased political responsibility did nothing either to cool Devonshire's temper or to abate the violence of his reaction to real or imaginary reflections on his honour. In 1676, standing in the doorway at a Whitehall ball, he obscured the view of a group of ladies who wanted to watch the dancing. An Irish soldier, thought to have been called Power,* observed, in a loud voice, that Cavendish would not have behaved so impolitely if it had been Mrs Heneage who stood behind him. Mrs Heneage was a famous actress and one of Cavendish's numerous mistresses. Both men claimed credit for initiating the duel which followed – Cavendish because a lady's honour had been impugned and Power because Cavendish had told him that, in mentioning Mrs Heneage by name, he had proved himself to be no gentleman. Whoever issued the challenge, it was accepted and – unusually for a Cavendish duel – the fight took place. It was concluded without injury to either party when Cavendish performed a manoeuvre which disarmed his opponent.

After the duel was over, more insults were exchanged. In the scuffle which followed, Lord Mohun, Cavendish's second, was wounded. In England, duelling – made fashionable again by Stuart exiles who had returned from the French Court – was illegal. But prosecutions were rare, unless one of the participants died. Mohun, fearing that he had suffered a mortal injury, nobly signed a declaration which absolved Cavendish from all responsibility for his death. Cavendish was grateful – not an emotion which he usually exhibited to excess. But he chose to express his gratitude, with characteristic insensitivity, by sending Mohun £100. It was returned with the observation that, until then, the recipient had believed himself to be a friend rather than a paid employee.

No doubt when William Cavendish fought with Power, he believed that he was defending his honour – a precious commodity which had to be protected more as a proof of courage rather than a demonstration of integrity. He was certainly neither offended nor embarrassed by the open recognition of his relationship with Mrs Heneage. His numerous liaisons were a feature of his life which he made no attempt to disguise. Thirty years after the duel and three days before he died he was happy – in the great Cavendish tradition of benevolence towards redundant mistresses from lower orders of society – to remember the actress in his will. 'I give to Mary Heneage, living in

---

* Alternative sources refer to him as Pore.

Dover Street, the Sum of one thousand pounds.'[5] He was even more
generous towards the two illegitimate daughters she had borne him.
Henrietta Huntingtower was gifted £2,000 without her parentage
being acknowledged.* Clare Anson was identified as 'daughter of the
said Mrs Heneage' and left '£500 more than what my father hath
anywaise given or provided for her'.[6] The reference to the Third Earl's
generosity confirms that, long after William Cavendish had reached
what should have been an age of responsibility, he was still being
indulged like a wayward child – or being protected against the consequences of continued immaturity. Where women were concerned he
never lost the insatiable appetite of his youth. It was rumoured that
Charles II forbade Nell Gwyn to meet him – a story which, true or
not, confirms a reputation which, in the aristocratic circles of Stuart
England, did him no harm.

There were, however, concerns about other aspects of his character.
Experience had encouraged the Court to believe that Cavendish blood
inhibited the anxieties about debt which influenced the behaviour of
ordinary people. But by 1680 – when he was forty years of age – it
seemed clear that he would never grow out of his youthful irresponsibility. A scheme was evolved to bribe him into better behaviour. Sir
Leoline Jenkins, the Secretary of State, wrote to Sidney Godolphin,
one of the King's favourites, with the idea for an initiative which, he
hoped, would encourage a change in attitude if not character. 'I had
a proposal made to me today to lay before his Majesty: that he would,
by his influence, dispose the Earl of Devonshire to pay the present
debts of his son and get him more liberal maintenance. The Lord
Cavendish will then return to his duty as pretended [claimed] to the
King as well as his father.'[7]

Substantial though William Cavendish's debts were, his father would
have found little difficulty in meeting them. His total income – largely
preserved by his prudent near-neutrality during the Civil War – was
not only immense but increased year by year. Among the accounts,
which are carefully preserved at Chatsworth, are records of profitable
acquisitions. 'Lands in settled on Earl of Devonshire in taile by deed
of settlement in August 1671' had a total 'yearly value' of £8,525 7s
2d. They included Stainsby Manor (£976 5s 9½d) and Hargett Lands
(10s). 'Lands comprehended in Deed of Settlement', drawn up seven
years later, had yearly values of £9,736 11s 7d.) The Third Earl was
as careful as his son was profligate.

---

* Mrs Heneage had been at first secretly married to Lord Huntingtower, the son of
the Earl of Dysart.

So no one feared that the Jenkins plan would fail because the Earl could not afford the cost of improving his son's behaviour. There were thought to be two obstacles in the path toward redemption. The Earl believed that a bribe was unnecessary because his son had already changed his ways. In March 1679, a Colonel Edward Cooke wrote to tell the Duke of Ormonde that his son-in-law Lord Cavendish 'has grown sufficiently moderate . . . and the darling of his father'.[8] Those who knew Cavendish best took the more realistic view. They regarded him as incorrigible.

Godolphin's reply to the Secretary of State showed that Charles II himself was, at best, sceptical about the chances of improving Cavendish's behaviour. 'The King harkes very favourably to the proposal which has been made to you concerning Lord Cavendish and would have it encouraged and when you shall be able to give him any assurance that Lord Cavendish will be more dutiful in future, the King will be very ready to use his endeavours to obtain the Earl Cavendish's desires.'[9] The doubts proved justified. The Jenkins plan, if it was even attempted, did not have the beneficial effect for which its author hoped. Nor did Cavendish remain his father's darling for long. In September of the following year, the Earl of Devonshire told the Duke of Ormonde that his son paid him no respect. His 'behaviour towards me . . . [causes] greater grief and trouble than my infirmities can bear'.[10]

The sort of conduct which caused his father such anguish was illustrated in a letter sent by the Duke of Ormonde to the felicitous Colonel Cooke during the year in which Christian, Cavendish's 'beloved grandmother, the truly pious and virtuous Countess Dowager of Devonshire departed this life in good old age'. It reveals that the grandmother was not as beloved as the memorialist suggests – at least by her grandson. Ormonde was 'glad that my good old Lady Devonshire's interment was so suitable to the whole cause of her life, full of honour and with the respect of all sorts of people' but added, 'If I had been in England, I think I would have supplied the place of Lord Cavendish. I am sure that it would have become me more to do it than it did him not to do it.'[11] For reasons which were never explained, William Cavendish did not attend his grandmother's funeral.

In 1675, during the House of Commons debate on the annual King's Speech from the Throne, Cavendish had proposed that parliament's Loyal Address of Thanks should include the request that 'his Majesty would be graciously pleased to order that no more of his subjects should enter into French service'. The motion was carried, but King Charles ignored it. The need to end the King's attachment to France became, for Cavendish, an abiding preoccupation which he pursued with such passion that those who did not share his views became his enemies. The personalisation of the issue combined with his aggressive nature to produce an incident which revealed the inherent brutality of his character.

On the afternoon of 13 October, Cavendish – while walking in Saint James's Park with a Sir Thomas Meres – was approached by an acquaintance who told him that Colonel John Howard, a man whom he barely knew, had been killed fighting for the French King. Cavendish replied 'that the Colonel was rightly served and that he wished that every Englishman might fare no better that acted against the will of parliament'.[12] Meres agreed. When Thomas Howard, the dead soldier's brother, was told of what the two men had said, he published an open letter which denounced their character and conduct. His description of them as 'incendiaries' was, by far, the least offensive noun in the whole document.

On the following day, a Member of Parliament, who had received a copy of the letter, read it to the House of Commons in the belief that its contents constituted a breach of privilege. The 'point of order' was the first that Cavendish had heard of Thomas Howard's letter, but he did not wait to discover if the breach of privilege complaint had been upheld. Instead he left the Commons chamber 'in a steaming heat'[13] in order to demand swift and direct redress. Assuming, on the basis of his reputation, that Cavendish was bent on violent retribution, the assembled Members immediately carried a resolution which forbade him to leave the precincts of the Palace of Westminster. It was supplemented by a parliamentary order which forbade both Meres and Cavendish to pursue their quarrel with Howard. It also instructed that the High Court of Parliament set up a committee to investigate the whole affair.

Howard was found not guilty of publishing a scandalous libel, but was, wholly unreasonably, convicted of a breach of parliamentary privilege. As part of his defence, he accused Cavendish – quite wrongly – of hiding behind the protection provided by his special status as a Member of Parliament. 'His Lordship had heard of the paper before the meeting of Parliament and yet did not think it proper until now to call him into account for it.'[14] Cavendish responded to the clear implication of cowardice with a form of retaliation that schoolboys have employed for centuries. He claimed that it was Howard, not he, who lacked courage. His accusation was nailed to the main gate of the Palace of Westminster. It was then the turn of Cavendish to be 'named' for committing a wilful breach of privilege. He was committed to the Tower, where he remained for two days. The offer of release was contingent on his 'acknowledging by a Petition his offence and begging the pardon of the House'.[15] To general surprise Cavendish gave preference to convenience over pride and made the apology. It was not the behaviour of a picture-book cavalier. But as Cavendish after Cavendish demonstrated, picture-book cavaliers are most often found in picture books.

The apology did not end the quarrel. Cavendish and Howard issued a series of challenges to each other. Parliament debated their conduct several times more and was rightly accused of interrupting 'the business of the nation' by the discussion of an essentially private quarrel.[16] But parliament, then as now, enjoyed the examination of personal failures and some Members regarded the demeaning fracas as an opportunity to further the more general objective of prohibiting duelling. When the House was eventually satisfied that Cavendish would obey the King's injunction and 'not send any challenge to Mr Howard or anyone else',[17] it 'proposed to bring in a Bill to render everyone who should fight a Duel incapable of pardon. But this proposal was no sooner mentioned than it was laid aside.'[18]

Cavendish continued to respond to what he regarded, often with no justification, as the demands of honour. On 12 February 1682, Thomas Thynne of Longleat was shot through the window of his coach as he was driving past Charing Cross. He died the next day. It was assumed that the murder had been instigated by Count Königsmark, a Swedish nobleman who had gallantly, and probably platonically, come to the aid of Thynne's wife when she ran away from the brutal husband who had been forced upon her. Königsmark had offered the deserted husband 'satisfaction'. Thynne had chosen to ignore the challenge, preferring to gain revenge by paying six men to kill the Count. They failed. When Thynne himself was murdered, it was taken for granted that Königsmark had struck back with hired assassins of his own. He was charged, together with three men who confessed to committing the crime, but, unlike them, was acquitted. William Cavendish, who had numbered Thynne among his best friends, decided that it was his duty to remedy the failure of the courts and see justice done. Königsmark was challenged to a duel – anywhere at any time. The Swede declined the invitation on the grounds that his employment by the King of France obliged him to live lawfully.

Cavendish's frustration that he had been denied the chance to gratify his passion for violence did not last for long. While acting as a second to Lord Plymouth, he picked a quarrel with Lord Mordant, an onlooker, and shot him in the shoulder. Nobody died. So William Cavendish avoided both punishment and censure. But he was soon to become embroiled in a conflict with consequences from which his rank could not save him.

When the Third Earl of Devonshire died in 1684, the terms of his will were immediately contested. Some of them were vexatious. Some were justified. All were robustly contested by the Fourth Earl. The most contentious and least reputable was made by Colonel Thomas Colpeper* – a figure on the edge of the Court and a distant relation of a Civil War hero whose disreputable reputation resulted from his attempts to capitalise on the family connection and habit of currying 'favour with the government by affronting the opposition'.[19] Colpeper's wife – the daughter and initially the heiress of Lord Frecheville of Staveley – had been disinherited by her father after marrying against his wishes. Shortly before his death, Lord Frecheville had repented and given his errant daughter £300. Colpeper argued that the gift demonstrated Lord Staveley's wish and intention to bequeath his daughter all his worldly wealth and that, had he not sold the town of Staveley to the Third Earl of Devonshire, for far less than its real value, he would have wished, and chosen, to leave her far more. On that flimsy pretext Colpeper petitioned that the sale be set aside and the whole town and its manor awarded to him. Before William Cavendish, by then Fourth Earl of Devonshire, had time to react to the allegation that his father was, in effect, a thief, the King intervened. The allegation had been made in the Royal Presence Chamber and was, in consequence, regarded by James – King since Charles II died in 1685 – an outrage against his royal person. It is not clear if James made Colpeper a *persona non grata* there and then or if the Earl, in a moment of what he no doubt regarded as forbearance, offered to ignore the insult for as long as Colpeper accepted voluntary exile. But, whatever the terms of his banishment, he returned to Court. He had chosen the time with care. The Duke of Monmouth's rebellion had just been put down at the Battle of Sedgemoor. And Colpeper expected that James would be particularly indulgent towards anyone who was known to be an enemy of the Protestant cause. Colpeper and Cavendish actually met. But once again the Earl was uncharacteristically calm. Respect for the King prohibited a direct confrontation. So instead of challenging Colpeper to a duel, he opened 'hostilities that seemed to belong to a ruder age'.[20]

Mrs Colpeper claimed that her 'house had been assaulted by ruffians in Cavendish livery'[21] and Devonshire retorted that 'he had been fired

---

* Some contemporary documents refer to him as Culpeper.

at from Colpeper's window'.[22] Emboldened by the skirmishes, Colpeper ventured back into the Presence Chamber and, seeing the Earl of Devonshire there, loudly observed that he was surprised to find such a vehement anti-Catholic so close to the King so soon after the failed rebellion of a Protestant pretender. Devonshire realised that the comment came very close to an accusation of treason if the remarks were directed towards him. Colpeper said that they were. So, restraint abandoned, Devonshire 'demanded satisfaction'. When the challenge to a duel was ignored Devonshire knocked Colpeper down.[23] Gentlemen-at-arms intervened, inevitably on the Earl's side, and Colpeper – although the victim of the assault – was taken, under arrest, to the Marshalsea prison. He remained there until March 1686 and passed much of his time writing apologetic (and unacknowledged) letters to Devonshire. However, on his release, he received an invitation to meet the Earl. He ignored what might have been an overture for peace. Again affronted, the Earl resumed the street warfare and sent his servants to break all the windows in Colpeper's house – an exercise which they found so rewarding that they repeated it as soon as the glass was replaced.

There followed several months of quiet. Then the two men met again at Court. On the pretext that he had been offended by an insulting look, Devonshire took Colpeper by the nose and led him from the Whitehall Withdrawing Room into the street, where he struck him in the face with his cane. Despite the disparity in rank and status, it was impossible to pretend that the affray – begun at the margins of the Court – was not instigated by the Earl. The claim that parliamentary privilege protected a peer from prosecution was dismissed and Devonshire was arraigned and convicted of assault. James II – as ingenious as his father in the invention of schemes for raising royal revenue – consulted the Keeper of the King's Conscience about the appropriate size of the fine. The Keeper, George Jeffreys – the presiding judge at the Bloody Assizes which had followed the Monmouth Rebellion – was noted for the severity of his sentencing. Devonshire was fined £30,000 and, as if to emphasise that he was not above the law, was committed to the King's Bench Prison where he was required to remain until the fine was paid.*

His mother – a Cecil by birth – proposed that he discharge his debt by a scheme which she should have realised was more likely to cause

---

* Devonshire neither forgave nor forgot. In 1697 he happened to meet Colpeper in the Auction House, St Alban's Street, London. The fifty-seven-year-old Duke tweaked the sixty-year-old Colonel's nose.

offence than be regarded as an acceptable alternative to a cash payment. She offered the King bonds with a face value of £60,000. They had been given to her husband by Charles I in return for money 'lent' to finance the Stuart cause during the Civil War and, in consequence, were – as he well knew – worthless. The offer was refused. Devonshire, unwilling to endure either restraint or indignity, announced his intention of leaving prison. No attempt was made to stop him. He left behind a letter to Lord Middleton which he asked should be shown to the King. It displayed a strange combination of resentment and subservience.

> My Lord, three weeks since I was obliged to make a journey into the country as well as for my health as to look after my private affairs, still retaining and paying for the lodging in the prison which I hope may free me from the imputation of escape. Since when the Lord Chancellor (whom I conceive has nothing to do with this matter, being foreign to his jurisdiction) has not only reviled the Marshal of the King's Bench with the most opprobrious language and threatened to hang him, but likewise processed a warrant to be sent after me signed by a privy judge, which as your lordship knows is not in force all over England.[24]

Outrage then gave way to defiance. 'Had it been signed by the Lord Chief Justice himself, I cannot but insist upon that which I insist to be the right of all the Peers of England not to be imprisoned for debt.' A not very convincing assurance of loyalty followed. 'I think I have pretty well shew'd my willingness to submit to His Majesty's pleasure.' But then he repeated the unacceptable offer of 'the great sums which my father lent' being regarded as 'at least as just a debt as any which arise from the last scandalous judgement given'. With which near ultimatum he turned his attention to rebuilding Chatsworth.

Of course the King was not prepared to allow a mere earl to flout his authority. So 'upon the news of his arrival [at Chatsworth], the High Sheriff of Derbyshire had precept to apprehend him and bring him, with his posse, to London'.[25] But in those days the Peak was wild and lawless country in which the King's writ was not as powerful as a Cavendish instruction. According to one version of what followed, the High Sheriff ignored his orders. In Devonshire's own account, he 'invited the Sherriff to keep him a prisoner of honour, till he had compounded his own liberty by giving a bond in payment of the whole sum'.[26] The bond was, of course, worthless. If it was offered and accepted, the arrangement only served to emphasise what the High

Sheriff's failure to act had already made clear. In Derbyshire, James ruled by courtesy of the Cavendish family. And if, as Cavendish claimed, the King endorsed what Cavendish and the sheriff had agreed, James tacitly admitted that he was powerless north of the Trent.

King James's agreement to what were essentially the Earl's terms was also an indication of his constitutional insecurity. He knew that shortage of funds might soon oblige him to recall parliament and ask for 'Supply'. When the House of Lords reassembled, Devonshire would be able to issue a writ of error, reiterating his belief that, even with the sovereign's backing, the courts could not convict a peer of the realm either for assault or failure to pay a fine. And the House of Lords could not be trusted to reject it. Devonshire had won but his 'political friends thought it best for himself and his cause if he remained in the background'[27] – to protect him from the King's vengeance or themselves from the consequences of his, undoubtedly only temporarily submerged, intemperance. Whatever the reason for their call for caution, surprisingly their advice was accepted.

At Chatsworth, 'reflecting in his mind on the deplorable state of the country', Devonshire read for the first time – and despite Hobbes's advice to his mother – 'the most celebrated Roman authors'. In particular, he 'drew from Tacitus many useful reflections in respect of power and liberty'.[28] His reading convinced him that only 'a Prince who ruled by law deserved his obedience' and that there should never be 'a passive reaction to tyranny'. Gradually what had been his instinctive and personal opposition to the behaviour of the Stuart kings coalesced into a theory of government. And once he had an idea to live by, his nature forced him to do all he could to put his theory into practice. For two years, he brooded. And while he brooded, like a true Devonshire, he built.

The Reverend White Kennet – a not altogether reliable witness whose biography was originally a supplement to the address that he gave at the Earl's funeral – attributes the apparently sudden urge to William Cavendish's indomitable character. 'It was during this Load of Difficulties' – the fallout from the Colpeper affair – 'that he first projected the glorious pile of Chatsworth, as if his mind rose up upon the depression of his fortunes.'[29] In fact, he had been considering the project for some time. On his accession to the earldom, almost a year before the Colpeper troubles began, he had been told that Elizabethan Chatsworth was 'decaying and weake'. According to James Whildon – who had already supervised attempts at renovation – it was 'for this and other reasons [that he] determined to pull downe the same or great part thereof'.[30] Kennet believed that his intentions were more modest, that he only intended to rebuild the south side and that 'when he had finished that Part, he [meant] to go no further'.[31] He changed his mind because of his 'expansive nature' – and the fear that Chatsworth was about to fall down.

The limits of his original aspiration were illustrated by his choice of architect. 'Mr Sturgess the Surveyor' was paid £5 for his plan for altering the east front of the house. Before the work was done he was discharged and replaced by William Talman, Controller of the King's Works at Hampton Court and architect of Thoresby, just across the border in Nottinghamshire. He lasted longer than Sturgess but he too was discharged long before the work – house and gardens – was completed. In all it took twenty-two years.

At first the building progressed quickly and smoothly. The earliest work was the least complicated. Most of the materials were available locally and there were plenty of gifted craftsmen who were happy to serve the Earl as contracted employees – at the time, this was a novel form of engagement. Whether or not it was the most efficient and cost-effective form of employment it was certainly an arrangement which the Earl – when he realised its significance – found intolerable. Accounts for the time include £500 received by a master mason 'in part payment upon the bargaines for the new buildings',[32] and 'bargaines' for 'joyners worke . . . plaisterworke . . . carved work' and for 'making figures'.

The Earl was not used to bargaining with workmen. His employees were normally hired on his terms and fired at his discretion. Part of their wages was always described as 'gifts' – invariably paid, but a perpetual reminder that they depended on grace and favour. That was the only relationship which the Earl would tolerate. As soon as he understood the full implications of the new arrangements, he cancelled the contracts. The bitterness which naturally followed reduced the craftsmen's enthusiasm and slowed down the work. But the greatest delay was attributable not to resentment which followed the changed conditions of employment but to other aspects of the Earl's autocratic nature. He constantly changed his mind about the sort of house he wanted the new Chatsworth to be. In one letter he first instructed William Poole, his London agent, to inform the master mason that he would not receive any payment 'Until the stairs in the hall are pulled down and begun again', and then went on to order that 'the stairs [are to be] left alone until further directions'.[33] He expected every change to be incorporated immediately into the ongoing work. Worse still, he believed that he was capable of designing some of the changes which he demanded.

Inevitably, he was encouraged in that delusion by his friends. Even before he got to the biographical supplement, Kennet claimed, in the funeral oration, that Devonshire had all the 'politer arts'. He referred to painting and poetry rather than good manners but, even allowing for that limitation, the obsequy relied a great deal on the licence which is allowed in such an address. Certainly Devonshire collected paintings. But the quality of his poetry can be judged from one of his printed works, *A Poem Occasioned By the Archbishop of Cambray's Telemachus.*

> Cambray! Whilst of Seraphic love you write,
> The noblest Image is the clearest Light!
> A Love by no self-interest debased
> But in t'Almighty high Perfect placed.

Kennet's final contention – 'in architecture [he had] a Genius and Skill beyond any one Age' – was justified with the explanation that when he came to rebuild Chatsworth House, 'he contracted with workmen in a plan he gave to them'.[34] That is the charitable interpretation of the role he performed in the rebuilding as well as a misunderstanding of his relationship with the builders. The alternative version of contribution he made to the work was that in 'the early 1690s a mighty confusion reigned at Chatsworth'. Its cause was the Earl's habit of 'embarking upon new schemes before finishing the old'.[35]

The outcome of the often interrupted rebuilding was a square three-storey house, built round a courtyard with giant Ionic pillars along the south front and its west front highly decorated. It may be that the rough ideas did emanate from the Earl himself. He had taken great interest in the emerging east front of the Louvre when he visited Paris in 1669. But he was not an architect in any real meaning of the word. The real work was done first by William Talman and then, after his arbitrary dismissal in 1696, by Thomas Archer, contemporary, though hardly rival, of John Vanbrugh and Nicholas Hawksmoor. By the time that Archer arrived in Derbyshire, Devonshire's fame did not depend on what part he had played in the redesigning of his family home. By then he had played a conspicuous part in deposing one king, enthroning another and establishing, for England, a Bill of Rights which took second place only to Magna Carta in the history of civil liberties.

CHAPTER 11

Dare Call it Treason

During his early years as a Member of Parliament, William Cavendish – yet to become the Fourth Earl of Devonshire – took the view that he had better things to do with his time than sit in the House of Commons. Had he chosen to spend his days at Westminster – rather than idling in Ireland after his marriage to Lady Mary Butler and fighting the Dutch at sea under the command of the Duke of York – he would have been party to what was, initially, a remarkably peaceful transition from Commonwealth to monarchy. During the early days of the Restoration, the 'Convention Parliament' was satisfied with the constitutional authority which it had established by 'inviting' Charles II to assume (or, as his supporters insisted, resume) the throne rather than allowing him to 'summons' Members at his pleasure. The King, anxious 'not to go on his travels again', chose to act as if he accepted the limitations that the new relationship required. The Prerogative Courts – an alternative system of justice which had been under the control of Charles I – were abandoned and, crucially, tax increases – the occasion if not the cause of the Civil War – were only be implemented with the agreement of the House of Commons. The King had undertaken not to seek revenge for his father's death and the Acts of Indemnity and Oblivion had, to an acceptable extent, fulfilled that promise. Although twelve regicides and Sir Henry Vane (a young firebrand who, it was assumed, would raise a revolt against somebody) were executed, the feared blood bath was avoided. Compromise over life and death was possible. Agreement about ownership of land – a subject which normally preoccupied the Cavendishes – was not.

Under the guidance of Edward Hyde* – Earl of Clarendon, Lord Chancellor and Charles's wise counsellor during the years of exile – King and parliament tried to satisfy both extremes of interest and opinion. Church and Crown lands and estates which had been confiscated and sold by the Commonwealth were returned to their old owners without compensation being paid to the new. Lands which Royalists

---

* He was also the father-in-law of the Duke of York and therefore, in consequence, grandfather of Queens Mary and Anne.

had sold to pay whatever indemnities were necessary to buy peace with parliament remained the property of whoever had bought them. The Cavendish family had secured its future by coming to an early accommodation with the Commonwealth. What was known as the Cavalier Parliament inevitably spent much time debating the level of reparations. William Cavendish was either absent or silent. He was not in a mood to spend time and effort fighting for payments to recompense Royalists who had sacrificed their lands by obdurate support of Charles I.

Throughout the early years of the Restoration William Cavendish was detached from the great issues of the day to the point of indifference. He supported, without exertion or passion, the Act of Uniformity – which reasserted the primacy of the Anglican prayer book – and the Conventicle Act, which prohibited the holding of services which observed different liturgy. Both measures were intended less to defend the doctrine and liturgy of the Church than to defend England against subversive Popish influences. Cavendish expressed no strong view on either subject.

For a while King and parliament lived in peace. In 1664, the year after the Restoration, the Speaker of the House of Commons felt able to record his pleasure at having presided over 'unparalleled unanimity'. The King's response was fulsome in its recognition of the support he had received from parliament and, before it was prorogued, Charles told the assembled Members that he could not thank them enough for their generosity. He went on to describe his gratitude in profoundly unwise language. 'I must confess to you, you complied very fully with me and have gratified me in all that I desired.' Gratifying the King's desires was the way in which only the most ardent Royalists in the Commons defined their role. And even they were shocked first to suspect and then to discover that the King was augmenting his income with subventions from Louis XIV – in return for which he supported Catholic France in its wars against Protestant Holland.

Success in the war against Holland – while it lasted – encouraged parliament, exiled in Oxford because of the plague, to act with unusual generosity towards both the King and his brother, the Duke of York, who was regarded as the architect of victory. But in the following year, although distracted by the Great Fire of London, the Commons had second thoughts about its indulgence. Members had come to suspect that, despite his protestations, Charles harboured 'Popish' sympathies. And the Duke of York – the heir presumptive to the throne – had been so emboldened by his brief popularity that he no longer hid his Catholicism. Parliament decided that it had been torpid for too long and began to use the one weapon which it possessed. Supply would be withheld until Charles implemented the laws which outlawed Popery. The King agreed to act – and did nothing.

In 1666, during one of his occasional visits to the House of Commons, William Cavendish supported the call for the suppression of 'Roman practices'. But it was not until the following year that he began to take a real interest in parliament and its proceedings. Then his Whig conscience – always more active in the defence of political liberty than in support of religious tolerance – began to stir. It was a good time to become a trouble-maker. Parliament had turned against Lord Clarendon – Lord Chancellor, Keeper of the Great Seal and by far the most powerful of the King's ministers – for the second time. The Second Dutch War had ended with New Amsterdam – from then on New York – being ceded to England. But even as the terms of peace were being negotiated, the Dutch fleet had sailed up the Medway and sunk English warships at anchor. Clarendon, the King's first minister, was held responsible. In parliament the big splash is most easily made in troubled waters.

Clarendon's survival depended on the King's patronage. Charles abandoned him in the hope that his sacrifice would appear a sign of willingness to reduce his royal authority. So Clarendon – ironically like Strafford whose execution he had supported – was impeached by the King for the sin of enthusiastically defending the royal prerogative. When parliament debated Clarendon's fate, Cavendish did not argue against the House of Commons bringing in a bill of attainder. For once, he lived up to the motto *Cavendo Tutus*, which is carved on the west front of Chatsworth House, and proceeded with caution. Instead of protesting Clarendon's innocence, he demanded that there should be no vote until the accused man had been given an opportunity to defend himself. When he seconded the procedural motion that provided for that protection, he asserted – in a proposition which we now take for granted – that it was 'contrary to all the rules of justice and equity to condemn [a man] unheard'.[1] That precept was rejected and the Cavendish conscience hibernated again. A complacent parliament worked on in the hope it would avoid a head-on conflict with the King – always without comment from William Cavendish and, more often than not, without even his presence.

Despite what the House of Commons had persuaded itself to believe, Charles – far from bending to parliament's will – appointed new ministers who were sympathetic to his natural autocratic instincts. Their names were Clifford, Arlington, Buckingham, Ashley and Lauderdale and, collectively, they became known as the Cabal. During the six years in which they retained power, parliament grew increasingly uneasy about the open revival of a Catholic monarchy in fact if not in name. It was still to express its concerns. So when it raised its doubts with the King, the Humble Address began with a hypocritical expression of gratitude towards 'His Majesty's constancy towards the Protestant religion at home and abroad'. But the message continued with a warning, thinly disguised as concern for Charles's safety. Parliament held itself 'bound by conscience and duty' to warn against 'the dangerous growth of Popery in His Majesty's dominions and the ill consequences whereof needs must be prevented'. The King always responded with the promise to take the action which his Commons demanded. And he always planned to do exactly the opposite. The Whigs were beginning to grow suspicious and to consider what might be done to force the King's hand. They planned and plotted without the support and advice of William Cavendish who spent much of the time abroad – including the visit to Paris in which the fracas at the Opera took place.

The residual animosity against the Dutch – England had been intermittently at war with Holland since the Commonwealth – enabled Charles to renew his alliance with France. The Treaty of Dover, negotiated and signed in 1670, united the two nations in a plan to invade and partition the Low Countries. A secret treaty was signed at the same time and endorsed by the Catholic-sympathising members of the Cabal. It promised to provide Charles with the 6,000 French troops and the £150,000 that he estimated would enable him to declare that England was a Catholic nation ruled by a Catholic monarch. What little chance there was of that coming about was extinguished by the Dutch people who rose up against the French invader, breached the walls of their dykes and flooded their meadows in the face of the advancing enemy forces. To complete their victory, the Dutch navy defeated the English fleet at the Battle of Sole Bay.

The Commons – at last suspecting that Charles still harboured hopes of re-establishing a Catholic monarchy and believing that the defeat by the Dutch had weakened the King's authority, flexed its financial muscles. 'Supply' – parliament's agreement to raise revenue – would only be granted if the King acted, rather than promised to act. So Charles accepted – with neither objection nor complaint – the Test Act. It obliged all public servants and office-holders – though not Members of Parliament – to add to the oath of allegiance a vow to take communion according to the rites of the Church of England and renounce all belief in transubstantiation. In recompense, the Commons voted a generous Supply.

William Cavendish had no objection to parliament's buying the King's betrayal of his true faith. But he believed that it had paid too much for what would be a bogus apostasy. Struggling to construct an aphorism but not quite succeeding, he told his friends, 'When so much money was granted to buy a law against Popery, the force of the money would be stronger to bring it in than the law would be for keeping it out.'[2]

The Duke of York, more passionate in his beliefs than his brother, resigned from all his offices of state rather than counterfeit a conversion to Protestantism. That open admission – or proud proclamation – of his Catholicism was not followed by a promise to renounce the succession. Indeed his resignation was intended to demonstrate that there were no circumstances which would induce him to abandon his faith or deny his royal destiny. William Cavendish reacted by prophesying 'awful consequences' and, what for him was an admission, by declaring that 'he had begun to reflect very seriously upon the matter'. The sad conclusion that he could 'look neither on the Duke nor Court in the same favourable light as he had done before'[3] made no sense. He had always treated them with undisguised contempt.

The King's Speech from the Throne, at the opening of the 1675 parliament, contained the promise that the sovereign would 'leave nothing undone that might show the world his zeal for the Protestant religion, as established in the Church of England, from which he would never depart'. The House of Commons pressed home its advantage and carried a resolution that required the recall of 'the English forces in the French Service so that they might no longer be encouraged to ruin us and the rest of their neighbours'. Charles replied with the dismissive insistence that he 'could not recall his forces without derogation of his honour and dignity'.[4] That was not William Cavendish's view. Indeed it was his opposition to English soldiers fighting for France which turned him into an assiduous politician with passionate opinions he could not moderate.

William Cavendish attacked Charles's continued support for France – and his willingness to allow and recruit Englishmen to fight in the French army – with a determination that amounted to an obsession. In consequence he joined the ranks of those Members of Parliament who ingeniously relate every issue before the House of Commons to the one cause which they believe takes precedence over all others. At the conclusion of a debate to raise £600,000 from land taxes, he announced – with no relevance to what had gone before – that 'there continued still creatures and pensioners of France' in the King's councils. He then proposed that the Earl of Lauderdale – a surviving member of the Cabal who had become Scottish Secretary of State and was, in Cavendish's view, the chief miscreant – should be excluded from the House. The motion was overwhelmingly defeated.

An uneasy agreement between King and parliament produced a declaration that those who agreed to serve, or arranged for others to serve, in the French army were 'enemies of the King and kingdom'. It made no reference to Englishmen already in King Louis's service. It was enough of a concession to satisfy most of the House of Commons – but not William Cavendish. However, rather than try to swim against the tide, he chose to make waves by raising a related complaint. Relying on suspicion rather than evidence, he announced that the King was not using Supply for the purposes which parliament intended. So he proposed that 'an enquiry should be made touching the money that has been raised by granting wine licences'. The Commons easily becomes impatient with Members who exhibit single-minded obsessions. It was probably irritation, as much as loyalty to the Crown, that brought an ignominious end to the expedition into the undergrowth of court finance. The motion was seconded but received so little support that it was withdrawn before it was put to a vote.

William Cavendish was incensed but not disheartened. For the next two years, he and the King played an elaborate, and increasingly bitter, game of political battledore and shuttlecock. The King pretended that he played within the rules, but broke them when he could. Devonshire claimed that he was doing no more than providing Charles with some necessary constitutional exercise. But, as the shuttle crashed backwards and forwards between Court and House of Commons, both men knew that the outcome of their competition would help to shape the form of English parliamentary democracy.

In a message to parliament the King claimed that 'alterations in affairs abroad' made it necessary for him 'to make such preparations as should enable him to defeat the designs and machinations' of England's enemies. Preparations cost money. Cavendish voted against the granting of additional Supply with the explanation that, although the King asserted that 'there had been alterations in the affairs abroad, he does not tell us what they are nor what influence they have on our own councils'.[5] The King explained that he had reason to believe that France would occupy all Flanders and threaten the Channel Isles and, without apparent embarrassment or shame, announced his intention to reverse his policy and form an alliance with Holland. When Charles added that the new obligations could only be met if the Commons voted more Supply, William Cavendish – instead of welcoming the conversion – announced that, believing the threat from France to be an invention, he would vote against. The vote on Supply was lost.

The King accepted a humiliation and agreed to explain himself and his decision in an address to both Houses of Parliament. William Cavendish, no longer able to oppose the policy, complained that 'as a result of ill council . . . money is demanded yet we do not see an alliance entered into'. He could not agree 'further to charge the people before war is declared'. Then, in an ironically titled Humble Address, he proposed 'that an Alliance should be forthwith entered into with Holland and Spain against France'. The Address was approved by the Commons but the treaty was not signed. William Cavendish, prevented by the laws of parliamentary propriety from accusing Charles of bad faith, blamed ministers. 'Application has been made to the King to enter into an alliance, but we find that nothing has been done in the matter.' The complaint that 'we have several reasons to question their veracity' was, formally, laid against royal advisers. But nobody doubted that, in truth, the King himself was included in the indictment for bad faith.

Emboldened by the reception of his proposal to tie the King's hands, Cavendish resuscitated what – because of the frequency of its appearances on the Order Paper – came to be called Cavendish's 'favourite bill'[6] – the proscription of Englishmen serving in the French army. Persistence was rewarded. The bill was passed. King Charles was so affronted by its acceptance that he ordered the prorogation of parliament. Cavendish and a dozen other Members attempted to revoke the order, but the Speaker left the chamber before the vote was put. When the House reassembled it was Cavendish who complained about the Speaker's conduct. By then it was not clear how many other Members regarded him as a guardian of English liberties and how many thought of him as a self-opinionated bore.

An alliance with Holland was made and to reinforce the partnership, Princess Mary – the King's niece – was given in marriage to William, Prince of Orange. But nothing satisfied William Cavendish. He complained that the terms of the treaty had not been shown and objected to a vote on Supply that allowed 'ministers to employ [in] either a short war or no war at all'. The longer the controversy continued, the more the protagonists talked about constitutional propriety and the clearer it became that their immediate concern was money. Parliament's anxiety was reinforced by the fear that Charles was gradually creating what amounted to a standing army. Memories of absolute monarchs – including the one who called himself the Lord Protector – had made parliament fearful of soldiers in barracks waiting for the King's order to suppress dissent.

England, in and outside parliament, was on edge. Only a state of near national hysteria could have induced parliament and people to believe in the existence of a 'Popish Plot' which, far from being aimed at enabling Charles to be true to his Catholic faith, proposed to assassinate him and crown a new monarch who had never temporised about his faith. There was no doubt who that new monarch would be. Prudently the Duke of York – who had increased Protestant concern by marrying the Catholic daughter of the Countess of Modena – went into temporary exile. Suspicions that he had been implicated in the plot against his brother were unjustified. No plot had ever existed.

The Popish Plot was the invention of Titus Oates, an obvious fraud who had feigned a conversion to Catholicism to enable him to enrol in the seminaries in St Omer and Valladolid. After exposure and expulsion he had invented a story which, despite its improbability, was seized upon by Protestants as proof of Rome's undiminished determination to recapture England for the Pope. Oates's allegations were given a spurious credibility by the publication of letters from the Duke of York's private secretary to Louis XIV's confessor – a connection which should have surprised no one. The King's reaction to the stories of a plot was certainly craven but was not, by some distance, an endorsement of Oates's accusation. He had 'been informed of a design against his person by the Jesuits', but would forbear 'to give his own opinion on the matter, lest he should say either too much or too little'. However, the Lord Chief Justice was instructed to examine Oates on oath. As a result, five peers were found guilty of plotting treason and parliament resolved to consider how the realm was to be protected from what, it chose to assume, would be continued attempts by Rome to suborn a free people.

Cavendish – whose acceptance of Oates's claim must have been influenced by his inclination to believe the worst about the Roman Catholic Church – was appointed to the House of Commons committee which examined what new powers parliament should take to resist the supposed rebellion. Whatever doubts he felt about the existence of a conspiracy, he subscribed to a report which began with the lie that the King's life was in danger and the safety of the realm imperilled by a 'hellish plot' which, had the infamy not been exposed, would have been 'carried out by Popish recusants'. Relying on that invention the committee recommended the introduction of a Ten Mile Act which excluded all practising Catholics from London unless and until they took an oath of allegiance to the King and the faith he claimed to protect. But the committee was working, albeit deviously, to achieve a more fundamental protection against Rome and the powers of Europe that supported its ambition. Fearful that the Duke of York – the heir presumptive – had never accepted the constitutional implications of the Reformation, parliament was determined to frustrate his ambitions to re-establish a Catholic monarchy in England. Some Members wanted to impose legal limitations on the powers which James was anticipated to inherit. Others were determined to prevent him from ever being King.

A series of 'Loyal Addresses' was presented to King Charles. One invited him to prohibit all recusants from taking permanent residence within five miles of an incorporated borough. The King agreed, with the provocative reservation that the restriction should not apply to the servants of the Queen and the royal duchesses – an extraordinary comment on their religious allegiance. The House of Lords proposed that a bill be brought in 'for the more effectual preserving the King's Person and Government by disabling Papists from sitting in either House of Parliament'. The peers added that 'nothing in the Bill should extend to his Royal Highness the Duke of York'. The amendment – moved and carried as a sign of loyal respect – was another public admission that James was a Catholic.

In the Commons, the Protestant outcry against the Duke of York's exclusion from the penal clauses of the bill was loud and immediate. Cavendish reacted with more subtlety than most Members had enough guile to employ. He was not, he claimed, prepared to accept the addendum because he could not 'agree to have the Duke declared a Papist by Act of Parliament'. Despite Cavendish's reservation the bill was passed by 158 votes to 156.

It was then that parliament discovered the value of the King's promises. Thomas Osborne, a Yorkshire squire who had become Charles's chief adviser and been created Earl of Danby, had – despite the King's assurances and it was assumed on his behalf – been engaged in secret negotiations with France. A motion to impeach Danby was making its contentious way through parliament when the King brought to an end the eighteen-year life of the Long Parliament. Danby was officially pardoned by the King for what amounted to carrying out royal instructions. But, since Charles placed survival above loyalty, he was then dismissed. As added proof of his Protestant sincerity the King replaced his entire Privy Council with thirty new members. Among them were William Cavendish and Lord Russell. It was the beginning of a partnership that was to play a crucial part in changing the constitution of England.

Neither Russell nor Cavendish was of the disposition that allows preferment to stifle the expression of long-held opinions. So Charles was foolish to hope that their support would bend parliament to his will. He discovered his mistake when he presented his legislative programme to the House of Lords without consulting the Commons. There was never any chance of either man even attempting to reassure the Commons that the King meant no disrespect. Immediately the House of Commons reassembled it went through what had become an annual ritual. Cavendish demanded Lauderdale's dismissal. The House then turned to serious business – 'That a bill should be brought in to disable James, Duke of York from inheriting the Crown of this Realm'. The resolution added that Members would defend King Charles's person and the Protestant religion 'with their lives and fortunes' – as if King and faith could be protected under the same banner.

The bill was introduced into parliament on May 15 1679. As well as disinheriting the heir presumptive, it made 'all acts of sovereignty and royalty that the Duke should exercise, in case of the King's death be not only be declared void but be High Treason and punishable as such'. It was the first and only time at which parliament anticipated circumstances in which it would call for the execution of a prince of the blood royal. Cavendish 'though enemy of Popery and of arbitrary power, was averse to extreme courses [and] had been willing to agree a compromise'.[7] But his moderation was neither supported nor rewarded. What came to be called the Bill of Exclusion passed its second reading, unamended. Once again, the King – against the advice of his Privy Council – frustrated the will of parliament by proclaiming prorogation before the bill became law. Charles, emboldened by the passive acceptance of his arbitrary intervention, recalled his brother from exile. That was too much for even instinctive Royalists to bear. The moderate Cavendish and the irreconcilable Russell both asked the King to accept their resignation from the Privy Council. Charles replied that he would do so 'with all his heart'.

From then on the dispute – King versus Cavendish – was personal and the dislike which Cavendish felt for James, Duke of York, was even more intense. A few months after his resignation he was given the opportunity to demonstrate his feelings and he accepted it with uninhibited zest. By chance, the Duke of York and Cavendish visited Newmarket Races on the same day. Cavendish's conduct was described by the Earl of Ossory in a letter to his son. 'The conduct of my Lord Cavendish I cannot enough admire. Coming here after his leaving the Court and being here several days in the rooms where he met the Duke [of York] and never took notice of him . . . or went to kiss his hand.'[8] It was a gesture of contempt which, a century earlier, might well have led to his execution. King Charles, whatever his instincts, was content merely to exile Cavendish from his presence.

Weeks later, Cavendish was a member of a House of Commons delegation which visited the King at Windsor. Told by Charles that he had been banished from his sight, Cavendish answered with the combination of personal arrogance and political cunning which sustained him throughout his turbulent years as both a Royalist and a critic of royal power. He had, he replied, been dismissed from His Majesty's service, but not even the King had power to dismiss his loyalty or his determination to be a good subject. It was in that capacity that he had come to advise the King of the wisdom of recalling parliament.

The King accepted the delegation's advice. Cavendish greeted the King's agreement with the usual formula which allowed him to criticise Charles without breaching the rules of court etiquette. He celebrated 'the happy' day on which the King had cast aside the advice of 'evil Counsellors'. But hopes of a new constitutional dawn did not prevent him from continuing his attempts to secure the Protestant succession by disqualifying the Duke of York from inheriting the throne. Ten months later – after much fruitless and discreditable debate on the continuing threat which parliament chose to pretend still emanated from the Popish plotters – a bill which proposed, explicitly, to disbar the Duke from the succession was again laid before the House of Commons. Charles again dissolved parliament before the bill became law.

The extraordinary process – the House of Commons expressing its determination that the Duke of York should never occupy the throne and Charles II using his prerogative to dissolve or prorogue parliament before that expression of opinion was given legislative effect – went on for two more years. Resolutions were proposed which aimed to revive the penalties which were imposed on Catholics during the reign of Elizabeth. A Bill of Exclusion actually passed all its stages in the Commons. But the Lords did not agree. That enabled the King effectively to veto the proposal. In an Address to the House he asserted his willingness 'to comply with all reasonable desires' but expressed his regret that 'their thoughts were so firmly fixed on a Bill of Exclusion'. He was 'confirmed in his opinion against that Bill by the judgement of the House of Lords who rejected it'. He therefore concluded that 'there was nothing more for him to say . . .'.

Charles's recalcitrant determination to defy the House of Commons was immortalised in John Dryden's *Absalom and Achitophel*, a satire but also a clear statement of royal policy. Its author had celebrated the Restoration by writing *Astraea Redux* – dedicated to 'His Sacred

Majesty' – and he was, in consequence, dismissed by his critics as 'the court poet'. Even had the opening couplet of *Absalom and Achitophel* ('In pious times, ere priest craft did begin, / Before polygamy was made a sin') not made an obsequious reference to Charles's amorous inclination, it would have been accepted as warning that the King's tolerance was almost exhausted. At the end of the poem Absalom and Achitophel (clearly representing the Duke of Monmouth, the King's illegitimate son, and the Earl of Shaftesbury) are told by King David (equally clearly Charles II):

> Thus long have I by natural mercy sway'd,
> My wrongs dissembl'd, my revenge delayed . . .
> That one was made for many, they contend:
> But 'tis to rule, for that's a monarch's end . . .
> For lawful pow'r is still superior found,
> When long driv'n back, at length it stands the ground.

The Whigs had never believed that 'one was made for many' – a proposition which came dangerously close to an endorsement of democracy. But they did believe in the power of parliament. At its height, the battle in its defence was led by Lord Russell with William Cavendish as his second-in-command. It was to prove a dangerous post to occupy.

Convinced that only rebellion could prevent the succession of the Duke of York, the most irreconcilable Protestants plotted to murder both the King and his brother in what was called the Rye House Plot.* The conspirators included Lord Russell (Cavendish's political mentor), Lord Shaftesbury, the Earl of Essex and the Duke of Monmouth, Charles's illegitimate son who, had the plot succeeded, would have been proclaimed King. Cavendish himself had the wisdom or cunning to avoid the slightest association with the plotters. At a time of doubt and accusation, he was never suspected of being a party to the plot and the likelihood is that he was not even invited to join them. Cavendish's detractors attributed his loyalty to base motives. He was known to be heavily in debt and it was rumoured that loyalty to the King was the price that he was required to pay for his father's agreement to meet his creditors' demands. But there is an alternative and more creditable explanation of his conduct. Cavendish did not believe that the country would rise in support of Monmouth and he was – as

---

* So named since the assassination was planned to take place on the road past the Rye House Inn in Hertfordshire.

the plotters well knew – not the man to become implicated in an insurrection which might not succeed.

The plot did fail, though not because the country failed to respond to the assassination of the King. The King and his brother not only survived, their lives were never in jeopardy. The plan was to assassinate the King and Duke of York as they passed along the road near Hoddesdon on their way home from Newmarket Races. By chance, the royal party left Newmarket earlier than they had originally planned and had passed the Rye House before the assassins were in place. Failed conspiracies test the loyalty of the conspirators to each other, and half a dozen minor participants in the Rye House Plot chose to confess in the hope of escaping conviction. The leaders – Russell and the Earl of Essex among them – were charged with complicity to kill the King. Essex committed suicide before he could be brought to trial. Russell – insisting on the right of free men to resist tyranny – went before the court to protest justification rather than innocence. The principal witness for the defence was William Cavendish. He chose, perversely, to argue that the defendant had played no part in the attempted murder – thus contradicting the defendant's own evidence. In a demonstration of his insensitivity he chose to refer to a man facing the death sentence in the past tense. 'It has been my honour to be acquainted with my Lord Russell for a long time. I always thought of him as a man of great honour and too prudent and wary a man to be concerned in so desperate a design as this and from which he could receive so little advantage.'9

Russell was convicted. While he was awaiting execution, he was – at least, according to folklore – 'sent a message by a worthy person, Sir James Forbes, that [Cavendish] would come and change clothes with him in the prison and stay there to represent him if in such a disguise he could make his escape'. The plausibility of Cavendish offering to play Sydney Carton to Russell's Charles Darnley is undermined by the dissimilarity of their appearance. But we know for certain the nature of the last message that Russell sent to Cavendish. It begged him to lead a more religious life. Russell would, he assured his friend, be comforted, on his way to the scaffold, by the knowledge that his martyrdom, as well as lighting a candle for freedom, had served to help a poor sinner find redemption and salvation. It was a few weeks later that Cavendish demonstrated his own conversion to godly ways by attacking Colonel Colpeper for the second time. His subsequent retirement to Derbyshire – more the result of discretion than of repentance – temporarily removed him from the political battlefield.

In January 1685 Charles II died as he had lived, a secret Catholic. Certain that his brother's stroke would prove fatal, the Duke of York had locked the dying King's bedroom door while Father Huddleston, the priest who had been the King's companion and confessor since the Battle of Worcester, administered the last rites. By then William Cavendish had become the Earl of Devonshire and had sat in the House of Lords since his father's death two months earlier. In James II's parliament, the Commons – from which virtually every Whig had been excluded – was simultaneously supportive of the King and antagonistic to his Catholic sympathies. Members were, naturally enough, united in their agreement to the suppression of the Monmouth Rebellion – by which Charles's illegitimate son hoped to seize the throne. But there was nothing like the same agreement about the barbarity with which the West Country rebels – many of them fierce defenders of the Protestant faith – had been suppressed.

It was probably more by good fortune than careful design that William, Fourth Earl of Devonshire, watched most of the turbulence of the new reign from Chatsworth. He made one speech in the House of Lords about the importance of maintaining the Test Act and another which advocated triennial parliaments as an antidote to corruption. There was a memorable phrase in the second speech: 'A little dirty borough might be bought for a certain price as easily as a bullock in Smithfield.' But apart from that, for three years he neither said nor did anything of note. He did not even own a house in London. At first he rented a house from Lord Montagu. But it seemed that he did not mean to stay there long. When it burned down on the night of January 20 1686 much of his property – damaged or destroyed in the fire – was packed in preparation for leaving.

From then on Devonshire's absence from parliament and Court was so conspicuous a sign of alienation that James demanded that he return to London. He rejected the demand without excuse or explanation. His cousin, the Second Duke of Newcastle, was sent to persuade him to comply. Persuasion failed. It was too late. There could be no reconciliation with a Catholic king. But kings are mortal. James's heir presumptive was his daughter, Princess Mary, a staunch Protestant and the wife of Prince William of Holland. Cavendish, like half a dozen other peers, was already in correspondence with Dykvelt, Prince William's emissary to the conspiratorial English Protestants. During the summer of 1687 letters sent to The Hague openly stated that they were content to wait for the natural death of James and the establishment of a genuine Protestant monarchy.

How long their patience would have lasted must – in the light of the

King's increasing antagonism to the Church of England – be in doubt. But on June 10 1688, a proclamation announced that Queen Mary had given birth to a son. At the age of fifty-five King James had acquired – or, as some Whigs claimed, pretended to acquire – a Catholic heir to an increasingly unapologetic Catholic throne. Before the month was out, a letter – written in a suitably conspiratorial cipher – had been sent to William, Prince of Orange, by 'the Immortal Seven' – the Earls of Danby, Devonshire and Shrewsbury, Viscount Lumley, Edward Russell (the executed peer's son), Henry Sydney and Henry Compton, the Bishop of London.* It invited the Prince to assume the English throne. Devonshire, Lord Delamere and the Earl of Danby – once impeached on a parlia-mentary motion moved by Devonshire but now a fellow revolutionary in the fight against Rome and an absolute monarchy – had met twice, first in Yorkshire and then at the Cock and Pynot on Whittington Moor in Derbyshire.† Their plan was for William of Orange to land on the east coast of England in easy marching distance from the northern counties which were judged to be home to his strongest potential supporters. London opponents of James II argued for the revolution to begin in the south-west – Monmouth country – which was equally sympathetic to the Protestant cause and, because of the barbarity with which the rebellion had been put down, had special reason to hate the King. In the end the decision was taken by the wind.

The English fleet was loyal to King James. Classical naval tactics required Prince William to destroy it before his troops landed. He decided, instead, to by-pass the enemy rather than fight. On the morning of November 11 1688, the wind provided him with an opportunity to sail south down the Channel while – miles away at Gunfleet off the Essex coast – King James's ships waited to intercept the navy which had already passed them by. William landed, unchallenged, in Devon, the beneficiary of his own daring and the unpredictable English weather.

The message that William had landed at Torbay was brought north in a letter hidden in the heel of the courier's boot and was barely readable by the time it reached Derbyshire. Once he was convinced that the revolution had begun, Devonshire began to secure the north for the new King.

On the twenty first of November 1688 the Earl of Devonshire came to Derby with a retinue of five hundred men. He invited many

---

* Perhaps we should speak of the Immortal Eight. Rear-Admiral Arthur Herbert, disguised as an ordinary seaman, took the letter to The Hague.
† It is preserved by English Heritage and now known as Revolution House.

gentlemen to dinner and openly declared his sentiments in favour of
the Prince of Orange . . . After reading . . . the declaration of the
Prince, he read another made by himself . . . declaring 'that they
would, to their utmost, defend the protestant religion, the laws of
the kingdom and the rights and liberties of the subjects'.[10]

Noble though the sentiments were, they did not have the desired
effect. 'Through fear, the inhabitants of the town did not immediately
declare themselves the supporters of the Prince.' Devonshire decided
it was expedient to move on to Nottingham where the citizens were
both more noble and sufficiently independent to compose a declaration
of their own. 'That though they owned it rebellion to resist a king
who governed by the law, yet was he always accounted a tyrant who
made his will the law and that to resist such a one they justly esteemed
no rebellion but a just and necessary defence.'[11] They were echoing Sir
John Harrington's epigram which, although written seventy years
earlier, exactly suited the times:

> Treason doth never prosper, what's the reason?
> For if it prosper none may call it treason.

A copy of 'The Association' – the pledge of loyalty to William of
Orange and the constitutional government which he promised – was
sent to Devonshire from London. By then, James had fled, been captured
in Kent, returned to London and been persuaded to go into voluntary
exile, voluntary of a sort, in St Germain, near Paris. The Earl of
Devonshire – as arrogant in victory as he was unyielding in defeat –
would only condescend to accept signatures from men who had
supported the revolution before its success seemed assured. His temper
was not improved by the knowledge that William was planning his
campaign and making new friends more than 300 miles away. He did
not have to wait long for the opportunity to become a central figure
in the bloodless and therefore Glorious Revolution.

In London, the Princess Anne – James's daughter and William's
sister-in-law – told her friends, 'I would rather jump out of the
window than be found here by my father.'[12] Claiming that she feared
for her own safety, she decided to leave the Court and find refuge
in the north. Her critics insisted that she deserted the capital because
she was irreconcilably opposed to her sister's and brother-in-law's
being offered the throne of England. At the beginning of the journey
she was under the protection of the Bishop of London – once her tutor
and, in his time, a Cornet of Horse in the Household Cavalry.

Devonshire was summoned to ride south to meet the royal refugee and escort her to safety. Nottingham, he knew, was loyal to the Protestant cause. Anne established her Court in the castle and remained there until Oxford – the home of lost causes and dilatory in its desertion of Catholic James – was, like Anne herself, reconciled to William's inevitable victory. Devonshire saw the Princess safely to her new home and then rode on to London to be received in audience by the man he would help to make King.

In January 1689, parliament invited William of Orange to act as temporary regent and head of state while it considered what more permanent status he should be accorded. Some Tories claimed that James was still the king. Whigs argued that when he fled the country he had, in effect, abdicated. Devonshire was loud in his agreement and added that James's conduct, as well as his sudden departure, had robbed him of all claim to the throne. 'King James not only endeavoured to subvert the constitution of the kingdom by breaking the original contract between King and people but, having violated the fundamental laws and withdrawn himself out of the Kingdom, had abdicated the Government and the Throne was thereby vacant.' The general acceptance of that proposition still allowed moderate Tories – led by Danby – to argue that, since the throne could not be vacant, Mary was already Queen in her own right. That absolved them of complicity in treason. The question was settled by the couple who were to make up England's only joint monarchy. William pronounced himself unwilling to become his wife's 'gentleman usher' and Mary refused to be crowned without her husband.

The Convention Parliament, which offered William and Mary the throne, also presented them, as a condition of their succession, with the Declaration of Rights. It promised free (though hardly representative) elections, regular meetings of parliament, freedom of speech and limits on the power of the monarch to raise taxes, suspend statutes and raise a standing army. The Declaration was translated into law by the Bill of Rights. Devonshire and the other Glorious Revolutionaries did far more than change one sovereign for another. They moved England a little nearer to becoming a democracy. Seventeen years later – when Joseph Addison wrote *Campaign*, a panegyric to commemorate the victory at Blenheim – he began his heroic couplets with praise for the men who had brought William to England. His encomium, though florid, was near to being justified.

> Thus would I fain Devonshire's virtues rehearse
> In the smooth records of a faithful verse . . .

Devon's exploits appear divinely bright
And proudly shine in their own native light.
Rais'd of themselves, their genuine charms they boast,
And those who paint 'em truest praise 'em most.

King William seems to have felt much the same. The Earl of Devonshire was made a Privy Councillor, a Knight of the Garter, Lord Lieutenant of Derbyshire, Lord Steward of the Household* and Colonel of a reserve regiment of foot. At the coronation – acting, for the day, as Lord High Steward of England – he carried the crown before it was placed on the King's head. His daughter, Elizabeth, was one of the Queen's train-bearers.

Devonshire – recognised as a true adherent who had supported the Protestant cause when it was dangerous to oppose a Catholic-sympathising king – became a trusted servant. In 1690 – despite having little or no experience of naval matters – he shared with the Earl of Pembroke the task of inquiring into the cause of the English defeat off Beachy Head by the French. Next year, he accompanied the King to Holland. The old impulses had not completely deserted him. Impatient at the time it took to berth the royal ship, he insisted on going ashore in a shallop which almost foundered in the waves that broke over the beach. Once established in The Hague, he indulged his natural extravagance – as well as proclaiming his independent magnificence – by entertaining on a scale which would have been lavish for a prince of the blood royal. The enquiry into Beachy Head having made him an expert on maritime warfare, he was sent to inspect the fleet at St Helens and determine if it was ready to invade France. The attack was called off after the French won the land-battle at Steenkirk. But the English navy was victorious at La Hogue. King William knew that, since he commanded the sea, it was only a matter of time before a reinforced army in Flanders restored England's fortunes. So there was time to spare for more gratitude.

Devonshire was made Lord Lieutenant of Nottingham and Chief Justice in Eyre, north of the Trent, and – at his initiative and as a sign of the favour in which he was held – King and parliament gave a posthumous pardon to his old friend, William Russell. Then on May

---

* It was far more than a sinecure. Lord Steward was 'Grand Master of the Household' and presided over the 'Board of green clothe' which was responsible for auditing royal accounts, arranging royal travel and acting as a court to try offences committed 'within the verge of the palace'. He also presided over the Marshalsea and Palace courts.

12 1694 came the ultimate accolade. William Cavendish was created Marquis of Hartington and Duke of Devonshire. The letters patent which accompanied the Cavendish elevation described the achievement which had brought it about. The citation was written in language which a more humble man might have found excessive.

> The King and Queen could do no less for one who has deserved the best of them: one who in a corrupted age, sinking into the basest flattery, had constantly retained the manners of the ancients and would never suffer himself to be moved either by the threats or insinuations of a deceitful court; but equally despising both, like a true asserter of liberties, stood always for the laws . . .

The encomium ran on and on. It was only to be expected that such a paragon would remain a trusted servant of the head of state. And so it proved. Queen Mary died from smallpox in the December of the year that Devonshire became a duke. From then on, when King William was out of the country, he shared with the Earl of Pembroke and Archbishop Tennison what amounted to the joint regency. So Arbella Stuart's distant cousin briefly rose to rule England – and enjoyed, albeit vicariously, the power which she, albeit secretly, believed should have been permanently hers by right of birth.

The accolade 'Freedom's Champion' – awarded to the Duke of Devonshire by Whig historians – was, perhaps paradoxically, more justified by his conduct after the fall of James II than by his behaviour during the reign of the last two Stuart kings. Before 1688 he spoke out, with undaunted courage, against the arbitrary rule of sovereigns who were his natural enemies. After the Glorious Revolution he opposed divergence from the rule of law with equal determination. In 1696 parliament set down rules to govern treason trials. One of them was the right of the accused to be defended by counsel – in principle the demand that Devonshire had made on Clarendon's behalf back in 1667. When an assassination plot was suspected almost thirty years later, Devonshire was one of the peers who were deputed, under the new procedures, to examine the defendants. He had no doubt that their plan had been to kill the King. But – in a defence which was more common in the twentieth century than the seventeenth – he argued, in the House of Lords, that John Fenwick should not be attainted on the grounds that his trial had not followed the correct procedure. His motion to acquit was defeated by seven votes and Fenwick hanged. But Cavendish's reputation for independence of mind – some would say arrogance – remained intact. In 1699 when Lord

Somers, the Lord Chancellor, was indicted for treason – in theory because he signed a treaty which agreed to the partition of Spain but in fact because he was a Whig in a parliament which Tories had come to dominate – King William, anxious not to antagonise the ruling party, refused to resist impeachment. Despite that, Devonshire, the 'king's man', spoke and voted against the motion. He carried the day and Somers retired in honour to Cheshunt and the presidency of the Royal Academy.

It was argued by Devonshire's critics that he chose to defend a would-be regicide and a failed minister not because of his reverence for justice but in order to show that – despite being weighed down with patronage – he was more than the King's creature. Whether his behaviour was prompted by ethics or hubris, the way in which King William reacted to what amounted to his insubordination was both admirable and extraordinary for the time. The Duke of Devonshire remained Lord Steward of the Household and the King's representative in Derbyshire and Nottinghamshire. When King William died, after being thrown from his horse, Queen Anne – no doubt remembering the man who had given her shelter in Nottingham – immediately asked Devonshire to retain all his many offices of state, and invited him to be one of the 'supporting mourners' at the royal funeral. She then made him (as her sister and brother-in-law had done) Lord High Steward for the coronation.

One appointment owed less to his ability and independence of mind than to his loyalty. Jacobite sympathisers had claimed that King William's posthumously revealed papers confirmed that he had opposed the succession of Anne, his sister-in-law, and supported the claim of James Edward Stuart, the only surviving son of James II and soon to be known as the Old Pretender. The claim was examined by a committee of peers, including the Duke of Devonshire. No incriminating papers had ever existed. The committee – packed with members as staunchly Protestant as Devonshire – was, therefore, spared the obligation of lying for the Queen.

Devonshire remained a champion of liberty – but liberty narrowly defined. He had no hesitation in limiting the rights of Catholics. It was not Rome's theology which antagonised him but fear of the Pope's imperial pretensions. Protestants, on the other hand – even when they were outside the Established Church – could be allowed to worship in whatever way they chose without the risk that they would attempt to interfere in affairs of state. When the overwhelmingly Tory House of Commons began to discuss the Occasional Conformity Bill, which proposed to inflict penalties on all Nonconformists who did not take the sacraments of the Church of England, Devonshire presented 127 Dissenting ministers to the Queen in order that they could offer their belated congratulations on her accession. The occasion was organised to remind parliament that the Queen's consort, Prince George of Denmark, was a Lutheran. If the bill was passed he would have to choose between forswearing his faith and being prosecuted. His dilemma could have been solved by the Prince's explicit exclusion from the bill's provision – the remedy proposed to protect the Duke of York from the Test Act. That embarrassment was avoided by Devonshire rallying opposition to the bill with the not-altogether-liberal cry that Protestants of every denomination should unite against the common Catholic enemy.

It was not only the First Duke's political energy which remained irrepressible to the end. In 1705, at the age of sixty-five, the Duke fathered a child by Mary Anne Campion, the seventeen-year-old daughter of his valet. Thanks as much to patronage as to talent Mary Anne had become an actress. Devonshire set her up in a house in Bolton Street and, in proper Cavendish tradition, proposed to keep her there in comfort. But the birth was difficult and, although the baby survived, the mother died. Equally true to the Cavendish tradition, the child was well provided for – brought up at Chatsworth and left £10,000 to be paid upon her marriage or majority. No attempt was made to hide either the relationship or its issue. The Duke did not attend Mary Anne's funeral. But he marked a grave with a tablet that was signed 'W – D of D':

> Here lie the mortal remains of Mrs A. C–n . . .
> The virtues of her mind excelled the beauties of her body
> That was admired with so many charms . . .

There were still a few more political battles to be fought. The Earl of Nottingham – Secretary of State and once an ardent supporter of James II – asked the Queen to remove Devonshire from the Privy Council. Anne refused and appointed him to the commission that negotiated the union of England and Scotland. In the spring of 1707 – the year in which the Act of Union was passed – he made his last public appearance when he accompanied Queen Anne to Cambridge, where they were both awarded honorary doctorates.

William Cavendish First Duke of Devonshire died – not how he had lived, but peacefully – at nine o'clock on the morning of April 18 1707. He had written his own epitaph. It appears on his tomb in what is now Derby Cathedral:

Willelmus Dux Devon
Bonorum Principum Fidelis Subditus
Inimicus et Invisius Tyrannis.

It is as accurate a description as it is reasonable to expect an epitaph to be.

CHAPTER 12

Eternal Vigilance

Freedom, the eighteenth-century Whigs believed, could not be left – with any guarantee of safety – in the hands of venal politicians, dependent for power on popular support. Only men of wealth and position – neither debased by the demands of democracy nor corrupted by the attractions of fame and the hope of new fortunes – could be trusted to protect the liberties which the Bill of Rights enshrined. But Whigs were also careless of the rules which governed the behaviour of respectable society and that combined in some of them with the temptations of wealth and position to prolong the excesses of youth into middle age. The Second Duke of Devonshire – another William Cavendish and known as the Marquis of Hartington after his father's elevation in 1694 – was unusual in that, during his early manhood, he was regarded as neither a reformer nor a rake, but a noble nonentity.

In youth, Hartington had been dominated by his uncompromising and headstrong father. His betrothal, at the age of fifteen, to fourteen-year-old Rachael – daughter of the executed William Russell – was arranged by the First Duke as a symbol of his commitment to the memory of the martyr to constitutional government who had been his friend. Cavendish marriages were usually arranged with the object of extending the family's land and property and were only confirmed after a period of hard bargaining. The union with the Russells – although preceded by lengthy financial negotiations – was also influenced by sentiment. 'The jointure may be so settled as there may be no room left for the slightest colour of hesitation.'[1] The proposal itself ended with the admission that the Duke of Devonshire was 'so desirous of the conclusion of this match that [they] would pass over no small difficulty to effect it'.[2] That was not the *de haut en bas* way in which the Cavendish family normally determined its affairs.

The wedding ceremony took place on June 21 1688 and despite its inauspicious origins seemed to grow into a love match – even transcending the contempt which the young groom's domineering father felt for his son's self-indulgent desire to spend time with his bride. Poignant letters from Chatsworth to Woburn House confirmed

Hartington's frustrated fidelity. 'Yesterday my father gave an order to hire a yacht and set out next Wednesday for Brussels. Thus, according to my father's commands, I must go away without seeing you. I assure you it is quite contrary to my desire.'[3] It was the year of the bloodless Glorious Revolution, so the young man might have been despatched from England for his safety or his education. But great things were afoot which he was able to observe from a distance. 'The Dutch fleet passed between Dover and Calais last Saturday by break of day. The English fleet passed next day to follow . . . We have no news of the Great Expedition.'[4] Back home, he filled with country sports what time he could spare from pining for his wife. 'I am so taken up with Hunting that I shall not see Newmarket until Saturday night.'[5]

In 1695 – the year after his father became a Duke – he was nominated as one of the Knights of the Shire for Derbyshire although he possessed no qualification to represent that, or any other, county except a brief involvement, four years earlier, in the Flanders War, and the distinction of his birth. Most Cavendish candidates for parliament thought – not always correctly – that the family connection was enough to guarantee their success. In 1701 when it was time for him to seek re-election, Hartington had doubts about his prospects – though not about the way to win. 'Please tell [my father] that Lord Rutland has given his son five hundred pounds for the cost of the election. I do not find that there is any order for any money for me and I am sure that, without it, we shall not get the poor Freeholders to the election. I cannot yet give any certain judgement of our strength: but I am pretty sure that if we could get all the Freeholders for the election we would carry it.'[6] Whether or not his father obliged remains uncertain. If he declined to help, he must take some of the blame for his son losing the contest.

The Devonshires had limited experience of defeat, but on the rare occasions when it could not be avoided, they usually proved adept at mitigating its consequences. In Hartington's case the setback worked to his advantage. He moved on to Castle Rising, under the patronage of a Lady Diana Fielding, and shared the two-member seat with the young Robert Walpole, before moving on to become one of the Knights of the Shire for Yorkshire. Walpole and Cavendish struck up an immediate friendship, which turned into a partnership from which, over the years, they both greatly benefited. Walpole, the son of a Sussex squire, was instinctively adept in the arts of corrupt politics – a talent which allowed him to become the first Prime Minister of England and survive financial scandals which were gross even by the standards of the eighteenth century. Hartington – although the more ineffectual sort of aristocrat – was an adornment of society and provided a conduit to all the opportunities for patronage which went with membership of the Establishment. His status was exemplified by his membership of the Kit Kat Club.

The Kit Kat, founded in 1703, took its name from the landlord of the Shire Lane inn in which its founding members met. Christopher Kat was famous for his mutton pies which, in tribute to him, were called kit-kats. When the club moved its meetings to the Fountain Tavern in the Strand it kept its name and its habits. It drank libations to the society beauties of the day – declaring its members to be Knights of the Order of Toasts – before moving on to elevated discussion and deep drinking. All the Whig grandees, as well as active politicians who grubbed about in the daily business of the House of Commons, attended Kit Kat meetings. So did the fashionable painters and writers – Vanbrugh, Steele and Congreve. Kit Kat was the sort of club which, unaccountably, the more gregarious politicians take seriously. It certainly provided an opportunity for what today would be described as 'networking'. Walpole, though an outsider, was a sufficiently valued member to be reproved for missing a meeting. 'I am commissioned', the letter read, 'by a full committee to expostulate with you . . . My Lord Hartington, Lord Halifax, Mr Smith, Lord Sutherland are painfully solicitous about it.'[7]

The intimacy of Walpole and Hartington – and perhaps the superficiality of Hartington's interest in politics – was illustrated by the nature of their private correspondence. It more often contained gossip than comments on affairs of state. Walpole, in London, told Hartington, in Derbyshire, 'Foreign post surprised the world with a letter, under the Duke of Shrewsbury's own hand, giving an account of his being married to an Italian widow.'[8] The casual approach to politics was reflected in Hartington's House of Commons' voting record. For years he did nothing except rebel against Whig legislation when it offended against his father's view that Protestant dissent ought to be tolerated rather than suppressed. He opposed the first Occasional Conformity Bill which penalised Nonconformists who, having taken Church of England Communion and thereby qualified (under the Test Act) to hold public office, attended Dissenting meetings. And until his father's death in 1707, his private life – like his public – was as dominated by the old Duke. 'I believe that you could not have made anything of my last letter for I was half asleep when I wrote it. My father kept me up at Wisk every night until twelve o'clock.'[9] It was therefore to general amazement – as well as the enthusiastic approbation of the Whigs – that he played such an energetic part in the dispute between Ashby and White and produced a defence of equality before the law in language of which Pym and Hampden – the standard-bearers of the fight against Charles I's autocracy – would have been proud.

William White, a Constable of the Peace, had prevented Matthew Ashby, an active Whig, from voting in the 1702 general election on the pretext that Ashby was not a 'settled inhabitant' of Aylesbury. Ashby was not the only victim of what he believed to be a calculated attempt to guarantee a Tory victory. There were so many other complaints about malfeasance in the same election that the case which followed was said to have been brought on behalf of the 'Aylesbury Men'. Ashby was merely the one complainant who possessed enough courage and self-confidence to go to law and initiate what was to become the defence of the rights of freeborn Englishmen.

The Chancery Court upheld Ashby's case. But, despite the dissenting opinion of the Lord Chief Justice, the decision was overturned by the King's Bench, on the grounds that questions affecting elections were matters for the House of Commons alone. The Commons judged that White had no case to answer. Ashby, clearly a man of determination, applied for the House of Lords to issue a writ of error which challenged the Commons' judgement. The writ was issued after the Lords had examined the case in Committee where the motion supporting Ashby's application was carried by a majority of fifty to sixteen – more or less the Whig majority. The writ was duly sent to the Commons where the nature of the Queen's Bench ruling on the limited jurisdiction of the courts allowed Members to elevate Ashby versus White into a matter of constitutional principle, not just the investigation of alleged electoral fraud. Speakers who supported the writ of error were explicit about its importance. It not only remedied a single injustice. They insisted that it established 'the right of every Englishman who has been arrested that he had been injured to seek redress in Her Majesty's courts'. Although many of the speeches were impressive examples of party prejudice dressed up to look like principle, Hartington showed every sign of believing what he said.

His speech in support of the writ began – dangerously but not unreasonably – by questioning the sincerity of his opponents. There was, he said, 'not much reason in their case' but vested interest that made it 'necessary to find fault with them one way or another'. The writ of error ought to be endorsed because 'the liberty of the cobbler ought to be as much regarded as that of anybody else. That is the happiness of our constitution.' His view on the rights of the court to adjudicate on matters affecting parliament were expressed in language which many MPs must have thought intentionally offensive.

When a person offers his vote in an election and is not admitted to give it and on such refusal (as in the present case) brings his action to the Courts, if judgement upon it be contrary to the Privileges of this House, then it is pretty plain that our Privileges do interfere with the rights of people who elected us . . . If, over the years, the Commons alone had decided such matters, the governing party could permanently maintain its majority. By the influence of officers they might have filled up the House with what Members they had pleased and then could have voted them duly elected.[10]

In the House of Commons, undeniable logic does not always win the day. A majority of Members supported the view that the legitimacy of an election was not a question to be decided by the courts. To emphasise the strength of their conviction, they passed a resolution which instituted proceedings against Ashby for breach of privilege. The indictment cited, in evidence, his effrontery in challenging the Commons jurisdiction.

It was then that five other Aylesbury men issued writs accusing the borough's returning officers of the malfeasance of which, according to Matthew Ashby, William White was guilty. The House of Commons, fearing that the challenge to its authority was becoming dangerously popular, attempted to put down the insurrection with the use of the weapon which illustrated its archaic determination to preserve its ancient privileges. The Sergeant at Arms was instructed to arrest the complainants. They were remanded in custody while a suitable punishment was determined. An application to the King's Bench for their release – citing habeas corpus – was rejected with the Chief Justice again entering a dissenting opinion. So, like Ashby before them, the Aylesbury Men invited the House of Lords to issue a 'writ of error'. The Commons sent an Address to Queen Anne reasserting its rights. She replied that she thought it necessary, before replying, to 'weigh and consider very carefully the liberty of the subject and the rights of parliament'. Either because of carelessness or careful calculation, she let her Tory followers believe she sided with the courts by describing the whole argument – Sergeant at Arms arrest and all – as 'judicial proceedings'.

When the question returned to the House of Lords, the First Duke of Devonshire continued the work which his son, the Marquis of Hartington, had begun in the Commons. He was appointed to the committee in which, it was hoped, the two Houses would resolve their differences. Neither side was willing to yield. Devonshire drafted a humble request for the Queen to issue a writ which ordered the

Aylesbury Men's release. The Queen – again balancing inclination against discretion – implied that, had it been necessary, she would have done so. However, she was about to prorogue parliament, in consequence of which the House of Commons would lose its judiciary powers and the Aylesbury Men would be free. With which consolation she left for Cambridge, where she bestowed a knighthood on Isaac Newton. Jurisdiction over all matters concerning elections was left in the hands of a corrupt parliament. The Devonshires had lost the battle for civil rights by default.

It was a time of shifting alliances within the House of Commons – Whig, High Tory and Moderate Tory. John Churchill – a friend and fellow exile of James II who had both commanded the Royalist forces at the Battle of Sedgemoor and, three years later, marched to join William of Orange when he landed at Torbay – had been made an earl, dismissed from all offices on suspicion of Jacobite sympathies and regained a foothold in the royal household by agreeing to be governor to the Duke of Gloucester, Princess Anne's son. When the Princess became Queen Anne he had been made captain general and commander of the British forces in the Low Countries. The First Duke of Devonshire – initially, equally valued because he had held the north for William while Churchill secured his landing in the south – inevitably became caught up in the changing fortunes of Whigs and Tories. But, although Anne adroitly shifted her support from faction to faction, the old Duke remained in favour until he died in 1707, the year that separated Churchill's victories against the French at Blenheim and Ramillies from his triumphs over the old enemy at Oudenarde and Malplaquet.

For a while the Second Duke of Devonshire prospered at Court. He had been Captain of the Yeomen of the Guard before his succession and new distinction was added to old by his appointment in his father's place as High Steward of the Household and member of the commission which was negotiating the Act of Union between England and Scotland. More important in terms of his long-term prospects, he also received assurances of Anne's goodwill. At his first audience – arranged for him to return his father's Garter regalia – the Queen told him: 'My Lord, I have lost a loyal subject and a good friend in your father, but I do not doubt but to find them in you.'[11] The Queen then confirmed her confidence in the new Duke's fealty by awarding him yet another distinction. When the Act of Union had amalgamated the Privy Councils of England and Scotland, the Second Duke of Devonshire immediately became a member.

The good times were not to last. By 1710, the Tory Party dominated the House of Commons, propelled into power by the people's reluctance to pay even for a victorious war and the impeachment of Henry Sacheverell, a fire-raising preacher and hero of the High Church. During a sermon, preached in Devonshire's church in Derby, Sacheverell had claimed that Dissenters threatened the Established Church and that moderate Tories and Whigs were too cowardly to support their proscription. Devonshire – implicated by association – denounced the bigotry, in the family tradition of defending any form of Christian faith except Catholicism. But it was the swing of the political pendulum, rather than his robust defence of Dissent, that brought his political career to an abrupt end. The Tories were in the ascendancy and Queen Anne yielded to their pressure. Devonshire was removed from the Privy Council and 'resigned' as High Steward of the Household – though whether the resignation was forced upon him and accepted with the reluctance that his friends claimed, remains in doubt. His detractors alleged that the Queen had dismissed him on the grounds that his attitude towards his opponents had been 'peevish and distasteful' and that when he was asked to hand in the High Steward's staff of office, he 'flew into a passion which did little credit to his dignity'.[12] But, whatever the cause of his departure from office – and the manner of his leaving – Devonshire found himself in the position from which his father had escaped in 1688 and which the head of the Devonshire family rarely occupied for the next 300 years. He had become a person of no influence either at Court or in the councils of state.

Much to his credit, the Second Duke of Devonshire chose – rather than retire to Derbyshire and a life of indolent luxury – to follow the example set by his father and champion the rule of law. When the Lords Tyrawley and Galway were impeached on the grounds that they were responsible for the defeat of the British army in Spain, Devonshire – echoing his father's demand that William Russell should not be condemned unheard – told the Lords that 'censure might ensue' but both generals must be given time and opportunity 'to make their defence'.[13] Most of his guerrilla forays ended in triumph for the superior ministerial forces, but in 1712 he won a notable – if vicarious – victory.

The Act of Settlement of 1701 had set aside all the Stuart claims to the Crown and made George Ludwig, Elector of Hanover, the heir to the English throne with the justification that he was the most plausible Protestant claimant.* Queen Anne's sensitivies were indulged by a tacit agreement that he should remain out of England until after her death. Devonshire believed that one consequence of this concession by

---

*The Queen's seventeen children had all predeceased her.

the ministers was the creation of doubt about how long the Hanoverian succession would last. To avoid any ambiguity he asked leave of the Lords 'To bring in a bill to settle the Precedence of the Duke of Cambridge', the Elector of Hanover's eldest son. Guaranteeing that Prince George would become George II established the Hanoverian dynasty and – despite the animosity between father and son – was highly welcome to the future king. No doubt Devonshire's motives concerned the national interest rather than personal advancement. But at a single stroke Devonshire had renewed his Whiggish credentials and prepared a place for himself in the Hanoverian Court.

In terms of both personal advancement and public policy, the stratagem was more successful than the Duke could have imagined possible. The Earl of Oxford, the Lord Treasurer, responded with a bill of his own. It established the rights of precedence of the Elector's whole family, 'children and nephews of the crown'. In his *History of My Own Time*, Gilbert Burnet – Bishop of Salisbury and effectively Chaplain General to John Churchill who had become the Duke of Marlborough – may have exaggerated Devonshire's appeal when he described him as 'a gentleman of good sense, a bold orator and zealous asserter of the liberties of the people. One of the best loved people in . . . England.' But he was undoubtedly right to explain, after Oxford's bill had been hurried through parliament, that 'notwithstanding all this haste, it is plain that the court did not design any such bill until it had been proposed by my Lord Devonshire, out of whose hands they thought to take it'.[14]

Queen Anne died on August 1 1714. George I, the new King, immediately appointed the Second Duke of Devonshire as Lord Steward of the Household and, more important in terms of power rather than prestige, President of the Council. Walpole – who in 1712 had been impeached for corruption – returned to office as Chancellor. Catholics were again plotting for the restoration of a Catholic monarchy and throughout the autumn of 1715 there were risings in the Scottish Highlands in anticipation of James Stuart, the son of James II, landing to claim the thrones of England and Scotland. The rebellion – a controversial description of the assertion of hereditary rights – was easily put down. But even the calm of Chatsworth House was disrupted. Devonshire exhibited his anxiety in the letters which he sent to London. 'Must wait for another express from Scotland. For one this day [says] that the rising has now in a manner begun, the Highlanders appearing in great numbers with drums swords and tents.'[15] Parliament was once more convulsed with fears of Popish plots and Catholic conspiracies. Proposals to strengthen the laws which penalised Papists – obliging them to register their residence and real estate – were passed with virtually no opposition. But a bill which was designed to achieve 'more easy and speedy trials of such persons who have levied or shall levy war against His Majesty' was vigorously opposed on the grounds that the limitations which it imposed on the due processes of the law were contrary to Magna Carta. True to the ambivalent – some would say hypocritical – Cavendish tradition, the Duke of Devonshire did not argue that the rights of man should be available to Catholics. He voted and spoke in favour of the bill.

During the early years of George I's reign, Devonshire's interventions in the House of Lords demonstrated either the breadth of his interests or the capricious nature of his mind. On April 10 1716, he moved a bill which proposed to replace triennial with quinquennial parliaments – a 'reform' which, he argued, avoided the 'inconvenience' of frequent elections. At a time when the nation needed to stand united, triennial elections served to accentuate party divisions. They 'raised and fermented feuds and animosities in private families' and 'gave a handle to the cabals and intrigues of foreign powers'.[16] Parliament was in a mood to protect itself against the dangerous influence of public opinion – even though voting rights were limited to men of property and therefore persons of formal respectability – and agreed in principle. In 1718, after Admiral Byng's victory over a marauding Spanish fleet, Devonshire refused to support the Lords' resolution of congratulations because 'applauding a sea fight before war is declared has dangerous consequences'.[17] Two years later he had the distinction of being one of the few men of property to oppose the South Sea Bubble scheme – a device for raising the funds to pay the national debt without increasing taxes. His argument, that it would burst and undermine the whole economy, was completely vindicated. But although he was the enemy of orthodoxy, he was so deeply entrenched in the establishment that he remained a confidant of the King. Like his father, he was appointed one of the Commissioners who administered the kingdom during George I's absence abroad and, for the last two years of George's reign, he was – for the second time – President of the Council.

The Second Duke was not by nature a diplomat but he became a successful courtier. 'The Prince of Wales approved of Devonshire. He was a frequent and welcome visitor at Leicester House.'[18] And he remained a favourite of George I, 'even though he was a friend of his son'. Popularity with both King and heir apparent was a rare distinction. The two men were temperamentally incompatible – a state of affairs which became public after a dispute over the trivial question of who should be principal godparent for the Prince of Wales's infant son. The Prince's choice was the child's uncle, the Duke of York. The King insisted that it should be the Duke of Newcastle. The Prince bent to the royal will but – while the christening was taking place – insulted his father's choice by telling him that he officiated at the ceremony against the wishes of the infant's parents. On the King's orders, the Prince was immediately confined to his quarters and, on the following day, after his children had been removed from his care, expelled from St James's Palace. While he lived in the manner of a private citizen in Richmond and Leicester House, the Court was torn apart by rival factions and its members were warned, 'If any of them should go to Their Royal Highnesses the Prince and Princess of Wales, they should forebear coming into His Majesty's presence.'[19] The Duke of Devonshire, not a man to allow even the King to choose his friends, ignored the injunction.

After the schism divided father from son, Whigs who supported the Prince met regularly at Devonshire House. The Second Duke of Devonshire 'was regarded as at least the titular head of their faction'.[20] But he remained sufficiently in the King's favour to lead the move for reconciliation. It was achieved in 1720. Lady Cowper recorded in her diary that on May 24, 'the Whigs . . . all met in Devonshire House to wait upon the King as it had been agreed the night before. The Duke of Devonshire made the King a short speech (which had been made for him . . . God having made him a very honest man but no speechmaker)'.[21] Neither his loyalty as a friend nor his good offices, as peacemaker and conciliator, were rewarded. After the death of George I, he fell from the new King's capricious favour. He remained High Steward of the Household. But the days of real power and influence were over. So, in the best Cavendish tradition – he retired to Chatsworth.

The First Duke of Devonshire had looked for solace and entertainment in rebuilding the house. The Second found his pleasure in filling it with treasures. The panegyric which followed his death in 1729 congratulated him on his collection of 'oriental Onyx and Sardonyx' and – in a moment of aesthetic bathos – 'portraits and real resemblances of Poets, Historians and Philosophers'. It was on safer ground when it added that 'a Raphael, Titian, a Guido Paulo, a Domenichino, a Correggio, a Claudio . . . are to be seen in his noble collection'.[22] As well as his works of art, he left behind a family of an unusual size even for a seventeenth-century duke. His surviving children included his son and heir, James (a Colonel of the Foot Guards and MP for Malton) and Charles (MP first for Wiltshire and then for Westminster). Four of his daughters – Mary, Catherine, Anne and Diana – died unmarried, an extraordinary dereliction of duty in a family which was famous for the wealth it had acquired by the arrangement of judicious unions. But Rachel married a Knight of the Bath and Elizabeth became the wife of Sir Thomas Lowther of Holker Hall in the County of Lancashire – a house which, a century later, was to be at the centre of Devonshire hopes and ambitions. In each generation, one marriage always added to Cavendish wealth and prestige.

CHAPTER 13

Noblesse Oblige

When the Third Duke of Devonshire – yet another William Cavendish – succeeded to the title in 1729, it was taken for granted that the head of the Cavendish family would always hold some office – if only honorific – at the Court of St James's and in the county in which his great house was situated. During the audience at which his father's Garter regalia was surrendered, George II – King since 1727 – addressed him in terms which were almost as affectionate as the language used by Queen Anne when the Second Duke had performed the same service 20 years before. It was only fitting that a period of time elapsed before the new Duke received the Garter but, within weeks of inheriting the title, his sovereign 'was pleased not only to make His Grace one of his Privy Council but also Lord Lieutenant of Derbyshire'.[1] No doubt, he expected nothing less. Each Cavendish heir was – from generation to generation – markedly different in temperament. In consequence, the Dukes led startlingly different lives. But throughout the eighteenth and early nineteenth centuries, one thing was common to them all. Immediately following their inheritance, they all became favourites at Court. Some of them did not remain close to the sovereign for long. But royal patronage was, for a new Devonshire Duke, as automatic as Membership of Parliament had been when he was young.

At Oxford, the William Cavendish who was to become the Third Duke became President of the Constitutional Club. So he was – as compared with his father and grandfather – a political prodigy. However, his election to parliament – as soon as he graduated – owed nothing to that early enthusiasm. His political career began in the usual Cavendish way. He represented, in turn, Lostwithiel, Grampound and Huntingdonshire because of who he was, not because of what he had done or was likely to do. His father had been a friend of the young Robert Walpole and had frequently acted as intermediary between the Whig leader and the often antagonistic Court. His son kept up the tradition by carrying messages between Walpole and Caroline of Anspach, Queen to George II and a reliable friend to the Whigs. After he became the Third Duke of Devonshire he was also willing (because of his family allegiance) and able (because of his wealth and prestige) to ensure a steady flow of Whig MPs from constituencies which were susceptible to flattery and bribes. With such a record of service, it was not surprising – despite doubts about his ability – that his political career prospered.

Doctor Johnson – who disliked Whigs with a passion – made an exception for the Third Duke – not, he said, 'a man of superior abilities, but a man faithful to his word'.[2] Johnson elaborated his point with a typically overblown example of the paragon's merits. 'If he had promised you an acorn and none had grown that year in his woods, he would not have contented himself with that excuse. He would have sent to Denmark for it.' Horace Walpole – son of Robert and writer of effete distinction – disliked the Devonshires because they were a different sort of human beings as well as a different sort of Whigs. So his description – 'outside was unpolished and his inside unpolishable' – may be biased.[3] The same may be said of the barbed compliment that he possessed 'the dexterity of raising his son to . . . Master of the Horse during his own lifetime and obtaining a peerage for his own son-in-law'.[4] James, Second Earl Waldegrave – a shrewder judge of ability than Walpole, and, with two weeks in office, the briefest Prime Minister in British history – agreed that the Third Duke was 'plain in his manners and negligent in his dress' but clearly admired his character. 'He was sincere, humane and generous . . . had a sense, learning and modesty with solid rather than showy parts.' And Waldegrave had no doubt about his leadership qualities. 'Many would have followed him had he given the least Encouragement, particularly those who subscribed to the purest Whiggism.'[5] Counterfeiting a distaste for power was to become, alongside a passion for building, another Cavendish characteristic. It was not the only attribute which the Third Duke inherited with his family name. Like so many of his ancestors, he had a highly eventful private life – though, in his case, the turbulence was the result of an excess, rather than a shortage, of affection towards his eccentric wife. Although he exhibited a most un-Cavendish belief in marital fidelity, he remained true to family tradition by playing some small part in the suppression of the Second Jacobite Rebellion and thereby assisting in the frustration of the last attempt to secure the throne of England for a Popish monarch.

In 1733, the Third Duke was made Lord Steward of the Household – an appointment theoretically of great importance because the incumbent was so close to the sovereign's private affairs, but in reality a task of little consequence. His responsibilities were reflected in a letter which, in November 1734, Walpole spared time from more important business to write in response for a request for information. 'I know nothing of Mr Rawlinson being discharged . . . but what I privately heard at court. Lord Delamere has since told me that it was on the King's express orders and he thinks solely upon account of the badness of his wine.'[6] The charitable interpretation of Devonshire's original question is that it concerned household management. The more likely explanation is that the whole correspondence was gossip of the sort that Walpole used to exchange with Devonshire's father.

Most Cavendishes were pathological builders who felt an emotional need to alter and enlarge the great houses that they owned. The Third Duke built out of necessity. The original Devonshire House, built for his grandfather at what is now the west (Knightsbridge) end of Piccadilly, burned down in 1733. The Third Duke employed William Kent – architect of the Horse Guards in Whitehall, designer of everything from furniture to wedding dresses and the Duke's special 'friend' – to build the ugliest house in Georgian London at a cost of something in excess of £20,000. It stood at what was then the western boundary of the city and would have commanded a view of Hampstead's wooded hills in one direction and across Green Park to the Thames at Westminster in the other, had it not been surrounded by a wall, 10 feet high.*

During the years of its construction there were only occasional appearances in the House of Lords. Few of his interventions were either memorable or distinguished. During the debate on a motion to set up an inquiry into the South Sea Bubble scandal – a combination of incompetence and corruption against which his father had warned parliament – he 'bounced up in opposition, spoke of his honour and conscience and sat down again'.[7] But, when questions of preferment were being considered, the procession of parliamentary aptitude was less important than noble lineage and Whig connections.

Devonshire's serious public service began in 1737 with his appointment as Viceroy, General Governor and Lord Lieutenant of Ireland with emoluments of £20,000 a year – despite the general assumption that he was exceptional in only one particular and that was the amount he drank. Fortunately for Devonshire it was a time when that country was preoccupied with arguments about tariffs and trade, rather than

---

* The external double staircase – the one feature that interrupted the monotony of the flat, square façade – was demolished in 1740 and the gates of Chiswick House were inserted into the wall seven years later. The whole house was demolished in 1925 and replaced by an eight-storey apartment block. The wine cellar became the ticket office of the Green Park tube station. The site is now occupied by several hotels and shops.

demands for freedom and the franchise. Walpole sent him on his way to Dublin with advice that he was entitled to resent as unnecessary. 'The weight of carrying the King's government in Ireland is left upon you. Your Grace must . . . only act as you think will best be conducive to the whole and not, therefore, to the few.'[8] Whether or not he took that advice, he seems to have been a success. Lord George Sackville, the son of his predecessor, judged that his first Speech from the Throne was 'very well liked'[9] – though that compliment was slightly diminished by the explanation that he 'spoke it so low that few people could hear it', and the gratuitous addition that 'as yet, he does not look worse for his drinking'.[10]

It may be that eighteenth-century Ireland did not expect the English King to send men of ability to Dublin and was, in consequence, easily satisfied. Dublin Castle, the Viceregal Lodge and the substantial emoluments which went with them were usually a reward paid to politically reliable nonentities whose loyalty to the government was beyond question and who would not hesitate to suppress, with suitable ferocity, any rebellion against the Crown. When, two decades earlier, the undoubtedly able John Carteret was appointed Viceroy and had begun to audit accounts which were three years out of date, Jonathan Swift had asked him, 'What vengeance has brought you among us?' And he had added – with a flippancy which was surprising in the Dean of St Patrick's Cathedral – 'Pray God to send us boobies back again.'[11] When Devonshire arrived in Dublin, Dean Swift was still at the height of his power and popularity. *Gulliver's Travels* had made him both famous among the general public and the hero of High Tories. His *Drapers' Letters* had been instrumental in forcing the Westminster government to abandon its plan to debase the Irish coinage. He clearly hoped that the habit of appointing boobies had been renewed.

Devonshire was too grand to indulge in the jobbery of which the Whigs were accused, although he was not above ensuring that the rotten boroughs, which he regarded as his property, returned Members of Parliament who supported Walpole. After he left a dinner of the Boyne Club, an institution created to celebrate King William's victory in Ireland, a drunken young aristocrat announced that he would duel to the death anyone who suggested that the new Viceroy was just as corrupt as his predecessors.[12] But although Devonshire convinced the Irish of his personal integrity, he had neither the power nor the inclination to influence government policy on Ireland's behalf. When the Westminster parliament turned its attention to the Irish gold coinage for a second time and decided that it should be devalued against the English pound sterling, he behaved as other Viceroys had done, and represented the English government, not the interests of the Irish people. Swift – by then in his seventies and an ancient by the standards of the time – returned to the fray, ordered the cathedral bells to be muffled as a sign of protest and distributed leaflets which called for demonstrations that the Viceroy regarded as riots. Devonshire was, by birth and upbringing, ideally suited to deal with the Dean – whose vocation, age and fame meant nothing to a Cavendish. Swift was told to choose between unmuffling the bells and immediate arrest. The bells of Dublin Cathedral rang out again.

During Devonshire's tenure, Ireland was passing through one of its periods of dormant anger. But events during his seven years as Viceroy served to illustrate why the anger would soon awake. It was the consequence of a relationship in which Ireland and England were supplicant servant and begrudging master. In preparation for asking that his nominee should become the Viceroy's chaplain, the Archbishop of Dublin reminded the Duke, without irony or embarrassment, 'You are in a Post in which, from a soliciting nation, you must expect to be often solicited.'[13] The 'Post' also had a judicial dimension.

It was reported to the Duke that Lord Sandys 'was drinking at a Common Ale House' when, seeing Loughlin Murphy, a former servant, he ordered him to drink a large glass of brandy and to break the glass. Murphy 'stayed for a short time' after Sandys left.[14] This apparently offended His Lordship who returned and 'without further provocation, drew his hanger and stabbed him in his side'.[15] Devonshire was advised that the accused was entitled to be judged by his peers who were 'unanimous in bringing him guilty of murder'.[16] Devonshire confirmed both their jurisdiction and their verdict. Lord Sandys was executed. The Viceroy's judgment mentioned the religious affiliation of neither the victim nor the accused. But it did not take long for Devonshire to adopt Irish ways. Three months later he was required to rule on the propriety of a magistrate's punishment of a vagrant. In his letter to the justices, which confirmed their sentence, he described the miscreant as 'one Michael Molloy, a papist carrying arms'.[17] The first task of the Viceroy was the suppression of Catholic revolt.

By 1739 he had been caught up in the fear – justified or not – of imminent Irish rebellion. His apprehension was heightened by a letter from Legge, private secretary to Robert Walpole. 'The pretender's son has not yet put himself into motion, but there are most sanguine hopes of bringing something to bear shortly. It is universally believed abroad that some attempts will be made in his favour either upon Ireland or England this summer.'[18] Six years were to pass before Charles Edward Stuart, the Young Pretender, raised his standard at Glenfinnan. But

Devonshire began to take extra precautions against subversion. A request to be allowed to open suspicious letters as they passed through the Dublin Post Office received a reply from Thomas Pelham, Duke of Newcastle and Secretary of State for the South, which contained respect for the rule of law and acceptance of hard necessity in equal measure. 'It cannot regularly be done without a Warrant from the Secretary of State . . . I send you herewith a Warrant directed to the Postmaster General for Ireland.'[19]

Occasionally, Walpole – Secretary of State for the North but effectively head of the government and the first man to be afforded the, then pejorative, title of Prime Minister – wrote directly on policy matters. His letters suggest that, in the modern jargon, his approach was surprisingly consensual. 'Although I have omitted giving Your Grace my opinion directly concerning Beer and Ale imports into Ireland, I have been mindful of learning people's opinion here . . . I think there is a disposition to concede any reasonable proposition.'[20] Most of the correspondence which dealt with official business was signed by private secretaries and written with reference to ministers in the third person, as messages between departments of state are written today. When Devonshire proposed that England should retaliate against the Irish parliament's 'misbehaviour over the wool bill'[21] Walpole's secretary replied in a model of civil service discretion. 'Sir Robert will consider Your Grace's proposals for suspending that part of the English Act which takes the duties off English yarn for two years longer.' Both the wool and the yarn duties were removed during Devonshire's tenure as Viceroy. But much of the correspondence between London and Devonshire suggests – even when it conforms to the usual conventions – that the day-to-day business of government was less important than the friendship which had helped Walpole to triumph over his numerous adversaries.

The impression of intimacy is particularly strong in letters sent from Downing Street by Edward Walpole, the Prime Minister's second son and secretary. Sometimes they did no more than give Devonshire news of events back home. 'I write to inform Your Grace that there is a ship now arrived from Admiral Vernon with the account of his having taken Porto Bello',[22] an encounter in the sporadic war with Spain which began, or at least was occasioned, by the removal of Captain Jenkins's ear for the crime of transporting English goods to South America. On other occasions they were a clear indication that two public men wanted to maintain a private relationship that transcended their official existences. 'Sir Robert has been very ill but is now, I think, quite well again . . . These details are a more just account than may come into your hands.'[23] And there were blatant indiscretions – without doubt, gossip between trusted friends of the sort that Walpole had exchanged with the Duke's father. George II was getting on with his son no better than he had got on with his father. 'The K–, a few days ago, sent Lord Cholmensely to Bishop Secker, authorised by him to desire the Bishop would go to the P– of W– and let him know . . . that if he would return to his duty and lay himself at his feet, asking his pardon and in writing acknowledging his offences (in general only) he would give him the other £50,000 a year.'[24]

In the following year, there was sterner news to report. It came, initially, from Lord Hartington, the Duke's son. The war against Spain, Porto Bello notwithstanding, had not gone well. 'I was with Robert Walpole this morning. He desired me to write to you to beg of you not to determine yourself in any way till he has spoke with you. He seems to have borne his change of circumstances with great spirit.'[25] The change of circumstances to which Hartington referred was Walpole's removal from the office of King's principal minister.

Walpole fell because the war with Spain had been expensive as well as unsuccessful. And there were fears that he would be impeached – ironically for incompetence rather than the corruption of which he had been undoubtedly guilty for most of his ministerial career. Devonshire was relieved to hear from his son that his old friend had 'received the strongest assurance from the Prince of Wales . . . and others that he will not be molested in Any Shape or upon Any Account . . . His Majesty hast done something or other, I don't know what, in the most affectionate and generous manner.'[26] Walpole himself supplied the details a week later. 'It is determined that the King should, this morning, when he passes the Malt Act, direct the two houses to adjourn themselves for a fortnight to give him time for settling a new administration. I shall go up immediately to the House of Lords with the title of Lord Orford.'[27]

After his resignation Walpole 'still had enough influence . . . to secure a government composed of men of his own choice'.[28] So Devonshire stayed in Dublin and, much against expectation, devoted himself to improving the cultural life of the city. During his last year as Viceroy, Handel was his guest and, at his invitation, gave six concerts to audiences of 500 or more. Thanks to Devonshire, the first performance of the *Messiah* took place in Dublin.

With the fall of Walpole, the ministry passed into the hands first of Carteret and Spencer Compton and then the Duke of Newcastle and his brother, Henry Pelham. Foreign affairs overshadowed every other issue and letters from London – some formal, some merely friendly

– kept the Viceroy of Ireland abreast of changes in policy and prospects. War with France had to be accepted as a continuing possibility and neglected alliances revived. Supply had to be voted to meet the cost of an expanded army and – more controversially – to pay the wages of the Hanoverian mercenaries who, on the initiative of George II, were recruited to fight for England. Hanoverian influence on British policy had been bitterly attacked in the House of Commons by William Pitt – one of Walpole's 'boy patriots' who was to become the Saviour of the Nation. Despite the King's dislike, the Pelham brothers had insisted on appointing him Paymaster General to the Forces and, in consequence, imperilled the life of a divided ministry.

The Administration survived. Hartington wrote to tell his father that the Whigs 'were very victorious on our army' though 'Pitt was against, opposing and refusing to speak in the debate. I am afraid it will be much worse next Wednesday on Hanoverian troop.'[29] In fact the motion to pay for the Hanoverian mercenaries was carried by a majority of 226. Hartington's prediction was a rare lapse into pessimism. Most of his letters were irrationally optimistic. He described the exploits of the splendidly named Admiral Haddock in more typical – and more ebullient – style. One English squadron, commanded by 'Haddock himself, attacked the Spaniards who behaved extremely well'. Another engaged the French who 'in a very short time ran away in a very cowardly and inglorious manner'.[30] In fact, Haddock was unable to prevent the combined fleet, and the troops that it carried, from reaching Italy.

The fear of French invasion haunted Devonshire's last two years in Dublin. Pelham himself wrote with the admission, 'We were all much alarmed here at the account of the French Fleet being so near our own coast and not a little so to find from the [captured] seaman that they thought their steerage was for Ireland.'[31] The fears proved groundless. Pelham sent reassuring news. 'I can now have the pleasure of informing you that in all probability you are in no danger of having a visit from the French.'[32] But a week later the French fleet was again, according to unverified reports, sighted off the Irish coast[33] and there was a rumour that Charles Edward Stuart's agents were recruiting soldiers among the Catholic population. Then there was a message from a Court official – reassuring about the prospects of invasion but disturbing in its implications about Devonshire's relationship with the government – which 'imagined' that the Viceroy had been told of the King's decision to cancel plans to move troops from England to Ireland.[34]

Letters telling Devonshire of decisions which 'it was assumed' he already knew were a feature of the correspondence between London and Dublin – suggesting that discreet bureaucrats were remedying the omissions of their masters. It was left to Hartington tell his father that the King wished him to remain in Dublin for a year longer than was originally intended. 'The Duke of Newcastle will, no doubt, inform you that the French have declared . . . that they are under the necessity of declaring war. The Duke did intend to have sent you an order to come home, but now seems to think that it is proper that you should stay.'[35] He stayed until January 1745.

On his return to England, the Third Duke of Devonshire was immediately appointed Lord Steward of the Household – an office that had so regularly been held by a Cavendish that it seemed to belong to the family by hereditary right. However – despite the power, prestige and intimate relationship with the King which the appointment provided – the Duke chose to spend most of the year at Chatsworth. It was there that he received the message from the north that Charles Edward Stuart had landed in Scotland and that 'the Rebels, who are about 2000 strong and almost all Highlanders and, in consequence, devilish good marchers, have slipped by [General] Cope and are marching towards Edinburgh'.[36] London saw the situation differently. 'Sir John Cope is Marching from Inverness round by Aberdeen from whence the force under his command will be brought by Transport to Leith.'[37] A footnote added that 3,000 men had been recruited to the rebel colours in the Duke of Athol's county and that Lord George Murray was to become effective second-in-command to the Young Pretender himself.

For some unaccountable reason, George II still believed that 'If the French make any attempt it will probably be in the south. That consideration will occasion troops to be chiefly garrisoned to the south of London. So I think we must consider how to keep things quiet in the northern counties where there will be scarcely any regular troops.'[38] The Duke was given the task of organising the defence of the Midlands. The captains of the local militias reported on their preparedness. 'We have 1220 Artillery Muskets, Bayonettes, Swords and Drums in Derby.'[39] Three weeks later it became clear that they might have to use them in different circumstances from those that King George anticipated. The threat came from the north.

A message from London, dated September 19, reported that 'the rebels have passed the Forth a few miles above Stirling. It is imagined that they will make their route to Carlisle.'[40] Three days later there were rumours – repeated by the Earl of Malton[41] and, it was claimed, endorsed by the Archbishop of York[42] – that 'the rebels have entered

Edinburgh'. By September 24 the location of the Pretender's army was
not in doubt. It was in Prestonpans. 'The account came this morning
that Sir John Cope's Forces were all cut to pieces and dispersed last
Thursday night.'[43] The Duke of Devonshire was sent the names of all
Cope's officers who were thought to be the Pretender's prisoners –
presumably, since negotiated release was unlikely, in order that he
could reassure any relatives who were known to him. They were
identified individually by name. A footnote added that 652 private
soldiers – 188 of whom were believed to be wounded – were thought
to be in enemy hands.[44] There was, however, some reassuring news
from one of Newcastle's secretaries. 'I am persuaded that it will be
agreeable to your Grace to be informed that a body of Troops,
amounting in the whole to near Ten Thousand Men with a sufficient
train of artillery, under the command of Marshall Wade, will move
northwards.'[45] The regular troops were to be reinforced by local volunteers. In September 1745, two proclamations were published warning
that 'the eldest son of the Pretender' together with 'numbers of
Rebellious and Traitorous Persons'[46] were moving south and giving
Lord Lieutenants 'Power and Authority . . . to form men into Troops
and Companies'.[47] Much of the midland and southern nobility –
including the Dukes of Bedford and Rutland as well as Lord Montague
and Lord Halifax – began to recruit. It seems that the Duke of
Devonshire was slow to follow suit. A letter from Lord Charles
Cavendish to the Marquis of Hartington, his elder brother, gently
implied that their father had not completely fulfilled his obligation to
heed the call to arms.[48] It was swiftly followed by another which was,
directly, critical of the family's neglect of its personal interests. 'You
say nothing about packing up your medals. If the French should land
there would probably be a rising here. In which case, I very much
doubt that there would be time to carry things away.'[49]

Whatever precautions were taken to protect Cavendish property,
the Duke eventually accepted his military responsibilities and attempted
to mobilise his county. On September 28 1745 he organised – and to
the clear astonishment of the other participants, attended with his son
– a meeting in the George Inn in Derby. It attracted 'the greatest
appearance of gentlemen ever seen'[50] in the city. After they had signed
a Declaration of Association, designed to frustrate the 'rebellion of . . .
the Popish Pretender', and subscribed sufficient funds to finance their
resistance, 'a grand entertainment was provided for the whole
company'[51] at the expense of the Duke and the Marquis of Hartington.
The Duke presided over a second meeting which was held, a week
later, in the King's Head. The proposition to raise two companies of

volunteers did not receive unanimous approval. But the objections were 'heard with much dissatisfaction and speedily overruled' before 'the Marquis of Hartington and Sir Nathaniel Curzon, the countie's representatives in parliament, were appointed colonels'.[52] The meeting estimated that the cost of a regiment of 600 men would be £1,205 9s 0d a month.[53] The Duke of Devonshire, who undoubtedly contributed to the county levy by which the militia was to be financed, also made some private provision. The Chatsworth household accounts record 'Money Paid by Alex'r Barker on raising men in the Rebellion: the 19th year of George Second, 1745.'[54] The total cost was £1,214 19s 6d. Captain Johnson received £52. Sergeants were paid £11, corporals £10 and drummers £4 12s 6d. The 122 privates were paid a daily rate. It cannot have been much above a penny. One received £1 for 141 days' service.

The Duke of Devonshire's volunteers cannot be said to have played a notable part in the suppression of the Jacobite rebellion. The Young Pretender received a rapturous reception in Manchester, but only 100 Englishmen joined his colours. He had intended to march south to Oxford or Birmingham before his final assault on London. But, hearing that an army recently returned from Flanders – under the command of the Duke of Cumberland, George II's second son – would block his path, he swung east and, after taking Macclesfield and Congleton, made for Ashbourne where the Duke of Devonshire, the Marquis of Hartington and 'near six hundred men lately raised by a subscription of gentlemen of that town and one hundred and twenty raised by the Duke and kept at his own expense'[55] were awaiting him or, as one contemporary account had it, 'hovered near the left flank of the advancing army'.[56]

The Derbyshire irregulars – after inspection by the Duke of Devonshire in the market square – waited in the expectation that they would augment the Duke of Cumberland's army which, they had been told, was 'near the rebels' and 'expected to do battle next day'.[57] So they were 'thrown into the utmost confusion on hearing . . . of the approach of the rebel vanguard'[58] while Cumberland was reported to be no nearer than Lichfield, 40 miles away. Several times, they mustered in the square and several times they were sent back to their lodgings whilst their commanding Duke decided what 700 amateur soldiers could do to hold back several thousand fierce Scottish clansmen and their English allies – all of whom believed that they were fighting a holy war. Wisely the Derbyshire volunteers 'all marched off in torch light towards Nottingham, headed by his Grace the Duke of Devonshire Etc.'[59]

When the Jacobite generals arrived in Ashbourne, they demanded lodgings for 9,000 men 'The longer they stayed, the more insolent they became.'[60] The loyal townspeople suffered their final humiliation when 'the pretended Prince', mounted on a stolen horse, and 'riding across the Market Place, went through Rotten-row . . . and followed the main body of his army to Derby'.[61] It was as far south as they advanced. When he reached the town, the Young Pretender's generals – despite news of panic and talk of capitulation at Court – refused to march on towards London. So began the long retreat to Scotland where, after an unexpected victory for the Young Pretender at Preston, the meeting between the Jacobites and Hanoverians – which the Derbyshire volunteers had anticipated would take place north of Ashbourne – eventually came about on Culloden Moor. There ended for ever the hopes of the Stuarts and the prospect of Britain's being ruled by a Catholic king.

By the time of the Young Pretender's defeat, Devonshire was preoccupied with family matters. His court and public life was drawing to a close and he spent his declining years in a fruitless attempt to reconcile his wife and his eldest son and heir. In 1718, ten years before he became the Third Duke of Devonshire, the Marquis of Hartington had married Katherine Hoskyns. Her father, a city businessman who was universally known as 'Miser Hoskyns', had inherited land in Kent and Surrey which had been in his family since the reign of the Tudors. But most of his wealth came from trade. He had become financial adviser to the Duke of Bedford to whom – at the time of his daughter's betrothal – the Devonshires were heavily indebted. Cavendishes traditionally married into the aristocracy with the intention of obtaining land. And it seems that at a time of financial difficulty, the Second Duke raised no objection to his son's marrying into the mercantile middle classes if the match brought money into the family. Money was not, however, Hartington's object. He married for love.

His affection – as well as his aristocratic self-confidence – left him unmoved and unaffected both by his wife's middle-class ways and by the stir that her occasionally outrée habits caused in fashionable society. Hugh Walpole was suitably horrified. 'The Duchess of Devonshire has her secular assembly . . . She was more delightfully vulgar at it than you can imagine; complained of a wet night and how the men would dirty the room with their shoes; called out at supper to the Duke, "Good God! My Lord, don't cut the ham, nobody will eat any!" and relating her private ménage to a Mr Obrien, she said, "When there is only my Lord and I, besides a pudding we have always a dish of roast!"'[62]

Her Grace retained 'the common touch' into old age. It was her habit to go into the skittle yard and keep the score for the working men who competed there and she was known to persuade fiddlers, who were playing in the servants' hall, to come into the drawing room and accompany her dancing. But in one particular, she held a rigidly aristocratic view. Her seven children were not free to make their own choice of whom they would marry.

The Duke, on the other hand, was indulgent to a fault and exhibited his sentimental affection by giving all his children pet names – Mrs Hopeful, Mrs Tiddle, Grundy, Puss, Cat, Toe and Guts, his eldest son. So he raised no objection when Guts – aged twenty-eight and therefore well into the age of discretion – announced his intention to marry Charlotte Boyle, the sixteen-year-old second daughter of the Earl of Burlington. Perhaps the Duke's agreement was influenced by the fortune that Lady Charlotte, heiress to the vast Burlington wealth, would bring into the family. But that did nothing to reconcile the Duchess to her son ignoring the list of eligible young women which she had drawn up for his consideration. Despite her opposition, the wedding took place on March 28 1748. In consequence, the Devonshires made the greatest of all the matrimonial additions to their property.

The Burlington wealth originated with Richard Boyle, the 'Great Earl of Cork' whose Irish estates had been bought – at fire-sale prices – from Sir Walter Raleigh, while he was in prison. Robert Boyle, the scientist, was his son and one of the few members of the family who could – even by the louche standards of the time – be regarded as respectable. Charlotte Boyle's mother had an open affair with the Duke of Grafton. That was acceptable. Her father's relationship with the architect William Kent was not. Nor was it excused by his status as one of the great aesthetes of the age. The Third Earl of Burlington had succeeded to the title at the age of nine and, by the time he was nineteen, he was regarded as an arbiter of taste and style. Handel was effectively his 'house musician' for three years. He was a patron of Alexander Pope, and was rewarded for his support by a dedication in one of the *Moral Essays*. John Gay paid him tribute, of sorts, in *Trivia: or, the Art of Walking the Streets of London*:

> There Handel strikes the Strings, the melting Strain
> Transports the Soul, and thrills through ev'ry Vein;
> There oft I enter (but with cleaner Shoes)
> For Burlington's belov'd by every Muse.

However, it was not only the Earl's interest in literature and music that excited gossip in London society. A mystery surrounded the death of Dorothy, his oldest daughter.

At the age of sixteen, Dorothy had married Lord Euston, one of her mother's many lovers. She died in childbirth less than a year later. Such deaths were not unusual in eighteenth-century England, but – according to rumour – her husband had brutalised her during the pregnancy with the intention of killing both mother and child. After the funeral, her mother wrote a brief obituary on Lady Dorothy's portrait. 'Married October 18th 1741 and delivered by death from misery May 2nd 1742.' It was followed by a poem which was dedicated to her daughter's memory – largely at the expense of her former lover:

> View here ye Fair the Ghost of Female Life
> The faultless virgin and the faithful wife.
> Once her proud parents comfort, joy and pride
> Who never gave them pain till made a bride . . .
> Till Love and Honour, gave her all to one –
> To one – Alas! – unworthy such a Prize,
> His soul to virtue deaf, to beauty blind his Eyes.[63]

Whether or not Dorothy was murdered, her death guaranteed the inheritance for the Devonshires. Lord Clifford – the Boyles' only son – had died in infancy. So on the death of Lord Burlington, the family's whole estate passed to their one surviving child and, through her, to her husband the future Fourth Duke of Devonshire. It included Burlington House in Piccadilly – which was more appropriately called a palace – a great Palladian villa on the Thames at Chiswick, land at Londesborough in the East Riding of Yorkshire and Bolton Abbey in the West, and several thousand acres in the south of Ireland with a castle, built by King John, at Lismore in County Waterford.

On March 28 1778, the Third Duke attended the wedding of his eldest son and Charlotte Boyle. His wife did not. Despite that emphatic sign of disapproval, Devonshire attempted to broker peace by drafting a conciliatory letter for the Duchess to send to 'Guts', her son. It implied, as was unavoidable, an admission of possible guilt. 'I am determined to believe that you never meant the least disregard to me . . . I shall be infinitely happy to find myself in the wrong in having given opposition to your inclinations.'[64] The Duchess refused to sign. Her son then attempted to heal the breach with a letter which revealed what he believed to be the best way of justifying his disobedience – an appeal to his mother's dynastic and acquisitive instinct by denying that he was motivated by love rather than his family obligation. 'I was aware that in the particular situation of my family . . . I was not merely to consider the dictates of my own passion but was to have a regard for what was a Benefit for my Family . . . Had I thought only of myself, my inclinations might have led another way.'[65] His mother did not believe him. 'I know very well', she wrote, 'what was the inducement and could say a deal upon it.'[66]

The Duke left for London, to attend to his duties as Lord Steward and receive treatment for a bad attack of gout. He was also suffering from a severe allergy to the strife which engulfed Chatsworth as a result of his wife's belief that, by siding with their son, he had betrayed her. The Duchess, beyond reconciliation, took up residence in the rectory in nearby Eyam from where she wrote dramatic letters to the Duke which combined a refusal to obey his wishes with renewed vows of obedience. The Bishop of Kildare, a family friend, persuaded her to forgive her husband, but she would still not 'think of returning to see and receive' her children 'while the remembrance of their behaviour was so fresh in [her] mind'.[67] In a last desperate attempt to heal the wounds, 'Guts' Hartington sent his mother a fulsome – if insincere – apology for his behaviour and an invitation to join him in the capital. He was rewarded by the reply that she would 'Infinitely rather beg my bread than return to London and suffer what I did before I left'.[68] Noting that it was the ridicule of London – rather than his company – that his wife now found repellent, the Duke decided to resign the Lord Stewardship and leave London for what Horace Walpole called 'the unaccountable and unenvied pleasure of shutting himself up in Chatsworth with his ugly, mad Duchess'.[69]

The ugly, mad Duchess survived her husband, son and daughter-in-law. Charlotte Boyle never became the Duchess of Devonshire. She bore four children but, while anticipating a fifth, complicated a condition, now thought to be smallpox, by playing shuttlecock. She died at the age of twenty-three, a year before her husband succeeded to the title. The Fourth Duke – who never remarried – mourned her death for twenty years. After his funeral, he was found to have kept her comb, silk bag and handkerchief in his desk drawer. Whether or not he was justified in telling his mother that he had married for land, at some time – before or after the wedding – 'Guts' had fallen in love with Charlotte Boyle.

CHAPTER 14

Brothers in Arms

Prime Ministers rarely leave office at a time or in a way of their own choosing. Nor, when they step down, are they usually held in as much regard as they enjoyed at the time of their appointment. William Cavendish, the Fourth Duke of Devonshire, was spared both the humiliation of dismissal and the ignominy of perceived failure. But he occupies an exceptional place in the Prime Ministers' pantheon for reasons which were wholly unrelated to either his ability or his achievements. He had never wanted to be made First Lord of the Treasury. Indeed, he is the only Prime Minister in English history to have taken the job both reluctantly and on approval. In 1756, invited by George II to lead his government, he 'did not accept until His Majesty had given his word that if he came to dislike his employment he should be at full liberty to resign at the end of the approaching session of parliament'.[1]

From the Fourth Duke's point of view, the impertinence was wholly justified by events. The job proved as uncongenial as he feared and, despite being advised to avoid the uncertainty of change, the King felt obliged to keep his word and let him go. Devonshire's tenure had been 'distinguished by faction and perplexed with difficulties'. But according to his friend, James, Earl Waldegrave, he left office with his reputation intact. No one had been disappointed because 'great things had never been expected of him as a minister'.[2] That, combined with his reluctance to accept office, explains why his younger brother, Lord John Cavendish, had a less exalted but more influential political career.

The Fourth Duke was, in some ways, the most idiosyncratic of the Cavendishes. David Garrick remarked on 'the great prudery of his dress'[3] and when the actor wrote to him from Venice – offering to buy pictures and statues on his behalf – he replied that, although much obliged, he could not take advantage of the kind suggestion. 'I have no money.'[4] Yet his income was estimated at £40,000 a year and he spent vast sums on Chatsworth.

He enjoyed all the privileges which were heaped upon Cavendish heirs apparent. In 1741, immediately on coming of age, he had become the Member of Parliament for Derbyshire and he represented the constituency until 1751 when, as was possible at the time, he was elevated to the Lords in the name of Baron Hardwick, one of his father's subsidiary titles. His ten years in the Commons were generally noted for their genial inactivity. But he did demonstrate his true Whig inclinations by opposing the promotion of foreign 'adventures' and doing so in a fashion which showed dash and daring but neither sympathy nor respect for any views other than his own. Pelham, First Lord of the Treasury, had decided to reduce the navy's establishment from 10,000 to 8,000 seamen. This was the time when William Pitt, as Paymaster General to the Forces, objected to the economy with such vehemence that Pelham lost his nerve and was on the point of capitulation when young Hartington put down a Commons resolution which limited the size of the navy to the total which Pelham had originally intended. When Hartington pressed it to a division, Pitt voted against. But he was supported by only fourteen other Members. A by-product of Hartington's impertinent initiative was the approbation of George II, for whom any humiliation of Pitt was a cause for rejoicing.

Four years passed before Hartington did anything else of political note. Most of his time was passed in planning, and eventually executing, his plans for the improvement of Chatsworth – not the house itself but the surrounding park and associated service buildings. His father, the Third Duke, had removed the offices and stables from the west front which – despite the view it offered of the River Derwent – had, up to that time, been regarded as the rear of the house. In 1758, the Fourth Duke employed James Paine to design and build a monumental stable block on the slope of the hill below the Hunting Tower.* The work took four years.† Two years later, he built a new bridge across the river. And he changed, out of all recognition, the view over the Derwent from the west front.

The bridge was, and remains, substantial – the product of the architect's majestic style and a necessity made unavoidable by the nature of the river over which it was built. Defoe, riding across Derbyshire during his journey through England, had treated it with uncharacteristic caution. 'We kept the Derwent on our right but kept our distance, the Derwent being out, for the Derwent is a frightful creature when the hills load her with water . . . We contented ourselves

---

* The stags carved in the lintel above the entrance bear the Bruce coat of arms. They represent a graceful gesture of thanks to the family who bequeathed the money with which the stables were built.

† It included a brewery to replace the one exiled to Burton by the Earl of Shrewsbury. The beer was aged in oak barrels known as The Twelve Apostles and then piped, underground, to the house. Beer was included in the servants' wages until 1931.

with hearing the rise of its waters.' By the end of the eighteenth century bonds had been straightened out and the river flowed more predictably, no matter how severe the weather. But in Paine's time it was still 'subject to rapid floods which . . . frequently rise in a few hours to great heights and the violence of these torrents render it extremely dangerous'.[5] So its course was changed and a new bridge was built to withstand both time and the torrent.

The changes to the park were made not out of necessity but in response to the demands of fashion. At a cost of £40,000, Grillet's formal gardens – designed for and built by the First Duke – were swept away and, in their place, Lancelot 'Capability' Brown created what he believed to be the landscape of Arcadia. Terraces became steep slopes. Parterres were grassed over. Ponds were drained and filled in and fountains were destroyed. The whole west garden was turned into a sweeping lawn which ran down to the river. An idealised version of nature took the place of a sophisticated interpretation of art. And – in a curious way, consistent with the greater informality of the landscape – the Fourth Duke announced that on 'public days' the state rooms and gardens would, for the first time, be open to anyone who chose to call.

The decision to open Chatsworth was just one mark of the Fourth Duke's geniality. Although, unlike his father, only a moderate drinker, he led an active social life which was not confined, as was the case with most of his family, to persons of equal status. Caroline Girle, a doctor's daughter who visited Chesterfield in 1757 – the year after he succeeded to the title and while he was still a power in the land – described, with awe and wonder, his apparently enthusiastic participation in local festivities. 'At about ten we went to the Assembly Rooms, where the Duke of Devonshire always presided as Master of Ceremonies and, after the ball, gave an elegant cold supper where, by his kindness and affability it would be unnecessary for me to say how affable he made himself to the company.'[6] Doctor Girle invited the Duke to take tea with the family who were the physician's hosts in Derbyshire. The invitation was graciously accepted.

In 1755 – the year in which his father died – the future Duke received an invitation which it was assumed he would decline. He was offered the office which was so regularly put at the disposal of the Devonshires that it seemed almost to be theirs by right. To general surprise, he agreed to become Viceroy of Ireland. As always, the highly remunerative appointment owed nothing to the new incumbent's achievements and ability. Nor was it his impeccable Protestantism – and his consequent alienation from the majority of the Irish population – which qualified him for the position. His preferment was the reward for jobbery. His family 'owned' twelve parliamentary seats which it was assumed they could deliver for his party.

Like his father, the Marquis of Hartington went to Ireland unburdened by the weight of high expectations. But it was assumed that he could not do worse than his predecessor, the Duke of Dorset, and it was hoped that he might do better. Dorset – who had succeeded the Third Duke of Devonshire in Dublin Castle – had interfered in the working of the Irish parliament and, by doing so, had disturbed the compliant consensus among the Protestant minority, which had been obtained by bribery, jobbery and the suppression of the smaller factions. In concert with George Stone, the Primate of Ireland, he had attempted to replace the Speaker – Henry Boyle, the leader of the Whig faction. Dorset was dismissed and Hartington was sent to Dublin 'partly to inspect military affairs . . . but more particularly to compose the civil dissentions which had raged with uncommon violence during the latter part of the Duke's Administration'.[7]

According to Horace Walpole's feline judgement, the appointment was prejudiced by his 'close connections with a certain family, who I fear will endeavour to attach him more to their private interests than to the true interests of the kingdom'.[8] Hartington was related by marriage to the Boyles and it was from them that, after the death of his wife, he had inherited the power and title of Governor of Cork. But that was not the connection which Walpole suggested might influence the new Viceroy's judgement. The problem, in Walpole's estimation, arose from Hartington's sisters having married into the Ponsonby family, which had been active in support of George Stone in his machinations against Henry Boyle. Walpole's complaint was a rare example of the suggestion that a Cavendish was disadvantaged by his influential relatives.

Walpole, in a moment of uncharacteristic fair-mindedness, accepted that 'Some there are who think from the honesty of the marquis, that he will not be biased'.[9] Fortunately the new Viceroy did not need to rely on the goodwill of those Irishmen who gave him the benefit of the doubt. The Ponsonbys had turned against Archbishop Stone before he arrived in Dublin. But it was still necessary to secure a permanent peace. This was accomplished by Hartington's arranging for Boyle to be elevated to the peerage with the title of Lord Shannon and a pension of £2,000 a year. The Speakership then passed to John Ponsonby. Nobody complained about the nepotism. It was an accepted feature of Irish government. Stone lost both power and influence, leaving the Viceroy to tell the Irish parliament, in his valedictory address, that Christians of every denomination should be united in their allegiance to George II. A year later, the Fourth Duke of Devonshire, as he had become, was the King's First Minister.

The Seven Years War formally began in 1756. It was a year of disaster for Thomas Pelham-Holles, Duke of Newcastle,* and, after the death of his brother in 1756, First Lord of the Treasury. The French were winning the colonial war in North America. The alliance with Austria and Holland had broken down when Austria began to regard Prussia as a greater threat than France. Britain, alone, was so unprepared to repel the anticipated French invasion that troops were hired from Hesse and Hanover to guard the south coast. The failure of the Newcastle Administration was symbolised by the loss of Minorca. Public outrage at the humiliation had been so great that, in response to the clamour, Admiral Byng had been tried by court martial and found guilty of dereliction of duty which amounted to treason. He was executed.

Henry Fox (father of Charles James) resigned from the government. Then William Pitt – dismissed from the ministry for outright refusal to support its policies – turned on his former colleagues with devastating ferocity. The Administration was near to collapse. Newcastle – after the relative failure of two naval encounters and fearing that he faced the same fate as Byng – left, or lost, office. The Fourth Duke of Devonshire – still Viceroy of Ireland – was, technically, a member of the discredited Administration. But he had spent the years of disaster in Dublin and, as Waldegrave wrote in his diary, the return to England 'had been subsequent to the loss of Minorca. Consequently he was clear of the obloquy to which other ministers were deservedly exposed. When the administration was changed he seemed the most proper person to succeed Lord Newcastle on account of the King's favour and the number of his friends.' The friends were reinforced by even more numerous political relations – the reason for Horace Walpole's complaint that the Cavendishes were 'almost a political party of their own'. In politics, popularity is a great substitute for ability.

If Waldegrave is to be believed, Cavendish was qualified by more than good connections alone. 'Pitt . . . paid great court to him.'[10] To have been cultivated by the Great Commoner, even before he became the Saviour of the Nation, was a qualification in itself. So Devonshire received the King's commission to form a government and – with the proviso that he would leave at a time of his own choosing – he became titular, if not quite effective, First Minister.

---

* The dukedom was a new creation and the Duke was no relation to William Cavendish, Lord General of the North during the Great Civil War.

The invitation to lead a new administration was made in the hope that Devonshire would make an alliance with Henry Fox. But the Duke chose William Pitt to become Secretary of State for the South – even though he only agreed to serve on the understanding that places would be provided for his numerous friends and relations. The concessions were more than acknowledgement that Pitt – who was to become the architect of victory in the Seven Years War – was indispensable. They amounted to the acceptance that, despite being unsparing in his expressions of contempt for Whigs and Whiggism, Pitt had become Prime Minister in fact if not in name.* Devonshire's act of self-abnegation was not universally admired. Waldegrave described his decision as being 'unjustly censured by some unreasonable friends'[11] who did not realise that he 'joined with Pitt rather than Fox not from any change of friendship or any partiality . . . but because it was more safe to be united with one who has the nation on his side than with the man who is the most unpopular in the country'.[12] The Administration of which Devonshire was nominal head lasted until July 1757. Then – when an alliance between Pitt and Newcastle was again possible – he resigned with absolutely no reluctance and with the King's grateful thanks. 'The Duke of Devonshire has acted by me in the handsomest manner and is in a very disagreeable situation entirely on my account.'[13] His friends were equally felicitous about his time in office. Waldegrave congratulated him on being 'made Lord Chamberlain [of the Royal Household] several weeks before he quitted [as First Lord of] the Treasury',[14] and thus remaining, in form if not in fact, a significant member of the government. But the best that he could say of him was that 'he had shown great punctuality and diligence and no want of capacity'.[15]

The years that immediately followed were, in terms of power and world esteem, some of the most glorious in British history. In India, Clive's victory at Plassey completed the conquest of Bengal, and in Canada Woolf's capture of Quebec established Britain as a great imperial power. The French were defeated on land at Minden and at sea on Quiberon Bay. Pitt's power was beyond limit and question – even by George II, who had once been so determined to deny him a place in government. Devonshire – who had so disliked and despised office – moved effortlessly into the role of elder statesman who saw it as his duty both to reconcile the incompatible grandees within the

---

* Pitt's power was so overt that in the Oxford *History of England* he is credited with the Administration's formal leadership: 'On 15 November 1756, Pitt's own ministry was formed.'

cabinet and to advise the King on the best way of keeping his leaky ship of state afloat.

Devonshire left no official record of his brief sojourn as George II's First Minister, but he left lengthy *Memoranda on State of Affairs* – describing the conflicts within the ministry – written in the manner of a twentieth-century political diarist. He noted the petulance. 'Pitt told the Duke of Newcastle that he did not say that he would resign but that he had heard himself declared an unfavourable minister.'[16] He recorded the resentments. 'The Duke of Newcastle came to me full of complaints about the way he was used by the King, also by Lady Yarmouth',[17] the last royal mistress to become a peeress in her own right. And he chronicled the confidences which had been reposed in him:

> The King took me into his closet and asked me whether I had seen the minute of the Council which had met on the Friday before. I told him that the Duke of Newcastle had shown it to me. You see, said he, my situation is a very delicate one . . . My ministers tell me that I cannot maintain my army . . . England was bound in honour as well as duty to maintain the troops

which were necessary to support Prussia in its battle with the Austro–French alliance. Pitt offered a simple solution to the King's dilemma. He 'acquainted Lady Yarmouth that the making of the militia perpetual would be moved immediately at the opening of the session'[18] of the next parliament. To Whigs, the idea of a standing army, at the King's disposal, was anathema.

George II died in 1760 and his grandson, who succeeded him as George III, told the first meeting of his Privy Council that he was opposed to what he called 'this bloody and expensive war'.[19] Lord Bute – who had been no more than 'groom of the stole' – was appointed the King's secretary and became his unofficial but most influential adviser. Bute, who had been the King's tutor, owed his position to his 'friendship' with George's widowed mother, the Dowager Princess of Wales – a type of relationship which has often been the secret of a nonentity's rise to power and is always described as a moral outrage by the rivals who were overtaken along the way. Bute, unlike Pitt, was for peace – even if it could only be obtained at a high price. When the Russian Ambassador offered to mediate with France, he convinced the King that the offer should be accepted. Pitt agreed, but insisted on minimum terms which – according to a note made by Cavendish at the time – were far less favourable to France than the King thought reasonable. Pitt formed his own opinion and came to the definite conclusion that nothing should alter that . . . [Britain] must keep all of North America and the [fishing] banks of Newfoundland or [he would] resign . . . He would not make war to save or regain Hanover but would never consent to give up acquisitions that he thought necessary to the country.[20]

Whatever might be negotiated with Paris, Madrid – he insisted – was preparing to invade England. He proposed to pre-empt their plans by declaring war on Spain at once.

Newcastle was still enough of a Whig to doubt the wisdom of the 'foreign adventures' but – partly because of a pathological need to remain in office – he decided, despite his doubts, to side with the King. Devonshire did the same – a judgement which he admitted was certainly influenced by the 'bonds of class and tradition'.[21] But he wrote, with real feeling, 'I wish to God that some expedient may be found out to prevent the continuation of the war. If the war is to continue I, for my part, see no light of day.'[22] His duty was, as he saw it, to preserve what was left of the Whig hegemony. So he urged Newcastle to swallow both his pride and principles – the first being less easily digested than the second – and accept that Bute was, in fact if not in form, the King's First Minister and work with him towards a negotiated peace. It was not an easy task. 'Never was there a time', Devonshire told Newcastle, 'when it was more necessary for two persons to agree than it is for you two at present. And therefore for God's sake keep your temper . . . I can't be gone for four and twenty hours but you must all be quarrelling. Pray be friends, for the public will suffer if it is not so.'[23] By then Devonshire was also advising Bute who, after a particularly quarrelsome Privy Council, was near to despair and asked him, 'Did you ever see such a day as yesterday?'[24] Bute's anguish ended in 1762 when the King made him First Lord of the Treasury, Pitt resigned and Newcastle was forced out.

Although Devonshire remained, as Lord Chamberlain, a member of the Administration, he claimed to be in a constant state of doubt about whether or not he could justify holding even a prestigious sinecure in an administration which he despised and which had treated Newcastle so badly. Horace Walpole described him as 'fluctuating between his golden key [the formal symbol of his office] and disgust'.[25] He retained the key but abandoned his duties at Court and took refuge in Chatsworth House from where he wrote to his friend, the Bishop of St Asaph, 'Having declined to attend Councils all this summer how long I shall be able to remain in office is uncertain. I should rather think that my continuation will be short, for if I was to appear one of the present Administration, I should lose the little credit I have in the world. At the same time I detest opposition.'[26] He added, by way of explanation if not excuse of his conduct, that his 'health has, for some time, been rather shattered' and that, in consequence, he was going to spend the autumn in Bath.

Lord Egremont, Secretary of State for the Southern Department in the new ministry, made it impossible for the vacillation to continue. 'Notwithstanding your having of late declined attending the Cabinet, yet, as the final Decision of the Peace is to be taken at one that will soon meet, on which the fate of the Country may depend, His Majesty has no doubt that you will give your personal attendance and your advice freely on so great a point. And so, to this end, the King has ordered me to desire you to come to Town as soon as you can.'[27] The Duke had no intention of obeying the royal summons. Following orders – even if they came from the King – was not the Cavendish way. And – less characteristic of the family – he was still not sure what path duty, honour and self-interest required him to follow. Perhaps unwisely, in his reply to Egremont, Devonshire attempted to justify his future negligence by explaining that it had been made unavoidable by negligence in the past. 'I hoped that His Majesty would excuse my not coming to Council as it was impossible for me to give an opinion in the uninformed situation I was in . . . and that I should not make myself responsible for measures I had no share in and was in a manner unacquainted with.'[28]

Even before he 'took the waters' and meditated upon his insult to the King, Devonshire must have realised that the decision about his future had already been taken out of his hands. So he pre-empted the announcement of his dismissal by resigning all offices. Despite his disenchantment with the King and his ministers, he behaved as propriety required and went to Court to surrender his symbols of office. But although the Duke was prepared to respect the rituals of resignation, George III was not. The page through whom he requested audience returned from the royal presence chamber with the news that the King would not see him. So the Duke asked for guidance about how he should deliver up his golden key and staff of office. The page again consulted his master and returned with a message which he conveyed with some embarrassment. His Majesty would send his orders to the Duke at a time of his royal choosing. That was a rebuff which Devonshire was not prepared to accept. So he took his staff and golden key and gave them to Lord Egremont with the injunction that they should be passed on to the King when he was in a mood to accept them. Whatever the whereabouts of the key and staff, the Duke was no longer Lord Chamberlain. The King had already sent for the Privy Council Register and, after demanding that he be given a pen, had himself – with evident savage pleasure – crossed out the name of Devonshire.

The Duke resigned all his English appointments and office but, in order to safeguard his Irish property, remained Governor of Cork. An exodus from the government of Cavendish friends and relations followed. The Earl of Bessborough, Devonshire's brother-in-law, resigned from the Post Office. The Marquis of Rockingham asked to be excused his duties as Gentleman of the Bedchamber. Only Lord George Cavendish, the Duke's brother and Comptroller of the Household, was granted a valedictory audience. Other departing ministers received the brusque message that 'Whoever desires to quit his staff, the King did not desire that he should keep it'.[29]

The Duke of Cumberland, who was close to the Cavendish family, did not hesitate to express his patronising disagreement with his nephew George III. 'I own on this occasion that I must pity the poor young King that hath bereft himself of the most useful and zealous subject . . . through the instigation of the most dangerous and wicked advisers that a young King had.'[30] Cumberland went on to predict that it would not be long before the Duke was recalled to service. He was wrong. The career of the man his mother had called the Prince of the Whigs was over. Devonshire never held office again. There was one last flurry of independence when he argued that – blasphemy and seditious libel notwithstanding – it was for the electors of Aylesbury to decide for themselves whether or not John Wilkes should represent them in parliament. Then, in August 1764, Cavendish was suddenly struck down with what doctors of the period called the palsy. The following month he 'took the waters' at Spa. When he showed no signs of improvement there were plans for him to take another cure at Aix-la-Chapelle, but before he could move on, a second stroke paralysed his left arm and leg. Within a week he was dead. For once, Horace Walpole drew the correct moral. 'But five and forty, with forty thousand pounds a year and happiness wherever he turned him! My reflection is that it is folly to be unhappy in anything, when felicity is such a phantom.'[31] He did not say, for such things did not concern him, that the serious business of politics – and what was left of the Whig tradition – had been bequeathed to the Fourth Duke's brother John. The Cavendish family had temporarily finished with government. But they had not yet finished with politics.

CHAPTER 15

All the Brothers Were . . .

The story of even a noble family is more than the history of its eldest sons and each of the Fourth Duke's brothers played a part in the history of England. Lord George Augustus was briefly Member of Parliament for Weymouth and Melcombe Regis. Then he announced that he would not contest the constituency a second time if the candidature was passed on to his brother. Of course, the electors – such as they were – were pleased to keep their votes in the Cavendish family. Lord George had not abandoned the Commons. He just preferred to represent Derbyshire, in which county he continued a parliamentary career that was characterised by what looked like self-sacrifice but was really blatant nepotism. In 1781, after twenty years as Member for Derbyshire – during which he resigned as Comptroller of the Household in sympathy with his brother, the deposed Lord Chamberlain – he again stood aside in favour of another Cavendish, his nephew, Lord Richard Cavendish. The young man died within a year and Lord George returned to be elected in his place. He remained a Member of Parliament until he died – thirteen years later, in 1794. Lord George had been bequeathed Holker Hall in Lancashire. The childless Sir William Lowther of Marske, grandson of the Second Duke of Devonshire, had left it to Katherine, his spinster sister, on the understanding that Lord George inherited it on her death.

Lord Frederick, the third of the brothers, was a soldier – a profession which few Cavendishes favoured and one which he combined with being Member of Parliament, first for Derbyshire and then for Derby. He rose, by rank, from ensign in the Foot Guards to field marshal and played enough of an active part in the Seven Years War to be captured during the campaign in St Malo. Offered parole, he declined to promise never to bear arms against France lest, as a Member of Parliament, he was required to vote Supply for the War Office. Told by the gallant enemy, 'We would no more object to you voting in Parliament than to your begetting children who might one day fight against France'[1] he accepted the offer and, on arrival back in England, quickly adjusted his opinion on what the obligations of honour demanded. He returned to battle in command of an infantry brigade.

In October 1774, he caught the attention of Georgiana, wife to the Fifth Duke. During a Chatsworth ball, she met him on the stairs 'extreemly drunk'.[2]

As a young man he had, together with James Wolfe, taken an oath not to marry until France was no longer a threat to England. It was said to confirm that he was a real soldier. But at the end of his career, he allowed his Whig sympathies to transcend his martial instincts. Sympathy with the colonists made him decline to serve in North America and it was said that, had it not been for his oath of allegiance, he would have fought on their side. Like all well-connected young officers he served, for a time, as an ADC – in his case to the Duke of Cumberland, commander-in-chief of King George's army in Germany. But his promotion was as much a result of proficiency as of patronage. He died, a bachelor, in 1803, with no house to bequeath. Twickenham Park had been left him with the proviso that, if he died without issue, it was to revert to the original owner's natural heirs. So he had only a fortune to leave to his nephew, George Cavendish, First Earl of Burlington. As a result – and thanks to vagaries of birth and death – it was eventually inherited by the Seventh Duke of Devonshire.

Lord John Cavendish, the youngest of the brothers, was one of fortune's favourites – pampered, flattered and indulged. He built his career on Cavendish self-confidence and the help that came with the Cavendish connection. His three years at Cambridge ended with an event which was rarely experienced even by graduating noblemen – the publication of an elegy written, and dedicated to him, by his tutor. In the same year, 1754, he inherited his seat in the House of Commons from his elder brother. During his five years as Member for Weymouth and Melcombe Regis, he did little of note. But after he moved on to Knaresborough – perhaps as a result of the way in which the King had summarily removed his brother's name from the Privy Council roll – he became active in the group of Whigs who were known as the Duke of Newcastle's 'young friends'. His manner – which was thought to reflect his temperament – caused great offence to senior Members. But arrogance is often the product of conviction. And there is no doubt that Lord John Cavendish was a man of strong beliefs. He made his name in parliament the hard way by following his great-grandfather's example and fighting his battles from the back benches of the House of Commons. By assuming the role of parliamentary buccaneer, he postponed promotion to high office but not – as he was dramatically to demonstrate – the chance to influence the course of great events.

When the Fourth Duke of Devonshire died in 1764, his son and successor was only sixteen. Lord John – the boy's uncle but the youngest of the three surviving brothers assumed the political leadership of the family by force of personality rather than order of precedence. He found it so much to his liking that, even when his nephew came of age, Lord John remained the Cavendish who distributed patronage and made sure that the constituencies which the family controlled returned Members on whom the Whig leadership could rely. He also, by his *de haut en bas* behaviour, incurred the undying enmity of Horace Walpole who, as well as describing him as 'the most obstinate conceited young man I ever saw', complained that Lord John believed that 'the house of Cavendish ought to have the exclusive right of choosing the Prime Minister'.[3] Walpole had identified the qualities that made Lord John an irresistible parliamentary force.

In 1765, the government, under George Grenville, determined – with the acquiescence, and probably on the initiative, of George III – that arrangements should be made to create a regency in the event of the King's death or incapacity. The pretext – that the heir apparent was a child – was less important than the subtext. The King was already suffering from bouts of profound depression which, his physicians feared, would turn into madness. Preparations had to be made for his possibly permanent incapacity. Such arguments as there were about the proposed regency council concerned its composition – particularly the inclusion of the King's mother. Augusta, Dowager Princess of Wales, was unacceptable to the leadership of both the Whigs and the Tories because of her close relationship with the, by then, discredited Lord Bute. After a struggle, the King agreed to her exclusion, but her name was added by a snap vote of parliament. Reluctant further to embarrass the King, ministers agreed to let the argument rest. Only a handful of Members of Parliament voted against the bill. Lord John Cavendish was among them.

Later that year, when the Marquis of Rockingham – leading a close association of Members of Parliament who called themselves Rockingham Whigs – replaced George Grenville as Prime Minister, Lord John joined the Administration as a junior Lord of the Treasury. Like his brother before him, he found office tedious and was 'tired in the confinement of [his] employment'[4] long before the premiership changed hands again and William Pitt (by then Earl of Chatham) returned to power. He resigned in November 1766. From then on, in government and out, Lord John was an irreconcilable and exclusive 'Rockingham Whig' who opposed co-operation with other Whig factions and was intolerant of any views other than his own. In consequence he was defeated at Lancaster in the 1768 general election.

Rockingham came to his rescue and arranged for him to be returned unopposed at York.

Edmund Burke – then a Whig himself – treated him with tolerant condescension. The ironic advice that his foibles should be endured with good grace was probably intended as a comment on the less than intellectual enthusiasms of most political grandees. 'He ought to be allowed a certain and reasonable portion of Foxhunting to put him into wind for the Parliamentary Race he is to run – but anything more is intolerable.'[5] In fact, inside the House and in the country, Lord John worked harder than most of his colleagues, almost always in support of traditional Whig causes which he advanced, not as matters of principle but as pragmatic necessities. He championed the rights of the elected legislature against an increasingly powerful executive, advocated the creation of permanent parliamentary alliances (a nascent party system) as the only way of ending the hegemony of the King and his advisers, argued for religious tolerance and opposed the Royal Marriages Act with the argument that a future monarch who wished to ignore its provisions would always do so.* His condemnation of the Gordon Riots owed nothing to religious toleration. He objected, not to the persecution of Roman Catholics, but the destruction of private property. The appeal to practical necessity rather than high principle was a technique which he employed in his most prolonged and important campaign – opposition to the war against the American Colonies.

In 1773, the British government agreed that the East India Company could dump its surplus stocks of tea in America. When the first consignment arrived in Boston, the colonists – outraged by the affront to their sovereignty as much as by the undercutting of their own produce – emptied the ship's cargo, 340 chests of tea, into the dock. Lord John was openly in sympathy with the perpetrators of 'the Boston Tea Party' and, in response to the British government's campaign to subjugate the rebellious colonists, moved an amendment to the Loyal Address with which the parliament of 1774 opened. It called for an end to repression in North America. It was defeated, but it was the opening shot in an eventually successful guerrilla war.

Some Whigs regarded support for the American colonists as a moral obligation. To them the rising against an arbitrary monarch was nothing less than a second Glorious Revolution. Others saw the rising as an opportunity to humiliate the hated George III and demonstrated their

---

* His judgement was vindicated when the Prince of Wales married Mrs Fitzherbert, a Catholic, without his father's permission.

contempt by parading London in 'Buff and Blue', the colours of George Washington's army.⁶ Lord John Cavendish endorsed neither approach. It was the practicality not the propriety of government policy which he attacked. And he proceeded with caution. The Custom House Bill – which would have closed Boston Harbour to shipping until the East India Company was compensated for its losses – he dismissed as unenforceable. But it was passed into law. His second (1775) amendment to the Loyal Address proposed not the abandonment of all repressive measures but their postponement until parliament had a clearer picture of the extent of the revolutionaries' support. The proposal was ignored. When a bill was introduced to exclude all of New England (as well as the Newfoundland fishing grounds) from trade with Great Britain, Ireland and the West Indies, Lord John did not argue that it was wrong in principle, but that the government could not be certain that all the states to which it was to apply were in rebellion. His criticisms were brushed aside as was his warning that the employment of German mercenaries in North America was needlessly provocative.

Lord John was not disheartened. His amendments to the Loyal Address became an annual event. In 1776 Hugh Walpole recorded the speech in his journals. 'The idea of marching through the continent of America was absurd . . . Distant provinces with their minds alienated would be a burden, not a benefit.'⁷ The amendment was again defeated. Disheartened by their continual failure, the Rockingham Whigs boycotted all debates on the war against the colonists. For a while Lord John fought on alone. In 1777, he attempted to force an inquiry into the accounts which set out the cost of the war in North America. Then it seemed that he too had lost the will to fight. In the following year, his only noteworthy contribution to the debates was a speech that illustrated his generosity of spirit. He spoke in favour of granting Chatham a pension of £4,000 a year. He then, in typical Cavendish style, lay dormant for almost five years.

In fact Lord John was waiting for the impracticality of the war to make its continuation impossible. On February 22 1782, the Whig motion that called for an end to hostilities – seconded by Lord John – was defeated. But on March 8 he moved the first of a series of motions which, in turn, censured the government for the cost of the North American War, the extent of British losses and the folly of fighting simultaneous wars with France, Spain and Holland, and called into question the general incompetence of ministers. Lord North's government survived the first vote, but with its majority cut to ten. The Prime Minister resigned in the knowledge that he faced certain defeat before the day's voting was done. In February 1783, having carried a Commons amendment which changed a motion on the peace preliminaries from approval to censure, Cavendish successfully moved the resolution which brought down the whole government.

Rockingham became Prime Minister. Lord John Cavendish served as a brief and reluctant Chancellor of the Exchequer and immediately added his name to the long list of Treasury ministers who announce the need to compensate for their predecessor's profligacy by reducing government expenditure. He included in his economies a saving which few of his succesors dared to propose: he cut the Civil List. Rockingham died after six months in office. The years of political instability which followed were ended by a cynical Whig and Tory alliance between Charles James Fox and Lord North formed around the repudiation of the North American peace agreement. The speech which made the alliance possible was given by Lord John Cavendish in 'terms so guarded, with a view to secure as many votes as possible, that it might rather be termed a hesitation in approving than a censure on the peace'.[8] The whole exercise was so obvious a contrivance that Lord John's reputation for plain dealing only survived because even those who condemned the opportunism which he defended took his previous good conduct into account.

Lord John – a man of generally recognised probity – was employed to sanitise a political union which had no other purpose than power. Fox and North built the legitimacy of the new government on Lord John's reputation. Thomas Townsend, a Tory, said that they only succeeded because of 'the most implicit reliance on the integrity and honour of that noble person who, from the dictates of his own generous mind',[9] could be relied upon 'never to advocate an unworthy cause'. Some of his critics argued that by supporting the coalition, Lord John had sacrificed his good name. But Townsend argued that the blame lay with the politicians who 'knew how to choose their man whenever they want any business to be effected which is not evidently right in itself'.[10] Lord John stood guilty of no more than gullibility, the result of the 'surfeit of respect' which he felt for his friends.

When Lord John became Chancellor for a second time – as reluctantly and briefly as before – his budget again showed a proper Whig indifference to the Court and its presumptions. He refused, point blank, to increase the Prince of Wales's allowance to a level which would finance his extravagant lifestyle. But government was not Lord John's natural habitat. Indeed, in both office and opposition, he was most successful when he followed his own conscience and instincts rather than working as either the leader or member of a team. He paid the price which is often demanded of politicians who give their support to men and measures with whom and which they do not agree. In 1784 he lost his seat at York – one of 'Fox's Martyrs', the name given to Whigs who were defeated because of their association with a politician who had tarnished his reputation by abandoning principles for power.

Despite his election for Derbyshire ten years later, Lord John's political career never recovered but he joined the elite ranks of politicians who are more admired after defeat than before it. Edmund Burke, who had bitterly quarrelled with Lord John, celebrated their reconciliation by publishing a series of laudatory essays.

> If any one were to ask abroad who were the men now living upon whom this nation valued itself and whom we were bound to hold out as specimens of what this country could produce to give an idea of its virtue, every man would certainly name Lord John Cavendish . . . a man who would have adorned the best commonwealth at the brightest periods.[11]

Lord John possessed 'great integrity, great sensibility of the heart . . . disinterestedness and an ancient English reserve'. His 'only fault' was the 'singular modesty and moderation of his nature' which denies 'the energy and lustre to his virtues which are necessary to give them full effect'.[12] Lord John recorded the renewal of their friendship in a more practical way. He left Burke a substantial bequest.

The always acerbic Horace Walpole – intending only to be critical – caught Lord John's character more accurately and, in consequence, described his achievements more accurately. 'Under the appearance of virgin modesty' Lord John 'had a confidence in himself that nothing could equal and a thirst for domination more extraordinary'.[13] Beneath the hyperbole lies the truth that Lord John was a Whig who thought it his duty to oppose the Court and its favourites when – as he suspected was regularly the case – they acted out of malice, ignorance, or greed. But he did not want to assume power in the miscreants' place. His job and the duty of his class was to point the way and clear the path for others. In doing so in the cause of the North American colonists, he had a far greater influence on the life of the nation than his brother, although briefly called Prime Minister, ever enjoyed.

CHAPTER 16

The Outsider

In the autumn of 1798, Henry Cavendish, grandson of the Second Duke of Devonshire, published a paper in the *Journal of the Royal Society* under the title 'Experiments to Determine the Density of the Earth'. It guaranteed the author's position at the head of a long list of distinguished scientists, beginning with Isaac Newton, who had sought to establish the specific gravity (relative density) of the earth. That paper remains – despite the extraordinary scope of his scientific achievements – the work for which Cavendish is most famous. In the hundred years which followed the 'discovery', his findings were said to be endowed with a variety of attributes which the author never suggested they possessed. Chief among them was the claim that Henry Cavendish had constructed a formula which enabled him to weigh the world – an essential addition to the understanding of the solar system. He certainly hoped and believed that his work would be of value to geologists and astronomers. But he performed the experiment which bears his name because he was personally curious about the nature of the universe.

To Henry Cavendish, scholarship was an end in itself. In consequence much of his work on the nature of electricity, the composition of water, latent heat and the identification of gases was not published until years after his death. Had he been less reticent about his discoveries, he would have been even more exalted in his own lifetime. But, because of his reclusive nature, his achievements were known only to his scientific peers. In his memorial lecture, Sir Humphry Davy made the comparison which Cavendish would have most welcomed. 'Since the death of Newton . . . England has sustained no scientific loss so great.'[1] Davy's prediction that 'his name will be an object of more veneration in future ages than at the present' – correct though it was – would have left Cavendish unmoved. Misanthropic is, perhaps, an exaggerated description of his view of life. But he was not so much detached as alienated from the world around him. And he was terrified of women.

Henry Cavendish was the son of Lord Charles Cavendish, a younger brother of the Third Duke, and was thus first cousin to the Fourth Duke. His mother was Lady Anne Grey, the daughter of the Duke of

Kent. His mother suffered from chronically poor health and at the time of Henry's birth (October 10 1731) was in Nice to avoid the rigours of an English autumn. She died, two years later, shortly after the birth of Frederick, her second son. Both brothers – like so many Cavendish boys of the period – attended a school in Hackney which specialised in providing the rudiments of a classical education for the scions of noble families. In 1749 Henry entered Peterhouse, Cambridge but – like his brother, Frederick, who followed him to the same college – left without taking a degree. Frederick's early departure from the university had an obvious and painful cause. For reasons which were never fully explained, he fell from an upper window of his college. He landed on his head and never completely recovered from his injuries. Happily, Henry had no such excuse for abandoning his studies. Some of his contemporaries suggested that, because of his scientific detachment from religion, he chose not to graduate in order to avoid the necessity of confirming his membership of the Church of England. Others assumed that he could not face the ordeal of a conversation with the examiners. The likelihood is that he, like so many young Cavendish men down the ages, did not condescend to be examined. But he did not retain conventional Cavendish attitudes for long. Indeed he was, by common consent, an outsider – a role which made him profoundly suspect in the opinion of those members of his family who thought that soiling their hands with science was beneath their dignity. The Fifth Duke of Devonshire – in many ways not a fastidious man – forbade his wife, Georgiana, to visit her kinsman. Henry Cavendish, he said, 'is not a gentleman. He works.'[2]

So many stories were told to illustrate his eccentricity that it is difficult to separate fact from fiction. He wore clothes which were old, worn and long out of fashion, shuffled along rather than walked and spoke in a high shrill voice. Not that he spoke very often. Lord Brougham believed that 'he probably uttered fewer words in the course of his life than any man who lived to four score years, not excluding the monks of La Trappe'.[3] The claim that he only communicated with his housekeeper in writing may be apocryphal. So may be the account of the night, during his Grand Tour, when he and his brother shared a bedroom with a corpse but did not mention it to each other until the following morning.[4] But there is no doubt that, in order to avoid the embarrassment of meeting housemaids on the stairs, he had a second flight built at the rear of his Clapham villa and it is equally certain that when he was forced to attend a family christening, instead of giving the attendant nurse the usual sovereign, he emptied the whole contents of his pocket into her lap and ran away before she had the chance to thank him. Money seems not to have concerned him. For a time that was just as well. After he came down from Cambridge his father – far from wealthy himself – made him a meagre allowance. But he neither spent, nor made the most of, what he got. When his bank manager approached him with news of his credit balance and suggestions about how a higher rate of interest might be earned he replied, 'Don't come here to plague me about it or I will move [banks].'[5] It was, in part, due to his frugality that he was able to leave a fortune to Lord George Cavendish, his second cousin.

Henry Cavendish was slightly more comfortable with scientists than he was with men and women who knew little or nothing of physics and chemistry. That was only to be expected. His life consisted of little else except the study of those two subjects. When he came down from Cambridge he chose to live with his father, Lord Charles Cavendish, and there he remained – completing most of his best chemical investigations – until his father died in 1783. Lord Charles was, himself, a scientist of sufficient distinction to become a member of the Royal Society and for years his son acted as his assistant as he performed 'experiments' – including 'the curious invention of making thermometers showing respectively the greatest degree of heat and cold which have happened in the absence of the observer' which won his father the Copley Medal. Much of Lord Charles Cavendish's research – heat, electricity and terrestrial magnetism – anticipated work which his son was to continue later with greater distinction. But a letter dated February 20 1762 from no less a scientist than Benjamin Franklin praised Lord Charles's academic rigour and regretted his reluctance to describe his work to the rest of the scientific community – two attributes which his son inherited. 'It were to be wished that this noble philosopher would communicate more of his experiments to the world, as he makes many and with great accuracy.'[6]

It was at his father's suggestion that, in 1758, Henry Cavendish began to attend meetings of the Royal Society. He was elected Fellow two years later. To the surprise of all who knew him he regularly – if silently – dined with the Royal Society Club at the extremely unacademic-sounding Crown and Anchor or Cat and Bagpipes. He paid for his supper with the five shillings which his father gave him explicitly for that purpose each week. But he usually left when the evening turned from scientific to social. At a *conversazione* in the home of Sir Joseph Banks – then the President of the Royal Society – Doctor Ignatius, a visitor from Holland, tried to introduce Cavendish to a fellow guest who, it was said, had come from Austria in the hope of meeting him. The object of admiration fled. On a rare occasion when he attempted to reciprocate his colleagues' hospitality, his housekeeper suggested that he needed to provide more than a shoulder of lamb. He replied, 'Order two.' He was probably most comfortable looking at the stars, high in a tree in his garden – a practice he had facilitated by building a structure which allowed him easy access to the lower branches.

When his father died, Henry Cavendish moved to a house on the corner of Montague Place and Gower Street, opposite the British Museum in Bloomsbury. A second house, in Dean Street, Soho, became his library in which other scientists were encouraged to work. His villa on Clapham Common was, in fact, an observatory from which – despite the smoke that hung over central London – he could, on a clear night, see the stars.

Cavendish lived in an age when it was possible for a man of genius to be several sorts of scientist. So he became – with almost equal distinction – a chemist, physicist, astronomer and geologist who conducted simultaneous 'experiments' in different disciplines. His choice of subject was so eclectic that, today, it seems to border on the capricious. His first two investigations, carried out in parallel, were reported in papers which read as if they were intended for publication, but were not published until ten years after his death. One, which examined the properties of arsenic in its various forms, was undertaken in order to discover more about phlogiston, now defined as 'a substance formerly supposed to exist in all combustible bodies and to be released on combustion'. As a by-product of the experiment he speculated about the nature of the 'red fumes' which some of his investigations produced. They were, he rightly concluded, related to nitrous oxide. It was the beginning of his examination of gases and the composition of the air.

Side by side with his analysis of arsenic, Cavendish – in what his notebooks suggest was work originally written up for the amusement of a friend – wrote a paper entitled 'On the Congelation of Quicksilver'. It examined the changes in temperature which follow vaporisation, liquefaction and solidification. The paper was not published for almost twenty years. Had it been sent to the Royal Society when it was written in 1764 or 1765, Cavendish would have competed with Joseph Black for the credit of setting out the laws of specific and latent heat. As it was, Cavendish – at the time – received no more than an acknowledgement that he had extended the work by continuing the examination of the subject. The new work was carried out, during the 1780s, with the assistance of the Hudson Bay Company. Thomas Hutchins, governor of Fort Albany in the far north of Canada, agreed to record the congelation point of alcohol and various mineral acids. His results led

Cavendish to dismiss as a myth the notion that polar temperatures sank to minus 300 or 400 degrees Fahrenheit. The true extreme, he rightly concluded, was about 10 per cent of the lower figure.[7]

There seems to have been no particular reason why, a year or so after the quicksilver paper was finished, Cavendish broke his silence by sending to the Royal Society a paper entitled 'Factitious Air'. It amounted to three separate but related essays on hydrogen, carbonic acids and the gases released during the decay of animal and vegetable matter. Cavendish did not 'discover' the existence of the gases. But he was the first scientist to analyse their properties – probably a greater achievement. He concluded that the 'inflammable air' which was obtained from metals (hydrogen) was a different substance from that which followed the putrefaction of flesh. A fourth paper, written at the same time but published a year later, was an analysis of pump water in London's Rathbone Place. When boiled it produced large deposits of calcareous earth – the result of the carbonic acid, which retained the chemical in solution, being evaporated. Long after he was dead, the manuscript of the fourth paper was found to be annotated 'Communicated to Doctor Priestley'. Their close co-operation suggests that Cavendish may well have 'discovered' – or co-operated in the discovery of – nitrogen. He certainly takes credit for analysing what he called 'mephitic air'. His work was filed under the heading 'experiments and observations made in and before the year 1772'. Lavoisier and Priestley examined 'phlogisticated air' well after that date and Rutherford, to whom the credit was given, published his work that same year.

More and more of Cavendish's work was being devoted to demonstrating that what had previously been regarded as single unified gases or liquids were several distinct substances, each one possessing more constituent parts than his contemporaries recognised. But electricity was the intellectual vogue of the age and even the most unfashionable of scientists could not resist turning his attention to the subject that preoccupied a visitor to England, Dr Benjamin Franklin. In 1771 the *Philosophical Transactions of the Royal Society* included a paper entitled 'Attempts to Imitate the Effects of the Torpedo'. It described the construction of apparatus which reproduced the distinguishing feature of the fish that gave its name to the underwater missile – the discharge of an electric current. Speculation about the nature of the 'ray' was only one, though the most graphic, of the ways in which Cavendish examined the fundamental attributes of electricity – voltage, resistance, insulation, positive and negative charges.

It was probably because of Franklin's influence that Cavendish made one of his rare forays into public service. In 1796 – prompted by a catastrophic explosion at the powder mill at Brescia in Italy – the Board of Ordnance asked the Royal Society to provide advice on possible ways of avoiding a similar disaster at the munitions magazine at Purfleet. Franklin and Cavendish joined with a local man, known to scientific history as Wilson, in deciding how to avoid a lightning strike. Cavendish and Franklin recommended a sharp-ended conductor which, despite Wilson's advocacy of the blunt alternative, was installed. The magazine was struck by lightning five years later. By then Franklin had gone home. The new committee excluded Wilson but included Joseph Priestley. It again recommended that a new conductor be installed and that it should be 'as acutely pointed as possible'.[8] Wilson, although possibly right in his prescription, was a builder and house painter by trade. There was never any question of his advice being taken in preference to the recommendation made by two Fellows of the Royal Society.

Cavendish next turned to the study of air. For 200 years, thanks to Bacon, scientists had – more or less correctly – argued that burning bodies were 'fed' by the air around them and that some inflammable materials actually increase in weight as a result of combustion. Then the theory of phlogiston – which asserted that the agent of combustion was transferred from burning material to the air – returned the study of combustion to its pre-Elizabethan ignorance. The myth was shattered by the identification of oxygen by Priestley, Scheele and Lavoisier; Priestley, since he recognised its power to support combustion, called it 'dephlogisticated air'. In the autumn of 1784 he employed John Jeffries, an American balloonist, to take specimens of air at various altitudes. Some of his experiments were more productive than others. They were most rewarding when they were analytical rather than attempts to find a previously unidentified substance. The examination of nitrogen – in his judgement 'phlogisticated' because it inhibited burning – was a classic example of the importance of recognising and defining constituent parts. Cavendish had observed that if a candle was lit in a confined space over water, by the time it had burned out, the amount of air had diminished and the volume of water increased. He determined to discover where the water came from, where the air went to and if there was a constant relationship between the reduction and the increase.

Hydrogen and air were confined in a closed container, in varying amounts. When the vessel contained one part of air to two of hydrogen, combustion resulted in the quantity of air being reduced by 20 per cent. The air that remained did not contain oxygen but nitrogen. The overall weight of the vessel and its contents had not changed. The loss of air had been matched by the creation of liquid. As Cavendish described it, 'all the inflammable air and about one fifth of the common air . . . condensed into dew'.[9] He – in a primitive form of analysis – tasted the 'dew'. He concluded that all the inflammable air and pure air had become 'pure water'.[10]

The result of this experiment was not made public until Cavendish, after some persuasion, read a paper on the subject to the Royal Society on January 15 1784. James Watt, in his northern fastness, did not hear of the Cavendish exposition until March. He immediately sent the Royal Society his 'Thoughts on the constituent parts of water etc.'. It included the claim that the Cavendish analysis had originally been carried out by him. At the same time, Lavoisier told the French Academy of Sciences that his work on the same subject preceded all the other discoveries. Cavendish, after some persuasion, published the contents of his notebooks. They would have confirmed that he was the first in the field had they not included notes added to the original text. Cavendish insisted that even the additions pre-dated Watt's work. Neither man contested the claim to originality with much passion. Cavendish actually visited Watt to promote reconciliation. His initiative clearly succeeded for Watt proudly showed him an improved model of his steam engine. But after their deaths – Cavendish in 1810 and Watt in 1819 – their intellectual heirs (and in Watt's case his son) joined battle to establish who had first conducted the experiment. Cavendish undoubtedly deserved the accolade. That he did not receive it in his lifetime was the result of his perverse reluctance to share his findings with his fellow scientists.

An extension of the original experiment, with a combination of free oxygen and hydrogen exploded by an electric spark, produced, as well as pure water, a substance which we would now call nitric acid – the result, Cavendish concluded, of pure air polluting the mixture. It enabled him to define the composition of what, until then, was an unknown chemical. Together with his discovery of argon, that, in itself, would have guaranteed his reputation as a chemist of historical importance. But he moved on to new fields of enquiry. Meteorology and astronomy were disciplines which were studied by all self-respecting eighteenth-century 'natural philosophers'. Cavendish took the study to new latitudes if not new levels with the publication, in *Asiatic Researches*, of a paper devoted to what he called the Sanskrit view of the solar system – 'The Civil Year of the Hindoos'. Work on the shape and size of the universe was a prelude to what was to become the 'experiment' that confirmed his place in the pantheon of English scientists.

In *Philosophiae Naturalis Principia Mathematica*, Isaac Newton had asserted that the relative densities of the sun, Jupiter, Saturn and Earth were, respectively, 100, 94½, 64 and 400 and that the density of the earth – based on his observation of rocks from the surface crust and the deepest mine-shafts in England – was five or six times that of water. The figures were more guesses than calculations. But the guess about the relationship of the earth and water was inspired. From 1687 onwards – when *Principia* was published – scientists made numerous attempts to improve on the figure which Newton had conjured out of his extraordinary intellect. Their work always consisted of attempts to calculate what Newton called 'the power of gravity proportional to all bodies' – usually by comparing the movement of a pendulum, suspended close by a mountain, with a calculation of what the movement would be if the pendulum had swung on low ground, or by comparing pendulum movements at the top of a mountain with the movement which would have been likely at the same latitude if the mountain had not been there. Not surprisingly, their efforts did not end in triumph. But they failed in good company. Newton himself had written that spheres 'of like nature to the earth' placed a quarter-inch apart, and subject to no other pressures, would not exert sufficient mutual gravitational attraction to cause them to move together in less than a month. In fact they would touch each other in barely five minutes. Henry Cavendish improved on Newton's work. It is a gigantic claim but one which is wholly justified.

Cavendish did not construct the apparatus on which the experiment was conducted. Ironically – since friendship was not his forte – his most famous work was made possible by the bequest of one of his few friends. Only two men were allowed to invade his privacy, both of them scientists. Doctor (later Sir) Charles Blagden resigned as Physician to the Army in order to become Cavendish's assistant and travelled on his behalf when geological specimens or chemical substances had to be obtained from outside London – which Cavendish rarely left. The Reverend John Michell, a professor of Geology in the University of Oxford, was his usual companion at Royal Society club dinners. It was, as Cavendish made clear in his paper, Michell who 'contrived a method of measuring the density of the earth'. But the work was not completed before his death. The apparatus on which the calculation was to be made became the property of his Cambridge successor, Professor the Reverend F. J. H. Wollaston who – believing that the intellectual heir was Cavendish – passed it on. So the work was continued and completed.

The apparatus consisted of two small lead balls – one at each end of a thin wooded rod which was suspended, from its mid-point, by a slender wire. The rod was able to rotate as well as swing, which it was encouraged to do by the placing of larger balls, which Cavendish called 'attracting spheres', in positions which exerted a 'gravitational pull' over the smaller ones. In order to avoid extraneous forces influencing the result Cavendish enclosed the apparatus in a mahogany case and 'resolved to place [it] in a room which should remain constantly shut and observe them by means of a telescope and to suspend the leaden weights in such a manner that I could move them without entering the room'. Cavendish then observed the movement of the balls and the speed at which they moved through a telescope which gave him sight of the proceedings without risking a deep breath, a footfall or a sigh upsetting the delicate balance of the apparatus.

The experiment was repeated seventeen times. Each result was fractionally different. So the conclusion was based on the mean average. Being a meticulous scientist he made sure that the result was not affected by variations in the apparatus by repeating it with different materials. He concluded that 'with the first wire used . . . the density of the earth comes out 5.48 times greater than water . . . With the second wire it comes out the same.' The careful recalculation was typical of his working methods. All his achievements were notable for – perhaps even dependent upon – the meticulous care with which he worked. But, Homer nods. Although Cavendish had conducted the experiment with exemplary skill, he made an elementary mathematical error in the calculation of the final figure. The Cavendish experiment had conclusively proved that the earth's specific gravity was 5.45 not 5.48 greater than that of water.

The error – not being noticed at the time – did nothing to diminish a sudden surge in Cavendish's reputation which was so great that the Tory government abandoned its hostility to a suspected Whig and recruited him to its service. Gold coins were losing weight and value – worn away, not by thieves but simply as a result of their being passed from hand to hand. Cavendish, together with a chemist and an instrument-maker, was employed to find a solution. He became a manager of the newly created Royal Institution and was elected to the Institut de France. Only death saved him from becoming part of society.

Two distinct accounts of his death, on February 24 1810, survive. Both agree that the cause was a 'seizure' that he immediately recognised as fatal but which took several days to complete its work. In both descriptions of his final days, he was, to the end, determined to remain as aloof from the conventions of death as he had been detached from the courtesies of civilised behaviour. According to one account, he summoned his valet and gave strict instructions that immediately he was dead, Lord Frederick Cavendish had to be informed but, until then, his brother was to be given no indication that the end was near. A few hours later, he sent for the valet again, told him to repeat his instructions and asked for lavender water. When the valet returned he was dead. The alternative version includes Sir Everard Home, an eminent surgeon, being persuaded by the valet to rush to Clapham Common and see if it was possible to save the dying scientist. Cavendish was said to reject all offers of help on the premise that to prolong his life would only result in an extended sojourn in the vale of tears. In the surgeon's presence, but without the acceptance of his offer to ease the pain, Cavendish died in the early hours of the following morning.

The valet asked Sir Everard to oversee his examination of the dead man's effects. In one chest of drawers they found parts of various women's dresses, and a great deal of valuable jewellery. One piece, a stomacher embedded with diamonds, was said to be worth, at the time, £20,000. There must have been speculation about what those effects revealed. Was it lost love or sexual ambivalence that made Cavendish feel, in exaggerated form, the need for social seclusion which he had inherited from his father? What gossip there was concerned the discovery of unexpected fortune. He was revealed to be the holder of £70,000 of bank stock (probably more than anyone else in England), freehold property which earned annual rents of £8,000 a year, £50,000 in cash and a canal with a value which was beyond calculation. Blagden, his loyal assistant, received a legacy of £15,000. The rest went to his second cousin, Lord George Cavendish, and through him – eventually the Second Earl of Burlington – back into the mainstream of the Cavendish dynasty. In 1839, Burlington repaid his benefactor by arranging for the Reverend William Harcourt to examine, edit and publish most of the papers which Cavendish had chosen not to submit to the Royal Society. It was the beginning of the full acknowledgement of a previously little-recognised genius. Twenty years later, James Clerk Maxwell, professor of Experimental Physics in the University of Cambridge, published – with even more acclaim for the author – Cavendish's papers on electricity. The final accolade was a donation of £6,500 made – in 1870, by the Seventh Duke and Chancellor of the University – for the establishment of a laboratory of experimental physics in Cambridge. Naturally, inevitably and properly its name evolved through several references to his distinguished forebear to 'the Cavendish Laboratory'. The social outsider had been immortalised by the university from which he chose not to graduate.

CHAPTER 17

The Misalliance

During the autumn and winter of 1774, Georgiana Spencer, Duchess of Devonshire, wrote to her mother almost every day. Her mother, Lady Spencer, replied almost as frequently. Sometimes Georgiana's letters described, with childish glee, life at Devonshire House. 'I was Dressed in *demi saison*. Silk. Very like the one I bought from abroad and wore at Bath. Pink. Trimmed with Gauze and Green Ribbon.'¹ Just as often they offered childlike apologies for minor misdemeanours. 'I write to you with a heavy heart for I am not at all pleased with the manner in which I have spent the Day. After dinner I really forgot it was Sunday and proposed playing cards.'² Lady Spencer's letters were often admonitory: 'Always date your letters to me at the top.'³ Sometimes Georgiana wrote in French. Other letters contained stanzas of doggerel verse. But they all had one feature in common. Georgiana's husband, the Fifth Duke of Devonshire, was never mentioned. It was a strange omission. Georgiana, not yet eighteen, had been married for barely three months and was, on the evidence of both her behaviour and correspondence, excitable to the point of hysteria. But there is nothing in her letters to suggest that she was even remotely enthused by her new state.

There was very little for her to be excited about. Her new husband, who had become the Fifth Duke of Devonshire when he was sixteen, was one of the dullest men in society. Before he set out on the almost obligatory Grand Tour, the Reverend John Hinchcliffe, his tutor at Cambridge, had told him, 'Tho' there is not a Duke in Christendom that I have more confidence in than your Grace, yet in this climate, from eighteen to eight and twenty, the odds are certainly on the side of passion against prudence.'⁴ If by passion the pious clergyman meant commitment to a cause or enthusiasm for a great issue, he was destined to be disappointed. If he used the word as a euphemism for sexual licence, he was right to fear that the young duke would find the temptations of France and Italy too strong to resist. It was believed that, while in Paris, he had a brief relationship with Madame du Barry, one of the greatest courtesans in history. But in later life, he seemed hardly able to show real enthusiasm even for the sexual adventures which interrupted his only true joy – gambling at Brooks's Club. Every other activity was a bore. In his *Handbook to Chatsworth* the Sixth Duke described his father's indifference to what went on around him. The Fifth Duke chose to sleep in a bedroom 'exposed to the noise and shaking of the noisiest of passages . . . When informed, one night by his servants, that the house was on fire, he turned round to sleep on his other side, observing that they had better try to put it out.'

Perhaps it was as well that the Fifth Duke and his Duchess were calm about the nature of their marriage – the alliance of the most introvert man and the most extrovert woman in late eighteenth-century London society. Within weeks of his wedding, a note, left with his valet, informed his wife, 'I am going to sup at St James's Place. I have sent you the carriage so that you may come in it if you wish.'⁵ There is no record of how the Duchess responded. But it is clear, from a letter sent by the Countess Cowper, her maternal grand-mother, what her family would have regarded as the proper reaction. Georgiana existed to meet the Duke's needs. There is, Lady Cowper wrote, 'so much intrinsic worth in him that he deserves your utmost endeavours to make yourself always an agreeable companion, even as it is for life. Outward attractions will not be sufficient.'⁶ The Countess went on to apologise for 'writing in the style of a grand-mother' – a forgivable offence and a much more comprehensible feature of her letter than the description of the Duke as a man of intrinsic worth.

The most charitable way in which to describe the Fifth Duke's nature was 'pathologically reserved'. A less well-disposed observer claimed that 'constitutional apathy forms his distinguishing characteristic',⁷ but even that was a euphemism for cold, egocentric and lacking in humour. He did not even possess the superficial graces of the aristocracy. Mrs Delany – in one of her many commentaries on contemporary society – called him 'a jewel which has not been well polished'.⁸ Contemporaries attested to his latent – indeed submerged – talent. Charles James Fox was attempting to persuade the Prince of Wales to moderate his demands on the Privy Purse when he urged him to accept the Duke's advice about the folly of insisting that parliament increase his allow-ance. So the Prince was probably right to react with scepticism to the assurance that Devonshire was 'a man whose generous and feeling heart and right head and understanding may be reposed in without fear, a man whom – if indolence did not overcome him – ought to govern the country'.⁹ But there is more evidence to justify the claim that 'on all the disputes that occasionally arose between members of [Brooks's] club related to Roman poets and historians, appeal was commonly made to the Duke and his decision or opinion was regarded as final'.[10] But whatever disagreements there may be about his abilities, one thing is clear. Devonshire was sublimely unsuited to his seventeen-year-old bride. He was – an almost unknown trait among the Cavendishes – even dull in his debauchery. Yet, by an irony of fate, he married the most flamboyant of all the Devonshire duchesses. In consequence – despite the world of masculine supremacy in which he lived – he is only remembered because of his wife.

Georgiana Spencer was a spoilt child. Her father – Earl Spencer, the great-grandson of Sarah, Duchess of Marlborough – had married for love. Together with his wife – Margaret Poyntz, the granddaughter of an upholsterer – he lived, for many years, in a state of hysteria about money and status, and of Lear-like anxiety about the affection of his daughters. The level of emotion at which her parents existed undoubtedly had an adverse effect on Georgiana. When she was barely six years old, she was left with her maternal grandmother while her parents travelled in Europe Then, when her younger brother and sister died, the Spencers were overcome with a remorse that drove them to religion, gambling and an obsessive concern about Georgiana's health. Their indulgence encouraged her precocity. By the time she was fourteen, she had been fêted by Paris society during her parents' second Grand Tour and there was already much public speculation about whom she would marry. In a moment of rare common sense her mother expressed her anxiety about Georgiana's life moving on too quickly for her own good. 'My fear is that she will be snatched from me before her age and experience makes her in any way fit for the serious duties of a wife, a mother and the mistress of a family.'[11] It was too late.

Georgiana possessed a complicated charm. Horace Walpole wrote that 'she effaces all without being a beauty, but her youth, figure, flowing good nature, sense and lively modesty and modest familiarity make her a phenomenon'.[12] No doubt those qualities attracted the twenty-four-year-old Duke of Devonshire when they met at Spa in 1773 – for while he regarded Georgiana as an 'appropriate' bride, the decision to marry her was not imposed on him as a dynastic duty. At the time of their meeting, the Duke's feelings were undoubtedly influenced by what amounted to his rejection by Lady Betty Hamilton, the step-daughter of the Duke of Argyll. Whatever the reason, before he left Spa he had made up his mind to marry Georgiana and she had either fallen in love with him or, in a fit of girlish infatuation, convinced herself that she had. Thus came about the marriage of two incompatibles.

The new Duchess of Devonshire was already such a figure in society that the wedding had to be held in secret at Wimbledon, with only close members of the family attending, to avoid the attention of unmanageable crowds of sightseers. The bride, in a white and gold dress, had pearls in her hair and was excited by the idea of a clandestine ceremony rather than offended by her parents' decision to keep the date of her marriage from her until two days before she became Duchess of Devonshire. Inevitably attempts to divert attention from the ceremony encouraged the suspicion that Georgiana had been forced to marry the Duke against her will. One gossip, who believed that 'her delight was chasing butterflies', claimed that 'the Housekeeper, breaking a lath over her head, reconciled her to the match'.[13] Such stories were the price she paid for becoming a celebrity. The *Public Advertiser* of June 15 1774 was nearer to the truth in its report that 'happiness was never more marked in a countenance in hers'[14] when – as protocol required – the new Duchess was presented at Court. But the auguries were not encouraging. The Duke arrived just before four o'clock, after his wife had been kept waiting for several hours – almost too late to witness the presentation.

In the following year Devonshire embarked on building the Crescent in Buxton Spa, one of the few creative endeavours in which he ever engaged and probably the result of no more than a whim. In November 1774, the Duke and his new Duchess had stayed with Lord Rockingham at Wentworth Woodhouse in South Yorkshire. The visit was most notable for Georgiana's first meeting with Edmund Burke, then no more than a secretary but soon to become the intellectual force behind the Rockingham Whigs and one of the men who inspired the Duchess's wayward interest in politics. It was there that the Duke met John Carr of York, the architect who was designing extensions and improvements to Wentworth Woodhouse. The Duke decided, during a casual conversation, that his healing waters in Derbyshire deserved a more elegant setting than the decaying bath-house. Carr was commissioned to provide it. There was little or no financial incentive to stimulate the Duke into making Buxton the Bath of the north. In 1795 the Hall at Buxton (rebuilt by the Earl of Shrewsbury for the convenience of Mary Queen of Scots) was earning him £1,200 a year in rent and the annual revenue from the ancient baths themselves totalled £1,400. Those sums were not, in themselves, an immense addition to Devonshire's already enormous wealth and the considerable Buxton investment was likely to make only a marginal increase to his income. But the wonder is that he agreed to build even the crescent and its stables, not that he chose to ignore the example of Bath. All that could have induced him to beautify the whole of Buxton was innate enthusiasm for a more extensive and ambitious development. And innate enthusiasm was not a quality which the Fifth Duke of Devonshire possessed.

The Fifth Duke failed – through lack of either interest or imagination – to make the most of natural resources. It was the age of spas – most notably Bath which, like Buxton, had dispensed healing waters since Roman times. In 1727, Daniel Defoe, on his travels through England, had written that both towns were squalid but that Buxton – being situated in high open country – had the greater potential as a health resort. Forty years later, Bath began the greatest urban redevelopment in English history. Under the leadership of John Wood, a whole new town was created. In 1775, seven years after the foundations of Bath's Royal Crescent were laid, the Fifth Duke of Devonshire financed the creation of his crescent in Buxton. It was, and remains, a noble building, and the circular stable block which compliments it is crowned by one of the most spectacular domes in England. But the Duke intended to do no more than provide facilities for a better class of bather. Bath's Royal Crescent – like the other less famous crescents in the town – is mostly composed of houses built on a hillside for the pride and pleasure of permanent residents. The Crescent in Buxton was designed as a series of hotels, built in the valley close to Saint Anne's Well for the convenience of the new bathers who, it was hoped, would be attracted by the healing waters. But even the intention to rehabilitate the spa was not pursued with any real imagination or vigour. The plans did not include a Pump Room, a public Assembly Room, or a Reading Room – amenities essential to a successful spa. The Duke was not sufficiently engaged in the project even to consider building the best spa in England.

Despite his remarkable capacity for detachment, the Duke did not altogether lack feelings. By the time of his marriage he had already fathered a daughter by a young milliner called, by coincidence, Charlotte Spencer. That sort of behaviour was routine for the Georgian aristocracy. But, in this one particular, Devonshire joined the ranks of the reckless and romantic – if not wholly responsible – minority by both acknowledging the child as his and maintaining an affectionate relationship with her mother. But he became notorious for his lack of care and compassion for his wife whom he increasingly regarded not as an object of affection but as a necessary accessory to his dynastic duty. One night he remained both literally and metaphorically unmoved at one end of the ballroom when he was told that she had fainted at the other. But he did his formal duty. A letter, sent to Lady Spencer on October 1 1775, was exactly what was to be expected of a responsible son-in-law. He understood that she was already 'acquainted with the Duchess's miscarriage . . . I only write to assure you she is as well as can be expected . . . Mrs Denman tells me that she has not often seen women in her situation where health seems to have suffered so little.'[15] The Duke was, undoubtedly, deeply disappointed that his wife had failed to perform her primary duty by giving birth to a male heir. But the cold formality of the message was typical of the Fifth Duke's apparent inability to express – or perhaps to feel – any deep emotion. His apologists attributed his character – taciturn, pedantic and uncompromising – to the lonely childhood which followed his mother's death when he was six. Whatever its cause, his indifference was something approaching a disease.

The Fifth Duke's emotional impotence made him a wholly unsuitable husband for a seventeen-year-old bride who expected and needed constant demonstrations of her husband's affection. Two days after their marriage, the Duke was back in Chelsea Pleasure Gardens, doing not very much and accompanied by his cronies. The notion that his wife might be both friend and companion never occurred to him. On evenings when there were no soirées, grand balls, or great dinners to attend, he always abandoned her and went to Brooks's Club, where he invariably ate the same supper – broiled breast-bone of mutton – and played cards until four or five o'clock the next morning.

Brooks's Club had been founded in 1764 by twenty-seven gentlemen who included the Dukes of Roxborough and Portland, the Earl of Strathmore, Mr Crewe (who was soon to become a marquis) and, more importantly, Charles James Fox. Originally it was run – or 'farmed' in the contemporary language – by William Almack, the proprietor of the Almack Assembly Rooms, but it was taken over by Brooks, a wine merchant and money-lender. In 1778, it moved to St James's where it remains open to its members today. Its character has changed in two respects. It has become less aristocratic but more respectable with age. The gaming tables are still there but the nobility no longer gamble huge sums on games of whist and hazard or make bizarre wagers with each other on contests that are created purely to enable large sums of money to be won and lost. Nor is it now the centre of political activity. In the eighteenth century Brooks's was a Whig club.

It was the gaming, rather than the politics, that attracted the Fifth Duke of Devonshire to Brooks's. He enjoyed the male ambience and subscribed to the unstated agreement that men went to the club to avoid the tedium of female company. Georgiana, on the other hand, was, by her nature, unable to sit patiently at home waiting for her husband's return from his club. So she accepted every invitation which she received and, because she possessed few moral or intellectual resources, committed all the social indiscretions of her age. The most innocent was a penchant for wearing exotic decorations in her hair – including stuffed birds, galleons in full sail and waxed fruit. Her most exotic accessory was ostrich feathers. At one royal reception she wore one which was 4 feet high. The Queen forbade their display at Court. But by then they had become the Duchess's trademark. For the rest of her life, cartoons – whether they pilloried her politics or exalted her elegance – always depicted her with extraordinary structures on her head. And they were always surmounted by ostrich feathers.

Had Georgiana's indiscretions amounted to no more than a bizarre choice of dress, she might have lived, lonely and unfulfilled, but peacefully reconciled to her status as a fashionable, political hostess. It would have taken some time for her to grow into her responsibilities. Her talent was not for entertaining but for being entertained. She found her duties at Chatsworth – presiding with the Duke at the weekly 'open day' and entertaining dozens of guests at dinners which began in the early afternoon and went on into the evening – particularly difficult. Routine soirées were barely more congenial or successful. 'I could not have much to say for myself' she told her mother after one morning reception, 'and some of the company were talking of things I knew nothing of. I made the silent figure you can conceive and . . . I broke all the rules of Hospitality in forgetting to offer them some breakfast.'[16] But it was in London – where the Devonshires spent half their lives – that, according to her mother's informants, she was guilty of 'unsuitable behaviour'. Georgiana was gambling and losing money which she did not possess.

Apologists blamed, and continue to blame, what undoubtedly became an addiction on the lonely nights spent in the sepulchral Devonshire House. No doubt the Duke's neglect, like the weakness of Georgiana's character, was a contributory factor. But there was also a genetic element. Both her parents gambled obsessively at times of stress and Lady Spencer maintained the habit into old age. However, neither her mother's own indiscretions, nor the thought that her daughter might have inherited the habit, prevented the liberal provision of maternal advice. It began with the proposal that Georgiana should not gamble at all. 'Let me entreat you . . . if it is mentioned to you any more to decline the taking part in it.'[17] The call for total abstinence having failed, Lady Spencer fell back to the proposition that if Georgiana could not resist gambling, she should be careful to avoid the most pernicious games. 'Play at whist, commerce, backgammon, tritrac or chess but never at brag, faro, hazard or any game of chance and, if you are pressed to play, always make the fashionable excuse of being tied up.'[18] Then, in what sounds like the voice of hard experience, Lady Spencer retreated to the hope that, although her daughter could not resist gambling, she would take precautions to ensure that she was unable to gamble excessively. 'Pray take care, if you play, to carry in your pocket as much as you can lose and never go beyond it.'[19] All the advice was ignored.

The Spencers always came to their daughter's rescue. They paid her gambling debts, though – claiming to be motivated more by respect for the Duke than the hope of repayment – they invariably told their son-in-law what they had done. For a time, the Duke – waiting for production of a heir – at least tolerated his wife's excesses. And Georgiana constantly anticipated that the goodwill that a son would guarantee would be a sure way of obtaining the Duke's forgiveness for all her misdeeds – as well as the liquidation of her debts. The extent of her losses was unknown even to the Duchess herself. Keeping careful accounts was not her style.

Unfortunately the longed-for event proved more elusive than either Georgiana or her husband had imagined it would be. The first miscarriage occurred after a little less than a year. The attendant physician, while explicitly not speculating about the cause of her disappointment, diagnosed the Duchess's subsequent lassitude as the result of physical exhaustion which could only have been the consequence of her active social life. The prescribed remedy was a rest cure in Spa. Georgiana sufficiently recovered to allow the party – both Devonshires and Spencers – to stop in Paris on the return journey where she renewed the acquaintance, made when a girl, with Marie Antoinette. But the waters of Spa did not have the desired effect. A second miscarriage followed the return to London. Shortly afterwards *The Morning Post* reported: 'The Duchess of Devonshire is dangerously ill and we hear that the physicians have attributed her indisposition to the reigning fashionable irregularities of the age.'[20] Lady Spencer was remarkably unsympathetic about her daughter being publicly accused of a dissolute lifestyle. 'You must expect to be classed with the company you keep.'[21] The company she kept became known – because of where they most regularly met – as the Devonshire House Circle.

Their preoccupation was politics but their relaxations were gambling and adultery. A Miss Pamela Fitzgerald asked her niece Emily, 'Does it ever strike you that vices are wonderfully prolific among the Whigs? There are such countless illegitimates, such a tribe of children of the mist.'[22] Because of its louche reputation, older and wiser Whigs treated the Devonshire House Circle with caution. Edmund Burke only attended its gatherings when Lord Rockingham, his patron, was present. But Georgiana was entranced by the 'dazzling, haphazard confusion'[23] of the society which she inhabited, in turn, as an adornment, an asset and eventually a liability.

Richard Brinsley Sheridan – now better known as a playwright, but then a politician who amused himself by writing plays – combined enthusiastic membership of the circle with amused contempt for some of its adherents. *The School for Scandal* is a gentle satire on their conduct. Georgiana appears as the spendthrift Lady Teazle. Other observers were less cultivated in their criticism. Lord Greville was both censorious and – in terms of the circle's effect on Georgiana – remarkably prescient. He described the circle as 'Very amusing as a scandalous chronicle, an exhibition of vice in its most attractive form, full of grace, dignity and splendour but, I fancy, full of misery and sorrow also'.[24] Perhaps even that description did the circle more than justice. 'Beneath the shining surface seethed always a turmoil of yearning, of jealousy, crisis and intrigue, gnawing hope and unavailing despair.'[25] Almost everything that happened in Georgiana Devonshire's early life contributed to her doom. Life at the centre of the Devonshire House Circle made it certain.

True to her character, Georgiana chose to outdo other members of the circle in their pursuit of excess. She gambled with such abandon that, for a time, she was even more notorious than the circle itself. The anonymous author of the 100-page pamphlet 'An Interesting Letter' called on the Duchess to 'give Vice and Folly a very considerable check by becoming yourself an example of Christian virtue' and prophesied, unless she changed her ways, that historians would conclude that 'Discretion and Good Sense, finding themselves deserted and unnoticed, abandoned their care and of all the Virtues that once possessed an interest in her, Chastity alone refused to abandon her'.[26] Chastity did not remain her guardian for long.

Encouraged by the excesses of the Devonshire House Circle, Georgiana became a heavy drinker. She was not pregnant again for a year and the Duke began to fear that his wife was unable to conceive or was intentionally avoiding conception. His remedy was a visit to Brighton where the sea water was said to promote fertility. It was there that Georgiana met Mary Graham, the object of her first – but by no means greatest – infatuation with another woman. All that can be certain about the nature of their relationship is the level of emotion that it engendered in Georgiana. After the Brighton trip was over, the Duchess's letters to her new-found friend expressed anguish at their separation and joy at the pleasure of meeting a mutual acquaintance who mentioned Mary's name. The obsession may have been no more than the product of loneliness. Gossips – perhaps motivated by malice – suggested otherwise.

Whatever Georgiana's feelings for Mary Graham were, in the summer of 1777 they were submerged under the sudden development of devoted admiration for a visitor to Chatsworth – Charles James Fox, a figure whose complicated character made him the object of wonder as well as affection. Fox, the second son of Lord Holland, was to become the great – though idiosyncratic – radical of his age as well as one of its most reckless gamblers. Georgiana seems to have been attracted by his intellect – 'his amazing quickness in seizing any subject. He seems to have the particular talent of knowing more about what he is saying and with less pains than anyone else.'[27] She might have added that he only turned his capricious mind to subjects which interested him. He was an acknowledged authority on the obscure Greek poet Lycophron, but – although he called one of his racehorses Jean-Jacques Rousseau – he admitted that he found *The Social Contract* unreadable, had never even opened Adam Smith's *Wealth of Nations*[28] and returned a presentation copy of Wordsworth and Coleridge's *Lyrical Ballads*, because he did not like that sort of poetry. His erudition and élan – combined with his willingness to treat her as an equal – were enough to convince Georgiana that he exemplified the better life that she should follow. In 1778 she told her mother 'I have many things I wish to repent and my heart is determined to mend.'[29]

Georgiana's path to redemption led, at first, not to politics but literature. The new life began with the composition of an anonymous novel, *The Sylph*. It was the story of a country girl who marries a rake and is sold by her husband to his creditors before he shoots himself in a fit of remorse. Fanny Burney, the famous author of *Evelina*, was deeply offended by the discovery that some uninformed readers had attributed the book to her and instructed her publishers not to advertise the two works side by side.[30] Significantly, Georgiana's favourite novel was *Les Liaisons Dangereuses*.[31]

On July 4 1776, a new excitement distracted the Duchess from both literature and the vices which it was supposed to hold at bay. The American colonists' Declaration of Independence was supported by the more romantically inclined Whigs – with whom Georgiana instinctively identified. But the colonists – although in rebellion against an absolute monarch as their heroes of 1688 had risen up against James II – were not universally popular in Britain. Supporting a revolutionary army in revolt against the Crown was, in itself, a dangerous position for politicians to take up. Continuing that support after France entered the war as an ally of the colonists was suicidal. Francophobia was so extreme that Lady Elizabeth Foster – destined to become, successively, the Duchess of Devonshire's bosom friend, the Duke's mistress and, after Georgiana's death, his second wife – was publicly upbraided for employing a French maid.[32]

When the inevitable fear of a French invasion reached the point of hysteria, the Duke, as Lord Lieutenant of Derbyshire, reorganised the county militia and led it to camp at Cox Heath in Kent. Georgiana – dressed in an adaptation of military uniform – accompanied her husband and did her best to act like a daughter of the regiment. Although a nearby house had been rented for her accommodation, she chose to live in a (lavishly furnished) group of tents and – after trying, unsuccessfully, to form a female battalion – asked permission to command a company. Her actual participation in martial affairs amounted to no more than walking one step behind the Duke during inspections. But she revelled in the excitement of it all and, in so doing, exposed the essentially silly aspect of her character. 'I rather think there will be an invasion', she told her mother, 'and I shall see something of it to complete the extraordinary scenes I have been present at this year.'[33]

The camp – with its tented ranks of aristocrat-led militia – provided ample opportunity for the promiscuity which was the fashion of the time. Lord Egremont fathered a child with Lady Melbourne. Lady Claremont had an abortion after a brief affair with a local apothecary. Lady Derby scandalised society not by openly consorting with the Duke of Dorset but by deserting her husband in order to be with her lover. The Duke of Devonshire conformed to fashion by having a brief liaison with Lady Jersey. Georgiana seemed to raise no objection, but her mother's forcible complaints convinced the Duke that he must mend his ways. However, Lady Spencer did not possess the power to prevent the accelerating disintegration of the marriage which – in five and a half years and with recourse to both genuine and quack medical treatment – had failed in its purpose. There was still no heir.

Some time in 1778, Charlotte Spencer died and the Duke – who had remained her lover to the end – asked his wife to accept the child of the irregular union in the Devonshire household. The fact that her husband had kept a mistress could not have come as a surprise. *Town and Country Magazine* had already published a story about 'the D–e of D–e and a Miss C–e S–r' and expressed astonishment that His Grace was not satisfied with his 'blooming, blithe and beautiful' wife.[34] Whatever her feelings, Georgiana had little alternative but to accept the arrangement. So the news was spread abroad that Chatsworth was to become the home of Charlotte Williams, the orphan daughter of a distant Cavendish relative. Lady Spencer – who undoubtedly knew the truth about the adoption – showed no sign of believing that stepmotherhood would assist in the Duchess's redemption. When Harriet, Lady Spencer's second daughter, became engaged to Frederick Duncannon, the future Lord Bessborough – and was, therefore, about to emerge into society – she wrote to Georgiana imploring her not to lead her sister into bad ways.[35]

Other distractions diverted the Devonshires' attention from domestic disappointment. Lord North – a Whig of the less romantic sort – had been carried along by the hardline ministers who wanted to suppress the rebellious colonists by military force. Whatever the merits of fighting a war in North America, losing it was an indisputable political disaster. Unrest in Ireland was being met with neither coercion nor conciliation. The renewed call for parliamentary reform was continually ignored. The Administration was doomed. Carried along by the excitement, Georgiana began to spend afternoons in the gallery of the House of Lords. And, at last, the Duke made his maiden speech. Such events often receive more praise than they are due. So Edmund Burke's gushing compliments about 'unrivalled authority' must be treated with caution. But there is no doubt that his encomium ended with an error of judgement. 'It will become a habit more disagreeable to him to continue in silence on an interesting occasion than hitherto it has been to him to speak upon it.'[36] The Duke only spoke in the House of Lords once more during the next thirty years.

In Britain, the fear of revolution began to moderate the enthusiasm for reform. Fox made wild speeches but, in private, urged caution and propriety. Edmund Burke, regarded as less radical than the more flamboyant advocates of change, remained steadfast in his advocacy of more honest government. He sponsored a series of parliamentary resolutions which, by abolishing sinecures, barring government contractors from the House of Commons, revising the Civil List and closing down the (allegedly corrupt) Board of Trade, would, he claimed, ensure 'the independence of Parliament and the economic reformation of the civil service and other establishments'. The motion to abolish the corrupt Board of Trade was carried and the proposal to revise the Civil List was defeated but subsequently revived and approved. John Dunning's resolution – summed up in a phrase which, with slight revisions, has been regularly repeated for 200 years – encapsulated the whole Whig case. 'The influence of the Crown has increased, is increasing, and ought to be diminished.' It was not a proposition which, on the face of it, seemed likely to appeal to the heir apparent. But the Whig policy possessed one attribute which the Prince of Wales found irresistibly attractive. It offended his father, George III. So he supported the critics of Lord North's dying, but not yet dead, Administration. The Prince of Wales was edging his way towards membership of the Devonshire House Circle.

The Duchess of Devonshire's first impression of the Prince was not altogether flattering. 'He is inclined to be too fat and looks too much like a woman in men's clothes' but she thought that 'the gracefulness of his manner and height certainly' made him 'a pleasing figure'.[37] True to the spirit of 1688, she initially disapproved of his 'inclination to dabble in politics'.[38] But, like other Whigs, she soon put aside her principles in favour of friendship with 'the First Gentleman of Europe' and when the Prince of Wales made clear that he was a true Whig at heart, members of what was called the 'ton' – fashionable and hedonistic society – did not reject the prospect of royal patronage. The Prince was established in the glittering centre of the Devonshire House Circle and took a lively interest in its ideas as well as its entertainment. The Prince grew to worship Fox – which was recommendation enough for most of Fox's followers and certainly for Fox himself.

Association with Fox did nothing to encourage Georgiana to take a more serious view of life and politics. Her rise to social eminence came at a time when anti-Catholic feeling was endemic in England. On June 2 1780, the London mob – provoked by parliament's refusal to repeal the Relief Act, which reduced the legal discrimination against Catholics and Dissenters, and incited to greater violence by Lord George Gordon – marched on parliament to demand increased penalties for those who indulged in 'Popish practices'. Rebuffed, they attacked the houses of prominent Catholics and Whig politicians who had argued for religious toleration. Devonshire House escaped but the Duke joined the 'garrison' which defended the besieged Lord Rockingham and, on his way home, his carriage was stopped in Piccadilly and detained until he agreed to shout 'No Popery!' The riots lasted for ten days. Georgiana was 'very much frightened . . . but kept quiet and preached quiet to everybody'.[39] She also, in a letter to her mother, provided another illustration of her innate silliness. All she had to say about a riot in which a thousand people were killed was 'I could not go to the Birthday – my gown was beautiful, a pale blue with the drapery etc., of embroider'd gauze in *paillons*'.

There was some compensation for her disappointment. The Prince of Wales had expressed his regret that he had been denied the chance to dance with her.[40] Although Georgiana and the Prince grew ever closer, the likelihood is that their relationship remained that which their letters proclaimed when they began 'Dear Brother' and 'Dear Sister'. The Prince's habit of insisting on dancing with the Duchess, to the exclusion of all other ladies, combined with his reputation, encouraged the assumption that they were lovers. But the likelihood is that their relationship was platonic – leaving Georgiana occupying a more dangerous position than a royal mistress. She was expected to share the Prince of Wales's secrets and assist in the execution of his most reckless plans. Georgiana never even calculated the embarrassment which even platonic association with him was bound to cause.

Despite the rumours, Georgiana's supposed relationship with the heir apparent caused less of a stir within the 'ton' than her public reversion to the old habits which had caused her so much anguish and her husband such a drain on both his tolerance and his fortune. As always her apologists claimed that circumstances conspired to undermine whatever determination she possessed to break with her addiction to gambling. After her marriage to Frederick Duncannon, the future Lord Bessborough, Georgiana's sister Harriet quickly became pregnant – a 'happy event' which provided a deeply depressing reminder of her own supposed failures. And it was claimed that Harriet's treatment at the hands of her violent husband incapacitated her sister with fear that the baby would be lost. Then her mother suffered a stroke. There can be little doubt that the Ladies Duncannon and Spencer did share some of the blame for Georgiana's relapse. But it was their example, not their health, that caused the problem. They too had become addicted to gambling. To meet the whole family's needs, professional croupiers – charging 50 guineas a night to preside at a faro table – were employed in Devonshire House. Georgiana continued to persuade herself that all excesses would be forgiven if she produced an heir.

In pursuit of another 'cure', the Duke and Duchess of Devonshire spent the spring of 1782 in Bath where the waters were said to be yet another sovereign remedy for infertility and there were all sorts of fashionable amusements, including Sarah Siddons at the Theatre Royal playing Shakespeare, to entertain them. A Doctor Moore, famous for prescribing pregnancy-inducing unguents, was called in to assist the process as the need to conceive became more urgent. When Lord George Cavendish – Devonshire's uncle but only six years his senior – announced that his wife was pregnant, the need for a son became more urgent. The Duke faced a real risk that his title would pass to posterity through a cousin rather than through him. Fortunately, during the dying days of the year, Georgiana was able to announce that she was pregnant again.

Sentimentalists attributed the new pregnancy to the happiness which Georgiana had found in a new woman friend. While in Bath she had met – and become deeply attached to – Lady Elizabeth Foster, the estranged and almost destitute wife of an Irish Member of Parliament. Something like harmony broke out in the Devonshire household. It seems unlikely that, during the sojourn in Bath, the Duke became Lady Elizabeth's lover. But he was so enthusiastic for her company that he agreed that she should join the Devonshires during their summer holiday in Devon – in form, if not in fact, as governess to Charlotte Williams on a salary (excessive for the time) of £3,000 a year. From Devon onwards, they were a permanent and established trio – alternating their relationship as Lady Elizabeth moved to and fro as the Duchess's best friend, the Duke's mistress and both simultaneously.

Elizabeth Foster was the daughter of the Earl of Bristol, an itinerant peer who had given his name to numerous continental hotels. Before he inherited the title from his brother he had been an ordained priest of the Church of England and had become Bishop of Derry on the nomination of his friend the Lord Lieutenant. At the age of eighteen Elizabeth had married John Thomas Foster of Denleer and, with remarkable despatch, gave birth to two boys. Shortly after the birth of the second, she was deserted by her husband and denied access to her sons. From then on she survived as an adventuress – a role which she was able to occupy with great success because of her pathetic state, petite good looks, high intelligence and capacity to change, like a chameleon, to accommodate her immediate environment. Georgiana told her mother – in response to Lady Spencer's refusal to invite Elizabeth to Althorp – 'she is the quietest little thing in the world and will sit or draw in the corner of the room or be sent out of the room or do whatever you please'.[41] That was not always the case. During the early days of her relationship with Georgiana, she was sufficiently self-confident to give the trio nick-names – 'Canis' for the Duke, because of his love of dogs, 'Racky', for herself, on account of her chronic cough and (unflattering and inexplicable) 'Mrs Rat' for the Duchess. In private conversation that is what they called each other for the rest of their lives.

It was agreed, as much in the hope of curing the Racky's cough as in the interests of propriety, that Elizabeth should take Charlotte Williams on a European tour which would begin during the final weeks of Georgiana's pregnancy. Lady Spencer, recently recovered from a stroke, took advantage of her daughter's lonely confinement to express what she believed to be home truths. 'In your dangerous path of life you have, almost unavoidably . . . gathered weeds instead of flowers'[42] and 'I see you running with eagerness to those . . . who are constantly talking to you on subjects which are best avoided'.[43] The accompanying good advice included the warning that, if there was another miscarriage, her social life would lead to the accusation that she liked parties 'better than a child'.[44] It may have been that fear that prompted Georgiana to announce that there would be no more involvement in politics until the baby was born. She did not mean it.

During the political turbulence of 1783 – when Lord John Cavendish first resigned and then returned, briefly, to the Treasury and became the last Cavendish to experience high office for nearly 100 years – the Duke was invited to become Lord Lieutenant of Ireland. Had he accepted, his wife would have been expected to go with him. So acceptance of the invitation would have meant separation from Elizabeth Foster who was forbidden, because of her estrangement from her husband, to enter Ireland. Georgiana was distraught at the thought of a prolonged separation from Elizabeth. But because of her infatuation with politics she urged her husband to do his duty and serve his country. The Duke rejected his wife's advice and the Lord Lieutenancy. His wife was gratified to receive a letter from France in which Lady Elizabeth announced that she faced life without Georgiana with the deepest foreboding. 'How necessary' her letter ended 'are you to my heart.'[45] Georgiana was also necessary to her financial security. After Elizabeth moved on to Naples – and was rumoured to be sharing a house with two lovers – she received both a remittance and reassurance from Georgiana: 'I send £50 tonight. That's a hundred. Canis will give me, the day after tomorrow, 200 which I will send.'[46]

Georgiana's baby, safely delivered after a difficult birth, was a girl. Georgiana was much criticised by her mother for feeding the child herself and therefore, according to the beliefs of the day, reducing the prospects of another swift pregnancy. More serious, John Heaton, the Duke's agent, thought fit to accuse the Duchess of keeping for her personal use money which should have been paid to tradesmen. He also claimed that tradesmen who were renovating and repairing Chatsworth were receiving, in lieu of payment, the promise that the Duchess would secure them the Prince of Wales's patronage – an offer which Heaton claimed she was only able to keep because she had become a royal mistress. The Duke accepted Georgiana's protestations of marital fidelity and financial propriety but, despite his wife's pleading, refused to dismiss the agent who, he accepted, had slandered her. His decision was purely pragmatic. 'I do not look enough into my own

affairs . . . I should be mad to quarrel with him. It would ruin me.'[47]
Heaton was wrong about the Prince of Wales. But allegations about
Georgiana's misconduct were becoming the common currency of
London society. Lord George Cavendish believed, or claimed to believe,
that she was having an affair with Fox.

Rumours about Elizabeth's conduct were equally common and more
plausible. It was said that in Rome she had an affair with Cardinal
Bernis and in Naples with Count Fersen, a Swedish diplomat who had
been the lover of Marie Antoinette. She certainly had lost her wish
swiftly to return home. Georgiana, pregnant again despite her mother's
foreboding, was still desperate for a reunion. What pleasure she might
have felt at the thought of fulfilling the Duke's hopes was eroded by
the pressure of debt 'so very, very large' that, on her own admission,
she 'never had courage to own it [to her husband] and try'd to win it
at play by which means it became immense'.[48] The discovery by her
widowed mother that the Spencer family were almost bankrupt as a
result of their gambling provided the consolation that her addiction
was 'innate'. But another twist of fate was about to complicate her
life. The Duke – a man who, it was supposed, had no emotions – had
fallen in love with Elizabeth Foster. And, as is often the case with
emotionally late developers, he was in love with the idea of love itself.
At the end of 1783, he wrote to her from Bath: 'There are many places
that so much put me in mind of you that, when I walk about the town
I cannot help expecting upon turning the corner of a street, to see you
walking along it.'[49]

However, the emotionally unstable Georgiana was increasingly
diverted from thoughts of her absent friend by her renewed enthusiasm,
politics. The turbulent circumstances of the time – Lord John Cavendish's
years of glory as Crown Prince of the Whigs – all conspired to catch
her febrile attention. At the end of the eighteenth century, political
power resided in whoever could attract the support of the King and
rely upon the loyalty of whatever unstable alliance temporarily dominated the House of Commons. The King, desperate to keep Fox out of
office, had invited the young William Pitt – then aged twenty-four – to
form an administration but Pitt had declined with the explanation that
he could not command a majority in the House of Commons. During
the following year, more and more Members rallied to Pitt's colours.
But the precarious state of the new Administration did nothing to
dampen the Devonshire House Set from celebrating the return to office
of Fox and the Whigs who were their friends and allies.

Georgiana was hostess at the numerous balls which were organised
as victory galas and treated with such reverence that a performance

at the Opera House was ended early in order to free the Prince of Wales to join his Whig subjects in their evening of rejoicing. As was the custom, friends of the new ministers were rewarded with honours. The Duke of Devonshire, made a Knight of the Garter, was said to have 'advanced up to the Sovereign' to receive the accolade, 'with the phlegmatic, cold, awkward air of a clown'.[50] Georgiana, on the other hand, rose to every occasion and was treated as if she had not so much contributed to the triumph as come to embody it. She had become even more of a celebrity than she had been on her secret wedding day and – perhaps not surprisingly for a woman of her character – she confused fame with importance. 'I came into the world at 17 and am now five and twenty. In those eight years I have been in the midst of action . . . I have seen parties rise and fall.' She announced that from then on, she would be a 'faithful historian of the secret history of the time'.[51]

Late eighteenth-century governments depended for their survival on pensions, peerages and patronage and George III refused to endorse any of the Whig proposals for rewarding their allies and seducing their enemies. The great issue of the day was the future of the East India Company which, according to William Pitt, the Administration proposed to turn into its own fiefdom. In fact Edmund Burke's plan to overhaul the governance of the company, enthusiastically promoted by Fox, was intended to end the corruption, incompetence and brutality which were its defining feature. The sinecures which would become available to Whig supporters were only a subsidiary consideration. Despite a spirited campaign against the reforms – including cartoons which lampooned Fox as Carlo Khan, the new Great Mogul – the Commons supported the reforming bill by a majority of two to one. But the Lords – encouraged by the King's announcement that he would ostracise peers who voted in its favour – defeated it. The government was dismissed without consultation or the courtesy of audience and Pitt – at the age of twenty-four – became the Prime Minister at the head of a minority administration.

Pitt's high-minded claim that he would remain 'unconnected with any party whatever [and] should keep himself reserved and act with whatever side he thought to be right'[52] was swiftly replaced by promises and proposals which made him a political hybrid – part King's Friend and part Tory. His willingness to remain First Minister – legitimised only by the support of George III – incited Whigs to new levels of sanctimonious contempt. Lord John Cavendish was typical. 'With the temper and disposition of Pitt and the Systems of the K[ing] and his friends, it is not possible for a man who has the feelings of a

Gentleman to continue for any time to act with them.'[53] So, for some months parliament behaved as it had done during the Whig assault on the Stuart autocracy. Motions critical of the King's conduct were carried and the vote on Supply delayed. But, gradually, the tide of opinion turned to such an extent that by March 1784 the majority against Pitt was reduced to a single vote. The inevitable outcome was the general election of 1784.

Fox was the candidate for Westminster, a two-member constituency which was also contested by Sir Cyril Wray, an erstwhile Whig who had become one of Pitt's most devoted followers. The turncoat, as the Whigs called Wray, received particularly brutal treatment. In one leaflet he was said to be better known as Judas Iscariot and was putting up for sale – 'in the Prerogative Arms in Westminster' – his honour and integrity. Admiral Hood, a naval hero who was the third candidate, escaped excoriation either as a result of his distinction or because his rivals did not think him a threat. The attacks on Wray set the tone of the campaign. Fox concentrated on publicity and personality rather than policy and programme. His hustings always took the same form. He addressed the assembled Covent Garden crowd from a platform, and there he remained while titled ladies – with fox-tails in their hats – first approached the immediate audience and then ventured into the nearby streets to accost passers-by. His canvassers included the Duchess of Portland, the Viscountess Duncannon, the Countesses of Derby and Carlisle, Lady Jersey, and no fewer than three Lady Waldegraves. But it was Georgiana, Duchess of Devonshire, who stole the headlines.

It was Georgiana's enthusiasm that resulted in her fame turning into notoriety. A Mrs Boscawden told Lady Chatham, 'She is in the street almost every day and this is her sole employment from morning till night.'[54] Hugh Walpole almost admired the way in which she 'made no scruple of visiting the humblest electors, dazzling and enchanting them by the fascination of her manner, the power of her beauty and the influence of high rank'.[55] But in his *Posthumous Memoirs* Nathaniel Wraxall was censorious. 'Neither entreaties nor promises were spared. In some instances even personal caresses were said to have been permitted.'[56] There is no certainty that Georgiana ever 'exchanged kisses for votes'. She certainly denied it. But the Pittite newspapers insisted that she did – sometimes elevating the story with expressions of regret that she was degrading her rank and sex and sometimes debasing it with the allegation that she was Fox's mistress. The pamphleteers – always a feature of eighteenth-century elections – combined ridicule with disgust.

Hired For the Day
SEVERAL PAIR OF RUBY POUTING LIPS
OF THE FINEST QUALITY
To be kissed by rum Dockers, queer Dukes, Butchers, Draymen
Dustmen and Chimney Sweepers.[57]

No mention was ever made of Lady Salisbury campaigning for Pitt.
But a song, of sorts, was composed about Georgiana:

> I had rather kiss my Mol than she
> With all her paint and finery.
> What's a Duchess more than a woman?
> We've sounder flesh on Portsmouth Common.[58]

Although one cartoon did Georgiana the compliment of depicting her
in the arms of an infatuated butcher, while his companion rejected the
advances of the Duchess of Portland, it was not the sort of exposure
to which Georgiana was accustomed and – to her mother's relief – she
retired from the fray. But with Fox's re-election in the balance the
Whig leadership urged her to return and even warned of the consequences which might follow a refusal. 'The censure and abuse has
already been incurred . . . If any votes are lost for want of similar
application' Georgiana would be blamed.[59] Were she to agree to return,
her renewed participation in the campaign would be more ladylike.
There would be no need – nor would she be asked – to leave her
carriage. Georgiana complained but acquiesced. On her return to
Westminster, far from resisting suggestions that she should do more
than wave decorously from her coach, she insisted on descending to
the streets and arguing the Whig case with individual voters. And she
augmented the power of persuasion with what amounted to bribery.
The Duchess went from shop to shop, demonstrating the righteousness
of Fox's cause by paying far more than the asking price for the goods
which their owners had on display and she neither needed nor wanted.

In eighteenth-century elections votes were counted as they were cast.
The fortunes of the candidates ebbed and flowed. But in the end, Fox
was placed second to Hood and declared elected.* Other Whigs were

---

* Fox did not take his seat as Member for Westminster until the spring of 1785. Claims
of malpractice – almost certainly malicious – delayed the declaration of the result until
the House of Commons voted to abandon a protracted investigation. Fortunately he
had also been elected Member for Orkney and Shetland and he represented that
constituency during the investigation.

not so fortunate. Lord John Cavendish lost his seat in York and throughout the country only 114 Whigs were elected while supporters of Pitt and the King numbered over 300. Pitt announced his intention to introduce an India Bill which created a Board of Control to replace the East India Company – more or less replicating the Fox proposals which he had denounced.

Despite the defeat of 200 'Fox's Martyrs', the Whigs, as is the habit with defeated politicians, looked for reasons to rejoice. In 1784 the best they could do was celebrate Fox's victory. A triumphant procession – several thousand strong and led by twenty-four horsemen in blue-and-buff livery – marched from Saint Paul's Cathedral down Fleet Street, along the Strand and through Piccadilly to Devonshire House. A brass band preceded the conquering hero himself who, garlanded in laurel leaves, waved from a decorated carriage which was driven, not by coachmen, but by prominent Whig politicians. Carlton House, home of the Prince of Wales, was circled three times in confirmation of His Royal Highness's political allegiance and when the cavalcade arrived at its destination, the Prince himself was there to greet it. Georgiana was by his side. She had acquired a political status in her own right and, at the same time, become dangerously close to the Prince of Wales.

In May 1784, the Prince had caused a minor scandal by, on his arrival at a ball, announcing publicly – what had previously been his unspoken intention – that he would dance only with Georgiana. She did not arrive until after midnight. So a gaggle of titled ladies had to endure not only the indignity of being passed over in favour of the Duchess but also the humiliation of being told that he would rather dance with no one than with them. Not surprisingly, they retaliated by whispering that the suspicions were confirmed and that it was now beyond doubt that Georgiana was the Prince's mistress. In fact – foolishly but perhaps unavoidably – Georgiana was conspiring with the Prince against his father, parliament and the laws of England. She had become the go-between in his doomed, but increasingly intense, relationship with the twice-widowed Mrs Maria Fitzherbert who was too respectable to sanction a relationship outside marriage and who, because she was a Roman Catholic, was prevented by the Royal Marriage Act from ever becoming the heir apparent's wife. Dancing with Georgiana allowed the Prince to pursue his latest infatuation by arranging for Georgiana to carry messages and arrange assignations. It was a task which she performed with reluctance and the constant fear that it would end in catastrophe. Six weeks after the Prince's flagrant discourtesy at the ball, it very nearly did.

One night in July 1748, Georgiana received an unexpected visit from two agitated men whom, although barely known to her, she recognised as the Prince of Wales's cronies. The Prince, they said, had discovered that Mrs Fitzherbert had decided to leave the country. In his anguish on hearing the news he had stabbed himself and was on the point of death. His dying wish was to see Mrs Fitzherbert, but – proper to the last – she had only agreed to go to Carlton House if she was chaperoned by the Duchess of Devonshire. She was waiting in her carriage, outside Devonshire House, for Her Grace to join her. Georgiana agreed. The two women found the Prince bleeding but obviously not mortally wounded. He still claimed that he was dying and begged Mrs Fitzherbert to go through an act of marriage there and then. Georgiana gave him one of her rings which he placed on Mrs Fitzherbert's finger. The Duchess of Devonshire had become an accomplice in what – by defying the Royal Marriage Act – amounted to high treason.

The Carlton House courtiers panicked and had to be persuaded by an unusually composed Georgiana not to report the incident to the King. Their anxieties were partly assuaged by both the Duchess and Mrs Fitzherbert signing an affidavit which swore that they had acted under moral duress and regarded the 'marriage ceremony' as meaningless. Much to their relief, Mrs Fitzherbert then fled to France, leaving Georgiana to break the news to the Prince. The esteem in which his Royal Highness was held was illustrated by the Duke of Devonshire's reaction when his wife confessed that she had played a part in the melodrama. He had no doubt that the Prince's 'suicide attempt' had been a charade and was even dubious about the existence of the supposed wound. Georgiana – being of a more romantic disposition – not only accepted that the blood was real but continued to act as an intermediary. The Prince visited Devonshire House so often – bearing messages, letters and gifts for despatch to France – that the gossips suggested that not only was Georgiana his mistress, but that she was about to give birth to his child.

Mrs Fitzherbert returned from France in November 1785 and agreed to marry the Prince of Wales in a more orthodox ceremony than the one which had been performed during the previous year. Georgiana was invited to be one of the witnesses. It may have been the Duchess who told Fox of the plan. However he found out, his reaction was predictable. The marriage would, at the very least, result in the Prince's disqualification from the succession and replacement by the Duke of York, an avowed enemy of the Whigs. Georgiana pleaded with the Prince to talk to Fox. He did, but only to assure him that he had no intention of defying the King.[60] He lied. The Prince of Wales and Mrs Fitzherbert were married in the front room of the bride's house in Richmond. The validity of the ceremony was not in doubt. It was performed, as the law required, by a priest of the Established Church. A week later, relying on the Prince's assurances, Fox told the House of Commons that stories of a secret wedding were a malicious invention. Georgiana – torn between loyalty to Fox and the Prince – turned on Mrs Fitzherbert as a preliminary, in a rare moment of common sense, to refusing all future invitations to play either Cupid or Pandarus and told her, 'I search into nothing and only wish to keep entirely out of it.'[61]

The Prince helped her wish come true by taking his wife to Brighton and spending a year in isolation from the persons of fashion, licence and extravagance with whom he usually passed his time. Then, after his return to London society, periods of estrangement from Maria were followed by brief reconciliations until the pressure of debt and responsibility caused him to repudiate the marriage in order to reingratiate himself with his father. During the inevitable recriminations which followed, Mrs Fitzherbert blamed Georgiana for not supporting her cause and the Prince's several mistresses complained that she had done nothing to protect their interests. The Duchess of Devonshire was becoming a pathological victim. Nothing that happened in the world by which she was surrounded turned out right for her.

CHAPTER 18

Games of Chance

It was only to be expected that Georgiana – a woman in her mid-twenties who was neglected by her husband – would grasp, with pathetic gratitude, the brief opportunity to star in a long-running political drama. But the moments of glory – called back from Chatsworth to revive Fox's flagging campaign and receiving the acclamation of the Whig crowd side by side with the Prince of Wales – soon passed and she was again faced by the demons of self-doubt and loneliness. She longed for the companionship of Lady Elizabeth Foster and urged her to return to England in the language she thought most likely to achieve that result. 'As much as I long to see you, it is not for myself I write. I am certain that poor Canis's health and spirits depend on your soothing friendship.'[1] Elizabeth was growing tired of wandering and, in preparation for her homecoming, responded to Georgiana's letter in a way she thought guaranteed to ensure a warm welcome. 'I cannot live away from you. I am miserable without you. Our hearts are formed for each other. I've lost the most precious time of our lives by being away.'[2]

So it was agreed that she should return to England. But after a brief sojourn at Chatsworth the Duke announced that she was so worn and pale that she should spend the winter in a warmer climate at his expense. It was in France that Elizabeth first heard of the growing suspicion that she and Georgiana were partners in an actively lesbian relationship. Elizabeth was scandalised by the accusation – though she implied that the allegation was made against Georgiana not her. 'Does the warm impulse of two hearts want an excuse to be accounted for, and must your partiality for me be ushered in by another connection?'[3] Once in Paris – with her social status guaranteed by letters of introduction from the Duchess – she began to forget her longing for England, home and Georgiana and, as if to demonstrate her heterosexuality, became the mistress of the Duke of Dorset, the British Ambassador, thus joining a ménage which included the Countess of Derby, La Baccelli (a principal dancer with the Paris ballet) and a courtesan, described by the diarist Nathaniel Wraxall as 'the celebrated Nancy Parsons'.[4] However, when she wrote to Georgiana to confess and ask forgiveness for her betrayal it was not the liaison with Dorset for which she apologised. The cause of her regret was a previous relationship about which she, wisely, gave no details. She was pregnant. The Duke of Devonshire was the father of her unborn child.

Elizabeth's confession was made in a letter which crossed in the post with one from the Duchess of Devonshire. It bore the news that Georgiana too would soon give birth again. Perhaps, in the light of her own pregnancy, Georgiana thought Elizabeth's 'betrayal' was a matter of no consequence. Or she may have already known the answer to the question which she chose not to ask. Whatever the reason, the point about paternity was never pursued. As Georgiana waited to give birth, the only emotion she admitted to Elizabeth was distress caused by her friend's continued absence. 'Oh my Dearest Bess, how I do love you! I cannot live without you.'[5]

Newspapers announced that the Duchess's new baby was a son. They were wrong. Georgiana gave birth to a daughter in a nursery which was decorated in white and gold to welcome the new Marquis of Hartington. By then Lady Elizabeth, ignoring both the Duke's and Duchess's entreaties to come home, had moved on to Italy where – in a squalid hotel on the Gulf of Salerno – she too gave birth to a daughter. The child was left with a local family so that Elizabeth could occupy, with the appearance of respectability, more salubrious lodgings with her brother in Naples. By then it was the Duke's turn to press Elizabeth to return – insisting that his wife was unaware that he was the father of her child and claiming that, even if Georgiana knew, she would not mind. 'The Rat does not know the chief causes of your uneasiness, and I, of course, shall never mention it to her unless you desire me. But I am certain that if she did, she would not think you had been to blame about it, particularly after I explained to her how the thing happen'd.'[6]

The Duke was clearly right to argue that Bess could return to London without fear of wrath or recrimination. For, although – after her baby was weaned – Georgiana was told of her husband's infidelity, she resumed her social life, not as an escape from a loveless marriage but with the enthusiasm of a genuine hedonist. She was in Grosvenor Square to witness a demonstration of hot-air balloons, at Drury Lane to see Mrs Siddons and at Covent Garden to watch Mary Robinson – the ballerina Perdita. Georgiana became such a social success that Lady Elizabeth decided to return to London, less because she was homesick than because she was jealous. She arrived shortly after the Duchess's excesses had caused a particularly violent example of the outbreaks of anger which punctuated her normally sullen relationship with her husband. Georgiana had never given up gambling and was in such debt with most of her regular faro dealers that she had begun to play with (and against) a known confidence trickster called Martindale. He claimed she owed him £100,000 – about £7 million at 2013 prices – and threatened to send her to a debtors' gaol unless she repaid him. Georgiana was left with only one option. She confessed all to her husband and threw herself on his mercy. The Duke immediately demanded a separation.

Georgiana knew, or ought to have known, that her husband was unlikely to fulfil his threat. Bess was about to return to England and, if the Duchess were not at Chatsworth or Devonshire House, the presence of Lady Elizabeth at either place would create a public scandal. And the 'ton' recognised the importance of keeping scandals private – or at least known only within their own close-knit group. More important, the Duke retained hopes of fathering an heir and only Georgiana could provide him with one. But the full extent of Georgiana's debt – far beyond what she owed to one crooked faro dealer – was increasing day by day as she continued to repay old debts by incurring new ones at exorbitant rates of interest.

Mary Graham was restored to the rank of close personal friend and made Georgiana gifts of money until her husband found out and forbade her to distribute any more largesse. In 1787, Richard Arkwright, Junior – whose father had invented the spinning frame and employed five thousand men and women to make cotton thread in his mill at Cromford on the outskirts of Matlock – made the Duchess a personal loan of £5,000. Arkwright, who made a business of lending cash to the impoverished nobility of Derbyshire, acted not out of friendship or kindness but with the intention of earning 5 per cent interest on what must have seemed a wholly secure investment. He was soon to discover his mistake.

On January 21 1788 Arkwright wrote Georgiana a letter in which respect came second to regret. 'I flattered myself with the hope that things might have turned out as you expected. I am immensely sorry to find that I was mistaken.' His mistake was the belief that the Duchess would keep her promise to make regular repayments and liquidate her major loan. He also enquired if he could 'rely upon the other notes having been regularly been paid as they became due respectively'.[7] He listed the dates on which payments should be made and the amounts which he expected to receive: '£200 due 20 Feb. 400: 1 March. 1021: 25 March. 1033: 22 June. 1579: 25 September.'[8] It is not known whether or not Georgiana replied. She certainly failed to make the payments. Nor is it clear if, by the end of the year – when she was even deeper in debt – she had the good sense to ask for advice from a candid friend. Unsolicited or not, on October 9 she received wise counsel from James Hare, friend, Whig MP and close associate of Charles James Fox. 'If you are in any scrape about money, it will be impossible for you to conceal it from the Duke and, therefore, the sooner he knows the better. But for God's sake, if you tell him anything, tell him all. Let Elizabeth or me tell him. There is no situation so desperate where there is not something to be done.'[9] Some time in 1790, she did make a confession to her husband – but not of the full amount of her debt.

Thomas Coutts came to Georgiana's financial rescue – though he was not motivated by altruism alone. After he heard one of the regular rumours about George III's 'distemper', he wrote to the Duchess in the hope that would persuade her to safeguard his future. 'If the king dies, I lose a good friend, but I hope that I may still be employed by his Successor, for I was his first banker and he always approved of my conduct. I should wish much that Your Grace would speak to the Prince in case this melancholy event proves true.' He went on to name members of the Devonshire House Circle with whom he had ingratiated himself. 'Mr Fox, I believe, Your Grace will find much my friend . . . Mr Sheridan will not dislike to be useful if Mr Fox is not returned [to parliament] . . . I was told that Mrs Fitzherbert, though I do not know her, has expressed herself favourable to me.'[10] Even with Coutts still willing to risk cash in the hope of favours, Georgiana's credit had run out. She was even excluded from a new faro bank which had been set up by the Prince of Wales and the Duke of Rutland.

Naturally enough Coutts soon began to regret having thrown his bread upon such unreliable waters. He sought consolation in the mistaken conclusion – briefly harboured by so many of her friends – that if Georgiana could be persuaded to acknowledge the full extent of her debts she would realise the necessity of repaying them. But the Duchess was not in denial. She realised how perilous her position was. The self-delusion was the certainty that she could charm her way to safety. For a while, she succeeded. Coutts was told that her debts totalled about £61,697. 'I don't know this is exact, near, I think: there are a few more little things of 100 or 50 & etc.'[11] And for a while – not knowing that she had intentionally omitted the Arkwright debt of £5,000 from the list – he believed that she was making a real attempt to pay her creditors. Ten years later, she was still negotiating repayments with both men and using each one both as a reason not to pay the other and as a witness to her credit-worthiness.

In October 1801 – when she realised that she could not hide the extent of her debts any longer – she told Coutts. 'To you alone I trust names. The 5000 is [owed to] one of the most interesting as well as most respectable characters in the country, a man who unites great talents with great simplicity . . . You already Guess I mean Mr Arkwright.'[12] She did not add that the object of her counterfeit admiration was pressing for repayment of his loan. In November she made Arkwright an offer which he accepted, despite its brazen inadequacy. 'I have been at Messrs Smith and Paynes where I have agreed to pay 50 more in the course of the next ten days and afterwards £100 monthly.'[13] It ended with what Georgiana clearly imagined to be reassuring news, though it was an admission that there were numerous other debts to repay. 'This is entirely independent of the arrangements which my friends are making for me and which my Mother & Sister expected to be in place on October 15th.'[14] The inadvertent admission that the rescue operation had not begun on schedule may have been the reason why Arkwright adopted a more stern, but equally fruitless, approach. First he sent a letter which was firm but couched in suitably obsequious language. 'I am disappointed in observing that the money is not to be paid me in interest tho I am glad to find that a plan is found for the purpose and till that is executed interest is to be paid monthly . . . I have to beg the favour of a [promissory] note for the *exact* balance, dated 10 Oct with *interest*.'[15] Some days later Georgiana's mother paid Smith and Payne £300 to reduce the capital debt and 'for 5 day's interest 4s 2d'. Arkwright responded with a formal demand for a promissory note for £5,441 6s 6d 'with interest for the same'. He received the note but not the money. Georgiana died in his debt.

At times of doubt and despair, Georgiana always took refuge in the arms of the only friend she thought she had left in the world – Lady Elizabeth Foster. Georgiana became so dependent on her 'Bess', and so detached from the Duke, that the discovery that little Caroline was his daughter did nothing to destabilise what had become a triangular relationship. Ironically it was Lady Elizabeth who had begun to complain that the Duke was not being sufficiently attentive, although – having publicly repented her affair with the Duke of Dorset – she had taken up with the Duke of Richmond. Her relationship with the Duke of Devonshire was improved by the news that she was pregnant again and the insistence that he, not Richmond, was the father. Bess was again despatched to France, so that she could spend her confinement in comfort if not luxury. The Devonshires saw her off at Dover and the two women made such emotional farewells that it would have been easy to believe that they were the lovers and the impassive Duke was the platonic friend of one or both rather than the father of the boy who was born three months later.

The complications of the family's private lives multiplied. Lady Spencer was on the verge of a nervous breakdown because of her estrangement from her daughters. Elizabeth Foster demanded that she be allowed to bring her newborn son to England. Duncannon was accused of trying to murder his wife, Georgiana's sister Harriet. So the distraction of Warren Hastings's impeachment may have come as a welcome relief. Even the Duke was diverted. Instead of going to Chatsworth he remained in London to attend the House of Lords.

Warren Hastings, after long service in India, had returned home to retirement and what he hoped would be rest. But in 1786, Edmund Burke – claiming that the Governor of British India had been both corrupt and tyrannical – had moved a House of Commons motion for his impeachment. Burke was undoubtedly motivated by a real belief that Hastings had misappropriated East India Company funds, brutal-ised the people of Bengal, fought unnecessary wars against neighbouring states and disposed of local rulers who opposed his hegemony. Other Whigs remembered that Pitt had brought down their government by opposing its plans for reforming Indian governance. But their hopes of doing the same to his administration were frustrated by his decision to put principle aside and back the impeachment resolution. Hastings was put on trial before the House of Lords where debates on such exotic subjects as the treasury of the Begums of Oudh, the execution of the Maharaja of Nandakumar and the rebellion of the Zeminder of Benares attracted an unusually high attendance. Hastings was acquitted. The Duke of Devonshire was one of the few peers who chose neither to speak in the House of Lords nor express an opinion at any time during the whole impeachment proceedings. They lasted for seven years.

Georgiana, still feeling bruised by the broad-sheets and cartoons, confined her political activities to meetings in Devonshire House, though the processions that celebrated Whig by-election victories always made the detour that enabled the participants to raise a cheer as they passed her gates. She had however found a new, and initially platonic, protégé. Charles Grey – the son of an admiral whose family Georgiana had visited when he was an Eton schoolboy – had been elected the Member of Parliament for Northumberland at the age of twenty-two. He immediately joined the Devonshire House Circle and was proclaimed – as much for his good looks and witty conversation as for his advanced Whig views – the 'coming man'. He demonstrated his own belief that he deserved that description when, with the Whigs anticipating a return to power, he announced that he would expect to be made Chancellor of the Exchequer.

The Whig hopes of victory were based on the news – delivered in November 1788 by an excited Prince of Wales – that George III's condition had deteriorated from morose confusion to violent insanity. He was clearly unfit to reign. All parties agreed that a regent must be appointed and that it could only be his heir apparent. If the regency was permanent and the Regent was given full regal powers, he would be expected to appoint a new Administration and it would certainly be Whig. The Whigs therefore – in defiance of their traditional demands for parliamentary limitation on sovereign power – demanded that the Prince of Wales be granted absolute authority and, in anticipation of carrying such a resolution in parliament – began speculative arguments about the distribution of portfolios.

The Duke of Devonshire, who had never even contemplated becoming a minister, was told that he could occupy any office which took his fancy. He replied that none did. Grey was put in his place by the promise that the best he could hope for was appointment as a junior Lord of the Treasury. All the plotting and planning was in vain. Pitt's resolution which proposed the creation of a regency with limited powers and life was supported in the House of Commons by 240 votes to 204. Blame for the defeat was shared between the two leading advocates of a permanent regency. Fox made a disastrous speech which forswore every Whig belief by denying parliament's right to impose limitations on the Regent's powers. Sheridan further alienated waverers with a threat that, once the Prince of Wales was given vice-regal powers, he would exact a terrible revenge on those who had attempted to deny them to him. The whole squalid episode was brought to a farcical end with the announcement, in February 1789, that the King had regained full health and would return to the throne.

Both Georgiana and the Prince of Wales himself had taken it for granted that the Whig day had dawned. On the day that parliament debated his regency, the Prince had waited to hear the result with the Duchess in Devonshire House. In anticipation of a triumph she had invented a 'Regency cap' which had a cockade of three feathers and bore the motto *Ich Dien*. The defeat of the Whigs subjected Georgiana to the fate of all flamboyant enthusiasts for lost causes. She was subjected to public ridicule. When she arrived at an assembly arranged by Lady Buckingham she was greeted with groans and hooting.[16] Georgiana refused to be intimidated. A month after the announcement of the King's recovery, a Queen's Drawing Room was arranged to give thanks for his deliverance. To exact revenge for Georgiana's impertinence in designing 'Regency caps', the women were instructed that their hats must be embellished with the slogan 'God Save the King'. The Whig ladies had no choice but to attend. They went bare-headed, with bad grace.

The *ménage à trois* had settled down into something approaching stability with the Duke of Devonshire, the Duchess and Lady Elizabeth Foster equally reluctant to risk what they saw as the benefits of the irregular relationship. The Duke still hoped for an heir. Lady Elizabeth had the material advantages, if not the status, of a duchess. Georgiana had what she saw as the incomparable benefit of Bess's friendship – a boon which she feared would be sacrificed if she refused to share her friend with her husband.

In the spring of 1789 the unusually extended family set off for France. The two legitimate Devonshire daughters could stay, without comment, in London with their grandmother, Lady Spencer. Charlotte Williams, the Duke's first illegitimate daughter, and his children by Lady Elizabeth (Caroline St Jules and Augustus Clifford) would have to travel with them. Georgiana had been temporarily disconcerted by the news that even Thomas Coutts had lost patience and was demanding both the repayment of her debts to him and a full confession to the Duke of her other liabilities. But she regained her spirits, and a brief respite from his harassment, by the invention of an ingenious scheme by which she bought more time. Two Coutts daughters were learning French in Paris. They could be provided with introductions to French society in return for a little more tolerance. Her brother lent her £500 and with that – and the continued belief that all her troubles would be ended when she gave birth to a son – she left England, confident that the waters of Spa would enable her to conceive again.

The party arrived in Paris just at the moment when France was changing the course of world history. The Third Estate had declared itself to be the National Assembly, announced that no taxes could be raised without its authority and, when it was locked out of its chamber, met in the indoor tennis court nearby. Georgiana loved the excitement of it all. 'The king made a speech to the *tiers*. After he left they all stayed and voted to annul everything he had said.'[17] During the lull which followed days of rioting they decided that it was safe to drive to Versailles. King Louis looked less agitated than Georgiana expected but Marie Antoinette was 'very much out of spirits'.[18] Back in Paris the Devonshires held a series of dinners, sumptuous enough in themselves to provide the sans-culottes with a justification for the revolution which was to come. During one soirée, Lafayette spoke up for the

National Assembly – no doubt expecting his Whig hosts to be as opposed to absolute monarchy in France as they were in England. But Georgiana – whose politics were less cerebral than social – told him, 'I am for the Court.'[19] On the way to Spa the Duke and Duchess heard the news that the Bastille had fallen.

The half-sisters – Charlotte and Caroline – remained in Paris, but the Devonshires received reassuring messages about their safety and health from the Duke of Dorset. His despatch from the British Embassy – dated July 14 1789 – reflected enthusiasm for the turmoil around him that suggested that he was more radical than Whig.

> The greatest revolution that we know anything of has been affected with, comparatively speaking – if the magnitude of the event is to be considered – the loss of very few lives. From this moment on we may consider France a free country, the king a very limited monarch and the nobility reduced to the level of the rest of the nation.[20]

It is unlikely that the Duke of Devonshire shared Dorset's pleasure at the demotion of the monarchy. But at Spa his always limited interest in politics was soon dispersed by the discovery of an impending event which was far more important to him than the fall of a monarchy. Georgiana was pregnant again.

The Duke immediately decided that the Duchess must not risk losing the baby on the bumpy ride home. His original intention was to remain with her, but events in England called him home. Duncannon had discovered that his wife, Harriet, was having an affair with Sheridan. It was Devonshire's duty, as head of the family, to return to England and mobilise the family campaign of threats and promises which eventually saved his sister-in-law from disgrace. So Georgiana and Bess stayed, without male protection, at Spa. On days when evening riots were anticipated, they made the gentle journey across the Franco-Belgian border and spent the night in peace.

The family was reunited in Brussels. When the Duke returned to the Low Countries, he brought with him Lady Spencer, Georgiana's two daughters and the Duncannons, who were not reconciled, but had been coerced into putting on a show of amity. While they all waited for the baby to be born, Georgiana tried – in some cases successfully – to borrow money. The Prince of Wales was subject to moral blackmail. His response to Georgiana's urgent request would be 'A great test and trial of [his] affection'[21] and, if his reply to her entreaties 'once more enclosed £300, tranquillity during [her] lying in would be secured'.[22] Cornelius Denne, the Duke's private banker, was prevailed upon to provide £5,000. Having learned nothing, Georgiana wagered most of Denne's loan on the Oaks and the Derby because 'the risk is so little and the gain might be so much'.[23] Her horses lost.

Georgiana was barely a month away from giving birth when the whole party was expelled from the Low Countries. As always she had voiced her opinions without much thought or inhibition and expressed her surprise at the expulsion with what she thought to be a witticism. 'You know I am a good Royalist in France. In Brussels I am a good Patriot.'[24] It was less the expression of not very profound sentiments that worried the authorities than the knowledge that the Devonshires were guilty of friendship with the Bourbons. Lafayette, an aristocrat who was popular with the Jacobins, promised them a safe conduct through France. After a traumatic beginning to their journey – the children were sickly and Georgiana had cystitis – they met, by chance, the Duc d'Ahrenberg who was on the point of fleeing from the country. He offered them the use of his house in Passy.

Exiled from the relative anonymity of Brussels, the motley group began to attract the wrong sort of attention. Some stories suggested that it was Bess not Georgiana who was pregnant and that, in the event of her giving birth to a boy, the child would be passed off as the Duke's heir as well as his son. There was also the suggestion that, if the Duke's wife, rather than his mistress, had been pregnant, she would have been attended by a more senior surgeon than Doctor Croft – a theory which was consistent with the social mores of the Georgian aristocracy but in contradiction to the suggestion that, whoever was the mother, a boy would immediately be declared the Marquis of Hartington. In fact Croft was the son of Doctor Denham, the Devonshires' regular obstetrician. In addition to being as well qualified as his father, he was young enough to travel across Europe. Lady Spencer did not intend to allow suspicion to grow into accepted wisdom. Elizabeth Foster was instructed to ride from Passy to Paris and show herself at the Opera. She was there on the night before the birth – according to Lord St Helens, in whose box she sat, looking 'as thin as a rake'.[25] After the baby was delivered, a dispute arose about how many witnesses attended the birth. According to one – almost certainly fraudulent – account, there were nine persons of repute willing to testify and two of them made written dispositions.[26] A message to the embassy which requested the presence of Lord Robert Fitzgerald was never delivered. But the Dowager Duchesse d'Ahrenberg was outside the bedroom door with Bess during the delivery.[27] Just before two o'clock on the morning of May 21 1790, the Duchess of Devonshire gave birth to a boy.

Back in London, the Whigs were sharply divided over the merits and morality of the French Revolution. Edmund Burke was irrevocably opposed. His *Reflections on the Revolution in France* denounced the notion of the rights of man as 'extravagant and presumptuous' and more likely to lead to chaos than the carefully circumscribed liberty which had been the inspiration of 1688. It was a thesis in which he believed with such passion that, a year after its publication, he interrupted a House of Commons debate on the constitution of Quebec to denounce supporters of the revolution in such strong terms that the Whigs were split for ever. Burke's *Reflections* were written in reply to a sermon preached by Richard Price, a Dissenting minister who applauded the French 'ardour for liberty'. Price was, by some standards, a moderate. The Reverend John Warner, in his time a confidant of the Devonshires, was dismissed as chaplain to the British Embassy in Paris after reacting to the escape of King Louis and Queen Marie Antoinette with the admission 'that they may be brought back before evening and guillotined before tomorrow morning are the two wishes next to my heart'.[28] With such a wide swathe of opinion among his supporters, it is not surprising that Fox prevaricated – first extolling the virtues of the new French constitution and then, after the royal family's flight to Varennes, announcing his support for the old monarchy. He was exhibiting the inevitable ambivalence of the aristocratic Whig, a belief in reform complicated by identification with the people who opposed it.

Georgiana suffered from a similar, though more trivial, conflict of emotions. She was attracted by the romance of revolution but her real sympathies – compassion mixed with class loyalty – were with the *émigrés* who flooded into London. They were regular guests at Devonshire House where, according to her children, 'shoals' of eager Frenchmen surrounded 'Monsieur'[29] – their name for the man who was to become Charles X of France. Chateaubriand was her most famous visitor. Her silliest escapade was the involvement with Fox and Sheridan (who should have known better) in a fantasy built around a plan to rescue Marie Antoinette and the Dauphin from the Jacobins. The idea was abandoned when a suitable Scarlet Pimpernel could not be found. In the process of her good work she acquired a new 'special friend', Madame de Coigny. For months the *émigrée* aristocrat was inseparable from the Duchess and Lady Elizabeth Foster.[30]

Nothing made Georgiana happy for long. A letter to her mother – composed as a rebuke to Lady Spencer's continued antagonism to Lady Elizabeth – revealed the self-doubt which was usually hidden under the bravado alongside the self-pity and self-deception. Bess was not, she insisted, the Duke's mistress. On the contrary, she had saved rather than imperilled the marriage which might have foundered on her own inadequacy. 'I am born to most complicated misery. I had run into errors which would have made any other man discard me . . . Her gentleness and affection sooth'd the bitterness which misfortune had brought upon me.'[31] The misfortunes were about to multiply. During her pregnancy, Georgiana had been able to use her delicate condition as a reason to postpone demands for a full statement of her finances. Her husband, she knew, would be particularly anxious not to imperil the birth of a healthy heir. So she asked him, 'Why do you force me, my dear Ca, to an avowal which agitates me beyond all measure and which is not necessary now? . . . I dread the opening of an explanation I should not dare encounter in my present situation.'[32] So the Duke had agreed not to cross-examine his wife until after the baby was born. Then he had extended the truce until the boy was weaned. Georgiana extended it again by insisting on feeding the baby herself – an eccentricity which had been attributed to sentimentality when she had suckled her daughter but was suspected of being no more than an excuse to postpone retribution when she chose to do the same for her son.

Inevitably the Duke lost patience and insisted on no more prevarication and renewed his demands for a full list of her creditors and the amount each one was owed. He got neither. Georgiana did admit debts of almost £62,000 – appreciably less than the true total – but she did not reveal that she had borrowed money from the Prince of Wales or that she owed Richard Arkwright £5,000. There was, however, the admission that she had suffered great losses on the Stock Exchange, as part of a syndicate that included Sheridan and her sister Harriet, and that – intolerable to a man of the Duke's character and upbringing – she owed more than £2,000 to the brother of one of their servants.

The Duke's sister Dorothy, by then the Duchess of Portland, urged him to banish his wife immediately and reinforced her advice with the threat that, whatever her brother decided, she would never speak to Georgiana again. Whether or not he was attracted by the idea of separation, he was still prevented from sending the Duchess into exile by the fear that, in the absence of his wife, Lady Elizabeth's presence in his household would become a public scandal. But he was growing increasingly attracted by the idea of finding a way of putting Georgiana in quarantine. Before he finally made up his mind another catastrophe added a new complication to the already fraught relationships within the family. Georgiana's sister, Harriet, suffered a stroke. The bronchial pneumonia which followed was said to be the result of the consequent paralysis and was assumed to be fatal. The Duke's reaction was not characteristic but it was decisive. Thoughts of separation were abandoned and financial recriminations were postponed. When – to general surprise – Harriet recovered some of her faculties, he hired a house in Bath for her convalescence. His wife and children, as well as Bess, went with her.

Georgiana was pregnant again when she left for the West Country. Her husband was not the father. During the months which immediately followed the return from France, her relationship with Charles Grey had begun to shock even the notoriously louche Devonshire House Circle. He had become so reckless that he followed her to Bath and Georgiana was so infatuated that she encouraged him to visit her – without either excuse or subterfuge – at all times of night and day. Fanny Burney met Georgiana outside the Pump Room and was struck by her high spirits. Whether they were the result of Grey's gallant attention or, the novelist later believed, joy at the discovery that she was bearing his child, must remain in doubt. But she was certainly sufficiently besotted to regard her pregnancy as a triumph rather than a potential disaster. Nevertheless, she wanted to keep the news from her husband for as long as possible. By October her condition was so obvious that, when her mother visited Bath, the truth could not be denied. At Lady Spencer's insistence Grey was told to keep well away until something – no one was sure what – was decided. In order to gain time, Georgiana suggested that, instead of returning home, Harriet should spend some weeks in the warmth of Cornwall and that she should accompany her. Someone – possibly his mother-in-law – told the Duke of the real reason for the proposal. He drove at once to Bath where he confronted his wife with a ferocity that intimidated even the naturally resilient Lady Elizabeth. Then he turned on her for being a party to the deception.

The Cavendish family – certain that their advice had been vindicated and convinced that Georgiana was beyond redemption – attempted, once more, to persuade the Duke to exile his wife. For a while he was tempted to agree. But although the problem of an heir had been solved, there remained two insuperable obstacles to separation. In the prolonged or permanent absence of Georgiana, Bess's position at Chatsworth would become intolerable. And – despite his own infidelity and detached relationship with his wife – a combination of jealousy and pride made him profoundly reluctant publicly to admit that he was a cuckold. He conveyed his final decision to Harriet in a letter which confirmed his concern for his own reputation. 'If you wish to save your sister and me from the most unpleasant disclosure, break off your going to Penzance and go abroad immediately.'[33] The ultimatum encompassed both the sisters. Georgiana and Harriet had to leave the country at once and stay abroad until the baby was born. The Duchess was also required to agree never to see Charles Grey again and to give up the baby for adoption within days of its birth. The alternative was divorce and a threat which he hoped would force Georgiana into accepting his terms – the permanent denial of access to her legitimate children. Georgiana agreed, consoling herself with the not entirely accurate thought that she had given up the man she loved so that she could bring up her son and daughters.

The Duchess of Devonshire left for Montpellier, accompanied by the usual retinue of women. But, after a few weeks' stay, it was thought that warmer weather was necessary for Harriet's health and most of the party travelled on to Nice. Only Elizabeth and her six-year-old daughter, Caroline St Jules, remained with Georgiana. They were there when the baby was born in late January 1791. A few days earlier, perhaps fearing death in childbirth, she had written letters to each of her other children. They were all dramatic in tone. Little Lord Hartington received a particularly theatrical farewell.

> As soon as you are old enough to understand this letter it will be given to you; it contains the only present I can make you – my blessing written in my own blood. The book that will also be given you is a memorandum of me you must ever keep. Alas I am gone before you could know me, but I lov'd you. I nursed you nine months to my breast . . . For my sake, observe my last wishes.

A litany of family obligations followed. The Duke had to be obeyed, the sisters treated with generosity and the cousins with kindness. The letter ended with what amounted to advice about how to achieve perfection. 'Make piety your chief study, never despise religion, never break your word, never betray a secret, never tell a lie.'[34]

The blood was barely dry on the paper when Georgiana gave birth to a daughter. She was called Eliza Courtney – a name chosen, as was the habit of the time when bastards were baptised, to reflect the relationship with one of the parents. Georgiana's maternal grandmother, a Poyntz, was vaguely related to the Courtneys. The baby was immediately farmed out to a wet-nurse and, when she was judged to be strong enough to travel, was sent back to England and delivered to Charles Grey's parents at Falloden. They brought her up to regard her father as her brother. Georgiana was told by the Duke that she must, on pain of permanent separation, remain abroad until he invited her back home.

Georgiana's periodic concern about her children's welfare was increased by the news that their father ignored them. They lived in Devonshire House under the supervision of Selina Trimmer, their nurse, whose relationship with their mother had been prejudiced by her habit of reporting Georgiana's behaviour to the Duke. Bess remained Georgiana's companion and comfort, although she feared that the Duke's apparent indifference to their whereabouts hid a desire for her to return which he was too proud to express but which would turn into resentment that she had failed to read his mind. The Duke, who normally noticed neither praise nor blame, condescended to express surprise that some of the 'ton' blamed him for his wife's wayward behaviour. One member went as far as to say that the only man in London who was not in love with her was her husband.

As soon as Grey's child was despatched to its grandparents Georgiana and Elizabeth set off for Aix-en-Provence, where they attempted – without success – to persuade the dying Comte St Jules formally to adopt Bess's daughter Caroline. During the journey, Elizabeth received a message from the Duke that, because of her prolonged absence, her annual allowance was in jeopardy. Nevertheless she agreed to accompany Georgiana to Nice to join Harriet and Lady Spencer – adding a new bizarre dimension to the already convoluted relationship by rejecting her lover's company in favour of his wife's. Whether or not the two women were in a lesbian partnership, they lived together in a permanent state of high emotion.

On the way to Nice, the party abandoned their coach and travelled on horseback rather than advertise their wealth to bandits who terrorised the road. Another hazard was waiting for them on their arrival. Mary Graham had taken up residence in the city, hoping that the climate would cure her consumption. There was a brief emotional tear-stained reunion before the Devonshire party moved on to Lake Geneva where they stayed with Edward Gibbon and spent some weeks disturbing his scholarly peace with parties, to which they invited guests of their own choice, and noisy games in which the children took part without restraint. They were still in Switzerland when they heard that Louis XVI had been executed. Harriet, once more in search of healing sun, left for Italy. Georgiana and Elizabeth remained behind in what they claimed was the belief – in truth, it was no more than a hope – that the Duke's permission for his wife to return home was imminent. By the time they accepted that there was nothing to gain by waiting for Georgiana's recall, fighting in the Savoy forced them to cross the Alps through the snow-covered Saint Bernard Pass. The whole party was reunited in Naples where they were joined by Lord Duncannon,

Harriet's husband, who – much to his mother-in-law's surprise – treated his wife with respect if not affection.

Duncannon did not stay for long. In March 1793 the Earl of Bessborough died and Duncannon inherited the title. The new Earl thought it necessary to return home, leaving his wife and her companions to enjoy the pleasures provided by the Court of King Ferdinand and Queen Maria Carolina, the sister of Marie Antoinette. Hospitality was provided by Sir William and Lady Hamilton who had yet to welcome Horatio Nelson into their lives. Georgiana began to learn Italian and attended meetings at which visiting English scientists discussed the eruptions of Vesuvius.

Georgiana enjoyed the febrile pleasures of Neapolitan society. But in May 1793, she received the Duke's letter, calling her home, with real delight and almost reprehensible gratitude towards the husband who had exiled her – even though she knew that Thomas Coutts was waiting for her with demands that his loans be repaid. She told her daughter, 'Little Georgiana', that her 'dear, dearest Papa' had told her to 'return in the middle of the summer' and added, 'God of heaven bless him for his kindness to me.'[35] The journey back to England, like Georgiana's whole life, stumbled along from excitement to emergency. Once again Harriet was too ill to travel. The Duchess and Lady Elizabeth arrived at Ostend shortly after the Duke of York – denied reinforcements by the government's sloth in ordering the despatch and payment of already recruited Prussian mercenaries – was defeated at Tourcoing by the French revolutionary army. The evacuation of British civilians had just begun and no boat was available for hire. So it seemed that the crossing to England would have to be delayed. But, once again, the aristocratic connection proved its worth. By chance they met Lord Wicklow who put his 'pleasure boat' at their disposal and they sailed, in state, back home to debts and the Duke.

The Duke and the Devonshire children were waiting on the quay at Dartford. Much to Georgiana's dramatically demonstrated distress, her son – the Marquis of Hartington, known affectionately as Hart – did not recognise her. Not quite sure by whom he was being so fondly embraced, he rejected his mother's affectionate advances. It was months before he would allow her to touch him. Georgiana herself did not find it easy to adjust to what passed for normality in the Devonshire household and stayed indoors for days. London renewed memories of happy days which would never return. She was still in love with Charles Grey, but determined to keep her promise not to see him, and the Whigs – hopelessly divided over the French Revolution – seemed unlikely, ever again, to think of her as their irresistible public face. Fox, once her hero, had reluctantly given his support to Sheridan's Association of Friends of the People, a movement which espoused the new radicalism of Tom Paine, and he had retreated – with Mrs Armistead, his mistress – to St Anne's Hill. The Prince of Wales no longer visited Devonshire House. So Georgiana had lost all claim to be even a political hostess and confidante of the powerful. Encouraged by Henry Cavendish – who was said, despite his misogyny, to be 'delighted with her'[36] – she ignored her husband's prohibition and turned to the study of science in general and geology in particular. Whether or not – had life maintained its unexciting equilibrium – the new interests would have become a permanent enthusiasm is highly doubtful. But in the summer of 1794 the precarious balance was disturbed by the first of new upheavals from which, it seemed, no recovery was possible.

The news that Charles Grey was engaged to be married should not have come as a shock to Georgiana. It was inconceivable that an up-and-coming, highly personable politician would remain single for long. But Georgiana's pain was certainly increased by the shock of reading the announcement in the newspapers and was probably intensified by the knowledge that her sister, now the Countess of Bessborough and greatly recovered from her stroke, had acquired a twenty-year-old lover. Grey's marriage to Mary Ponsonby came so quickly after the engagement that it increased the original pain rather than created a new agony. But soon physical suffering was to be added to emotional trauma. Georgiana, who had for years suffered from head pains, virtually lost the sight of her right eye. In the hope that proper vision could be saved, the Senior Surgeon Extraordinary to the King removed the ulcer which protruded from beneath her eyelid. The operation was excruciatingly painful but only a partial success. Some sight was restored but her right eye drooped in a most unattractive way. Then life changed again.

John Foster died. So, much to Elizabeth's delight, her sons were free to join her – a prospect that Georgiana was happy to facilitate. But Bess's prospects were totally changed by the death of the Duchess of Richmond – wife of her occasional lover. That meant that she had at least a chance of becoming a real, rather than a surrogate, duchess. It also put the long-established *ménage à trois* at risk. Even the Duke of Devonshire's usually phlegmatic progress through his turbulent family life was suddenly disturbed. Lord John Cavendish – his father figure and one of the few people for whom he really cared – died. Grief was compounded by disappointment when Georgiana miscarried yet again – confounding the hope of a second son to safeguard the inheritance. And private chaos was matched by political crisis. The French were winning the war in Europe and Ireland was on the verge of civil war. Ireland was one of the few political subjects which engaged the Duke's interest. He owned most of County Waterford and had an obvious vested interest in putting down Irish rebellion. Despite – or perhaps because of – that, he once more deviated from the usual pattern of Cavendish conduct. He argued for the rehabilitation of Catholics in British society.

There were three political factions in Ireland, none of them sufficiently cohesive to be called a party, each of them associated with a religious denomination and all of them antagonistic to the London government. The Catholics, with every justification, regarded themselves as a persecuted majority. The Presbyterians, although not subject to such draconian penalties, were also denied a political role. And even the Episcopalians resented English domination of Irish affairs. Ireland's real problem was poverty and its causes economic. But the French Revolution inspired Irishmen of every stripe to cry liberty. The United Irishmen openly advocated revolt. Henry Gratton – the most distinguished of Dublin's politicians – phrased his hopes for the future in language more appropriate in France than Ireland. 'Let the kingly power which forms one estate of our constitution continue . . . But let it be, as by the principles and laws of this country it should be, one estate only.'[37] When the French made a landing at Fishguard on the South Wales coast, its defeat by the loyal Pembrokeshire militia did nothing to extinguish the fear that, had an earlier attempt to land at Bantry Bay not been frustrated by the weather, the local population would have risen up in its support.

Georgiana – whose enthusiasm for revolution and reform had been overlaid by concern for the Devonshire finances – told her daughter, 'If any misfortune should happen in Ireland, we should be very reduced in our circumstances.'[38] However, although she had lost her political influence, she had not lost her political interest. So she began to offer unsolicited advice to her brother, Earl Spencer, the First Lord of the Admiralty in Pitt's Government. When it seemed that his portfolio was in danger, following the mutiny of the fleet at Spithead and the Nore, she persuaded her husband to make a rare visit to the Lords and vote in his defence. Spencer, fearful that he would be ridiculed for calling on his sister for support, was furious. His sister responded with the defence which she so often employed when caught out in an indiscretion. She lied. Spencer knew her well enough to realise that she would not have been content, as she claimed, with doing no more than inform her husband that malign forces were plotting to make Admiral Lord Hood the First Lord.

Spencer's anger did not deter Georgiana from continuing to offer him advice. It included the complaint that he was too easily influenced by other people's views. There was a moment when she believed that she had converted him to her judgement about how the Irish could be pacified and that he, in turn, had converted the whole Administration. 'I believe the Government is coming over to the opinion of the Duke of D, and indeed all reasonable people, about emancipation to the Catholics.'[39] The expression of any political opinion by the Duke always came as a surprise. But, even after the passage of the Catholic Relief Act had given Papists the vote, his advocacy of full emancipation – the call coming from the head of a family whose rank and reputation were built on championing the Protestant cause – must have generated general astonishment. But it was a reform in which he undoubtedly believed. Six months later he spoke in the House of Lords in favour of a motion which called for an inquiry into the governance of Ireland. His speech,* brief because he was nervous, included the Duke's prescription for peace – the replacement of coercion with conciliation.

Domestically, little had changed for Georgiana. She was still being pursued by her creditors and begging the Duke to meet her debts while deceiving him about their full extent. Despite her drooping eye – a deformity that made her consider wearing a mask – Sir Philip Francis, a married Whig politician who had made a fortune in India, announced that he was in love with her. Their relationship never progressed beyond an emotional correspondence about what he regarded as her infatuation with Fox – still boycotting politics and parliament at St Anne's Hill. When news of Nelson's victory in the Battle of the Nile reached Britain, Georgiana told her mother that she and her friends intended to wear laurels on their hats on the day of official rejoicing.[40] With the Duchess, celebrations always required her to put something exotic on her head. And her rejoicings never lasted for long before they were overtaken by despair.

It seems unlikely – whatever her intention – that Georgiana's spirits were lifted for long by the friendship she carefully courted with Mary Grey after the whole family were invited to Devonshire House. Mary, unaware of Georgiana's previous relationship with her husband, was flattered by the affection that the Duchess showed towards the Grey children. Georgiana was anxious, though ambivalent, about Elizabeth Foster's future. The Duke of Richmond continued to talk of marriage but never proposed. Georgiana wanted Bess's hopes to be realised but

---

* It was the one speech he made in the thirty years which followed his maiden speech.

feared to lose her from the Devonshire household. The occupations to which she turned for distraction were not pursued with complete success. Her ambitious plan to renovate Chiswick in a way that restored its original Palladian design came to not much more than planting honeysuckle and roses. Excursions into drama and literature were more rewarding. She wrote a song for inclusion in Sheridan's *Pizarro*, a play which was so successful that it briefly relieved the author of the debts he had incurred in an attempt to build a new theatre to replace Drury Lane. An autobiographical poem, *The Passage of the Mountain of St Gothard*, followed. Its heroine made the perilous journey in the hope of being reunited with her children. Initially, it was privately printed for circulation to friends, but a copy appeared in the public prints. It was received with acclamation until Samuel Taylor Coleridge published a parody which ended 'O Lady nursed in pomp and pleasure / Where did you learn this heroic measure.' Even then it retained enough public esteem to be published in French, Italian and German.

Georgiana rarely triumphed over adversity. But she had the capacity to put her troubles behind her and enjoy, with exaggerated gratitude, the joys which life provided. When the Prince of Wales chose once more to cultivate Whig society, she and her daughters accompanied him to the Haymarket Theatre. Her confidence briefly restored, she offered Lady Spencer[41] her considered view on the strategic failings of the younger Pitt's war effort. He should, she said, have fought less on land and more at sea. A letter to Sir Philip Francis explained – apparently in seriousness – how much she wished she had been born a man so that her 'talents', as well as her hopes, could have been united with Fox's genius in the government of England.

However successful Georgiana might have been in management of public affairs, she was clearly incapable of managing her private life with either discretion or discipline. As soon as old debts were discharged by generous friends or her exasperated husband, new ones were incurred. When her mother told her 'the last 27 years has repeatedly given me reason to fear that you are incorrigible',[42] she was describing, as a possibility, what all her circle knew to be a certainty. Georgiana's only excuse was that almost all the 'ton' behaved with a similar irresponsibility. At the turn of the century, both her brother, George Spencer, and her sister, Harriet Bessborough, were declared bankrupt just as Harriet was about to give birth. The father of the child was Leveson Gower. The Duke of Devonshire, Lord Frederick Cavendish and Lord Fitzwilliam offered to subscribe to a trust fund which would manage – that is to say liquidate – the three siblings' debts. Harriet and Georgiana accepted with good grace though no real intention of reducing their expenditure. Lord Spencer rejected the scheme as an indignity. Georgiana was left to stumble on with the help of a £6,000 loan from the Duke of Bedford.

Bedford, although thirty-five, was considered a possible husband for the Devonshires' sixteen-year-old daughter, Georgiana – 'Little G'. The other candidate was the twenty-seven-year-old George Howard, the future Earl of Carlisle. Earlier generations of Devonshires would have chosen the Duke and his money. Georgiana – there is no evidence that her daughter was consulted – preferred and argued successfully for Howard. The Duchess's visit to London to buy the young bride's trousseau required Lady Elizabeth to assure the Duke of Richmond that, although she would be alone with Devonshire at Chatsworth, no impropriety would occur. It also enabled Georgiana to take advice from Doctor Erasmus Darwin about the hope of restoring some of the sight to her right eye. He prescribed electric shocks – electricity being the scientific preoccupation of the time. The electrodes, attached to her temples, were painful though ineffective. But comfort, of the most effective sort, was at hand. Fox was about to end his voluntary exile from politics. And Georgiana had no doubt that, if he regained his place at the centre of the Whig firmament, she would again shine in his reflected glory.

In November 1799 – the year of Little G's betrothal – Napoleon Bonaparte had returned from Egypt and declared himself First Consul. Pitt's tactic of attacking the French on several fronts at once had, as Georgiana warned, not brought victory. But England's superior sea power had, as she predicted, convinced France that, until its navy could challenge the allies' at sea, it could not win the war. So in December, Napoleon sued for peace. Pitt did not trust him. 'If peace affords no prospect of security: if it threatens all the evils we have been struggling to avert . . . then I say it is prudent for us not to negotiate at the present moment.'[43] Fox did not agree and divided the House of Commons. Pitt won the vote by 265 votes to 64. For a year his dominance of parliament was unchallenged and unchallengeable. Then, convinced that rebellion in Ireland could be prevented only by full Catholic emancipation, Pitt told his cabinet that he intended to introduce the necessary legislation. Half a dozen of his ministers – including Portland, the Duke of Devonshire's kinsman – objected. One of them reported Pitt's intention to the King who denounced the initiative as 'the most Jacobinical thing [he] ever heard of' and promised that 'any man who proposes any such measure' would become his 'personal enemy'.[44] Pitt resigned and Addington, the Tory Prime Minister, cobbled together a new (mostly Tory) administration. The Prince of Wales himself told Georgiana the news. In the fragmentation and realignment which followed, Devonshire House again became the meeting place for fashionable Whigs. One of the consequences of the change of fortune was regular visits by Charles Grey.

Georgiana was breaking her promise, made to the Duke, never to see Grey again. But she insisted that their renewed relationship was wholly innocent and entirely political. Her claim was slightly undermined by the parallel claim that nobody knew that they ever met.[45] But, if she was a woman with a guilty secret to hide and they were lovers again, she was sharing Grey with Hecca, Richard Sheridan's second wife. Sexual adventures were always a feature of the 'circle' to which only the betrayed wives and husbands took exception. But political perfidy was taken more seriously. Sheridan was suspected of wanting to join the Addington coalition. Georgiana, who always clung to the illusion of power, boasted that she had prevented him from persuading the Prince of Wales to give the new political alliance his blessing. Addington, more trustful of Napoleon than Pitt had ever been, signed the Treaty of Amiens and was wildly popular until French perfidy was exposed.

Georgiana was not old even by the standards of her time. But – despite the reinvigoration that a renewed, albeit vicarious, political role stimulated – she was growing tired. When, at last, she began to make the full list of all her debts that Coutts required before he would consider a rescue operation, she told the banker that, when she died, the inventory was to be sent to her husband for payment with the plea that her 'children's welfare be taken into consideration'.[46] Thoughts about death led her to religion. On Christmas Day 1801 she wrote to her recently acquired spiritual adviser what amounted to a barely coherent, but highly qualified, admission of a lifetime's guilt. 'I shrink from the task before me – the task of viewing myself with the Eye of severe Truth – of ever having made engagements upon the slight grounds of hope in fear of hurting others . . .'[47] The task was made more difficult by a temporary parting from Elizabeth.

The Duke of Richmond had announced that he did not intend to remarry and Georgiana undoubtedly shared the pain of Elizabeth's rejection. It is impossible, 200 years on, to understand the true nature of the two women's complicated relationship. But there is no doubt that – in one way or another – they had a protective love for each other. Bess's decision to hide her humiliation in France left Georgiana without the support which, although not always as freely given as she supposed, was essential to her well-being. Georgiana was left in Derbyshire to nurse the Duke through a bad attack of gout – a task that she performed with some reluctance but which was, surprisingly, reciprocated when she was incapacitated by a gallstone.

Just before Georgiana collapsed, she wrote to Fox – recently married to Mrs Armistead – urging him to accept a plan that had been put in her mind by George Canning and endorsed by the Prince of Wales. Pitt and Fox should work together in the national interest. When Addington's administration fell in April 1804, Pitt spoke to the King about including Fox in the new government. Perhaps he welcomed the royal veto. He certainly agreed to go ahead without Fox. For once the Whigs, from whom Pitt was increasingly detached, were solid. Each faction – Foxites, Addingtonians, Grevillites and the Prince of Wales's coterie – all resisted Pitt's blandishments. Georgiana's plan failed. But a Gillray cartoon, *L'Assemblée National*, portrayed her at the heart of a seething mass of Whigs. She was once more the centre of Whig attention. Frail though she was, that sustained her for the next two years.

It was not only Georgiana whose health was deteriorating. The King's life was assumed to be drawing, far from peaceably, to its close and it was taken for granted that when the Prince of Wales became George IV he would take a terrible revenge on those ministers who had sided with his father against him. Pitt sought to forestall his summary ejection from office by first attempting to reconcile father and son and then establishing a new relationship with the Prince. The Whigs, basing their prediction on what they knew of the Prince's character, assumed that, if Pitt's offer contained anything to his advantage, he would betray his old friends. After an agonised discussion, they agreed that Georgiana should write to him and explain that Pitt only wanted a swift rapprochement because he knew that the day was fast approaching when the Prince would inherit the power to appoint his own ministers. The Prince took the point and agreed to arrange a meeting at which he, and Fox, would discuss the political prospect with the King. Georgiana helped Fox to rehearse his lines.

The reconciliation meeting was not a success. George III was in one of his manic phases and listened to neither his son nor Fox. But the Prince decided that he had nothing to gain by perfidy. So Pitt's hope of ingratiating himself with the heir apparent was confounded. Fox told Grey that the opposition *seemed* restored to robust health. His letter ended with a note which might have indicated no more than his gratitude for the way in which Georgiana had brokered the agreement with the Prince. Or it may have been added in the sadly mistaken belief that Grey still harboured feelings of regret. 'You will be glad to hear that the D– of D– is doing something kind and handsome about the D–s debts.'[48] And so it proved. After much anxious thought, Georgiana told the Duke almost the truth about the size of her debts. He had expected them to total about £6,000. They amounted – even on a conservative estimate – to over £50,000. It took the Duke so long to decide how to react that, by the time he had made up his mind, the figure had increased by £800 – the amount that his wife had borrowed from the Prince of Wales to see her through her husband's deliberations. But in the end, the Duke agreed to double her annual allowance from £1,000 to £2,000 and employ a firm of solicitors to plan the gradual liquidation of her total debt.

A life divided between elation and anxiety was beginning to take its toll. An attack of jaundice accompanied by severe stomach pains was attributed to more gallstones. The right eye continued to deteriorate and began to disfigure half of her face. There were still balls to be organised and soirées to host, but although the enthusiasm remained the energy was running out. Pitt's popularity had risen to new heights after Nelson's victory at Trafalgar on October 21 1805 guaranteed England safety from invasion, but on January 23 1806 – twenty-five years to the day after he had entered the House of Commons at the age of twenty-one – he died, muttering his anxiety about the country's future. Georgiana's valediction was one of her rare expeditions into political analysis. Pitt, she told her son, 'came into place against the constitution and supported himself in place by exercising the power of the throne'.[49] Despite his talents – the greatest of which, she wrote, was his eloquence – that denial of the rights of parliament made him anathema to Whigs.

Pitt's death left King George with no choice but to send for Grenville and Fox and accept the creation of what came to be called, with dubious justification, the Ministry of All the Talents. Georgiana enjoyed the return to power and popularity for barely two months. On March 26 1806, after another attack of jaundice and several days of agonising but fruitless treatment, she was convulsed with a seizure which lasted for most of the night. Four days later – the abscess on her liver painful beyond endurance – she died in her sister's arms. The Duke was said to have 'shown more feeling than anyone thought possible',[50] Fox wept without inhibition and the Prince of Wales was incoherent with grief. Crowds congregated outside the gates of Devonshire House waiting to witness what amounted to a lying-in-state.

Some time during her final attack of jaundice, Georgiana had written the last of her frequent valedictory letters to her son and eldest daughter. She had congratulated Hart on inheriting all her 'fervours and cheerfulness' but must also urge him to avoid the 'follies which marked, with giddiness, [her] introduction . . . into the vortex of dissipation'.[51] To her daughter Georgiana, she expressed 'most unfeigned repentance for many errors' and enjoined her 'to be exact about expenses' and 'never to run into debt about the most trifling sum'.[52] The Duchess of Devonshire died, as she had lived, trying to borrow money. Her last letter was written to her mother. It solicited a banker's draft of £100.

Lady Elizabeth Foster was left with the melancholy duty of clearing up the Duchess's affairs. 'Four Gentlemen' had been asked by the Duke to determine what his late wife owed to whom. But the debt to Richard Arkwright was beyond question. So Lady Elizabeth wrote him a holding letter. 'The Duke desires that I should write to you to say that he received your letter and he hopes to have it in his power to settle everything with you. I found the letter & the statement of debt among the D's papers.'[53] Arkwright had been more fortunate than he realised; £4,396 of his £7,300 debt (including interest) had been paid. The Four Gentlemen calculated that, on her death, the Duchess's total indebtedness was £109,135 17s 5d.

That Georgiana, Duchess of Devonshire fascinated the society in which she moved is not in doubt. The causes of that fascination are more difficult to describe. It was possibly her eager – almost childlike – energy that made her most attractive to the men and women who shared her enthusiasms. She certainly worked hard at becoming popular. 'Networking' was not a word which came into popular use until 200 years after she was dead. But it was a practice that she adopted with great success. In consequence she can be described in language which, although anachronistic, is wholly accurate. Georgiana was a celebrity who was famous for being famous. Her reputation has been immensely and irrationally improved by accounts of her husband's failings. The Fifth Duke of Devonshire was undoubtedly an insensitive and autocratic brute. That may have made his wife a martyr. But she was not a saint. She lied. She cheated. She neglected her children and she exploited her friends – sins which history has suggested that her vivacious personality absolved.

CHAPTER 19

A Great Deal to Spend

Whatever the Fifth Duke of Devonshire thought of his children – and he thought of them very rarely – he kept to himself. His wife on the other hand – being emotionally incontinent – spilled out her opinions in letter after letter. By the time of her mother's death, Little G was – as measured by the unexacting standards of her time and class – happily married and, at the age of twenty-two, was the mother of three children. Her sister Harriet (known to her mother as Harryo) married Leveson Gower – after some hesitation on his part, but surprisingly little on hers. Lord Granville, as Leveson Gower had become, was her Aunt Harriet's lover and father of two of her aunt's children. The 'good match' dispelled Georgiana's fears that her second daughter was too fat to be a social success. The Duke, who was certainly unconcerned by his new son-in-law's romantic history, gave Harryo a dowry of £10,000. Its limited size confirmed the true recipient of the little affection of which he was capable. Caroline St Jules, his daughter by Lady Elizabeth Foster, received £30,000.

It was William (known to his mother as Hart), the son and heir, who caused Georgiana most concern. On her return from exile she had written to Lady Spencer, 'Hartington is very pretty but very cruel to me. He will not look at me or speak to me.'[1] Towards the end of her life, his attitude, and perhaps his feelings, began to change enough for him to welcome and encourage his mother's habit of sending him a political commentary, written in the form of a journal and entitled, by its author, 'A Secret History of the Times'. But whether or not he ever felt a real affection for his mother, there is no doubt that his strange upbringing – for which she bore a major responsibility – scarred him for life. The partial deafness was congenital. But the obsessive reserve was the result of a childhood spent in the lonely company of a governess in a house in which the atmosphere was heavy with guilt, deceit, fear and intrigue.

After Georgiana's death, Lady Elizabeth Foster, motivated by both compassion and self-interest, made herself indispensable to the family, first by nursing Hart through an unidentified illness and then taking charge of Chiswick House when Fox made it his home as he slowly died of dropsy. Few people in the Cavendish circle doubted what the result of her devotion would be. But it took the Duke three years to make up his mind that he wanted to regularise their union. Then Bess plighted her troth in unconventional, not to say rationally incomprehensible, language. It was, she insisted, her 'severe duty to be the Duchess of Devonshire'.[2] Whether or not the Duke shared that view, or even understood what Bess was talking about, he accepted the proposal. They were married in October 1809. The three Cavendish children were horrified. At the time of the wedding, Hart invariably referred to his stepmother as 'the crocodile'.

Long before then, a characteristic which defined and determined his personal relationships had been established by his boyhood at Chatsworth. Those early years had not encouraged the notion that love – at least of the marital variety – conquers all. The result was the acquisition of one of his mother's most enigmatic qualities. Georgiana needed to strike up emotional, indeed dependent, relationships with persons of her own sex. Hart, the Sixth Duke of Devonshire – the Bachelor Duke as he came to be called – needed to do the same.

Hart – Marquis of Hartington from birth – had been brought up under the influence of women, all of whom (unlike his father) chose not to conceal their feelings. As well as his mother and Elizabeth Foster, Chatsworth was home to Caroline St Jules, the issue of the Duke's irregular union with Elizabeth Foster, and the two legitimate Cavendish daughters. Georgiana ('Little G', who became the Countess of Carlisle) and Harryo (the future Countess Granville) were respectively seven and five years older than their brother. And the female influence on his early years was increased by the appointment of a governess, Miss Selina Trimmer.* His sisters felt and expressed an admiration for their brother which lasted through the years. 'How happy you are', wrote Harriet, 'in the power of being such a blessing to those about you . . . Believe Hart you are a blessing to us all.'[3] The boys on the margins of the family might, had they been his early companions, have changed some of his attitudes to life. But Augustus Clifford – his natural half-brother who was occasionally admitted to Chatsworth as the orphan son of one of the Duke's close friends – was sent off to sea as a fourteen-year-old midshipman. And Elizabeth's sons – Frederick and Augustus Foster – were first forbidden, by their father, to visit their mother and then, when the Duke died, were found to have acquired

---

* Among her qualifications was a distinguished lineage. Her mother was the author of *Sacred History Selected from the Scriptures with Anecdotes and Reflections Adapted for the Comprehension of Young Persons.*

such wild Irish characters that they did not suit Chatsworth and Chatsworth did not suit them.

At the age of eight Hart entered Harrow. That was a break in family tradition. The Devonshires were, and remain, an Eton family. George Gordon, Lord Byron – two years his senior but, like him, a member of the school's Whig Club – described Hart as possessing a 'soft, milky disposition', which made him 'insensible of ill-treatment'. Byron also claimed that he exhibited 'a happy apathy which defies deeper emotions'.⁴ Whether that judgement was made in praise or censure, the implication of delicacy proved justified. After a year Hart was taken ill – almost certainly with some sort of nervous disorder – and Harrow was abandoned in favour of the Reverend Smith, a 'crammer' who dispensed education in Woodnesborough, Kent. It was at that establishment that he met John Russell Tavistock, who was to become the Duke of Bedford and a lifelong friend. In the years ahead, they regularly consulted and consoled each other about the delicate state of their finances and the absolute necessity of spending money, which they did not possess, on rebuilding their houses and redesigning their gardens.

It was to Tavistock that Hart made the almost certainly fraudulent claim that he preferred women's company to men's. One of the few incidents in his life which supported that assertion was the hysteria with which, at the age of fifteen, he greeted the news that his cousin, Lady Caroline Ponsonby, had become engaged to William Lamb. He was said to have claimed that he 'looked upon her as his wife' and 'gone into violent hysterics' which lasted so long that Doctor Farquhar, the family physician, was called to sedate and calm him.⁵ The episode was altogether out of character. Normally Hart showed no emotion other than despondency and dissatisfaction. At his mother's funeral, the Fifth Duke – who had been neither a faithful nor an affectionate husband – was near to collapse. Hart, her loving son, exhibited neither grief nor regret.

Hart came of age on May 21 1811 and celebrated his majority with a suitably lavish ball at Devonshire House – during which, according to gossip, he was clearly smitten by Charlotte Campbell, the daughter of Lord Lucan. Nothing further was heard of the supposed infatuation. But Hart was, almost certainly, the most eligible bachelor in England. So it was taken for granted that it would not be long before he found a suitable wife. Two months after his twenty-first birthday, the death of his father made title and riches become his by right rather than in anticipation. The Fifth Duke of Devonshire left his son property even more extensive than that which he had inherited. To Chatsworth House and Hardwick Hall, Bolton Abbey in the West Riding of Yorkshire and Londesborough Hall in the East, Lismore Castle in County Waterford, Devonshire House and Chiswick House he had added land in Huntingdon, Nottinghamshire and Cumberland, and in or near to Buxton, Hartington and Chesterfield in Derbyshire, and an additional new property in Ireland.

At first Hart seemed to lack the Devonshires' contempt for financial prudence. At the age of seven he had written home with the suggestion that if the ownership of a watch made him liable to tax, the demands of the exchequer should be met by his father. But the financial caution which seems to have been a brief feature of his childhood did not survive adolescence. Since he was encouraged in his extravagance, that is hardly surprising. In his *Handbook to Chatsworth*, he expresses his gratitude for his father's 'most generous and noble feelings'. Mindless profligacy would have been a better description of the Fifth Duke's attitude to money in general and his son's extravagance in particular. One anecdote illustrates his attitude. John Heaton, the old and crabbed auditor, was said to have told Hart's father, 'My Lord Duke, I am sorry to inform your Grace that Lord Hartington appears disposed to spend a great deal of money.' And the Duke was said to have replied, 'So much the better, Mr Heaton; he will have a great deal to spend.'

Throughout Hart's life there were brief periods of enforced economy when he was obliged to take the dramatic action which was the only alternative to bankruptcy and disgrace. But as soon as the sale of land had manoeuvred his affairs into temporary solvency, he returned to his profligate ways. The diary that he began to keep on Sunday August 26 1821 – ostensibly because he was 'sure to forget obligations and things which are expected of me from others' – records that in four years his 'debts increased by £20,000'. The rest of the entry explains why. He had spent £32,000 on his current enthusiasm – renovating and rebuilding. The diary then becomes specific if not precise – '10,000 laid out on D[evonshire] house. 15,000 at least on work already done. 7,000 at a guess for my purchase of marble.'[6]

Extravagance rarely bought him lasting contentment. He was the most restless of all the dukes of Devonshire. Towards the end of his life, he was plagued by guilt and remorse – particularly for the self-indulgence that he never made a serious attempt to overcome. In his later years he found some comfort in an evangelical faith which alarmed his friends and family even more than it comforted him. But he never ceased to express regret about the bachelor status which, had he wished, he could easily have ended by marrying any one of the rich and eligible women who – as well as attracted by his undoubted charm – would have gladly shared his wealth and status. His reaction to the death of his brother-in-law, the Earl of Carlisle, illustrates both his morbid self-absorption and his longing for the settled life which, perversely, he chose not to have. 'O happy end to die surrounded by that most numerous loving family of children and grandchildren, blessed and tranquil and . . . at peace with God and secure in futurity. And here am I, vile slave of indulgence and worldly passion.'[7] With which lament he returned to his old ways.

Nothing in life ever quite satisfied him. 'I have lost my taste for Paris,' he wrote. 'I am bored to that degree that I think it will be impossible for me to stay a month.'[8] But he stayed – complaining continually about the place and the people. It was his restless disposition which made him, in turn, an obsessive builder who felt an irresistible need to improve and extend the great houses which he owned, an avid collector of fine art and a passionate advocate and patron of innovative horticulture. He claimed to be devoted to Chatsworth, where – surprisingly to those who are familiar with North Derbyshire – he found the summers filled with what he called 'true Italian days'[9] blessed with 'hot Italian weather'.[10] But although he wrote 'I love this place', he spent long months on foreign expeditions – sometimes in the hope of adding to one or another of his collections and sometimes just seeing the sights, taking the waters and meeting and seeking out people he regarded as his social equals.

According to his own account, the Sixth Duke's happiness was constantly impaired by a variety of physical disabilities. Although in old age he spent happy hours listening to piano music, there were times during his early manhood when he was, or appeared to be, stone deaf, a condition which some of his friends believed that he affected as a protection against unwelcome conversation. His whole life was punctuated by 'cures' and 'purges' – remedies for illnesses which were often imaginary. Hart was a hypochondriac. However, it was the circumstances of his birth and upbringing which must take the blame for the years of needless anxiety about his health as they must accept responsibility for his other strange attributes.

After his father's death, it took some weeks for Hart to discover that he had not inherited a fortune. Mortgage repayments and interest on borrowed money – totalling almost £600,000 a year – swallowed up over 60 per cent of the income from the estate which he had inherited. Hart brushed his debts and liabilities aside, believing – as innumerable Cavendishes had believed before him – that dukes can live on aristocratic credit. But, although he was not oppressed by the burden of his new liabilities, he was irredeemably despondent about almost every other aspect of his life. When he wrote to his sister, 'My own G[eorgiana] I cannot tell you how much I love you and how much I hope you will be kind to me now that it is one of the things that can make me happy',[11] he was expressing the gloom that – except when he was caught up in one of the obsessions which later ruled his life – engulfed his whole existence. The gloom became notorious. After passing through Chatsworth Park, Catherine Booth – then the wife of an itinerant Nonconformist Methodist minister who had yet to found the Salvation Army – moralised that 'the Duke ought to be a happy man if worldly goods can give felicity. But alas we know they cannot and, by all accounts, he is one to whom they have failed to impart it.'[12]

Superficially Hart was the typical Regency buck – so anxious to remain what he describes to his sister Harriet as 'beautiful to look at' that he dieted to avoid putting on weight and employed a Parisian dentist to keep his teeth straight and white. He enjoyed – or at least led – a sometimes frenzied social life. Although he took no great pleasure from racing he regarded ostentatious patronage of the sport as essential to the preservation of his reputation. An incident at one meeting reveals the conduct of his set to be so extravagant that, had an account of such behaviour appeared in a novel by Georgette Heyer or Baroness Orczy, it would have been dismissed as romantic novelist's fantasy. To make 'a show' he arrived at a Doncaster race meeting in a coach-and-six with twelve outriders in Cavendish livery. Next day, his neighbour, Lord Fitzwilliam – not to be outdone – arrived with two coaches-and-six and sixteen outriders. Nothing had prepared Hart to meet the obligations of his inheritance.

His first duty, which he did not enjoy, was to decide if part of his inheritance should be passed on to other members of the family. Elizabeth Foster – whether Hart liked it or not, the Dowager Duchess of Devonshire – clearly had a call on the estate. But the marriage to their father had made her even more disliked by her stepdaughters, Lady Georgiana and Lady Harriet, than she had been when she was merely the Duke's mistress. Initially – by agreement between all her stepchildren – she had been told to leave Devonshire House within a week of her husband's death. But she insisted that she had been promised Chiswick as a dower-house, together with a substantial lifetime pension and a settlement on her son, Augustus Clifford, which would pay the young naval officer £3,600 a year. While Hart pondered his obligations, and listened to his sisters' expressions of outrage, the Dowager acted. Two weeks after his father's death, the new Duke – having completed the sad duty of sorting out his father's clothes – found his stepmother already installed at Chiswick.[13] Happily – as is so often the case when difficult decisions about money are needed – it was decided that moral duty and financial self-interest coincided.

Hart concluded that it was necessary for Elizabeth to receive less than she thought her due. But he told his sisters that his decision was unrelated to a desire to keep as much of the estate as possible for himself. The Dowager was to be denied much of what she had claimed because of his Christian duty to ensure that she did not benefit from 'employing art and falsehood at such a time'.[14] It is even possible that Hart was sincere in his determination not to reward Elizabeth's insensitivity. Once she had been punished for contesting her husband's will before his corpse was cold, her stepson treated her with consideration, kindness and generosity which it was hard to distinguish from affection. His sisters were unyielding in their animosity. But Hart was of a gentler disposition.

Elizabeth was allowed to remain at Chiswick for only one year but, in compensation for that limitation on her lease, Hart's original cash offer – an annuity of £3,000 – was increased to £4,000. That enabled his stepmother to rent accommodation in Piccadilly while she built a house of her own on the bank of the Thames at Richmond. Augustus Clifford, her son, was given an annual allowance of £2,000 which would be increased on his marriage or when he left the navy. But he was to be told nothing about the eventual improvement in his prospects – lest it should encourage him to indolence. Either the trick worked or Clifford did not find indolence a temptation. He became an admiral and was Gentleman Usher of the Black Rod, the sovereign's representative, and constable, in the House of Lords.

There were other settlements of undisputable generosity. Hart's sisters both received £30,000. The original gift of £20,000 to Harriet was supplemented several times. An old tutor, who was thought to have fallen on hard times, was paid a pension. William was obeying his mother's injunction to make other people happy. But he was not respecting her advice on the subject of careful housekeeping. During the days which immediately followed his father's death he certainly ignored and probably actively avoided John Heaton – the agent and auditor whose struggles against the Fifth Duke's profligacy, although by no means successful, had enabled the family to avoid bankruptcy. The Sixth Duke was just as reluctant to discuss income and expenditure as his father had been. When Heaton finally obtained audience, he found his new master no more prudent than his old. He was probably as much relieved as saddened when he was replaced by James Abercromby, the Devonshires' steward – a man who rose to become Speaker of the House of Commons, not least because – in Westminster as in Chatsworth – he avoided the expression of inconvenient truths.

Like his father, Hart had no wish to serve his sovereign. He was happy to be the Prince Regent's occasional friend and carry the orb at his coronation – a task he subsequently performed at the coronations of William IV and Queen Victoria. After the death of George III, he visited the new King in Brighton with the hope of reconciling him to the Whigs who – because of their opposition to the plots against his father – George IV had come to regard as his enemies. It was a risky venture, for the Whigs had felt an obligation to oppose the new King's attempt to divorce his wife. Despite the auguries, the Brighton visit – planned with the apparently hopeless ambition of convincing George IV that the Whigs were still his friends – was, in personal terms, a success. Hart's diary records that because he was both late in rising and nervous about the meeting, he missed breakfast. But he 'went to the New Chapel with the king . . . This is the first day I met with the king, I believe owing to it being Sunday.'[15] There were other meetings which were jovial but politically inconclusive.

Neither the King nor the Whigs changed their minds about the desirability of a royal divorce. When the House of Lords considered the Bill of Pains and Penalties – the impeachment of Queen Caroline in preparation for the coronation – Hart made a rare appearance in parliament. He found his fellow peers uncongenial companions. In what he had wrongly believed to be private, he described them as 'old and fat and stinking'.[16] That was more a comment on their opinions than an observation about their physical state. But it was still deeply offensive. Hart remained unrepentant. His judgement was influenced by attendance at the trial which had preceded the proposed legislation*and he felt only distaste for the way in which the Queen had been systematically humiliated. The Bill of Pains and Penalties – against which Hart voted – was carried in the House of Lords by a majority of eleven. Lord Liverpool, the Prime Minister, concluded that it would be defeated in the Commons and sensibly abandoned the whole squalid enterprise. According to the Duke of Devonshire, 'Brooks's [club] was such a scene of rejoicing as I never saw.'[17] The jubilation celebrated more than justice done. Brooks's was a Whig club and the Tories, as well as George IV, had been humiliated.

Despite his undoubted Whig inclinations Hart wanted to remain in favour with the King. But his wish to please was not strong enough to persuade him to make the personal sacrifices which a life of public

---

* In fact the marriage could probably have been dissolved as an illegal union. But that would have required the King to confess that, because of his earlier, secret, marriage to Mrs Fitzherbert, he was a bigamist.

service requires. Out of a sense of obligation – first to Canning and then to Melbourne – he twice accepted the office of Lord Chamberlain. But he resigned in 1828, never to become a courtier again. In 1835 – when he was offered the choice of becoming Lord Chamberlain for a third time or being appointed Lord Lieutenant of Ireland – his sister, Lady Granville, reproved his declining both offices and thereby refusing to do his duty and ignoring the Whig obligation to serve the nation. The affectionate, though clearly heart-felt, rebuke chided him for 'sitting under a red rhododendron at Chatsworth, under the shade of palms and pines [with] no thought of the country's weal and woe'.[18] The criticism was not entirely justified. He had responded to the second invitation to become Lord Chamberlain with the despairing conclusion that although he 'abhorred' the House of Lords, he would be 'obliged to accept from ties to the king and the good of my party'.[19] A third term of office would have been beyond endurance.

Although Hart had no interest in the practice of politics, he held firm and fearless political convictions which included Catholic Emancipation. When his father had advocated the same course as necessary to peace as well as justice his demand for conciliation rather than confrontation had been assumed to be an aberration. Support for the same view by a second Cavendish – the head of a family which had built its fame and fortune on defending Protestant England against Rome and 'Popish' subversion – was treated with a combination of disbelief and alarm. That was not a response that concerned the Sixth Duke. In November 1825, he had presented a petition to parliament which called for 'our Roman Catholic fellow subjects' to be granted the civil liberties which were theirs by right and which provided 'the best and only means of really promoting the peace and tranquillity of Ireland'.*[20] Fourteen months later, after the defeat of the Emancipation Bill†, he 'expressed regret at the condition into which the Catholics of Ireland have been thrown as a result of the decision which has been taken' by the House of Commons and added that, 'apart from principle and justice, I have always felt the strongest conviction of the expediency of supporting these claims'.[21]

Hart's support for limitation on the hours of child labour was less surprising. But the language, if not the sentiment, of his speech on slavery to the burghers of Derby was – by implying an equal status to all races – ahead of the opinions of all but the most advanced

---

* The speeches were all carefully recorded in the Duke's diary – some on the day, some on the day before they were made.
† It was passed in 1829.

abolitionists. It also contained an implied rebuke: 'I shall indeed rejoice if, late as the interests may have been excited, the County of Derby shall be found to be among the first to take up the cause of humanity, the cause of so many of our fellow creatures living in misery and degradation.'[22] And it was in Derby that, after the defeat of the 1831 Reform Bill, he attacked the Tory who had opposed it in language which some of his peers must have regarded as class treachery. 'Members of the aristocracy have sometimes been considered in an unfavourable light by people [of lower rank]. For much of this they are indebted to the manner in which the present representation in parliament has allowed them to interfere in and dictate the method of that representation.'[23] The vote was reversed in 1832, and Hart was so determined that the franchise would be extended that he reluctantly conceded that since 'The Reform Bill is through the Commons' he 'must go up soon'[24] to London to see its safe passage through the Lords. It was clearly a great sacrifice. When he heard the news of the bill's passage, he was 'in the library upstairs arranging books' and, far from thinking of London, felt only that 'here I could live always'.

It was not only his attitude towards politics and his sovereign's service that made Hart a different sort of Devonshire. In absolute distinction both to his forebears and his successors, he felt no enthusiasm for racing. His diaries – recording his obligation to attend a meeting at Doncaster – described the sport of kings as 'hated'.[25] He was, however, wholly typical of his family in one respect. He felt an irresistible compulsion to spend more than he could afford and, like his predecessors, he built – not always to the aesthetic advantage of the houses which he aimed to extend and improve. Building – and filling what he had built with rare and exotic collections – were the two greatest obsessions of a life in which new obsessions developed almost every year.

A year after he succeeded to the dukedom he visited Lismore in Ireland and immediately concluded that his castle needed reroofing and general restoration. He was already indulging the other aspect of his extravagance, collecting for collecting's sake. The enthusiasm's first manifestation was a desire to own antique coins and medals. It was a transient and costly passion. A collection which he bought for £50,000 was later sold, together with several years' additions, for £7,500. But by then he had moved on to a more lasting preoccupation. He had become a bibliophile in the true, and initially in the limited, sense of the word – interested in books as objects rather than as opportunities to read and learn. Later in life he acquired the reading habit.[26] But there is no reason to believe that when, in May 1812, he paid £10,000 for the Bishop of Ely's whole library, he was remotely interested in what was inside the books' covers. Later in the same year he bought forty-six antique volumes – including one printed by Caxton – from the Duke of Roxborough. Normanville, a French bookseller, sent books from Paris – some of them obtained on the pretence that they were destined for the Emperor Napoleon. All his acquisitions were regularly rearranged by his own hand. Such was his enthusiasm that when, in 1815, the collection grew too big for his library to accommodate, he housed them in the gallery which the First Duke had built along the east front. The reconstruction required the removal of the William and Mary panelling. 'By doing so', the Duke confessed, he 'not only endangered the security of the walls, but approached certain flues much too nearly'.[27]

It was not his spendthrift ways or even his sudden lurches from one enthusiasm to another that worried his family. They were concerned that his romantic associations always ended in what other young men would have regarded as disappointment. There were plenty of eligible women who enjoyed his company. The Prince Regent was said to be so concerned by Hart's flirtatious relationship with his daughter, the Princess Charlotte, that he told the young Duke to 'recollect the difference between' nobility and royalty.[28] More suitable companions seemed to make brief appearances in his life before they married men of less wealth, inferior position and, most of his acquaintances agreed, inferior charm. When Lady Elizabeth Bingham announced her engagement to Granville Harcourt, MP, she reassured friends that, despite rumours about Hart's secret affection for her, she did not 'think it necessary to feel alarm for him'. Lady Elizabeth was one of the several young women on whom the family had rested its hopes of Hart's making a suitable match. The explanation of her decision to marry Harcourt was also a comment on Hart's character – he cared 'for none of them and is far too babyish in his manner to and about them to give them any reason to hope or complain. He feels a real relief as they go off his hands.'[29] There were occasional rumours of 'affairs' – including a relationship with Fanny Arkwright, daughter of the Richard Arkwright who had been his mother's reluctant benefactor. But the evidence of their letters suggests that the friendship was platonic. Nobody thought – or feared – that the young Duke of Devonshire was not attracted by women in general. Evidence of his close associations abounded. It seemed that he was simply opposed to formal commitment or legal attachment.

There was plenty of evidence to confirm that, from time to time, he felt the inclinations of a normal, healthy, young man. At the end of 1825, the list of problems which he recorded in his diary as being endured during the year included 'the worry of Harriette Wilson'. Unlike the Duke of Wellington, Hart was not prepared to tell the notorious courtesan 'Publish and be damned.' So he feared that her memoirs would excite 'the licentious personalities of the newspapers'.[30] In fact their publication did nothing more damaging than repeat the accusation that Hart had cut her in Piccadilly – an allegation to which he was said to have already responded, 'Don't you know that I am blind as well as deaf and a little absent too.'[31] His relationship with Elizabeth (Eliza) Warwick was, at once, more straightforward and more mysterious. For years she was less his mistress than his wife and, while she lived in The Rookery at Ashford in the Water, seemed to make the Duke as contented as his strange character allowed. At the end of 1827 she appeared in the year's 'causes of happiness' for which he gave thanks. Two months earlier he had described her as 'perfect for me' and proclaimed, 'Every day I like her better.'[32] But, for the next two months, the diary records a series of events which might have presaged either the end of the affair or its transformation into the marriage for which Mrs Warwick hoped. 'At 5 I paid a visit which may have great influence on my whole life.'[33] More mysteries followed. The entry 'I called on Eliza Rodd and returned to no 50 Gloucester Place'[34] was accompanied by an inexplicable marginal note: 'Mrs Warwick who lived with me for ten years.' The next day, the Duke confessed to a subterfuge that most Devonshires – who lived by moral laws which they decided for themselves – would have scorned. 'Managed so that my servants, except Ross, ignored my absence.'[35] The relationship staggered on. But, inevitably, Mrs Warwick – who wanted to be more than a paramour – grew increasingly disenchanted with her status. The gift of £1,200, 'so that she may feel a measure of independence',[36] did little to reconcile her to life in the demi-monde. During one anguished discussion of her future she 'worked herself into a dreadful state and was by way of making to stab herself with a knife'.[37] The Duke, 'disgusted and worried to death', as well as attributing his increasing dependence on drink to Harriette Wilson's behaviour, did what nineteenth-century dukes always did at such inconvenient moments. He instructed the family solicitor to pay her off. It cannot have been an easy decision. With Elizabeth, Hart undoubtedly enjoyed moments of something approaching domestic bliss. Perhaps he needed someone on whom to lavish affection.

Even before Mrs Warwick had gone from his life, his need for a vicarious family had been met by the marriage of Blanche Howard – daughter of his sister, Georgiana, the Countess of Carlisle – and

William Cavendish, the future Lord Burlington and his likely successor. Hart welcomed, enjoyed, loved and perhaps needed a ready-made family which allowed him, spasmodically, to indulge his need for affection, but did not prevent him from gratifying the obsessions which his strange temperament induced. But his affection for Blanche and, after her early death, his concern for her bereaved husband combined to influence many years of his life.

Hart's avuncular concern was not limited to the nephews and nieces who were destined to guarantee the future of the dynasty. When the Countess of Granville's daughter (yet another Georgiana) proposed to marry Captain Aubrey Fullerton, an attaché in the British Embassy in Paris, he thought it his duty to enquire into the soldier's suitability. He concluded that Fullerton was 'not the wisest of men but has good sense and is uncommonly amiable'.[38] Further investigations left the Duke 'quite satisfied [that] if he is well off and has money', he would make a satisfactory husband.[39] So, in order to discover the truth about that possible financial impediment, he advised the young officer 'to write to his father to know what his expectations are'.[40] We must assume that the reply did not suggest that the future Mrs Fullerton would be able to live in the style to which she had been accustomed. Her uncle, the Duke of Devonshire, made her an annual allowance of £2,000 for life.

His early life was all gaiety, much of it forced. There were dinners and balls at Devonshire House and Chiswick, shooting parties at Hardwick Hall and Bolton Abbey and weekend gatherings of sumptuous splendour at Chatsworth – all of which were punctuated by proud expositions of the works of art which he had recently added to his collection. But to his credit, he was always looking for more creative ways in which to occupy his time and mind. The greatest opportunity to enlarge his horizon had come by chance, but a chance that only his aristocratic status made possible. Lord Granville, his brother-in-law, was the British Ambassador to Russia. Largely due to that connection, in November 1816, Hart had dined at the residence of the Russian Ambassador to the Court of St James's. The guest of honour was Grand Duke Nicholas, the youngest of the Tsar's three sons. The two men struck up an instant rapport – based, they both believed, on similarities which included the identical weight of 13 stones 7 pounds. The Grand Duke accepted an invitation to visit Chatsworth and reciprocated by asking the Duke to accompany him to Berlin, where Princess Charlotte of Prussia was to join him first for the journey to Saint Petersburg, and then in marriage. Hart was invited to the wedding. He found the ceremony and its attendant celebrations a disappointment and, over-sensitive about status, he imagined that he had been treated with less respect than his exalted position demanded.

Grand Duke Nicholas had not been there to greet him on his arrival in the capital and had been continually inattentive during the days which followed. Hart made up for the disappointment by making the return home a Grand Tour and visiting Munich, Stuttgart, Vienna, Venice, Padua, Verona and Paris. In each city he visited the great houses as well as meeting the great families. He had always enjoyed noble company. It was during the return journey from Russia that he developed a taste for noble buildings and the classical statuary which went with them.

Hart's romantic biographers suggest that, during that European tour, he experienced a moment which can best be described as an architectural epiphany and that the decision to rebuild followed a sudden dissatisfaction with Chatsworth House. The story is romantic but untrue. Soon after his accession to the dukedom he had decided to remedy some of the errors in design which had resulted from the First Duke's capricious conviction that he was an architect – errors which made some parts of the house inconveniently inaccessible. But once Hart had set out on the work of rectification, he had felt – like his illustrious ancestor – an irresistible compulsion to go on and on. It all began with the conversion of the east front into a library. But once he had started, he could not stop. The work went on at Chatsworth for twenty-four years – longer than it had taken the First Duke to create the building which the Sixth originally intended only to improve.

John Russell Tavistock had celebrated his succession to the Bedford dukedom by extending Woburn Abbey. He had commissioned Jeffry Wyatt – a highly fashionable architect who changed his name to the more aristocratic-sounding Wyatville after he had supervised the rebuilding of Windsor Castle – to design a sculpture gallery and Temple of Muses in the neo-classical style. Hart had become neo-classically inclined and Wyatt was a good salesman of his own wares. So the architect who was initially commissioned only to submit plans for an extension quickly evolved from employee to muse, confidant, inspiration and friend who, in Hart's opinion – though few other people's – was 'a delightful man, good, simple like a child, indefatigable, eager, patient, easy to deal with, ready to adapt a wish if practicable [but] firm to resist a faulty project'.[41] He was certainly eager to rebuild as much of Chatsworth as the Duke believed, wrongly as it turned out, he could afford.

Work started on what can now be described as the first stage of the redevelopment in 1820. Wyatt had designed a new north wing (which contained bedrooms and bathrooms), a theatre, a ball room, a dining room, kitchens and offices. The old east front was to be refaced. In 1827 the Duke commissioned additional work which included a new staircase in the Painted Hall. Seven years later, the rebuilding of the south front and the west wing began. In 1839 the new Chatsworth – basically what the house is today – was declared finished. While the work was in progress, William Wordsworth visited Derbyshire and composed a sonnet which – as well as making the usual contrast between art, as represented by Chatsworth, and nature, as depicted by the surrounding country – moralised about contentment.

> Chatsworth! thy stately mansion, and the pride
> Of thy domain, strange contrast do present
> To house and home in many a craggy rent
> Of the wild Peak; where new-born waters glide
> Through fields whose thrifty occupants abide
> As in a dear and chosen banishment,
> With every semblance of entire content . . .

The poem goes on to argue that wise peasants will realise that 'not for Fancy only pomp hath charms' as those who live a 'favoured life' do, or should, protect others from 'lawless harms'.

In 1819 – the year between the submission of the first plans and the work beginning – Hart had set out for Rome with James Brougham as his companion and, as a result of his real or imaginary poor health, a Doctor Eyre to act as personal physician. The doctor's contract of employment illustrated the difference in status which separated him from Hart's companion. Eyre, unlike Brougham, was firmly told that 'The Duke cannot undertake to introduce him or to promise his introduction to any courts which he may visit'.[42] It seems that the unfortunate doctor missed a great deal of the fun. For, socially, the visit to Rome was a great success – largely as a result of efforts by the Dowager Duchess of Devonshire, then sixty-one years of age, who had taken up residence in the Eternal City and become a figure among the artistic cognoscenti. Stendhal, in his *Pages from Italy*, described the Dowager Duchess and the Duke, her stepson, as 'the only English in my knowledge for whom the Romans make an exception in the profound hatred they bear towards their countrymen'.[43]

In the year that the Fifth Duke died, Elizabeth, Dowager Duchess of Devonshire – perhaps because she was released from her husband's thrall – had begun to blossom as a devotee and patron of the arts.

She had become one of those women who knows every writer and makes confident judgements on their writing without ever writing anything of note herself. She sent Augustus Clifford (her sailor son) a message about the consequences, for its author, of the rapture which surrounded the publication of *Childe Harold*. 'The subject of conversation, of curiosity, of enthusiasm, almost one might say of the moment is not Spain or Portugal, Warriors or Patriots but Lord Byron! His poem is on every table . . . He has a pale sickly but handsome countenance and a bad figure . . . The men [are] jealous of him, the women of each other.'[44] It was the development of such interests that endeared her to the Roman artistic society. They also helped to change her stepson's attitude, through tolerance, to outright affection. On New Year's Eve, 1821 – summing up the year in his diary – Hart recorded, among the other 'Causes of Happiness', Elizabeth's 'satisfaction with my attendance to her'.[45]

It was during his visit to Rome that Hart developed 'the love of marble [which] possesses most people like a new sense'.[46] He was happy to confess that the taste awakened an insatiable taste, from which he 'did not scruple'. Indeed, marble and Antonio Canova, its greatest nineteenth-century exponent, became his next all-consuming passion. The collection of Canova's work held his interest for years. Some of his acquisitions had, as was fashionable at the time, ancient classical associations. An early purchase was a representation of Petrarch's Laura. But Hart, like Canova, had a weakness for imperial splendour in all its many forms and he sympathised with the sculptor's admiration for the faded glory of Napoleon Bonaparte – by then exiled. Hart wrote – certainly in approval and possibly with admiration – that 'Canova kept the large bust of Napoleon in his bedroom until his dying day'.[47] The Duke was given it, after Canova's death, by Lady Abercorn. A Paris bookseller negotiated the purchase of *Madame Mère* – 'the unfortunate mother of the greatest of men' – a lady who 'used to receive [the Sixth Duke] in Rome and rather complained of [Hart] possessing her statue'.[48] Napoleon and his mother aroused – if arousal was necessary – all of Hart's romantic yearnings. Once *Madame Mère* was safely installed in Chatsworth he 'used to come down [from the state rooms] and look at her by lamplight'.[49]

In Hart's opinion, the most important sculpture in his collection was Canova's *Endymion*. It was certainly the one he most loved – perhaps because it represented eternal youth. He remained remarkably calm when it was suggested that the work had been finished by an apprentice in Canova's studio. The claim was refuted by documentary evidence

– after Hart had insisted that none was 'required when you contemplate the admirable perfection of the work'.[50] That commendation was typical of the extravagant praise that Hart always heaped on his hero of the moment. Canova was 'the most talented, the most simple and the most noble minded of mankind'.[51] It all seemed a long way from contemporary England, the land of the Peterloo Massacre and the Six Acts which suspended habeas corpus, gave magistrates summary powers to prohibit seditious gatherings and speeches and enabled them to imprison anyone whom they believed to be a threat to the established order. The Sixth Duke was certainly one of the most gentle Devonshires. But he was also the most detached from the world around.

When, in 1822, news of Canova's death reached England Hart's immediate concern was for his yet undelivered sculpture and, with Wyatt at his side, he set out for Italy to ensure that the recently completed *Endymion* was ready to be despatched safely to Chatsworth. Paying tribute to the sculptor's memory was, essentially, the subsidiary purpose of the journey. Neither enterprise was wholly successful. *Endymion*'s spear was broken in transit and the monument which Hart thought should be erected in Rome was built in Venice, the city of Canova's birth. In consequence, he subscribed only £50 towards its cost. But once again, largely thanks to the Dowager Duchess, the visit was an unqualified success. Elizabeth had become an amateur archaeologist and spent much of her days excavating the ruined Forum. Her detractors were not mollified by her sudden devotion to classical scholarship. Lavinia (by then the Dowager) Lady Spencer – biased by her affection for the wronged Georgiana – wrote to her other daughter, 'That witch of Endor, the Duchess of Devonshire has been doing mischief of another kind to that which she has been doing all her life, by pretending to dig up for the public good in the Forum. She has, of course, found nothing, but has brought up a quantity of dirt and old horrors and will not be at the expense of carrying it away.'[52] But other, less prejudiced judges took her work more seriously. Amongst them was Cardinal Ercole Consalvi. After a period out of grace he had again become one of Pope Pius VII's closest advisers and was busy retrieving works of art which Napoleon had stolen from Italy. He had commissioned a new gallery – the Braccio Novo extension to the Museo Charamonti – in which to house them. Hart was taken by his stepmother to view the building. He immediately decided that Wyatt's design for the extension of Chatsworth must include a reproduction of the Braccio Novo ceiling.

The passion to build extended beyond Chatsworth itself and in 1839, when work on the house was finished, Hart embarked on a new project. After a visit to Blaise Hamlet, John Nash's Gloucester model village, he determined to have something similar on the Chatsworth Estate. First he commissioned Decimus Burton – Nash's pupil – to design a new farmhouse and stables on the hill opposite Edensor. Then Wyatt was employed to build two lodges, one Italianate and one Tudor, for the entrance to a village that did not yet exist. Behind them the Duke built a new Edensor, with houses in every known style. It remains an architectural paradox – a practical but picturesque folly.

Edensor had existed as a village in Saxon times and had grown into what, immediately before the Sixth Duke decided to rebuild it, was large enough to be called a town. It included a church and a parsonage. A new inn had been built to accommodate travellers on the coach road which, along the stretch from Matlock to Baslow and Tideswell, had been renewed as recently as 1777. In his geographical eulogy, *The Gem of the Peak*, W. Adams described what, in 1838, he clearly regarded as a blot on the landscape. Compared with the beauty of its surroundings, Edensor 'presented a far different feature – unsightly houses and plenty of dirty, ragged looking children generally appearing to open the gate on the passage of a carriage' into Chatsworth Park.[53] By then, the demolition of houses in the old town, west of the road, had begun. 'The Duke had most of these removed by building the poor cottagers better and more substantial houses, with good gardens attached, on an eminence by the roadside about a mile away at Pilsley.'[54] In fact he demolished all but one, which was spared for no reason anyone knew or knows. It still exists today. So does the inn to the north of the old town in which Doctor Johnson lodged in 1774. According to Adams, the houses of the old town, west of the road, were to be made 'more ornamental'. Some of them were. What is now called the Swiss Cottage and the old alehouse were renovated and the church was left untouched. But the rest of Edensor – a village again – was in materials and construction, if not in concept, new.

Wyatt was either too busy or too grand to design the houses. So John Robertson of Derby was hired. He based his designs on one of the 'pattern books' of domestic architecture which, at the time, were a popular way of deciding on the appearance of rural houses. No two are the same and those at the front, facing onto the road, have the slightly unreal appearance of scenery constructed for the production of a fairy story or an idyll of Olde England. But most of them were built as the habitations of practical men who worked for the Devonshires but were also smallholders. In the fields above the village there are stone sheds where a cow or a pig can be, or could have been, kept in winter. There is no record of the Sixth Duke boasting of Edensor as a social innovation intended to improve the lives of working men and women. It is now a social phenomenon of a different sort – a whole village with one owner. But it is not unique in that. Outside Chatsworth Park, Beeley and Pilsley are still, in every sense, Devonshire villages.

It says much for the Sixth Duke's energy – both physical and intellectual – that while he was engaged on rebuilding Chatsworth and its environs he was also travelling in continental Europe with the regularity common to nineteenth-century aristocrats. Usually it was at his own unlimited expense and undertaken with some cultural object in view. But in 1826 he had accepted, with undisguised delight, the suggestion that he should become Ambassador Extraordinary to the Russian Court and represent England and its King at the coronation of his old friend the Grand Duke Nicholas who was about to become Tsar of all the Russias. Nicholas had ascended to the throne in circumstances which were unique. The oldest of the three brothers, who had been crowed Tsar Alexander I, had decreed in his will that the next in line – his brother the Grand Duke Constantine – should not succeed him. After Alexander's death, and a brief period of indecision, Constantine agreed and preparations were made for the coronation of Tsar Nicholas I. On May 10 1826, the Duke of Devonshire – accompanied by a suitable body of retainers including his nephew and successor – set out to attend what, to Hart's delight, he rightly expected to be a ceremony of extraordinary grandeur. The whole expedition was, however, beset by unexpected difficulties. Vicissitudes did not bring out the best in Hart.

The voyage to Russia – always likely to be difficult for a hypochondriac – got off to a bad start. In the absence of a following wind, HMS *Gloucester* had to be towed out of Sheerness by a steam boat. It was continually becalmed for the next ten days – an inconvenience for which the Duke blamed the captain, who incurred the hatred of his illustrious passenger by refusing to obey the orders to ignore the absence of wind and set sail. The 'disobliging beast'[55] also retired to his cabin early each evening instead of attending to Hart's needs. Surprisingly he escaped blame for the many illnesses – new as well as old – which afflicted Hart throughout the journey.

Hart was pleased with the reception that he received when they arrived at Cronstadt – one ship was 'dressed overall'. But he felt that his party was not greeted with sufficient enthusiasm in St Petersburg. Then he had to endure the inconvenience of the coronation being postponed because of the death of the new Tsar's mother, the Empress Elizabeth. Hart occupied his time visiting and being visited by the assorted grandees who were also waiting for the great event. Although

Peter the Great had made St Petersburg the temporal capital of Russia, the religious capital had not changed. So there followed the uncongenial necessity of travelling to Moscow for the religious ceremony. But the excitement of each day – meeting heirs apparent and presumptive as well as Princes, Arch Dukes and Grand Dukes – compensated for some of the hardship. One of the Duke's qualifications for becoming Ambassador Extraordinary had been his anticipated willingness to spend large sums of his own money on entertainment. He did not disappoint. He spent £60,000 of Devonshire money – three times more than the government's grant in aid. Meticulous accounts were kept in both sterling and roubles. 'Postillions for coach' cost 100 roubles. Expenditure on that scale allowed Hart, in his own estimation, to entertain more lavishly than any of the other plenipotentiaries. The ball which was the climax of his visit was, he boasted, a generally agreed triumph – 'leaving my colleagues . . . far behind'.[56]

There were periods of debilitating apprehension during which he feared that he was being neglected. But after waiting overlong for a meeting he was able joyfully to record 'Instead of today being the coronation it has been the first day of seeing the Emperor. One glance showed me that he was unaltered to me. Oh God bless him. He did not greet me as an Ambassador but as *un ami* Devonshire.'[57] There was, however, a major disappointment to come. He left Russia without being awarded the Order of St Anthony and on his return to England, after four months' absence, he was not immediately made – as he hoped and expected to be – a Knight of the Garter. For that honour he had to wait, much to his impatience, until the end of the year. Yet he had already experienced the event which, then unbeknown to him, was to change his life and to secure his place in the history of the age of improvement. On May 9 1826 – the day before the Sixth Duke of Devonshire left for Russia – Joseph Paxton, his new head gardener, arrived at Chatsworth.

CHAPTER 20

Ermine and Enterprise

Joseph Paxton was born on August 3 1803 in Milton Bryant, a village on the edge of the Duke of Bedford's Woburn estate. Legends about his boyhood abound. They were encouraged by his own oblique references to hardships which he had once endured – including the casual comment to his daughter, 'You never know how much nourishment there is in a turnip until you have to live on one.'[1] When his father – a tenant farmer – died, Joseph was sent to live with his elder brother, the bailiff and superintendent at Battlesden Park, the home of Sir Gregory Page Turner. Thanks more to nepotism than natural aptitude, he was employed on the estate as a gardening boy. According to some accounts, he rebelled against the harsh discipline to which he was subjected and ran away. The story was elaborated by nineteenth-century myth-makers who claimed, without any hard evidence, that during his wandering he met a Quaker who convinced him of the importance of industry and self-improvement. Whether or not the meeting ever took place, Paxton certainly came to believe that work purifies and ennobles. He could have been the inspiration of the Ford Madox Brown painting that extols 'Work' as a sign of virtue as well as the path to prosperity with a quotation from the Book of Proverbs. 'Seest thou a man diligent in his business? He shall stand before kings.'

Converted to the importance of acquiring the qualifications that would enable him to rise above the labouring classes, Paxton obtained an apprenticeship at Woodall where William Griffin, author of *Culture of the Pineapple*, introduced him to the world of fashionable horticulture. By 1822, Paxton was sufficiently accomplished to return to Battlesden Park, where he was employed in the construction of an ornamental lake – the first recorded example of his fascination with decorative water. Sir Gregory was made bankrupt shortly after the job was finished and Joseph was forced to find new employment. He may have worked briefly for the Duke of Somerset at Wimbledon House or for Lee and Kennedy, the London nurserymen. But on November 13 1823 he began work as a labourer in the Horticultural Society's 'experimental gardens' in Chiswick. When he signed the society's register he gave his date of birth as 1801. He was born in 1803 but he was afraid that, if he told the truth, he would be regarded as too young for both the heavy work and intense study which lay ahead.

The Horticultural Society was essentially a child of the English Enlightenment, founded at the suggestion of John Wedgwood – son of Josiah – in part to fill the vacuum in horticultural scholarship which had been created by the neglect of the Botanical Gardens at Kew. Its purpose was to encourage the greater understanding of plants and shrubs – both those which were native to Britain and the increasing number of exotic foreign species which were being imported – and to train future master gardeners. John Lindley, the assistant secretary of the society, made its purpose clear in his first annual report. 'The head gardener will be a permanent servant of the society, but the under gardeners and labourers will be young men who, having acquired some previous knowledge of the first rudiments of the art, will . . . become entitled to fill situations as Gardeners in private or other establishments.'

The experimental garden had been established on land leased from the Sixth Duke of Devonshire. The Duke thought of himself as one of the *savants* who explored and exhibited the mysteries and wonders of the natural world. So he was the society's ideal landlord. When Hart had inherited Chiswick House from his father he had immediately created a formal Italian garden and a huge conservatory to house the camellias which were the floral vogue of Regency England. And, to the horrified wonder of his sister Harriet, he had not limited his acquisitions to rare plants. The animals in his collection were even more exotic than the flowers. Among them were 'a few kangaroos – who, if affronted will rip anyone up as soon as look at him – elks, emus and other pretty, sportive, death-dealers . . . The lawn is beautifully variegated with an Indian Bull and his spouse, and goats of all colours and dimensions.'²

After six months with the society, Paxton was placed under the supervision of Donald Munroe, the curator of new plants. It was a good year to train in that speciality. The aspidistra had just been introduced from China, the fuchsia from Mexico and the petunia from South America. Their cultivation required the construction of frames, greenhouses and 'stoves'* in which they could be protected from the English weather. But Paxton was not to spend long on learning the part of his trade which initially made his name. While still – in his own admission – with much to learn, he was offered the chance to

---

* Stoves, as distinct from greenhouses, rely on artificial heat rather than the warmth of magnified sunlight.

become under-gardener in the society's arboretum. Again it was a fortunate appointment. England's appetite for new trees – particularly conifers – was boundless.

It may have been Paxton's training in the nurture of trees which attracted the Sixth Duke of Devonshire or perhaps Hart – a man of sudden impulses and instinctive attachments – met the young gardener during the months in which the apprentice walked to work over Cavendish land. Whatever the reason, the minutes of the Horticultural Society's council meeting on May 4 1826 record that 'on April 22nd, Joseph Paxton, under gardener in the arboretum left: recommended a place'. He had been appointed 'superintendent of gardens' at Chatsworth with a salary of £65 a year and a rent-free cottage in Edensor village. He gave two weeks' notice of his intention to leave the arboretum – during which time he was appointed a Fellow of the society. That in itself was a tribute to the prodigious speed at which he had learned his trade. On May 8 he received his instructions from his new employer. At the age of twenty-two, he had become head gardener at one of England's greatest houses.

Not surprisingly, employer and employee had different views about the importance of the appointment. The Duke – about to leave for Tsar Nicholas's coronation – did not even mention it in his diary. Paxton set off immediately for Derbyshire.

I left London by Comet Coach for Chesterfield and arrived at Chatsworth at half past four in the morning of the ninth of May 1826. As no person was to be seen at that early hour, I got over the greenhouse gate by the old covered way, explored the pleasure grounds and looked round the inside of the house. I then went down to the kitchen gardens, scaled the outside wall and saw the whole place, set the men to work there at six o'clock; then returned to Chatsworth and got Thomas Weldon to play me the water works, and went to breakfast with poor dear Mrs Gregory and her niece. The latter fell in love with me, and I with her and thus completed my first morning's work at Chatsworth before nine o'clock.[3]

Joseph Paxton married Sarah Bown and remained devoted to her throughout his lifetime. But she was in every way subordinate to his work and often required to take second place to the Duke, his employer. That was, in part, because Paxton was driven by ambition. But the greater cause of what – at least in terms of time – amounted to neglect was the insatiable desire for Paxton's advice, support and company which Hart developed with the years. The relationship which resulted – more friends than master and servant – grew out of the two men's different, but equally passionate, attitudes to gardens and gardening.

For almost 300 years, the garden which Joseph Paxton was employed to manage had reflected the horticultural tastes and necessities of the time. In Bess's day there had been arbours and shady walks – which might have been designed for Shakespearean conversations – in front of the house, with orchards and beds of herbs, which supplied Chatsworth's medical as well as culinary needs, at the back. The Fourth Earl's (First Duke's) radical changes to the landscape reflected the view that there was a distinction between art and nature and that art was superior. London and Wise – the leading British exponents of the Dutch School of landscape architecture – designed complicated parterres with symmetrical flower beds in geometric patterns, removed a hill which obscured a sylvan view and replaced it with the 'canal' of still water which was essential to their idea of a perfect garden. The Fourth Duke had altered the course of the river but – influenced by the theories of William Kent, who rebuilt Devonshire House after the fire in 1733 – became a devotee of 'natural' landscape. Lancelot 'Capability' Brown was employed to make Chatsworth Park look as if it was untouched by human hand. Flower beds were removed from parterres and precise horizontal lawns were turned into grassy slopes. Ponds were drained, fountains removed and trees were planted in clumps to resemble the pattern of distribution that God would have chosen. Walpole, visiting Chatsworth in 1760, attributed the change in the landscape less to new aesthetic sensibilities than to the old prejudices. He was impressed by 'rich turf to the top of the mountains and fine old oaks in the park'. But he was depressed by the absence of trees on other parts of the estate. 'The second Duke, having planted some and neglecting to fence them from cattle who destroyed them, there was an idle notion that trees would not grow there. The [Fourth] Duke is making vast plantations.'[4] It fell to Joseph Paxton to make the garden a reflection of Victorian values.

The Sixth Duke was infatuated by trees. Oak, ash, beech, elm, sycamore and poplar turned the hill to the east of the house into an incipient forest. Together with the saplings which were planted in other parts of the park they won the Duke a Gold Medal from the Society for the Encouragement of Arts, Manufacture and Commerce. Since they were all planted exactly 4 feet apart, they may provide evidence that Hart was turning away from 'natural' horticulture. Wyatt – while supervising the extensions to the house – was certainly urging him to make the garden 'picturesque' as the proper complement to his design.

A gravel path, almost a third of a mile long and flanked by trees, had already been constructed and it was clear that Paxton was expected to be no more than a working gardener who implemented plans which were presented to him. However, whatever the intentions for the future, in 1826 – as the Duke himself ruefully noted – the kitchen garden contained only '4 pine houses, bad; two vineries which contained 8 bunches of grapes; 2 good peach houses and a few cucumber frames. There was no house at all for plants and there was nowhere a plant later introduced than about the year 1800. There were 8 rhododendrons and not one camellia.'[5]

Paxton could not have effected much fundamental improvement before the Duke's return from Russia. But during the seven months that his employer was away, he certainly made a start. Hart, who 'arrived [back] at Chatsworth *de gioia*' was 'enchanted by the progress' of the rebuilding. Praise for the new gardener was less ecstatic. But he was commended for having made 'a great change'.[6] The new regime had imposed rigorous discipline on the under-gardeners and labourers who worked twelve-hour days (with half an hour break for breakfast and an hour for lunch) in the late spring, summer and early autumn, and as long as weather and light allowed, within those times, for the rest of the year. They were fined for lateness, lounging and failure properly to clean their tools. The gathering of fruit, flowers or vegetables was punished, on the second offence, with instant dismissal. Yet, such were the standards of the time that the Duke and his head gardener were regarded as benevolent employers.

For the first year of Paxton's employment, the Duke was a reluctant Lord Chamberlain and rarely at Chatsworth. Benjamin Currey, the Devonshires' London solicitor, was given effective control of all the Duke's affairs – one of the earliest examples of the aristocracy handing the management of their wealth and estates to the professional middle classes. He immediately advised the Duke that his only hope of solvency lay in the sale of his West Riding estate. The Earl Fitzwilliam, hearing that a sale was possible, immediately urged the Duke not to betray his heritage in the name of false economies. After several paragraphs of statistics, which concluded with the unsubstantiated assertion that the sale would only raise £500,000, he asked what he regarded as the crucial question. 'What do you lose in order to gain this small proportionate addition to your disposable income? Why, you lose greatly in station . . . The alienation of one of the great masses of your landed property . . . cannot fail to make a sensible inroad upon your influence and the position you hold in the great national community.'[7] The Duke accepted Fitzwilliam's advice and decided to spend some of the inadequate disposable income – which he had decided not to increase – on a 'pinetum', a copse of every known variety of conifer.

In the autumn of 1827 – the year in which he married Sarah Bown – Paxton went to London to buy the seed of a Douglas fir and, for its safety, carried it back to Derbyshire in his hat. After the successful planting of the conifers, Paxton was made forester as well as head gardener and his salary increased, threefold, to £226 a year. Social elevation followed promotion. Paxton was taken to shoot with the Duke at Bolton Abbey. It was the beginnings of his elevation from servant to friend. Upwardly mobile by nature, he took advantage of his new status in a way of which, he knew, the Duke would approve. In 1831, together with the head gardener at Wortley Hall, 25 miles away in South Yorkshire, he founded the *Horticultural Register and General Magazine*. Three years later he launched *The Magazine of Botany and Register of Flowering Plants*, a magazine which was intended to have popular, rather than professional, appeal and therefore a more ambitious publishing project. By then he had taken another giant step up the social ladder. He and the Duke had made a tour of great house gardens – travelling in the same carriage.

Paxton's standing with the Duke had been further enhanced by the contribution he had made to the undoubted success of Princess Victoria's visit to Chatsworth. The heir presumptive's tours of England were, for her hosts, hazardous events. William IV disapproved of his niece anticipating her succession and Sir John Conroy, who accompanied the party on the King's instruction, was in constant, and often public, disagreement with the Duchess of Kent, the Princess's mother. So was Victoria's governess, Louise Lehzen – the Princess's own choice of companion whose power and influence the Duchess of Kent openly rejected. Fortunately there were no scenes at Chatsworth and the Princess was deeply impressed by everything she saw, including the kitchens which she commended for their cleanliness.[8] The highlight of the visit was the evening entertainment with the restored and renewed fountains, described as 'illuminated waterworks'. Thousands of Russian lights shone on and through what were to become the famous Chatsworth cascades. And the explosions of colour – which the young Victoria regally described as 'most imposing'[9] – was not Paxton's only contribution to the triumph. He kept a gang of labourers working all night to sweep and roll paths which, he insisted, must be immaculate when the Princess first saw them in the morning.

During Paxton's early years at Chatsworth, the garden's reputation largely rested on the Duke's desire to make a show. Rare species were avidly collected. A forty-year-old weeping ash – weight 8 tons, trunk 28 inches in diameter and branches spread 37 feet wide on either side – was bought in Derby and pulled north by six horses in a cart specially designed by the Duke. At the end of its four-day journey, the gates into the park had to be lifted from their hinges in order to let it through. Gradually Hart developed a more genuine love of gardening. John Claudius Loudon, a rival gardener and once one of Paxton's fiercest critics, had no doubt how the change had come about. 'The Duke of Devonshire has stated to us that he owes his taste in botany entirely to Mr Paxton. A few years only have passed since Chatsworth, as far as gardening was concerned, was below mediocrity. Its noble owner bestowed neither money nor patronage in advancing the art. In fact he had no taste for gardening. Now he has become its most faithful friend.'[10]

As the Duke's enthusiasm for gardening grew, so did his dependence on his gardener. It became so great that, during a visit to Paris to collect rare seeds, he suddenly felt such need for Paxton's company that he sent an urgent call to Chatsworth. It was answered by a dash from Derbyshire which was completed in the near record time of three days. When Hart returned home, Paxton remained in France to make purchases at a Russian horse sale – a task for which he was wholly unqualified. Santi, the Duke's Russian servant who also remained in Paris, persuaded him to visit a gambling house. He watched Santi lose £70, but did not place a bet himself. Paxton was prudent by nature. It was a characteristic which faced him with a continual dilemma. He wanted Chatsworth to boast the biggest and best garden in England. But he was always reluctant, and sometimes unwilling, to endorse the Duke's extravagance. He was happy enough to create a new arborctum, with 1,670 different species of trees, because the cost could be met by the sale of felled timber. But when he was sent to buy a collection of orchids from a horticulturally inclined clergyman, the Vicar of Kimbolton, he wrote back to London with the sort of message that Hart found hard to understand. 'With all my anxiety to have a collection for your Grace unsurpassed by anyone, I cannot recommend your Grace to spend so serious a sum.'[11] Nevertheless the Duke paid the asking price. Paxton's only consolation was that he had persuaded the vicar to part with an almost worthless collection of cacti at no extra cost.

Orchids – fashionable and, in consequence, the plants which the Duke desired most – needed protection from English weather. For several years Paxton, a gardener by instinct and training but also an ingenious, though untutored, engineer, had been experimenting with ways of building a more efficient hothouse at a reasonable cost. His initial idea – metal instead of wood – had proved too expensive. But he had developed the idea of setting the glass at an angle which caught the sunlight – a notion which originated with his old adversary, Loudon – and it was incorporated into a glasshouse to hold the Chatsworth orchid collection. Its giant size – 97 feet by 26 – required that its weight be distributed over fifteen bays. The front row of supporting cast-iron columns accommodated pipes through which rainwater was drained from the roof. That was only one of the ingenuities that reduced cost and increased convenience. The hothouse was judged a complete success by all who saw it. That stimulated Paxton's ambition to design and build an even bigger and indisputably better glasshouse. The eventual result was a structure 227 feet long, 120 feet wide and 67 feet high with its roof made of curved glass arches – each one set at an angle to the sky in order to maximise the attraction of sunlight.

For once the Duke, urged by Currey to be prudent and chastened by the failure of similar schemes in other great gardens, took expert advice before agreeing that the scheme could go ahead. But all of the authorities who were consulted – genuine, rather than amateur, engineers – judged the design to be practicable. A hothouse, smaller but of similar design, was erected in the kitchen garden to confirm their assessment and the building of the 'Great Stove' – artificially heated by water pipes so as to accommodate the most delicate orchid – was begun. It was designed to be a thing of beauty in itself. So its less elegant elements had to be hidden away. The boilers, accommodated in a basement beneath the stove, were fed by coal which was transported through a tunnel buried deep beneath the garden. Paxton insisted that sheet glass – rather than small crown-glass panes – was essential to both appearance and efficiency. Chance Brothers of Birmingham, who had just developed a new production technique, agreed to supply sheets which were 48 inches square – the largest ever made – at cost price. Almost four years after its conception the Great Stove was ready.

It was not destined to house orchids alone. Expeditions were sent to distant places with commissions to find and bring to Chatsworth the rare specimens of plants which would flourish under the curved roof. John Gibson, a Chatsworth gardener, was despatched to Calcutta where, with the assistance of the curator of that city's Botanical Garden, he collected, successfully packed and, with some relief, brought home 300 plants, including two specimens of *Amherstia nobilis* (an evergreen with red and yellow flowers) and *Musa superba* (a dwarf banana) as well as more than a hundred previously unknown orchids. One of the *Amherstia* had died during the journey, but the East India Company, co-sponsors of the expedition – who might have claimed the survivor

– graciously agreed that it should go to the Duke. Paxton went down to London to see the precious cargo safely on its way to Chatsworth and, after breakfast in the Painted Hall at Devonshire House, stowed it aboard the Duke's long boat and – enjoying the benefit of a canal which had been cut to protect fragile merchandise from the rigours of rough English roads – sent it north to Cromford where, in the sight of Arkwright's great mill, the plants were loaded onto sprung wagons for the 12-mile drive home. John Gibson was able to tell the family, with whom he was reunited, that the Duke had made him foreman of the Chatsworth garden's newly created historic plant department.

Not all the expeditions had such happy endings. The Duke rejected an invitation to invest in the botanical exploration of Panama and Guatemala and sponsored, instead, an expedition to the west of North America to collect firs and pines. Paxton proposed that they should travel overland across the continent. The Horticultural Society regarded the journey as too dangerous to be contemplated and suggested co-operation with the Hudson Bay Company which was sending a ship round the Horn to Fort Vancouver. Paxton's will prevailed. Four days before the expedition reached the Pacific, two Chatsworth gardeners were drowned in the rapids of the Columbia River. It fell to Paxton, the man who had planned the route, to break the news to their families.

By then Paxton's fame had spread far beyond Derbyshire. In January 1838 he had received his first public appointment – membership of a committee to enquire into the cost and management of the royal gardens. Within the space of a fortnight, the committee visited the gardens at Buckingham, Kensington and St James's Palace, Hampton Court, Windsor Castle and the Brighton Pavilion – and found them, according to Paxton, 'in an excellent state of wretchedness'.[12] The committee recommended that 'the most miserable places ever seen' should either be opened to the public or sold off. The report was largely ignored, but Paxton had attracted Victoria's notice. She described him as the 'gardener to the Duke of Devonshire at Chatsworth who never thought of what was economy'.[13] It was the Duke, rather than his gardener, who was, in Her Majesty's opinion, unacceptably extravagant. For Paxton was sure that when the royal gardener was dismissed – the inevitable outcome of the report – the job would be his for the asking. Much to his wife's displeasure, he believed it his duty to stay loyal to the Duke.

Over the years, Paxton's subservience evolved into deference and deference became respect that did not require obedience. From the earliest days of his employment at Chatsworth he had always been his

own man. He had never felt any obligation to hide – at least from his
wife – his occasional exasperation with the Duke's conduct. After one
relapse into religion, Paxton described his employer as 'a ranting,
canting saint', in a condition 'some think a species of insanity' which
provoked him into attending chapel along with 'the rag tag and bobtail'
of humanity.[14] Success increased his confidence. His patent machine
for cutting the struts of the Great Stove's sash windows won him the
silver medal of the Society of Arts. He was working with John Lindley,
the secretary of the Horticultural Society, on the *Pocket Botanical
Dictionary*. And when the two men began to plan the *Gardeners'
Chronicle*, he exhibited a new independence by ignoring the Duke's
'great objection and dislike' of one of his employees 'being connected
with a newspaper'[15] – a very different proposition from editing a
learned, or even a layman's, botanical journal. Paxton was beginning
to think of exploring the world beyond horticulture.

It took him some time to leap over the garden wall. So, despite his
burgeoning reputation and outside interests, Chatsworth was still the
centre of Paxton's attention when, in 1842, the Duke learned that
Victoria – by then queen rather than princess – was to make a second
visit. The house and estate ignited an explosion of preparation. Twelve
men were hired to prune the lime trees at Edensor and another dozen
employed in renewing the white and yellow gravel on the path to the
arboretum. The Queen and Prince Albert – together with Lords
Palmerston and Melbourne and the Duke of Wellington – drove through
the Great Stove in their carriages. The early evening was again illuminated by Russian and Chinese lanterns which were supplemented by
red, white and blue Bengal lights. At ten o'clock, the sky was once
more lit up by a firework display.* Paxton, the impresario, was
rewarded by a visit, to his house, of Victoria herself, where she was
presented with the first nine volumes of *The Magazine of Botany*. The
Queen pronounced herself enchanted by all that she had seen but gave
no assurances about what she would read. The 'fairy-lights' had given
particular pleasure. It all encouraged Paxton to look for new worlds
to conquer.

When Tsar Nicholas announced his intention to visit Great Britain,
the Duke of Devonshire took it for granted that his itinerary would
include an excursion to Chatsworth – a prospect which, according to
the Duke, made him 'excited and Paxton frantic'.[16] The great event

---

* Lanterns and fireworks became the traditional Devonshire way of celebrating great
occasions. In 2000, the Fiftieth Anniversary of the 11th Duke's succession was marked
in that way.

was to be marked by the creation of a fountain – a single jet which, by rising 260 feet into the air, became the biggest gravity-fed fountain in the world. Paxton turned himself into a civil and hydraulic engineer. He organised the excavation of a 9-acre lake, laid a 2½-mile conduit to fill it with water from a hill stream and perfected a pneumatic valve by which the fountain could be turned on and off. Then the Russian Embassy announced that the Tsar would not travel outside the capital. Paxton's disappointment was as great as the Duke's. He was consoled with an audience with the Tsar in London at which he presented Nicholas with the eleventh volume of the *Magazine of Botany*.

Preparations for the Tsar's visit had required the Duke to spend what he accepted was more than he could afford. Indeed had he been restricted by the rules of credit that restrain ordinary men, he would have been adjudged able to afford nothing. His debts included £269,000 for the extension and renovation of Chatsworth, £97,000 for the removal and rebuilding of Edensor village and £36,000 for the creation of the stove. The capital expenditure was financed by borrowing, which the Duke seemed to believe was unrelated to his current account. The cost of maintaining the various Cavendish houses and the financial demands of the Duke's extravagant lifestyle – which approached £100,000 a year – would, in normal circumstances, have been covered by his income. But the Duke's financial circumstances were not normal. The cost of the compound interest, which he paid on his combined debt – liabilities which he had incurred or inherited – was £1 million a year.

Benjamin Currey, the Duke's lawyer, decided that it was his duty to force the Duke to face up to his precarious financial position. Paxton – whose increasing influence he recognised with mixed feelings – was consulted in the hope that he would become an ally in the cause of retrenchment. His character made recriminations inevitable. But after he told Currey that he should have acted sooner, Paxton admitted his own, albeit unconscious, responsibility. He told the Duke, 'I have been the cause of your Grace spending a great deal of money. Had I been at all aware of your real position, I certainly never would have done so.'[17] Then, after unctuously adding 'The great pleasure I have had in adding to your pleasure of this princely seat is my only excuse', he got down to the serious business of suggesting ways of liquidating the debt. His recommendations were accompanied by the dire, but entirely justified, warning, that the repeal of the Corn Laws – abolishing the tariff on imported grain – would severely reduce the Duke's annual income.

Paxton wanted to cut deeper than Currey thought necessary. Initially the Duke was impressed. 'Currey so good, but not quite up to what I want done. Only Paxton keeps suggesting a grand plan for paying off my mortgages.'[18] Paxton's proposals, delivered on June 16 1844, included the sale of Lismore Castle and estate. That desperate expedient was opposed by Currey (who predicted a rise in Irish land values) and rejected by the Duke. Paxton, in a letter to his wife, made the best of his defeat. 'The Victory is gained. All the debt is to be paid off . . . Mr Currey had not a word to say against my plan except for the sale of Ireland . . .'[19] The solution – far more Currey's idea than Paxton's – was the sale of land in Yorkshire to George Hudson, the draper who had become the 'Railway King'. It was a shrewd decision. Hudson – reckless and anxious to improve his social status – could be relied on to pay an inflated price for ducal land. And the deal could be promoted, at favourable terms, by an agreement over rights of passage for future railway lines. Land at Baldersley was immediately sold for £100,000. The Londesborough estates went for £450,000 a year later.

Although Paxton's advice to sell Lismore was rejected, the confidence with which he advocated a comprehensive solution to the Duke's dilemma enhanced his reputation. He was elevated, in fact if not in form, to rank which was equal to Currey's. And in the introduction to the *Handbook to Chatsworth and Hardwick* which the Duke wrote that year, Paxton was exalted in extravagant language which typified his employer's invariably excessive reaction to every situation. 'Unspoilt and unaltered, he has risen to something like command over all persons who approach him . . . Beloved and blessed by the poor, considered and respected by all, to me a friend if ever a man had one.'

Horticulture and its attendant disciplines were no longer enough to satisfy Paxton. He had become a public figure and was in public demand. During one of the long absences from home that she clearly resented, Sarah wrote that he had 'got into the London papers, travelling with the Duke of D . . . They call you Mr Paxton the celebrated florist and gardener.' Then she added, in what sounds more like bitterness than pride, 'Well you have a nice time of it. Long may they last.'[20] Her wish, sincere or not, was amply granted. *The Gardeners' Chronicle* prospered and Paxton's association with William Bradbury, its printer, grew into a friendship. Bradbury was one of the investors who had rescued the floundering *Punch* and through him Paxton met the literary figures of the day – Thackeray, Dickens and Trollope. Social advancement was matched by professional recognition. Edwin Chadwick sent him a copy of the report into *The Sanitary Conditions of the Labouring Poor*. The cholera maps, on which its conclusions were based, confirmed the obvious truth that contagious diseases were more likely to spread in towns than the country, but Paxton sent him a note about the underestimated health hazards faced by rural labourers and suggested that gardens and gardening might help to clear urban air of the 'vapours' which were thought to promote epidemics. He was soon to be given an opportunity to put his theory into practice.

Richard Vaughan Yates, a Liverpool councillor and businessman, had bought 97 acres of land from the Earl of Sefton, on which he proposed to build houses for the fast-increasing middle classes. He proposed that 47 acres should be made into a park for the enjoyment of the surrounding householders. It was be dedicated to the recently born Prince of Wales. Paxton was commissioned to draw up the design. But the days of personal involvement in shifting soil and planting shrubs were over. A senior gardener at Chatsworth was deputed to supervise the implementation of the plan.

New commissions quickly followed. Birkenhead – expanding across the Mersey at a pace which even Liverpool itself could not match – invited Paxton to design the first wholly public park in Britain and offered a fee of £800. Ten years later, the men who were to win the competition to design Central Park in New York visited Birkenhead and found that 'In democratic America, there is nothing to be found comparable to [that town's] People's Garden. Gardening has here reached a perfection, never before dreamed of.'[21] Then Coventry invited Paxton to supervise the landscaping and drainage of its municipal cemetery. He accepted the invitation as he accepted every opportunity to do more, earn more, be more. And, thanks to his prodigious energy, he always managed to extend his responsibilities without diluting his power to discharge them. In 1849, a year after he joined the Midland Railway board, he travelled to London overnight, lay down for two hours' sleep and then got up and began business.

> Our meeting at the Isle of Wight lasted for two hours. I had between one and two to see Cannon. At two we commenced upon the Southampton project which lasted until five. Without getting a morsel of food, I started off again for Derby . . . Got to Derby at about half past eleven, where I found the Sheffield deputation waiting to see me. We sat discussing matters over until three o'clock in the morning. I had to be at breakfast at seven o'clock to be ready to start . . . to Gloucester and Bristol.

By then Paxton, although still Chatsworth's gardener, was one of Victorian England's great entrepreneurs. The Duke of Devonshire's ungrudging support for his private enterprises was, by the standards of the time, extraordinary. Paxton – acknowledging that talent alone might not have allowed him to rise so high – expressed his gratitude for the Duke's 'fostering hand' and – in a moment of affectionate *lèse-majesté* – described his patron as a partner in 'Paxton and Company'.[22]

Paxton became rich. Total earnings were large enough to enable him to become – with a subscription of £25,000 – the major investor in the projected *Daily News* and, when it almost foundered, to shrug off his losses and maintain his hopes of sharing the ownership of a radical newspaper. How radical Paxton really was is open to question. The Duke, his master, had certainly supported the progressive causes of the century's beginning. But his attitude towards the poor was that of the typical Whig. They were to be always pitied and sometimes helped. But they were not allowed to help themselves – a process which might well end with a change in the proper social order. Geography and the casual benevolence of earlier generations had insulated the Devonshire estates from the upheavals which had imperilled the lives and property of other landed families. In Derbyshire, most arable common land had been enclosed by agreement before the first General Enclosure Act (1801) empowered commissioners to determine the pattern of new ownership. And in 1832 common pasture was enclosed at Ault Hucknall and Heath without resistance.[23] According to Samuel Glover – author of the nineteenth-century *History and Gazette of the County of Derby* – the prospect of alternative employment in mills and mines reconciled the peasantry to losing rights over poor-quality land. So did the new settlements. 'On recently enclosed lands . . . there are small allotments in which clusters of comfortable cottages with appropriate garden-grounds . . . are superior to the old cottages.'

Derbyshire did not escape the agitation which, for ten years, followed the publication of the People's Charter in 1838. But although there were 'a significant number of National Chartist Associations in the county' – like all Chartist activity, demanding political representation as a prelude to social and economic justice – the disturbances seem to have escaped the notice of the Sixth Duke of Devonshire who never mentions them in correspondence until they came to a climax and an end in 1848. Derby was 'most shamefully disgraced by the blasphemous bills that are going on walls . . . defying all that is virtuous and holy.'[24] Glossop alone added 5,600 signatures to the Great Charter. In August 1842, when 400 men marched from Duffield to Derby and were joined by 400 colliers and lime burners from Buxton and 700 weavers from New Mills, the Dragoons, called out to protect property and restore order, had to be reinforced by the local yeomanry, militia and a troop of regular hussars. Yet – if diaries and letters are to be relied upon

– the turmoil was barely noticed by either Paxton or the Duke until failure of the final march signalled that it was all over. 'Fearful defeat of the Chartists. There will now be an end of all the destruction of rank and property in England.'[25]

Paxton was in London on the day that the Chartists attempted to deliver their petition to parliament and wrote home to describe the precautions which had been taken against their sacking the capital. He was so confident that the positioning of special constables at the House of Commons and soldiers at the Bank of England was unnecessary that he went to his stockbroker and bought shares which had fallen in value because of the fear of revolution. Within the day – the great rally on Kennington Common having ended peacefully – he had made a profit of £500.

One more great horticultural achievement lay ahead. Since 1840 Paxton had been attempting to propagate the Great Amazonian Water Lily. It had been discovered in Peru at the beginning of the century. But no attempt was made to send specimens to England until it was rediscovered, years later, in Guyana. None of the plants survived the journey. But in 1840 seeds were sent to Chatsworth and Kew. Paxton attempted to germinate them at once. Kew, where their cultivation started later, succeeded first. But the Kew lily, named *Victoria Regina*, refused to flower. In an admirable show of scientific solidarity, Kew offered Chatsworth a seedling and the chance to overtake their achievement. Paxton travelled to London to pack the precious specimen and bear it north himself. It was housed in a specially constructed tank within a new Lily House, which was made almost entirely of glass – a development made affordable by the repeal of the glass tax. A water wheel simulated the motion of the lily's native river and the wonderful new discovery, generated electricity, replicated the heat and light of Guyana. Prudence still ruled. 'If Electric light was not so expensive, I should use it for two or three hours, morning and evening.'[26] His efforts were amply rewarded. In October 1849, three months after the lily's arrival at Chatsworth, its leaves measured 4 feet across, though its sibling at Kew had not grown at all. It flowered in November. Paxton went to Windsor to present Victoria with a bud. And the achievement was celebrated at Chatsworth by Annie, Paxton's seven-year-old daughter, standing on a leaf to prove that it was strong enough to bear 100 pounds in weight. The *Illustrated London News* printed an engraving of the occasion and *Punch* published a poem in praise of both the girl and the flower. By September 1849, *Victoria Regina* had produced 140 leaves and 112 buds. It had also provided inspiration for his greatest achievement. Speaking to the Fine Arts Society on

November 13 1850, he explained that 'Nature has provided the leaf with longitudinal and transverse girders and supports that I, borrowing from it, have adopted in this building'.[27] The building of which he spoke housed the Great Exhibition of 1851 and became known – thanks to Douglas Jerrold of *Punch* – as the Crystal Palace.

The Society of Arts had held regular exhibitions in London since 1756 and in 1847 it attracted over 20,000 visitors to its displays of English craftsmanship. Inspired by that success – and after a visit to Paris where there had been regular exhibitions since the dawn of the French Revolution – they decided, in conformity with the spirit of the time, that the next London exhibition should be international. The Corn Laws had been repealed and free trade was extolled as the guarantee of industrial innovation, economic expansion and lasting prosperity. England would demonstrate what it could make, confident that foreign competition would only stimulate the increased exertion that produced greater success. And the goods of the world would be on display to educate, encourage and inspire. Prince Albert was convinced of the merits of the enterprise and added a royal dimension to its objectives. Increased commerce was the sure way to achieve lasting peace. Queen Victoria – rumoured initially to be sceptical – gave the enterprise her blessing. In January 1850, she announced the formation of a commission to supervise the creation of a Great Exhibition of the Works of Industry of all Nations to take place in London from May to October 1851. The chairman was the Prince Consort himself and its members included Lord Russell, the Prime Minister and Sir Robert Peel, the Leader of the Conservative Opposition. Robert Stephenson, Charles Barry (the architect of the Houses of Parliament) and William Cubitt respectively represented engineering, architecture and construction. The Society of Arts must have believed that, with such distinguished men as its patrons, the Great Exhibition would make uninterrupted progress towards a glorious opening. If so, they were wrong.

The Times dismissed the notion that trade would promote peace as the whimsical fantasy of men who did not understand the causes of war. *Punch* was amused by the idea of the Prince Consort appealing for funds and published cartoons of him, cap in hand. The *Evening Standard* merely anticipated a fiasco – not an unreasonable prediction in the light of what it regarded as a thoughtless announcement that opening day would be a mere sixteen months from the first meeting of the commission. Conscious that time was short, the commission's building committee (which included Brunel, Stephenson and Barry) announced that the building in which the exhibition was to be housed must be capable of swift construction – as well as being of moderate cost and designed to display British art and science at its modern best. Despite those exacting requirements, within three weeks of the invitation being issued, the committee had received 245 rival designs. Eighteen submissions were first commended and then rejected as too expensive. The committee decided to prepare a design itself.

There was still no agreement where the – as yet undesigned – building should be erected. Hyde Park was the commission's preference. But, while the opponents of the exhibition in general disliked every possible venue, they were particularly opposed to its being sited in Kensington. Colonel Charles de Laet Waldo Sibthorp, MP – a bitter opponent of the principle of free trade on which the exhibition was founded – was typical. The exhibition, he said, was 'one of the greatest humbugs, frauds and absurdities ever known' wherever it was located. But he was especially incensed by the idea of 'an industrial exhibition in the heart of fashionable Belgravia' which could only 'enable foreigners to rob us of our honour'.[28] Arguments about where the building should be erected were temporarily abandoned in favour of expressions of horror about the design which it seemed that the commission – having supervised the drawings itself – was certain to approve. A long, low building – constructed from 20 million bricks and surmounted by a cast-iron dome which, at 200 feet in diameter, was twice as big as the dome at Saint Paul's Cathedral – would not only be monstrously ugly. It would be permanent.

On June 11 1850, Joseph Paxton dined in the House of Commons with John Ellis, MP, the chairman of the Midland Railway Company. According to an article in *Household Words* of January 1851 – anonymous but, it is now believed, written by Charles Dickens – it was Paxton himself who suggested that the exhibition should be housed in a glass pavilion. There is no way of knowing if Paxton was angling for an invitation to submit a design or if he merely – with characteristic self-confidence – observed that a building constructed like his Great Stove and the subsequent Chatsworth lily house would be superior, in every particular, to the brick pavilion. It is, however, certain that, before the end of the dinner, Ellis had become determined that Paxton's ideas should be put to the commission. Ellis tried to arrange a meeting with Lord Granville, vice-president of the Commission and the Duke of Devonshire's nephew. Granville was, or said he was, unable to see him. Another commissioner, Henry Cole, was more obliging. Ellis was accompanied at the meeting by Paxton who spoke less as an applicant than as a benefactor. If, and only if, he was assured that his design would receive serious consideration, he would submit completed plans within nine days. The work had to wait until he had returned to Derbyshire from Bangor, where he was to witness the third tube of Robert Stephenson's Britannia railway bridge being floated across the Menai Straits.

Paxton hurried back from Wales to take the chair at a Derby meeting of the Midland Railway's Works and Ways Committee. It decided to fine a pointsman for indiscipline. While the members deliberated about the miscreant's fate, Paxton made rough sketches of his plans for an exhibition building on a sheet of blotting paper.* Next day – after taking advice on the strength of girders and columns from the Midland Railway's chief engineer – he drew up his detailed design, assisted only by employees of the Chatsworth estates office. On the train to London, to submit his plans to what, he had been warned, was a sceptical commission, he met Robert Stephenson who was travelling back south after a longer stay in Bangor than Paxton's crowded life allowed. After pleasantries about the Britannia bridge, he showed Stephenson his drawings. By the end of the railway journey, at least one member of the commission was enthusiastically on his side. More lobbying followed. Granville at last made himself available and then arranged a meeting with Prince Albert. Hopeful of success, Paxton sent copies of his design to Fox, Henderson & Co. of Smethwick, potentially the suppliers of the iron work, and Chance Brothers of Birmingham who had rolled the special glass for the Great Stove and would do the same for the Exhibition Building. Both companies agreed to enter into partnership with Paxton. The commission confirmed that it still preferred brick to glass by publishing detailed drawings of its favoured plan in the *Illustrated London News*.

The more the public saw of the commission's choice of design, the less they liked it. Paxton thought of delivering a *coup de grâce* by publishing descriptions and engravings of his alternative which, he had no doubt, would capture popular imagination. But – fearful that his invention would be plagiarised – he decided to wait until the ridge-and-furrow roof, which had been employed with such success at Chatsworth, had been patented. When the details of his scheme were published, the reaction was exactly what he had anticipated. The public was awe-struck by the sheer size and complexity of what he proposed. The building was to be 1,848 feet long, 408 feet broad – which made it six times as large as Saint Paul's Cathedral – and 66 feet high. Its appearance delighted commentators who thought the exhibition would

---

* The blotting paper is now in the Victoria and Albert Museum.

herald the dawn of a new era* but appalled critics who looked back to an imaginary golden age. So did the method by which it was constructed. To ensure that the work was finished on time its component parts were – in the language of a later age – 'mass produced'. That required the girders, columns, sash bars and guttering to be identical throughout the building, an obligation that excited John Ruskin's contemptuous comment that it was neither crystal nor a palace and convinced Edward Burne-Jones that, if it was ever finished, Paxton's pavilion would be 'monotonous' as well as 'cheerless'.[29] It was, according to its devotees, 'in keeping with the age' in that it successfully combined art and science. 'The aesthetic bloom of its practical character' reflected both the romance and 'the practical character of the English nature'.[30] Disraeli's encomium had to wait until the exhibition had opened and been pronounced an indisputable success. Then he described the building in which it was held as an 'enchanted pile . . . raised for the glory of England and the delight and instruction of two hemispheres'.

The argument about location was ended by the House of Commons resolving that it should be Hyde Park – thus relieving the Duke of Devonshire from the obligation to make good his offer to provide a site, free of charge, at Chiswick.† But there was still no agreement about design. Commissioners visited Chatsworth to examine the lily house. Brunel announced that, while he still hoped for the success of the scheme that incorporated his cast-iron dome, he was impressed by Paxton's ingenuity. Stephenson was resolute in his support. On July 15, Paxton, having been asked if the job could be done for £75,000, concluded that he was the commission's choice and telegraphed the station master at Derby, 'My plan has been approved – Send this to Chatsworth.'[31] Not surprisingly, he was 'triumphant, being chosen for this great building'.[32] The official decision to adopt Paxton's plan – amended to incorporate a 108-feet-high transept to accommodate Hyde Park elms which could not be felled – was agreed on July 26 1850 – leaving ten months before the Great Exhibition was due to open.

Two thousand workmen were employed on the site. The building which they assembled – watched, most days, by the Sixth Duke of Devonshire – was made up of 33,000 iron columns, 2,000 girders, 60,000 feet of timber and 9,000,000 square feet of glass. That it was

---

* In one particular, the claim was literally true. Had the glass tax not been abolished a 'crystal palace' would not have been possible.

† Sir Robert Peel, who had supported the choice of Hyde Park, was killed, in a riding accident, while returning home from the debate.

finished on time was a miracle comparable to its design. Paxton – who always wanted to do more – was attentive. But he had other duties to perform. There were visits to Lismore to supervise Augustus Welby Pugin's recreation of medieval splendour in the great hall of the castle and conversations with Baron Mayer de Rothschild about what, in its way, was Paxton's most ambitious enterprise – the design of Mentmore, the Rothschilds' country house in Buckinghamshire. The untutored architect proved so satisfactory to his client that he was commissioned to design a second Rothschild house, Ferrières, 20 miles from Paris.

The *Builder* magazine – representing the views of the whole industry – continued to express outrage that the building of the century – which was intended to exhibit British craftsmanship – should have been designed by a gardener rather than an architect. It took consolation from the undoubted fact that it could not have been constructed without the assistance of men with formal qualifications. But nothing could diminish the glory of May 1 1851. Thirteen thousand exhibitors were crowded into Paxton's crystal palace and – as the Duke of Devonshire proudly noted – when, during her opening address, Queen Victoria mentioned the designer's name, she 'turned towards him in a gesture of approbation'.[33] Perhaps more significant of Paxton's rising status, onlookers were heard to exclaim, '"Look. There's Mr Paxton" in a very loud voice, and then more gently "and there's the Duke of Devonshire"'.[34]

Other aristocrats struggled to come to terms with his new eminence. After Paxton's proposal of free entry to the exhibition was rejected by the commission, he wrote to *The Times*, repeating the importance of making attendance available to 'the sinews of the land'. His persistence was dismissed by Earl Granville with an explanation of his impertinence. 'Mr Paxton's head had been turned by the events of the last five months. It is not surprising that they should have had such an effect on a self made man.'[35]

During the 1850s Paxton seemed to be everything and everywhere and to meet – as an equal member of society – all the famous figures of the day. Charles Dickens, a collaborator in the *Daily News* venture, travelled to Chatsworth to discuss the progress of the project and it was there that the Duke of Devonshire met the most popular of all English novelists. Dickens told the Duke that finishing *David Copperfield* had made him 'really unhappy'[36] – not as was the case with the death of Little Nell because he sympathised with the character he had invented but because the story was autobiographical. The Duke was notoriously susceptible to the blandishment of artistic and literary celebrities. He had lent Leigh Hunt £200 to pay his debts – despite his own perilous financial position and the poet/essayist's conviction for criminal libel against the Prince of Wales. And, when the loan was repaid on time, he had been so gratified by his debtor's punctuality that he had rushed round to Hunt's house and insisted on transforming it into a gift.[37] So, at about at the time when the Great Exhibition opened, Dickens asked the Duke – with every hope of success – to support the Guild of Literature and Art – a charity which he and Bulwer-Lytton had founded to provide help for destitute writers and painters.

Dickens had a penchant for amateur dramatics. He had written a play, *Not So Bad As We Seem or Many Sides to a Character*, in which he proposed to star during a series of performances which devoted their profits to the guild. He suggested to the Duke that the premiere should be staged in Devonshire House – if it could be arranged, in the presence of Queen Victoria and the Prince Consort. The Duke gave his enthusiastic agreement after assuring Paxton, 'I never missed reading a number of his beginning with *The Pickwick Papers* and I told him that I could pass an examination on all his histories.'[38] The Queen and Prince accepted the invitation and the premiere took place on May 16 1851. Victoria, as well as paying £50 for her ticket, donated £150 to the guild's funds.[39] Dickens's status improved. When he visited Chatsworth in October 1851 his host was not Paxton but the Duke.

By then Paxton too had made another great leap up the social ladder. Two weeks after the Great Exhibition closed on October 15, he was knighted – a tribute not only to his talent but also to a lifestyle which, according to Charles Dickens in *Household Words*, would 'kill a man of fashion with its hard work'.[40] Sometimes he tried to do too much. He declined to stand for election in Nottingham, but then accepted nomination in Coventry and duly became a Liberal Member of Parliament. He was not a success in the House of Commons, but, with the outbreak of the Crimean War and following a speech about the need for better roads to Balaclava and Sevastopol, was appointed to create a Corps of Navigators – 800 navvies and 200 craftsmen – who would act as pioneers. His activities as a member of the Select Committee on Barrack Accommodation were not confined to attending meetings. He designed a folding bed for use in the front line, tents with hollow poles to act as flues for stoves and a cheap felt ceiling lining by which army huts could be insulated. While Paxton enjoyed exhibitions of his ingenuity, the Duke of Devonshire was trying to reconcile himself to war against Russians or, more exactly, what he saw as war against his friend the Tsar.

That difference in approach – indeed difference in temperament and character – was an illustration of the changing times. The aristocrat was making way for the entrepreneur. In the last year of the Sixth Duke's life the conflict between old money and new was illustrated most dramatically by his disagreement with Paxton over the creation of the Devonshire hospital in Buxton. E. W. Wilmot, the Duke's agent in the town and a popular figure in the area who gave an annual oyster supper to the local clergy and a New Year's ball to the town's tradesmen, was an influential patron of the Bath Charity. He was therefore actively engaged in raising funds to pay for the lodgings of patients who visited the Poor Man's Bath. In 1857 he sponsored an appeal for £6,000 to finance the building of a lodging house which would accommodate eighty-four 'sick mendicants'. The Duke donated a suitable piece of land and paid his architect to prepare plans. Normally the endorsement by the Duke guaranteed a rush of subscribers to any scheme which he approved. But Buxton was not enthusiastic about the prospect of an influx of paupers. The appeal raised only £3,326.

Wilmot knew that the Great Stables were rarely ever used and were falling into disrepair. Indeed, on his own initiative, he had allowed the annual show of the Buxton Agricultural Club to occupy one of their dilapidated rooms. He put his plan to the Duke who – without much thought – agreed. The outburst of opposition with which the news was greeted was not confined to the lodging-house keepers who could have been expected to resist an assault on their livelihoods. Doctor Robertson, the local physician, believed that 'no human creature could be healthy where horses had lived'.[41] Paxton's opposition was based on commercial, rather than medical, considerations. 'So many lame, poor and ill-dressed people infesting the Hall Gardens and using the seats would be very disagreeable to visitors.'[42] The Duke, admitting that he had 'overlooked the great objections there might be',[43] reluctantly changed his mind.

However, Wilmot – believing that the Duke remained sympathetic to the idea – proposed a compromise which met Paxton's point. If his predictions about the results of the influx of eighty-four sick paupers 'proved to be so – which he doubted – they must have enclosed grounds of their own and except in bathing hours be confined to them as in other hospitals'.[44] The Duke agreed and leased the charity – on a peppercorn rent – as many stables as were necessary to accommodate 100 beds, all of the circular exercise yard and its colonnade and an adjacent piece of land to be used as a hospital garden. Five patients were accommodated in the following year. From then on the hospital grew in scope and size – first accepting admissions beyond membership of the Bath Charity and then taking over, piece by piece, the whole stables. It was the Sixth Duke's last show of contempt for financial prudence – and perhaps his best.*

Sentimentalists suggested war with Russia, and his consequential alienation from Tsar Nicholas, contributed to the Sixth Duke of Devonshire's decline and death. That is, at least, a more likely explanation than Paxton's own superstitious alternative – thirteen for dinner with the main dish a swan. Whatever the reason, on the morning of January 18 1858 the Duke's footman found him dead in bed. Immediately after the will had been read, Currey announced that bankruptcy could be averted only by major cuts in expenditure and the family lawyer's plea for economies was supported by his employer, the Seventh Duke, whose response was more draconian than those who knew his gentle nature had anticipated. Paxton, who had been the agent of so much extravagance, could not be expected to supervise the destruction of what he had created. He would have to go. Happily, the Duke was spared the agony of discharging the Devonshires' most devoted and most distinguished servant. Perhaps Paxton anticipated the purpose of the urgent meeting to which he had been summoned. Before a word was spoken, Sir Joseph handed the Duke a letter. 'You will readily believe that it is not without a feeling of great sorrow that I make this communication. My close and intimate association with Chatsworth and the late Duke for a period of upwards of thirty years cannot be severed without a pang. But my other engagements are now so varied and important that I feel a duty to both Your Grace and myself to make this proposal.'⁴⁵ So ended the improbable partnership of 'Paxton and Company' in which ermine and enterprise worked hand-in-hand. Although neither of them knew it – and would have been shocked to be told – it was men like the gardener of genius who brought to an end the exotic world of men like his profligate master.

---

* The stables became a fever hospital. In 1882, the courtyard was covered over by the biggest dome in Britain – bigger in its circumference than the dome of Saint Paul's Cathedral.

CHAPTER 21

The Railway Comes to Rowsley

The coming of the railways made Great Britain a United Kingdom. Steam reduced the price of travel to a level which could be afforded by passengers described by the Great Western Company as 'persons within the lowest stations of life'[1] and in 1844, William Ewart Gladstone, President of the Board of Trade, required all railways to run at least one train a day on which tickets cost no more than 1d a mile – the 'parliamentary trains' about which Sir William Schwenck Gilbert was to write so derisively. Railways also brought together men of power, wealth and ingenuity by combining the fascination of the new with the irresistible attraction of a huge, and apparently guaranteed, profit. The great landowners, over whose acres the railways were to run, suddenly discovered that, by co-operating with the entrepreneurs, new fortunes could be made. Some of them – motivated by excitement as much as by greed – could not wait to seize the opportunity. Others – sceptical about the merits of what the railway engineers called progress – were not prepared to sacrifice the tranquillity of their estates.

When Robert Stephenson and Joseph Paxton proposed the creation of a line to link Manchester (and therefore Liverpool) to the existing Derby-to-London line, the Sixth Duke of Devonshire announced that it was 'welcome to come through any part of his park' as long as it was 'not within smell of the house'.[2] That requirement could, he thought, be met by the excavation of a tunnel of the sort which was being blasted – at great expense and with reckless loss of life – through the Pennine rock at Woodhead, 30 miles away. The Duke of Rutland, in nearby Haddon Hall, took a different view. There was no expedient which would reconcile him to the railway crossing his land.

The Duke of Devonshire was conscious of the benefits that a local railway system would provide for him. Stations conveniently situated at Rowsley on the south of the Chatsworth estate and Baslow on the north would provide easy access to a line. It would even be possible for the two villages to be designated 'halts' at which the train only stopped when requested in advance to do so because a local grandee was waiting to board. During journeys which did not include distinguished passengers the locomotive could speed on without polluting the countryside with the smoke and grime which were spewed out by stationary steam engines. However, the Duke's main interest was financial. The men whose advice he trusted had no doubt that locomotion was a gilt-edged investment.

Although by nature not a reckless man, Paxton had invested in railway shares ever since the late 1830s – initially in Robert Stephenson's Birmingham-to-London line. It may be that his interest had been encouraged by the entrepreneur's father. For George Stephenson – who had, for some years, been buying and leasing property all over North Derbyshire – had developed such an affection for the area that in 1838 he took up residence in Tapton House on the outskirts of Chesterfield. Stephenson was virtually in his retirement and had become an amateur horticulturalist. He built ten greenhouses at Tapton, heated them with hot-water pipes and announced that it was his ambition to 'knock over those at Chatsworth' by growing bigger pineapples and pumpkins than were grown by the Duke. He failed. So he turned to the pursuit by which he hoped to demonstrate his superior skill – the cultivation of a straight cucumber. He succeeded. However, it was generally agreed that he paid a terrible price for his horticultural victory. One obituary attributed his death to 'spending too many years in a hot house in a praiseworthy, but imprudent, rivalry with the Duke of Devonshire in the cultivation of certain exotics'. It then went on to suggest that his competitive instinct was one of the qualities that had made him great. 'Whether peer or commoner, Stephenson could not bear that any other man should be his superior or equal in whatever he undertook.'[3] In that he was at one with Paxton. The engineer-turned-gardener and the gardener who was to become an architect exhibited a competitive impulse, a breadth of interest and ability which was typical of their age. It was through Stephenson that Paxton met another man of similar temperament – Isambard Kingdom Brunel, engineer of the Great Western broad-gauge line, designer of the mighty, iron-built SS *Great Britain* and the director of numerous nascent railway lines. One of them was the Sheffield, Bakewell and Midland and North Derbyshire Union.

Parliamentary debates on bills authorising the development of new lines were preceded by reports from a select committee on the effect that the cuttings, viaducts and tunnels would have on local landscapes and husbandry. Stephenson and Brunel employed Paxton as an expert, if not entirely objective, witness to give evidence to the consequences of the lines which they proposed. It was probably the examination of proposed railway lines which changed him from a speculator into a participant. For until he became professionally as well as financially involved both he and his wife were ambivalent about risking their money on railways. As early as 1839, writing home from the Adelphi Hotel in Liverpool, he left no doubt that he understood the type of man with whom he had to do railway business. 'I saw from the manner of the reports, from the manner of the [company] officers and the manner of the directors that they were anxious to depress the value of the shares to the lowest possible value, intending no doubt, to buy largely now.'[4] Not that he wholly disapproved of their conduct. 'I would buy 100 shares tomorrow if I could find the money to pay for them.'

Sarah Paxton – clearly more emancipated than was usual for women of her class in the middle years of the nineteenth century – was party to most of the transactions. She wrote to tell him that most 'shares are horribly low' and that, since she was 'looking for a line to have a bit of a private go at', she wished that she 'could have been in the city today'[5] and had the opportunity to move some of her money into railways. Sometimes the Paxton shares, individually or jointly owned, fell in value. Then she offered her husband comfort and consolation. 'All this will come right when this little panic is over.'[6] Occasionally she expressed horror at what she clearly believed a reckless decision about which she had not been consulted. 'I am quite flabbergasted you have sold Birkenhead for such a price.'[7] But the overwhelming impression created by their correspondence is that of a close couple united, amongst other things, by a near obsession with railway shares.

> September 1845. In the supplement to the Railway Chronicle I found a very satisfactory report on the Birmingham and Gloucester directors, held Aug 23rd. They have declared a dividend of £1.16s. for £100 shares (ours amount to £300), but I have an idea that the last was £2 per share. Was it? The Bradbury is due today. I see in Paper a prospectus of the Southern Manchester and Oxford Junction Railway.[8]

In 1843 Joseph Paxton – having established a relationship with the town by designing its public park – became a director of the Birkenhead Railway and Docks Company and began his lifelong friendship with Thomas Brassey, the engineer who built a third of England's railway lines. In 1848 Paxton joined the board of the Midland Railway, an amalgamation of the Midland Counties, the North Midland and the Derby and Midland Railways. He certainly accepted the appointment with his employer's blessing and probably with his encouragement. It was not an indulgence which landowning aristocrats would normally extend to their employees. But, by then, Paxton had secured an extraordinary status at Chatsworth and enjoyed an extraordinary relationship with his employer which enabled him to introduce the Duke to George Hudson, the company's chairman[9] – an initiative of which his wife, who never trusted the 'Railway King', heartily disapproved. As early as 1845, when Joseph Paxton still thought that everything Hudson touched turned to gold, she had begged her husband to consider his associate's character and credentials with more sceptical care. 'See if you can detect anything to alter your opinion of this man and his dubious dealings.'[10] But in 1848, Hudson was still regarded with the awe which follows spectacular success. His 'accession to a director's seat in any particular company, immediately gave value to the line'.[11] And the Duke of Devonshire was anxious for the Midland line to prosper. So he was happy to meet the social-climbing draper who longed to be accepted in society, but was usually shunned by the well-connected speculators who hoped to make fortunes from investment in railway lines about which they knew little and cared less.

The Midland – much to the delight of the North Derbyshire towns which felt keenly their isolation from the railway network – decided to make a second attempt to link Manchester and Derby with what the company proposed to call the Manchester, Buxton, Matlock and Midland Junction Railway. Its hopes of success were encouraged by the Duke of Rutland's change of heart. The private bill authorising construction of the line was passed by parliament, accompanied by much rejoicing, in the year that Paxton became an M.B.M.M.J.R. director. News that the Duke of Devonshire – by then an infrequent participant in parliamentary business – had given evidence in support of the bill was greeted with unrestrained joy in the towns and villages which believed that they were about to be connected to the great world outside their parishes. Sarah Paxton wrote to tell her (as usual) absent husband that Chatsworth was 'in an uproar'.[12] In Castleton, Hope, Bamford, Hathersage and Chapel-en-le-Frith, church bells rang, town bands paraded through the streets and inns gave away free beer. In Chapel, pupils were given the day off from school to make a solemn visit to the place where, it was believed, the station would be built and in Bamford a cannon (origin unknown) was fired in salute. Even in an age in which carrier pigeons were released from outside parliament to speed the joyous news of a railway bill's passage,[13] the Derbyshire celebrations were exceptional. Unfortunately, the rejoicing was not wholly justified.

Parliament – impressed by the news that Chatsworth received 60,000 visitors each year – accepted the Duke's advice and agreed that the new line could be built along the proposed route. But agreement came too late: 1848 was the Year of Revolution in Europe. In England the repeal of the Corn Laws had reduced the price of wheat and barley to a point at which many farms were no longer viable. As always, psychological and economic depression went hand-in-hand. The optimism, which had joined with greed to intensify railway mania, had vanished. Even Hudson, on paper still prosperous, could not raise new capital. So the best that the new company, the Manchester, Buxton, Matlock and Midland Junction Railway, could do was build what it hoped would be the first 11½ miles of the proposed track and link Rowsley – just south of Bakewell and almost equidistant between Chatsworth and Haddon – to the main line at Ambergate. The branch line, along Monsal Dale to Buxton, was not completed until 1863. So the Sixth Duke was spared denunciation by John Ruskin who thought the necessary viaduct – now a protected national treasure – a desecration of the landscape.[14]

The Rowsley-to-Ambergate line was opened on June 4 1849. The Duke's coach overturned just as it arrived at Rowsley station. No one was hurt but the coachman was instantly dismissed. Nobody regarded the accident as an augury of disasters to come. George Cavendish, MP – by then chairman of the M.B.M.M.J.R. – opened the proceedings with a speech which included a tribute to the 'irresistible energy and indomitable perseverance of Mr Paxton' and Paxton replied with an encomium to the Duke of Devonshire who had sold rights of way to the company for the price normally charged for agricultural land. He did not behave with such public spirit when it was proposed that a railway be constructed between Newark and Chesterfield. He successfully opposed the application on the grounds that the line would run too close to Hardwick Hall. But on the great opening day, Paxton spoke as if the Duke of Devonshire was a railway pioneer. Had other landowners, he said without mentioning the Duke of Rutland, behaved with similar public spirit, the whole line would have been completed four or five years earlier. But his strongest criticism was levelled against the government. It had, he claimed, 'done everything bad'[15] and must be prevented, at all cost, from extending its influence over the development of future railways. By then Paxton had become almost as engrossed in the creation of new lines as he had been, ten years earlier, in the propagation of exotic plants. Dickens probably overstated his power when he described him as possessing 'command of every railway influence in England and abroad except the Great Western'.[16] But he was right to say that Paxton's emotional and financial commitment put him 'in the heart and purse' of the whole industry.

The Ambergate-to-Rowsley line was an immediate success. Thomas Cook, from down the line in Melbourne, had devised a scheme by which train tickets were bought in advance by weekly instalments. Day trippers, taking advantage of the offer, poured into Chatsworth. The first visitors came from Derby and were carefully supervised as they toured the house and garden. Two thousand teetotallers from Sheffield were trusted to explore the gardens alone. Since visitors were not charged for entry, the increased popularity of Chatsworth did nothing to reduce the Duke's debts. But the revenue from rent and sale of land adjacent to the railways did, although the increase in value was less than he had expected. The return on his railway investment was similarly welcome and disappointing.

Paxton, on the other hand, had bought all the right stock. It was the railways which made him a fortune which at the time of his death was more than £180,000 – the equivalent of £10 million today. Yet Sarah was never quite reconciled to what she believed was his exploitation by the moguls of the industry. She had cautioned him to take care in his relations with 'the overgrown Nabob', George Hudson. 'I fear he only uses you as a tool.'[17] And she had complained that his real vocation and his family were being sacrificed to his fascination with the speculators in lines, sleepers and rolling stock. 'The railways have harassed you for years and I certainly think that you are acting improperly in giving up so much time to them.'[18] Even work on the North Derbyshire line – from which a profit was rightly expected – was regarded as a health hazard and an example of how lesser men benefited from his endeavours, 'I wish you would take this Peak railway easy. Do not encumber yourself till you have not breathing time. Look at George Cavendish. He won't act. Look at old Hancock; he won't stir. But they have no hesitation in partaking of the profit when you have been the slave.'[19] Of course her husband took no notice. Paxton was not a man to bother about such trifling considerations as being exploited. Being the personification of Victorian values, the railways – romance as well as remuneration – were in his blood. The Sixth Duke of Devonshire – in spirit a man of an earlier era – could remain more detached from the great innovation. But his successor was, like Paxton, enthralled by the power and potential of steam. As a result he was to lose as much as Paxton made.

CHAPTER 22

Moving with the Times

William Cavendish the Seventh Duke of Devonshire was a serious man who – unlike his predecessor – found his pleasure in family, religion, scholarship and gainful employment. He was the child of wealth and power. But he was denied, or escaped, the opulence of Chatsworth and Devonshire House and was brought up in the restrained, though hardly austere, surroundings of Holker Hall, in the Vale of Furness. He inherited the title because the Fifth Duke fathered only one son and the Sixth remained a bachelor. So the line had to be traced back 100 years to the birth of Lord George Augustus Henry Cavendish, First Earl of Burlington (by the second creation) and second son of the Fourth Duke of Devonshire.

Burlington – a Member of Parliament for fifty-six years who successfully petitioned for the restoration of the title which had been dormant since the death of his paternal grandfather – had followed the Cavendish tradition and married money. His wife, Lady Elizabeth Compton, was the daughter of the Seventh Earl of Northampton and had inherited Compton Place and its Sussex estates surrounding Eastbourne. In 1812, their eldest son, William Cavendish, died at the age of twenty-nine after being thrown from his carriage in Holker Park. At the time, his heir, another William, was four years old. Fifty years later, he became the Seventh Duke of Devonshire.

Before the religious conversion which had filled his final years with guilt and remorse, the Sixth Duke had personified the elegant decadence of Georgian England – even after the spirit of the times had changed. By force of circumstances, his successor came to represent the sterner ethos of the Victorian age, the industries on which it was built and the competitive economy which thrived on the idea that progress depended on accepting that, in both life and business, some people win and some people lose. The Seventh Duke of Devonshire usually lost.

The William Cavendish who became the Seventh Duke, was – true to family tradition – sent to Eton. It was the brutish period in the history of English public schools, during which bullying by older boys and physical assaults by the masters were thought to be essential to the proper education of gentlemen. William – a sensitive and intelligent boy – took refuge in work and worship. As a result he went up to Cambridge as a genuine scholar, graduated as second wrangler and was placed eighth in the classical tripos. In the same year, at the age of twenty-one, he was elected Member of Parliament for the university and married Blanche Howard, fourth daughter of the Earl of Carlisle and granddaughter of the famous Georgiana Devonshire. He must have felt that fortune smiled on him. It did not smile on him for long.

In 1831 William Cavendish supported the first attempt to pass a Reform Bill. The university did not. In the general election which followed the bill's defeat, Cavendish lost his seat. He moved on, thanks to family connections, first to Malton in Yorkshire and then to Derbyshire. In the meantime, the University of London – perhaps as a rebuke to Cambridge for rejecting so distinguished a scholar – elected him Chancellor of the University at the age of twenty-six.* As soon as he took up residence in Holker Hall in 1836 – two years after he inherited the Burlington earldom – he agreed to become chairman of the local Board of Guardians. It was a mark of his instinct for public service. But he was far too introverted to make much of a mark in parliament and force of circumstances required him to concentrate most of his time and energy on commerce. Despite his mother's inheritance, the family was near to bankruptcy. Unfortunately he tried to build the restoration of his fortunes on an enterprise that was doomed from the start. In 1838 he ruefully wrote in his diary: 'My ordinary expenses are, I fear, barely within my income and I have two large extra claims for money.' One 'claim' was 'the addition to Holker Hall'. That was a liability which was only forced upon him by the Cavendish family's building gene. The other was 'the new slate works',[1] an enterprise which he anticipated would make a profit that he would use to reduce his debts. It made losses which increased them. Worse still, the hope that it would one day be successful encouraged the development of a variety of related enterprises which – after at best briefly flourishing – made heavy losses. Twenty years later, when he was promoted from earl to duke, he inherited new debts to add to the old. He reacted to his even more precarious condition by increasing his investment in the activities which had, during the previous two decades, brought him to the brink of bankruptcy. He could not be shifted from the laudable, though vain, belief that the prescription for financial salvation was expansion not contraction. In that, he was a child of his time, the first

---

* Cambridge made amends by electing him Chancellor of the University in 1861.

Cavendish to realise that the future lay in industry and commerce. But he continued the aristocratic habit of building and rebuilding houses which were better described as palaces, because he was a Cavendish and building was an ancient family addiction.

Often his errors were compounded by the boyish wonder that always engulfed him when he entered the new world of enterprise. It was territory into which the aristocracy rarely ventured and for which he was profoundly unsuited. In January 1838, after a gloomy assessment of his financial prospects he 'went to see the Electric Telegraph at Exeter Hall' and was immediately excited by its commercial potential. 'The mechanism seems perfect to attain its purpose . . . I think there is no obstacle against adopting it on a large scale.'[2] The notion of a large scale was to prove his undoing. Whenever one of his ventures began to lose money his inclination was to do more rather than less and to invest in related endeavours which, he believed, would turn the loss into a profit. He was encouraged in his profligacy by men who were willing to gamble his money on schemes of their own invention. Although he was far too clever not to worry about the quality of advice that he received, he was far too indecisive to reject it.

The land east of Holker Hall, its minerals and its potential port, were not the only possible source of Burlington revenue. In 1833, his grandfather had been convinced by Decimus Burton that the family land in and around Eastbourne could be developed into a prosperous holiday resort. Burton was the architectural prodigy who had designed the layout of Hyde Park when he was twenty-five and the Wellington Arch at Hyde Park Corner, the Athenaeum and Regent Park's Cornwall Terrace before he was thirty. His plan for Eastbourne was simply explained and, he believed, infallible. Brighton had prospered, thanks to the patronage of George IV. Southend, although less fashionable, was near enough to London to attract the holiday trade which – because of the example set by the Prince Regent – grew year by year. Eastbourne – then a small town with a population of 3,000, one lawyer, one brewery and five inns – languished. The First Earl of Burlington had been reluctant to risk time and money on the hope that it could become the third south coast dormitory and resort. Three years after he died, Burton approached the Second Earl and future Seventh Duke of Devonshire with the same idea.

The Second Earl was interested. Burton suggested that he begin by constructing no more than infrastructure – roads, sewers and a sea wall – at the cost of £2,200.[3] Sixty acres of land could then be opened up for building. A second more ambitious scheme would have cost £7,500, but while the new Earl was pondering the alternatives, Burton

Henry Cavendish
Weighing the world

William Cavendish,
Fifth Duke of Devonshire
'The only man in society
who did not love...'

...his wife, Georgiana

Charles Grey
Father of both the Great Reform Bill
and Georgiana's illegitimate son

Lady Elizabeth Foster
The Fifth Duke's mistress,
his wife's friend and 'the quietist
(sic) thing in the world'

Georgiana gambling at Devonshire House
'Discretion and good sense, finding themselves deserted, abandoned her'

Babble, Birth and Brummagem
Gladstone, Hartington and Chamberlain on the Liberal front bench

William Spencer Cavendish,
Sixth Duke of Devonshire
'A great deal to spend'

Sir Joseph Paxton
'Do more. Earn more. Be more'

Spencer Compton Cavendish, Eighth Duke of Devonshire
'The last of the golden age'

Lord Frederick Cavendish
'Full of love for the country'
in which he was killed

Unknown to his assailants and killed by chance

Hardwick Hall
'More glass than wall'

Chatsworth House
The Tsar, for whom the Emperor Fountain was created, cancelled his visit

offered another option – using land known as the Meads. Burlington accepted the third proposal. Trinity Chapel, designed as the first building on the site, was actually begun. But three months after the work started, Burton transferred his skills to the development of St Leonards along the coast. And without the constant encouragement of the architect, Burlington lost interest. The creation of a holiday resort had never stirred his imagination. Even when Burton was still preparing the last of his plans for what should have been a project too exciting to neglect, Burlington had set out with his wife on the Grand Tour of Europe. When, in June 1839, they returned to England after an absence of almost two years, the first commercial news that he received concerned Furness not Sussex. 'A cargo of slate has been tried [for sale] in Ireland and . . . the failure is complete.'[4] Six months of declining income and increasing gloom followed. In 1840, Burlington's depression turned into despair after a tragedy which scarred him for life and made him a temporary recluse.

On April 27 1840, the Countess of Burlington – twenty-eight and the mother of four small children – died. It now seems that the cause of death was too frequent pregnancies. The first symptom of what turned out to be her fatal illness was no more than lethargy. Her doctors diagnosed nervous debility and prescribed a hemlock-based sedative.[5] Not surprisingly, her condition deteriorated. What was meant to be a restorative carriage ride ended when she began to cough blood. Her death was almost as traumatic in its effect on the Duke of Devonshire as it was on Burlington. The old Duke had begun to regard Blanche as a surrogate daughter for whom, according to her husband, 'all the alterations and projects at Chatsworth were done very much in the feeling that she would come after him and take pleasure in them'.[6] That was almost certainly the invention of a bereaved husband. But the intensity of the Duke's grief is not in doubt. In its extreme form it accepted Blanche's death as divine retribution for his years of sinful excess. At the Countess's funeral he told a friend that 'An avenging God' had forced him to ask himself, 'How dare I complain?'[7] The mourning widower – to whom religion had not come so suddenly – described emotions which, while equally intense, were less irrational. The night Blanche died, he wrote in his diary: 'All is over. I have lost the joy of my heart – my Blanche is taken away from me for ever. The will of God be done, but it is bitter grief.'[8] From then on, 'shyness and desolation settled down upon him. His bowed figure tacked into a room like a vessel finding an intricate channel.'[9]

Burlington turned for comfort to his children – Spencer Compton, the first to survive, Louisa, Frederick and Edward. Moved by his kinsman's desolation, the Sixth Duke suggested that the whole Burlington family move to Derbyshire. 'Many circumstances of my younger days combined to prevent me marrying. You are my heir, be my son . . . Your children would be the delight of my life.'[10] The widower declined in the certainty that his children would be unlikely to reflect their mother's saintly image if their formative years were spent in Chatsworth. He chose to educate his three surviving sons himself at home, rather than subject them to the rigours of Eton. Between his wife's death and his succession to the Devonshire title and estate, parental duty combined with personal inclination to ensure he rarely left Holker Hall. When forced to visit London he wrote long letters home which included complaints that his sons wrote too rarely to him.

The affection in which he held his children was reciprocated. The boys – two of whom became central figures in the politics of nineteenth-century England – welcomed his advice, as well as his financial assistance, well into middle age. Indeed Spencer Compton – one of the great figures of the Victorian parliament – rarely took a political decision without consulting his father. But it was Louisa, the only daughter of the too-brief marriage, who displayed most selfless devotion. At the age of fourteen she assumed command of the Holker Hall housekeeping – a responsibility that she kept even after her marriage to an amiable admiral who agreed to move into his father-in-law's house.

If Burlington failed as a father, it was because he was over-indulgent towards his sons. Since he could see little wrong in anything they did, he found it hard to correct and criticise. Spencer Compton – a country sportsman rather than a scholar who had little or no interest in learning – he described as a 'delightful boy full of life and animation' and added, almost wistfully, 'I trust he has strong religious feelings, but he is certainly fond of amusement.'[11] As the years passed he began to believe that he had a greater duty to his sons than merely teaching them Latin and Greek and the other essential elements of a good education. Like all Devonshires he felt an obligation to leave behind a tangible inheritance – more land, improved houses, new titles. His hope was that he could also bequeath to the next generation an inheritance which, to earlier members of the family, must have seemed a modest aspiration. He wanted to leave his sons solvent. That daunting task assumed additional importance as the years passed – not least because of the Earl's feeling of obligation towards the people of the Holker estate and the town of Barrow 20 miles away. But it was family feeling that drove him on – sometimes recklessly – to find new ways of making money.

Even before his return from the Grand Tour in 1839 Burlington had lost most of his illusions about the prospect of turning the slate quarry accounts from red to black. In early 1838 he methodically listed the initiatives which had to be taken and the problems which had to be overcome if they were to be made viable. '1. Shipping the freight by sea, using flat bottomed boats. 2. Using water power to turn a powerful wheel. 3. The expense of carrying the railway to the higher ground. 4. The cost of working the quarry and mill under present circumstances.'[12] Nevertheless, he agreed to go ahead before the necessary changes were made, even though he also put his anxiety on record. 'I have been most perturbed about my affairs today . . . I have borrowed £34,000 in the last three years, partly to buy land, partly to carry on a slate quarry which I fear will never answer.'[13]

Benjamin Currey (the Cavendish family solicitor who had been recruited to provide advice which he was not qualified to give) suggested that the slate quarry should be leased to a mining company. But that would only be possible if new money was invested in a railway with a branch line to a deep-water port, allowing the slate to be transported by steamer rather than flat-bottomed boats. Burlington agreed to put up the money but, almost immediately, decided that it was 'a very wild scheme'. His willingness to invest in such a dubious venture was encouraged by advice he received about the possibility of mining and exporting iron ore. There was no certainty of success. Some of the mineral rights on the land with the best potential yield were owned ('usurped' in Burlington's opinion) by the Duke of Buccleuch and there was little chance of negotiating a partnership or obtaining legal title. But he behaved in a way which came to typify his reaction to business propositions. He feared that the venture would fail but still agreed to go ahead. At the same time he decided that Jopling, the slate quarry manager, employed 'too many over-lookers and the men are suffered to waste their time'.[14] Again, he reacted in a way which exemplified his failings as an businessman. He identified the problem but made no attempt to rectify it.

In July 1839 the first of the 'experts', on whose advice Burlington so often relied, came into his life. 'Mr Schneider, a London merchant' reinforced the suggestion that 'opening some [iron ore] workings' would be profitable.[15] The hopes of long-term solvency ebbed and flowed – at least in Burlington's mind – as disconcertingly as the prospect of slate quarrying making a profit waxed and waned. In August 1839 Schneider was said to have 'met very promising appearances in his search for iron ore'.[16] But in March of the following year 'the iron ore [was] not turning out as well as Mr Schneider expected'.[17] Explorations were, however, continued on three sites. Then plans were laid to build a dam at Standish Colt to drive the necessary water wheel. By December 1840, hopes were not so much revived as thought to be realised. During the previous twelve months 40,000 tons of high-quality haematite iron had been extracted from mines on Burlington's land. It had all been transported to the coast in farm carts and then shipped out from the shallow-water port of Barrow, 80 to 200 tons at a time, in flat-bottomed boats.[18] The argument in favour of a railway branch line seemed irresistible.

The unexpected good news about iron ore was followed by renewed 'despair about the [slate] quarry ever succeeding'.[19] Burlington was convinced that 'Jopling must go'.[20] But Jopling stayed and in a last desperate attempt to make both minerals earn much-needed revenue Burlington took the decisions which precipitated events that guaranteed him a place in the history of the Industrial Revolution. In 1842, Captain Eddy, a mining expert, was employed to modernise the quarries and later in the same year, James Walker, an engineer, was commissioned by Burlington, the Earl of Lonsdale and the Duke of Buccleuch to consider how increased production of both slate and iron ore could be exported to the expanding economies of Britain, Europe and the New World. On October 31 1850 Burlington noted in his diary: 'Schneider and Davis found ore on my farm at Parkhead and are going to put up an engine.'[21] That increased the ambition to transport the ore – new finds and old – to the iron and steel works of England. The result was the Furness Railway – initially intended, according to the prospectus published in November 1843, only to run from the quarries and mines to a possible deep-water port at Roa Island at the mouth of the Walney Channel, south of Barrow-in-Furness.

In the years before the railway plan was launched, the performance and prospects of the slate quarry and works added to Burlington's melancholy to the point at which he was 'almost in despair about [them] ever succeeding'.[22] But he continued to subsidise their losses. And he was 'more than ever convinced that Jopling must go'[23] even before he discovered that 'he had all along grievously misled and deceived the company'.[24] But Jopling stayed. Burlington took refuge in another plausible panacea. The productive potential of both the port and the slate work would be released and realised if a railway connected them to the industrial North and Midlands of England.

The Furness Railway Company was launched with a subscribed capital of £750,000 – almost all of it provided, in a number of different forms, by Burlington, Buccleuch and Currey. It was expected to earn revenue from passenger as well as freight traffic. The first order for passenger rolling stock – placed in December 1845 – was limited to four carriages with first- and second- though no third-class compartments.[25] The idea of day trippers to the sea was to come later. By January 1846, the company was sufficiently well established to build, 'as cheaply as can be', ten cottages for its employees – 'price not to exceed £100'.[26] Later that year four houses were built, at a cost of £210 each, to accommodate foremen and managers. Among the occupants was James Ramsden, the new locomotive superintendent. He was to become a major figure in all of the Burlington enterprises and is now regarded as the founding father of modern Barrow-in-Furness.

In what was the age of railway mania, other companies were being created in north-west England and promoting the necessary parliamentary bills. Some seemed likely to further the Earl's interests. 'A line is projected from Barnard Castle to Tebay which is likely to be very useful to us and which, therefore, we shall further as much as we can.'[27] Some competitors were so big that they had to be accommodated. In November 1856 a group of men described as 'Westmorland gentry and railway promoters' met at Kirkby Stephen to discuss if it was possible to connect 'the ironstone of the East with the ports and the manufactures of the West'.[28] Amongst them was Henry Pease of the Stockton and Darlington Railway Company and the founder of modern Middlesbrough. That alone was enough to make the enterprise a serious proposition. When the directors of the Furness Railway met on December 17 they responded with a resolution to assist in the completion of the (until then) rival Ulverston and Lancaster Railway. Burlington and Buccleuch acted as guarantors of the required £50,000 new capital. Eventually the line was extended north to Broughton and a line from Ulverston to Lancaster linked it to the main rail network. From then on a north-western rail network existed in a complicated state of co-operative competition.

Building the railways helped to revive Burlington's spirits. After May 1845, when Benjamin Currey persuaded him of the wisdom of 'continuing our line to Ulverston, Greenodd and Newby Bridge',[29] his life was filled by inspections of embankments and cuttings, examination of earthworks which protected low-lying stretches of line from tides and floods, drainage schemes for the stretches of track which ran along the sands, discussion of plans to complete the inclined plane to the slate works and debates about the need to build a pier. Two or three days each week were occupied with railway business. By June 18, the therapy was complete and he could triumphantly announce. 'The railway is nearly ready for opening.'[30] For once the prediction was only slightly over-optimistic.

Two months later 'the inclined plane to join the railway [to the slate works] had made little progress and altogether everything connected with the railway is behind what I expected'.[31] But the line was opened on October 11 1846, barely four months later than planned. A handful of travellers from Skegness – who made the journey just to experience the wonder of locomotion – confirmed its potential as a passenger line. The inaugural dinner on October 20 – featuring a speech from the Duke of Buccleuch and a vote of thanks from Burlington – 'had been intended to take place much earlier'.[32] So small an inconvenience did nothing to reduce Burlington's irrational faith in the eventual triumph of enterprise. But his determination to fill the gap left in his family's life by the death of his wife prevented the full exploitation of his entrepreneurial instinct. In December 1846, he received a letter from Earl Russell, the Prime Minister, 'offering to place [him] at the head of the Railway Board'. He declined. 'It would totally disarrange my plans with regard to my children.'[33]

In March 1848, Benjamin Currey died and was replaced as chairman of the Furness Railway Company by Burlington. Another gap left by the lawyer's death was harder to fill. Burlington – although an aristo-crat with genuine intellectual credentials – so lacked confidence that he needed an adviser to provide constant, if sometimes counterfeit, reassurance. Paxton, on whom the Sixth Duke of Devonshire had once relied so heavily, was the obvious man to fill the old solicitor's place. But it is clear that Burlington neither completely trusted him nor treated him with the awe and reverence to which he was accustomed. However – in an act of admirable humility – the Duke invited him to return and – in an act of equally laudable grace – he accepted. The first busi-ness meeting which he attended got off to a predictable start. The Furness Railway was discovered to be in a worse state than Burlington 'was prepared for'. Possibly prompted by Paxton, he attributed his ignorance to the fact that Currey 'had grievously misled him'.[34]

For the next two years there were regular meetings – sometimes two a week – to discuss possible extensions. The Broughton-to-Coniston Line was a particular favourite as it was 'cheaply constructed . . . £16,000 to cover all expenses'.[35] Other estimates were proving consist-ently unreliable – the Lindal extension 'cost much more than we expected'.[36] However – despite the damage to confidence done by the fall of George Hudson, 'the Railway King' – railway mania, which had made its belated arrival in the north-west, raged on. Other companies – notably, Lord Lonsdale's Whitehaven-to-Furness line – had begun to compete for what, in 1850, was limited business. Paxton caused irritation by failing to hide that he had other things on his mind. In July 1850, Burlington made his first visit to Chatsworth in three years. Paxton was there, 'full of his great glasshouse for the Exhibition of 1851'.[37] The concession – 'I suppose it is a great triumph for him'[38] – was clearly made through clenched teeth and the rejection of Paxton's proposal to lease part of the railway to independent contractors was treated as a minor triumph since its advocate was 'nettled and disconcerted'.[39]

By then Burlington had revived his interest in the Sussex estate. The catalyst that caused the sudden explosion of enthusiasm was the news that the London, Brighton and South Coast Railway was to open a branch line to Hastings, passing through Polegate, 6 miles from Eastbourne. James Berry, the Sussex county surveyor, was commissioned to prepare a plan, based on the assumption that a building boom would follow the railway. He advised that a sea wall was the first essential. Simpson, Burlington's local agent, was keen for him to start building at once, but he hesitated.[40]

The caution, if caution it was, did not last for long. At Burlington's request, a new version of Berry's plan was prepared. It proposed a sea wall and a promenade with squares of houses behind them. Between 1850 and 1853, seventy building agreements were signed and for a couple of years all seemed to be going well. Fifty large houses were completed and ready for let or sale by the end of 1851.[41] But long before the whole scheme was finished, the early contractors ran out of money. Some houses were left unfinished, denying Burlington the income, from either sale or rent, on which he relied. Between 1850 and 1855, he subsidised Eastbourne builders by at least £37,000[42] and, as a result, by 1859, all the houses in the first development scheme had been finished and sold. And westward, the land also looked bright. The ore mines were prospering. In 1857 he was receiving 1s 3d a ton in royalties and Schneider calculated: 'I shall pay to Lord Burlington upwards of £8,000 this year.'[43] H. W. Schneider and Robert Hannay had begun to create the Barrow Haematite Steel Company. The Earl never held more than a minority stake in the company. But it was the steel works – founded in 1858, the year in which Burlington became the Seventh Duke of Devonshire – from which more than a decade of Cavendish (and Furness) prosperity flowed.

The income from industry helped to pay the bills which, paradoxically, were the price the Duke was forced to pay for the ownership of nine grand properties in addition to Holker Hall – Hardwick Hall and Chatsworth House in Derbyshire, Bolton Abbey in Yorkshire, Compton Place in Sussex, Lismore Castle in Ireland, Beaufort House in Newmarket as well as Chiswick House, Devonshire House and Burlington House in London. Burlington also acquired title to exten-sive lands in Lancashire, Derbyshire and Yorkshire. So perhaps he should not be blamed for discovering, with astonishment, that 'the income is large, but by far the greatest part of it is absorbed by the payment of interest, annuities and expenses of Chatsworth'.[44] It was, he wrote, with admirable restraint, 'a worse condition of affairs than I had expected'. At a loss to know how to make his books balance, he asked the Duke of Bedford – by reputation, a shrewd businessman – for advice. His total indebtedness was, he said, 'very little less than a million'. His gross annual income was £200,000, but after repairs and maintenance, principally at Chatsworth, it was reduced to £115,000. More than half of what remained was absorbed in interest payments and the discharge of annuities. In a good year there was additional income of as much as £20,000 from lead and iron mines. But in a bad year he believed that the mines earned virtually nothing. His dilemma was how 'out of an available income of £55,000 and which, more probably than not may be reduced to £40,000 or £45,000, I can safely calculate on being able to meet my expenditure ordinary and extraordinary and at the same time set apart a considerable sum annually (which I think ought not to be less than £20,000) towards paying off the debt[45] . . . I have been very busy looking over the agent's estate accounts.. The result shows that great economies are everywhere necessary.'[46]

The Duke of Devonshire's first instinct – being, by the standards of his elevated status, a modest man – was to sell one or more of his houses. 'I have so many', he told Bedford, 'that to get rid of them would be a relief rather than a sacrifice.'[47] But for all his natural reticence he was a Cavendish. So he feared that the sale 'might lower the position of my family'.[48] No doubt Lismore, being in Ireland, could be sold without damage to his reputation in English society. But he was conscious that, if he resorted to that desperate expedient, 'the number of people to be dismissed must be very great and great discontent is inevitable'.[49] Bedford's advice was based on Devonshire's aristocratic obligations rather than his apprehensions about Irish unrest. 'The duties and responsibilities of such an estate as yours and mine are very great. We must discharge them as best we can and make a good amount to look back on at close of life.'[50] The Duke accepted that to sell land would be a betrayal of his heritage – a noble precept which he and his descendants were forced, as the crisis deepened, to abandon. So he turned to other ways of re-establishing the family fortunes.

One expedient was reducing the cost of running Chatsworth. There, unlike Lismore, staff could be discharged without the fear of rick-burning and riot. Joseph Paxton – by then a knight, a Member of Parliament, an acknowledged expert on all things horticultural and the director of numerous public companies but still in the employment of the Devonshire family – had already been 'let go'. His last advice to his employer had encapsulated the ruthless spirit with which he epitomised the values of Victorian enterprise. Mendicants, he told the Duke, were being treated too indulgently at the Buxton spa and 'the result of that generosity was a complete absence of initiative [which] put a premium on lazy indifference'.[51] Paxton was an early critic of welfare dependency.

Like all good Victorians, the Seventh Duke of Devonshire thought of 'industry' as a virtuous attribute and, when defined as the alternative to agriculture, the commercial activity on which prosperity could be built. He was a man of his times and the times were what patriots thought to be the apogee of Britain's greatness. The mightiest empire the world had ever known was widely believed to be the birthplace of the Industrial Revolution and still the most successful manufacturing nation in the world. In fact Britain was running a poor second to Germany and the national balance sheet only showed a surplus because of 'invisible exports' to India. But Devonshire proved himself in tune with the spirit of the age by investing his hopes of future prosperity in steel and ships – as well as demonstrating that he was a man with an eye to the future by reviving his belief that, despite the Eastbourne disappointments, sooner or later the new middle classes would, by imitating the behaviour of their betters, create demands for goods and services to which their parents and grandparents did not even aspire. So he divided his eggs between two baskets. Heavy industry would be hatched in Barrow on the coast of his Holker Estates and houses and associated amenities germinated in and about Eastbourne on the 11,000 acres of Sussex land which the family had acquired when his grandfather married Elizabeth Compton.

Whatever his other shortcomings as investor and proprietor the Seventh Duke was neither quick to blame nor swift to fire. Indeed, he usually tolerated failure for far too long. James Berry, the county surveyor who drew up the first Eastbourne development plan, was generally agreed not to possess the imagination which the scheme demanded. But he was discharged only when Burlington inherited Henry Currey, the nephew of the Devonshires' long-serving family solicitor – along with the dukedom in 1858 – and gave him the job of project director out of tribal loyalty. He produced a new development plan which was ready in the following year. It immediately provoked an argument between the Duke and a Mr Gilbert – a rival developer – over the water supply. The dispute was settled on the Duke's terms and the two men drew up a plan for roads and sewers which effectively opened up all Eastbourne to speculative building and would, they both agreed, stimulate a housing boom. For a while it did. 'New building meets the eye on every side,' wrote the *Eastbourne Gazette*.[52] 'Fields are turned into streets, squares and other construction.'

The catastrophe, which the Duke should have realised was inevitable, was largely the result of the need to economise. Currey's town plan was, on the Duke's instruction, less expensive to implement than Berry's original scheme. Part of the savings were made by modifying the plans for a fresh-water supply and arterial drainage. At the height of the development's apparent success the town was struck by a scarlet fever epidemic. The *Eastbourne Gazette* reported the 'great injury inflicted on our trade and lodging house keepers'.[53] Funds were raised to construct a new drainage system. Before it was completed the contractors went bankrupt. The Duke of Devonshire paid all the outstanding bills and the remaining cost of the scheme. Eastbourne had caught him in the same web of diminishing hope and escalating payments that had ensnared him in Barrow. But Barrow absorbed more of his time than Eastbourne – and much more of his money.

The romance of steel caught his imagination. By the end of December 1858 Schneider had begun to smelt steel and, in the first month of the New Year, Devonshire, as he had just become, 'went to Barrow and saw the iron run out of Schneider's furnaces'. He found it 'a sight worth seeing particularly after dark'.[54] In November 1863, the Duke and James Ramsden had their first serious discussions about creating a major steelworks at Hindpool, close to Schneider's smelters. The Duke invested £40,000 and the work began in the following March. There were the usual setbacks – shortage of labour, inadequate management and the sudden breakdown of machinery – but by 1866 the Haematite Company was operating in a building 750 by 250 feet which contained reheat furnaces, rail, bar and tyre mills. The instinct to expand and innovate was irresistible. In 1863, the Duke had been a guest at the opening of John Brown's rolling mills in Sheffield and witnessed – as well as the rolling of 5½-inch armour plate – 'the Bessemer process for making steel'.[55] Ten years later, the Hindpool smelting works was the most efficient Bessemer plant in the world. In 1873 its 3,000 workmen produced 250,000 tons of pig iron and 100,000 tons of steel – most of it going to its sister enterprise the Haematite Company.

Thanks to the increased demand for iron and steel, the Furness Railway, which transported it east, began to prosper and expand – despite all the vicissitudes which had characterised its early development. It extended its line north to Broughton and east to Ulverston. The Ulverston and Lancaster line – a bargain because it had been rescued by Devonshire capital and important because it provided an indirect link to the national rail network – was absorbed into the company. A subsidiary, the South Durham and Lancashire Junction Company, connected the steelworks to the coking coalfields of the north-east and, as confirmation of its eminent position in the industrial life of the country, direct lines were established to the Midland and the London and North-Western Railways. The region's horizons seemed boundless. The Furness Railway bought the Ulverston Canal and Barrow Island Company. Once again the optimism far exceeded the bounds of reality. Plans were made for the steelworks and the railway – and even the slate quarries – to be opened up to world markets by the construction of a port to rival Liverpool.

In the rush to build the best and biggest steelworks in England, the second 'shed' was begun before the first was in full operation. That allowed time for neither caution nor careful calculation. Contractors were paid exorbitant prices to complete the buildings. Even so, 'scarcity of labour' meant 'less progress than expected'.[56] The chosen remedy was the offer of higher wages which, it was hoped, would attract workmen from all over the country. The need to recruit from far afield – Barrow grew from a hamlet of 140 inhabitants in 1846 to a town with 3,000 citizens in 1861 and over 73,000 in 1873 – established the pattern. When the steelworks was built and working, it was impossible to reduce wages to the level paid by competitors or to revise conditions of employment which were far more favourable than those which regulated neighbouring industries. The company did try. In 1872, the Barrow Trades Council had negotiated – on behalf of the local steelworkers – a nine-hour working day. Two years later – at the first sign of reduced demand – the company announced an increase in the working week from 54 to 57½ hours and a 5 per cent reduction in wages. The workers, organised in the Associated Society of Engineers, rejected the proposal point blank. The result was a ten-month lockout which ended with the compromise of a wage cut but no extra hours. The damage that the stoppage did was only a prelude to the steady decline of the company for the rest of the decade. Sidney Gilchrist Thomas had perfected what he called the 'basic' steel-making process which, since it allowed the smelting of phosphoric iron, reduced industry's demand for haematite. Cheap Spanish and Swedish non-phosphoric iron, easily transported to the steelworks of the North-East and Midlands of England, had begun to compete with the ore mined in and about Furness and the expensive steel products which it produced.

The American railway boom had ended and with it the demand for 'Bessemer rails'.

Even if retrenchment had been the Duke of Devonshire's way, by the time that the iron and steel began to show a loss it was too late to husband his dwindling resources. New enterprises were being developed which, it was hoped, would complement the old. When Devonshire confirmed that 'the proposed Jute and Flour Mill will be commenced very shortly', he was able to add that 'there seems no doubt that a Shipbuilding Yard will follow'.[57] The project was even more ambitious than the Duke revealed, though he described the planning of the gigantic enterprise in alarmingly inconsequential language – 'a good deal of talk about starting a shipbuilding company and also a company for building and owning a line of transatlantic steamers'.[58] On January 27 1871, the 'provisional meeting of the Barrow Shipbuilding Company' was held at the home of James Ramsden and, before the evening was concluded, the participants – Ramsden, David Duncan of Clydeside Shipping, Devonshire and Frederick Cavendish, his son – had agreed to found the Eastern Steamship Company 'to trade with China and India, by way of the Canal'. Devonshire bought £25,000 of shares in the two companies. His younger son, Lord Frederick Cavendish, already a director of the Jute and Flour Mill, joined the board of the shipping line.

The high hopes survived for a couple of years, then the building of the shipyard – like construction of every other development with which the Duke of Devonshire had been associated – was found to be so behind time that there was no immediate hope of its earning any income. Schneider was asked to devise a plan which would avoid bankruptcy. He produced two. Both required the Duke of Devonshire to provide £630,000. Neither offered any real prospect that the capital would ever earn a dividend or be repaid. The only alternative was the sale of the Furness Railway and the use of the receipts to keep the yard in business – a desperate expedient which was seriously considered and only abandoned when the Midland and North-Eastern Railway – a major shareholder on which it depended – declined even to discuss the idea. So Devonshire accepted, with noble resignation, that the shipbuilding company ('being in a deplorable state') could only be kept going if he 'provided very large sums'[59] and the Barrow Shipbuilding Company stumbled on from crisis to crisis. In 1882 it was obliged to buy *The City of Rome* from another yard 'in order to escape from the risk of action which the Inman Company are bringing . . . for the non fulfilment of a contract for building a ship'. Ruefully the Duke had added his agreement – 'although it will oblige me to find large sums of money'.[60] As always, the price of avoiding insolvency was paid by the Duke of Devonshire.

Four years later, nothing had changed. Devonshire had no doubt that 'unless matters improve shortly a catastrophe cannot be long averted'.[61] It was then that the directors of the Barrow Shipbuilding Company at last realised that their yard, managed by the wrong people, was building the wrong ships. In February 1888, 'negotiations which had been going on for some time' were completed.[62] For once, an attempt to change the shipyard's fortunes did not require an injection of Cavendish capital. A novelty of equal proportions was the transfer of control to experienced shipbuilders, a syndicate led by Bryce Douglas and Nordefeldt. The new share issue was over-subscribed. 'Many times the amount required might have been obtained without difficulty.'[63] Potential investors had realised that at last the yard had been put on a businesslike footing. The construction of merchantmen was abandoned and replaced by specialisation in the building of warships. Two years later, the Duke attended the launch of HMS *Latonia*, a 3,400-ton cruiser which had been built for the Royal Navy by what he called 'the naval armaments company'. The shipyard was, at last, a success. And so it remained.

So, for a time, was Eastbourne. The sinking of new sewers convinced both developers and potential residents that it was the place to breathe the healthy Sussex air. The formal opening of the main drainage works took the unusual form of a civic procession, led by the Duke himself, to 'the outfall where the valve was opened and the drain discharged its contents most successfully'.[64] The town's respectability, and permanence, was confirmed in 1870 when the foundation stone of Eastbourne College ('a place for the education of gentlemen') was laid. In the same year the Duke's diary recorded – with more relief than triumph – that the pier was half finished.[65] In 1875, the *Eastbourne Gazette*, although inclined to exaggerate both triumph and disaster, reflected the mood of the town. 'Brilliant as has been the last ten years of Eastbourne's existence, the sun of success has only just dawned and will rise higher and higher as the years move on, bathing its enterprising inhabitants in a flash of golden light.'[66] The quality of the prose is explained, if not excused, by the demographic statistics. By 1871, the population of Eastbourne – just over 3,000 thirty years earlier – had risen to over 100,000 and occupied 1,800 houses – most of them built during the previous decade.

For the next ten years Eastbourne built all the amenities that were to be expected in a south coast holiday resort. Many of them bore the name and arms of the family which financed them. In addition to the Queen's and the Grand, there was a Cavendish Hotel. There were

Devonshire Parks and Baths and a Devonshire Club. The baths, the theatre and floral hall took other titles and, although the Duke financed its extension to the west, the promenade was called 'Royal'. But Eastbourne was the Devonshires' town. Its first mayor was George Ambrose Wallis, the Duke's local agent. And it was to them that the town looked to promote what the *Eastbourne Gazette* thought no more than its natural due. 'Scores of boroughs, far less important than Eastbourne, enjoy the right of selecting their special representative in parliament.'[67] Eastbourne, largely thanks to the Seventh Duke of Devonshire, had arrived on the political map.

During the periods of apparent financial success – or at least respite from immediate emergency – the Duke was able to resume the types of pursuit which, in his youth, had seemed (and probably were) more consistent with his natural inclinations. He commissioned the first and only catalogue of the Chatsworth library to which he added books of his own taste – most notably, John James Audubon's *Birds of America*, the rage of fashionable artistic society. He also committed what today would be regarded as an act of unforgivable vandalism. The fourteenth-century church which had been preserved in Paxton's village at Edensor was demolished and rebuilt, in Victorian-Gothic style, by Sir Gilbert Scott. The old family vault at All Saints, Derby, had been closed. It was necessary to create a suitable burial place for the Duke and his descendants.

The need to restore the Cavendish fortune was, however, never out of his mind for long. He was equally obdurate in his determination not to learn by his mistakes. So he continued his attempts to compensate for old failures by launching new enterprises. The greatest mistake of all was the belief that the best way to revive the fortunes of a failing industry was to establish a related enterprise which would provide work for its ailing partner. The next expedient was the establishment of a shipping line which used ships that were built in the local dockyard which, in turn – no matter who owned it – would use steel from the local factory. A local steamer company, with a regular service to Belfast and the Isle of Man, prospered in the boom years of the 1870s and provided some work for the shipyard. In the following year, two more ambitious projects followed – the Eastern Steamship Company in 1871 and a line from Barrow to Canada. The Canadian enterprise was supported by influential and experienced backers. Ironically, despite the involvement of the firm of Clyde shipbuilders and a Montreal millionaire, Devonshire was 'doubtful whether to embark as so much would be necessary in the project'.[68] Several alternative schemes were considered. They included the outright purchase of the Allen Company, the leading Anglo-British shipping line. In the end a new enterprise, the Barrow Ocean Shipping Company, was created. Devonshire was one of the two main investors. A regular service to Canada was started in March 1872. The plan – which could not be said to lack ambition – was for Barrow to replace Sheffield as England's premier steel town and then to transport more freight and passengers than Liverpool and become England's largest northern port.

When trade began to decline, Devonshire immediately proposed to extend his commercial empire in the hope of stimulating the whole Barrow economy. The early experiment in Keynesian economics involved the purchase of two steamships from a competing yard, the inauguration of a more frequent transatlantic service and the use of the extra revenue to build yet two more steamships in Barrow. 'This plan', he concluded, 'would probably be of much advantage to Barrow interests generally' but, he wearily added, 'it involves the immediate payment by me of a very large sum'.[69] It was the second time that he expressed justifiable doubts about investing in what was, at best, a dubious prospect and the second time that he overcame his anxieties and provided the necessary capital.

By then he had come to feel – and to express his belief – that having pointed Barrow in the direction of an industrial future he had a duty to lead its people towards the lasting prosperity that it could, eventually, provide. He felt a special obligation to the hundreds of workmen who, with their families, had moved to the town because, thanks to him, it seemed to be the land of promise. So he suggested a new way of priming the pump. 'The only prospect of holding out anything like encouragement is with respect to a project of establishing a line of steamers between New Orleans and Barrow . . . The ships would bring Texas cattle and Indian corn.'[70] A Liverpool shipowner, named Fernie, drew up the plan. Naturally enough it required the Duke to contribute one third of the capital on which it would be founded. Devonshire told Fernie 'with all my Barrow investments I am reluctant to lay out more'.[71] But he did – £40,000 in all. He took the risk on the assumption that 'If the scheme succeeds . . . Barrow can hardly fail in many ways to gain a great advantage'.[72]

Within twelve months he gave his name and support to an even less promising scheme – a steamer line to Baltimore. The shipyard was to build the steamers and the Furness Railway Company would build cattle sheds and slaughter-houses in anticipation of the new trade. Unfortunately, no one had realised that recent legislation – designed to prevent the spread of disease – regulated the import of cattle. So the scheme had to be abandoned. Nothing daunted, the Barrow Steamship

Company proposed, in co-operation with the Anchor Line, to inaugurate a regular passenger service to New York. During the brief boom, which began in 1880, the shipping line more than paid its way. But then it foundered leaving, unused, a floating dock – built at a cost of £55,000 to bear a load of 3,000 tons.[73] By 1886, even the ever-hopeful Devonshire feared that 'there seems a great risk of Barrow and all its works becoming an utter and complete failure'.[74] His melancholy was increased by the gloomy conclusion that 'owing to the general depression which has largely reduced [his] income in all its sources',[75] he would never again be able to come to the town's assistance.

The depression was not confined to the north-east or to industrial England. The Duke himself conceded that, in Eastbourne, 'there is certainly much less prosperity than there has been recently' and that he, in part, was responsible. 'The place has, for the present, been rather overbuilt.'[76] The *Eastbourne Gazette* confirmed his judgement and added that 'those who own houses find them a drag on the market'.[77] It was worse than that. There were so many bankruptcies and so much unemployment that a relief committee was set up. For once the *Eastbourne Gazette*'s colourful language described, rather than exaggerated, the situation. 'Large numbers of honest able-bodied men seek in vain, for week after week, work out of town. As a result our industrial population is being gradually decreased . . . Empty houses tell the sad story of domestic suffering and want of means.'[78] The town, which had thought of Devonshire and Gilbert as the architects of its fortunes, called upon them to create jobs for the, now unemployed, men who had been attracted to the town. It was not an easy demand to meet.

The developers had planned to build Eastbourne's appeal on its sylvan tranquillity. *Powell's Popular Gazette* had boasted that the resort 'may claim a purer atmosphere than generally falls to the share of larger towns on account of the almost total absence of manufacturing industry'[79] and the *Eastbourne Pictorial* rejoiced that Eastbourne 'keeps up its rural and ornamental aspects. The streets are boulevards, the highways wooded avenues almost as green as country lanes.'[80] It was too late, successfully, to change the prospectus. So instead of attempting to attract manufacturing industry, the now suspect benefactors published a plan which stimulated the economy by promoting public amenities – a steamboat service, a public library, an art gallery and a marina. The council undertook to extend and improve the roads and the Duke's Drive was constructed to provide easy access from the town to the splendid view from the summit of Beachy Head. In 1890, the demand for labour began to rise again. Eastbourne was about to become profitless but genteel.

It now seems extraordinary that the Duke of Devonshire should have sacrificed so much of his family capital on enterprises that, a more discerning man would have realised, were doomed from the start. His folly must, in part, have resulted from a combination of arrogance and naivety. He believed that a combination of blood and brains equipped him to determine which enterprises – and, perhaps more crucially which entrepreneurs – were likely to succeed in the hard world of nineteenth-century commerce. But another motive also influenced his reckless spending and turned it from profligacy into generosity. He had come to accept that it was his duty to improve the lot of the people he regarded, proprietorily, as 'his' and he had no doubt that the best way to help them was to allow whatever he earned from the new enterprises to trickle down into their pay packets. There is no doubt that their welfare concerned him. In a letter to the Marquis of Hartington, which invited his eldest surviving son to become chairman of the Bryce Douglas and Nordefeldt shipping syndicate, he emphasised that if the new venture was successful 'it is almost certain that Barrow generally will derive great advantages'.[81] Hartington – a passionate opponent of Irish Home Rule, who had just declined to serve in Gladstone's cabinet – was himself part of the reason why the Duke was so determined to make the slate quarries, the railways and the shipyard succeed. He felt a deep sense of obligation to his children. It was his duty to pass on to them more prosperous estates than those which he had inherited. And because he was a man of his time, he chose to pursue that objective, not through the traditional increase in land and property, but by speculation in the industries of Victorian England.

None of the projects liquidated the Cavendish debt. In 1886, Lewis 'Lulu' Harcourt recorded in his diaries gossip to the effect that 'mortgages to the extent of £200,000 have been foreclosed on the Duke of Devonshire's estates . . . He talks of selling something to raise the money and as Chiswick will not realise well, thinks of parting with Devonshire House for building lots.'[82] That dreadful prospect was avoided. So, when he died five years later, yet another Cavendish inherited the family debts along with the family title. But the failure of Barrow, and to a lesser extent of Eastbourne, to raise enough revenue to make the Devonshires solvent again does not reduce the importance of the way in which the attempt was made. It was an early example of a growing inclination for aristocrats to 'turn from pomp and circumstance to investment and income as the bulwark of status'.[83] Perhaps, had he not inherited the debts, the Seventh Duke of Devonshire would have been happy to accept the old ways. But, whether or not the decision to innovate was forced upon him, he accepted the role of entrepreneur with genuine enthusiasm. His belief that he had a duty to protect the interests of the men and women who lived on his land and accepted his wages can be dismissed as no more than a nineteenth-century adaptation of the Whig obligation. But his belief in industrial expansion – often misdirected though it was – made him the most progressive of the Devonshires. It was the Seventh Duke who began to drag that ancient family into the modern world.

CHAPTER 23

The Reluctant Statesman

Spencer Compton – the Seventh Duke of Devonshire's oldest son – was, according to his indulgent father, 'a most delightful boy full of life and animation'.[1] None of his youthful contemporaries ever wrote or spoke of his charm. But then, thanks to his social and intellectual limitations, none of them even suspected that one day he would enjoy the distinction of being the only man in British history to be invited, three times, to form a government and to have declined, even the attempt, on each occasion.

The three invitations and their rejection confirmed his reputation as the embodiment of the Whig belief that the aristocracy had a duty to scorn delights and live laborious days – spurred on, not by wish for fame or lust for power, but by the belief that only politicians who neither hoped to rise nor feared to fall could provide honest government. In fact his reasons for rejecting the premiership were more complicated – and less altruistic – than his friends claimed. But Spencer Compton, the Marquis of Hartington – the Eighth Duke's title during most of his thirty-four years in the House of Commons – assiduously cultivated the notion that, for him, service was a sacrifice. Perhaps, after years of protestation, he actually believed it.

The Marquis of Hartington was a man of his time – wholly unsuited to a life in politics after the Reform Bill of 1867 extended the franchise to the property-owning lower middle classes and required candidates for election to ingratiate themselves with those they aspired to represent in parliament. Cavendish regarded making concessions to other people's wishes and convenience as demeaning. And on the rare occasions when he attempted to show sympathy or understanding, he found the task beyond him. Sir Frederick Ponsonby, private secretary to Queen Victoria, expressed surprise and regret that Hartington 'never by chance said "thank you" to any servant who helped him'.[2] Sir Almeric FitzRoy, Secretary to the Privy Council, described him as 'standing in that particular way of his as if half inviting and half forbidding conversation'.[3] His expression was 'habitually dreary and if by chance he said he was glad to see you, you would have some difficulty in believing it . . .'[4] and his appearance – tall, stooping and heavily bearded

– contributed to the impression that he was not a man to be approached or interrupted. His conversation often amounted to no more than a series of grunts. But he was not retiring or reclusive. He chose to be aloof and remote because of his profound conviction that men of his rank were under no obligation to conform to the civilities of polite society. In defence of Hartington's perpetual bad manners his friends argued that he lacked conviviality not sympathy and urged his critics not to confuse his pathological insouciance with contempt for the lower orders of society. That he bored easily was not in doubt. But, said his apologists, his boredom was indiscriminate. Whatever the cause of his air of superiority, it earned him a nick-name that remained with him for all of his life. He was for ever Harty-Tarty.

Hartington was born at Holker Hall in Lancashire on July 23 1833. He was spared Eton – where his father had been deeply unhappy – and, after years of learning at his father's knee, was sent to a tutor for a brief period of private education, which he heartily detested. At Cambridge – Trinity, the Cavendish college – he 'scarcely lived up to expectations'. His lack of academic success was attributed to rejection of 'the restraint which hard reading requires',[5] but Lord Welby – a Trinity contemporary – admired his 'utter absence of ostentation' and insisted that, 'while he did not shine in talk', his friends all 'recognised [his] sound male common sense'.[6] Half-way through his second term, he told his father, 'I heard from Michealson the other day. The yeomanry are going out exactly during the time of the May examinations. I think it would be a good idea if I were to cut the Mays in favour of the yeomanry as I shall do very badly.'[7] Six months later, he sent his father what he clearly believed to be a reassuring message. 'I have begun to read a little and I hate it.'[8] The admission that his 'affairs [were] not quite so prosperous as [he] thought'[9] received a response from the Duke that moved him to gratitude. 'Thank you for the 50£ without a lecture on extravagance.'[10] When, on achieving his majority a year later, his maternal grandfather made him an allowance of £2,000 a year, he 'hardly knew what to say'.[11] Nor did he know how to spend his allowance wisely.

Financial prudence was not a Cavendish characteristic and Hartington was true to the family tradition. In 1876 – forty-three years old and leading the Liberal Party in the House of Commons, while Mr Gladstone brooded on his future – he had still to ask his father for money. It took the Duke some time to respond and the cheque for £25,338 was preceded by a message of reproach. 'I am sorry of course to hear of the state of your finances and it is certainly a pity that you have allowed things to go on for so long.'[12] The reproof did not induce his son to change his ways. In 1881, while Hartington was defending the introduction of the 'closure'* as a necessary protection against the Irish Party's abuse of parliament, he again had to call on his father to clear his debts. The Duke responded with a cheque for £40,776.[13]

Although the Eighth Duke of Devonshire never repented his extravagance, he certainly came to regret that he had spent so little time and effort in sharpening his wits. In an address to the undergraduates of Cambridge University – where he became an unlikely Chancellor – he confessed, 'All through my life I have had to work with men who thought three times as quickly as I did and I have found it a great disadvantage.'[14] Whether or not he was held back by failures of intellect, he was certainly propelled forward by his aristocratic connections.

In August 1856 Alexander II was crowned Tsar of All the Russias in Moscow. Earl Granville was made special ambassador to the Romanoff Court for the duration of the celebrations. Lord Spencer Cavendish (his father had not then inherited the dukedom, so he was not yet the Marquis of Hartington) was invited to accompany his cousin as honorary ADC – just as his father had accompanied the Sixth Duke of Devonshire to the coronation of Nicholas I. He was not impressed. 'The coronation on Sunday, I am afraid, a little disappointed me. The cathedral is so small . . .'[15] In the years which followed, little – except the country pastimes – lived up to his expectations. Back home he had to endure the ennui of the 1857 general election – called after Palmerston's government was defeated in a vote of censure which condemned its defence of opium dealers who were trading under the British flag. The Duke of Devonshire proposed that Cavendish be found a seat in Ireland. He chose instead North Lancashire and was returned to parliament unopposed, a luxury he enjoyed in every election until 1868. If the message which he sent to his father, on the eve of his first poll, is to be believed, he did not enjoy the campaign. 'I am most heartily sick of the business. However it will all be over tomorrow thank goodness.'[16]

Palmerston and his supporters triumphed, but – within a year – the Whigs were beaten again and a minority Tory administration (with Lord Derby as Prime Minister and Benjamin Disraeli as Chancellor of the Exchequer) took office. It too survived for barely a year before another general election renewed Palmerston's mandate and majority. Derby, as was the Victorian habit, waited to resign until he had been defeated in the House of Commons. Cavendish had only made one

---

* A device introduced into parliamentary procedure to curtail debates which were prolonged by filibustering.

short speech in parliament – around which was built the myth that he had found the event so boring that he had interrupted himself with a yawn. But he was chosen to propose the amendment to the Loyal Address that brought the Derby government down.

Palmerston sent Cavendish what amounted to a draft speech with a note which instructed him that, even if he did not repeat it more or less verbatim, he must follow its line of argument. 'The greater part of it is copied from Peel in 1841.'[17] The essential point was that in the general election, the Tories had been denied the majority for which they asked and their position was therefore unsustainable. Whoever had won, they had lost. Hartington more than justified the confidence which, so unexpectedly, had been placed in him. The Speaker wrote to his father with the surprisingly partisan message that he had 'thoroughly succeeded and justified all my expectations'. The Duke must have found his postscript particularly gratifying. 'While I am writing, Disraeli has spoken of the manly and promising speech of the noble lord.'[18] Gladstone was equally complimentary. 'Anybody would be glad to make such a speech.'[19] The amendment was carried by 323 votes to 310.

Surprisingly, when the new government was formed, no place was found within it for the hero of the amendment. Palmerston thought it necessary to explain and justify the omission not to Cavendish himself but to his father, the Duke. There were, he wrote, 'a great number of persons whom general reconciliation of sections brings onto the list of candidates'. He offered, by way of compensation, the suggestion that the young man would be 'better employed by taking part in general business'.[20] Cavendish did not grasp the opportunity. He did not speak in the House again until May 1861, when he supported the abolition of excise duty on paper and attacked the House of Lords for attempting to retain it. The following year he spoke of the distress in the Lancashire textile industry, for which the shortage of cotton (caused by the American Civil War) was responsible. Four months later, he set sail for the United States. By then his father was the Seventh Duke and he was Marquis of Hartington.

It is clear from Hartington's letters home that he regarded his visit to America as more an adventure than a study tour. He deeply regretted missing and not witnessing the Battle of Antietam – the bloodiest single day in the whole Civil War – from the safe vantage point of a convenient hill. But, despite having missed the theatre of 23,000 casualties, he made himself an expert on the conflict. That notwithstanding, he decided that he would not take part in any House of Commons debates on either the merits or progress of the war. That may have been because his views were in conflict with the position which his party, after some doubt and agony, had taken up and the cotton workers, in the county which he represented, had supported with righteous neglect of their own economic interests. His sympathies were so strongly with the South, which he believed was being ravaged by the Union army, that at a New York dinner party he wore the colours of the Confederacy in his buttonhole. Whether riding over rough country or meeting the grandees of both North and South, he exhibited rare signs of enjoying himself. He was experiencing the joy of freedom. One reason for the trip was to escape from the possessive embrace of Skittles Walters.

Hartington had met Skittles in 1860 and their correspondence – and we must assume their relationship – began then. Skittles – the daughter of a Liverpool shipping clerk and, as well as a great beauty, an accomplished horsewoman – was the mistress of the Honourable George Fitzwilliam. She was elevated from whore to courtesan when Fitzwilliam took her to a meet of the hunt of which he was master. She became a celebrity of sorts when, because of her status within the hunting fraternity, she began to ride in Hyde Park's Rotten Row. When Fitzwilliam ended the relationship in 1861 – with a pension of £300 a year for life – Hartington became her 'protector'. There is no doubt that what, for both of them, began as no more than a commercial arrangement deepened into a love affair. Not that Hartington imagined that the relationship could last. 'Sometimes I think that it would be better for you if you could forget me and leave off loving me . . . Someday you ought to find someone who will take care of you for the rest of your life . . . which I am afraid I shall never be able to do.'[21] But the messages which he sent her showed that, from the first, he treated her with great respect. His notes 'requested' assignations which could be declined if 'inconvenient'. He was too terrified of his father's discovering the liaison to allow her anywhere near Chatsworth, but in London she was accepted as one of his 'set'. He bought her a house in Park Street and, as a sign of his fearless affection, took her with him to the Derby.

There is no doubt that Skittles thought that his visit to America was a prelude to the end of the affair. That was why she followed him across the Atlantic – travelling with an Irish squire of her acquaintance who had abandoned his wife so that they could appear on the ship's passenger list as Mr and Mrs Aubrey de Vere Beauclerk. Skittles was left to languish in New York while Hartington went south to gain a Confederate perspective on the Civil War. After they were reunited, they spent a couple of weeks together. But that was only a stay of execution. The end came in July 1862. Skittles received a parting gift of £400 and a guaranteed £400 a year for life. The letter in which his decision and her recompense were set out also contained a reproach. Because of her visit to America, his father had been 'told about the whole thing'.²² It ended with the afterthought that he was 'very unhappy'. But he had been provided with the consolation that reconciled Anthony Trollope's Plantagenet Palliser to the discovery that his wife loved Burgo FitzGerald more than she loved him. Hartington had been 'elevated to the Treasury Bench'.

Once again, Lord Palmerston preserved the aristocratic proprieties. He had apologised to the Duke of Devonshire for not including his son in the government when it was formed and, when a sudden resignation provided a vacancy, he wrote to the Duke 'to know . . . whether he might look to Lord Hartington'²³ to fill it. Hartington was asked, and agreed, to become Lay Lord of the Admiralty. But before he took office, he was switched to another junior post – Under-Secretary for War. That required him to move the second reading of the Volunteers Bill. His late arrival in the chamber obliged other ministers to waste the House's time until he appeared. But despite what other men might think of as an embarrassment his performance was 'cool as a cucumber and civil at the same time'. Granville concluded that there was 'no reason why, if he chooses, he should not, at some future time, lead the House of Commons'.²⁴ He was still at the War Office when the general election of 1865 increased the Whig/Liberal majority and there he remained until the death of Palmerston in the autumn of that year. Lord John Russell, the new Prime Minister, promoted him to Secretary of State for War. He was thirty-three. He celebrated his prodigious elevation with the weary claim that he would have preferred to be passed over for a year or two. His boredom was brief. Six months later, the government was defeated.

Russell's administration was dominated by William Ewart Gladstone, the Chancellor of the Exchequer, and it was due to him – in alliance with the old Radical, John Bright – that a limited measure of parliamentary reform was introduced into the House of Commons. Hartington remained true to his practice of never believing or opposing anything too strongly. He was not enthusiastic for extending the franchise, but he told the cabinet that 'whether they considered their pledges rash or not, they had to be fulfilled'.²⁵ The proposed reduction in the property qualification from £10 to £7 of rateable value added barely 400,000 voters to the electoral list. But it was enough to enable Disraeli – like Gladstone the real, though not titular, leader of his party – to encourage fear of revolution. The old Whigs on the government benches joined him in bringing down the Russell administration – enabling the Tories to take office and introduce a far more extensive Reform Bill of their own.

The defeat of Russell marked the beginning of the slow decline of the Whigs as a political force. It was a sea change in British politics which Hartington was slow to recognise and unwilling to accept. One of the extraordinary features of his career was his willingness and ability to hold high office while swimming against the tide. His apparent reluctance to devote himself to affairs of state made it possible to reconcile the divergence between his ideas and the obligations of his appointments. A more eager politician would not have been allowed to disagree but yet survive so often.

Hartington, in opposition, spent much of 1866 in Prussia,[26] witnessing the celebration of victory over Austria and discussing military matters with the generals who had led the King's apparently invincible army. Back in Britain – much to the delight of the Duke of Cambridge, the Queen's cousin and commander-in-chief of the army – he spoke against proposals to end the purchase of commissions and abolish flogging as military punishment. But most of his time was spent in the field, not the Commons. The centre of his sporting activities was Kimbolton Castle in Huntingdon, the home of the Duke of Manchester. The Duchess, born Louise von Alten, had become his mistress.

In April 1868, Gladstone moved in the House of Commons a resolution which was the first manifestation of what was to become his obsession. It proposed the disestablishment and disendowment of the Church of Ireland. The motion was carried by a majority of sixty-five. The general election which followed was fought on new constituency boundaries, and an electoral roll which, thanks to Disraeli's Reform Bill, included the new middle classes. The result was a Liberal majority of 112. But Lancashire swung towards the Tories. Gladstone was defeated in the south-west constituency of the county but, as was the habit of party leaders at the time, was a candidate in a second seat. Greenwich elected him. Hartington lost his seat in what he told his father was 'more complete defeat than [he] had expected'. It was not, he admitted, 'pleasant to be beaten in this way' but, typically, he added, 'I cannot say that I am very unhappy about it.'[27]

Gladstone expressed his regret that the 'gallant fight' in Lancashire had ended with Hartington's 'exclusion from parliament' but felt that until he found a new constituency to represent, he could not return to the War Office. Instead he proposed to make him Lord Lieutenant of Ireland. Hartington declined. The Prime Minister then offered him the Post Office on the understanding that he found a constituency before parliament met – three months after the general election.

Aristocratic hauteur did not prevent Hartington from accepting what amounted to a demotion. Indeed he searched for a seat with a determination that was the first indication of his undoubted, but concealed, enthusiasm for office. Lord Clarendon was approached 'on a personal matter' and agreed to find out if there was any truth in the rumour that Mr Green Price, Member of Parliament for the Radnor Boroughs, had said 'a short time ago . . . that he was willing to resign his seat'.[28] The rumour was confirmed and Hartington took Green Price's place in the House of Commons and laboured for two years at the Post Office while Edward Cardwell, Secretary of State for War, introduced the programme of military reforms which, together with the 1870 Education Act, defined Gladstone's First Administration. Flogging was abolished for crimes committed in peacetime and the purchase of commissions prohibited – practices which Hartington had defended. Service with the colours was reduced from twelve to six years followed by another six in the army reserve. The infantry – reorganised in county regiments to encourage territorial pride and *esprit de corps* – was rearmed with the breech-loading Martini-Henry rifles. There is no record of Hartington, former Secretary of State for War, taking part – publicly or privately – in the inevitably passionate debates which ended only when the government by-passed an obstructive House of Lords with the procedural device of abolishing the purchase system by royal warrant rather than legislation.

Throughout all of Gladstone's Administrations, Ireland was always on the Prime Minister's mind. Hartington, to the Prime Minister's surprise, was not wholly unsympathetic to the Land Act of 1870 – which regulated rents and introduced a scale of compensation for improvements as well as disturbance. But he was bitterly opposed to the disestablishment of the Irish Church. Indeed he opposed the proposal so strongly that he wrote to the Prime Minister with the request that, despite his absence from the cabinet on the day when it was discussed, his dissent should be noted.[29] And when Lord Spencer, Gladstone's second choice as Lord Lieutenant, threatened to resign unless stronger powers were taken to combat Feinian violence, he seriously considered – or told friends that he considered – resigning with him. The serious consideration of resignation – concluding with a decision not to resign – became a feature of Hartington's long political career. But his passionate belief in the need to suppress all manifestations of Irish nationalism was genuine and permanent. Over the next decade, Hartington and Gladstone were to disagree over many things. None of them was as deep as the gulf which divided them over the governance of Ireland and the merits of Home Rule.

Yet despite their disagreements, on December 23 1870, Gladstone invited Hartington to become Chief Secretary for Ireland and Hartington, who might have immediately grasped the chance to slow down the rush to Home Rule, declined next day, giving as his reasons the inability to 'reconcile [himself] to giving up almost the whole year to official duties'. Pressed to reconsider, he asked to be given 'another day or two to consider'[30] and combined that request with the hope that the appointment would not require permanent residence in the country he would govern. After a couple of days' thought the invitation was again declined, the result 'more of inclination than reason or argument'.[31] But Gladstone persisted and on New Year's Eve, Hartington wrote to his father, 'I suppose you cannot be more surprised than I that I was bullied into accepting.'[32] Thus began one of the most ambivalent relationships in the history of British politics. Gladstone and Hartington were both incompatible and inseparable.

Like many secretaries of state – before and after his tenure – Hartington was, immediately on his appointment, confronted with demands for stronger action against the insurgents who, in 1870, seemed to be as concerned with the ownership of the land as they were with the government of Ireland. The Peace Preservation Act (passed six months before Hartington moved to the Irish Office) was proving inadequate. Terrorists, who called their gang the Ribbon Society, pioneered in West Meath what came to be known as 'agrarian outrages' – acts of violence which, in their ugliest form, included the maiming of cattle. Hartington's proposal to suspend *habeas corpus* was greeted by Gladstone with 'horror and dismay', but on the insistence of the new Irish Secretary the proposition was put to cabinet. The compromise to which ministers agreed was a Select Committee of the House of Commons to inquire into 'the nature, extent and effect of certain unlawful combinations and confederacies'. Hartington was required to support the cabinet compromise in a speech which he described as 'defending a course which I did not think adequate to the occasion'. After it was made he concluded, with more satisfaction than regret, that his disagreement with the policy he defended 'showed all too plainly'. Dissembling was not in Hartington's nature. So he used the speech to express opinions which were diametrically opposed to the Prime Minister's conviction that a political solution was possible. It would, he said, 'be the height of insanity to suppose that the establishment of religious equality or the passing of a land law regulating tenure would' pacify Ireland.[33] From then on, he was in open conflict with almost every item of Gladstone's Irish policy. But – despite his professed distaste for office – he did not resign.

It was in the year 1870 that Isaac Butt, a Dublin lawyer, founded the Home Rule movement. Hartington did not hide his dismay at Gladstone's reaction. 'Much too Liberal in my opinion . . , If [the nationalists] will only profess to maintain the supremacy of the Imperial Parliament, he does not much concern what they go in for.'[34] The great schism was still a decade away. But, as a rehearsal for the final act, Gladstone and Hartington spent three years disagreeing over smaller things. Ironically, there were two items of reform which Hartington advocated but Gladstone felt were of little consequence – the creation of a system of genuine local government to replace the feudal hegemonies in the Irish counties and the public acquisition of Ireland's sixty-six railway companies. Hartington let the issues rest, but he did fight a losing rearguard battle against the creation of an Irish university which, unlike Trinity College Dublin, Catholics would feel able to attend. As Hartington predicted, the proposal irritated Irish Protestants and Liberals, failed to enthuse Catholics and presented Disraeli with an opportunity to assemble an anti-government majority in the House of Commons. The bill was defeated by three votes. Gladstone resigned, but Disraeli refused to form a government. Queen Victoria, instead of dissolving parliament and condemning Disraeli to certain defeat, sent for Gladstone again and Hartington wrote to Lord Spencer, the Viceroy of Ireland, 'We are in again. I am sorry to say that, not without an attempt on my part to get free . . . I have really come to detest office.'[35] But again, he did not resign.

Hartington's wish, or what he claimed to be his wish, came very near to being granted. Spencer gave the Prime Minister notice that he intended to resign at the end of the parliament. Gladstone mistook the warning for an immediate resignation and, no doubt hearing rumours of discontent, mistakenly believed that Hartington wanted to leave office at the same time. He pre-empted the second resignation with a plea for Hartington to remain, accompanied by the offer of a different portfolio – the Post Office. Hartington declined to be demoted for a second time and told Spencer, 'I am, therefore, so far as I know out altogether, at which I shall greatly rejoice.'[36] But Gladstone, once again, was determined that Hartington should remain in the government and made a direct appeal to his Whig conscience with a disclaimer which – since to him duty was all – he clearly did not mean. 'I put aside', the Prime Minister wrote, 'my own personal conviction about the claim which the Crown as well as the country has on the services of men born into great positions and properties and the hereditary rights of legislation.'[37] Put aside or not, that obligation – *noblesse oblige* – accounts for Gladstone's determination that Hartington should serve and goes some of the way to explaining why, in the end, Hartington always agreed. The cabinet was reorganised, but there was no change at the Ireland Office.

Hartington looked a serious, indeed gloomy, man. But life for a Whig grandee was, by its nature, unavoidably punctuated with events of extravagant frivolity. Throughout the mid-1870s he was part of, though not at the centre of, the Marlborough House Set whose members built their social lives around the Prince of Wales. Perhaps the Duchess of Manchester – his increasingly frequent companion – dragged him towards louche royal company in her 'fast' wake. Or it may be that the heirs apparent to the throne of England and the Devonshire dukedom were united by their mutual love of cards and the turf. Whatever the reason, the two men were regular companions if not ever quite friends. In December 1872, the Prince and Princess of Wales made the first of many visits to Chatsworth. The preparations caused the Duke of Devonshire – a genuinely serious man – much anxiety. He appealed to his son for help. 'Glad you are staying at Sandringham for you will be able to get answers to several things I need to know. How long do they stay? How many servants do they bring? How many servants for the Princess? Do you think they could bring any horses? Fear ours would not stand the cheering.'[38] No doubt the Chatsworth staff were anxious about the visit too. There was only one bathroom in the house and that, naturally enough, was made available for the Prince of Wales's exclusive use. Other guests had zinc baths brought into their bedrooms and filled from pitchers of boiling water.

Sometimes the Prince of Wales and Hartington met in less formal, if equally exotic, circumstances. At one Marlborough House fancy-dress ball, Hartington was invited to dress 'in the Venetian manner' and obliged by wearing lavender-coloured doublet and hose. The authenticity of his costume was compromised by a medallion which bore the portrait of Henry VIII, which he insisted was a gift from Henry himself to a Tudor Cavendish. It is not clear how far Hartington mirrored the Prince's irregular lifestyle – particularly as it related to young women. He certainly gave the impression that he was faithful and devoted to the Duchess of Manchester. But the Austrian Ambassador claimed that when, in the summer of 1875, he told Hartington that 'with whist and the Turf and morning visits', he wondered how time was found for politics, the Marquis responded, 'So do I.'[39] That may have been a joke. Though the extent of Hartington's sense of humour is best illustrated by what his friends quoted as an example of his wit. Asked by the Prince of Wales if he had considered the effect of smoking on his health, he had replied, 'I never anticipate the future.'

He could not have possibly anticipated either the extent or the nature of the turbulence which was to disturb his equitable existence throughout the final years of the decade. On January 24 1874, still oppressed by defeat of the Irish Universities' Bill and disagreements among ministers about the religious content of elementary education, the Prime Minister advised the Queen to dissolve parliament. In the general election, held in the following month, the Tories were returned to power with a majority which (thanks to the vagaries of the various Irish members) was alternatively computed as forty-eight and eighty-three. At the last cabinet meeting of the defeated government, Gladstone told his colleagues that he 'would no longer retain the leadership of the Liberal Party nor resume it until the party had settled its differences . . . He would sit as a private member and occasionally speak for himself, but he would not attend the House regularly or assume any one of the functions of leader.'[40] Significantly it was Russell, the oldest-fashioned of old-fashioned Whigs, who immediately wrote to Hartington. 'I look to you in the Commons . . . to lead the business of our party . . . I can never look to Gladstone any more as a leader. With great abilities, he and Granville have led the Whig Party of Lord Grey to destruction and dispersion.'[41]

Hartington had become the hope of the Whigs – the man they thought most likely to stem the onward rush of radicalism which Gladstone was too preoccupied with his own obsessions to resist. But it was almost a year before Gladstone's expected resignation letter reached Lord Granville, the Liberal Leader in the House of Lords. The new parliament was preoccupied with church business – the Scottish Church Patronage Bill, the Endowed Schools Bill and the Regulation of Public Worship Bill. And Gladstone was not prepared to lay down the burden of leadership until he was sure that the interests of the Anglican Communion had been properly protected. But, true to his word, he took no interest in other subjects. So it fell to Hartington to speak for the opposition on Isaac Butt's motion proposing Home Rule for Ireland. 'In honour and honesty, the Imperial Parliament is bound to tell the Irish people that . . . whatever might be the effect upon the internal affairs of that country, it could never give its consent to the proposal.'[42] Russell must have felt that his judgement was vindicated. The Whig Party of Lord Grey had found its champion.

It was not only the survivors of past administrations who wanted Hartington to lead the Liberals in the House of Commons. William Harcourt – a contender for the Liberal leadership thirty years later – was an early supporter. 'I hope there is no doubt and hesitation about you being the man to lead us in the Commons.'[43] The reply – 'I would not accept the leadership of the Opposition unless the proposal met with general agreement'[44] – was clearly not meant to be an outright rejection of the idea. However, Hartington remained publicly reluctant. 'The party seems to be occupying itself in deploring, not its own position, but the deficiencies of possible leaders . . . I do not think that I could endure the treatment I was required to put up with.'[45]

Lord Frederick Cavendish – Hartington's younger brother – agreed that 'the position is not a very attractive one' but did not think that it was possible to defy what might become the unanimous wish of the party.[46] It became the unanimous wish when W. E. Forster – the only other credible contender – unequivocally refused to accept nomination. On February 3, John Bright wrote to Hartington from the Reform Club, 'A resolution has been passed offering you the honourable position of leader of the party in the House of Commons.'[47] Gladstone's endorsement had already been obtained, though it was provided in the form of a reproof, again expressed in the language of the Whig obligation. 'You have not been a good attendant in parliament relative to your parliamentary rank . . . and you will be disposed to admit that the public and your country has some unpaid claims upon you.'[48] Clearly, there was trouble ahead.

It is at least possible to argue that Disraeli's 'one nation' domestic policy was more progressive than the programme of the government that lost office in 1874. The Artisan Dwellings Act, the Sale of Food and Drugs Act and the Public Health Act all initiated intervention in the economy which Gladstone would not have contemplated apart from in the always exceptional Ireland. But it is for its foreign and colonial policy that the Administration is remembered – the purchase of Suez Canal shares, the annexation of the Transvaal, the attempted pacification of Afghanistan, the Zulu War, the addition of 'Empress of India' to Queen Victoria's titles and, above all, the involvement in the balance of power in the Balkans. On all of these areas of policy, save only the imperial crown, Hartington and Gladstone disagreed.

Gladstone was guided by unshakable principle. Hartington was more inclined to judge issues on what he saw as their individual merits. Gladstone disapproved 'both financially and politically'[49] of the acquisition of shares in the Suez Canal company, Hartington had 'no doubt the measure [was] generally approved' and 'saw no reason for committing [the opposition] prematurely to an opinion upon it'.[50] Both men had reservations about creating Victoria 'Queen Empress'. Gladstone opposed the bill on principle, Hartington as a matter of taste. 'If you put to an old English castle a Grecian portico or an Italian façade, I venture to think that there will be a change . . . to that noble structure.'[51] Inevitably, Disraeli accused him of suborning his own opinion to the demands of his less patriotic colleagues. But it was the Eastern Question that opened up an unbridgeable gulf between the Grand Old Man of the Liberal Party and his temporary successor. In the summer of 1875 Bosnia and Herzegovina rose up against Turkish oppression. In the House of Commons, Hartington joined with Disraeli in urging upon the Sultan 'the expediency of adopting such measures of administrative reform as may remove all reasonable cause of discontent', but warned against 'undue impatience in regard to events which have recently occurred'.[52] That was not enough for Gladstone. The battle lines were drawn between *realpolitik* – which, its adherents insisted, required support for Turkey as a bastion against Russian expansion – and principle, which was said to demand unqualified endorsement of the Balkan Christians in their struggle to be free.

The struggle intensified. Serbia and Montenegro declared war on Turkey. Russian forces crossed the Turkish border. A rising in Bulgaria was put down with a campaign of murder, torture and rape. Twelve thousand Christians died. Disraeli, relying on Britain's passionately pro-Turkish Ambassador to the Sublime Port, described the stories of atrocities as 'to a large extent inventions'. Within a week of the news reaching England, Gladstone had written and published his pamphlet *The Bulgarian Atrocities and the Question of the East*. Forty thousand copies were sold within three days. 'From that time forward', Gladstone wrote, with surprising disregard of Ireland, 'until the final consummation in 1879–80, I made the Eastern Question the main business of my life.'[53] To Hartington's distress, it also became the main focus of Liberal anxiety. The party was determined to oppose, root and branch, Disraeli's determination – despite public opinion having swung against the Turks – to defend Turkey in 'Britain's national interest'. The radicals did what radicals often do. They called a national conference. Rather than approach Hartington directly, the organisers asked Lord Frederick Cavendish to ask his brother to participate. They should have anticipated what the outcome would be. Hartington was emphatic. 'Such a conference would almost be sure to get into the hands of men of extreme opinion.'[54] And so it turned out, though 'with the exception of Gladstone . . . they did not obtain the adherence of men of much weight'.[55] The conference did, however, help to define the deepening gulf which divided the two Liberal leaders – one in name and one in fact. Gladstone always stood, or claimed to stand, on principle. 'What', he asked, 'is to be the consequence for public order if British interests are to be the rule for British agents all over the world?'[56] Hartington thought of himself as the apostle of hard necessity. And Lord Spencer's advice – meant to be a comfort – only served to emphasise the difference in temperament that divided the two men. 'It is useless to try and gauge Mr Gladstone's conduct by any ordinary test. He is governed by impulsiveness and enthusiasm.'[57] Some of Hartington's critics explained Hartington's contrary position in more human terms. Charles Dilke – the rising star of the Liberal Party who was to be brought down by sexual scandal – had no doubt why he had taken up such a deviant position on the Eastern Question. 'He fell more and more under the somewhat stupid influence of [those] surrounding the Duchess of Manchester.'[58]

Hartington continued to insist that he led the Liberals in the House of Commons because it was his duty, not because it was his wish. Gladstone was equally disingenuous. Although he refused even to consider resuming the party leadership, he invariably behaved in a way which made the party rank and file long for his return and sometimes conducted himself as if he had already assumed the role. His publication of a pamphlet which demanded that reform be forced upon the Turks was a clear challenge to the leadership's policy if not to the leader himself. Its demands were replicated in a series of House of Commons resolutions which Gladstone did not move but endorsed. Hartington was as near to despair as his character allowed. 'On the Eastern Question, Mr G has taken the lead and is looked upon by a large section of the party as their leader . . . He does not cease to be leader of the party by merely saying that he will not be leader.'[59] As the crisis deepened, Disraeli prepared – or pretended to prepare – for war. He was encouraged by the changed national mood.

> We don't want to fight
> But by jingo if we do
> We've got the men, we've got the ships
> We've got the money too
> The Russians will not have Constantinople.

The British fleet sailed through the Dardanelles and anchored in the Bosporus. Indian troops were deployed to Malta. When parliament 'voted on account' £6 million to finance possible military operations, Gladstone called it 'a step towards violence and barbarism'. Hartington, on the other hand, was so sympathetic to the mobilisation that he warned Lord Granville, by then the Liberal Leader in the House of Lords, 'Not only am I unable to move an amendment negativing the vote, but also I could not vote for it.'[60] Retirement to the back benches was the obvious, and some would say only honourable, way out of the dilemma. Hartington chose not to take it.

Gladstone did not resume the Liberal leadership and Lord Hartington did not resign it. The amendment to negate the vote on account was defeated by a majority of 328 to 124. Lord Hartington abstained, Gladstone voted with the minority. Whatever else might be said about Lord Hartington's conduct, it could not plausibly be described as heroic. Reginald Brett,* his secretary, wrote that 'a less calm, less self-controlled, vainer man than he would have given up long ago and most assuredly last week'.[61] Lord Derby, writing from the elevated position occupied by those who resign as a matter of principle, attributed the abdication of political responsibility to natural insouciance. 'He talks of politics sensibly but without animation and leaves in one's mind the impression of thinking the whole concern a nuisance.'[62] Neither of them was quite right.

A new Liberal Party was beginning to grow from within the old. The driving force for change was Joseph Chamberlain, a screw manufacturer and Unitarian Sunday School teacher who – as leader of the Birmingham Liberal caucus and Lord Mayor – had persuaded the town council to buy the local gasworks and use its profits to rebuild the sewers. Chamberlain, always suspected of what Hartington implied was the *sin* of ambition, was attempting to amalgamate local Liberal parties into a federation which, his critics feared, would certainly support his radical ideas and might well support him in a bid, one day, to become leader. Chamberlain's letter inviting Hartington to address a meeting dedicated to bringing that amalgamation about was a model of loyalty. Hartington's reply was a cautious refusal dressed up as if it was tinged with regret. 'I cannot give you a definite answer. I must therefore ask you to make your arrangements without reference to me.'[63] Chamberlain interpreted the reply as proof that Hartington – more ambitious than he pretended – was not in a mood to alienate party members on whose support his eventual leadership might depend.

Hartington was an old Whig leading a rapidly changing Liberal Party in which the radicals were gaining ground that could never be recaptured. What few attempts he made to hold back the tide of change were half-hearted and ineffectual. Yet he remained its unhappy leader, protesting that a return to high office – far from being the hope that kept him struggling with both his conscience and his colleagues – would

---

* Brett was to become Lord Esher – the supreme Victorian courtier. Despite his eventual eminence, he remembered his duties to his old chief. On the death of the, by then, Eighth Duke of Devonshire, he destroyed Skittles' letters.

be a penance rather than a pleasure. The Eastern Question was resolved by the Treaty of Berlin – 'Peace with honour' according to Disraeli, but 'an insane covenant' in Gladstone's estimation. In the debate which celebrated Disraeli's perceived triumph, Hartington typically predicted that the ultimate solution to the Balkan crisis would be the result of 'internal and natural . . . rather than external and artificial causes', but rejoiced that 'a temporary solution [had] been found that will leave scope for those natural causes to work'.[61] Then he retired to Holker Hall to attend a sale of shorthorn cattle.

More than disagreement over the Eastern Question separated the titular and de facto leader of the Liberal Party. The Afghan War – another consequence of England's fear of Russian expansion – revealed divisions which were just as deep. In 1876, a new Viceroy of India was appointed with instructions to invite Sher Ali, the Amir of Afghanistan, to co-operate with Great Britain to forestall Russian ambitions. The Amir agreed, but a year later it was discovered that, before his agreement, he had been planning an alliance with Russia and that a military mission from Moscow was expected in Kabul. Britain insisted on being afforded similar access. It was refused and three British armies invaded Afghanistan and won spectacular victories. Mr Gladstone called upon the people of Britain to remember that 'the sanctity of life in the hill villages of Afghanistan is as inviolable in the eyes of Almighty God as can be your own'[65] while Hartington, despite his private doubts, took up a more conventionally responsible position. 'Our position in parliament ought not to take the form of direct opposition to the war or giving the government the means of continuing it.'[66] He took the same 'responsible' view of the Zulu War – even when it ended in absolute disaster with the massacre at Isandhlwana where almost a whole British battalion and the supporting native levies were wiped out. Gladstone advanced onto the moral high ground. Zulus had been slaughtered 'for no other offence than the attempt to defend against your artillery, with their naked bodies, their hearths and homes, their wives and their families'. But Hartington insisted that, while the conflict continued, it was not right to attack ministers for their strategic failures. 'I cannot conceive of anything more disastrous than that the House of Commons should in any way attempt to regulate the conduct of a campaign for which it does not possess the required military knowledge.'[67] That remained his view when, after a period of uneasy peace, Afghan soldiers mutinied and murdered the whole British legation in the capital. Their deaths were avenged when General Roberts stormed Kabul. But the general public had lost its taste for imperial glory. The time had come for a general election.

Gladstone accepted nomination in Midlothian – a constituency of 3,600 electors – and Leeds, where the electoral roll was nearer 50,000. Both seats elected him – Leeds with a majority of 24,000. But it was in Midlothian – where his backers promised him no more than a narrow victory – that he chose to raise his standard. During the opening week of the first Midlothian campaign – meant to establish his reputation in Edinburgh – he made nine speeches. His largest audience was 20,000, his smallest 2,500. In the second Midlothian campaign he took his message out into the neighbouring Scottish towns and cities. After another twenty-one meetings he calculated, with his usual implausible precision, that he had addressed 86,930 men, women and children. His themes had been invariably uplifting – the repudiation of Mammon, the 'intellectual dignity' of Christianity and the primacy in all things of 'truth, charity, dignity and reverence'.[68]

The dying months of 1879 – throughout a triumph for Gladstone – were, for Hartington, a period of almost constant anxiety. In anticipation of the general election, his supporters gave him advice which he should not have needed. Harcourt told him, 'You must give up Newmarket and all your favourite sins and give yourself up entirely to your Manchester speech',[69] an event which was intended to demonstrate his leadership credentials. However Hartington reacted to that injunction, the outcome was not encouraging. 'I have never looked at the reports of my Friday speech', he confessed, 'but it was not a success at the time. It was exceedingly dull and the audience showed that they thought so.'[70] Like most of the party leadership he was thrown off balance by doubts about Mr Gladstone's intentions. Hartington was, or claimed to be, ready to step aside. 'The best course would be that I should, in whatever way may be thought most desirable, resign the leadership . . . I do trust that Mr Gladstone may find it in his power to resume the leadership at all events until the crisis is over.'[71] Lord Granville was horrified by the suggestion. 'Gladstone has got up a tremendous head of steam which, if it does not evaporate during the next three months, will do tremendous damage . . . Your resignation would throw much cold water upon the party.'[72] W. E. Forster – who had stood aside in favour of Hartington's leadership – was particularly alarmed by Gladstone's behaviour. His return to the leadership would alienate traditional Liberals, 'large masses of whom don't want a radical, dissenting, ritualist'.[73] But he also warned Hartington of what he already knew. 'A large part of the party would think, even say, that he ought to be leader, so making your task of leadership harder and perhaps impossible.'[74]

Hartington – out of patrician perversity or uncompromising principle

– reduced his chances of leading his party by setting out rules of political conduct which made it virtually impossible for him to form a government. Charles Stewart Parnell – the Protestant who had persuaded Home Rule factions in the House of Commons to unite in an Irish Party and, initially, led it in a programme of parliamentary disruption – had announced that there were 'other ways to bring the Whigs to reason' than obstructing business in the House of Commons.[75] Hartington immediately retorted that 'if he means that we should be ready to purchase his support with concessions which we think fatal to the integrity of the empire' he should realise that politicians who did so 'would thereby condemn themselves to lasting exclusion from office'.[76] Ten days later, he made the same point more simply. 'I would never be a party to the legislative separation of England and Ireland.'[77] From that solemn undertaking there could be no retreat.

Disraeli, deceived by the results of two by-elections, asked for the dissolution of parliament on March 8 1880. A week later, Gladstone returned to Midlothian, pausing en route from London to address huge crowds at railway stations along the way. At his eve-of-poll meeting in West Calder – already certain of victory for both himself and the Liberal Party – he told his audience that England, 'its interests mismanaged, its honour tarnished and its strength weakened', had 'resolved that this state of things shall cease and right and justice be done'.[78] His claim on the leadership of the Liberal Party was so clear that Queen Victoria told her private secretary 'she would sooner abdicate than send for or have any communication with that half mad firebrand who would soon ruin everything and become a dictator . . . Others but herself may submit to his democratic rule but not the queen.'[79] She was spared that distasteful duty, at least for some days, by operation of the democratic conventions which she had threatened to ignore. Hartington was still nominally the leader of the opposition in the House of Commons and Disraeli, quite properly, advised the Queen to invite him to form a government.

The period between Disraeli's defeat and his resignation had provided an ideal opportunity for the Liberal Party to decide who should lead its new government. Unfortunately a clear decision had been prevented by Gladstone's conduct. Not only was he uncertain where his duty lay. He expressed his uncertainty in language which was so obscure that it was impossible even to guess whether or not he intended to come out of retirement. Hartington came to the right conclusion about his wishes but the wrong calculation about the likelihood of their being gratified – a misjudgement which he expressed in the letter to his father which destroyed the self-created myth that he had no personal ambition. 'He is quite determined that he will take no place except the first and would, no doubt, take that if it was forced upon him. In fact as Granville says, he really wishes to be Prime Minister, though I suppose he would not admit it. As I don't think it likely to be pressed upon him, it does look a very hopeful prospect for me.'[80] A hopeful prospect for me! Those are not the words of a Victorian Cincinnatus, determined to return to his plough.

The summons to Windsor cleared Hartington's mind. When he left London for his audience with the Queen, he was reconciled to reality. It was set out in the careful notes which he had prepared before his departure. 'No strong Liberal Government could be formed which did not receive the support of Mr Gladstone . . . I have no reason to suppose that Mr Gladstone would accept a subordinate post in the Cabinet . . . If the government should fall Mr Gladstone would become the only possible Prime Minister . . . relying on the support of the more advanced sections of the party.'[81] The idea that it was better to have a moderate Gladstone now than an extreme Gladstone later did not appeal to Victoria. Hartington was told to instruct Gladstone that she would not send for him under any circumstances and enquire if he would serve under another Prime Minister. Hartington was instructed to return to Windsor with a report on how the G.O.M. reacted. Wisely, Hartington delivered only the second part of the message. Even that was prefaced by the apology, 'This is a question which I would not have put to you except when desired by the queen.'[82] He then returned to Windsor with a second – equally carefully prepared – speaking note.[83] Only one man could form a government.

So Gladstone received and accepted the Queen's commission – adding gratuitously that he could not understand why, in the first instance, she had sent for Hartington rather than Granville. Hartington's letter to his father resumed the pretence of reluctant statesman. 'I have just got back from Windsor and am happy to say that my troubles are ended . . . I believe that Mr Gladstone wants me to take the India Office, but it is not settled.'[84] He had established his reputation as the man who had declined to accept the Queen's invitation to become Prime Minister by doing no more than accept that forming a government had never been within his power.

CHAPTER 24

The Faithful Apostate

It was, and it remains, the habit of Prime Ministers to welcome each member of a new administration with an exaggerated account of the crucial influence his (or in more modern times her) appointment will have on the future of the government. Gladstone could not resist telling Hartington that Secretary of State for India was the second most important portfolio in the cabinet. The real reason for his appointment was more concerned with unity than seniority. The India Office was responsible for the one area of policy in which Hartington's views were very close to Gladstone's own. After Hartington accepted the offer – with the usual reluctance and regret – their almost identical position was represented in a report he wrote about the situation in Afghanistan. It could well have been composed by a minister in the Blair, Brown, or Cameron governments. 'The result of two successful campaigns, of the employment of an enormous force and the expenditure of large sums of money . . . is the disintegration of the state which we wanted to see strong, friendly and independent.' The new Liberal government was determined to withdraw as soon as it was 'possible to entertain the hope that the prospect of a stable government has been secured'.[1] The prospect of that hope being soon realised was shattered when Ayub Khan – a rival to Abdurrahman, the British favourite in Kabul – attacked and overwhelmed the ruling Amir's forces in Kandahar. A British brigade marched out to meet him and was heavily defeated. Of the total force of 2,476 officers and men, 1,039 were killed or recorded as missing during the battle and retreat. Queen Victoria sent the first of the angry messages which were a feature of her relationship with Hartington during his tenure of the India Office. 'The honour and name of the Empire, as well as its safety, must be maintained. We cannot afford to be defeated.'[2] Both royal objectives were achieved by General Roberts's second forced-march to Kandahar. An army of 10,000 men covered 313 miles in 23 days. Victoria remained suspicious about the government's intentions. 'To give up Kandahar solely because the members of the present government, when in opposition and unaware of the real causes of the war, were unfavourable to the policy of their predecessors, would be a most deplorable course to follow.'[3]

Hartington remained solid for withdrawal – supported by the stability that General Roberts's victory had brought about and in agreement with the generals who, on the instructions of the Queen, had been asked to approve the policy. General Roberts – again anticipating opinions expressed a century later – advised that 'the less the Afghans see of us, the less they will dislike us'.[4] Despite pressure from both Victoria and the government of India, the cabinet agreed that it was time to go. Gladstone, chastened by reality, did not insist that the British grant to Abdurrahman should be dependent, as was his original intention, on social reforms within Afghanistan. When Hartington set out the principle on which the decision to withdraw was based, *Punch* congratulated him for describing the merits of the proposals 'as if he were himself convinced'.[5] For once, pragmatism and principle combined. 'We go away now', Hartington told the House of Commons, 'because we do not want Kandahar and because we have no right to be there, but if we go back, we shall do so with the assent and goodwill of the Afghan people to defend them against some other power.'[6]

Hartington's speech on the withdrawal from Afghanistan sounded remarkably like the product of a conversion to Gladstone's high-minded view of British foreign policy. It was not. Afghanistan, friendly and at peace, was an essential team mate in 'the great game' of keeping Russia out of India and Hartington saw the country's future purely in terms of what best served Britain's interests. Ireland was different. Although he argued that Home Rule would diminish England's status in the world and damage the economy in the no longer United Kingdom, his passionate opposition was not the result of a careful calculation of advantage. His attitude towards Ireland was as intemperate as Gladstone's and, since the two men held diametrically opposed views, was a constant source of friction within the cabinet. Hartington told Reginald Brett, his secretary, that 'the attempt to govern by a combination of Radicals and Whigs is to ride two horses'. Brett offered an extension of the image. It is like an 'attempt to drive two horses, one a sluggard and the other a runaway'.[7] Hartington took offence at neither the correction nor the metaphor. He wanted to be the great restraining force on the 'old man in a hurry'.

At the beginning of the new parliament, the government had allowed the Coercion Act of 1875 to lapse and introduced a Land Bill which aimed to end some of the undoubtedly justified grievances of tenant farmers. Hartington was in favour of coercion but against land reform. In a moment of admirable self-awareness he had told the Prime Minister, 'Perhaps I look at the question from the landlord's point of view, but the confiscation of the right of property seems to me even more serious than the heavy levy on the Exchequer which is the consequence of the proposal.'[8] But the bill passed its second reading in the House of Commons with a majority of seventy-two, despite four dozen Liberals voting against it. Then the House of Lords threw it out by a majority of 232. The violence which followed – murder, arson and the campaign of isolation which took its name from its first victim, Captain Boycott – was unprecedented, even in Ireland. The Land Bill was sent back to the Lords and became law on April 7. Hartington described it as a 'hard morsel to swallow' – a metaphor which suggests dislike without rejection. He was willing neither to fight its introduction nor to accept the discipline of collective responsibility. The day before the bill became law he wrote to the Prime Minister, expressing the hope that he would not be 'asked to take part in its defence more than can be helped'.[9] He was gradually edging his way to a position in which the demands of honour and conviction left him no opportunity to compromise. Reluctant though he was to resign, he must have known that Gladstone was committed to policies which would eventually make it impossible for him to stay in the government.

W. E. Forster, the Chief Secretary for Ireland – a Quaker who, nevertheless, was nicknamed 'Boom Boom' because of his belief in the pacifying influence of shotguns – believed that the renewal of violence, which followed the Lords' initial rejection of the Land Bill, justified a new Coercion Act that included the suspension of *habeas corpus*. John Bright (the Chancellor of the Duchy of Lancaster) and Joseph Chamberlain (the President of the Board of Trade) announced that they would resign if such legislation was introduced. Forster threatened to go if it was not. Hartington added to the crisis by telling the Prime Minister, 'I do not see how it would be possible for me to remain in the government if Forster is forced to leave it . . .'[10] On the whole of our Irish policy, there has not been (with the sole exception of the prosecution of the Irish Land League) a single important measure on which I have been in agreement with the Cabinet.' He had almost resigned 'over the powers deemed necessary for maintaining order . . . The time must come when further concessions are impossible . . . We have throughout been too sanguine in our estimate of the fairness and sense of justice of the Irish people.'[11] Gladstone was equally adamant. 'I will not go back on the past decisions to which you refer.'[12] Forster resigned, Hartington did not. He had become the sort of minister whom colleagues find most tedious – one who constantly talks of resigning but never resigns. Instead he announced that he would support the government à la carte.

Not surprisingly, he pronounced himself satisfied with the Property

Protection Bill, a measure introduced 'for hundreds of thousands who desire to gain honestly their living but do so in fear of their very lives'.[13] It became law on March 2 1881, assisted by the invention of the closure. Hartington defended, with great conviction, the power to limit the length of debates. 'The time of the House belongs not to every individual Member of the House, but to the House itself.'[14] But disagreements between Hartington and Gladstone over Ireland were becoming both more frequent and more profound. It was a subject about which the two men were separated by background, temperament and philosophy. Hartington rejected Gladstone's didactic certainty that establishing peace in Ireland was his unique mission. 'It seems to me that in such an alarming condition as Mr Gladstone described . . . some effort ought to be made to unite the two great parties in Irish policy and to establish a truce in all other questions until the Irish issue is settled.'[15] Origins and upbringing made Hartington instinctively in favour of co-operation with his peers in other parties. But on Ireland, he was coming increasingly to believe that the Tories were right and the Liberals wrong.

Forster's resignation from the Irish Office had set the scene for a private tragedy which can only have increased Hartington's profound antipathy to Irish nationalism. On May 6 1882, Lord Frederick Cavendish – on his first day as the new First Secretary for Ireland – was murdered in Phoenix Park, Dublin.* The murder of his brother broke one of Hartington's few remaining links with the Prime Minister. Lord Frederick, a Gladstone favourite and protégé, thought it his duty to reconcile two temperamentally irreconcilable men. Once the link was broken, it was only a matter of time before their ways parted and the party split. Gladstone, feigning reluctance to continue in government, encouraged speculation about who should succeed him. Hartington confirmed his increasing alienation from his party by warning that he would find it difficult to 'take charge of [Liberal] legislation, especially in regard to Ireland'.[16]

Gladstone had no intention of abandoning the premiership, but he lightened his load by resigning from the Treasury. Granville told the Prime Minister that Hartington had no wish to become Chancellor. He proposed that the job go to Hugh Childers – previously the Secretary of State for War[17] – and that Hartington should move back to the War Office. The change amounted to demotion. He was to return, at the age of fifty, to the office which he had held when he was thirty-three. But Hartington accepted the indignity without complaint.

---

* Lord Frederick's life and death are examined in the chapter which follows.

The Queen's Speech of 1883 promised the extension of representative local government to Ireland. It was advocated with passion by Joseph Chamberlain – no less opposed in principle to dismembering the empire than Hartington – in the belief that while Dublin was denied what was available in Birmingham, 'the seeds of discontent and disloyalty will remain'.[18] Hartington changed his position, ignored the obligations of collective responsibility and denounced the policy as 'madness . . . unless we can receive from the Irish people the assurance that the boon will not be used for the purposes of agitation'.[19] Gladstone was more shocked than angry. 'I console myself with thinking that it is hardly possible that he could have meant to say what both the *Times* and *Daily News* make him seem to say.'[20] Hartington's explanation accepted his detachment from the government but showed no sign of remorse. 'I confess that I had forgotten that the subject . . . had been mentioned in the Queen's Speech.'[21]

Ministers who are fundamentally opposed to one aspect of the government's programme often find that their disenchantment spreads to other items of policy. Hartington had always believed that he had an obligation to speak on behalf of the great landowners. But even his most faithful Whig followers were surprised by the vehemence with which, in cabinet, he opposed a mild Agricultural Holdings Bill which proposed to extend the rights of tenant farmers. After the cabinet meeting of April 21 1883 Dilke noted that Hartington had attacked the measure in language which was particularly offensive to the Earl of Derby – who, having left the Tories, had become Gladstone's Colonial Secretary. 'All my lords very radical indeed today except our Marquis, who was ferocious to the highest point being thoroughly at bay. He gave us to understand that Derby was a mere owner of Liverpool ground rents who knew nothing about land.'[22] Ireland and William Ewart Gladstone had begun to disturb Hartington's usually glacial calm.

Although Hartington had no doubt that he was right about Ireland, even his patrician certainty could not have prevented the occasional feeling of doubt about the wisdom of the enthusiasm he had shown for the purchase of shares in the Suez Canal Company. Incontinent spending by the Khedive – the Governor General appointed by the Turks – had brought Egypt near to bankruptcy. So the great powers of Europe had decided that the Cairo government must – willingly or not – accept their guidance. Detailed intervention in the affairs of a foreign country must have been anathema to a Whig – even one who had felt (and expressed) some sympathy for Disraeli's 'forward' foreign policy. But, as always, Hartington acquiesced. After a series of military revolts, attempted coups and failure of puppet khedives nominated by the European governments, Egypt became what amounted to an Anglo-French condominium. A change of government in Paris produced a change in policy in Cairo. Emboldened by the decision that France would henceforth concentrate its influence and forces inside Europe, the nationalist leader, Arabi Pasha, installed his nominee as Prime Minister, declared himself Minister of War and announced his intention to extract Egypt from the Ottoman Empire.

Radical opinion in Britain was sympathetic to Arabi's hopes of freeing his people from Turkish rule. Gladstone – who was, for a time, much influenced by Wilfrid Scawen Blunt, Arabist and by then the protector of Skittles Walters – closed his mind to the reality of Britain's obligations. 'I wonder', wrote Hartington, 'whether any human being (out of Downing Street) could believe that not a word has been said in the cabinet about Egypt for a fortnight and I suppose will not be said for another week, if then.'²³ On June 11 1882, the subject forced its way onto the agenda. Some of Arabi's wilder supporters rioted in Alexandria and killed sixty Europeans, the British consul general among them. Arabi's soldiers then began to fortify the harbour and install artillery in positions that threatened the Anglo-French fleet in the bay. The French ships were ordered by Paris to sail home. The British bombarded the Alexandria redoubt and reduced it to rubble. Gladstone's cabinet agreed that the best way to secure stability was invasion. On September 13, a British expeditionary force, under the command of Sir Garnet Wolseley, destroyed Arabi Pasha's army at Tel-el-Kabir. The Liberal government had become more embroiled in the governance of Egypt than even Disraeli's Tories had considered either feasible or right and Hartington became more embroiled in the internal affairs at Windsor than he could have either anticipated or wished.

The fault lay with Queen Victoria. After she heard of the victory at Tel-el-Kabir – instead of sending her congratulations via the War Office, as protocol required – she sent a personal message directly to Sir Garnet Wolseley. Hartington, waiting to see the Queen's encomium before he sent his own, did not realise for several days that he had been by-passed. Believing that he was left to look as though his thanks were merely an afterthought, he complained to the Palace and received a reply, again direct from the Queen, to the effect that she would write to her generals how and when she chose. It was followed by a highly indiscreet note from a private secretary. It apologised that yet again, a telegram sent from Windsor – without thought or consultation – had caused unnecessary and justified offence. Hartington was soon required to turn his mind to matters of greater substance.

In 1883, a slave trader from Dongola, capital of the Northern Sudan, had proclaimed himself Mahdi, or Messiah, and raised a revolt against the undoubtedly corrupt and repressive Egyptians who had ruled the Sudan, with tacit British support, since 1819. His success against the enfeebled Khedive created an aura of supernatural invincibility and swelled his army of fanatical supporters. But the Egyptian government unwisely decided to confront him head on. A punitive expedition – led by Hicks Pasha, a British officer – was annihilated by the Mahdi's forces. The British cabinet decided to revert to the traditional Liberal position on colonial adventures. The Sudan, south of Wadi Halfa, would be evacuated.

Whether or not that strategy was justified, the decision to give General Charles George Gordon command of the withdrawal was a fatal error. Correspondence between General (by then) Lord Wolseley and Hartington confirms that ministers should have realised that Gordon's appointment could only end in disaster. They had already agreed that 'looking at the fanatic character of the man',[24] it would be unwise to permit him to serve the King of the Belgians in the Congo. But he knew the Sudan. Ten years earlier he had pacified most of the country and suppressed the slave trade. And because of his reputation as an evangelical Christian, popular opinion – led by W. T. Stead the campaigning journalist – had made him a hero waiting to lead a new crusade. The government's decision was finally determined by the sort of bureaucratic considerations which so often influence the course of great events. Gordon had ignored advice and accepted employment in the Congo without resigning his commission. Hartington wrote to Granville to say 'we ought to retire him' but explained, with obvious reluctance and regret, that 'under our admirable regulations, he will retire with nothing'.[25] Another note on the same day added, 'I understand that Gordon would postpone his Congo employment if asked to go to the Sudan.' Preserving Gordon's pension rights became more important than an orderly evacuation of the Sudan. Sir Evelyn Baring, the British Consul General in Cairo, had wisely warned that appointing a British officer would mean that, if he got into trouble, British forces would have to be sent to the rescue. His advice was ignored and he was persuaded that the risk of defeat was small and therefore worth taking.

According to Evelyn Baring, Gordon always accepted that his orders were to evacuate the Sudan. But the account of a meeting in the War Office, sent by Hartington to Gladstone, was much more equivocal. 'He was unable to indicate the nature of the advice which he would give the government until he had learned the state of things on the spot.'[26] Gordon's own notes (which were attached) were precise about only two aspects of his commission. He was to 'proceed to Suakin and

report on the military situation' and he was to receive in expenses
'£500 to be accounted for'.[17] It seems that neither undertaking was
honoured. When, a few hours after his appointment had been confirmed,
Gordon left from Charing Cross Station, he had no ready money.
Granville, the Foreign Secretary, bought his ticket and General Lord
Wolseley, Adjutant General and effective head of the army,* gave him
all the notes he had in his wallet and his gold watch to sell if he was
in sudden need of cash.[28]

On the advice of Evelyn Baring, Gordon 'proceeded' not to Suakin
but to Cairo, where the Khedive appointed him Governor General of
the Sudan. He thus became a servant with two masters – as well as a
Soldier of God who, from time to time, received orders from a higher
authority than the Army Council. It was not long before his telegrams
to the War Office revealed a dangerously independent view of Sudanese
policy. On February 2 Wolseley reported to Hartington that Gordon
had come to the conclusion that evacuation, leaving the country to
local tribal leaders, 'would be preferable to . . . handing it over to a
government of Egyptian Pashas'.[29] But withdrawal was not his preferred
option. He wanted to create a government which was built on Sudanese
gratitude for release from Egyptian bondage. If he could 'make it
known that henceforth [the Sudan] was to be governed by British
officers, the Mahdi's power would soon melt away'.[30] Three days later,
dervishes – apparently unimpressed by the presence of a British officer
– attacked and defeated a contingent of Egyptian gendarmerie under
the command of General Baker. Hartington responded by wisely anticipating that an orderly evacuation might not be possible and that a
general uprising would prevent even a scramble to safety. So he told
the Prime Minister, 'I know that the cabinet would not agree to any
effectual measures for the support of Gordon . . . But it would be as
well to settle what line to take both in and out of the House.'[31]

Much to his credit – and despite his disenchantment with office –
Hartington attempted to focus the Prime Minister's attention on the
impending crisis in the Sudan. He failed and without Gladstone's guidance the government had no hope of steering a steady course. Wolseley
was left to accommodate whatever he imagined its policy to be and
– as is so often the case with generals and civil servants – told ministers
what he thought they wanted to hear. On February 6 he had given
Hartington his opinion on the feasibility of reinforcing or rescuing
Gordon. 'If you want it done, I think it could be effected by troops

---

* The titular head was the geriatric Duke of Cambridge, Queen Victoria's cousin.

now in Egypt.'[32] Two days later he had warned the Secretary of State for War that 'the defeat of Baker Pasha . . . alters materially the position of affairs generally in the Sudan . . . I think that the time has come for a revision of policy . . . I would advise that Gordon, in announcing his appointment as Governor General, should announce his intention to retain possession of the country to the east of the White Nile.'[33] But on February 10 he reassured Hartington that Gordon knew that he was on his own. 'I told him most emphatically that the cabinet would not consent to the use of British troops in the Sudan.'[34] That view was certainly endorsed by the Prime Minister, though it was expressed in less uplifting language than that which he usually employed. Indeed his statement of policy sounds like an apology. The government intended to 'evacuate the territories, not incur the very onerous duty of returning to the people of the Sudan a just future government'.[35]

Arguments developed about Gordon's willingness to be rescued. Gladstone asserted that he must take his own decision on the timing of withdrawal without waiting for explicit instructions from London or Cairo. Hartington, no doubt influenced by Wolseley's wish to order a partial withdrawal, had begun to change his mind and hoped to change Gladstone's. Plans for a relief expedition were prepared[36] and circulated to the cabinet, on Hartington's instructions, on March 8. Queen Victoria had no doubt about where the government's duty lay. On March 23 she told Hartington, 'You are bound to try to save him . . . You have incurred a fearful responsibility.'[37] Hartington – despite his own increasing doubts about government policy – replied with a remarkably robust rejection of the royal recommendation. 'However critical may be General Gordon's position and however strongly the Government would desire to render assistance to him, the risk and difficulty of dispatching a military force [would be so great] as to make the attempt an unjustifiable one.'[38]

Still Gladstone prevaricated. On April 7 Gordon telegraphed London. 'You state your intention of not sending any relief up here to Berber. I shall hold out here as long as I can and if I can suppress the rebellion I shall do. If I cannot I shall retire to the Equator and leave you the indelible disgrace of abandoning the garrison.'[39] The telegram stimulated in Hartington a previously unknown capacity for irony. Gordon's message was sent to the Prime Minister with an accompanying note. 'We can scarcely say any longer that we know that he does not want troops.'[40] And when Gladstone replied that a decision to mount a relief expedition depended on Gordon's answer to a number of 'carefully prepared questions', Hartington responded that the situation had already become so grave that it was 'doubtful if we can

receive replies to any questions, carefully prepared or not'.[41] By then
he was reluctantly coming round to the unequivocal view that Gordon
must be rescued. No doubt, despite his contempt for populism, he
shared the view expressed to him by W. E. Forster, the recently resigned
Irish Secretary. 'The country would certainly demand [a relief expedi-
tion] if Gordon was shut up.'[42]

Preparations for a relief expedition continued with the general staff
drawing a sharp distinction between the difficulties which would be
encountered if the object was relief of the entire garrison rather than
removal of its English officers. The opposition did not wait for a decision to be made before moving a vote of censure on the government.
Sir Michael Hicks Beach had never heard 'a more disgraceful suggestion than the proposal that a British soldier and Christian hero should
desert those who had placed themselves in peril for his sake'.[43]
Gladstone, putting his own gloss on the Sudanese campaign, rejected
the idea that Britain should 'wage a war of conquest against a people
struggling to be free'. When Forster responded that the G.O.M. 'could
persuade most people of most things and himself of anything',
Hartington loyally defended the Prime Minister against the 'bitter
personal attacks'.

The adventure in the Sudan ended in chaos as well as tragedy. In
cabinet, Hartington complained that the use of the term 'removal . . .
went against the grain' since government policy was to allow General
Gordon to decide for himself whether to go or stay. But on May 26
1884, the Mahdi captured Berber and Gordon was cut off. Hartington
told the Queen that he proposed to ask Lord Wolseley to assume
temporary command of the troops in Egypt – 'not necessarily [to mount]
an expedition but to supervise and direct the organization of the force'.[44]
But a rescue attempt had become unavoidable. New orders which were
sent to Wolseley made clear that the Sudan was to be abandoned and
that 'the primary object of the expedition up the Nile is to bring away
General Gordon and Colonel Stewart', his chief of staff.

Gordon held out until December. The last entry in his diary was on
the 14th. The relief expedition arrived in Khartoum on January 21
1885. News that it was too late reached London on February 5. The
message was passed on to Hartington at Holker Hall where, by chance,
Mr Gladstone – less at odds with the Seventh Duke of Devonshire
than with his son – was staying. The Prime Minister and his Secretary
of State left at once for London. At Carnforth Junction they received
a telegram from the Queen which was more historically accurate than
grammatical. 'These news from Khartoum are frightful and to think
that all this might have been prevented and many lives saved by earlier

action is too fearful.'[45] Hartington shared the Queen's view and, much to his credit, expressed it – in a modified form – during the House of Commons autopsy which followed. There was no mention of his eventual dissent from the decision to delay, simply the statement that he had 'no hesitation in saying that the justification or excuse or whatever term you prefer of the Government has rested mainly on the fact – which we have never attempted to conceal – that the Government were not, until comparatively recently, convinced of the absolute necessity of sending a military expedition to Khartoum.'[46]

The admission was all the more extraordinary in the light of telegrams which Hartington and Wolseley had exchanged the day after the doleful news from Khartoum had reached England. 'We consider', Hartington had written, 'from your want of instructions that after the fall of Khartoum and the death or capture of General Gordon, [you might have concluded that] the reason for any offensive operation against the Mahdi had ceased and we might wish, as soon as possible, to fall back, abandon the Sudan and restrict the defence of Egypt to the Wadi Halfa frontier.' But nothing could have been further from the truth. Gordon's death had made the conquest of the Sudan more, not less, desirable. 'In addition to saving the life of General Gordon', the forces under Wolseley's command had been assembled to 'Check the Mahdi's advance in the provinces of the Sudan'.[47] The general's reply was an elegant reproof. 'This week has been one of surprises all round . . . You had so frequently announced your determination to clear out of the Sudan that this piece of news was the most astounding of all.' Then he explained, in plain soldier's language, that 'to undertake a summer campaign against the Mahdi with British troops would be simply impossible'.[48] Hartington had become an incompetent, indolent or simply detached minister who had not exercised – or because of Gladstone's caprices could not exercise – authority over the policy of his own Department of State.

Subsequent correspondence with Queen Victoria confirms the weakness of his grasp. The government was rescued from the folly of attempting to conquer the Sudan by Russian troops occupying disputed territory on the border of Afghanistan and the consequent fear that every available British soldier might be needed to defend the Indian border against 'the bear'. The Queen, hearing rumours of the Egyptian withdrawal, told her Secretary of State for War that 'no changes should be made until you have the opinion of Lord Wolseley and Sir E Baring'.[49] The implication of respect for Wolseley's judgement signified a change in the Queen's opinion. On March 19 1881 she had written to Hartington opposing his appointment as Adjutant General[50] – largely because of the contempt in which she, rightly, feared he held the ancient Duke of Cambridge, who remained the Commander-in-Chief.

The Queen ended her telegram with a rhetorical flourish about the new contention that the Sudan could be left to itself. 'How can you answer for destroying so many lives, if you had no object?' Hartington's response amounted to the admission that the Secretary of State for War was a cipher who endorsed policies about which he was not even informed and for which[51] he took no responsibility. 'Lord Hartington begs to inform your Majesty that until very recently he had no knowledge of any change of policy in the Sudan.'[52]

Hartington – detached to the point of indifference – must take some of the blame for the slaughter in Khartoum, but the major culprit was Gladstone. During the three months which preceded the triumph of the Mahdi's forces, the Prime Minister neither took any decisions about General Gordon's future nor allowed any minister in his government to do so. Gladstone, preoccupied with new proposals for franchise reform, simply ignored the impending crisis in the Sudan. He proposed to extend the electorate from 3 to 5 million, revise constituency boundaries so as to make every parliamentary division roughly the same size and give Irishmen the same voting rights as those which were enjoyed in England. But, influenced by his usual valetudinarian concerns about his health and physical well-being, he doubted his ability simultaneously to pilot both bills through the Commons at the same time. So he proposed to extend the franchise in one year and revise the boundaries in the next. Hartington, fearing that a general election might intervene and that new voters within old boundaries would increase the radical vote, told Gladstone that both measures must be passed simultaneously. The dispute was resolved as all disagreements between the two men were concluded, until their fundamental differences over Home Rule split the government. Gladstone won and Hartington agonised to his friends about the attractions of leaving office – but did not leave. In December 1883 he told Granville – anticipating correctly that news of his disenchantment would be passed on to the Prime Minister – 'I have not at all made up my mind that I will agree to a single barrelled reform bill. I am terribly sick of office and seldom find myself in real agreement with my colleagues.'[53] Granville faithfully relayed the *cri de coeur* to Gladstone but added his own warning about Hartington's position. 'If he is not convinced as to his public duty, there is no other temptation for him. He dislikes office, still more his present office and above all he dreads the brilliant success which some day may fall upon him.'[54] His comment to Hartington himself was more robust. 'What are you going to do if you give up politics? Nothing but horse racing?'[55]

Although as a young man he had hunted with reckless daring, by early middle age, racing was one of the few interests that Hartington retained. Despite his enthusiasm and the resources he invested in his stable, he was a singularly unsuccessful owner. His horses won only one classic, the One Thousand Guineas in 1877. Thanks to his rank and eminence, he became Steward of the Jockey Club and was said to have admitted, 'I have six houses and the only one I really enjoy is the House at Newmarket.'[56] Indeed the story which, although probably apocryphal, best sums up his character is the claim that 'The proudest moment in my life was when my pig won first prize at Skipton fair'.[57]

On June 8 1885 the Tory opposition – assisted by the abstention of 76 dissident Liberals – defeated the government by 264 to 252 votes. Gladstone resigned at once. Salisbury – who had succeeded Disraeli as Tory leader – chose, rather than call a general election, to form a minority administration. Hartington made his increasing disenchantment with the Liberal Party public. 'I should feel both inclined and bound to give the new government all the support I possibly can as long as they do not make any unnecessary changes to policy.'[58]

At the same time as Hartington was growing increasingly disenchanted with the party, rank-and-file Liberals – except those of the diminishing Whig persuasion – were growing increasingly disenchanted with him. It was again time for him to find a more convenient and reliable constituency and on January 12 1885 – just as General Gordon was preparing to meet his Maker by reading, for the last time, John Henry Newman's *Dream of Gerontius* – he had been offered a new candidature. The letter in which the offer was made illustrates how much the relationship between Members of Parliament and their constituency parties has changed with the years. 'I hope you will excuse me troubling you but I have been required by several leading Liberals in the future Division of Rossendale to ask you if you will kindly consent to receiving a deputation whose object is to try and induce you to become a candidate for this division.'[59] It is not known whether or not the request for a preliminary meeting was granted, but Lord Hartington did graciously agree to represent the Liberal interest in Rossendale.

More than Hartington's constituency had changed. The 1885 Franchise Act had extended the vote in a way that made Irish Nationalists a major force in parliament. Parnell announced in Dublin on August 24 that, after the election, there could be no dispute about the principle of Home Rule, 'only about how much self government they can cheat us out of'. The Irish Party would fight the election on a 'programme with only one plank and that one plank is national independence'.[60] Hartington was not only offended by Parnell's effrontery. He was profoundly concerned that his determination to 'preserve the unity of the empire' would be undermined by both the cynicism of political expediency and the naivety of misguided principle. One party or the other would, he feared, pay the price that Parnell charged for supporting a minority government. The prospect of that party being the Liberals was enhanced by Gladstone's increasing obsession with Home Rule.

According to some of his closest associates, Gladstone remained open to persuasion that he was wrong about Ireland. John Morley, his acolyte and biographer, argued that for some years, his speeches on Ireland had been 'open to more than one interpretation'.[61] Hartington took the more realistic view that the only possible interpretation of Gladstone's admittedly prolix texts was the support for some form of self-government. Principle and expediency would, he feared, coincide in Gladstone's need for Parnell's parliamentary support. He attacked the notion – again with a hint of irony – from what he clearly believed to be the high ground of political probity. 'I cannot believe that there exists in this country any political leaders . . . [who] will consent either to acquire or retain office by conceding the terms by which alone Mr Parnell says his alliance can be purchased.'[62] Joseph Chamberlain expressed identical sentiments, thereby creating one of the most extraordinary alliances in British politics. During the battle over the future of Ireland, Chamberlain and Hartington agreed over the absolute necessity of preserving the Union. At the time, they disagreed, fundamentally and passionately, about everything else.

During the election campaign of 1885, Hartington seemed more worried about the emergence of Chamberlain than the eventual result. In August he wrote to Granville, in obvious anguish, that Chamberlain 'says he is going for graduated taxation and that Mr Gladstone agrees with him . . . He is also for free schools. In short we are going as fast as we can in the socialist direction.'[63] By October the campaign had become as much of a contest between Whigs and radicals as between the Liberal and Conservative parties. Hartington's message to Granville combined anger and despair that he was fighting the Home Rule battle alone. 'Where are the Whigs? I thought you were going to make a speech . . . If I cared a rap about my own prospects or if I thought that there was any possibility of a united Liberal Party being again formed, I should be disgusted at the want of support I have received . . . I see nothing for the Whigs but to disappear or turn Tories. I think I shall prefer the former.'[64] Granville's reply was calculated to appeal to both Hartington's higher instincts and his baser emotions. Gladstone deserved support because he had 'made an honest and successful attempt to unite the party' and a Whig resignation, while Chamberlain remained loyal, would 'place him on a pedestal'.[65] By the beginning of November, Hartington had reached such a pitch of anxiety that he thought it necessary to raise his concerns with Mr Gladstone himself. 'I feel that my position within the party is becoming every day more difficult.'[66] An almost daily exchange of letters followed. Gladstone, although never hiding his determination to make some changes in the governance of Ireland, gave no hint that he was discussing with Parnell – through an intermediary – a 'scheme' of Home Rule which, if adopted by the Liberals, would secure them Irish Nationalist support. But he was temperamentally incapable of concluding the deal without weeks of detailed discussion. Parnell was impatient. Forty-eight hours before polling day, he urged the Irish in Britain to vote Conservative.

Rossendale returned Hartington to parliament with a more than respectable majority of 1,832 after a campaign which ended with his 'intense relief' and the profound hope that he would 'never have to go through anything of the sort again – making bricks without straw'.[67] Distaste for political life, which had been the pose of his youth, was becoming the reality of his middle age. The Liberals – enjoying new support from the recently enfranchised counties – won 86 more seats than the Tories but could still not command a majority in the Commons. Parnell's supporters won 86 seats in Ireland. Gladstone expressed the genuine hope that the Tories would offer to 'settle the Irish question' on terms he could support. But on December 17 an article in the *Pall Mall Gazette* – replicated in other papers – announced that 'Mr Gladstone has definitely adopted the policy of Home Rule'. It forecast that Lord Hartington, among others, would 'come round to Mr Gladstone's view'. Hartington's outrage was increased by the discovery that the prediction had been prompted by an interview with Herbert Gladstone – son and effective secretary to the party leader. The following day he published a letter affirming his undying opposition to Irish self-government. The scene was set for the split which his critics thought he would never have the inclination or energy to bring about. It moved on to its dramatic climax when the Tory government, abandoned by Parnell and his party, failed to defeat an amendment to the Queen's Speech which regretted its failure to introduce measures that improved the lot of rural labourers. Salisbury resigned and Gladstone returned to Downing Street with the promise 'to examine whether or not it is practicable to comply with the desire, widely prevalent in Ireland, and testified by 85 [*sic*] out of 103 representatives, for the establishment by statute of a legislative body to sit in Dublin'.[68] It was set out in a

memorandum which he sent to colleagues from his previous administration. The covering note to Hartington read, 'Please come to me as
soon as you can. The Queen has sent me her commission.'[69]

CHAPTER 25

Full of Love for the Country

Although the Marquis of Hartington was destined to spend his political life at odds with William Ewart Gladstone, Lord Frederick Cavendish – his younger brother by three years – was delphically described by the Liberal leader as 'the son of his right hand'.[1] The reason why the G.O.M. felt such affection for the Seventh Duke of Devonshire's second son is not easily explained. As a young man 'Freddy' was, in habit and interest, indistinguishable from Spencer Compton, his older brother. 'On the whole they were gentlemen, manly in pursuits and ideas, insouciant, taking life easy as it came, without ambition and with little culture.'[2] Most of their undergraduate evenings were spent in the Cambridge's Athenaeum gaming club where they played cards. Both were said, after they left, to be cleverer than they appeared.

In 1864, Lord Frederick had married Lucy Lyttelton, Mrs Gladstone's niece and – after the death of her mother – virtually the Gladstones' adopted daughter. Lucy was admirably unimpressed by the noble family of which she had become a member. 'None of the family seem to be quick or brilliant, but they have a most wonderful accuracy, thoroughness and grasp of a subject.'[3] Dinner parties at Chatsworth were so boring that she wondered how she managed to stay awake rather than 'roll off [her] chair with a crash'.[4] Freddy, being a Cavendish, was found a seat in the House of Commons – in his case the North-west Riding of Yorkshire, the constituency which encompassed the Cavendish land around Bolton Abbey. But he was not expected to be a parliamentary star. Lord Frederick had a slight speech impediment which, it was said, was why he spoke in public with such an obvious lack of confidence. *Punch*, describing one of his more lucid performances in the House of Commons, wrote that 'in his calmest moments his words tumble out, fourteen to the dozen'.[5] It claimed that his colleague, Sir William Harcourt – listening with obvious apprehension to Cavendish 'trembling in every limb at the dispatch box and pouring out torrents of speech' – believed that 'all his words are conjunctions'.[6] Yet Gladstone – notably exacting in his judgement of others – not only loved him like a son, but regarded Lord Frederick as the rising hope of the Liberal

Party. Gladstone was notorious for favouring – in speech, writing and preferment – members of his own family. And he had a well-known weakness for the nobility. Lord Frederick passed both tests.

Despite the disparities in age, Frederick Cavendish and William Gladstone became close friends. In 1875, when the Gladstones were moving out of Number 11 Carlton House Terrace and their house in Harley Street was not ready for occupation, they took up temporary residence with the Cavendishes at Number 23. Each family thought and spoke of the other with great affection. In May 1881, with distress and dissent in Ireland at its height, Lord Frederick – then a Junior Lord of the Treasury – returned from Dublin oppressed with concern about his mentor's state of mind and health. On his way home he had called on Mr Gladstone and, according to his wife's diary, he ended the account of the meeting by saying 'that he was greatly distressed by uncle W this evening – that for the first time things were getting too much for him and had advised him to give up the Exchequer'.[7] That was advice which would only have been given by a highly reckless or entirely devoted friend.

During the arguments about the great questions which separated Hartington and Gladstone Lord Frederick usually supported his brother – sometimes out of conviction and sometimes because, being the younger by three years, he felt an obligation to defer to his senior sibling. He often felt guilty about disagreeing with Gladstone but he overcame the conflict of loyalty by being absolutely frank with both protagonists and urging each one to compromise with the other. It fell to him to explain to Gladstone that his brother privately supported and would not publicly condemn the Tory position on the Eastern Question – adding that he shared the view that there was no realistic prospect of creating a Christian enclave within Turkey.[8] After the breakdown of the Constantinople Conference of the Great Powers – and the consequent end to all hope of reform within the Ottoman Empire – he reassured Hartington that Gladstone, although 'of course deeply disappointed', was not 'so much excited as I have sometimes seen him'.[9] And after the arrest of Parnell in 1881 he returned from Ireland with an account of the renewed violence, the panic it was causing among law-abiding citizens and the unwelcome advice that, after all, *habeas corpus* should be suspended.[10] Gladstone was happier with his recommendations on Irish land reform. His plan was admirably progressive in that it extended the rights of tenant farmers, but it was significantly different from the scheme advocated by Parnell. But whatever his proposal, Gladstone at least listened to what he had to say and listening was not the Grand Old Man's habit.

When W. E. Forster, unsuccessful in his demands for greater coercion, resigned as Chief Secretary for Ireland, it was assumed that Gladstone was only prevented from appointing Joe Chamberlain in his place by a reluctance to share his mission with so glamorous a figure.[11] Charles Dilke, Chamberlain's friend, wrote in his diary that the job was offered to Hartington – despite his emergence, since he had first occupied the office, as a bitter opponent of Home Rule.[12] Unlikely though that seemed, the story was confirmed by Lady Lucy Cavendish, who – after her husband was appointed – said, with more judgement than loyalty, that she thought his older brother 'the better candidate'.[13] Cavendish only went to Ireland because Hartington refused.

Lord Frederick was promoted from Financial Secretary to the Treasury to Chief Secretary for Ireland on May 1 1882. There is no evidence to suggest that he discussed the possibility of such an appointment with the Duke – until then, the invariable practice of both the Cavendish brothers when they were asked to accept new jobs in the administration. He did tell his father after it was too late to alter his decision and the Duke expressed 'misgivings' about 'inhabiting a place of such extreme difficulty'. The Duke wrote in his diary that, 'If the matter had not been almost settled before I knew about it, I would have strongly advised against acceptance.'[14] His forebodings proved prophetic.

Lord Frederick arrived in Dublin on the morning of May 6. That afternoon he and Lord Spencer, the Viceroy, worked on papers in Dublin Castle. Lord Spencer left his office at four o'clock, Lord Frederick an hour later. Normally he would have been driven to the Vice-Regal Lodge, but it was a fine spring evening and he recklessly decided to walk. He was overtaken – fatefully as it turned out – by T. H. Burke, the Permanent Under-Secretary and, according to Irish Nationalist extremists, the author of most of the laws which tyrannised them and suppressed their activities. They walked on together. A group of men – members of a secret society on the criminal fringes of the Home Rule movement, which called itself the Invincibles – were waiting in Phoenix Park. They had missed the Viceroy but, to their delight, they saw the hated Burke, on foot, in deep conversation with a companion and, unusually, unaccompanied by bodyguards. The assassins hacked both men to death using surgical knives. Lord Frederick was not even recognised. He was killed merely because he was there.

That night the Prime Minister was dining with the Austrian Ambassador. So was Sir William Harcourt, the Home Secretary, who received the news from Dublin after both Mr and Mrs Gladstone had left the embassy. Mr Gladstone walked home. So he arrived back in

Downing Street after his wife, even though she had made a brief call at the Admiralty where Lord Hartington, his sister Louisa and her husband, Admiral Egerton, had spent the evening. By the time that the Prime Minister got to Number 10, Mrs Gladstone had already heard the dreadful news. 'When his secretary told him of the horrible thing that had been done, it was as if he had been felled to the ground.'[15] Indeed, according to some reports, he literally went down on his knees in the hall and extemporised a prayer for the departed soul of his young friend.

Quite rightly, the Prime Minister believed that it was his duty to tell Lucy Cavendish that her husband was dead. So he composed himself and hurried off to Carlton House Terrace. According to Lord Thring, who claimed to have witnessed the terrible moment of revelation, Mr Gladstone 'Went to Lady Cavendish. Knelt down by her side, offered a prayer and then went back to work.'[16] If that account is remotely correct, Thring was wholly justified in describing Gladstone's conduct as 'grand but not human'. Lucy Cavendish recalled that his first words were 'Father forgive them for they know not what they do', to which he added 'Be assured it will not be in vain.'[17] The prayer was as much in character as his farewell words as he left Carlton House Terrace. Lucy Cavendish called out, 'Uncle William, you must never blame yourself for sending him' and Gladstone replied, 'Oh no, there can be no question of that.'[18] The Marquis of Hartington chose never to describe the strange emotions which he must have felt when he heard that his brother had been murdered while serving in a ministry which he had rejected.

According to her brother-in-law, Lucy Cavendish's behaviour was equally 'quite as extraordinary' as Gladstone's, but in a more admirable way. Hartington 'talked to her for a long time about her husband, when she was perfectly calm. She has not a shadow of doubt in her mind about him being right to go and most anxious that no one should be blamed for it.'[19] When the news was broken to the Duke of Devonshire he was, according to his youngest son, Lord Edward Cavendish, 'stunned by the blow but well in health. His grief [was] at times terrible, but he recovers and talks of him and of the crisis quite calmly.'[20]

Mr Gladstone, for whom return to work on the night of the murder had been a therapy, used the same remedy to overcome the grief which, he feared, would prevent him from adequately paying tribute to Lord Frederick in parliament. He worked with colleagues in Downing Street before and immediately after he spoke his encomium. In between, according to his diary, he 'went reluctantly to the House and, by the grace of God, forced out what was needful on the question of adjournment'.[21] In Chatsworth Park, a crowd of more than 50,000 people watched Lord Frederick's coffin carried into the Edensor village church. In the grounds of Bolton Abbey, the Duke erected a memorial fountain. On it were engraved words from the House of Commons eulogy which Mr Gladstone had found so hard to deliver. 'Devoted to the service of Ireland, full of love for that country, full of hope for her future, full of capacity to render her service.'

Mr Gladstone's letter to the bereaved father was less well fitted to the emotions of the moment. It began with regrets that the Duke had suffered such a 'terrible affliction', but went on to discuss in detail Lord Frederick's possible replacements.[22] Yet it was not the least sensitive letter written in consequence of Lord Frederick Cavendish's death. The surgeon who performed the autopsy wrote to assure Hartington that he had been 'careful to pay respect to the remains'.[23] And Queen Victoria could not resist ending her message of condolence with the comment, 'which shows what a terrible state Ireland is in'.[24] Nor could the two English political parties be wholly absolved of falling below the standard of conduct which the occasion demanded. In the consequent by-election, the electors of the North-west Riding constituency were urged to vote Liberal and 'avenge the death of Lord Frederick Cavendish'. The Conservative candidate won with a majority of over 2,000.

One man comes out of the whole tragic episode with an undiminished reputation – Charles Stewart Parnell. His near despair at the news of Lord Frederick's death was genuine and the result of personal sorrow about the mindless death and fear that every act of gratuitous violence set back Ireland's cause. He had, for some time, been carrying on secret negotiations with Mr Gladstone through two unlikely intermediaries – Joseph Chamberlain and Captain William O'Shea, the husband of his mistress and future wife. On the morning of May 7 1882 an anonymous message – which it was assumed had the usual provenance – was received in Downing Street. 'I am authorized by Mr Parnell to state that if Mr Gladstone considers it necessary for the maintenance of his position that Mr Parnell should resign his seat, Mr Parnell is prepared to do so immediately.'[25] The Prime Minister replied the next day. His 'duty did not allow him for one minute to entertain Mr Parnell's proposal' though he was 'sensible of the honourable motives by which it had been prompted'.[26] He told Lord Granville, 'If Parnell goes, no restraining influence will remain.'[27] Hartington must have known about both the offer and the reasons for its rejection, but he was not of a mind to give Parnell any credit.

Hartington remained irreconcilable. He supported, with undoubted enthusiasm, the Crimes Bill which was introduced into parliament at the beginning of 1887 and made its way through the Commons, with the assistance of a series of articles in *The Times*. They reached their hysterical climax, on the morning of the Second Reading, with the publication of a facsimile of a letter, allegedly signed by Parnell, which associated the Irish leader with the Phoenix Park murderers. The letter was a forgery which had been manufactured by Richard Piggott, a penniless and disreputable journalist, and touted from newspaper to newspaper by Edward Houston, a 'loyalist' fanatic who had convinced himself that it was genuine. Not surprisingly he had approached the brother of the assassins' most famous victim. But 'Lord Hartington refused to touch either Mr Houston or his letters'.[28] His aristocratic *de haut en bas* did not survive publication day. In the Commons debate on *The Times*'s 'revelations' he suggested that if Parnell was innocent he should seek redress in the courts – a proposal which he must have known could not clear Parnell's name. An English jury would have been prejudiced against him and vindication by an Irish court would be attributed to nationalist bias. Parnell asked for a select committee of the House of Commons to investigate the charges. The government responded by setting up a judicial commission which, while implicating other Irish leaders in campaigns of violence, acquitted Parnell of all charges. On the day that the commission's report was published, Parnell was greeted in the House of Commons by a spontaneous standing ovation. The only Member to remain in his seat was Lord Hartington.[29]

The best that can be said of Hartington's attitude to Parnell is that he was consistent in his hatred. When Parnell was cited as co-respondent in the O'Shea divorce case and the demands of Christian respectability required that he resign the leadership of the Irish Party, Hartington might have been expected to feel at least a twinge of sympathy. His life was far less respectable than Parnell's. He too had a permanent relationship with a married woman – though, outside the exclusive society in which he moved, it was kept a secret in conformity with the hypocrisy which was an essential part of Victorian morality. So, in the light of his own private life, Hartington's reaction to the news of Parnell's fall was particularly disreputable. His correspondence with the Queen was usually formal to a fault. But on the day of Parnell's resignation and disgrace he allowed himself a personal footnote. He told the Queen that he 'never thought that anything in politics could give him so much pleasure'.[30]

Perhaps there was no way in which Hartington's antagonism to Home Rule, and his hatred of the men who demanded it, could have been kept within bounds. But Lucy Cavendish – true to her husband's memory – believed that it was still possible to avoid the great schism.

She reposed her hopes in Mrs Gladstone. Hartington was known to relax in her company – even to the point of once kissing her on the cheek.[31] Catherine Gladstone tried and failed. But, to her obvious surprise, when she tried he was 'genial, not in one of his . . .'. Lucy Cavendish*expressed disappointment at the news and added – loyally though not altogether tactfully – that she had a 'feeling that Freddy would have drawn Uncle W and Hartington together as he had done before'.[32]

The Home Rule Bill was defeated in the House of Commons by 394 votes to 276. The majority included 78 Liberals who shared Hartington's 'unionist' position. If Lucy Cavendish was right to believe that, had her husband lived, he might have reconciled his brother to Gladstone's 'mission', the Phoenix Park murders changed history. Home Rule might have survived and Ireland would have been spared a century of troubles. By killing a man they did not know the Invincibles had made Ireland an even more 'distressful country'.

---

* Lucy Cavendish devoted her years of widowhood to promoting educational opportunities for women. She declined the offer to become Principal of Girton, but accepted the first honorary doctorate from Leeds University.

CHAPTER 26

The Last of the Golden Age

The Liberal government which was formed in 1885 did not include Lord Hartington. The day after victory was confirmed, Mr Gladstone had invited Hartington to call upon him, with the intention of offering him the place in the cabinet which his status and service justified. But he responded to the invitation with a letter that 'set out . . . the main reasons which made it impossible' for him to join the government. They amounted to the wholly justified contention that Mr Gladstone's behaviour made clear that he did not distinguish between 'an examination and the actual conception and announcement of the plan' for Irish Home Rule.[1] The rest of his letter was so emollient that a more thoughtful man would have realised that it was open to misinterpretation. 'While I reserve full liberty to form the best judgment I can . . . I hope and believe it may be possible for me, as a private member, to prevent obstacles being placed in the way of a fair trial being given to the policy of the new government.' A week later he thought it necessary to complain that, because of the moderation of his reply, it was being put about that he had 'been in general agreement' with Gladstone's Irish policy.[2] Dignity required him to make clear that he had chosen the back benches as a matter of principle. During the next four months he spoke in the House and country with unusual frequency. All the speeches were in opposition to Home Rule.

For a time, he was the one senior Liberal to defend the Union. But in March, when a Home Rule Bill was discussed in the cabinet, Joseph Chamberlain cross-examined the Prime Minister about what powers Irish Members would enjoy in the Westminster parliament and, being dissatisfied with the answer, resigned the Presidency of the Board of Trade on the spot. Because of their contrasting characters, Chamberlain became the leader of the Liberal revolt. But Hartington – in the long campaign which followed – made the more substantial, if less pyrotechnic, speeches. The Home Rule Bill was introduced on April 8 1886. During the second day of the debate, Hartington questioned the constitutional propriety of 'initiating legislation . . . of which the constituencies were not informed and of which, if they had been so informed, there is the greatest doubt as to what their decision might be'.[3] The passion with which he defended the democratic doctrine of the manifesto and mandate was enough to persuade Lord Randolph Churchill of 'the enormous desirability' of his moving the rejection of the Home Rule Bill's Second Reading.[4]

Hartington was not easily flattered, but Churchill convinced him that he was more qualified than anyone else to lead the fight against what he was to describe as 'a mischievous measure . . . injurious to the best interests of the nation'.[5] His enthusiasm to play the leading part was reinforced by figures of voting intentions supplied to him on the day before the debate. The prediction was '313 in the ministerial lobby: 252 Conservatives and 79 Liberals in the opposition lobby'.[6] For the government to win the day, 33 of the 43 declared abstainers would have to support the government. The firm prediction was that there would be a majority of 18 against the bill. Like all the best estimates, it erred on the side of caution. Home Rule was rejected by 343 votes to 313, with 93 Liberals in the opposition lobby. It was the second time in his parliamentary career that Hartington had moved the resolution which brought the government down. Back in 1859 he had begun the parliamentary process which routed his Tory opponents. Twenty-seven years later, he became spokesman for the rebellion which confounded his Liberal friends. They did not remain his friends for long.

In the country, the Liberal Party – which, despite his claims of loyalty, Hartington attempted to rally against the Westminster leadership – was less divided than it was in parliament. J. W. Ramsden, MP, wrote to Hartington from his home in Ferrybridge to report the mood in the West Riding. 'I have done as you thought advisable and held a meeting of my constituents. The hall, which accommodates 2,000 people, was nearly full . . . They passed a resolution, thanking me for my speech, but expressed complete confidence in Mr Gladstone.'[7] In Ramsden's opinion the vote did not reflect the slightest preference for Home Rule. 'The feeling was simply that whatever Mr Gladstone said must be right.'[8]

In the House of Commons, the vote split the Liberals irrevocably. Mr Gladstone was left with no real choice but to resign office. In the general election which followed, the Conservatives' decision not to nominate candidates in seats which were held by government rebels made the realignment of the parties equally inevitable. But it was not only Ireland that alienated Hartington from the increasingly radical Liberal Party. On issue after issue, he felt instinctive sympathy for Tory policy. And he certainly felt more at home with Lord Salisbury, the Tory leader, than he did with Mr Gladstone. But he was still not ready – nor were the other Liberals who had brought the government down

– to make a clean break with the past and turn old friends into new enemies. Sir William Harcourt, Chancellor of the Exchequer in the defeated government, wrote to describe the relief with which he heard the news that Hartington would not campaign against him. 'Anything which brought me into personal conflict with you would be the most painful thing in the world.'[9] Some of Hartington's constituents were not so emotionally fastidious. 'Many of my old constituents', he told his father, 'seem very angry and are working as hard as they can against me.'[10] Despite that, he held the seat – albeit with a reduced majority and Tory assistance. The Tories won 316, Gladstonian Liberals and Irish Nationalists combined 280, Hartington's Unionist Whigs 60 and Chamberlain's radical Unionists 12.

Before parliament assembled, the Liberal Unionists (meeting as a group with Hartington leading the Whigs and Chamberlain the radicals) refused to support Salisbury over any issue other than Home Rule. But the Conservatives, in the hope of leading an all-powerful coalition, made overtures to those individual Liberals who, it was thought, were most likely to cross the floor. Chamberlain dismissed the idea as absurd, but told Hartington – implying that the Marquis had been a Tory for years – his situation was 'somewhat different'. 'You might join and be perfectly consistent.'[11] A week later, Lord Salisbury offered to stand aside and advise the Queen to send for Lord Hartington in the hope that he might be able to form and lead a coalition which could command reliable and regular majorities. For the second time, Hartington rejected the chance of becoming Prime Minister.

Again the chance was slight. The letter in which he declined Lord Salisbury's offer was commendably frank. 'I have', he explained, 'come to the conclusion that the difficulties in the way of forming a Government are so insuperable that it would be useless for me to attempt it.'[12] He had a clear view of how Liberal Unionist MPs would react to the idea of coalition. 'They have represented themselves to their constituencies as Liberals and nothing will induce many of them to act with Conservatives.' The prospect was even more remote than Hartington had initially realised. Salisbury responded to his refusal with the admission that 'he was not certain that his friends would support such an Administration'.[13] In fact, once again, Hartington had been offered the chimera of the premiership. In 1886, just as in 1880, the glittering prize which was dangled before him was beyond his grasp. The Queen was convinced that, in or out of government, Hartington must support Lord Salisbury and thus avoid the 'perpetual changes of government which upset everything and give painful uncertainty at home and abroad'.[14] It was advice which suited his increasingly ecumenical instincts.

It might have been expected that, at a time of the breaking of parties, the House of Commons would avoid the creation of a parliamentary 'crisis' over an issue which, in the real world outside Westminster, would be regarded, at most, as a trivial dilemma. Not so. In the days before parliament recognised an 'official opposition', Privy Councillors who had served in defeated governments occupied the front bench to the left of the Speaker. Someone therefore had to decide whether or not it would be proper for the Right Honourable adversaries – Liberal Unionists and Gladstonians who had fought what amounted to a civil war during the general election – to sit side by side. Hartington's letter to Gladstone – describing the dilemma in dramatic terms – received the dismissive reply which it deserved. 'So far as places on the front opposition bench is concerned, your rights to them are identical to ours.'[15] Having disposed of what he clearly regarded as a matter of no consequence, he then turned to a question of substance. Was Hartington going to narrow or widen the gap which separated the two Liberal factions? It was a rhetorical question. Gladstone knew that sooner or later Hartington would align himself with the Conservative leadership. The ties of birth and breeding made the alliance inevitable. So did Hartington's politics.

He was soon presented with an opportunity to demonstrate the direction in which his instincts led him. Hartington – as devoted to the Union as any Tory – outflanked the Conservatives during the debate on the Tenants' Relief Bill – by discounting consideration of its merits and 'objecting to any concession to Parnell which he could use as proof of his power of coercing Parliament'. Having disposed of the danger inherent in granting tenant rights, Hartington decided to take a recuperative holiday in India. But the Queen, exhibiting remarkable prescience, told him that it was his duty to remain close at hand to assist in the resolution of any emergency which might arise. He was in Rome when the storm broke.

Lord Salisbury had appointed Lord Randolph Churchill – brilliant, mercurial and certain of his own destiny – as both Leader of the Commons and Chancellor of the Exchequer. At thirty-seven he was the youngest Chancellor in history. His first budget was one of the most complex and comprehensive on record. As well as inventing a number of new taxes, he changed the rate of almost all of those which he inherited. Most of the cabinet acquiesced – persuaded by the force of Churchill's personality and his proposal to cut income tax. But – as is so often the case – the service ministers rejected his calls for reduction in naval and military spending. Churchill told Salisbury that he would resign unless the Secretary of State for War accepted reduced estimates. The Prime Minister, believing he was bluffing, rejected the ultimatum but hoped to retain the Chancellor. Churchill, mistakenly concluding that Salisbury had already decided that he must go, was prompted by pride to resign before he was dismissed. Foolishly he published a resignation letter in *The Times* before he received any intimation of the Prime Minister's intention. The likelihood was that, in the end, Salisbury would have made whatever concessions were necessary to keep him in the cabinet. But the publication of the *Times* letter made it impossible for either man to adjust his position. Churchill's political career was over for ever and the government was in crisis.

Lord Salisbury thought that the best way to resolve it was to send for Lord Hartington who had just returned to England. The Prime Minister's telegram to Chatsworth – one gentleman to another – did not request an immediate return to London, but merely asked when the return would be and warned that on his arrival he would find a letter which renewed the proposal of the previous July. In fact it made two offers. Hartington could take his pick – either the premiership or the leadership of the House of Commons in a Salisbury coalition. Victoria – in a letter written on Christmas Day – urged him to form a new government.[16] For the third time Hartington turned his back on Downing Street.

It took him five days to reply to the Queen's invitation. He spent the time consulting his friends. His letter to Windsor – describing the result of those consultations – confirmed that he could not command enough support to form a government. Many of the Liberal Unionists to whom he had spoken had told him that ties of loyalty still bound them to the Liberal Party and – the one issue aside – were too strong to be broken. There was little doubt that he wished it could have been otherwise. The likelihood is that, had he been able to persuade the Liberal Unionists to follow him, he would have accepted the chance, his third, to become Prime Minister. His letter to his father, the Duke of Devonshire, insisted, 'I do not regret it at all.'[17] It was a protest which made clear that he regretted it very much indeed.

Hartington loyally followed Queen Victoria's injunction to support stability as personified by Lord Salisbury. So when George Joachim Goschen (a Liberal First Lord of the Admiralty under Mr Gladstone) was offered the Treasury, Hartington advised him to accept. The drift across the floor of the House of Commons had begun. But it was ten years before he felt that he was able, with honour intact, to take his place in a Unionist administration. So he spent four years in the Commons, for the first time in nearly three decades, not a shepherd but one of the sheep. He was not assiduous in his attendance. But he retained his record of public service by accepting the chairmanship of two Royal Commissions. One examined the Administration of the Naval and Military Departments. The other reported on Questions Affecting the Relations between Employers and the Employed. His duties left plenty of time for hunting, shooting and the activities which rank and wealth obliged him to perform. He enjoyed only the hunting and shooting. 'His duties as chairman of companies in which he was the largest shareholder were rather irksome to him. He distrusted his knowledge of business matters and consequently, as a rule, did not attempt to force his view on colleagues . . . Appointing clergymen to vacant livings was a duty he particularly disliked.'[18] It seems as if, until he was stirred to wrath by Irish nationalism, he saw the House of Commons as a convenient alternative to boredom. He left it, for a better life above, on December 21 1891, when – on the death of his father – he became the Eighth Duke of Devonshire.

An immediate consequence of his elevation was that Rossendale – which he had represented for the last six of his thirty-five years in parliament – was engulfed in a bitterly fought by-election in which Mr Gladstone intervened with the allegation that Hartington, the previous Member, speaking on behalf of Liberal Unionists, had 'promised a large introduction into the Irish Government of the representative principle and a fundamental reform of the system of administration known as the hated Dublin Castle'. To drive his point home, Gladstone added that 'nearly six years have elapsed, but not a single step has been taken towards the redemption of these pledges'.[19] That was hardly surprising as the pledges had never been given. Hartington was infuriated by the suggestion that he was, or ever had been, in favour of anything more inimical to the Union than an extension, to Ireland, of the form of local government which existed in England. 'I was not, in 1886, and have never since been, in a position to promise fundamental reforms and I made no such promises.'[20] Mr Gladstone's candidate won the by-election by a comfortable margin. But if the Liberal Unionist defeat distressed the new Duke, 1892 brought many consolations. In July he learned that he was to become a Knight of the Garter and in the following month he married the recently widowed Louise, Duchess of Manchester, making her – in reality rather than the society joke – 'the double duchess'.

The newspapers claimed to be surprised. Hartington's regular visits to the Manchesters at Kimbolton Castle – where he chose to keep his horses – was, they explained, thought to be no more than the result of Saint Neots' convenient situation in racing country. Fellow guests were said to be surprised by the intimacy of their conversation when, one morning while writing letters, the then Duchess of Manchester was heard to ask, 'Harty darling, stand me a stamp.'[21] But the closed society in which they both moved must have known the truth. And the Duke of Manchester must have known too.

Marriage to the Dowager Duchess of Manchester either released a previously subdued aspect of Devonshire's character or obliged him to accept, with good grace, the more gregarious lifestyle of the wife for whom he had waited so long. His regular amusements – shooting, hunting and cards – became great social occasions. There were dinners of lavish splendour at Devonshire House and long weekend parties in the country. Hartington's new enthusiasm for entertaining coincided with a period of close, if brief, friendship with Joseph Chamberlain who spent a weekend at Hardwick Hall. Lady Salisbury (whose husband had declined to accept a dukedom because he could not afford to live in a manner appropriate to the improved status) described a visit to Chatsworth – at which everyone played poker and bezique until midnight – in a letter which left no doubt that one section of society disapproved of the couple's lifestyle. 'No one has the slightest knowledge of or interest in the great treasures of books etc . . . But I think they are very happy which is a great thing – only [they] all [would] be so much happier in Monte Carlo.'[22]

The Duke of Devonshire – in middle age responsible, for the first time, for managing the assets on which he lived – had never been financially prudent. After 1891, his extravagance – on good works as well as self-indulgence – was wilfully reckless. For he had discovered on his accession that his father had not, as he had supposed, cleared off the debts incurred by the Sixth Duke. The attempts at building a new Devonshire prosperity on property in Eastbourne and heavy industry in Barrow-in-Furness had done worse than fail. Instead of compensating for the loss of estate income during the great agricultural depression, they had increased the debt by something in excess of £2 million.

Hartington, now the Eighth Duke, was as ruthless in his determination to pay off his creditors as he was to maintain the lavish lifestyle that his wife took for granted. Sentimental attachment, either to the men and women who lived on his estates or to the land which his family had owned for centuries, did not hold him back. The Furness ironworks and naval shipyard were sold to Vickers and Maxim for shares in those companies worth £300,000. Part of the Derbyshire estate had to be auctioned. Despite the slump in land values there was even talk of putting Devonshire House on the market and closing Chatsworth to visitors – an activity which, in the nineteenth century, made a loss. But one aspect of the agricultural depression provided its own compensation. Ironically the Irish land reforms – about which the Duke had expressed so many doubts – provided the major source of Devonshire's 1890 income. Assisted purchase schemes contributed £660,000 to the liquidation of the debt which, by 1899, had been reduced to £1 million.

Yet it was the Duke of Devonshire's destiny always to be regarded, outside his own gilded circle, as the recipient of vast inherited wealth. When the great political realignment was completed – he had joined with Balfour in an alliance of Tories and traditional Whigs – 'Harty-Tarty' became the favourite example of the unjustified power and privilege that opposed reform. David Lloyd George, defending proposals to disestablish the Welsh Church, reminded the Duke – a passionate opponent of the bill – that the Cavendish dynasty owed its power and position to the dissolution of the monasteries. 'The very foundations of his fortunes are laid deep in sacrilege.'[23]

CHAPTER 27

A Drag on the Wheel

A year after Lord Hartington became the Eighth Duke of Devonshire, Lord Salisbury – despite enjoying a majority of 66 in the House of Commons – advised the Queen to dissolve parliament. The announcement was followed by an offer from Chamberlain which marked the apogee of his close relationship with Hartington. He offered to arrange for Victor Cavendish – the twenty-three-year-old son of Lord Edward and the likely heir to the Devonshire title – to become the Liberal Unionist candidate in the Handsworth Division of Birmingham. Cavendish had inherited his father's seat in West Derbyshire, so the invitation to sup with the man who was soon to become the devil, was declined with thanks.

In Liverpool in November 1891, the Eighth Duke predicted that the Liberal Party was fractured beyond repair, a clear indication of both the hope and the anticipation that its Unionist wing would form a closer alliance with the Tories. His judgement on the Liberal future was clearly influenced by a speech which Mr Gladstone had made, three weeks earlier, to the National Liberal Federation. It had set out what, thanks to the town in which the federation met, became known as the 'Newcastle Programme'. Many of the policy proposals which it contained – employers' liability for industrial accidents, restriction of working hours in most manual industries, the payment of MPs and the threat to emasculate a recalcitrant House of Lords – were too radical for Gladstone's taste and the Liberal leader had only agreed to endorse them in order to ensure that its authors supported Irish Home Rule, the one policy about which he really cared. So it was not surprising that the rag-bag of promises must have convinced Devonshire that the Liberal Party had drifted to within hailing distance of the socialism which he had always feared. From then on it was only a matter of time before his part of it became – in one guise or another – an adjunct of the Conservative Party.

The election of 1892 produced a Home Rule majority – Liberals and Nationalists combined – of 40. Salisbury's government was defeated in the subsequent Vote of Confidence. In the second general election, both sides, in what became a bitter argument, made increasingly wild speeches, inside and outside the House of Commons. The Duke of Devonshire – wholly uncharacteristically – made one of the wildest. On April 15 1893 in the Corn Market in Dalkeith – the heart of Gladstone's constituency – he issued a genteel version of Lord Randolph Churchill's battle cry, 'Ulster will fight and Ulster will be right.' It began with a tribute to the Glorious Revolution of 1688 – modestly omitting to mention the part which the Cavendish family had played in bringing it about. He then moved on to what John Morley, the Secretary of State for Ireland, called 'the high watermark of the frenzy to which Unionist fanaticism and superstition can bring men of intelligence'.[1] Devonshire was undoubtedly attempting to justify, if not to encourage, armed revolt. 'We expect the inhabitants of Ulster will obey the law, but no subject is bound to obey a law which does not give him at least equal protection with that which is offered to every other class of his fellow subjects . . . How can the descendants of those who resisted King James II say that they have not the right, if they think fit, to resist – if they think they have the power – the imposition of a government put upon them by force?'[2] It was all in great contrast to his advocacy, five years earlier, of a permanent Coercion Act. 'We are here to amend if necessary but to support the government in the enforcement of the law. We are not here for preaching or condoning resistance to the law, either passive or overt.'[3] But his attitude to Ireland was neither consistent nor rational. He was, unavoidably, influenced by possession of Lismore Castle and the Boyle Estate in County Waterford which, like so much Cavendish property, had been acquired as the result of a fortuitous death and a provident marriage. But he felt a sincere and passionate attachment to the *idea* of the Union which he believed that his ancestors had saved from Papism.

Gladstone's will did not prevail only within the Liberal Party. On April 23 1893 the Second Reading of a new Home Rule Bill was carried in the House of Commons with a majority of 43. It was then rejected by the House of Lords and Mr Gladstone resigned though the government did not. His successor, the Marquis of Rosebery, survived in office for a year. Then it was Lord Salisbury again and an opportunity – justified by the old government's defeat on the second Home Rule Bill – for the new administration to be built around men of different political origins but a common view on the sanctity of the Union. Joseph Chamberlain became Salisbury's Colonial Secretary. Goschen, who had been Chancellor, moved back to the Admiralty. The Marquess of Lansdowne was appointed Secretary of State for War and Lord James Cavendish was made Chancellor of the Duchy of Lancaster. The Duke of Devonshire was offered the Foreign Office but said that he would prefer to be Lord President of the Council. His wish was granted.

The social extravagance, which had become a feature of his life since his marriage, continued unabated. On July 2 1897 Queen Victoria's Diamond Jubilee was celebrated by a Devonshire House Ball. For his description of the event, Bernard Holland – Devonshire's sometime private secretary and Edwardian biographer – abandoned the language of deference in favour of the prose of awe and wonder.

> The elect of the British aristocracy appeared in the Court costume of all times and countries. They were received at the head of the curving staircase by the Duchess, gloriously apparelled as Zenobia, Queen of Palmyra and the Duke as Emperor Charles V, adorned with the collar and badge of the Order of the Golden Fleece. Princess Henry of Pless shone as the beautiful Queen of Sheba, her train borne by four negro boys. Two English kings to be were present. The Prince of Wales appeared as Grand Master of the Knights of Malta, the Duke of York as Clifford, Earl of Cumberland in Elizabethan days. The Duchess of York came as the renowned Marguerite de Valois.

The description continued down the order of precedence through a variety of politicians ending with the Home Secretary, Herbert Asquith, a *soi-disant* intellectual but an inveterate party-goer, 'faithful to his lifelong convictions . . . attired in the riding dress of a Puritan or Roundhead'.[4] Holland's sycophancy was outdone by the correspondent of *The Times* who noticed that the Cavendishes and the Hapsburgs 'are curiously alike in features'.[5]

Devonshire's return to the political arena meant – whether he liked it or not – alliance with Joseph Chamberlain. They were united by a common view of Britain's place in the world but 'Radical Joe' argued for domestic policies which violated all the Duke's notion of privilege and property. In the end their shared belief in an imperial destiny was enough to bind them together. In their different ways – buccaneer and grandee – they both played crucial parts in last imperial adventure of Queen Victoria's reign, the Boer War. Its cause was the bitter dispute over who should gain most from exploiting the gold of the Transvaal. Its occasion was the refusal by the Afrikaans government of that province to allow British Uitlanders the full rights of citizenship. The Duke of Devonshire, chairman of the cabinet's Defence Committee, approved and signed the ultimatum that amounted to the formal declaration of a war which he described as 'undertaken in defence of imperial interests' and essential to maintaining British 'authority in every part of the world'.[6] But the Boers stole Devonshire's thunder with an ultimatum of their own.

The early successes of the South African campaign were thought to have enhanced the authority and increased the popularity of the Salisbury government. In September 1900, the Prime Minister – hoping to catch the tide of esteem – asked the Queen to dissolve parliament and precipitate the first of the two 'khaki elections' of the twentieth century. Devonshire refuted in the language of an English gentleman the allegation that the Unionists were exploiting the patriotism of the people. 'The captain of a cricket team, when he wins the toss, puts his own side in or his adversaries, as he thinks most favourable to his prospects of winning.' The Prime Minister had done much the same in choosing 'a moment which he thinks not unfavourable to his own side'.[7] The pitch was not quite the batting wicket that the Unionists' captain supposed. They increased their majority by only four seats. The Duke of Devonshire, more in conformity with convention than as a result of personal inclination, offered to return his seals of office. Salisbury asked him to remain Lord President of the Council and, of course, he agreed.

At the time his continued responsibility for education was thought to be just a formality. The Vice-President of the council would do all the work. But the Duke had developed a strong and genuine interest in one education policy. His concern combined two proper Whig principles – the obligation of the ruling classes to protect the interests of those they rule and the equal duty to ensure the primacy of the Established Church. The obligation and duty were in conflict with each other – a problem which the Duke seems not to have recognised even though education had been part of his theoretical responsibilities since the election of 1895, also the year in which a Royal Commission, chaired by James Bryce – scholar, lawyer and Liberal MP – had concluded that schools' policy was 'neither continuous nor coherent' and that the 'first problem to be solved must be that of organization'. Bryce's proposed solution was the creation of a 'central authority' under the direction of a cabinet minister and a network of 'local education authorities'.

The government's involvement in education was bedevilled by concerns about the nature of the religious instruction which the main-tained schools could, or should, provide. The Education Act of 1870 had been amended by the Cowper-Temple clause which required that 'no religious catechism or religious formulary which is distinctive of any particular denomination shall be taught in school' financed by the state. It was meant to ensure that religious instruction was taught from the Bible rather than a prayer book. But it satisfied nobody. The Nonconformists and the Catholics believed, correctly, that the Established Church regarded its brand of Christianity as non-denominational and the Church of England feared, with equal justification, that Nonconformists wanted to preach their own gospel in the maintained schools where children of their persuasion predominated. When the Bishop of London told the Royal Commission that 'education ought to be free of fluctuations of opinion'[8] he meant that the religious syllabus should be determined in York and Canterbury. The Duke of Devonshire was so incapable of distinguishing between the Anglican gospel and universal truth that he told critics of the Church of England's influence on the syllabus, 'I am afraid that there is some defect in my intellect which renders me incapable of even understanding the apprehensions of the advocates of denominational education.'[9]

In 1896 and 1898 bills had been introduced with the intention of reassuring Nonconformists that religious education in state schools would be taught from the Bible, not denominational prayer books. Both had been abandoned. In 1897, a rate relief bill – designed, said the Duke of Devonshire, to 'relieve the voluntary [i.e. church] schools from the intolerable strain of poverty and to relieve the oppressive burdens of rates in some of the poorer districts' – had been passed into law.[10] That apparently modest ambition confirmed the long-held suspicions of Nonconformists in both the Liberal Unionist and the Liberal Parties. A proposal to provide extra financial assistance for voluntary schools – a large majority of which were Anglican foundations – amounted, in their opinion, both to 'subsidising the Church of England' and guaranteeing that its schools proliferated. It was clear that opinion, even inside the Unionist coalition, was deeply divided. On March 24 1897, Devonshire wrote to the Prime Minister. 'I look forward with a good deal of anxiety to what may occur here. I think it has required all your influence in the Cabinet to keep us together and do not feel that those who have joined us unwillingly in the present policy will be equally amenable if further developments should arise.'[11]

Despite Devonshire's doubts, the government pressed on with its plans to create a Board of Education, which would be separate from the Privy Council. The Duke was asked, and (of course reluctantly) agreed, to add the new presidency to his other duties, though Sir John Gorst, the Vice-President, was expected to take effective charge. Gorst was not the ideal man to pilot a controversial bill through parliament. He had been a member of the so-called 'Fourth Party', a Tory ginger group led by Randolph Churchill, and although he had become less critical of the party leadership, he remained a controversial figure. It was a status which he enjoyed and encouraged by his abrasive manner, uncompromising opinions and habits of speech which had included describing the Duke of Devonshire as 'a wet blanket'. According to Sir Almeric FitzRoy, the clerk to the Privy Council, 'the Duke stood to a large extent between Sir John and the resentment he incurred, defending him . . . in the House of Lords with great vigour'.[12] It seems that in private the Duke was less supportive. Parliament first defeated a proposal to create local education authorities – an innovation which Gorst espoused with an enthusiasm that the Duke did not share – and then frustrated a second attempt by delaying the passage of the legislation. When the cabinet refused to spend any more parliamentary time on what they regarded as already a lost cause, Devonshire told his deputy, 'Your damned bill's dead.'[13]

Frustrated by Gorst's constant alienation of potential allies, Sir George Kekewich – the permanent secretary at the Education Department – suggested (it is not known how seriously) that he might be offered the governorship of a moderately sized colony. Devonshire replied that he could not 'imagine the government offering Sir John the governorship of a colony which it wished to retain'.[14] However irresponsible his character and conduct Gorst can take some credit for the introduction of the 1902 Education Act – an intrinsically admirable measure. He also transformed the Duke of Devonshire from an undoubted, but moderate, believer in modest extensions in the provision of secondary and technical schools to a determined advocate of wholesale reform in the entire education system.

In January 1900 – at the inception of the new education ministry – Salisbury found it necessary to warn the Duke of Devonshire that he was determined to protect the interests of the Church of England. 'I am afraid I shall have trouble with you about the denominational question. I cannot accept any measure which aids undenominational religion out of the public funds and refuses the same to denominational religion.'[15] Concern about the future of voluntary schools was so great that it is at least possible that no major change would have come about had not fate intervened, in the form of T. B. Cockerton, the auditor of the Local Government Board.

In June 1900, Cockerton upheld a complaint – made on behalf of the Camden School of Art by the Technical Education Board – that the London School Board had acted *ultra vires* in subsidising 'higher grade' education. Gorst supported the Camden Art School's claim and referred the whole issue to the Government Auditor, who found that 'instruction in science and fine art could not be described as "elementary education"' – all that the London Education Board was entitled to provide. After a series of appeals, the Master of the Rolls confirmed that judgment. As a result the government was forced to choose between introducing a new Education Act and prohibiting school boards, all over the country, from providing anything that could be described as 'higher' or 'secondary' education.

Arthur Balfour – heir apparent to the Unionist leadership and nephew to Lord Salisbury, the Prime Minister – saw the crisis as an opportunity to introduce a major reform which would provide general improvement and security for the voluntary schools. He had long believed in the need for a new education bill which both improved the quality of maintained schools, set up under the 1870 Act, and, by subsidising 'voluntary schools', guaranteed a continued place for the churches (particularly the Church of England) in the instruction of the young. But even he was overwhelmed by Devonshire's enthusiasm for the idea of education reform. 'I go to Chatsworth on Monday and Devonshire is sure to talk at length upon educational schemes. I confess they alarm me not because they are defective but because they are too complete.'[16]

A short 'holding bill' which temporarily legalised previously prohibited expenditure was introduced into the House of Commons with the intention that it should be piloted through its several stages by Sir John Gorst. Unfortunately, on July 15 1901, his rebellious past caught up with him. A Liberal MP quoted a speech which he had made in Bristol four years earlier. He had attributed Conservative neglect of education to the origins of the party leadership – 'selected from a class which was not altogether convinced of the necessity or desirability of higher education for the people. They held the opinion . . . that there were certain functions which had to be performed in the modern life of civilised communities which were best performed by people ignorant and brutish.'[17] It sounded so like a description of the class from which his chief, the Duke of Devonshire, came that he had no choice but to resign. Balfour accepted personal responsibility in the Commons for the major legislation which followed but wrote to the Duke of Devonshire to explain that, far from attempting to extend his empire, he had been 'dragged, much against [his] will into matters concerning education'.[18]

By then, Devonshire was much under the influence of Sir George Kekewich, an instinctive progressive who, according to Balfour, was 'most anxious that only Secondary education should be touched' and that comprehensive reform should be postponed until a government 'more favourable to his friends in the school boards and National

Union of Teachers' was elected. 'The poor old Duke' – a variation on a phrase which he was to use again three years later with lethal effect – 'did not realise' that Kekewich's reservations were politically motivated. Balfour did and insisted that the new bill should include the reform of primary education. To the astonishment of Sir Robert Morant, the civil servant to whom ministers turned after the fall of Kekewich, the Duke drafted the necessary cabinet memoranda 'all by himself'.[19] Until the papers were circulated, it had seemed a task to which he was wholly unsuited.

Almeric FitzRoy had thought that 'the details of educational administration, however interesting to the enthusiast, were frankly distasteful to the Duke's temperament'.[20] However, he 'surprised all his colleagues by displaying a considerable mastery of all the issues involved. He had unfolded his views with great cogency.'[21] Despite his genuine interest in the subject, the unexpected assiduity was probably more the result of his determination to keep the Unionist alliance alive than his enthusiasm for popular education. Victor Cavendish, his nephew and heir presumptive, wrote in his diary that 'Uncle Cav' was 'very worried about the education bill. Afraid there may be trouble. May break up the party.'[22] He was right to be concerned. The Liberal Nonconformists (Unionists included) were opposed to the bill root and branch and even had their spokesman – Joseph Chamberlain – inside the government. Indeed, Devonshire attracted much admiration by 'not allowing himself to be disturbed by the interventions of Mr Chamberlain' during cabinet discussions.[23]

The Nonconformist objection was best (or at least most vehemently) articulated, after some initial wavering, by a young Welsh MP called David Lloyd George. The predominantly Anglican church schools, which the Baptists and Methodists had hoped would wither and die through lack of funds, were not only being restored to healthy life. They were being offered the chance to propagate. Balfour's bill, the Nonconformists claimed, made that injustice permanent. Worse still, for a time it proposed that 'board schools' be allowed to offer whatever sort of religious teaching the parents wanted. And that, the Nonconformists feared, would most often be Church of England. In a concession to Joseph Chamberlain, the idea of parental choice was briefly abandoned and a clause was added to the bill which gave county and borough the 'local option' of not implementing its provisions. The concession was withdrawn while Chamberlain was out of the country.

In the House of Lords the Duke of Devonshire chose neither to trim nor to equivocate. He admitted that 'to many conscientious men, a denominational school – especially if it is supported out of public funds, whether those public funds be derived from taxes or rates – is an abomination' but added, before the gasps of opposition had died down, 'Certainly that is not the opinion of His Majesty's Government and we do not believe it to be the opinion of a majority of the country.' After insisting that the bill diminished rather than extended 'clerical control', he turned – with more courage than judgement – to the 'real Nonconformist grievance. The real grievance is that [the bill] does not extinguish Church Schools. They hoped, many of them, either to have those destroyed by legislation or starved out of existence. That is a grievance which we cannot undertake to remedy.'[24] His defence of the interests of the Established Church was in the great Cavendish tradition. So was his miscalculation of the consequences which followed from brushing aside opinions which were different from, but just as strong as, his own.

The Duke of Devonshire was probably right to say that most of the British people would have regretted the passing of church schools. But, being wholly insulated from the vibrant Nonconformist communities that enlivened so many parts of England and Wales, he had no idea how damaging their opposition would be. Joseph Chamberlain – for all his arrogance a man of the people and, in his time, a Unitarian Sunday School teacher – realised the consequences of offending every Methodist and Baptist chapel south of the Scottish border. On September 22 1902 he wrote the Duke a letter which was both blunt and aggressive. 'I told you that your Education Bill would destroy your own party. It has done so. Our best friends are leaving us by the score and they will not come back . . . We are so deep in the mire that I do not see how we can get out.'[25] His judgement was vindicated when Nonconformists rose up against the Unionist Coalition. But the Education Bill was not the only cause of Balfour's defeat. His government was effectively destroyed by a crisis in which the Duke of Devonshire played a particularly ignoble part.

The Duke cannot be blamed for causing the 1903 crisis. That accolade goes to Joseph Chamberlain. The year before, he had proposed that the 'corn tax' – a 'registration fee' of 3d per cwt levied on imported grain and 5d added to the price of flour, which had been imposed as a temporary expedient to meet the costs of the South African War – should be made permanent, with an important exception. Imports from the colonies should be given a 'preferential reduction' which effectively spared them payment of the tariff. Chamberlain was less concerned about the revenue that his proposal would raise than the effect that 'imperial preference' would have on the unity of the empire. Charles

Ritchie, the Chancellor of the Exchequer and a devout believer in free trade, was opposed to the scheme but, faced with a cabinet which was almost unanimous in its favour, appeared – at least to Chamberlain – to have grudgingly agreed to incorporate the proposal in his budget. Chamberlain, believing that the argument was over, left for a triumphant tour of South Africa, where the Boers – although beaten in war – had been reconciled to their defeat by a generous peace agreement. He returned home a hero, but found that, in his absence, the imperial tax concession had been dropped. The Chancellor had presented Balfour with an argument and an ultimatum. According to his recollection, he had agreed neither to make the 'corn tax' permanent nor, during its temporary life, to impose it only on grain imports from outside the empire. What was more, he would rather resign than introduce a fiscal regime with which he did not agree.

The Prime Minister had chosen to keep his Chancellor and lose imperial preference – therefore, according to his critics but not his friends, ignoring a cabinet decision in which he had acquiesced. The argument illustrated the wisdom of Lloyd George, thirteen years later, introducing what was then the innovation of cabinet minutes. It also revealed the blatant insouciance which characterised Devonshire's attitude towards the business of government. When Chamberlain asked for confirmation that the Chancellor had broken his undertaking to the cabinet, the Duke replied, 'I have myself no clear recollection of what took place . . . but I do not think it possible that Ritchie's protest against the pledge for the retention of the tax with a view to giving preference to [the empire] was in any way over-ruled. My impression was that the whole question was to be left till the Budget.'[26]

Ministers – sobered by Ritchie's repetition, at the pre-budget cabinet, that he preferred resignation to surrender – reacted to the Chancellor's defiance more calmly than is usually the case when a colleague breaks ranks. They accepted that the most they could achieve was a statement by the Prime Minister which speculated about 'the possibility of reviewing the [corn] tax if it were associated with some great change in our fiscal system'. Chamberlain gave notice of his intention to make a speech (naturally in Birmingham) which would say 'much the same thing'.[27] On April 23 1903, Ritchie announced that the grain duty was to be abolished. On May 15, relying on the familiar pretext of merely starting a discussion, Chamberlain ignored his promise to speak of imperial preference in only speculative terms and announced, 'I believe in the British Empire, an Empire which, though it should be its first duty to cultivate friendship with all the nations of the world, should yet, even if alone, be self-sustaining, self-sufficient and able to maintain itself against the competition of its rivals.' He ended with a question to which, it was obvious, he believed there could only be one answer. 'Do you think it is better to cultivate trade with your own people or let it go in order that you can keep the trade of those who are your competitors? . . . I believe in a British Empire . . . I do not believe in a Little England.'

Initially, Devonshire reacted to the clear breach of both faith and collective responsibility with the mildest of reproofs – reflecting his free trade agnosticism rather than his strong views on the subject of Joseph Chamberlain. His most stringent criticism was that 'Chamberlain had not given the least sustained thought to the consequences of his theories'.[28] He was much more affronted by the discovery that copies of the contentious speech had been distributed by the Liberal Unionist Association, though it did not embody the view of either the government or, as he put it, 'myself as President'. The association, he argued, could not be in 'active support of a policy' which the government had not endorsed 'without the serious risk, if not the certainty of it breaking up'.[29] It is not clear from the letter if the 'it' which he feared would fracture was the government or the association. But the avoidance of 'breaking up' was to become the chief objective of both Devonshire and Balfour. Both were to pay dearly for putting unity above principle.

Other ministers complained more strongly about Chamberlain's perfidy. But Balfour's response to the calls for punitive action was a model of urbane complacency. 'It must be admitted', he conceded in a letter to Devonshire, 'that Chamberlain's speech has not made either the Parliamentary or the Cabinet situation easier . . . Yet surely nothing has occurred which ought to make it difficult for all of us – whatever shade of opinion we may entertain on the subject of Colonial Preference – to act cordially together.'[30] Playing for time – in the manner adopted by Prime Ministers down the ages – he set up an inquiry. 'Remember this question is not a question that the House will have to decide this session or next session or the session after. It is not a question which this House will have to decide at all.'[31] The reassurance that nothing would be decided before the next general election was reinforced by support from the Duke of Devonshire – still accepted by all free traders as one of them. He told the House of Lords that he could not see 'How any convinced and rational Free Trader [could] take exception to the inquiry'. He believed that the result would be endorsement of 'the essential principles which underline [existing] policy'. Then he added what the free traders thought to be meaningless assurances meant to sooth the bruised egos of protectionists. It might be necessary to add 'some modifications and alterations of our arrangement [to] strengthen and consolidate . . . a system that met the needs of an empire with colonies which have manifested a desire to enter into closer political relations with each other and with the Mother Country'.[32]

The Duke's friends, encouraged by Balfour, described the speech as a display of admirable objectivity. No one, at least openly, suggested that the Duke – like the experienced racing man he was – had decided to hedge his bets. Less experienced ministers believed that the partisans on either side of the argument – the disciples of the 'Manchester School' who looked upon free trade as the basis of Britain's prosperity and the representatives of Britain's increasingly troubled agriculture – would be satisfied by a tightrope walk. But the Duke must have known better. Yet he acted like a neutral in a world of combatants, anxious only to preserve the unity of His Majesty's government. Perhaps the lofty detachment of his youth had become, in old age, no more than bored indifference. Or more likely – the reputation which he had so carefully cultivated notwithstanding – he was desperate to remain one of His Majesty's ministers and was a party to Balfour's cunning game.

Throughout the summer of 1903, ministers on each side of the argument put their case to the country. Balfour, in the hope of creating the semblance of party unity, prepared a paper – *Insular Free Trade* – around which he hoped ministers should rally. It proposed what Balfour called 'retaliatory tariffs' – a device which, he insisted, was not 'protectionist' in principle but a patriotic, and commercially essential, response to discrimination against British exports. The paper was discussed, inconclusively, at a cabinet meeting on August 13 along with a more formal document (known as the Blue Paper) which was drafted by civil servants. Free traders were horrified by what they regarded as the thin end of the tariff reform wedge and looked to the Duke to lead the last ditch fight against 'Chamberlain's policy'. Ritchie told Devonshire that, although 'it would be infinitely more agreeable to resign . . . he was quite prepared to remain in office'[33] and to carry on the fight. The Duke sent his strongest letter of the whole free trade saga to the Prime Minister. 'Mr Chamberlain, who advocates something which is not easy to distinguish from protection, finds the Prime Minister's paper sufficient authority to enter into his autumn campaign.'[34]

As a way of preserving the semblance of unity, the Duke suggested that the cabinet should discuss 'definite proposals . . . before the autumn agitations' began. Balfour's long and detailed reply interrupted his justification of 'retaliatory tariffs' with both an acknowledgement of Devonshire's selflessness and an appeal to his loyalty. Divisions in the Unionist Party would be a 'national disaster'. The Prime Minister concluded with a compliment that was also a stern reminder of duty's call. 'Much as you dislike office and justly as you may feel that you are entitled to some rest from your public labours', the Duke would – no doubt – give his obligations precedence over questions of personal comfort. Balfour had guessed that, in truth, Devonshire was desperate to avoid being forced to choose between resignation and the accusation that he placed power above principle.

In anticipation of the cabinet meeting, called for September 11, Charles Ritchie joined with Lord Balfour of Burleigh in the preparation of a memorandum which not only dismissed the Blue Paper's conclusions but went on to criticise – in trenchant language – the Prime Minister's attempt to find a mutually acceptable compromise. Before the papers were discussed, the meeting was adjourned until September 14. Balfour needed the time to plot – particularly to win over Devonshire, whose resignation would have brought to a sudden end the Unionist alliance. The Prime Minister's high hopes of keeping him on board were encouraged by the undoubted fact that, although a convinced free trader, the Duke's understanding of fiscal issues was less than complete.

When the adjourned cabinet reassembled it confirmed a decision to publish the official paper, but not the Prime Minister's musings. That decision amounted to the endorsement of retaliatory tariffs. Three ministers – including Charles Ritchie, the Chancellor of the Exchequer – expressed their formal disagreement. Stirred at last to anger, Balfour issued an ultimatum. Unless the ministers he dismissively described as 'Cobdenites' recanted, he would expect their resignations. The Duke of Devonshire had 'Never heard anything more summary and decisive than the dismissal of the two ministers'.[35] Chamberlain pressed home his advantage, by announcing that, unless his preferential proposal was adopted – a much greater step towards protection than a retaliatory tariff – he too would leave the cabinet.

The 'Cobdenites' had no alternative but to resign. They invited the Duke of Devonshire – the senior Liberal Unionist and, it was assumed, an ally – to meet them. They all took it for granted that Chamberlain's wishes would prevail, that he would remain in the cabinet to supervise the gradual introduction of imperial preference and that Devonshire – motivated by belief in free trade, loyalty to them and dislike of Chamberlain – would add his resignation to theirs. On that assumption they assumed that they were left with nothing to discuss but the timing and manner of their departure. They were wrong.

During the post mortem which followed – the corpse under

examination being the Duke's reputation – Devonshire contested that version of events. 'I certainly had not made up my mind to resign when we met . . . Neither did I undertake the commission on the part of us all to communicate the resignations to the Prime Minister. What I distinctly remember that I undertook to do was to ask the Prime Minister whether those Ministers who, as it were, had given notice to quit, were expected to attend the Cabinet next day.'[36] Whatever the truth about that meeting, there is no doubt about the sequence of events which followed. Balfour attempted, and for a time succeeded, in tricking Devonshire into remaining a member of the government. Since the Duke was secretly determined to stay – encouraged, said his critics, by his ambitious wife who believed that he still might become Prime Minister – it was not a difficult trick to perform.

On the evening of September 14, Devonshire met the Prime Minister to discuss his own future. The 'Cobdenites' certainly believed that the discussion would amount to the Duke's giving notice that the free traders intended to resign together. By then, Chamberlain, fired by an evangelical fervour for imperial preference, had privately confirmed to the Prime Minister that he proposed to leave the government as soon as the cabinet's tariff discussions were concluded, so that he was free to campaign for its full implementation. That crucial fact was not revealed to Devonshire. According to the Duke, Balfour 'again referred to the possibility of the resignation of Mr Chamberlain . . . though it was not presented to me in such a manner as to lead me to understand that a definite tender of resignation had been made, still less that it was likely to be accepted'.[37] It is not clear whether or not he reported 'the possibility' to the three ministers who had sought his help and advice. He may have thought the news too inconclusive to justify repetition. But an intriguing question – reflecting on the Duke's competence and Balfour's honesty – still remains. Did the Prime Minister tell, or attempt to tell, Devonshire of Chamberlain's resignation as soon as it was formal and definite?

According to Lord Stanley – the future Earl of Derby, Devonshire's stepson-in-law and therefore an impressive witness for Balfour's defence – on the night of September 15, the Prime Minister sent the Duke a note, confirming that Chamberlain would go. Devonshire and Stanley were dining in Gunnersbury with Leopold de Rothschild, so the note was sent by messenger in a ministerial 'red box'. The Duke had left his keys at home and in consequence, according to Balfour's apologists, the note remained unread until after the 'Cobdenite' had resigned the next day. In Stanley's version of events Devonshire 'jumped as if he had been shot' when he was told that Chamberlain had resigned before him and immediately began to speculate about the possibility of with-drawing his resignation. His hope was realised by his stepson-in-law interceding on his behalf with the Prime Minister. As a result the Duke stayed in the cabinet while his associates, unaware of his decision, left.

It is easy enough to believe that Devonshire, having been unable to unlock his box on the previous night, had not bothered to open it on the morning of his resignation. He had become the most casual of ministers. After Chamberlain – a politician whose nerve always exceeded his discretion – complained that Devonshire had failed to voice any objections when the cabinet had first discussed imperial preference, the Duke had replied, apparently without embarrassment, 'As you know, I am rather deaf and I am afraid sometimes inatten-tive.'[38] But the evidence suggests that Devonshire's decision to abandon his free trade friends was not merely the result of his negligent failure to keep abreast of the swirls and eddies of cabinet changes. Balfour wanted to keep the Duke and lose his 'Cobdenite' associates. So he provided him with an opportunity to abandon them.

The 'Cobdenites' and the Duke met to decide their future after the cabinet meeting of September 15, which they attended and at which routine business was discussed. The meeting ended with the decision that all four ministers – including Devonshire – would resign that afternoon, though the Duke made clear that he was to meet the Prime Minister again that evening and that it was 'possible, though not prob-able' that Balfour might offer assurances which would cause him to change his mind. A letter, sent to prepare the ground for his meeting with Balfour, was entirely consistent with that proviso. 'Before sending you my final decision, I should like to know, if possible, what you propose to say about preferential treatment of the Colonies involving the taxation of food. Though I understand you to doubt its practica-bility at the present time, I do not understand that you will say anything that will prevent Chamberlain from continuing to advocate it.' Reading that request for clarification, Balfour must have realised at once, had it not been clear before, that his fish could be caught on a familiar, if disreputable, hook. Personal animosity transcended political conviction. The Duke would be prepared for protection to stay as long as Chamberlain went. Indeed he would want to remain triumphantly in the cabinet from which Chamberlain had been forced to resign.

Minutes dictated by Devonshire to his private secretary after meet-ings with the Prime Minister confirm that Balfour realised that, for the Duke, the well-being of his friends was far less important than the discomfiture of his arch enemy, and encouraged his co-operation by telling him almost the truth about Chamberlain's intentions. As early as September 11, the Prime Minister 'Informed you that Chamberlain was almost certain to resign. Asked you not to mention it to anyone.'[39] The truth was rather different. Chamberlain's formal letter of resignation had been in the Prime Minister's possession since September 9. Devonshire's own – and undoubtedly honest – account of the conversation confirmed that Balfour had chosen to deceive him. The Prime Minister 'referred to the possibility of the resignation of Mr Chamberlain. But even at that time it was not presented to me in such a manner as to lead me to understand that a definite resignation had been made.'[40] Had Balfour told the truth, all four 'free traders' would have expected to remain in the cabinet. By giving the impression that Chamberlain's future was still in the balance, he made sure that the other 'Cobdenites' would go and that Devonshire could, eventually, be given the justification for staying which he craved. That justification depended on Devonshire's conduct being sharply distinguished from the behaviour of his three colleagues.

That was why Balfour changed his explanation of why the two most vocal free traders had left the cabinet. At first 'Mr Balfour's remarks led you to believe that Lord Balfour and Ritchie were dismissed on account of the memorandum on the fiscal question which they had recently circulated'. Later the Prime Minister 'further informed you that B of B and Ritchie were not dismissed on account of the memorandum which they had circulated but on account of the attitude which they had assumed toward the fiscal question throughout all its stages'.[41] The Duke's willingness to forget the first explanation and accept the second illustrated his eagerness to endorse the idea that his principled disagreement with the Prime Minister was quite different from the serial disloyalty of the free trade recidivists who, sooner or later, would bring down the government. It justified his breaking ranks or, as some of them saw it, his betrayal.

Balfour's assessment of Devonshire's character proved correct. But honour still required a gesture. The letter sent by the Duke to the Prime Minister on September 15 gave the opportunity to the Prime Minister to provide one. It was accompanied by a 'covering note' of 1,500 words which began with an admirable example of a plain man's impatience with the world of ideas. 'It might be possible for one more conversant with the abstract doctrines of political economy than I am, or who possesses more dialectical skills than I can pretend to, to support the position that you are going to take up while dissociating myself from the more advanced position that is going to be advanced by Mr Chamberlain.'[42] It ended with a statement of high principle. Devonshire felt 'the most profound conviction' that his continued membership 'could only bring discredit on the Government'. Had he stuck to that point of view, he would have ended his ministerial career with his reputation intact. But the evidence suggests that, even as he offered his resignation, he was hoping that it would not be accepted. His private secretary made a précis of the letter and underlined a crucial sentence which summarised the covering note's central message. 'If you had written under any misapprehension of the position, it would be for Mr Balfour to correct you should he desire to do so.'[43] Devonshire had secured his route of escape.

The following day, September 16, the Prime Minister visited Devonshire House – an unusually humble way for a Prime Minister to behave – and showed the Duke Chamberlain's resignation letter. Whether or not Devonshire noticed that it was dated September 9, there is no evidence to suggest that he expressed even surprise that it had been kept from him for so long. He simply agreed – without further argument – to remain in government and even accepted, with good grace, the agreement that, in return for Chamberlain's assurance of good behaviour, his son, Austen, should become Chancellor of the Exchequer. That obvious concession to protectionist sentiment would, he told his secretary, mean that his 'plumage would be rather ruffled, but he would survive'.[44] He did, however, suggest that the three 'Cobdenites' who, like him, had resigned under a misapprehension, should be invited to reconsider their position. The Prime Minister refused his request for reasons that the Duke himself set out to Ritchie in a letter of staggering insensitivity. 'He assured me that the promptitude with which he had acquiesced to the necessity of your resignation was not due or mainly due, as I had assumed, to anything contained in the memorandum recently circulated, but to your general attitude . . . which he considered had been different from my own.'[45] The Duke's volte-face was greeted with incredulity even by family and friends. Victor Cavendish – nephew and heir presumptive – reflected the general reaction in a heroically understated diary entry: 'Uncle Cav induced to stay at last minute. Impossible fully to judge what the result will be.'[46]

Devonshire had not thought it necessary to tell the 'Cobdenites' of his decision until Ritchie wrote to him to ask if 'the situation had altered after [the] interview' with the Prime Minister.[47] The Duke's reply was copied to Lord George Hamilton and Balfour of Burleigh. Initially, Hamilton was remarkably magnanimous. 'If you had refused to stay on, the Unionist Party would have been scattered to the four winds. You have treated me, as you do everybody else, with complete good faith.'[48] Ritchie, on the other hand, chose, understandably, to recriminate on the familiar pretext of needing to explain the true position to his friends. 'I am obliged to tell them what took place, namely that we separated on Tuesday with the understanding that all our resignations were to go in on that night, with the proviso on your part that Balfour wished to see you before you took the final step. You, however, said that there was no chance of his altering your determination.'[49] When the Duke replied that he had no recollection of 'any understanding that we should act together',[50] Hamilton thought it necessary to abandon the civilities and support Ritchie's version of events. 'I clearly understood that we were all acting together and that, in recognition of this cooperation the duke (on behalf of us four) conveyed our resignations to the Prime Minister.'[51]

To Balfour, the bitterness of the 'Cobdenites' was of no consequence. It seemed that he had papered over the cracks in the rest of the Unionist Party. *The Times* agreed. 'While Mr Balfour is backed by the Duke of Devonshire and the rest of the ministers, except the Cobdenite seceders, and while he has Mr Chamberlain's loyal and independent support, the reconstruction of the Cabinet need not be expected to involve any serious difficulties.'[52] The editor had not taken into account the Duke's response to the suggestion that he had behaved dishonourably. Although he had brushed aside Ritchie's allegation of bad faith, he had shown the accusatory letter to Lord Stanley with a bitter comment. 'To think that I have gone through all my life and then at the end of it to have these sort of accusations thrown at my head.'[53] Gradually, the damage to his reputation became too much for the Duke to bear. In his anguish he damaged it further by attempting to explain why he had initially believed it right to stay in the government and then, within weeks of taking that decision, had thought it right to leave.

On October 1 1903 the Prime Minister told a meeting of the Unionist Association that the nation 'would not tolerate a tax on food'. Despite what the Duke might have been expected to regard as a welcome adjustment – in the long term, corn, the commodity about which Chamberlain talked the most, would enter Britain tariff-free, whether it came from Canada or anywhere else – the Unionist Association speech became the *causus belli*. On the evening following its delivery, Balfour received a telegram from Devonshire announcing that the policy which the Prime Minister had laid out before the National Union had made it impossible for him to remain in the government. Two letters followed. One was the formal resignation. The other asked how soon the resignation could be announced. The usually urbane Arthur Balfour replied with a savagery which revealed his disappointment and questioned – according to how it was interpreted – either the Duke's integrity or his intelligence.

The principal reason for this transformation was, you tell me, the Sheffield speech. This is strange indeed. In intention (at least) there was no doctrine contained in that speech which was not contained in *Notes on Insular Free Trade* . . . If any man other than yourself had expressed so much inquisitorial subtlety in detecting imaginary heresies, I should have surmised that he was more anxious to pick a quarrel than to be particular as to the sufficiency of the occasion.[54]

The unkindest cut was left till last. Balfour expressed 'special regret' that the Duke had chosen 'at this particular juncture to sever [his] connection with the Unionist Party'. He had 'left it when (in the opinion at least of its opponents) its fortunes are at their lowest ebb'. What Devonshire regarded as the obligation of honour was regarded by the Prime Minister as the desertion of a sinking ship. The Prime Minister's continuing indignation was reflected in the contemptuous, and by convention inappropriate, language in which he wrote to the King to tell him that there would be changes in His Majesty's government. It amounted to the allegation that a vain old man was more concerned with the appearance than the reality of decent conduct. 'The Duke of Devonshire's conduct has been pitiable. Nor is it possible to excuse, or even to understand, his vacillations without remembering that he has without doubt somehow put himself in the power of Mr Ritchie and his friends. He is forced to behave badly to me lest he should be publicly taxed for behaving badly to them.'[55] The letter ended with an insult disguised as reassurance. 'His loss administratively is nothing . . . Mr Balfour's confidence that he can successfully carry on the government is in no way shaken by the Duke's defection.'

If Lord Stanley is to be believed, Balfour's anger was wholly justified. Devonshire's claim that the Sheffield speech had left him no option but to resign was an outright lie. The resignation letter was written before the speech was made. 'He did not fear any strides towards protection.' He was looking for, and Sheffield provided, 'an excuse for an exit from circumstances that had become distasteful'.[56] Within a fortnight he realised that his new circumstances were even more distasteful than the old. 'I have', he told Lord James of Hereford, 'made a mess of this and come out of it severely damaged.'[57] The damage was greater than he realised. He had become a figure of ridicule, the worst fate which can befall a politician. After he regained his composure, Balfour reflected the dismissive judgement of both friends and enemies. 'Silly old Duke. Fancy him resigning after all.'[58]

For the next three years, Devonshire limited his speeches in the House of Lords to the issue which had caused his downfall. Often he added a personal dimension which, at his prime, he would have thought beneath him. 'Mr Chamberlain says that I am content that my name should go down to posterity as "the drag on the wheel". If he will allow me a slight modification of that phrase, I am content to accept it. A brake is an important and sometimes necessary part of the mechanism of a locomotive.'[59] The danger posed to the established order by Joseph Chamberlain had become his new obsession. In his last speech in the House of Lords, he complained that every revision of the plan to introduce imperial preference 'contained more socialism than was embodied in the old'. They all increased the extent to which 'the state is to undertake and regulate the course of commerce and industry'.[60] But he no longer felt an obligation to spend long days in the service of the state. He declined an invitation to chair the Royal Commission on Unemployment and the Poor Law and thereby missed the opportunity of influencing a report that changed the course of social history.

When a Liberal Unionist Association was re-formed – a single body replacing the separate council and association – he declined the presidency and, no doubt to his chagrin though surely not his surprise, the honour was bestowed on Joseph Chamberlain. As he grew older, being a Cavendish became more important that being a Liberal or a Unionist. In the general election of 1906, one nephew, Victor Cavendish, contested West Derbyshire as a Balfour Unionist and won. Another, Richard Cavendish, stood in Lonsdale as a free trade Unionist and lost. Their uncle endorsed them both.

Thanks to his still energetic, if no longer youthful, wife, the Eighth Duke's social life became even more spectacular than it had been during the early years of their marriage. King Edward and Queen Alexandra visited Chatsworth three times within the space of three years and were entertained, among other delights, by the amateur dramatics which were performed, at almost every party, in the little theatre below the belvedere at the north end of the house. When, in 1907, the Duke heard that, during one of his visits, the King proposed to invest him with the Grand Cross of the Royal Victorian Order, he consulted Sir Frederick Ponsonby, the King's private secretary, about how the decorations should be worn at the Twelfth Night party which the subject had arranged for his sovereign that evening. His dilemma was how to reconcile his new insignia with that of the Garter. Told to wear 'not only the Riband and Star of the Victorian Order but also the Garter Star and diamond Garter on his leg', he described the obligation as 'tiresome' but agreed to observe the proprieties.[61] He was not always so polite. When he was called as a witness for a friend who was contesting a suit for divorce, he replied to most of counsel's questions with the monosyllable which had become such a dominant part of his conversation: 'What?'[62]

Despite his deteriorating hearing – which often produced gaps in conversation which were attributed to his legendary ill-manners – the Duke continued an active, and apparently no longer reluctant, social life. On June 5 1907 – the evening of the Derby – he dined with the Jockey Club at Buckingham Palace while the Queen dined with the Duchess at Devonshire House, where both parties met at a ball later in the evening. A week later – as Chancellor of Cambridge University – he made his last public appearance when he awarded an honorary degree to the Prime Minister, Sir Henry Campbell-Bannerman. Then, whilst a guest at Windsor Castle for Ascot week, he was taken ill and forced to return home. It was the beginning of a year's decline.

On October 24 1907 the Eighth Duke of Devonshire left England, never to return. The hope was that months in the warm clear air on the Nile would result in a revival. Barely improved, he began his journey home in early March 1908. On the 24th the party paused in Cannes. There the Duke died on March 28 1908. His last words, spoken as he floated in and out of consciousness, were noted down. 'Well the game is over and I am not sorry.' Perhaps, his friends suggested, the strange valediction was the result of an hallucination that he was playing cards. A more likely explanation is that he was pronouncing his judgement on a life in which pleasure had too often given way to the demands of duty – and the desperate need to prove that he deserved the admiration and respect that blood and birth had always guaranteed his family.

Afterword

In the House of Commons, Mr Asquith – leading for the government in the absence of the sick Prime Minister – chose to make his memorial tribute more precise than effusive. 'In the Duke of Devonshire', he said, 'we have lost *almost* the last survivor of our heroic age.' Whoever the other candidates for that accolade might be, one fact about the Duke's life was beyond dispute. He was *certainly* the last Cavendish to play a major role in the politics and government of England. After him, no member of the family exerted the influence or possessed the power which – for good or ill – had been its prerogative between Henry VIII's Declaration of Royal Supremacy in 1532 and the Unionist Party's conversion to tariff reform in 1904. Nor did his heirs and successors continue to be, like Hamlet's father, the mould of fashion and the glass of form. Cavendish men sat in parliament – more often in the Lords than in the Commons. Occasionally they held office. Invariably they were awarded the honours and places at Court which accompany rank and title. But usually – and by their own choice – they did not guide the destiny of the nation.

Victor Cavendish, the Eighth Duke's nephew and heir, was a whip in the Salisbury government, an appointment which carried the official title of Treasurer of the Royal Household. The day after Queen Victoria died he discovered that, although not a member of the Privy Council, he was required to attend the meeting which recorded the end of her reign. The invitation caused him great distress, not on account of its sad occasion, but because – as it was to be held at St James's Palace – he was expected to wear 'court dress'. His diary records his concern. 'My uniform was not finished.'[1] He asked for advice from the late Queen's private secretary – a Ponsonby and therefore distantly related. Ponsonby obliged. 'He lent me a suit but it was far too big.'[2]

A week later he received a telegram from the Duke of Norfolk, telling him that he was to march in the third rank of the funeral procession. For a second time in seven days he faced a clothes crisis. 'Full dress coat. Had to borrow one.'[3] A friend, by the name of Arthur Hill, obliged. Unfortunately, on the day before the funeral, Hill – having discovered that he too was to follow the coffin – 'came round and asked for it back. Tried to get another one. He was very nice about it.'⁴ Happily Hill felt unable to face the rigours of the march behind the gun-carriage and he decided to sit in the stand. The coat was returned to Cavendish and, properly dressed, he embarked on a 'long and exhausting day'.⁵

Seven years later he succeeded to his uncle's title and estate. The death of the Eighth Duke was marked by the Devonshires' first, though by no means most salutary, experience of death duties. The Exchequer was owed more than £500,000. Added to the debts accumulated by the Seventh Duke's heroic attempts to build an industrial and commercial empire, the taxes left his grandson with no choice but to embark on the biggest sale in Cavendish history – the antithesis of everything the family had believed in since Bess applied to the family of her recently dead first husband for a portion of his estate.

Holker Hall, the Seventh Duke's Lancashire home, was saved for the family but passed into the possession of Lord Richard Cavendish (the Ninth Duke's younger brother). His descendants still live there. Perhaps with less regret than a more culturally inclined man would have felt, the Ninth Duke concluded that the best way of satisfying the Revenue's demands was to raid the Chatsworth library. First to go were twenty-five books printed by William Caxton. Then the whole collection (1,347 volumes in all) which the Sixth Duke had bought from John Kemble was sacrificed. Although it included the four Shakespeare First Folios and thirty-nine Shakespeare quartos, the sale did not raise enough to pay the bill. But where literature failed, land succeeded. Land was sold in Derbyshire, Sussex and Somerset.

Twelve years later debts were again so great that it was decided that property – the houses which had been built or bought, improved and extended by generations of Cavendishes – would have to be sacrificed. There was talk, swiftly abandoned, of demolishing parts of Chatsworth to save running costs. Instead, in 1920 Devonshire House – the scene of so many triumphs and tragedies and the spiritual home of the Whig Ascendancy – was sold to 'developers' and swiftly demolished. The Duke bought 2 Carlton House Gardens as its replacement. The press baron, Alfred Harmsworth, the First Lord Rothermere, died in a hut erected on its roof. One of the symptoms of his madness was claustrophobia which was alleviated by temporary accommodation high above the Mall. There was a ten-year respite from property sales. Then, in 1929, Chiswick House was sold to the Middlesex County Council.

Financial pruning cut the cost of the Chatsworth gardens. The number of gardeners was reduced from eighty to forty and Paxton's great conservatory was demolished. Between 1914 and 1918 there had been no fuel available to charge its furnaces and most of the exotic plants which it housed had died in the cold. The family had neither heart, nor enough money, to start Paxton's work all over again. So, in 1920, the mighty structure was demolished by high explosive and the scattered iron debris sold for scrap. But, despite the demands of time and the Exchequer, the Duke of Devonshire was still able to live like a duke. 'After the Great War, footmen still powdered their hair when there was a party. The practice stopped in 1924. They wore full livery if there were more than six for dinner – lemon coats, dark blue britches and white stockings – till 1938.'[6]

The Ninth Duke – who had been a Civil Lord of the Admiralty during the early years of the war – was made Governor General of Canada. On his return to England in 1921 he became Mayor of Eastbourne and Derby in quick succession. A year later, when Andrew Bonar Law succeeded David Lloyd George as Prime Minister, the Duke became Secretary of State for the Colonies. When the Irish civil war began, anxiety about his property was recorded in his diary day-by-day. 'No news from Dublin. The evening papers tell of terror. But we hear nothing.'[7] Personal concern competed for his emotions with frustration at the ineptitude of the Protestant minority with whom he instinctively identified. 'The Irish loyalists are really the most hopeless collection of people I ever came across.'[8] To his surprise, and clearly to his un-patrician relief, when Stanley Baldwin replaced the dying Bonar Law, he remained in the government. 'Had a letter from Baldwin. Definitely wants me to stay at C.O. as a member of the cabinet.'[9]

The Ninth Duke was the last Devonshire to sit in the cabinet, but it was his misfortune to be remembered neither for that nor for the shire horses that he bred and whose foals he personally delivered in the stables at Pilsley – now that the Devonshires have gone into trade, the Chatsworth farm shop. His name is always associated, far beyond the High Peak grouse moors which he owned, with 'the Kinder Scout Trespass' – an adventure story in which he appears as villain. His grandson, the Eleventh Duke – wonderfully frank about his grandfather's autocratic ways – always insisted that a sudden stroke and the subse-quent change of character explained and excused the excesses of his final years when he developed the unfortunate habit of striking out with his stick at anyone who annoyed him. But that cannot wholly account for what happened on Sunday April 24 1932 – a small skirmish in the long retreat of feudal England.

The Kinder Scout Trespass – a carefully planned, badly executed and totally triumphant demonstration in favour of free passage across the Peak District moors – was undoubtedly politically motivated. The men and women who inspired and led it believed that 'God gave the land to the people'. Most of them were regular ramblers who, on Sundays, escaped from the northern industrial towns to breathe the clean air of rural England. On Easter weekend in 1932, one of the organisations which planned and led their expeditions – the Communist-inspired British Workers' Sports Federation – had arranged a camp at Rowarth on the western edge of Kinder Scout, the summit of a 2,000-feet climb and accessible to fit and healthy hikers from both Manchester and Sheffield. A party from the London branch of the BWSF chose to walk east towards Bleaklow. They were turned back by the Duke of Devonshire's gamekeepers who were said to be threatening and abusive. Benny Rothman, secretary of the Lancashire BWSF, later wrote that the hikers 'decided there and then to prove the point'.[10]

Some sort of direct action had been contemplated for more than a year. The idea was revived every time that a footpath was closed. But there were many hikers and ramblers – by nature a gentle breed – who were reluctant to break the law. Professor G. M. Trevelyan – sufficiently respectable to be appointed Master of Trinity College, Cambridge – certainly supported the militant approach and Professor Joad – then only a philosopher rather than a radio personality – had already told a rally at Winnats Pass, near Castleton, 'If you want the moors to be free, you must free them for yourselves.'[11] But it was the aggressive behaviour of Bleaklow gamekeepers on Easter weekend 1932 that provoked the decisive action.

Rothman, an unemployed motor mechanic, and 'Woolfie' Winnick, his best friend, decided that the demonstration would only be successful if it was sufficiently publicised to attract an army of protesters. The organisers assumed that, once their plans were known, the police would attempt to disband their protest before it began. So, to keep the rallying point secret, Rothman and Winnick cycled rather than took the local train to the village of the advertised rallying place at Hayfield. They joined 400 determined protesters and marched off to Bowden Bridge quarry, 5 miles from the Kinder Scout summit. There Benny Rothman addressed them from a giant rock before the final ascent began. Although an unlikely Henry V, he told them that hikers, then a'bed in Manchester, would think themselves accursed they were not there – or words to that effect.

For the first part of their climb they followed a footpath which had been public since 1897. About half the way up William Clough, they reached rough ground called Sandy Heys. At the word of command from 'Woolfie' Winnick, they turned off the legal route and began to scramble, like advancing infantry, up the hillside. They did not get very far. A line of gamekeepers with sticks was waiting on the brow of the hill. One gamekeeper – irritated by the trespassers' celebration of what he thought a failure, insisted that they 'only trespassed about 100 yards – they never got halfway up the clough'.[12] Benny Rothman agreed. But at the victory meeting, he told the cheering hikers – reinforced by a column of ramblers from Sheffield – that it was the fact, not the extent, of the trespass that mattered.

The combined forces of Manchester and Sheffield marched back in triumph towards Hayfield. The police were waiting for them. The five 'leaders' were arrested. So was a John Anderson who had chosen not to trespass but had gone to the aid of a gamekeeper who had fallen and hurt his ankle in the scuffle. All six were held overnight in the Hayfield lock-up and charged next day, at the New Mills magistrates' court, with disturbing public order and holding a riotous assembly. There were not and could not have been charges of trespass. Trespassing is not, and never has been, a criminal offence.

The days between charge and trial at Derby Assizes were spent in Leicester Gaol. Benny Rothman defended himself. 'We ramblers, after a hard day's work in smoky towns and cities, go out rambling for relaxation, a breath of fresh air, a little sunshine. But we find that the finest rambling country is closed to us, just because certain individuals wish to shoot for about ten days a year.'[13] The judge – no doubt influenced by the revelation that the collected works of Lenin had been found among the defendant's possessions – was unimpressed. Two of the trespassers were sentenced to six months' imprisonment. The other three served two months in gaol. Until then, even the ramblers' organisations had been divided on the wisdom, as well as the propriety, of direct action. In the weeks that immediately followed the convictions, the more 'responsible' leaders of the countryside movement feared that the Kinder Scout climb had set back the hopes of greater access by alienating the landowners on whom 'the right to roam' depended. They were wrong. The severity of the sentences caused general outrage – not least against the Duke of Devonshire who, it was assumed, had influenced the judge just as he had encouraged the police to initiate criminal proceedings. There is no evidence to suggest that he cared about the odium. He was not the sort of man who bothered about public opinion.

The Ninth Duke of Devonshire died in 1938. Edward Cavendish, his son and successor – a man who was known to wear paper collars – was noted for the unpretentious simplicity of his life. His interests were gardening, fishing and, a bad third, the House of Commons. He chose to spend most of the year at Compton Place in Eastbourne and when in Derbyshire lived in Churchdale rather than the much larger Chatsworth. Despite his modesty he was said to share the family doubts about the wisdom of Dorothy, his sister, marrying Harold Macmillan, a lowly publisher.[14] His brother, Lord Charles, was a man of altogether different habits and temperament. While at Cambridge he had fallen out of a window and severely damaged his head. The family attributed the accident to his heavy drinking. After an unsuccessful stint as a banker with Pierpoint Morgan, he married Adele Astaire – once the dancing partner of her brother, Fred – and retired to Lismore Castle where, even during the Second World War, he could enjoy a life of luxury while the Duke, his brother, worked away as a junior member of the Chamberlain and Churchill governments. The Tenth Duke had declined Winston Churchill's offer to make him Viceroy of India.

When war broke out, Chatsworth had been abandoned 'for the duration'. It became the evacuation home of a girls' boarding school, Penrhos College, and survived, surprisingly well, the transformation of its state rooms into dormitories. Six years of war were to prove less damaging to Cavendish interests than the election of a majority Labour government. The Marquis of Hartington was commissioned in the territorial army before hostilities began. But he had always hoped for a political career. After he had served for four years in the Coldstream Guards a seat was found for him. Colonel Henry Hunloke – son-in-law of the Ninth Duke and the latest of the family's nominees to represent West Derbyshire – resigned from parliament in 1944 and made way for 'Billy' Hartington, the Tenth Duke's heir.

The Conservative assumption that the seat was theirs for the taking was reinforced by the coalition's agreement that, until the end of the war, by-elections would not be contested and the candidate nominated by the party which previously held the seat would be returned unopposed. But in several seats 'Commonwealth' – in effect a loose alliance of independent socialists – had already denied the Tory Party the walkover that the pact allowed. In Derbyshire it nominated Alderman Charlie White, a pillar of the county council. White was accused by his opponents of making personal attacks on Hartington – including the allegation that he had accepted nomination in the hope of avoiding service. There is no doubt that supporters of the Commonwealth Party drew attention to Hartington's wealth and privilege.

Winston Churchill, told that White was fighting a class war, chose to join in and increased the likelihood of a Devonshire defeat by sending the Conservative candidate a letter which seemed to confirm Commonwealth's claim that Hartington thought of the seat as

Devonshire property. It reminded the electors that the Conservative candidate's family had been 'identified for about 300 years with the Parliamentary Representation of West Derbyshire'.[15] Alderman White won with a majority of 4,561. 'Billy' Hartington told the crowd, which had assembled outside Matlock Town Hall to hear the declaration of the result, 'Now I am going to fight for you at the front.' Before he left for France, he married Kathleen 'Kick' Kennedy, daughter of the former American Ambassador to the Court of St James's.

The Cavendish family were far too loyal, outside the bounds of their own close circle, to allow any suggestion that they disapproved of the match. But their opposition was not in doubt. Joseph Kennedy had built his fortune on bootlegging during the years of American prohibition and was a flagrant womaniser who could not conduct his numerous affairs with either the panache or the discretion of a gentleman. Worse still he was known, from his years as ambassador, to be certainly anti-British and probably sympathetic to Hitler. There was also a problem about his religion.

Joseph Kennedy and Rose, his wife, were pious Roman Catholics and had no doubt that, by marrying a man from a deeply religious Protestant background[16] in the church of his choice, their daughter was offending against her religion. There were agonised conversations between bride and groom about the consequences of a future Duke of Devonshire being married according to the rites of the Catholic Church and swearing – as Rome would require – to bring up his children in his wife's faith. The Duke gently reminded his son of the family's historic obligations by giving him, as a birthday present, an ancient leather-bound Book of Common Prayer.

Kathleen Kennedy found a Catholic bishop who was prepared to argue that a civil marriage was not a mortal sin and the wedding went ahead without Joe Kennedy's blessing and despite the unforgiving opposition of the bride's mother, Rose. It took place at Chelsea Register Office in May 1944. The bride's parents did not attend. The witnesses were the Duke of Devonshire and Joseph Kennedy, Junior, Kick's oldest brother, a US Navy pilot and the first of the ill-fated brothers to meet a violent and premature death. Two months after the wedding in 1944 he was killed while taking part in Operation Aphrodite – the perfection of a plane which, loaded with high explosives, would crash, unmanned, onto its target. Two months later still, Billy Hartington – back on active service – was shot and killed by a German sniper on the French–Belgian frontier.

Andrew Cavendish – a company commander in the same regiment who had won a Military Cross, fighting his way north in Italy – had left England expecting that, if he survived the war, he would become a publisher. After his brother's death, he returned with the prospect of becoming heir to an inheritance on which the Labour government intended to impose far heavier death duties than great estates had ever been charged before. On his death in 1938, the Ninth Duke had paid the Treasury £379,000. The Tenth knew that – unless a suitable arrangement could be made – when his surviving son inherited the title and estate, he would be levied at least ten times as much.

Accountants and lawyers prepared a plan to reduce the tax liability. It transferred £2,225,000 of shares from the Chatsworth Estates Company to a discretionary trust, the Chatsworth Settlement. There were financial advantages in postponing the transfer for as long as possible, but – to avoid death duties – it had to be made three years before the beneficiary inherited. However, there seemed no urgency to put the plan into operation. At the end of the war, the Tenth Duke of Devonshire was still only fifty and, as far as his doctors knew, in good health. So even when the Labour government extended the qualifying period for exemption to five years after the creation of the trust and the top rate of death duties was increased to 80 per cent, the documents were still not signed. The Duke was fit and still no more than middle-aged.

In May 1948 Kathleen Hartington was killed – together with the Eighth Earl Fitzwilliam – in an air crash on their way to spend a weekend together in the South of France. Opinions disagree about the likelihood of their affair evolving into marriage once the Earl was divorced. The Kennedys would certainly have been opposed. 'Ambassador Kennedy was the only member of the family able to get to the funeral. He wore a bright blue crumpled suit, which was all that he had with him and this surprising colour accentuated the anguished misery of his face.'[17] The notion that Rose Kennedy was unable to attend the funeral is a charitable interpretation of her absence. At home in Boston, the dead woman's mother sent her friends memorial Mass cards. On them was printed a prayer for souls in purgatory. Kick Kennedy was buried in Edensor churchyard – consecrated by the Church of England.

Whether or not the deaths of both the Marquis and Marchioness of Hartington concentrated Cavendish minds on mortality, it was taken for granted that the Tenth Duke of Devonshire had years to live. He died of a heart attack in November 1950, while felling a tree – three months before the Chatsworth Settlement would have qualified for exemption from death duties. Devotees of conspiracy theories and murder mysteries – always excited by the suggestion of crimes that involve the aristocracy – suggested that the failure to notify the Eastbourne coroner of the Duke's sudden death provided grounds for suspicion. Long after he was dead, the idea was revived when his general practitioner, Doctor John Bodkin Adams, was prosecuted – unsuccessfully – for the murder of elderly ladies who had made him the beneficiary of their wills. Years afterwards, the fires of scandal were fuelled by the Eleventh Duke's Delphic comment that 'it should, perhaps, be noted that the doctor was not appointed to look after the health of my two younger sisters who were there at the time'.[18] But that was no more than a typically laconic aside – an example of the insouciance which was to help him through the hard days ahead.

The death duties on the Tenth Duke's estate were, on the Treasury's initial estimate, £4,720,000. The Eleventh Duke appealed and the appeals were rejected. There was some thought of abandoning England altogether and making Lismore Castle the family home. Talk of selling Chatsworth was renewed. There was some talk of it becoming 'an outpost centre of the Arts' for Manchester University. Meanwhile interest on the unpaid duty was adding £1,000 a day to the Devonshire debt. But the Duke – an urbane man of sophisticated tastes – defied expectations and determined to save what he could. For those who know her it is hard to believe, but the Eleventh Duke's wife, Deborah – the most beautiful and least controversial of the Mitford Sisters* – always insists that she played no part in the long and arduous negotiations.

First to go was land – 12,000 acres in Dumfriesshire and then 42,000 acres in Derbyshire. Then the woods around, and houses within, Eastbourne were sold. Compton Place was let as a school. The eight greatest works of art – including Rembrandt's *Philosopher* and Rubens's *Holy Family* – were taken by the Treasury in lieu of cash. The British Museum acquired 141 rare books – 14 of them published by Wynkyn de Worde, Caxton's head printer. But the debt was still substantial. So Hardwick Hall, built by Bess – which was still as she designed it and had been Cavendish property for fifteen generations – was offered to the government as an alternative to cash payment. The offer was accepted and, in 1959, after long negotiations, the house – Bess's initials on the turrets now clearly visible from the M1 – became the property of the National Trust. But the debt was still not quite cleared. The last payment to the Treasury was made on May 17 1967 – partly from funds provided from the estate income of the Chatsworth Trustees.

---

* They included Nancy, the author of *The Pursuit of Love* and *Love in a Cold Climate*, Diana who married Sir Oswald Mosley, the leader of the British Fascist movement, Unity who shot herself in the head on the day that Britain declared war on Germany, and Jessica, a member of the United States Communist Party who wrote *The American Way of Death*.

The deficit on their account was liquidated in 1974, twenty-four years after the death duties were incurred.

Since then Chatsworth – a Trust run by a board of directors, a majority of whom may not be members of the Cavendish family – has become, at least for the foreseeable future, financially secure. Three-quarters of a million visitors pay to enter the house and garden. Twice as many walk and picnic in the park. Chatsworth has become the venue for pop concerts as well as game fairs and horse trials. It is supported by a farm shop and a garden centre.

The family that can trace its certain origins back to fifteenth-century London mercers is in trade again. The Fifth Duke, who would not let his wife meet Henry Cavendish because he was a scientist and therefore not a gentleman, would be profoundly shocked. So would Bess's grandson, the William Cavendish who left the country rather than face the humiliation that followed the Royalist defeat at Marston Moor. And there was not a Tudor peer, Stuart earl or Georgian and Victorian duke – not excluding the most modest among them – who would even have believed possible the event which became the climax of the Kinder Scout Trespass Seventieth Anniversary Celebration.

In April 2002, the ramblers had assembled in Bowden Bridge Quarry – where the trespassers had gathered seventy years before – to hear speeches in praise of the Right to Roam pioneers, when a Bentley, resplendent with ducal coats of arms on its rear doors, pulled up at the edge of the crowd. Andrew Cavendish, Eleventh Duke of Devonshire, had accepted an invitation to attend the celebration and, at his own suggestion, he 'took the opportunity to make a public apology . . . for the terrible wrong' that his grandfather had done seven decades earlier. And then he watched as the hikers spread out over the once forbidden grouse moors.

Andrew Cavendish was a famously generous man – generous with his time and his money and generous in his opinions of others. But his appearance at the Seventieth Anniversary of the Kinder Scout Trespass signified more than a naturally gracious disposition. It exemplified the way in which the world moves irresistibly on and the inability – even of those whose circumstances insulate them against change – to hold back the march of progress. The Twelfth Duke – a man who hates to be called 'His Grace' and holds 'advanced' views on art – happily emphasises how great the changes have been. He did not quite say – as one newspaper suggested – that the aristocracy was dead and that he proposed to renounce his title. But he does believe that, as it gradually lost its role in parliament, it has changed its character. Without power, titles are only an anachronism.

Of course the Devonshires retain some of the characteristics which have sustained them for five centuries – not the least of which is their wealth. And their wonderfully Whiggish willingness to describe (admit would be quite the wrong word) their own and their close relations' personal foibles and failings remains a sign of their self-confidence, not humility. Yet, as the Kinder Scout Trespass made plain, even the mightiest families are swept along in the tide of history. The Devonshires played a major part in changing the nation's history and then – like the humblest of Bess's housemaids and Paxton's under-gardeners – they too were changed.

Notes on Sources

ABBREVIATIONS

CHA – Chatsworth House Archives
Fogler – Fogler Library, Orono, Maine, USA

CHAPTER I
Before Bess

1 Bickley, Frances Lawrence, *The Cavendish Family*, Mifflin, New York, 1914, p. 2
2 Collins, Arthur, *Historical Connection*, 1752, p. 3
3 Round, J. Horace, *Family Origins and Other Studies*, Constable, 1930, p. 26
4 Oman, Charles, *The Great Revolt of 1381*, Clarendon Press, 1906, p. 104
5 Round, op. cit., p. 29
6 Ibid. p. 26
7 Cavendish, George, *The Life of Cardinal Wolsey*, Harding and Leopard, Pall Mall, 1827, p. 401
8 Ibid., p. 295
9 Ibid., p. 298
10 Riden, Philip, 'Sir William Cavendish, Tudor Civil Servant and Founder of a Dynasty', *Derbyshire Archaeological Journal*, vol. 239, p. 129
11 McKie, J. D., *The Early Tudors*, Oxford University Press, 1952, p. 376
12 Pearson, John, *Stags and Serpents*, Macmillan, 1983, p. 10
13 Bickley, op. cit., p. 11
14 Pearson, op. cit., p. 10
15 Riden, op. cit., p. 239
16 Lovell, Mary, *Bess of Hardwick: First Lady of Chatsworth*, Little, Brown, 2005, p. 42
17 Riden, op. cit., p. 240
18 Ibid., p. 241
19 Ibid., p. 262

CHAPTER 2
Four Weddings and . . .

1 Lovell, op. cit., p. 42
2 Durant, David M., *Bess of Hardwick*, Peter Owen (USA), 1999, p. 5
3 Lovell, op. cit., p. 9
4 Durant, op. cit., p. 4
5 Ibid., p. 6
6 Ibid.
7 Thompson, Francis, *History of Chatsworth*, Country Life, 1951, p. 22
8 Riden, Philip, 'The Hardwicks of Hardwick Hall in the C15th and C16th', *Derbyshire Antiquities Journal*, vol. 130, 2012, p. 137
9 Ibid., p. 2
10 Fogler Xd 486 (23)
11 Ibid.
12 Lovell, op. cit., p. 27
13 Ibid., p. 25
14 Fogler Xd 486 (15)
15 Riden, op. cit., p. 42
16 Ibid.
17 Durant, op. cit., p. 22
18 Lees-Milne, James, *The Tudor Renaissance*, Batsford, 1951, p. 101
19 Thompson, op. cit., p. 24
20 Ibid.
21 Durant, op. cit., p. 27
22 Riden, op. cit., p. 247
23 Lovell, op. cit., p. 106
24 Riden, op. cit., p. 249
25 Durant, op. cit., p. 33
26 Riden, op. cit., p. 249
27 Lovell, op. cit., p. 170
28 Ibid.
29 Ibid., p. 188
30 Ibid., p. 193
31 Bernard, E. W. (ed.) *The Tudor Nobility*, Manchester University Press, 1992, p. 193

32 Ibid., p. 267
33 Ibid.
34 Lovell, op. cit., p. 201
35 Somerset, Anne, *Elizabeth I*, Fontana, 1991, p. 360
36 Ibid.
37 Lovell, op. cit., p. 329
38 Bernard, op. cit., p. 268
39 Ibid.

CHAPTER 3

. . . And an Execution

1 Fogler Xd 428 (86)
2 Ibid. Xd 428 (78)
3 Ibid. Xd 428 (16)
4 Somerset, op. cit., p. 213
5 Lovell, op. cit., p. 205
6 Ibid.
7 Strickland (ed.), *Letters of Mary Queen of Scots*, Colborn, 1842, vol. II, p. 161
8 Guy, John, *My Heart Is My Own*, Fourth Estate, 2004, p. 449
9 Somerset, op. cit., p. 398
10 Lodge, Edmund, *Illustrations of British History*, John Chidley, Aldersgate, 1687, p. 239
11 Somerset, op. cit., vol. II, p. 398
12 Ibid.
13 Fraser, Antonia, *Mary Queen of Scots*, Weidenfeld & Nicolson, 2009, p. 479
14 Lovell, op. cit., p. 206
15 Rawson, P., *Bess of Hardwick*, Hutchinson, 2001, p. 156
16 Ibid.
17 Fraser, op. cit., p. 482
18 Dunn, Jane, *Elizabeth and Mary*, HarperCollins, 2003, p. 410
19 Ibid.
20 Durant, op. cit., p. 81
21 Fraser, op. cit., p. 504
22 Ibid.
23 Ibid., p. 488
24 Durant, op. cit., p. 76
25 Ibid.
26 Ibid.
27 Ibid.
28 Somerset, op. cit., p. 259

29 Ibid., p. 285
30 Heape, R. G., *Buxton under the Dukes of Devonshire*, Robert Hale, 1948, p. 15
31 Lodge, op. cit., vol. XVII, p. 217
32 Fogler Xd 428 (102)
33 Fraser, op. cit., p. 550
34 Durant, op. cit., p. 421
35 Guy, op. cit., p. 521
36 Lodge, op. cit., vol. II, p. 166
37 Bickley, op. cit., p. 22
38 Somerset, op. cit., p. 213
39 Guy, op. cit., p. 454
40 Ibid.
41 Durant, op. cit., p. 130
42 Somerset, op. cit., p. 101
43 Guy, op. cit., p. 455
44 Lovell, op. cit., p. 308
45 Ibid.
46 Dunn, Jane, *Mary Queen of Scots*, HarperCollins, 2005, p. 459
47 Fraser, op. cit., p. 550
48 Round, op. cit., p. 67
49 Lovell, op. cit., p. 329
50 Ibid.
51 Fraser, op. cit., p. 582
52 Lovell, op. cit., p. 371

CHAPTER 4

A Cavendish Queen?

1 Gristwood, Sarah, *Arbella: England's Lost Queen*, Bantam, 2003, p. 18
2 Ibid. p. 15
3 Ibid.
4 Ibid.
5 Ibid., p. 19
6 Fogler Xd 428 (130)
7 Ibid. Xd 428 (131)
8 Gristwood, op. cit., p. 27
9 Hardy, B. C., *Arbella Stuart*, Constable, 1913, p. 24
10 Durant, David, *Arbella Stuart: A Rival to the Queen*, Weidenfeld & Nicolson, 1998, p. 29
11 Steen, Sarah Jane (ed.), *Letters of Arbella Stuart*, Oxford University Press, 1994, p. 19
12 Durant, *Arbella*, op. cit., p. 121

13 Ibid., p. 129
14 Gristwood, op. cit., p. 66
15 Stewart, Alan, *The Cradle King: A Life of James VI and I*, Chatto & Windus, 2003, p. 91
16 Gristwood, op. cit., p. 68
17 Ibid.
18 Ibid., p. 74
19 Steen, op. cit., p. 162
20 Gristwood, op. cit., p. 67
21 Ibid., p. 75
22 Ibid., p. 81
23 Ibid.
24 Fogler Xd 428 115
25 Ibid., Xd 428 131
26 Hardy, op. cit., p. 68
27 Durant, *Arbella*, op. cit., p. 71
28 Gristwood, op. cit., p. 82
29 Ibid., p. 93
30 Handover, P. M., *Arbella Stuart: Royal Lady of Hardwick*, Harvard University Press, 1957, p. 115
31 Gristwood, op. cit., p. 110
32 Ibid., p. 97
33 Ibid., p. 133
34 Bradley, E. T., *Arbella Stuart*, Bentley, 1889, p. 92
35 Gristwood, op. cit., p. 147
36 Ibid.
37 Ibid., p. 150
38 Ibid.
39 Steen, op. cit., p. 126
40 Ibid., p. 134
41 Ibid., p. 141
42 Ibid., p. 161
43 Ibid., p. 170
44 Ibid., p. 145
45 Ibid., p. 142
46 Durant, *Arbella*, op. cit., p. 111
47 Ibid.
48 Gristwood, p. 185
49 Ibid., p. 200
50 Coote, Stephen, *A Play of Passion: The Life of Sir Walter Raleigh*, Macmillan, 1993, p. 306
51 Stewart, op. cit., p. 92
52 Gristwood, op. cit., p. 217
53 Coote, op. cit., p. 312
54 Durant, *Arbella*, op. cit., p. 128
55 Gristwood, op. cit., p. 240
56 Steen, op. cit., p. 228
57 Gristwood, op. cit., p. 257
58 Durant, *Arbella*, op. cit., p. 174
59 Ibid.
60 Ibid. p. 176
61 Steen, op. cit., pp. 234–5
62 Durant, *Arbella*, op. cit., p. 188
63 Ibid., p. 205

CHAPTER 5

The House Divided

1 Riden, Philip, *Henry Cavendish and the Cavendishes of Doveridge*, Occasional Papers of the University of Nottingham, p. 31
2 Bath (Marquis of) Manuscripts, Longleat, vol. V, 1533–1639 (HMSO), p. 131
3 Ibid.
4 Ibid.
5 Ibid.
6 Ibid.
7 Durant, *Bess of Hardwick*, op. cit., p. 169
8 Bickley, op. cit., p. 33
9 Bath Manuscripts, op. cit., p. 132
10 Ibid.
11 Riden, *Henry Cavendish*, op. cit., p. 16
12 Ibid.
13 Hunter, J. *History of Hallamshire*, p. 118
14 Ibid.
15 Camden Miscellany – Vol. XVII, Royal Historical Society, 1940, *Mr Cavendish and his Journey to and from Constantinople 1589 – by Fox his servant*
16 Ibid.
17 Hasler, P. W. (ed.), *The House of Commons 1558–1603*, HMSO, History of Parliament Trust, 1981.
18 Riden, op. cit., p. 18
19 Hasler, op. cit.
20 Ibid.
21 Riden, op. cit., p. 13
22 Ibid., p. 2
23 Ibid., p. 21
24 Ibid., p. 24
25 Bath Manuscripts, op. cit., 10.2.93, p. 119

26 Ibid.
27 Hasler, op. cit.
28 Ibid.
29 Bath Manuscripts, op. cit., p. 127
30 Trease, Geoffrey, *Portrait of a Cavalier*, Macmillan, 1979, p. 21
31 Saul, Nigel, *For Honour and Fame*, Bodley Head, 2011, p. 366
32 Lovell, op. cit., p. 411
33 Hasler, op. cit.
34 Lovell, op. cit., p. 457
35 Ibid.
36 Bath Manuscripts, April 1608, p. 134
37 Martinich, A. P., *Hobbes: A Biography*, Cambridge University Press, 1989, p. 25
38 Ibid., p. 27
39 Ibid.
40 Ibid., p. 59
41 Ibid., p. 31
42 Ibid., p. 28
43 Ibid., p. 59
44 Ibid., p. 77
45 Ibid., p. 84
46 Ibid., p. 87

CHAPTER 6

Wrong but Romantic

1 Clarendon, Earl of, *The History of the Rebellion*, Clarendon Press, 1826/27, book I, p. 78
2 Ibid.
3 Aubrey, John (ed. Richard Barber), *Brief Lives*, Bagdell Press, 1975, p. 68
4 Newcastle, Margaret (Duchess of), *The Life of William Cavendish, Duke of Newcastle*, John C. Nimmo, 1886, p. 112 note
5 Aubrey, op. cit., p. 68
6 Bickley, op. cit., p. 78
7 Newcastle, op. cit., p. 194
8 Trease, op. cit., p. 28
9 Newcastle, op. cit., p. 4
10 Ibid.
11 Newcastle, op. cit., preface, p. vii
12 Ibid., p. 20
13 Ibid., p. 22

14 Ibid.
15 Ibid. p. 5
16 Longueville, T., *The First Duke and Duchess of Newcastle-upon-Tyne*, Longman, 1910, p. 12
17 Trease, op. cit., p. 51
18 Ibid.
19 Ibid.
20 Longueville, op. cit., p. 14
21 Trease, op. cit., p. 67
22 Newcastle, op. cit., p. 197
23 Trease, op. cit., p. 73
24 Ibid.
25 Ibid., p. 74
26 Ibid.
27 Longueville, op. cit., p. 32
28 Ibid.
29 Ibid.
30 Ibid., p. 34
31 Ibid.
32 Ibid., p. 47
33 Ibid., p. 78
34 Ibid., p. 139
35 Newcastle, op. cit., p. 11
36 Ibid.
37 Trease, op. cit., p. 86
38 Newcastle, op. cit., p. 13
39 Ibid., p. 15
40 Portland Papers, Nottingham University, PW1 673
41 Newcastle, op. cit., p. 15
42 Bickley, op. cit., p. 88
43 Trease, op. cit., p. 91
44 Newcastle, op. cit., p. 19
45 Ibid.
46 Braddick, Michael, *God's Fury, England's Fire: A New History of the English Civil Wars*, Allen Lane, 2008, p. 223
47 Riden, Philip and Edwards, David (eds), *Essays in Derbyshire History*, Derbyshire Record Society, p. 155

CHAPTER 7

The Business of Yorkshire

1 Riden and Edwards, op. cit., p. 155
2 Newcastle, op. cit., p. 20
3 Braddick, op. cit., p. 277
4 Trease, op. cit., p. 95

5 Ibid.
6 Newcastle, op. cit., p. 30
7 Trease, op. cit., p. 101
8 Newcastle, op. cit., p. 36
9 Portland Papers, op. cit., PW1 125
10 Ibid.
11 Longueville, op. cit., p. 92
12 Ibid.
13 Bickley, op. cit., p. 87
14 Trease, op. cit., p. 100
15 Bickley, op. cit., p. 87
16 Ibid., p. 114
17 Newcastle, op. cit., p. 56
18 Aubrey, op. cit., p. 65
19 Aubrey, op. cit., p. 66
20 Bickley, op. cit., p. 49
21 Aubrey, op. cit., p. 66
22 Newcastle, op. cit., p. 52 note
23 Aubrey, op. cit., p. 67, quoting
   Cavalier Broadsheet
   MERCURIUS AULICUS
24 Newcastle, op. cit., p. 56 note
25 Ibid.
26 Ibid., p. 110
27 Bickley, op. cit., p. 94
28 Ibid.
29 Longueville, op. cit., p. 112
30 Newcastle, op. cit., p. 64
31 Ibid.
32 Portland Papers, op. cit., PW1 530
33 Trease, op. cit., p. 132
34 Ibid., p. 127
35 Newcastle, op. cit., p. 121
36 Ibid.
37 Ibid., p. 69
38 Ibid., p. 70
39 Braddick, op. cit., p. 528
40 Ibid.
41 Ibid., p. 329
42 Newcastle, op. cit., p. 74
43 Trease, op. cit., p. 134
44 Ibid.
45 Newcastle, op. cit., p. 77 note
46 Ibid.
47 Ibid., p. 76
48 Ibid., p. 77 note
49 Ibid., p. 78
50 Ibid., p. 112 note
51 Ibid., p. 80 note
52 Longueville, op. cit., p. 167
53 Bickley, op. cit., p. 103
54 Newcastle, op. cit., p. 87

CHAPTER 8

For King and Cavendish

1 Newcastle, op. cit., p. 287
2 Longueville, op. cit., p. 181
3 Ibid., p. 189
4 Newcastle, op. cit., p. 313
5 Ibid., p. 315
6 Pepys, Samuel, *Diaries*, Bell &
   Hyman, 1970–83, vol. 8, 11 April
   1667, p. 163
7 Ibid., 26 April 1667, p. 185
8 Ibid., 11 April 1667, p. 163
9 Newcastle, op. cit., p. 312
10 Pepys, op. cit., 30 May 1669, p. 217
11 Newcastle, op. cit., p. 109
12 Bickley, op. cit., p. 117
13 CHA, De L'Isle and Dudley
   Manuscript (copy), MSS 6 11
14 Grove (Mr) of Richmond, *The
   Lives of All the Earls and Dukes
   of Devonshire, William: Third
   Earl*, J. Coote, Paternoster Row,
   1764, p. 1
15 Ibid., p. 3
16 Aubrey, op. cit., p. 68
17 Bickley, op. cit., p. 117
18 Newcastle, op. cit., p. 110
19 Bickley, op. cit., p. 112
20 Newcastle, op. cit., p. 112 note
21 Aubrey, op. cit., p. 68
22 Newcastle, op. cit., p. 126
23 Ibid., p. 130
24 Ibid., p. 131
25 Ibid.
26 Ibid., p. 141
27 Ibid. p. 150
28 Ibid.
29 Pepys, op. cit., 11 April 1667,
   p. 163
30 Ibid., 24 April 1667, p. 196

CHAPTER 9

Leviathan Awakes

1 CHA, letters 160
2 Grove, op. cit., p. 4
3 Bickley, op. cit., p. 67
4 Pepys, op. cit., 18 March 1667,
   p. 243

5 *Correspondence of Thomas Hobbes* (ed. Noel Malcolm), Clarendon Press, 1997, vol. 1, p. 170
6 Martinich, op. cit., p. 323

CHAPTER 10
The Wayward Whig

1 Macaulay, Thomas Babington, *History of England*, Philip Sampson, 1857, vol. I, p. 532.
2 Ibid.
3 Grove, op. cit., (First Duke), p. 32
4 CHA op. cit. Broadsheet
5 Ibid., 18.14
6 CHA, Calendar of State Papers – Reign of Charles II, 29.9.80
7 CHA, Occasional Papers – copy of MSS held at Kilkenny Castle, Ireland, vol. 5 MS p. 291
8 Ibid., 25.11.80
9 CHA, Occasional Papers – copy of MS preserved at Kilkenny Castle, Ireland op. cit. v13 MS
10 Grove, op. cit., p. 37
11 CHA, Occasional Papers – copy of MS preserved at Kilkenny Castle, Ireland, op. cit.
12 Grove, op. cit., p. 40
13 Ibid.
14 Ibid., p. 41
15 Ibid., p. 42
16 Ibid.
17 Ibid.
18 Ibid., p. 43
19 Macaulay, op. cit., vol. I, p. 695
20 Ibid.
21 Ibid.
22 Ibid.
23 Evelyn, John, *Diaries*, Manning and Bray Edition, 1767, p. 227
24 CHA, Occasional Papers, op. cit. (undated)
25 Grove, op. cit., p. 54
26 Ibid.
27 Macaulay, op. cit., vol. 1, p. 691
28 Grove, op. cit., p. 193
29 Kennet, White, *Memoirs of the Family of Cavendish*, London, 1708, p. 139

30 Thompson, op. cit., p. 33
31 Kennet, op. cit., p. 139
32 Thompson, op. cit., p. 139
33 Ibid., p. 113
34 *Grove Dictionary of Art*, Grove, 2001, 1D 2D
35 Lees-Milne, James, 'Chatsworth and the First Duke', *Country Life*, 18 April 1968

CHAPTER 11
Dare Call it Treason

1 Grove, op. cit., p. 28
2 Ibid., p. 36
3 Little, David M. and Kahrl, George H. (eds.), *The Letters of David Garrick*, Belknap Press of Harvard Univesity Press, 1963, vol. III
4 Ibid., vol. III, p. 38
5 Ibid., vol. III, p. 51
6 Ibid., vol. III, p. 56
7 Macaulay, op. cit., vol. II, p. 533
8 CHA, Kilkenny Papers 5NS, p. 291
9 CHA, Occasional Papers – Letters of Lady Rachel Russell – origins in Woburn Abbey
10 CHA, ed. Rev. D. P. Davies, 'Memoirs of the Family of Cavendish Dukes of Devonshire', p. 164
11 Grove, op. cit., p. 11
12 Macaulay, op. cit., vol. II, p. 103

CHAPTER 12
Eternal Vigilance

1 CHA 2.87/8 18.1.29
2 Ibid.
3 Ibid., 51.0, 29.8.88
4 Ibid., 51.0 9.11.88
5 Ibid., 51.8 7.10.96
6 Ibid., 51.10 31.12.96
7 Plumb, J. H., *Sir Robert Walpole: The Making of a Statesman*, Cresset Press, 1956, p. 116
8 CHA 1140 22.9.03
9 Ibid., 51.11 1.8.99

10 Grove, op. cit. (Second Duke), p. 14
11 Ibid., p. 19
12 Pearson, op. cit., p. 62
13 Grove, op. cit., p. 38
14 Ibid., p. 47
15 CHA 51.22
16 Grove, op. cit., p. 71
17 Ibid., p. 85
18 Plumb, op. cit., p. 263
19 Grove, op. cit., p. 85
20 Plumb, op. cit., p. 116
21 Grove, op. cit., p. 92
22 Ibid., p. 115

CHAPTER 13

Noblesse Oblige

1 Grove, op. cit., (Third Duke), p. 2
2 Boswell, James (ed.), *Life of Doctor Johnson*, Oxford University Press, vol. III, p. 167
3 Wraxall, Nathaniel, *Posthumous Memoirs*, London, 1887, vol. 1/I, p. 16
4 Ibid.
5 *Memoirs and Speeches of James, 2nd Earl Waldegrave*, John Murray, 1754/58, p. 26
6 CHA 114.3 10.9.34
7 Williams, B., *The Whig Supremacy 1714-1760*, in the Oxford History of England, Oxford University Press, 1960, p. 278
8 CHA 114-11 31.12.34
9 Bickley, op. cit., p. 191
10 Ibid.
11 Williams, op. cit., p. 293
12 Bickley, op. cit., p. 192
13 CHA 246.0 30.7.37
14 Ibid., 261.2
15 Ibid.
16 Ibid., 261.1
17 Ibid., 228.76
18 Ibid., 257-8 12.2.39
19 Ibid., 182-15 8.11.39
20 Ibid., 114-17 17.11.41
21 Ibid., 257-82 23.2.39
22 Ibid., 257-40 15.3.39
23 Ibid., 245-9 6.110.41
24 Ibid., 245-11

25 Ibid., 260-18 4.2.42
26 Ibid., 260.5 6.2.42
27 Ibid., 144-19 12.2.42
28 Williams, op. cit., p. 208
29 CHA 266.29 17.1.43
30 Ibid., 260-43 13.3.44
31 Ibid., 249-15
32 Ibid., 260-32 4.2.44
33 Ibid., 294-11 23.3.44
34 Ibid., 294-14 4.2.44
35 Ibid., 260-45 22.3.44
36 Ibid., 163-6 3.9.45
37 Ibid., 320 12.9.45
38 Ibid., 163 9.9.45
39 Ibid., unclassified 14.9.45
40 Ibid., 320.1 19.9.45
41 Ibid., 320.0 19.9.45
42 Ibid., 323.0 22.9.45
43 Ibid., 290.12
44 Ibid.
45 Ibid., 182.29 25.9.45
46 Ibid., 163-98
47 Ibid.
48 Ibid., 211.2 3.10.45
49 Ibid., 211.3
50 Glover, Stephen, *History of the County of Derby* (quoting *Derby Mercury*), 1829, vol. 1, p. 221
51 Ibid.
52 Ibid.
53 Ibid., p. 290
54 CHA C21B
55 Glover, op. cit. (quoting Hutton's *Derby*), vol. 1, p. 390
56 Bickley, op. cit., p. 194
57 Ibid.
58 Ibid.
59 Glover, op. cit., p. 390
60 Ibid.
61 Ibid., p. 392
62 Toynbee, P. (ed.), *Letters of Horace Walpole*, Clarendon Press, 1903, vol. III, p. 101
63 CHA 228-14
64 Ibid., 3D 344
65 Ibid., 3D 444
66 Ibid., 3D 344.1
67 Ibid., 3D 348.0
68 Ibid., 3D 344.3
69 Toynbee, op. cit., vol. II, p. 389

CHAPTER 14

Brothers in Arms

1 *Waldegrave*, op. cit., p. 85
2 Ibid., p. 141
3 Little and Kahrl, op. cit., vol. I, p. 347
4 Ibid.
5 Thompson, op. cit., p. 23
6 Pearson op. cit. p. 79
7 *Waldegrave*, op. cit., p. 140
8 Toynbee, op. cit., vol. III, p. 292
9 *Waldegrave*, op. cit., p. 140
10 Ibid.
11 Ibid., p. 88
12 Ibid.
13 Ibid., p. 100
14 Ibid., p. 141
15 Ibid.
16 CHA 260–260 11.9.59
17 Ibid., 260–205 29.1.60
18 Ibid., 260–273 20.11.60
19 Williams, op. cit., p. 367
20 CHA 260–311 9.4.61
21 Bickley, op. cit., p. 292
22 Namier, Lewis, *England in the Age of the American Revolution*, Macmillan, 1963, p. 292
23 Ibid.
24 CHA 260–310
25 Toynbee, op. cit., vol. III, p. 272
26 CHA 466–387
27 Ibid., 640 2
28 Bickley, op. cit., p. 220
29 Toynbee, vol. IV, p. 21
30 Bickley, op. cit., p. 222
31 Toynbee, op. cit., vol. IV, p. 126

CHAPTER 15

All the Brothers Were . . .

1 Bickley, op. cit., p. 223
2 Stokes, Hugh, *The Devonshire House Circle*, Herbert Jenkins, Haymarket, 1944, p. 84
3 *The Last Journals of Horace Walpole*, 1916 edition, vol. II, p. 291
4 BL Additional Manuscript 32976 for 269 (copy in CHA)
5 Copeland, T. W., *The Correspondence of Edmund Burke*, Cambridge University Press, 1855, vol. III, p. 89
6 Mitchell, Leslie, *The Whig World*, Hambledon, 2006, p. 159
7 *Last Journals*, Walpole, vol. I, pp. 494, 580
8 Wraxall, op. cit., vol. II, p. 429
9 Bickley, op. cit., p. 234
10 Ibid.
11 Copeland, op. cit., vol. IV, p. 526
12 Ibid.
13 Walpole, H., *Memoirs of the Reign of King George III*, vol. II, p. 17

CHAPTER 16

The Outsider

1 Berry, A. J., *Henry Cavendish*, Hutchinson, 1960, p. 25
2 Bickley, op. cit., p. 202
3 Ibid., p. 201
4 Ibid., p. 199
5 Berry, op. cit., p. 15
6 Ibid., p. 24
7 Wilson, George, *The Life of the Honourable Henry Cavendish*, Cavendish Society, 1851, p. 33
8 Berry, op. cit., p. 23
9 Wilson, op. cit., p. 49
10 Ibid.

CHAPTER 17

The Misalliance

1 CHA 5–5 9.10.74
2 Ibid., 32 16.10.74
3 Ibid., 23 25.9.47
4 Pearson, op. cit., p. 86
5 CHA 59.2
6 Ibid., 19
7 Wraxall, op. cit, vol. III, p. 342
8 Foreman, Amanda, *Georgiana, Duchess of Devonshire*, HarperCollins, 1998, p. 17
9 CHA 508
10 Foreman, op. cit., p. 17
11 CHA 521

12 Toynbee, op. cit., vol. IX, p. 161
13 Stokes, op. cit., p. 68
14 Ibid.
15 CHA 97
16 Ibid., 43
17 Ibid., 17
18 Ibid., 66
19 Ibid., 163
20 Foreman, op. cit., p. 219
21 CHA 219
22 Cecil, David, *Melbourne*, Constable, 1930, p. 7
23 Ibid. p. 32
24 Reeve, Henry (ed.), *Memoirs of Lord Greville*, Project Gutenberg ebook treehouse project, vol. V, p. 308
25 Ibid.
26 Pearson, op. cit., p. 98
27 CHA 580
28 Mitchell, op. cit., p. 32
29 CHA 206
30 Stokes, op. cit., p. 161
31 Mitchell, op. cit., p. 42
32 Ibid., p. 81
33 CHA 246
34 Pearson, op. cit., p. 98
35 CHA 306
36 Ibid., p. 269
37 Foreman, op. cit., p. 79
38 Ibid.
39 CHA 289
40 Ibid., 297
41 Bickley, op. cit., p. 258
42 CHA 396
43 Ibid., 403
44 Ibid., 472
45 Ibid., 507
46 Ibid., 532
47 Foreman, op. cit., p. 128
48 CHA 607
49 Ibid., 569
50 Foreman, op. cit., p. 92
51 CHA 433
52 Hague, William, *Pitt the Younger*, HarperCollins, 2004, p. 355
53 Ibid., p. 124
54 Foreman, op. cit., p. 143
55 Ibid.
56 Ibid.
57 Hague, op. cit., p. 172
58 Ibid.
59 Foreman, op. cit., p. 149
60 Bessborough, Earl of (ed.), *Extracts from the Correspondence of Georgiana, Duchess of Devonshire*, John Murray, 1955, p. 88
61 CHA 712

CHAPTER 18

Games of Chance

1 CHA 614
2 Ibid., 621 2.6.86
3 CHA 584
4 Stokes, op. cit., p. 261
5 CHA 679
6 Ibid., 744
7 Ibid., unclassified 21.1.88
8 Ibid.
9 Fitton, R. S., *The Arkwrights: Spinners of Fortune*, Manchester University Press, 1989, p. 240
10 CHA 926
11 Fitton, op. cit., p. 240
12 Ibid.
13 Ibid.
14 Ibid.
15 Ibid., p. 241
16 Foreman, op. cit., p. 221
17 CHA 962
18 Ibid., 963
19 Ibid., 964
20 Stokes, op. cit., p. 266
21 Foreman, op. cit., p. 240
22 Ibid., p. 241
23 Ibid.
24 CHA 1019
25 Lees-Milne, James *The Bachelor Duke*, John Murray, 1991, p. 3
26 Ibid.
27 Foreman, op. cit., p. 244
28 Stokes, op. cit., p. 267
29 Ibid., p. 269
30 Ibid.
31 CHA 1720
32 Ibid., 1050–1
33 Foreman, op. cit., p. 263
34 CHA 1117
35 Ibid., 1121
36 Foreman, op. cit., p. 293
37 Watson, J. Steven, *The Reign of*

George III, in the Oxford History of England, Oxford University Press, 1960, p. 390
38 Foreman, op. cit., p. 308
39 Ibid., p. 310
40 Bessborough, op. cit., p. 229
41 CHA 1799
42 Ibid. 1601
43 Watson, op. cit., p. 381
44 Ibid., p. 401
45 Foreman, op. cit., p. 346
46 Ibid.
47 CHA 1609
48 Foreman, op. cit., p. 388
49 CHA 1845
50 Foreman, op. cit., p. 389
51 CHA 1873
52 Pearson, op. cit., p. 114
53 Fitton, op. cit., p. 241

CHAPTER 19

A Great Deal to Spend

1 CHA 1180
2 Maxwell, H. (ed.), *The Creevy Papers*, John Murray, 1903, p. 84
3 Markham, Violet, *Paxton and the Bachelor Duke*, Hodder & Stoughton, 1935, p. 17
4 McCarthy, Fiona, *Byron: Life and Legend*, John Murray, 2004, p. 65
5 Pearson, op. cit., p. 116
6 CHA D201x21
7 Ibid., D201x41
8 Ibid., D3x1121
9 Ibid., D1x33
10 Ibid.
11 Lees-Milne, *Bachelor Duke*, op. cit., p. 19
12 Hattersley, Roy, *Blood and Fire*, Doubleday, 2000, p. 81
13 Pearson, op. cit., p. 118
14 CHA 6D 16
15 The Sixth Duke's diary, CH6 27.i.22
16 Lees-Milne, *Bachelor Duke*, op. cit., p. 48
17 Ibid.
18 Markham, op. cit., p. 52
19 CHA, Diary, op. cit., 15.iv.27
20 Ibid., 17.xi.25

21 Ibid., 20.iii.27
22 Ibid., 12.i.26
23 Ibid., 22.iii.31
24 Ibid., 23.iii.32
25 Markham, op. cit., p. 15
26 Slater, Michael, *Charles Dickens*, Yale University Press, 2009, p. 225
27 Handbook of Chatsworth, Sixth Duke, 1844
28 Maxwell, op. cit., p. 183
29 Lees-Milne, *Bachelor Duke*, op. cit., p. 26
30 CHA, Diary, op. cit., 31.xii.25
31 Lees-Milne, *Bachelor Duke*, op. cit., p. 69
32 CHA, Diary, op. cit., 28.x.27
33 Ibid., 29.xi.27
34 Ibid., 8.xii.27
35 Ibid., 9.xii.27
36 Markham, op. cit., p. 81
37 CHA, Diary, op. cit., 13.x.38
38 Ibid., 3.vi.32
39 Ibid., 8.vi.32
40 Ibid., 9.vi.32
41 Lees-Milne, *Bachelor Duke*, op. cit., p. 42
42 Ibid., p. 44
43 Ibid., p. 45
44 McCarthy, op. cit., p. 159
45 CHA, Diary, op. cit., 31.xii.21
46 Handbook
47 Ibid.
48 Ibid.
49 Ibid.
50 Ibid.
51 Lees-Milne, *Bachelor Duke*, op. cit., p. 45
52 Markham, op. cit., p. 14
53 Adams, W., *The Gem of the Peak*, London, 1835, p. 77 note
54 Ibid.
55 CHA, Diary, op. cit., 18.vii.26
56 Ibid., 3 vi 26
57 Lees-Milne, *Bachelor Duke*, op. cit., p. 52

CHAPTER 20

Ermine and Enterprise

1 Markham, op. cit., p. 5

2 Colquhoun, Kate, *A Thing in Disguise*, Hodder Perennial, 2003, p. 22
3 Markham, op. cit., p. 30
4 Walpole Society, *The Walpole Journals*, 1932, vol. XVI, p. 28
5 Handbook, op. cit.
6 CHA, Diary, op. cit., 9.xii.26
7 Markham, op. cit., p. 47
8 Ibid., p. 48
9 *Gardeners' Magazine*, May 1835
10 Colquhoun, op. cit., p. 79
11 Ibid., p. 85
12 Ibid.
13 Lees-Milne, *Bachelor Duke*, op. cit., p. 125
14 Colquhoun, op. cit., p. 104
15 CHA, Diary, op. cit., 17.iii.44
16 Ibid., p. 132
17 CHA, Diary, op. cit., 8.v.44
18 Markham, op. cit., p. 158
19 Colquhoun, op. cit., p. 108
20 Ibid., p. 136
21 Briggs, Asa, *Victorian People*, Penguin, 1954, p. 43
22 Riden, P. and Fowkes, D., *Great House and Its Estate*, Phillimore, 2009, p. 65
23 *Derby Mercury*, 2 June 1841
24 Ibid., 15.v.42
25 CHA, Diary, op. cit., 14.iv.48
26 Markham, op. cit., p. 179
27 Ibid., p. 182
28 Briggs, op. cit., p. 43
29 Ibid., p. 44
30 Ibid., p. 45
31 Colquhoun, op. cit., p. 172
32 CHA, Diary, op. cit., 15.vii.50
33 Markham, op. cit., p. 218
34 Ibid.
35 Colquhoun, op. cit., p. 180
36 Slater, op. cit., p. 316
37 Holden, Anthony, *The Wit in the Dungeon*, Little, Brown, 2005, p. 295
38 Slater, op. cit., p. 324
39 Ibid., p. 330
40 Colquhoun, op. cit., p. 180
41 Heape, op. cit., p. 80
42 Ibid.
43 Ibid.
44 Colquhoun, op. cit., p. 186
45 CHA 100.44

CHAPTER 21

The Railway Comes to Rowsley

1 Woodward, L., *The Age of Reform*, in the Oxford History of England, Oxford University Press, 1962, p. 42
2 Lees-Milne, *Bachelor Duke*, op. cit., p. 171
3 Davies, Hunter, *George Stevenson*, Weidenfeld & Nicolson, 2002, p. 274
4 Markham, op. cit., p. 127
5 Ibid., p. 128
6 Ibid.
7 Ibid.
8 Ibid.
9 Ibid., p. 131
10 Ibid., p. 120
11 Baker, H., *The Railway Mania*, Letts & Sons, 1869, p. 15
12 Markham, op. cit., p. 132
13 Baker, op. cit., p. 24
14 Ruskin, John, *Praeterita*, vol. 3, George Allen, 1907
15 Markham, op. cit., p. 133
16 Ibid., p. 126
17 Ibid., p. 131
18 Ibid., p. 169
19 Ibid., p. 170

CHAPTER 22

Moving with the Times

1 CHA, Diary, op. cit., 22.i.38
2 Ibid., 23.i.38
3 Cannadine, D., *Lords and Landlords*, Yale University Press, 1980, p. 287
4 CHA, Diary, op. cit., 4.x.39
5 Pearson, op. cit., p. 28
6 Bickley, op. cit., p. 139
7 Ibid.
8 CHA, Diary, op. cit., 27.iv.40
9 Bickley, op. cit., p. 147
10 Ibid., p. 140
11 CHA, Diary, op. cit., 27.vii.50
12 Ibid., 16.iii.38
13 Ibid., 3.iv.38
14 Ibid., 5.vii.38

15 Ibid., 12.vii.39
16 Ibid., 28.xii.39
17 Ibid., 6.iii.40
18 *Economic History Review*, vol. 18, Pollard, Sydney, *Barrow-in-Furness and the Seventh Duke of Devonshire*
19 CHA, Diary, op. cit., 5.ii.41
20 Ibid., 30.ii.42
21 Marshall, J., *Furness and the Industrial Revolution*, Barrow-in-Furness Library and Museum Committee, 1958, p. 203
22 CHA, Diary, op. cit., 15.ii.41
23 Ibid., 30.ii.42
24 Ibid., 12.ii.43
25 Marshall, op. cit., p. 178
26 Ibid.
27 Ibid., p. 216
28 Ibid., p. 217
29 CHA, Diary, op. cit., 1.v.45
30 Ibid., 5.vi.46
31 Ibid., 24.vii.46
32 Ibid., 20.x.46
33 Ibid., 15.xii.46
34 Ibid., 22.v.48
35 Ibid., 22.ii.49
36 Ibid., 9.iv.51
37 Ibid., 25.vii.50
38 Ibid.
39 Ibid., 28.v.51
40 Ibid., 15.vi.49
41 Ibid., 11.xii.51
42 Cannadine, op. cit., p. 243
43 Marshall, op. cit., p. 208
44 CHA, Diary, op. cit., 26.i.58
45 Letters, Devonshire to Bedford, CHA 17.5.58
46 Ibid., 16.02.59
47 Ibid.
48 Ibid.
49 Ibid.
50 Bickley, op. cit., p. 278
51 Heape, op. cit., p. 27
52 Cannadine, op. cit., p. 243
53 Ibid.
54 CHA, Diary, op. cit., 24.i.60
55 Ibid., 9.iv.63
56 Ibid., x.xii.64
57 Ibid., 22.ii.70
58 Ibid., 31.ii.70
59 Ibid., 29.iv.75
60 Ibid., 27.vii.82

61 Ibid., 26.vii.86
62 Ibid., 23.ii.11
63 Ibid.
64 Ibid., 14.v.67
65 Ibid., 7.vii.71
66 Cannadine, op. cit., p. 246
67 Ibid.
68 CHA, Diary, op. cit., 23.v.71
69 Ibid., 26.ix.74
70 Ibid., 19.x.77
71 Pollard, op. cit., p. 220
72 Ibid.
73 Ibid.
74 CHA, Diary, op. cit., 20.iv.86
75 Ibid.
76 Ibid., 26.v.87
77 Cannadine, op. cit., p. 246
78 Ibid., p. 248
79 Ibid., p. 254
80 Ibid.
81 CHA, Diary, op. cit., 30.i.87
82 Cannadine, op. cit., p. 240
83 Thompson, F. L. M., *The English Landed Society*, Routledge & Kegan Paul, 2006, p. 191

CHAPTER 23

The Reluctant Statesman

1 CHA, Diary, op. cit., 23.vii.50
2 Vane, H., *Affair of State*, Peter Owen, 2004, p. 34
3 Ibid., p. 35
4 Jackson, Patrick, *The Last of the Whigs*, Associated University Presses, 1994, p. 17
5 Holland, Bernard, *The Life of Spencer Compton, Eighth Duke of Devonshire*, Longman, 1911, vol. I, p. 16
6 Ibid., p. 15
7 CHA 340 54
8 Ibid., 340 57
9 Ibid., 340 51
10 Ibid., 340 52
11 Ibid., 340 68
12 Ibid., 340 720
13 Jackson, op. cit., p. 25
14 Holland, op. cit., vol. I, p. 171
15 CHA 340 111

16 Ibid., 340 120
17 Ibid., 340 142
18 Ibid., 340 145
19 Ibid., 340 143
20 Holland, op. cit., vol. I, p. 34
21 CHA 340 161
22 Vane, op. cit., vol I, p. 65
23 CHA 340 187
24 Ibid., 340 199
25 Holland, op. cit., vol. I, p. 65
26 Ibid., p. 78
27 CHA 340 383
28 Ibid., 340 398
29 Ibid., 340 412
30 Holland, op. cit., vol. I, p. 83
31 CHA 340 447
32 Ibid., 340 450
33 Hansard 22.2.71
34 Holland, op. cit., vol. I, p. 96
35 Ibid., p. 120
36 CHA 340 537
37 Holland, op. cit., vol. I, p. 124
38 Vane, op. cit., p. 95
39 Ibid., p. 115
40 Holland, op. cit., vol. I, p. 132
41 Ibid.
42 Hansard 30.6.74
43 CHA 340 585
44 Ibid., 340 587
45 Ibid., 340 593
46 Ibid., 340 596
47 Ibid., 340 605
48 Ibid., 340 601
49 Ibid., 340 660
50 Ibid., 340 666
51 Holland, op. cit., vol. I, p. 164
52 Hansard 8.2.76
53 Morley, J., *The Life of William Ewart Gladstone*, Macmillan, 1903, vol. III, p. 179
54 Holland, op. cit., vol. I, p. 185
55 Ibid.
56 Ibid., p. 189
57 CHA 340 668
58 Jenkins, Roy, *Sir Charles Dilke: A Victorian Tragedy*, Collins, 1959, p. 105
59 Holland, op. cit., vol. I, p. 198
60 Ibid., p. 204
61 Holland, op. cit., vol. I, p. 206
62 CHA 340 732
63 Jackson, op. cit., p. 262

64 Hansard 29.7.78
65 Morley, op. cit., vol. II, p. 595
66 Holland, op. cit., vol. I, p. 230
67 Ibid., p. 239
68 Jenkins, op. cit., p. 427
69 Holland, op. cit., vol. I, p. 255
70 Ibid.
71 Holland, op. cit., vol. I, p. 262
72 CHA 340 856
73 Ibid., 340 860
74 Ibid., 340 862
75 Holland, op. cit., vol. I, p. 265
76 Ibid.
77 Ibid., p. 266
78 Morley, op. cit., vol. II, p. 611
79 Ponsonby, Arthur, *Henry Ponsonby*, Macmillan, 1943, p. 184
80 CHA 340 932
81 Ibid., 340 941
82 Jenkins, Roy, *Gladstone*, Macmillan, 1995, p. 437
83 CHA 340 942
84 Ibid., 340 943

CHAPTER 24

The Faithful Apostate

1 Holland, op. cit., vol. I, p. 299
2 CHA 340 977
3 Holland, op. cit., vol. I, p. 305
4 Ibid., p. 314
5 Hansard 30.3.81
6 Hansard 25.3.81
7 Holland, op. cit., vol. I, p. 332
8 CHA 340 1040
9 Holland, op. cit., vol. I, p. 340
10 Ibid., p. 329
11 Ibid., p. 335
12 CHA 340 1055
13 Hansard 11.1.81
14 Holland, op. cit., vol. I, p. 370
15 Ibid., p. 344
16 CHA 340 1278
17 Jackson, op. cit., p. 145
18 Holland, op. cit., vol. I, p. 383
19 Ibid., p. 384
20 CHA 340 1314
21 Ibid.
22 Ibid.
23 Jenkins, *Dilke*, op. cit., p. 166

24 Ibid., p. 414
25 Ibid., p. 416
26 Ibid., p. 418
27 Ibid.
28 Jenkins, *Gladstone*, op. cit., p. 511
29 CHA 340 1408
30 Ibid.
31 Ibid., 340 1410
32 Ibid., 340 1409
33 Ibid., 340 1411
34 Ibid., 340 1417
35 Ibid., 340 1813
36 Ibid., 340 1446
37 Ibid., 340 1435
38 Ibid., 340 1436
39 Holland, op. cit., vol. I, p. 437
40 Ibid., p. 439
41 Ibid., p. 440
42 CHA 340 1418
43 Hansard 12.5.84
44 Holland, op. cit., vol. I, p. 486
45 Guedalla, P. *The Queen and Mr Gladstone*, Macmillan, 1934, vol. II, p. 326
46 Hansard 27.2.85
47 CHA 340 1653
48 Ibid., 340 1674
49 Ibid., 340 1723
50 Ibid., 340 1099
51 Ibid., 340 1723
52 Ibid., 340 1726
53 Holland, op. cit., vol. I, p. 397
54 Ibid., p. 398
55 Ibid.
56 Ibid., p. 237
57 Ibid., p. 236
58 Holland, op. cit., vol. II, p. 63
59 CHA 340 1692
60 Lyons, F. S. L., *Charles Stewart Parnell*, Collins, 1977, p. 249
61 Morley, op. cit., vol. III, p. 224
62 Holland, op. cit., vol. II, p. 63
63 Ibid., p. 72
64 Ibid., p. 74
65 Ibid., p. 75
66 Ibid., p. 90
67 Ibid., p. 96
68 CHA 340 1921
69 Ibid., 340 1920

CHAPTER 25

Full of Love for the Country

1 Shannon, R., *Gladstone: Heroic Minister*, Allen Lane, 1999, p. 295
2 Holland, op. cit., vol. I, p. 14
3 Marlow, Joyce, *The Oak and the Ivy*, Doubleday, 1977, p. 118
4 Ibid.
5 Kee, Robert, *The Laurel and the Ivy*, Hamish Hamilton, 1993, p. 436
6 Ibid.
7 Shannon, op. cit., p. 295
8 Ibid., p. 139
9 Ibid., p. 193
10 Ibid., p. 282
11 Jackson, op. cit., p. 138
12 Jenkins, *Dilke*, op. cit., p. 152
13 Jackson, op. cit., p. 138
14 CHA, Diary (Seventh Duke), 4.iv.82
15 Morley, op. cit., vol. III, p. 67
16 Shannon, op. cit., p. 297
17 Marlow, op. cit., p. 214
18 Ibid., p. 215
19 Holland, op. cit., vol. I, p. 354
20 CHA 340 1148
21 Morley, op. cit., vol. III, p. 68
22 CHA 340 1161
23 Ibid., 340 1247
24 Ibid., 340 1148b
25 Morley, op. cit., vol. III, p. 70
26 Ibid.
27 Ibid.
28 Lyons, op. cit., p. 370
29 Ibid., p. 424
30 Curtis, L. P., *Coercion and Conciliation in Ireland*, Gill & Macmillan, 1988, p. 328
31 Marlow, op. cit., p. 243
32 Ibid.

CHAPTER 26

The Last of the Golden Age

1 CHA 340 1922
2 Holland, op. cit., vol. II, p. 125
3 Hansard 9.4.86
4 CHA 340 1979
5 Hansard 10.5.86

6 CHA 340 1997
7 Ibid., 340 1992
8 Ibid.
9 Ibid., 340 2015
10 Ibid., 340 2022
11 Ibid., 340 2021
12 Ibid., 340 2029
13 Ibid., 340 2032
14 Ibid., 340 2037
15 Ibid., 340 2034
16 Ibid., 340 2072a
17 Ibid., 340 2085
18 Holland, op. cit., vol. II, p. 224
19 Ibid., p. 208
20 Ibid., p. 209
21 Vane, op. cit., p. 82
22 Ibid., p. 192
23 Hattersley, Roy, *David Lloyd George*, Little, Brown, 2010, p. 333

CHAPTER 27

A Drag on the Wheel

1 Holland, op. cit., vol. II, p. 250
2 Ibid.
3 Hansard 18.4.87
4 Holland, op. cit., vol. II, p. 264
5 *The Times*, 3.7.97
6 Holland, op. cit., vol. II, p. 277
7 Ibid., p. 278
8 Royal Commission on Secondary Education, 1895, minutes of evidence, p. 492
9 CHA 340
10 Holland, op. cit., vol. II, p. 271
11 Ibid.
12 Ibid., p. 273
13 Ibid., p. 272
14 Mackay, Ruddock F., *Balfour: The Intellectual Statesman*, Oxford University Press, 1985, p. 86
15 Holland, op. cit., vol. II, p. 271
16 Mackay, op. cit., p. 86
17 Kekewich, Sir George, *The Education Department and After*, Constable, 1923, p. 92
18 Balfour Papers 49705 BL
19 Mackay, op. cit., p. 92
20 Holland, op. cit., vol. II, p. 274
21 Miunson, J. E., 'The Unionist Coalition on Education', *Historical Journal*, 1971
22 CHA, Victor Cavendish Diaries, 3.11.01
23 Miunson, op. cit.
24 Hansard 17.12.02
25 Holland, op. cit., vol II, p. 284
26 Ibid., p. 298
27 Balfour Papers 49776
28 Annual Register for 1903
29 Holland, op. cit., vol II, p. 305
30 Ibid., p. 307
31 Hansard (House of Lords) 15.06.03
32 Ibid.
33 CHA 340 2941
34 Ibid.
35 Holland, op. cit., vol. II, p. 340
36 Ibid., p. 341
37 Gollin, Alfred, *Balfour's Burden*, Blond, 1965, p. 153
38 Holland, op. cit., vol. II, p. 357
39 CHA 340 2929
40 Gollin, op. cit., p. 153
41 CHA, Eighth Duke – Mandeville Memorandum
42 Holland, op. cit., vol. II, p. 344
43 CHA, Eighth Duke – Mandeville Memorandum
44 Adams, R. J. Q., *The Last Grandee*, John Murray, 2007, p. 216
45 CHA 340 2954
46 CHA, Victor Cavendish Diaries, op. cit., 18.09.03
47 Holland, op. cit., vol. II, p. 347
48 Ibid., p. 350
49 Gollin, op. cit., p. 172
50 Ibid.
51 Ibid., p. 174
52 CHA, Victor Cavendish Diaries, op. cit., 18.08.07
53 Jenkins, Roy, *Winston Churchill*, Macmillan, 2001, p. 194
54 CHA 340 2985
55 Royal Archives, R23 No 103 4.10.03
56 Adams, *The Last Grandee*, op. cit., p. 218
57 Holland, op. cit., p. 368
58 Ibid.
59 Hansard 4.11.03

60 Ibid. 22.02.06
61 Vane, op. cit., p. 243
62 Ibid., p. 240

Afterword

1 Hattersley, Roy, *The Edwardians*, Little, Brown, 2004, p. 10 (quoting Victor Cavendish Diary)
2 Ibid.
3 Ibid.
4 Ibid.
5 Ibid.
6 Deborah, Duchess of Devonshire, *The House*, Macmillan, 1982, p. 58
7 CHA, Ninth Duke's Diary, 25.11.22

8 Ibid., 22.11.22
9 Ibid., 23.5.23
10 Smith, Roly, *Kinder Scout: Portrait of a Mountain*, Derbyshire County Council and National Trust, 2002, p. 91
11 Ibid., p. 89
12 Ibid., p. 93
13 Ibid., p. 94
14 Devonshire, Eleventh Duke of, *Accidents of Fortune*, Michael Russell, 2004, p. 65
15 Pearson, op. cit., p. 201
16 Personal conversation
17 Ibid.
18 Cullen, P., *A Stranger in Blood: The Case Files on John Bodkin Adams*, Elliott & Thompson, 2004, p. 176

Select Bibliography

ADAMS, R. J. Q., *The Last Grandee*, John Murray, 2007
ADAMS, W., *The Gem of the Peak*, London, 1835
BAKER, R., *The Railway Mania*, Letts & Sons, 1869
BERNARD, E. W. (ed.), *The Tudor Nobility*, Manchester University Press, 1992
BICKLEY, FRANCES L., *The Cavendish Family*, Mifflin, New York, 1914
BRADDICK, MICHAEL, *God's Fury, England's Fire: A New History of the English Civil Wars*, Allen Lane, 2008
BRADLEY, E. T., *Arbella Stuart*, Bentley, 1889
BRIGGS, ASA, *Victorian People*, Penguin
CANNADINE, D., *Lords and Landlords*, Yale University Press
CAVENDISH, GEORGE, *The Life of Cardinal Wolsey*, Harding & Leopard, Pall Mall, London, 1827
CECIL, DAVID, *Melbourne*, Constable, 1930
COLQUHOUN, KATE, *A Thing in Disguise*, Hodder Perennial, 2003
COLQUHOUN, KATE, *The Busiest Man in England*, Hodder Perennial
COOTE, STEPHEN, *A Play of Passion: The Life of Sir Walter Raleigh*, Macmillan, 1993
CRABTREE, J. H., *Richard Arkwright*, Sheldon Press
CURTIS, L. P., *Coercion and Conciliation in Ireland*, Gill & Macmillan, 1988
DAVIES, H., *George Stevenson*, Weidenfeld & Nicolson, 2002
DUNN, JANE, *Elizabeth and Mary*, HarperCollins, 2003
DURANT, DAVID M., *Bess of Hardwick*, Peter Owen (USA), 1999
DURANT, DAVID M., *Arbella Stuart: A Rival to the Queen*, Weidenfeld & Nicolson, 1998
FITTON, R. S., *The Arkwrights: Spinners of Fortune*, Manchester University Press, 1989
FOREMAN, AMANDA, *Georgiana, Duchess of Devonshire*, HarperCollins, 1998
FRASER, A., *Mary Queen of Scots*, Weidenfeld & Nicolson, 2009
GOLLIN, ALFRED, *Balfour's Burden*, Blond, 1965
GRISTWOOD, SARAH, *Arbella: England's Lost Queen*, Bantam, 2003
GUY, JOHN, *My Heart Is My Own*, Fourth Estate, 2004

HAGUE, WILLIAM, *Pitt the Younger*, HarperCollins, 2004

HANDOVER, P. M., *Arbella Stuart: Royal Lady of Hardwick*, Harvard University Press, 1957

HARDY, B. C., *Arbella Stuart*, Constable, 1913

HEAPE, R. G., *Buxton under the Dukes of Devonshire*, Robert Hale, 1948

HOLDEN, ANTHONY, *The Wit in the Dungeon*, Little, Brown, 2005

HOLLAND, B., *The Life of Spencer Compton, Eighth Duke of Devonshire*, 2 vols, Longman, 1911

KENNET, WHITE, *Memoirs of the Family of Cavendish*, London, 1708

JACKSON, P., *The Last of the Whigs*, Associated University Presses, 1994

JENKINS, ELIZABETH, *Elizabeth the Great*, Coward-McCann, New York

JENKINS, HUGH, *The Devonshire House Circle*, Haymarket

JENKINS, ROY, *Gladstone*, Macmillan, 1995

JENKINS, ROY, *Sir Charles Dilke: A Victorian Tragedy*, Collins, 1959

KEE, ROBERT, *The Laurel and the Ivy*, Hamish Hamilton, 1993

KEE, ROBERT, *The Green Flag*, Weidenfeld & Nicolson

LEES-MILNE, JAMES, *The Tudor Renaissance*, Batsford, 1951

LEES-MILNE, JAMES, *The Bachelor Duke*, John Murray, 1991

LONGUEVILLE, T., *The First Duke and Duchess of Newcastle-upon-Tyne*, Longman, 1910

LOVELL, MARY, *Bess of Hardwick*, Little, Brown, 2005

LYONS, F. S. L., *Charles Stewart Parnell*, Collins, 1977

MACAULAY, THOMAS BABINGTON, *History of England*, Philip Sampson, 1857

MACKAY, RUDDOCK F., *Balfour: The Intellectual Statesman*, Oxford University Press, 1985

MARKHAM, VIOLET, *Paxton and the Bachelor Duke*, Hodder & Stoughton, 1935

MARLOW, JOYCE, *The Oak and the Ivy*, Doubleday, 1977

MARSHALL, J. D., *Furness and the Industrial Revolution*, Barrow-in-Furness Library and Museum Committee, 1958

MARTINICH, A. P., *Hobbes: A Biography*, Cambridge University Press, 1989

MCCARTHY, FIONA, *Byron: Life and Legend*, John Murray, 2004

MCKIE, J. D., *The Early Tudors*, Oxford University Press, 1952

MITCHELL, LESLIE, *The Whig World*, Hambledon, 2006

MORLEY, JOHN, *The Life of William Ewart Gladstone*, 3 vols, Macmillan, 1903

NEALE, J. E., *Queen Elizabeth*, Penguin

NEWCASTLE, MARGARET (Duchess of), *The Life of William Cavendish, Duke of Newcastle*, John C. Nimmo, 1886

PEARSON, JOHN, *Stags and Serpents*, Macmillan, 1983

PLUMB, J. H., *Sir Robert Walpole: The Making of a Statesman*, Cresset Press, 1956

PLUMB, J. H., *England in the Eighteenth Century (1714–1815)*, Penguin

RAWSON, P., *Bess of Hardwick*, Hutchinson, 2001

RIDEN, P. AND FOWKES, D., *Hardwick: A Great House and Its Estate*, Phillimore, 2009

ROUND, J. HORACE, *Family Origins and Other Studies*, Constable, 1930

SAUL, NIGEL, *For Honour and Fame*, Bodley Head, 2011

SHANNON, RICHARD, *Gladstone: Heroic Minister*, Allen Lane, 1999

SLATER, MICHAEL, *Charles Dickens*, Yale University Press, 2009

SOMERSET, ANNE, *Elizabeth I*, Fontana, 1991

SOMERSET, ANNE, *Queen Anne: The Politics of Passion*, Harper Press

STEWART, ALAN, *The Cradle King: A Life of James VI and I*, Chatto & Windus, 2003

THOMPSON, F., *History of Chatsworth*, Country Life, 1951

THOMPSON, F. L. M., *The English Landed Society*, Routledge & Kegan Paul, 2006

TREASE, GEOFFREY, *Portrait of a Cavalier*, Macmillan, 1979

VANE, HENRY, *Affairs of State*, Peter Owen, 2004

WALDEGRAVE, SECOND EARL, *Memoirs and Speeches*, John Murray, 1754/58

WATSON, J. STEVEN, *The Reign of George III 1760–1815*, in the Oxford History of England, Oxford University Press, 1960

WILLIAMS, BASIL, *The Whig Supremacy 1714–1760*, in the Oxford History of England, Oxford University Press, 1960

WILSON, GEORGE, *The Life of the Honourable Henry Cavendish*, Cavendish Society, 1851

WOODWARD, L., *The Age of Reform*, in the Oxford History of England, Oxford University Press, 1962

Index

www.vintage-books.co.uk